WHEN POLITICS ARE SACRALIZED

Over the years, there have been increasing intersections between religious claims and nationalism and their power to frame and govern world politics. *When Politics Are Sacralized* interdisciplinarily and comparatively examines the fusion between religious claims and nationalism and studies its political manifestations. State and world politics, when determined or framed by nationalism fused with religious claims, can provoke protracted conflict, infuse explicit religious beliefs into politics, and legitimize violence against racialized groups. This volume investigates how, through hegemonic nationalism, states invoke religious claims in domestic and international politics, sacralizing the political. Studying Israel, India, the Palestinian National Movement and Hamas, Sri Lanka, Saudi Arabia, Serbia, Iran, and Northern Ireland, the fourteen chapters engage with the visibility, performativity, role, and political legitimation of religion and nationalism. The authors analyze how and why sacralization affects political behaviors apparent in national and international politics, produces state-sponsored violence, and shapes conflict.

Nadim N. Rouhana is Professor of International Affairs and Conflict Studies and Director of the Fares Center for Eastern Mediterranean Studies at the Fletcher School of Law and Diplomacy, Tufts University. His most recent (edited) volume is *Israel and its Palestinian Citizens: Ethnic Privileges in the Jewish State* (Cambridge, 2017).

Nadera Shalhoub-Kevorkian is the Lawrence D. Biele Chair in Law at the Faculty of Law–Institute of Criminology and School of Social Work and Social Welfare at the Hebrew University of Jerusalem, and Global Chair in Law at Queen Mary University of London. Her latest book is *Incarcerated Childhood and the Politics of Unchilding* (Cambridge, 2019).

When Politics Are Sacralized

COMPARATIVE PERSPECTIVES ON RELIGIOUS CLAIMS
AND NATIONALISM

Edited by

NADIM N. ROUHANA

Tufts University

NADERA SHALHOUB-KEVORKIAN

The Hebrew University of Jerusalem
Queen Mary University of London

CAMBRIDGE
UNIVERSITY PRESS

University Printing House, Cambridge CB2 8BS, United Kingdom

One Liberty Plaza, 20th Floor, New York, NY 10006, USA

477 Williamstown Road, Port Melbourne, VIC 3207, Australia

314–321, 3rd Floor, Plot 3, Splendor Forum, Jasola District Centre,
New Delhi – 110025, India

79 Anson Road, #06–04/06, Singapore 079906

Cambridge University Press is part of the University of Cambridge.

It furthers the University's mission by disseminating knowledge in the pursuit of
education, learning, and research at the highest international levels of excellence.

www.cambridge.org
Information on this title: www.cambridge.org/9781108487863
DOI: 10.1017/9781108768191

© Cambridge University Press 2021

This publication is in copyright. Subject to statutory exception
and to the provisions of relevant collective licensing agreements,
no reproduction of any part may take place without the written
permission of Cambridge University Press.

First published 2021

A catalogue record for this publication is available from the British Library.

ISBN 978-1-108-48786-3 Hardback

Cambridge University Press has no responsibility for the persistence or accuracy of
URLs for external or third-party internet websites referred to in this publication
and does not guarantee that any content on such websites is, or will remain,
accurate or appropriate.

Contents

List of Figures	*page* vii	
List of Maps	viii	
List of Tables	ix	
List of Contributors	x	
Preface and Acknowledgments	xv	

1	**A Comparative Perspective on Religious Claims and Sacralized Politics: An Introduction** Nadim N. Rouhana and Nadera Shalhoub-Kevorkian	1
	PART I ISRAEL	31
2	**Religion and Nationalism in the Jewish and Zionist Context** Amnon Raz-Krakotzkin	33
3	**Religious Claims and Nationalism in Zionism: Obscuring Settler Colonialism** Nadim N. Rouhana	54
4	**On the Uses and Abuses of Tradition: Zionist Theopolitics and Jewish Tradition** Yaacov Yadgar	88
5	**The Relations between the Nationalization of Israel's Politics and the Religionization of Its Military, 1948–2016** Yagil Levy	113
6	**Sacralized Politics: The Case of Occupied East Jerusalem** Nadera Shalhoub-Kevorkian	134

v

vi   *Contents*

PART II   INDIA   159

7   Hindutva: The Dominant Face of Religious Nationalism in India   161
Tanika Sarkar

PART III   SRI LANKA   185

8   The Genesis, Consolidation, and Consequences of Sinhalese
Buddhist Nationalism   187
Neil DeVotta

PART IV   SERBIA   213

9   Serbian Jerusalem: Inventing a Holy Land in Europe's
Periphery, 1982–2019   215
Vjekoslav Perica

PART V   IRAN   245

10   The Crossing Paths of Religion and Nationalism
in Contemporary Iran   247
Ali Banuazizi

PART VI   SAUDI ARABIA AND WAHHABISM   273

11   Saudi Nationalism, Wahhabi *Daʿwā*, and Western Power   275
Michael A. Sells

PART VII   NORTHERN IRELAND   307

12   Protestantism and Settler Identity: The Ambiguous Case of Northern
Ireland   309
David Lloyd

13   Does Religion Still Matter?: Comparative Lessons from the
Ethno-national Conflict in Northern Ireland   337
Liam O'Dowd

PART VIII   PALESTINE   363

14   Palestinian Nationalism, Religious (Un)claims, and the Struggle
against Zionism   365
Khaled Hroub

Index   387

Figures

12.1–12.5   Loyalist murals, Northern Ireland. Reproduced by permission
from Bill Rolston, *Drawing Support: Murals in the North of
Ireland* (Belfast: Beyond the Pale Publications, 1992), and
Drawing Support 2: Murals of War and Peace (Belfast:
Beyond the Pale Publications, 1998)   *page* 318–20

12.6   Republican murals, Falls Road, Belfast, Northern Ireland.
Reproduced by permission from the Palestine Poster Project
Archives. © 2009–13, Liberation Graphics   327

12.7   Loyalist flag incorporating Ulster Banner and Star of David.
© Cathal McNaughton / Reuters Pictures. Reproduced by
permission from Reuters   328

Maps

9.1	Historic Serbian monasteries in Kosovo	*page* 224
9.2	Proposed territory swap between Serbia and Kosovo	237

Tables

5.1	Four stages of nationalization and religionization of Israel's politics and military	*page* 129
11.1	Saudi-Wahhabi chronology	300
13.1	Average number of Belfast residents per church by religious denomination	349

Contributors

Ali Banuazizi is Professor of Political Science at Boston College and Director of the Program in Islamic Civilization & Societies. After receiving his PhD from Yale University, he taught at Yale and the University of Southern California before joining the Boston College faculty in 1971. He has held visiting appointments at the University of Tehran, Princeton, Harvard, Oxford, and MIT. He has served as the founding editor of the *Journal of Iranian Studies*, President of the Association for Iranian Studies (AIS) and the Middle East Studies Association (MESA), and Associate Editor of the *Encyclopedia of Islam and the Muslim World* (2016). He is the author of numerous articles on Iranian and Middle Eastern politics, society, and culture; coauthor (with Ahmad Ashraf) of *Social Classes, the State, and Revolution in Iran* (Nilufar Publications, 2008) and coeditor (with Myron Weiner) of three books on politics, religion, and society in Southwest and Central Asia.

Neil DeVotta is Professor in Politics and International Affairs at Wake Forest University. His research interests include Asian security and politics, ethno-religious nationalism, ethnic conflict resolution, and democratic transition and consolidation. He is the author of *Blowback: Linguistic Nationalism, Institutional Decay, and Ethnic Conflict in Sri Lanka* (Stanford University Press, 2004) and editor of *Understanding Contemporary India* (Lynne Rienner, 2010, second edition) and *An Introduction to South Asian Politics* (Routledge, 2016), in addition to authoring numerous articles. He has also consulted for a number of organizations, including the United States Agency for International Development, Freedom House, and Bertelsmann Stiftung.

Khaled Hroub is Professor of Middle Eastern Studies and Arab Media Studies at Northwestern University, Qatar. Previously, he taught history and politics of the Middle East at the Faculty of Asian and Middle Eastern Studies, University of Cambridge, where he founded and directed the Cambridge Arab Media Project (CAMP) between 2003 and 2012. He authored *Hamas: Political Thought and Practice* (Institute for Palestine Studies, 2000) and *Hamas: A Beginner's Guide*

List of Contributors xi

(Pluto Press, 2006), and edited *Political Islam: Context versus Ideology* (Saqi, 2011) and *Religious Broadcasting in the Middle East* (Hurst, 2012). In Arabic, he published *Fragility of Ideology and Might of Politics* (Saqi, 2010), *In Praise of Revolution* (Saqi, 2012), *The Anxious Intellectual versus the Intellectual of Certainty* (al-Ahlia, 2018), and three prose and poetry collections between 2008 and 2017. He obtained his PhD in international relations from the University of Cambridge, in addition to three masters in various fields from other universities.

Yagil Levy is Professor of Political Sociology and Public Policy at the Open University of Israel. His field of research is the theoretical and empirical aspects of relations between society and the military. Levy has published eight books, in addition to a coauthored work, textbook, and four edited volumes. His most recent book is *Whose Life Is Worth More? Hierarchies of Risk and Death in Contemporary Wars* (Stanford University Press, 2019). Levy served as President of the European Research Group on Military and Society (ERGOMAS) and Vice President of the Israeli Sociological Society. He serves on the Board of Editors of *Armed Forces & Society*. He has held visiting posts at Georgetown University, the New School for Social Research in New York, and the European University Institute. Levy also regularly publishes op-ed articles in *Haaretz*.

David Lloyd, Distinguished Professor of English at the University of California, Riverside, works primarily on postcolonial and cultural theory, critical race theory, and on Irish culture. His recent publications include *Irish Culture and Colonial Modernity: The Transformation of Oral Space* (Cambridge University Press, 2011), a study of Samuel Beckett's visual aesthetics, *Beckett's Thing: Painting and Theatre* (Edinburgh University Press, 2016), and a collection of essays on aesthetics, race, and representation, *Under Representation: The Racial Regime of Aesthetics* (Fordham University Press, 2019). He has also published numerous articles on Palestine and Israel, including "Settler Colonialism and the State of Exception: The Example of Israel/Palestine" in *The Journal of Settler Colonial Studies* 2, no. 1 (2012); the introduction (coauthored with Patrick Wolfe) to a special issue of *Settler Colonial Studies* (2015), "Settler Colonial Logics and the Neo-liberal Regime"; and "From the Critique of Violence to the Critique of Rights," in *Critical Times* 3, no. 1 (2020).

Liam O'Dowd is Emeritus Professor of Sociology at Queen's University, Belfast. He has published widely on borders, ethno-nationally divided cities, the sociology of intellectuals, and the Northern Ireland conflict. His most recent book (coedited with Martina McKnight) is *Religion, Violence and Cities* (Routledge, 2015). He is currently working on a coauthored book with James Anderson on a comparative analysis of ethno-nationally divided cities in contested states.

Vjekoslav Perica is a Croatian-American historian, author of, inter alia, *Balkan Idols: Religion and Nationalism in Yugoslav States* (Oxford University Press, 2002; Biblioteka XX vek, 2006), and Professor of History at the University of Rijeka,

Croatia. He is currently writing a book about using religious resources and institutions for postwar symbolic reconciliation of the faiths and peoples in the Western Balkans. Perica holds a PhD in history from the University of Minnesota – Twin Cities. He is a former Fulbright scholar (Belgrade) and research fellow at the Netherlands Institute for Advanced Studies (NIAS). Before coming to the United States in 1991, Perica was a basketball player, jurist, and journalist in the former Yugoslavia. He now lives in Baltimore and Croatia. In between, he spends time with his grandsons in New York.

Amnon Raz-Krakotzkin teaches at the Department of Jewish History, Ben-Gurion University of the Negev. He was a fellow at the Wissenschaftskolleg zu Berlin (2003–2004) and the Center of Advanced Judaic Studies, Philadelphia (2006, 2009–2010). He studies both early modern Christian-Jewish discourse and Zionist historical consciousness. His publications include *The Censor, the Editor and the Text: Catholic Censorship and Hebrew Literature in the Sixteenth Century* (University of Pennsylvania Press, 2007) and *Exil et Souverainete* (La fabrique, 2007).

Nadim N. Rouhana is Professor of International Affairs and Conflict Studies and Director at the Fares Center for Eastern Mediterranean Studies, the Fletcher School of Law and Diplomacy, Tufts University. His current research includes work on settler colonialism, collective identity and democratic citizenship, the questions of reconciliation, decolonization, and transitional justice. His research and writing focuses on the conflict between Zionism and the Palestinians and on Israeli and Palestinian societies. His publications include *Israel and Its Palestinian Citizens: Ethnic Privileges in the Jewish State* (Cambridge University Press, 2017, edited) and numerous academic articles. He has held various academic positions in Palestinian, Israeli, and American universities including at Harvard University, Boston College, and at Tel-Aviv University. He was a cofounder of the Program on International Conflict Analysis and Resolution at Harvard's Weatherhead Center for International Affairs where he cochaired the Center's seminar on International Conflict Analysis and Resolution from 1992 to 2001.

Tanika Sarkar is a retired professor of modern history at Jawaharlal Nehru University, Delhi. She has also taught at St. Stephen's College, Delhi, and as a visiting professor at the universities of Chicago, Yale, Göttingen, and the Witswatersrand. She was invited as a visiting fellow at Trinity College, Cambridge, Keele University, University of Washington, University of Pavia, Dublin University, and Zentrum Modern Oriental, Berlin. Sarkar has published several monographs on political and cultural nationalism in India, gender, and Hindu extremist movements. She has coedited, with Sumit Sarkar, Unrvashi Butalia, and Sekhar Bandypadhyay, several volumes on caste in India, social reform in India, women of the Hindu Right, and on colonial Calcutta. Her latest monograph is *Rebels, Wives and Saints: Designing Selves and Nations in Colonial Times* (Permanent Black, 2009). She is also writing a volume called *Gender in Colonial South Asia: India, Pakistan and Bangladesh, Late 18th Century to the 1980s* (Cambridge University, forthcoming).

Michael A. Sells is Emeritus Professor of the History and Literature of Islam and Comparative Literature at the University of Chicago. His research interests include pre-Islamic and classical Arabic poetry, the Qur'an, Sufism, comparative mysticism, and religion and violence. His works on religion and violence include *The Bridge Betrayed: Religion and Genocide in Bosnia* (University of California Press, 1996). His article "Holocaust Abuse: The Case of Hajj Amin al-Husayni" traces the history of the claim that the Palestinian leader was an architect of the Holocaust, exposes the manipulation of history behind it, and analyzes its influence on American attitudes toward the Middle East. His chapter "'Armageddon' in Christian, Sunni, and Shia Traditions" (in *The Oxford Handbook of Religion and Violence*, Oxford University Press, 2012) focuses on the mutual influence and rivalry between contemporary American Christian and Sunni Islamic "end times" apocalypticism.

Nadera Shalhoub-Kevorkian is the Lawrence D. Biele Chair in Law at the Faculty of Law, Institute of Criminology and the School of Social Work and Public Welfare, the Hebrew University of Jerusalem, and the Global Chair in Law at Queen Mary University of London. Her research focuses on trauma, state crimes and criminology, surveillance, gender violence, and law and society. She is the author of numerous books, among them *Militarization and Violence against Women in Conflict Zones in the Middle East: The Palestinian Case Study* (Cambridge University Press, 2010), *Security Theology, Surveillance and the Politics of Fear* (Cambridge University Press, 2015), and *Incarcerated Childhood and the Politics of Unchilding* (Cambridge University Press, 2019). Her articles appears in multidisciplinary fields including the *British Journal of Criminology*, *Feminist Studies*, *Ethnic and Racial Studies*, *State Crime*, *Violence Against Women*, *Social Science and Medicine*, *Signs*, *Law & Society Review*, and the *International Journal of Applied Psychoanalytic Studies*.

Yaacov Yadgar is the Stanley Lewis Professor of Israel Studies at the University of Oxford. He has written extensively on matters of Jewish identity, nationalism, secularism, modernity, and tradition in Israel. He is the author of *Sovereign Jews: Israel, Zionism, and Judaism* (SUNY Press, 2017) and *Israel's Jewish Identity Crisis: State and Politics in the Middle East* (Cambridge University Press, 2020).

Preface and Acknowledgments

Our initial interest in this project emerged from our research and personal involvement in the dynamics of the Israeli-Palestinian conflict and our observations of its historical evolution. Each of us has studied, separately, over the years, wide-ranging facets of both Israeli and Palestinian societies and politics. Our academic careers span teaching and research in Israeli, Palestinian, and American universities. We both have personally witnessed the settler-colonial project in Palestine unfolding and expanding. Consequently, it was natural to turn our intellectual and academic interest to examining Zionism, its intellectual representation, and the justificatory system that enabled it for so long to conceal the essence of its settler-colonial project that is called the "Jewish state" in Palestine. Of central interest to us is not only the fact that religious claims are foundational to the Zionist movement, but also their current manifestations in state politics and the rise of what we call the religiously legitimized sacralized politics. This required opening a space for a genuine critical analysis to investigate the nature of this process in comparative perspective.

We came to this project, not as scholars of religion and nationalism per se, but more as involved scholars of a conflict in which the intertwining between religious claims and nationalism are transforming its dynamics. While mainstream discourse across the globe often invokes religion as a major reason for the Israeli-Palestinian conflict, the majority of Israelis and Palestinians have historically understood the conflict as fundamentally secular in nature – either national or settler colonial on the Palestinian side, or a conflict of liberating *Eretz Yisrael* (read Palestine) from foreigners on the Zionist side. Yet, in the past few decades, the apparent invocation of religious claims and interpretations and the role of religious players in the conflict have been on the rise, as evidenced by the increased infusion of religious claims into the local and global discourse and into state politics, particularly on the Israeli side and on the part of Hamas. Therefore, it was vital to examine the role religious claims are playing in Zionism as a political project.

This project, generously funded by the Henry Luce Foundation, focused on a number of cases worldwide in which such fusion affected state identity and politics. In conjunction with the Israeli case, our volume examines the cases of India, Sri Lanka, Serbia, Iran, Saudi Arabia, Northern Ireland, and Palestine (with emphasis on Hamas). Under the auspices of the project, we invited leading scholars from different disciplinary positions and areas of expertise to engage in workshops or small conferences in Boston, New Delhi, Sarajevo, Johannesburg, Jerusalem, and Ramallah between 2014 and 2018 in order to develop a comparative research agenda about the cases selected for study. Out of these working meetings, the chapters that ultimately comprise this volume emerged.

We believe that this project has opened some space, as minor as it might be, for critical discussions among some international scholars on how the intertwining between religious claims and nationalism sacralizes the political. The project has facilitated a more nuanced, comparative analysis, with locally embedded and globally examined perspectives. If the sacralization of politics is about power relations where state policies use religious framing or religious claims to regulate some groups and entities and position others as exclusively entitled, how precisely are we to understand the way such ideological norms are produced and used to maintain and stabilize the material, psychological, and political apparatus of governance, and how can we engage with conflict studies under such complexities?

In the introductory chapter, we focus on the above questions and on how religious claims and nationalism are used by states to maintain and mobilize the machinery of power in general, and in certain types of conflict situations in particular. We argue that examining the sacralization of politics can expand our understanding of violations of human rights, violence of state and non-state actors, political justificatory systems, territorial greed, and colonial and settler-colonial structures and machineries of governance. Such an examination can help shed light not only on what happens when religious claims are invoked to promote racialized violence and enhance discriminatory systems of governance, but also on what is being constructed and affirmed politically.

The various chapters in this volume touch on all the above issues but not in any systematic comparative way. Different chapters focus on different manifestations of this fusion of religious claims and nationalism. The need for a comparative study with these manifestations at the center is still needed. The investigation provided new insights into the possibilities and pitfalls of conflict resolution efforts in sites afflicted by the interlocking of religious claims and nationalism manifest in the power structure. This volume doesn't address this issue directly, but our analysis might provide guidance for future efforts, because it raises critical questions about the role of sacralized politics in constructing the matrix of power, how it justifies exclusion and violence, and the way it mobilizes global support.

Throughout the work on this project that culminated in this volume, we have learned a tremendous amount and been supported by wonderful scholars, including the contributors to this volume. Our enduring appreciation for accomplishing this book goes to Kate Rouhana for editing the entire volume with characteristic

Preface and Acknowledgments xvii

generosity, good spirit, and valuable insights. We would also like to thank Stephanie Williams for her gracious and meticulous editorial assistance throughout and Nina Griecci-Woodsum for editorial support in the early stages. We were fortunate to have great colleagues from Australia, India, Sri Lanka, Palestine, Israel, South Africa, Bosnia, Croatia, the US, and Canada accompanying us on our intellectual journey. Their generous engagement with our project in various meetings and workshops and their friendship and support made this project a most gratifying learning experience. These include Dino Abazovic, Lila Abu-Lughod, Aijaz Ahmad, Basem Ezbidi, Gadi al-Gazi, Benjamin Beit-Hallahmi, Meir Buzaglo, Anuradha M. Chenoy, Kamal Chenoy, Steven Friedman, Nomboniso Gasa, Mark Gevisser, Ran Greenstein, Amos Goldberg, David Theo Goldberg, Rema Hammami, Dhammamegha Annie Leatt, Achille Mbembe, Hlonipha Mokoena, Esmail Nashif, Sarah Nuttall, Raef Zreik, Rada Drezgic, Selma Porobic, Gorazd Andrejc, Islah Jad, David Myers, Goldie Osuri, Suvendrini Perrera, Joseph Pugliese, Uri Ram, Rosemary Sayigh, Sherene Razack, Ghanyshyam Shah, and Achin Vanaik.

We are also indebted to many colleagues who contributed their intellectual insights as this project began to take shape, including Rachel Busbridge, Yossi David, Areen Hawari, Sarah Ihmoud, and Einas Odeh-Haj. Our students and assistants helped in research, writing, and in organizing the workshops and conferences: Danielle Angel, Christopher Blair, Nina Griecci-Woodsum, Inas Khatib, Revital Madar, Amir Marshi, and Stephanie Williams.

Nadim Rouhana would like to thank the Netherlands Institute for Advanced Studies (NIAS) for its generous support of his fellowship at the Institute during the academic year 2019/2020. The intellectual climate and institutional support provided by the NIAS were ideal for completing the project. He would also like to thank his colleagues at the Institute, in particular Jan Willem Duyvendak, NIAS's director, for their engagement and insightful feedback on his chapter during the Institute's seminars.

Nadera Shalhoub-Kevorkian would like to thank her colleagues at the Faculty of Law at Queen Mary University of London, especially Penny Green, Richard Falk, and Neve Gordon for their kind feedback and attentive engagement with this project.

This project was made possible by the generous support of The Henry Luce Foundation. It could not have succeeded without the major, long-term support of The Luce Foundation, especially its flexibility in accommodating the project's demands within the shifting circumstances in conflict areas. We would like to express our deepest gratitude in particular to the Director of Policy Initiatives, Toby Volkman, for all of her support and contributions in the various meetings and for her attentiveness, which helped us bring the project to fruition in the form of this edited volume. We also thank our editors at Cambridge University Press, John

Berger and Jackie Grant, for their support and patience throughout the development of this volume.

We are grateful also for the institutional and technical support of both the Fletcher School of Law and Diplomacy at Tufts University and Mada al-Carmel – the Arab Center for Applied Social Research in Haifa. Last but not least, we are deeply indebted to our families for their sustaining love and for our many dialogues over the years.

1

A Comparative Perspective on Religious Claims and Sacralized Politics

An Introduction

Nadim N. Rouhana and Nadera Shalhoub-Kevorkian

Over the past years, the various forms of intersection between religion and nationalism have increasingly been invoked as potent forces in framing and perhaps driving national and international conflicts. Accordingly, observers have examined the impact of these intersections on national and international conflicts – particularly in regard to political violence, and specifically as it relates to non-state actors. State politics, when determined by or framed in terms of nationalism fused with religious claims, have the potential to provoke protracted conflicts, infuse explicit religious beliefs and theories into politics and modes of governance, legitimize the exclusion of groups – including of fellow citizens – on the basis of interpreting sacred texts, and condone or instigate violence in the name of religiously embedded claims. In this introduction, we will examine the workings of such politics and discuss their implications for domestic, regional, and international conflicts. In this chapter, *we define such politics as religiously legitimated or framed politics of sacredness.*

Our central concern here (and in this volume as a whole) is not the relationship between religion and nationalism per se. We are interested in the influence of religion and religious claims, through their intertwining with nationalism, on state policies – domestically, regionally, and internationally. What stands at the center of our inquiry is the impact of the intertwining, particularly when religious claims and nationalism are fused to the extent that religious claims bestow sacredness on the state's working of power. Examples include establishing the state's identity; determining regime type, including governmentality and the questions of democracy and equality; codifying laws accordingly; defining the politics of state territoriality; endorsing particular perceptions of the "self" and the "other"; engaging in strategic and policy planning; and sanctioning state violence in the service of all of the above.

Scholarly discussions on the relationship between religion and nationalism and the emergence of the secularization paradigm and its critique have been exhaustive. Views range from suggesting that modern nationalism is distinctly secular, epitomizing modernity's replacement of religion – what is known as the secularization paradigm (e.g., Anderson 1991; Gellner 1994; Hobsbawm 1990; Taylor 1998) – to the view that nationalism has always been intrinsically religious (e.g., Asad 2003; Casanova 1994; Connolly 2011; Friedland and Moss 2016; Mahmood 2017; Norris and Inglehart 2010; Spohn 2003). The literature delves into the origins of the secularization paradigm, its historical determinants and influence of modernity, its functionality, impact on identity and conflict, and other implications.[1] Many scholars have convincingly argued that modern nations and nationalisms are interwoven, albeit to very different extents and in diverse forms, with religious myths, narratives, symbolisms, or rituals (e.g., Brubaker 2012; Friedland 2001; Friedland and Moss 2016; Perica 2002; Shenhav 2007; Soper and Fetzer 2018). The views that divorce nationalism from religion, reject the possibility that religious elements are integrated in nationalism, or consider nationalism as modernity's total replacement of religion have long been challenged in the literature on religion and nationalism.

We share the argument that has been broadly accepted in postcolonial literature that secularist and Eurocentric biases have shaped the view that nationalism replaced religion and became a distinctive category, as also highlighted by some contributors to this volume (e.g., Chapters 2, 4, 9, 10, and 13). Yet, while we accept this view, we also concur with Brubaker (2012, 16) that there remains the case that "the fundamental point of reference of nationalist politics is 'the nation,'" and that political claims are made in the name of the nation and its distinctive doctrine of sources of legitimacy and political authority. This is why Brubaker argues for approaching the two – religion and nationalism – as fundamentally different despite their discursive intertwining. We therefore argue that it is important to examine the impact of the fusion between religion and nationalism upon the state's ideological framing and its ensuing actions, because, in practice, it is the state that embodies the identity of the nation and acts on its behalf.

The term "fusion" of religion and nationalism that we use and that makes religious impact on state policies inevitable is similar to the term "intertwining" as defined by Brubaker (2012).[2] It describes a relationship between religion and nationalism in which religion simply becomes so interwoven to the extent that the two fuse. This takes place when the boundaries of religion and nationalism coincide or when religion supplies "myths, metaphors and symbols that are central to the discursive or iconic representation of the nation" (Brubaker 2012, 9). In many cases of fusion between religious claims and nationalism that we study in this volume, like Zionism and the Hindutva, the religious substance not only shapes and highlights the distinctiveness of the group's identity, history, and destiny (Smith 2008); the fusion

---

[1] For some reviews, see Beshara (2019); Cragun, Manning, and Fazzino (2017); Ebaugh (2002); Gorski (2000); Gorski and Altınordu (2008).

[2] Brubaker (2012) proposes four overlapping and non-exhaustive ways to study the relationship between religion and nationalism. In addition to the intertwining mentioned above, he suggests religion and nationalism as analogous phenomena – religion as an explanation of nationalism rather than an antithesis to it, and religious nationalism, which represents an alternative to secular nationalism.

of the two also provides the state with nationalism that integrates the vitality of foundational sacred texts, the assertions that the land is sacred (both in the political and religious sense), religio-national collective myths and symbols, and the very legitimation for state policies derived from religious claims embedded in this fusion.

At the same time, given the vast literature on the interactions, juxtapositions, and interlocking effects between religion and nationalism, we should address the question of what makes this intertwining or fusion different than other forms of interaction. This is particularly important in light of what we stated above – that we agree that all nationalisms have some sort of religious elements, roots, or traces. In this regard, narrowing this question to the inquiry posed by Brubaker (2012, 11) can help us: "What counts as religious message and imagery as opposed to religiously tinged or originally religious but subsequently secularized language and imagery?" This is a critical question, but one that is hard to address fully, because the answer, given the diverse historical contexts and multiple cases, often becomes a matter of interpretation influenced by power dynamics, including Western-centered intellectual and political predispositions and interests. Our answer goes to the heart of our concern and sidesteps the possible problematics of subjective interpretations: What counts as fusion is when religion and religious claims interact with nationalism in ways that are used to frame and/or legitimize the state's political ideologies, decisions, and governance. This is why, in our view, when it comes to the impact of religious claims on state politics, lumping all cases of nationalism together by arguing that "all nationalisms have religious influence" misses a potentially major theoretical input. It leads to overlooking cases in which religious claims or the invocation of religious text and interpretations have a vital hold on nationalism in ways that become apparent in framing state policies. A distinctive feature of the state in such cases, as detailed below, is *sacralizing politics embedded in religious claims and sacred religious texts*.

Thus, in many instances (particularly before the recent rise of populism in the US and some European countries), modern nationalisms have traces of religious-like influence on state policies – for example, in the US and Europe (e.g., Bellah 1998; Brubaker 2012; Gorski 2017). In other cases, the politics and political works of religion and religious claims come to play a major role in the state by, for example, legitimizing state ideologies, strategies, and policies, because religion *fuses* with nationalism as in Sri Lanka (DeVotta 2007), India (Kamat and Matthew 2003; Nigam 2006; Sarkar 2002), the former Yugoslavia (Perica 2002; Sells 1998), and Israel (Bishara 2005; Chapters 2 and 3 in this volume). This also applies to some states with regional stature, such as Iran (Chapter 10 in this volume; Moallem 2005) and Saudi Arabia (Chapter 11 in this volume; al-Rasheed 2014). The nuances of the political impact of religious claims in these (and other) sites are not put always into productive conversation with one another.

Witnessing the rise of this kind of sacralization in world politics, our substantive line of investigation is inquiring to what extent do religious claims, texts, and narrations regulate and legitimize state politics and shape state governance. To open the conversation, we take a comparative look at the contextualized role of religion and religious claims, analyze their impact on present hierarchies of power, and examine the resulting policies of ruling, control, and violent practices.

RELIGIOUS CLAIMS AND THE SACRALIZATION OF POLITICS

Our analysis seeks to examine how, through hegemonic nationalism, states invoke religious claims as being foundational for political and national claims in domestic and international politics, thus sacralizing the political. This sacralization bestows the certainty of religious sanctification even when invoked by nonreligious and secular actors. The emphasis on state policies in this regard is important because, as we show in this volume, states' reliance, often explicitly, on religious claims or texts for justifying and legitimizing contentious policies is on the rise, although it is rather the non-state actors that have occupied political attention and academic research.

The concept of sacralized politics has been almost exclusively reserved to secular politics in the sense of conferring religious-like forms and significances (but not religious legitimation) to the political. For example, Demerath (2007a, 66) defines sacralization as "the process by which the secular becomes sacred or other new forms of the sacred emerge, whether in matters of personal faith, institutional practice or political power. And sacralization may also occur gradually or suddenly, and may be sometimes temporary and occasionally reversible"; for example, sacralizing shared heritage in the form of "civil religion." Similarly, in his study of the relationship among totalitarianism, secular religion, and modernity, Gentile (2004, 327) defines sacralization of politics as "the formation of a religious dimension in politics that is distinct from, and autonomous from traditional religious institutions." This process happens all the time and becomes apparent when a political movement confers a sacred status on a political entity, such as the nation, the state, or the party (Gentile 2005). While Gentile studies the extreme manifestations of this process in totalitarian regimes, others discuss its prevalence in modern politics, including in democracies that developed their own "holy scriptures," such as the constitution and "prophets" in the form of founding fathers, foundational myths, and symbols (Augusteijn, Dassen, and Janse 2013; Beshara 2019; Burrin 1997). Similar definitions with a tinge of religious substance penetration into the process of sacralization are offered by scholars examining other cases such as Moallem (2005, 124), who defines sacralization in her study of Iranian politics as "the convergence of religious and political agendas." Similarly, examining the case of Turkey and the Justice and Development Party, Yabanci (2020, 95) shows that right-wing populism "spirals into sacralization of politics, particularly when populist actors fuse religious and nationalist appeals."

A Comparative Perspective on Religious Claims and Sacralized Politics 5

In his comprehensive work on religion and secularism, Beshara (2019), while tracing the process of sacralizing the political space – the space of the state and the statist values – alerts us that sacredness is not equivalent to religion and emphasizes that in these instances, sacralization (of secular values, institutions, or leaders) does not equate to religion:

> This applies to sacralizing individuals, institutions, or worldly values. Sanctification in itself does not produce an alternative worldly religion in this case. In addition, a minimum level of ritual worship is required .... As for the feelings of people towards the sanctity of the homeland or the sanctity of human life, as in some charters and constitutions, these are human characteristics, which bestow sacredness and elevation to some values. (Beshara 2019, 65)

It is precisely here that our intervention seeks to revert to the original meaning of religious sacralization and investigate how religious claims confer sacredness, in this original sense, to the policies of states and how they bring to the forefront the invocation of religious legitimation of such policies. Our emphasis on sacralization, by which we mean religious legitimation or framing, of official *state* policies is an effort to contribute to highlighting the dangerous impact of sacralization on national and international politics. Indeed, often when religious legitimation of state policies is examined, one finds either references to rhetoric that has historically religious traces but is now fully secularized – at least for its "consumers" – or openly religious legitimation efforts led by social or religious organizations that are acting in non-governmental capacities outside the state's official domain.

When religion is discussed as a force of legitimating social power, it has often been assumed that it does so as "a sphere of activity where efforts are deliberately made to influence, manipulate, and control people's thoughts, feelings, and actions in accordance with various religious values" (Beckford 2017, 58) but in the social and not official sphere by religious groups. The direct actions of religious groups, particularly among the religious right, point to another way of political influence. This is done through political activities such as lobbying, legislative efforts, intervention in public discourse, and so on. Indeed, after reviewing the literature, Billings and Scott (1994, 178) conclude that "there is little doubt that religious activism currently influences the legitimacy of certain policies, the shape of constituencies and coalitions, levels of participation, cultural climates, and the social definitions of public and private spheres in the United States." This activism seeks to influence public policy on related issues such as abortion, pornography, and violence in the media. In this sense, therefore, religion as a force of legitimation is mainly a reference to religious activists seeking to have their competing moral claims influence the public sphere (Gorski 2017).

Bellah (1987) maintains that religion and politics, both public and sacred, often needed each other for legitimation. In some cases, historically, "the political institution needed ideological justification and the assurance that its rule was legitimate or at least preferable to the alternatives from the church" (Bellah 1987, 89). Taking Japan and the US as his case studies, he argues that in many contemporary societies, this mutual legitimation is no longer effective. In both cases, religion and politics were privatized and secularized and therefore lost their ability to provide legitimacy. Thus, religion influenced public life in the US by using religious but nonsectarian discourse, through social movements motivated by moral convictions. He concludes that religious influence in the US or "the religious superstructure of the American Republic ... has been provided mainly by the religious community itself entirely outside of any formal political structure" (Bellah 1987, 197). This religious superstructure finds numerous ways to influence domestic policies, internal politics, and international policies. Riis (1998) provides a very similar European perspective in which the religious legitimation of states and their rulers is confined to European history. In recent history, when churches in Western Europe withdrew from the political space altogether, they tried to exert influence on issues related to the private sphere such as laws on divorce and abortion. The main sphere of visibility for religion in politics is within the private space, by the church itself. But even these attempts to influence policies do not often meet with much success, as demonstrated by the recent overturning of the long-standing prohibition on abortion in Ireland (Earner-Byrne and Urquhart 2018).

Gorski (2017) decries that some in the religious right in America want to "make America Christian again" (or at least it should be governed by Christians) out of the belief that America was founded as a Christian country. But this is an ideology of one religious group, not even a political or governing party (notwithstanding its influence and intimate political relationships with power centers in the US and elsewhere). It is not a state ideology.[3]

One area that has attracted considerable attention in the study of religious legitimation and justification of political behavior is political violence. But, with few noticeable exceptions in the field (such as Demerath 2007b; Perica 2002; Sells 1998; van der Veer 1994; and to a lesser extent Hall 2013[4]), the focus has been on non-state actors. For example, in the forty chapters of *The Oxford Handbook on Religion and Violence* (Juergensmeyer, Kitts, and Jerryson 2013), not much attention is paid to state religious legitimation of violence. Similarly, major scholars in the field have given little attention to religiously based state violence (see, for example, the works of Appleby 2000; Hoffman 2006; Jones and Smith 2014; Juergensmeyer 2003; Shah, Stepan, and Toft 2012; Stern 2004), even though many share the view pointed out by

---

[3] Gorski (2017) believes that the American democracy's goal of balancing unity and diversity can be achieved by dedication to "a civic unity" based on the ideals of "liberty," "equality," "union," and the "general welfare." This unity, he argues, should be based on the shared status of American citizenship. He then says that civic unity is not based on religious identities, although it need not conflict with them. Gorski is not even talking about religious values but rather of values of American citizenship based on the secular ideals he discusses.

[4] Hall (2013) had to go back to the Crusaders to demonstrate religiously legitimated state violence, but he also discusses the role of religion in colonization policies.

A Comparative Perspective on Religious Claims and Sacralized Politics

Toft (2012) that religiously motivated political violence can be more deadly and intractable.[5]

Both Lusthaus (2011) and Omar (2015) decry the neglect of state-sponsored violence when examining the religion and violence nexus, particularly by major scholars in the field. Each of the above researchers provides three examples of state violence with religious foundations. Omar examines three convincing cases: Bosnia-Herzegovina (1992–95); South Africa (1948–94); and the Gujarat state of India (2002). And Lusthaus examines Israel, Iran, and the US. While engaging with the particular arguments of each paper is beyond the scope of this chapter, the effort to refocus some attention on state violence is a welcome effort.[6]

Abulof (2014, 2016), who studies both Zionism and the concept of legitimacy, argues that Zionism has increasingly been using religion for the political legitimation of the (Jewish) state itself. Religious claims to legitimatize the very establishment and existence of the state fit well with the theme of this volume and with the chapters that examine similar cases. Like Aboluf, some chapters in this volume examine the roots and workings of the legitimation process, but we go further to examine how this legitimation in Zionism and other cases inevitably leads to a broad range of domestic governance and regional policies.

THE WORKINGS OF RELIGIOUSLY FRAMED SACRALIZED POLITICS

We do not claim that the religious discourse used in the process of sacralizing politics is simply a pretext or a ploy for achieving social and political goals, even if in some cases it might be. Furthermore, we maintain that the process of sacralizing politics is not considerably affected by whether religious claims represent sincere commitment emanating from religious convictions or is employed for purposes of political manipulation. Like Peter van der Veer (1994), in his study of religious nationalism in India, we maintain that the discourse as well as the use of religious claims in politics become constitutive and a defining feature of the political identity. Obviously, such discourse and its constituted identity enter a mutually reinforcing process. The performativity of the process itself, in the sense that it turns into a "discursive practice that enacts or produces that which it names," creates political realities and promotes discourses that become part of social consensus (Butler 1993,

---

[5] In studying the Israeli context, specifically the violence of "Price Tag" vigilantism, arrests of Palestinian children, and what she defines as the occupation of the senses, Shalhoub-Kevorkian (2015, 2017) suggests that state violence is legitimized by religious claims of biblical rights and chosenness.

[6] For example, in the Iranian case, Lusthaus (2011) fails to connect any of his general arguments about Islam to one single action undertaken by the Iranian state; and in the case of the US, the connection he makes to religiously legitimated state violence is based on rhetoric that can be traced to remote religious roots such as the term "crusade" or the term "axis of evil." Although important to investigate such rhetoric, it should be noted that the state actors who use it do not justify it with religious references, nor do the recipients of such rhetoric – the citizens – necessarily recognize it as religious.

13). Following Butler (1993, 13), we emphasize the extent to which the discourse gains "the authority to bring about what it names through citing the conventions of authority," considering that in this case it is religious authority, such as the biblical, that is at play. The various chapters show that this religious authority can be employed to justify state domination, as in the cases of India or Israel, or to resist domestic domination and Western intervention, as in Iran under the shah, or to defy military occupation.[7]

In making the claim that some forms of the interaction between religion and nationalism lead to sacralization of politics, we are aware of and agree with the body of research that criticizes the total separation between religion and nationalism and that underscores nationalism's underlying religious components (Asad 1993, 2003; Friedland and Moss 2016; Norris and Inglehart 2010). Indeed this volume's chapters share this view, and some contributors (e.g., Chapters 2, 4, 10, and 13) elaborate on why in the cases they study it is important to keep this perspective in mind. Yet there are cases of nationalism or national movements that represent or seek to create a full fusion of nationalism and religion, such as Zionism, the Hindutva, and Sinhalese Buddhist nationalism. The fact that all nationalisms have some sort of underlying religious components that were integrated into them during different historical processes should not blind us to the variance in the extent to which these components influence politics in each case, or to the fundamentally different types of nationalism in which religion or religious claims are not simply residues of a historical process, but are defining features of nationalism itself.

Religiously based sacralization of politics (hereafter sacralized politics) is the practice of appealing to religious claims, religious text, or religious beliefs to justify and legitimize policies, in any area, explicitly or in coded manner, regardless of the political actors' religious or secular worldview. In its various forms of political encounter with national, religious, or ethnic groups in the same homeland, the sacralization of politics serves to sanction the power of one group and establish not only its exclusive sovereignty (even in multiethnic states) but also its exclusive political authority and belonging to a homeland. The sacralization of politics helps understand the way religious or ethnic affiliations become a racialized marker of difference and not a signifier of a particular theological interpretation or just cultural difference. It creates a matrix of power within which political life can be lived or articulated through racialized religiously based national or ethnic affiliation, and therefore it constructs discriminatory practices that can constitute an identity of

---

[7] Indeed, the literature has extensively studied the "double function" of religion as a means of protest and galvanizer of liberation or as an apologetic force for an unjust status quo or even an instigator of communal violence (Appleby 2000; Berger 1967; Billings and Scott 1994). Turner (1991, 226) notes that "[o]n a global scale ... religion often assumes renewed vitality as the cultural medium of political protest against internal colonialism by subnational cultures or against external colonialism by subordinated nationalism."

A Comparative Perspective on Religious Claims and Sacralized Politics 9

privilege and the innumerable tangible and intangible advantages that can then flow from it.

The deployment of racialized discourses of sacredness and its religious distinctions are there to reaffirm the politics of religious exclusivity. Sacralized politics, we argue, depends upon particular racialized narrations that frame some as Others, confining them in spaces of difference – legally, culturally, and politically. Racialization, in this case, is an ongoing process reflected in structural relations of power, producing and maintaining the self and the Other – be it the non-Jew, non-Hindu, etc. – whose political rights can then be framed as violatable. Revealing the racialized contours of the sacralized politics and its governance and management can also show how resistance to it becomes inevitable.

Sacralization operates politically through numerous modes. To trace the matrix of power that sacralization of politics mobilizes, and when looking comparatively at the various case studies examined in this volume, we point to three main (among other) modes of sacralization's profound impact on politics. The first operates through **managing consciousness, including the construction of self-identity in relation to others;** the second, through **territoriality and the politics of land;** and the third via political governance, **using violence and a necropolitical regime of control.** While each mode can operate separately, all operate through mutual reinforcement and each with elements of sacredness, resulting in an emergent power structure that is self-sustaining and resistant to change. In what follows, we briefly describe the workings of each mode.

1. **Managing consciousness and the construction of self-identity in relation to others.** We here refer to the construction of politically and ideologically motivated imagination, embedded in religious claims to maintain the "purity" of the nation and its culture (see, for example, Chapters 4, 7, 8, and 9 in this volume), its religiously justified perception of "chosenness," its fulfilling the word of the Deity, or using religious texts to legitimize political acts – even if by secular agents. Such processes engage communities and nations in dynamics that not only rationalize and legitimate prejudiced ideologies that support privileges for one's own group vis-à-vis others, but also rationalize constructing a collective self that internalizes supremacy and exclusivity – at a minimum to justify the privileges endorsed by the sacred – and makes it commonly narrated and socially shared.

   Narrations of exclusivity founded on sacralized accounts function to produce affects, patterns of acting, and modes of thinking that consolidate a collective self-perception of being "chosen." Narrating exclusivity to construct the self in relation to the Other can be found in the case of the Hindutva in India, for example. As discussed in Chapter 7, the Hindutva, as apparent in the language, writings, and rhetorical passion used by Savarkar, not only makes Hindu and Indian synonymous, it also aims to construct Muslims as seeking to destroy the Hindu faith, and argues that non-Hindus may stay in the country only if they accept being subordinated, as non-deserving Others. Building an entire narration that constructs the sacred Hindu body as having been injured by non-Hindus, Hindutva accused Muslims of violence, including demolishing Hindu temples, killing cows (which are sacred to Hindus), abducting and raping Hindu women, and so on. This sensational narration against Muslims, aimed at searing the public consciousness and legitimizing racialized ideologies, positions the Hindu as superior and the Muslim as inferior. Hence, performativities of sacralized politics are not only about acting, speaking, using sacred scripts, and participating as having intrinsically been born with power. Such performativities are also about using sacralized politics to reproduce dominance and dominant structures.

In much the same way as supremacy comes to define the settler colonial, or as Memmi (1991, 56) maintains that "[t]he colonial situation manufactures colonialists, just as it manufactures the colonized"[8] – supremacy can come to define the groups, ideologies, or powers that sacralize politics to govern, as described in this volume in the cases of the Hindutva in India, Sinhalese Buddhist nationalism in Sri Lanka, and Zionism in Israel/Palestine. This can help explain how and why individuals, communities, and states maintain a sense or even entrenched conviction of "chosenness" and, by definition, of entitlement to privileges and superiority over others.

The processes of narrating exclusivity and accumulating privileges develop with time and come to affect the individual and collective selves, as well as the belief system. As Lloyd's Chapter 12 on Northern Ireland shows in reference to Ulster's Unionists, "What begins then as no more than 'an identification with British social and political institutions' devolves into a constitutive claim to what Edward Said termed positional superiority."

In this sense, managing and regulating consciousness affects both groups, the dominant and the dominated. Construction of superior rights with the help of religious claims leads to portraying the dominated, their collective voice, and their struggle in ways that serve the self-perceived moral superiority of the dominant (such as when they claim that Others are violent, savage, or terrorist) and their political superiority. This process is encouraged when the larger global politics is indifferent or even supportive. The dominant tries to manage and regulate the mode of thinking, the belief systems, the symbols, and even the existence and destiny of the dominated in such a way that they all become subordinated to a supreme, divine narrative.

Narrating exclusivity becomes a powerful political tool, including in land and territorial policies, as described next. But it is worth noting that the authority of narratives – religious or otherwise – becomes codes for power

---

[8] For the Israeli context, see Rouhana and Sabbagh-Khoury (2006).

A Comparative Perspective on Religious Claims and Sacralized Politics

politics. As Said (1993, xiii) argues, in many cases where the conflict is over land, "when it came to who owned the land, who had the right to settle and work on it, who kept it going, who won it back, and who plans its future – these issues were reflected, contested, and even for a time decided in narrative."

2. **Territoriality and sacralizing land.** In this regard, we discern two related routes that characterize most cases of sacralized state territorial politics and that have evident consequences for instigating interstate and intrastate conflicts. The first is claiming the right to undertake territorial expansion at the expense of other nations in the name of a religious text or tradition. The second, with potent implications for intergroup relations within a state (whether ethnic, religious, racial, or lingual groups), is endowing the land with some sort of sacredness. In the first route, states can seek territorial expansion on religiously based claims. Perica (Chapter 9) describes in detail how in the 1980s the Serbian nationalist elites assisted by the Serbian Orthodox Church portrayed Kosovo as the medieval seat of the Serbian Church with all its historic monuments leading to constructing it – consciously imitating Zionism – as "Serbian Jerusalem." The territorial expansion into Kosovo, or the "return" to Kosovo, the sacred land, is a cornerstone of religiously based Serbian nationalist claims. The case of Israel's expansion into the West Bank (and for some, the case of Zionism itself even prior to Israel's establishment) is a manifest case of territorial claims based on religious entitlements founded on a religious text. The claim of exclusive sovereignty over Jerusalem, east and west, as well as the claim that the West Bank – Judea and Samaria of the biblical text – are lands that belong to the entire Jewish people (not to Israeli citizens, 26 percent of whom are not Jewish, and not only to Jewish citizens of Israel but to Jews worldwide) is perhaps one of the most blatant present-day examples of claiming territorial expansion through settler-colonial machinery, legitimized manifestly on the basis of a religious text. Interestingly, as Rouhana argues in his Chapter 3, this explicit claim by "secularists" is now a last resort to obscure the settler-colonial in Zionism. In both cases – the Serbian and the Zionist – pursuing the religiously constructed claims is clearly conflict provoking.

The second route of territorial politics is sacralizing land. States employ such claims not only for land seizure and territorial expansion, but also for excluding fellow citizens – ethnic, national, or religious groups – on the grounds that the land, as being sacred for the privileged group based on religious scripture, belongs to that group only. Sacralized ownership over land secures the dominance and exclusivity of one group over another. Once the land gains the status of sacredness, or when the nation claiming the land sacralizes the claim by relying on religious rhetoric, the way is open to regarding others, including fellow citizens, as strangers, outsiders, foreigners, "not one of us," invaders, and even as the embodiment or reincarnation of "past invaders." As several chapters in this volume describe, this route operates on different levels of explicitness and is employed by ideologies for which religious claims play a central role in their belief systems, with natural differences among various factions within each ideology.[9]

We here describe one of the most extreme manifestations of this route of sacralizing the land, namely, rendering native fellow citizens as invaders or foreigners to the land. We choose to describe briefly how the four state-ruling ideologies in the multiethnic/multinational states discussed in this volume employ this route. The similarity in this regard among the four cases – Hindutva, Serbian Orthodox nationalism, Zionism, and Sinhalese Buddhist nationalism – is striking. In all four cases, fellow citizens who are native to the land are collectively considered as invaders or traitors if they don't accept the exclusive ideology that renders them unequal, inferior, or outsiders based on religiously grounded claims.

In the Serbian case, as Sells (1998) explains, the Muslims – Bosniaks and Albanians – were constructed through Christoslavism, the Serb religious national ideology that propagates "the belief that Slavs are Christians by nature and that any conversion from Christianity is a betrayal of the Slavic race." Thus, Slavic Muslims could no longer claim to be Slavic; in the Serbian social construction, they became the embodiment of the Turkish conqueror – the dreaded historic invaders. They were portrayed as the direct successors of the Ottoman invaders and therefore shared in the Ottoman guilt, especially for the murder of Prince Lazar and other "martyrs" of the 1389 Battle of Kosovo, which brought about the breakup of the medieval Serbian Kingdom.

In India, similarly, the sacralization of land is integral to constructing the Muslims and Christians as invaders. As Sarkar demonstrates in this volume, for the Hindutva, the land of India is "marked by rivers and mountains that have been mentioned in ancient Hindu holy texts. ... it is territory made sacred through its association with Hindu cosmogony and mythology." These holy texts and the religion it represents originated in India unlike other religions, and based on this logic, India belongs to those whose religion is indigenous to it. In this construction, Hindus are viewed as the "native" inhabitants and the Muslims, albeit native born, as invaders (see also Hasan 2002; Metcalf 1995). The "foreignness" and "inauthenticity" of the Muslim invaders was outlined in this narrative.

In Sri Lanka, the view propagated by Sinhalese Buddhist nationalism that "This is a Sinhala Buddhist country" or "the country belongs to the Sinhalese" (see Tambiah 1992; DeVotta 2007) is similarly based on the *Mahavamsa* (*Great*

---

[9] Obviously, land is also sacralized (in the secular meaning of the term as described above) as a national endowment. Such endowment, unlike the case of the religious sacralization of land, can be as exclusive or inclusive as the particular nationalism itself and operates through religious-like but not religious zeal.

Chronicle), a historical poem that documents events that date from the sixth century BC but was arguably compiled in the sixth century AD by Buddhist monks. While not a religious text, it covers the history of Buddhist religion in Sri Lanka. Based on the *Mahavamsa*, Sri Lanka is the island of the Sinhalese that is ennobled to preserve and propagate Buddhism. In this perception, others who came later – read non-Sinhalese – "invaded" the land. The explicit claim of Sinhalese Buddhist supremacy (also constitutionalized) designates all others as merely tolerated in the land of the Sinhalese.

In the case of Zionism, this process was two-sided, because the Zionist history in Palestine is relatively recent. So the process necessitated both the indigenization of the waves of settlers who came to Palestine from outside it, and the deindigenization of its native inhabitants. Both sides of this process are justified based on biblical claims that integrate the sacred with settler-colonial nationalism. It is precisely based on these claims that Jews wherever they live in the world, whether citizens or not, are considered natives with a birthright to the land, while the native Palestinians are framed as invaders, foreigners, intruders, infiltrators – the term varies depending on the historical and political context and the Zionist faction (see Rouhana 2015).[10]

Once land is considered through the lens of religiously based claims, many land-related policies, such as land ownership, land use, zoning, planning, and spatial policies that aim at evicting the "foreigners" or "invaders," come under the influence of sacralized hierarchies of power. (For how this works in Israel, for example, see Amara 2013; Forman and Kedar 2004; Jabareen 2017; Yiftachel 2006.)

3. **Using violence and a necropolitical regime of control.** The third mode of sacralization operates through political governance, including the use of violence and necropolitics (Mbembe 2003) that can take multiple expressions. When religious claims are integrated into the nationalism of the dominant group in a multiethnic state, it opens the door for religiously based legitimation for ethnic nationalism and other exclusionary ideologies and forms of governance. The political governance becomes the expression of discriminatory ideologies. Ethnic and religious nationalism, for example, can play the destructive role of promoting an ethnically exclusive state, and the religious claims can play a double purpose – not only to increase the extent of exclusivity, but also to provide legitimation for such exclusion (usually translated into political domination) and means of violence. These means can take extreme forms, precisely because of the religious legitimation.

Political governance, as we argue here, is reflected in the inbuilt discrimination and unequal citizenship and the domination system that it requires, and

---

[10] Although representative of Zionism in general, where this is clearest is in rabbinic discourse of the "goy" as possessing a different ontological and moral status than Jews. See Ophir and Rosen-Zvi (2018).

in a biopolitical order reflected in demographic policies and surveillance regime. It is expressed in multiple governing models, the most obvious being the ethnic state, sometimes referred to as ethnocracy (Chapter 8 in this volume; Yiftachel 2006), or in the flawed model developed by Zionist scholars known as "ethnic democracy."[11]

The terms "Sinhala Buddhist country," "state of the Hindus," "Jewish state" or "state of the Jewish people," "a Protestant state for a Protestant people" (in Northern Ireland prior to the Good Friday Agreement), "Greater Serbia," or "India as the sacred territory for the Hindu" (and equating Indian with Hindu) are manifestations of exclusively ethnic regimes of governance with religiously based legitimations that by definition are conflict instigating. Such states can claim to be democracies or enact governance that has the "formal" trappings of democracy, often translated to the tyranny of the majority, but this governance is in fundamental contradiction with democratic values and equal citizenship. In such regimes, ethnic privileges are encoded both in the official constitutional and legal systems and in socially sanctioned discriminatory practices, particularly on issues required for perpetuating ethnic domination such as state identity, citizenship and immigration laws, land control, and status of language (see Chapter 8 in this volume; Sultany 2017).

Regimes that legitimate domination, supremacy converted to ethnic privileges, and exclusion on the basis of sacralized politics are racialized systems. Governmentality performing sacralized racialities operates through various forms of violence that are legitimated on the basis of religious claims and maintains a system of ethnic control or expansion. The most dangerous forms of violence are those embedded in biopolitical and necropolitical arithmetic (Mbembe 2003) and statistics that "count" and "calculate" the sacred against "disposable" Others, defining those perceived as tolerated inhabitants, dangerous Others, or a demographic threat.

As Marvin and Ingle (1996, 1999) put it, both religion and nationalism have the potential to organize "killing energy" and promote blood sacrifice. A fusion of the two is thus likely to generate greater violence and willingness on behalf of individuals to sacrifice themselves in the name of the collective. In Serbia, for example, violence against the Bosniaks was not only nationally motivated but was religiously motivated and legitimated (Sells 1998) – at least in popular religion[12] (or what Appleby (2000) calls weak religion and Chuman (2006) calls "thick" religion).

---

[11] The model was developed by Sammy Smooha (1997) and gained popularity in Israeli academia but was also challenged by many scholars for justifying accumulated ethnic privileges and for being nondemocratic (see, among others, Bishara 1995; Ghanem, Rouhana, and Yiftachel 1998; Jamal 2002; Rouhana 1997).

[12] According to Michael Sells (1998, 89–90), "survivors of concentration camps report that during torture sessions or when they begged for water, they were made to sing Serbian religious nationalist songs, reworded to reflect the contemporary conflict."

A Comparative Perspective on Religious Claims and Sacralized Politics 15

Other social mores emerge, such as a sense of demographic threat (also shared by political class), stigmatizing disapproval of mixed marriages, control of reproductive capacity,[13] and anxieties about sexual interaction with members of excluded groups – particularly by women in the superior group – articulated and behaviorally expressed depending on the particular context. While such mores are common in other ethnic regimes, they become particularly venomous when they are justified on religious bases and supported by religious concerns. This moves the public discourse about them away from the social and political sphere to the considerations of purity and contamination as defined by the religious (see Chapters 7 and 8).

What should be kept in mind, as most of the contributions in this volume point out, is that political governance institutionalizes and constitutionalizes the ethnic privileges, with some differences determined by the particular domestic context and global politics of tolerance. The institutionalization of privileges produces new rationalities, technologies of control, as well as specific subjectivities that are conducive to this type of governance.

This volume explores how and to what extent religiously based claims interact with nationalism and sacralize politics in this particular sense. Our central concern is to focus on when and how religion interacts or fuses with nationalism in ways that are used to legitimize political actions, inactions, decisions, and governance. The various contributors delve into the details of each case and examine historical, domestic, and global factors that affect such sacralization. The volume looks at ways in which explicit invocation of religion and religious claims influence state domestic and international policies, regime legitimization, conflict dynamics, discourses on citizenship rights in multiethnic states, constructing oneself and the Other, legitimation of violence, territorial expansion, and state identity. By offering an interdisciplinary comparative approach to the challenges raised when religion and nationalism conflate in various ways, contributors pay particular attention to the religiously framed sacralization of politics across different political contexts and geographies, as the following chapter summaries demonstrate.

***

In "Religion and Nationalism in the Jewish and Zionist Context," Amnon Raz-Krakotzkin maintains the centrality of the political-theological aspect in defining and forming the Israeli state, positing that it is the theological with its apocalyptic dimension that stands at the heart of the definition of Israel as a Jewish state. He meticulously shows how Zionism is not simply a national identity supported by religious claims and argues that, "what makes the Zionist theological perspective unique ... is its direct relation to the Jewish-Christian messianic images and to the biblical images of Palestine." Thus, Raz-Krakotzkin argues that what makes the

---

[13] For example, the Israeli government has introduced over the years numerous reproductive measures to support the state's efforts to be a Jewish state (Kanaaneh 2002; Nahman 2013; Portuguese 1998).

Israeli case stand out is the relationship between messianism (and its political interpretations) and nationalism. The chapter explains how Western secularization of nationalism – including its colonial history and its defining characteristics of redemption and chosenness – was the context within which Zionism emerged and by which it was shaped. Consequently, Zionism – the nationalization of the Jews – has the inherent dimension of settler colonialism that characterizes other Western nationalisms.

Zionism was founded on the European secularist distinction between nation and religion, but the perception of the nation (allegedly secular) was deeply rooted in the theological, and based on an interpretation of the concept of redemption as political in the modern, Western, sense of the word. While Zionist secularism excluded God and religious dogma from its discourse (although God's promise has been used to legitimize Zionism), nationalism incorporated the religious-messianic conceptions, particularly transforming the messianic longing for redemption into a (secular-nationalist) political project. This is why Raz-Krakotzkin coined the saying that summarizes the (secular) Zionist outlook as being "God does not exist, but he promised us the Land" and why, in his view, the secular and the religious cannot be disentangled in Zionism (see also Chapter 3). While the Bible was secularized and defined as national, the Talmud was defined as "religious" and was therefore rejected by (secular) Zionism, in a way reproducing "the Christian fundamental ambivalence toward traditional Judaism and, by extension, the Jews."

Raz-Krakotzkin emphasizes that the idea of the modern political restoration of the Jews as a Western vision was first developed by Christian millenarians in the seventeenth century, as they believed that a precondition for the messianic scenario of the Second Coming was the return of the Jews to the Holy Land. It is in this context that the term "the state of Israel" first appeared, interestingly at the same period that the concept of the "state" became central to philosophical discussions. Thus Zionism, as the secularization of the Jews, is a realization of Christian millenarian perception – a Jewish secular realization of a Christian theological concept.

In **"Religious Claims and Nationalism in Zionism: Obscuring Settler Colonialism," Nadim Rouhana** examines how nationalism, religious claims, and settler colonialism enmesh within Zionism and how their interaction played a major role in sidelining or obfuscating settler colonialism as an appropriate frame of analysis for Zionism's encounter with the Palestinians. Anchoring the analysis in a settler-colonial framework, Rouhana first demonstrates why settler colonialism, an obvious framework for analyzing and understanding the unfolding of the Zionist project in Palestine, was sidelined in Israeli political and academic discourse.

While accepting the argument that nationalism and religion are neither totally separable nor mutually exclusive, Rouhana maintains that the intertwining of the two in Zionism is of a fundamentally different nature in the sense that religious claims are not only pervasively present in Zionism but also indispensable for

A Comparative Perspective on Religious Claims and Sacralized Politics 17

legitimizing the project among Zionists and the international community. This is so, because for Zionism, which is in essence the nationalization of a biblical story (or even further, as Raz-Krakotzin argues in Chapter 2, the nationalization of messianism), the overlap between religion and nationalism is inevitably total (Bishara 2005). Thus, while many scholars consider that up until the early 1970s, Zionism was a secular ideology, in truth, it was never so. Zionism always resorted to the biblical narrative to legitimize its project in Palestine. Furthermore, the nationalization of biblical narrative is inevitably settler colonial, regardless of whatever justification, legitimation, or intentions the settlers put forth. Therefore, while highlighting the characteristics of Zionism as a national movement, Rouhana argues that it is explicitly settler-colonial nationalism. However, due to global forces, the modern history of the European Jewish communities, and the power of the biblical narrative particularly in the West,[14] the essential settler-colonial nature of Zionism was obscured.

Finally, Rouhana argues that while secularization was possible in other settler-colonial contexts such as South Africa, Northern Ireland, and North America, it is impossible to achieve secularization within a Zionist regime in Palestine (although Rouhana argues it would have been possible to achieve secularization in other colonies considered by Zionism, such as Uganda). Rather, for secularization and democratization to take place, Israel has to recognize the settler-colonial reality of the Zionist project, a recognition that will make it possible to free Israeli Jewish nationalism from religionism and work toward decolonization.

In "**On the Uses and Abuses of Tradition: Zionist Theopolitics and Jewish Tradition,**" **Yaacov Yadgar** argues that the binary of "secular-religious" is a misleading foundational construction that makes it possible to endow the "Western, Protestant-in-outlook nation-state" with dominance and rationality as the site of secularism in this binary. This binary has historically been used by Zionism to construct itself as a secular ideology. Accordingly, Zionism then reimagines Jewish identity as secular and conceives of its national project of establishing the state of the Jews as "rebelling" against its religious members. In the process, as Zionism was used to establish a national project, Jewish identity was emptied of positive meaning. The limitation of this secularism is evident in the fact that neither Israel nor Zionism has a path for joining the nation "in the name of which it exercises its sovereignty" – that is, of course, the Jewish people, not the Israeli nation – except by the religious route. At the same time, because Israel's raison d'être as a Jewish state depends on having a Jewish majority, the question of inclusion and exclusion into the larger Jewish group that the state (with the "secular" worldview) represents is under the control of Orthodox rabbinical authorities – breaking with principles of liberal democracies.

---

[14] Israel could also have pointed to the UN General Assembly's partition of Palestine resolution from 1947 as a source of legitimacy (though not as a settler-colonial project).

Yadgar reveals how the division of labor justified as a "compromise" between the secular and the religious portrays the secular as allegedly being "forced" to concede to the demands of the religious. He reveals how the

> murky yet persistent sense of a fundamental distinction between matters that are secular and of-the-state's and matters that are religious and not-of-the-state's, which dominates the political (and, to a large degree also the social-scientific) discourse in Israel, allows the state to act on a racial logic of belonging and Otherness, while celebrating itself as democratic, liberal, and enlightened (as is "naturally expected" from a secular, or at least "not-religious" entity).

Therefore, the logic of the Israeli state, a logic embedded in secular ideology of the nation-state, is dependent on Jews comprising the majority of its population, which is racial at root.

Yadgar believes that Zionism failed or is unwilling to define a national identity that is independent of Jewish religion, which inevitably makes the state's – read the secular – definition of Jewish politics racial and exclusionary. He argues that the claim of fusion between religion and nationalism in the Israeli case emanates from a secularist epistemology, but he doesn't offer any suggestions for an alternative identity that is independent of religion or how such an identity can pose an alternative to the claim of total fusion between religion and nationalism.

In **"The Relations between the Nationalization of Israel's Politics and the Religionization of Its Military, 1948–2016," Yagil Levy** examines the process of rising religionization in the Israeli military following (but not necessarily caused by) the increased conscription of religious soldiers. Rising religionization is expressed in the military's ethics, culture, symbols, and conduct. Levy identifies four stages in the relationship between the religionization of the Israeli military and the country's politics. The first stage, which extends from 1948 when Israel was established until the 1967 War, corresponds to the period known as the period of secular Zionism. Levy argues that the idea was to shape the military as a secular organization, but the integration of religious soldiers in mixed units introduced observance of religious dietary laws and observance of the Jewish Sabbath and holy days.

In the second stage, after the 1967 War and the occupation of the West Bank (including Jerusalem) and Gaza, an ethno-national religionization process started to penetrate Israeli politics. During this stage, the renewed encounter with historically religious sites in the Occupied Territories increased identification with religious traditions and the power of religious nationalism. Levy calls the third stage, in the 1980s–1990s, "denationalization," because "weakened national values such as solidarity, patriotism, and localism" were eclipsed by the rise of the market economy, liberal discourse, and values of individualism, achievement, and consumerism. The military witnessed a decline in the motivation of its backbone of secular middle-class recruits. Thus, what Levy calls the "denationalization of politics" may have paradoxically led to the religionization of the military by opening up new opportunities of social mobility and expression of religious values for religious youth through the military, resulting in "a new version of the fusion between religion and nationalism." This paved the way for the fourth stage – "religionization of nationalism" in the 2000s.

Levy demonstrates how the rise in religious values in Israeli society was influenced by major developments related to the conflict with the Palestinians (the occupation of the West Bank and Gaza, the First and Second Intifadas, etc.), how global changes and domestic liberalization changed the motivation for army service, and how those factors contributed to changing the face of the military, with its incorporation of the society's religionization as an integral process.

In "**Sacralized Politics: The Case of Occupied East Jerusalem,**" Nadera Shalhoub-Kevorkian investigates the intertwining between religious claims and nationalism as evidenced in the Israeli settler-colonial regime of governance in occupied East Jerusalem (oEJ). She looks at the political work of the religio-nationalist modes of colonial governance performed by both global and local power holders and exposes expressions of theologized supremacy that stands at the core of land and life dispossession. Invoking two sets of theorization, settler colonialism and Foucault's theorization on governance, the author focuses on the intensification of violence that took place in oEJ from 2014 to 2019. In examining the authorization of state and non-state violence as a form of sacralized politics, the chapter looks closely at three sites within the colonized space of oEJ: state law and legal practices; "non-state" "Price Tag" (*Tag Mehir* in Hebrew) vigilante attacks; and state-sponsored incursions into the sensory and aesthetic experience of the colonized – what the author has elsewhere defined as the "occupation of the senses."

In discussing globalized sacralization, the chapter also addresses the Trump administration's policies and spotlights the ethno-religious exclusivist claims embodied in the US government support for Israel's position on Jerusalem. In doing so, the author quotes the remarks of the US ambassador to Israel, who stated that his country "recognized the unbreakable, historical truthful connection between the Jewish people and the city of Jerusalem." The adoption of a Zionist religious narrative regarding the history of the land in Friedman's remarks, as Shalhoub-Kevorkian claimed: "is presupposed by the historical uprootedness of the Palestinians and the denial of their historical roots and collective rights."

The story of oEJ, as exposed in the political and violent work of religious claims and nationalism, reveals the Israeli violence against Palestinian bodies, lives, land, and senses as a colonial story designed to create, govern, transform, and construct the colonized as a racialized Other. By exposing the various modalities of violence apparent in the ongoing Judaization of Jerusalem, Shalhoub-Kevorkian demonstrates how the sacralized politics is essential in the violent governance of the Palestinian body and space, and in turn, the maintenance and reproduction of racialized Zionist politics.

In "Hindutva: The Dominant Face of Religious Nationalism in India," Tanika Sarkar shows how Hindu nationalist ideology blurs the distinction between religion and state politics. Religious sentiments, she argues, are subsumed into the national and cultural discourse to the extent that for many contemporary Hindus, nationalism has overtaken the function of faith as a perspective through which to understand the world. She traces the current hospitable space in India for Hindu religious nationalism to the cultural nationalism in the late nineteenth century among both Hindus and Muslims that emerged in defense of self and identity against colonial cultural values. From its birth, she argues, the twentieth century anti-colonial nationalism (within both the Hindu and Muslim communities) used religious appeals heavily. Indeed, Hindu nationalism founded itself on exclusive claims that combined its recent resistance to colonialism with earlier resistance to Muslim rulers in the distant medieval past. Since then, Sarkar argues, nationalism and faith have never bifurcated completely, and exclusivity became a defining feature of Hindu nationalism. The late nineteenth-century Hindu-invented Goddess of the Motherland/Nation is now worshipped with adoration; the Goddess personifies the country as a Hindu divinity, to the exclusion of Muslims and Christians.[15] Sarkar traces the anti-Muslim violence to what she calls "the primary ingredients of the Hindutva ideological apparatus" and describes in some detail how the apparatus is used to incite communal violence against Muslims and Christians and justify it on a religious basis in the service of extreme Hindu nationalist goals.

Interestingly, Sarkar discusses the role played by the colonial power in creating this state of affairs with the 1920 colonial registration of voters in religious terms; this augmented a Hindu emphasis on demography and its related anxieties and bigotry.

Sarkar presents a penetrating analysis of how the Hindutva uses religion in intra-Hindu politics. She shows how Hindutva's accommodation of Hinduism's diversity insidiously maintains the primacy of particular rituals and myths that are employed to promote the concept of a monolithic nation with a "national soul" and in the service of uniting all Hindus in the name of the "Nation-God," while leaving the internal inequalities intact.

In "The Genesis, Consolidation, and Consequences of Sinhalese Buddhist Nationalism," Neil DeVotta shows why Sri Lanka, which appeared after independence in 1948 to have the capacity to transition to a democratic modern state, instead became "a reference point for ethno-religious carnage." He finds the answer in the triumph of Sinhalese Buddhist nationalist ideology at the expense of interethnic relations and democratic institutions. While the conflict in Sri Lanka between the

---

[15] Interestingly, Hindu nationalists perceive objection to such personification as hostility to the nation – not unlike the Zionist perception of Arab citizens' objection to defining Israel as a Jewish state or the state of the Jewish people as promised by the biblical God.

majority Sinhalese and Tamil minority is not religious, Buddhism was instrumental in legitimizing demands for Sinhalese domination.

Like Zionism and Hindutva and other cases discussed in this volume, Sinhalese Buddhism claims Sri Lanka, with the Sinhalese constituting 75 percent of the population, as the Sinhala Buddhist country and as the "chosen repository of Buddhism." According to this view, other citizens (about 25 percent of the population) live in the country by virtue of Sinhalese Buddhist tolerance. In addition, Sinhala language itself is inextricably linked to Buddhism, and thus language and religion as well as foundational religious texts are fused with Sinhalese nationalism and the notion that the historical destiny of Sinhalese Buddhist nationalism is to strengthen the faith, land, and race.

This nationalism stands in opposition to a Sri Lankan multiracial and multi-community nationalism inclusive of all Sri Lankans that seemed possible pre- and postindependence. "This is a Sinhala Buddhist country" is a common slogan that Sinhalese Buddhist nationalism promotes, in striking similarity to other cases in this volume. Obviously religion plays a central role in this exclusive nationalism (similar to the role religion plays, for example, in Hindu nationalism and in Zionism). As DeVotta explains, what follows from this ideology is "that all those who challenge the hegemonic Sinhalese Buddhist position seek to diminish the preeminence of Buddhism and Sinhalese Buddhist predominance and are, therefore, traitors."

DeVotta traces the historical and political processes that led to the rise of this nationalism to its current most potent level, where Sinhalese nationalism and religion have fused and it has become legitimate to invoke the need for violence, even within a Buddhist perspective, to ensure Sinhalese Buddhist domination.

In **"Serbian Jerusalem: Inventing a Holy Land in Europe's Periphery, 1982–2019," Vjekoslav Perica** traces how the concept of "Serbian Jerusalem," introduced in the early 1980s as a catchy slogan by nationalists in the Serbian Orthodox Church, became a hallmark of sacralized discourse and how the comparison between Kosovo and Jerusalem, Serbs and Jews, and Serbia and Israel became a Serbian nationalist strategic policy for territorial claims, similar to the case of Israel. Perica critically examines the influence of ethno-religious myths by focusing on the idea of glorified Kosovo-centered Serb history and its power to revive religiously based territorial claims.

In order to trace the concept of "Serbian Jerusalem," Perica shows the role that Kosovo, or what became known as the Kosovo myth – a mixture of history, memory, and religion that defined Serbian national identity since the nineteenth century – played in the emergence of this concept. Greater Serbia, which the Serbian Orthodox Church and nationalist intelligentsia in Serbia promoted in the late 1980s, perceived Kosovo – the medieval seat of the Serbian Church and state with its overwhelming Albanian majority – as a religious and national cornerstone site of an intense Serbian nationalism. The Serb nationalist movement, which actually began in Kosovo, was influenced by the Serbian Orthodox Church's view of history. This view sought to justify the borders of Greater Serbia in Kosovo (and elsewhere) by using historic sacred monuments as its markers.

Perica explains that modern Serbian nationalism claimed Kosovo as a sort of "holy land" to justify its "liberation." This is why, since the Balkan War of 1912, and later in post-Tito Yugoslavia, the claim to Kosovo was justified on the basis of religious sacredness to Serb culture and national identity. The author shows how the comparison with Israeli religiously based territorial claims helped Serb nationalists to justify their own expansionist policies. In this context, Perica explicitly examines what the Balkan nationalists borrow from Israel and Zionism as "Israel appears as a role model to follow in the nationalist struggles for land."

In **"The Crossing Paths of Religion and Nationalism in Contemporary Iran,"** **Ali Banuazizi** examines how nationalism and religion have served as ideological bases for state legitimacy and political mobilization in Iran's recent history, and how the relationship between religion and nationalism varied over time and in different political contexts. Banuazizi focuses on two recent historical periods: 1925–79 under two autocratic Pahlavi monarchs; and 1979 to the present under the theocratic political rule of the Islamic Revolution. Each period tells the story of the domestic circumstances and international politics that promote nationalism, political Islam, or their crossing path.

In the first period, Banuazizi traces the first expressions of nationalist sentiments to the late nineteenth century and observes the rise of secular Iranian nationalism after World War I, particularly under Reza Shah Pahlavi (1921–41). Iranian nationalism sought to build a modern state with modern administrative bureaucracy, public education for both sexes, and measures to limit the influence of the clergy in the public sphere. This continued through the reign of Mohammad Reza Shah (1941–77) and the socially progressive policies and emphasis on pre-Islamic Iranian identity (with a democratic window during the prime ministership of Mohammad Mosaddeq (1951–53), who was removed in a CIA-led coup). Secular nationalism was successful in achieving broad support, but domestic suppression of democratic participation was the main factor in galvanizing the opposition. The Islamic Revolution leaders' stance emphasized Iran's Islamic identity, but its stance toward nationalism has changed according to political domestic and international circumstances.

The two focal points of Iranian identity are most evident in its foreign policy. The Islamic Republic moved beyond its earlier support for Islamic movements in other parts of the world on the basis of religious solidarity to focus on its national interests. Even its support for the Hezbollah movement in Lebanon, Bashar al-Assad's regime in Syria, and the Houthis in Yemen, which might have started as sectarian solidarity, is now dominated by strategic interests and foreign policy priorities. These alliances are conceived through the prism of Iranian national interest rather than Islamic

A *Comparative Perspective on Religious Claims and Sacralized Politics* 23

solidarity. The question, of course, is whether these are not so closely intertwined that it is hard to disentangle their influence.

In "**Saudi Nationalism, Wahhabi *Da'wā*, and Western Power,**" **Michael A. Sells** examines how the rise of populist nationalism in Saudi Arabia interacts with Wahhabism[16] and the role of Western power in controlling the outcome of this interaction.

The current ruling Saudi family is bound by a foundational agreement from 1744, according to which 'Abd al-Wahhāb (and now his followers) decide on religious issues, and Muḥammad ibn Sa'ūd (and now his successors) control the state and its administration. Thus, the Saudi ruling family needs the support of Wahhabi clerks (who prefer the term Salafis[17]) for internal legitimacy and of the West, mainly the US, for technological help, and defense and security backing.

Since the 1960s, Saudi rulers have instrumentalized Wahhabism, disguising it as Salafism, to advance a pan-Islamic ideology (*da'wā*) in an effort to fight rivals at home and to combat Arab nationalism and liberal, socialist, and Marxist trends in the Arab region and Islamic societies. The pan-Islamic ideology was also used to achieve global influence by providing philanthropy, scholarships, and supporting social activism and jihadist movements worldwide.

The overlap between Western strategic interests – particularly in the Middle East and the Islamic world – and the Saudi instrumentalization of Wahhabism in the form of international jihad was best demonstrated in the American and Saudi support to Afghani *mujāhidīn* in the 1980s. Saudi rulers at once collaborated with the West, mainly the US, and with the Wahhabi doctrine in general. Neither the West nor the Saudi rulers seemed to mind the major role played by the Wahhabi clerics in the propagation process.

According to Sells, Saudi Arabia is a case in which an extreme interpretation of religious doctrine was needed to legitimize an authoritarian regime making the dogmatic religious teaching as an integral part of the official state and its political modalities. Furthermore, it became a tool not only for domestic governance but also for international outreach as tools of foreign policy.

In "**Protestantism and Settler Identity: The Ambiguous Case of Northern Ireland,**" **David Lloyd's** point of departure is that the form of conflict in Northern Ireland is determined not by religious convictions but by settler-colonial structures. Religion, he argues, "functions as an alibi for settler mentalities," and the "religious convictions" approach to studying the conflict ignores and even obscures the underlying settler-colonial structures. The political and the religious are not of

---

[16] Wahhabism refers to a movement of the eighteenth century with dogmatic religious teachings led by Muḥammad ibn 'Abd al-Wahhāb, an Arab preacher and activist from what is currently known as Saudi Arabia.

[17] Salafis are those who adhere to the teaching and practice of the Prophet and his followers. For an insightful study of Salafism, including the difference between Salafism and Wahhabism, see Beshara (2018).

equal weight in explaining the conflict, and the claim that they are intertwined is not helpful to understanding the conflict between two nationalisms. To be sure, there are religious differences between the two communities in conflict, but these differences became "a marker that performs the work that race does in other settler-colonial settings," including the compartmentalization of residential space and the sense of threat experienced by the colonizers about sharing their social space with the colonized.

To support his argument, Lloyd brings in some comparison with the Republic of Ireland to the South. He observes that there, with the Republic's liberalization of cultural policy centered around Catholicism, religion gradually lost its function as a critical marker of ethnic or national identity, while in the North, seeking "a Protestant state for a Protestant people," the loyalists employed the religious differential for highlighting their distinction in order to maintain supremacy and privileges.

Applying settler-colonial theorizing and some comparison with other settler-colonial settings, Lloyd points to the Unionists' sense of siege, supremacy, and disdainful superiority, anxiety about "demographic threats" posed by the Nationalists, and wishes for the colonized to disappear. Lloyd argues that the aftermath of the Good Friday Agreement shows that power sharing has ended decades of settler-colonial domination by "a Protestant people" and brought recognition of civil rights, laws against discrimination, and declarations of "parity of esteem" achievements. This demonstrates that colonial societies are not necessarily permanent or endemic, but capable of transformation if and when relations of domination are dismantled.

When comparing Northern Ireland to Israel, Lloyd claims that the achievements in post-1998 Northern Ireland are unlikely in present-day Israel, because Israel is a state that is "constitutively founded on and committed to discrimination" and because of the existing internal and external structures of power that help maintain this system. To achieve change, external support or its withdrawal can play a major role in moving power structures toward democracy and equality.

Also taking Northern Ireland as a case study, in "**Does Religion Still Matter? Comparative Lessons from the Ethno-national Conflict in Northern Ireland,**" **Liam O'Dowd** examines the relationship between religion and nationalism and how violence is impacted by this link. He draws on the intersection between popular religion and ethno-national conflict to advance deeper analysis of the relationships between religion, nationalism, and violence. Based on empirical research carried out in Belfast as a site of contention over memory in a post-conflict era, he examines two dominant perspectives in the literature. The first is that religion is irrelevant to post-conflict Northern Ireland, and that it is rather the competing nationalism of the two communities that matters. The second is that the religious differences are enduring, and that religious politics persists as a main factor in the interaction between the two communities.

O'Dowd posits that the two perspectives are inadequate. He argues for a more discriminating analysis by identifying different forms of religion – such as a category of practice rather than a category of belief – and how these forms interact with different forms of nationalism in Belfast to generate violent conflict. In post-Good Friday Belfast, O'Dowd finds that while religion and nationalism had formerly interacted, inscribing violence on the spatial and physical fabric of the city for thirty years, that dynamic has now been replaced by contestation over sites of memory – how and what to remember about the thirty-year conflict known as "the Troubles" – and over the meta-narratives about the conflict's outcomes. In this conflict, religion as practice served as the repository of collective memory, giving meaning to violence, sacrifice, and rituals and thus intersecting with the ethno-national parties. Thus, while he challenges the claims that religious differences are intrinsically violent, O'Dowd argues that "convergent and mutually supportive, religion and secular nationalism can sustain enduring violence and division."

One form of religion remains integral to the conflict, and that is religion as practice or as a set of lived experiences connected to place-making and territorial segregation. O'Dowd explains how "violence itself does much to sacralize cities by welding popular memories to particular places." Yet this form is substantively different from other modes described in this volume.

In **"Palestinian Nationalism, Religious (Un)claims, and the Struggle against Zionism," Khaled Hroub** focuses on the role of religious claims in Palestinian nationalism. He starts by comparing the latter to Zionism, highlighting the fundamental differences between the two, namely: function – i.e., the purpose for which religion and religious claims were used in Zionism and the Palestinian national movement; and centrality – i.e., the extent of significance religion and religious claims had within each movement.

In terms of function, for Zionism, the main concern was legitimacy for its claim of Jewish "ownership" of the land; while for Palestinians, the main issue was mobilizing resistance. In terms of centrality, Hroub argues that Zionism has employed religious claims as a *primary* force of mobilization, at least in terms of the national claim to Palestine. The Palestinian national movement, by contrast, invoked religion only *secondarily*. This secondary role remains marginal until now, except of course in Hamas, which Hroub discusses at length.

As to the role of religion and religious claims in the Palestinian national movement, Hroub identifies three periods: (1) pre-1948, when the movement emerged and developed in Palestine – before and after the British Mandate and while resisting the Zionist takeover of the country; (2) from 1950 to the 1980s, when the center of the movement was in exile and during which the PLO and its various institutions emerged; and (3) since the late 1980s, after the start of the First Intifada until now. The author shows that in the first two periods, the two main identities were the pan-Arab and the Palestinian identity. No strong religious identity presented any competition with those two national identities. But Hamas, founded in

December 1988, represented a major player challenging the historically marginal role of religion and religious claims in Palestinian political thought.

Hamas in 1988 embraced resistance and declared itself as the Muslim Brotherhood branch in Palestine. As reflected in its charter, blending religion and resistance, religion was central and functional to its worldviews, social norms, politics, means of struggle, and the claim of Palestine, resulting in religionizing the Palestinian cause. But Hroub traces the profound changes the group underwent: its Palestinization, nationalization, and the transformative journey that led to changing its charter in May 2017.

REFERENCES

Abulof, Uriel. 2014. "The Roles of Religion in National Legitimation: Judaism and Zionism's Elusive Quest for Legitimacy." *Journal for the Scientific Study of Religion* 53, no. 3: 515–33.

2016. "Public Political Thought: Bridging the Sociological–Philosophical Divide in the Study of Legitimacy." *British Journal of Sociology* 67, no. 2: 371–91.

Amara, Ahmad. 2013. "The Negev Land Question between Denial and Recognition." *Journal of Palestine Studies* 42, no. 4: 27–47.

Anderson, Benedict. 1991. *Imagined Communities: Reflections on the Origin and Spread of Nationalism*. 2nd ed. London: Verso.

Appleby, R. Scott. 2000. *The Ambivalence of the Sacred: Religion, Violence, and Reconciliation*. Lanham: Rowman and Littlefield Publishers.

Appleby, R. Scott, Atalia Omer, and David Little, eds. 2015. *The Oxford Handbook of Religion, Conflict and Peacebuilding*. Oxford: Oxford University Press.

Asad, Talal. 1993. *Genealogies of Religion: Discipline and Reasons of Power in Christianity and Islam*. Baltimore: Johns Hopkins University Press.

2003. *Formations of the Secular: Christianity, Islam, Modernity*. Stanford: Stanford University Press.

Augusteijn, Joost, Patrick Dassen, and Maartje Janse. 2013. "Introduction: Politics and Religion." In *Political Religion Beyond Totalitarianism*, edited by Joost Augusteijn, Patrick Dassen, and Maartje Janse, 1–11. London: Palgrave Macmillan.

Beckford, James A. 2017. "Religion and Power." In *In Gods We Trust: New Patterns of Religious Pluralism in America*, edited by Thomas Robbins and Dick Anthony, 43–60. 2nd ed. New York: Routledge.

Bellah, Robert N. 1987. "Legitimation Processes in Politics and Religion." *Current Sociology* 35, no. 2: 89–99.

1998. "Religion and Legitimation in the American Republic." *Society* 35, no. 2: 193–201.

Berger, Peter. 1967. *The Sacred Canopy: Elements of a Sociological Theory of Religion*. New York: Doubleday.

Bhargava, Rajeev, ed. 1998. *Secularism and Its Critics*. Oxford: Oxford University Press.

Billings, Dwight B., and Shaunna L. Scott. 1994. "Religion and Political Legitimation." *Annual Review of Sociology* 20: 173–202.

Bishara, Azmi. 1995. "The Israeli Arab: Readings in a Truncated Political Text." [In Arabic.] *Majallat al-Dirasat al-Filastiniyya* 24: 26–54.

2005. *From the Jewish State to Sharon: A Study in the Contradictions of Israeli Democracy* [in Arabic]. Beirut: Dar al-Shorouk.

Beshara, Azmi. 2018. *What Is Salafism?* [in Arabic]. Doha: Arab Center for Research and Policy Studies.

2019. *Religion and Secularism in a Historical Context*. Pt. 2, vol. 2. Doha: Arab Center for Research and Policy Studies.

Brubaker, Rogers. 2012. "Religion and Nationalism: Four Approaches." *Nations and Nationalism* 18, no. 1: 2–20.

Burrin, Philippe. 1997. "Political Religion: The Relevance of a Concept." *History and Memory* 9, no. 1/2: 321–49.

Butler, Judith. 1993. *Bodies That Matter: On the Discursive Limits of "Sex."* New York: Routledge.

Casanova, José. 1994. *Public Religions in the Modern World*. Chicago: Chicago University Press.

Chuman, Joseph. 2006. "Does Religion Cause Violence?" In *Religion, Terrorism, and Globalization: Nonviolence: A New Agenda*, edited by Karikottuchira K. Kuriakose, 15–30. New York: Nova Science Publishers.

Connolly, William E. 2011. "Some Theses on Secularism." *Cultural Anthropology* 26, no. 4: 648–56.

Cragun, Ryan T., Christel Manning, and Lori L. Fazzino, eds. 2017. *Organized Secularism in the United States: New Directions in Research*. Religion and Its Others 6. Berlin: De Gruyter.

Demerath, N. J., III. 2007a. "Secularization and Sacralization Deconstructed and Reconstructed." In *The Sage Handbook of the Sociology of Religion*, edited by James A. Beckford and N. J. Demerath III, 57–80. London: Sage Publications.

2007b. "Religion and the State; Violence and Human Rights." In *The Sage Handbook of the Sociology of Religion*, edited by James A. Beckford and N. J. Demerath III 2007, 381–95. London: Sage Publications.

DeVotta, Neil. 2007. "Sinhalese Buddhist Nationalist Ideology: Implications for Politics and Conflict Resolution in Sri Lanka." *Policy Studies*, no. 40. Washington, DC: East-West Center.

Earner-Byrne, Lindsey, and Diane Urquhart. 2018. *The Irish Abortion Journey, 1920–2018*. Cham, Switzerland: Palgrave Macmillan.

Ebaugh, Helen Rose. 2002. "Presidential Address 2001: Return of the Sacred: Reintegrating Religion in the Social Sciences." *Journal for the Scientific Study of Religion* 41, no. 3: 385–95.

Forman, Geremy, and Alexandre Kedar. 2004. "From Arab Land to 'Israel Lands': The Legal Dispossession of the Palestinians Displaced by Israel in the Wake of 1948." *Environment and Planning D: Society and Space* 22, no. 6: 809–30.

Friedland, Roger. 2001. "Religious Nationalism and the Problem of Collective Representation." *Annual Review of Sociology* 27: 125–52.

Friedland, Roger, and Kenneth B. Moss. 2016. "Thinking through Religious Nationalism." In *Words: Religious Language Matters*, edited by Ernst van den Hemel and Asja Szafraniec, 419–62. New York: Fordham University Press.

Gellner, Ernest. 1994. *Encounters with Nationalism*. Oxford: Blackwell.

Gentile, Emilio. 2004. "Fascism, Totalitarianism and Political Religion: Definitions and Critical Reflections on Criticism of an Interpretation." *Totalitarian Movements and Political Religions* 5, no. 3: 326–75.

2005. "Political Religion: A Concept and Its Critics – A Critical Survey." *Totalitarian Movements and Political Religions* 6, no. 1: 19–32.

Ghanem, As'ad, Nadim Rouhana, and Oren Yiftachel. 1998. "Questioning 'Ethnic Democracy': A Response to Sammy Smooha." *Israel Studies* 3, no. 2: 253–67.

Gorski, Philip S. 2000. "Historicizing the Secularization Debate: Church, State, and Society in Late Medieval and Early Modern Europe, ca. 1300 to 1700." *American Sociological Review* 68: 138–67.

2017. *American Covenant: A History of Civil Religion from the Puritans to the Present.* Princeton: Princeton University Press.

Gorski, Philip S., and Ateş Altınordu. 2008. "After Secularization?" *Annual Review of Sociology* 34: 55–85.

Hall, John R. 2013. "Religion and Violence from a Sociological Perspective." In *The Oxford Handbook of Religion and Violence*, edited by Mark Juergensmeyer, Margo Kitts, and Michel K. Jerryson, 363–74. Oxford: Oxford University Press.

Hasan, Mushirul. 2002. "The BJP's Intellectual Agenda: Textbooks and Imagined History." *South Asia: Journal of South Asian Studies* 25, no. 3: 187–209.

Hobsbawm, Eric. 1990. *Nations and Nationalism since 1780.* Cambridge: Cambridge University Press.

Hoffman, Bruce. 2006. *Inside Terrorism.* New York: Columbia University Press.

Jabareen, Yosef. 2017. "Controlling Land and Demography in Israel: The Obsession with Territorial and Geographic Dominance." In *Israel and Its Palestinian Citizens: Ethnic Privileges in the Jewish State*, edited by Nadim N. Rouhana, 238–55. Cambridge: Cambridge University Press.

Jamal, Amal. 2002. "Beyond 'Ethnic Democracy': State Structure, Multi-cultural Conflict and Differentiated Citizenship in Israel." *New Political Science* 24, no. 3: 411–31.

Jones, David Martin, and M. L. R. Smith. 2014. *Sacred Violence: Political Religion in a Secular Age.* New York: Palgrave Macmillan.

Juergensmeyer, Mark. 2003. *Terror in the Mind of God: The Global Rise of Religious Violence.* Comparative Studies in Religion and Society. Berkeley: University of California Press.

Juergensmeyer, Mark, Margo Kitts, and Michel K. Jerryson, eds. 2013. *The Oxford Handbook of Religion and Violence.* Oxford: Oxford University Press.

Kamat, Sangeeta, and Biju Mathew. 2003. "Mapping Political Violence in a Globalized World: The Case of Hindu Nationalism." *Social Justice* 30, no. 3: 4–16.

Kanaaneh, Rhoda Ann. 2002. *Birthing the Nation: Strategies of Palestinian Women in Israel.* Berkeley: University of California Press.

Lusthaus, Jonathan. 2011. "Religion and State Violence: Legitimation in Israel, the USA and Iran." *Contemporary Politics* 17, no. 1: 1–17.

Mahmood, Saba. 2017. "Secularism, Sovereignty, and Religious Difference: A Global Genealogy." *Environment and Planning D: Society and Space* 35, no. 2: 197–209.

Marvin, Carolyn, and David W. Ingle. 1996. "To Blood Sacrifice and the Nation: Revisiting Civil Religion." *Journal of the American Academy of Religion* 64, no. 4: 767–80.

1999. *Blood Sacrifice and the Nation: Totem Rituals and the American Flag.* Cambridge Cultural Social Studies. Cambridge: Cambridge University Press.

Mbembe, Achille. 2003. "Necropolitics." *Public Culture* 15, no. 1: 11–40.

Memmi, Albert. 1991. *The Colonizer and the Colonized.* Boston: Beacon Press.

Metcalf, Barbara D. 1995. "Presidential Address: Too Little and Too Much: Reflections on Muslims in the History of India." *Journal of Asian Studies* 54, no. 4: 951–67.

Moallem, Minoo. 2005. *Between Warrior Brother and Veiled Sister: Islamic Fundamentalism and the Politics of Patriarchy in Iran.* Berkeley: University of California Press.

Nahman, Michal Rachel. 2013. *Extractions: An Ethnography of Reproductive Tourism.* New York: Palgrave Macmillan.

Nigam, Aditya. 2006. *The Insurrection of Little Selves: The Crisis of Secular Nationalism in India*. New Delhi: Oxford University Press.

Norris, Pippa, and Ronald Inglehart. 2010. *Sacred and Secular: Religion and Politics Worldwide*. 2nd ed. Cambridge: Cambridge University Press.

Omar, A. Rashied. 2015. "Religious Violence and State Violence." In *The Oxford Handbook of Religion, Conflict and Peacebuilding*, edited by R. Scott Appleby, Atalia Omer, and David Little, 236–58. Oxford: Oxford University Press.

Ophir, Adi, and Ishay Rosen-Zvi. 2018. *Israel's Multiple Others and the Birth of the Gentile*. Oxford: Oxford University Press.

Perica, Vjekoslav. 2002. *Balkan Idols: Religion and Nationalism in Yugoslav States*. Oxford: Oxford University Press.

Portuguese, Jacqueline. 1998. *Fertility Policy in Israel: The Politics of Religion, Gender, and Nation*. Westport, CT: Praeger.

Al-Rasheed, Madawi. 2014. *A Most Masculine State: Gender, Politics, and Religion in Saudi Arabia*. Cambridge: Cambridge University Press.

Riis, Ole. 1998. "Religion Re-emerging: The Role of Religion in Legitimating Integration and Power in Modern Societies." *International Sociology* 13, no. 2: 247–72.

Rouhana, Nadim N. 1997. *Palestinian Citizens in an Ethnic Jewish State: Identities in Conflict*. New Haven: Yale University Press.

    2015. "Homeland Nationalism and Guarding Dignity in a Settler Colonial Context: The Palestinian Citizens of Israel Reclaim Their Homeland." *Borderlands* 14, no. 1: 1–37.

Rouhana, Nadim N., and Areej Sabbagh-Khoury. 2006. "Force, Privilege, and the Range of Tolerance." [In Hebrew.] In *Knowledge and Silence: On the Mechanism of Denial in Israeli Society*, edited by Kinneret Lahad and Hanna Herzog, 62–74. Tel Aviv: The Van Leer Jerusalem Institute and Hakibbutz Hameuchad Publishing House.

Said, Edward. 1993. *Culture and Imperialism*. New York: Alfred A. Knopf.

Sarkar, Sumit. 2002. *Beyond Nationalist Frames: Postmodernism, Hindu Fundamentalism, History*. Bloomington: Indiana University Press.

Sells, Michael A. 1998. *The Bridge Betrayed: Religion and Genocide in Bosnia*. Berkeley: University of California Press.

Shah, Timothy Samuel, Alfred Stepan, and Monica Duffy Toft, eds. 2012. *Rethinking Religion and World Affairs*. Oxford: Oxford University Press.

Shalhoub-Kevorkian, Nadera. 2015. *Security Theology, Surveillance and the Politics of Fear*. Cambridge: Cambridge University Press.

    2017. "The Occupation of the Senses: The Prosthetic and Aesthetic of State Terror." *British Journal of Criminology* 57, no. 6: 1279–300.

Shenhav, Yehouda. 2007. "Modernity and the Hybridization of Nationalism and Religion: Zionism and the Jews of the Middle East as a Heuristic Case." *Theory and Society* 36, no. 1: 1–30.

Smith, Anthony D. 2008. *The Cultural Foundations of Nations: Hierarchy Covenant and Republic*. Malden, MA: Blackwell.

Smooha, Sammy. 1997. "Ethnic Democracy: Israel as an Archetype." *Israel Studies* 2, no. 2: 198–241.

Soper, J. Christopher, and Joel S. Fetzer. 2018. *Religion and Nationalism in Global Perspective*. Cambridge: Cambridge University Press.

Spohn, Willfried. 2003. "Multiple Modernity, Nationalism and Religion: A Global Perspective." *Current Sociology* 51, no. 3–4: 265–86.

Stern, Jessica. 2004. *Terror in the Name of God: Why Militants Kill*. New York: HarperCollins.

Sultany, Nimer. 2017. "The Legal Structures of Subordination: The Palestinian Minority and Israeli Law." In *Israel and Its Palestinian Citizens: Ethnic Privileges in the Jewish State*, edited by Nadim N. Rouhana, 191–237. Cambridge: Cambridge University Press.

Tambiah, Stanley J. 1992. *Buddhism Betrayed? Religion, Politics, and Violence in Sri Lanka.* Chicago: University of Chicago Press.

Taylor, Charles. 1998. "Modes of Secularism." In *Secularism and Its Critics*, edited by Rajeev Bhargava, 31–53. Oxford: Oxford University Press.

Toft, Monica Duffy. 2012. "Religion, Terrorism, and Civil War." In *Rethinking Religion and World Affairs*, edited by Timothy Samuel Shah, Alfred Stepan, and Monica Duffy Toft, 127–48. Oxford: Oxford University Press.

Turner, Bryan S. 1991. *Religion and Social Theory.* Newbury Park, CA: Sage.

van der Veer, Peter. 1994. *Religious Nationalism: Hindus and Muslims in India.* Berkeley: University of California Press.

Yabanci, Bilge. 2020. "Fuzzy Borders between Populism and Sacralized Politics: Mission, Leader, Community and Performance in 'New' Turkey." *Politics, Religion and Ideology* 21, no. 1: 92–112.

Yiftachel, Oren. 2006. *Ethnocracy: Land and Identity Politics in Israel/Palestine.* Philadelphia: University of Pennsylvania Press.

PART I

Israel

2

Religion and Nationalism in the Jewish and Zionist Context

Amnon Raz-Krakotzkin

INTRODUCTION: RELIGION AND NATIONALISM IN THE JEWISH CONTEXT

There are still those who assume that it is possible to clearly distinguish between "nationalism" and "religion" in a comprehensive manner, to view them as mutually exclusive structured categories. However, even if this sort of distinction continues to frame the political discourse and some academic approaches, it seems as though the majority of scholars no longer accept these simplistic diagnoses. In many contexts, religion has been nationalized during the nineteenth century, and it is hard to see any political model that does not appropriate "religion" (sometimes as a national church, sometimes as a central factor of national identity) for the (re) shaping of "identity." Distinctions between "religion" and "ethnicity" are rather protean and often context dependent. At times, "religion" confers meaning to what in other contexts is dubbed "national consciousness" and vice versa.[1] Furthermore, there are a few cases where one can indicate a full separation of "religion" from the public sphere. José Casanova convincingly offers what he terms "public religion," namely, the role of religion in the development of the political sphere in both Western and non-Western societies, and consequently also pointed out the process of "de-privatization" (Casanova 1994).[2]

In this framework, one can agree in principle with those who claim that the connection between religion and nationalism or religion and state in Israel is not so unusual.[3] Arguing that Israel is not secular according to an ostensibly secular model is problematic, as the model featuring total separation between religion and state or nationalism hardly exists. Moreover, the theoretical articulations of this model stand at the core of a growing critical discussion: the concept of secularism

---

[1] See, for example, van der Veer and Lehman (1999), especially van der Veer's comments in the introduction. In the meantime, many scholars have contributed to the literature on this topic.

[2] Casanova's "de-privatization" process may be divided into two parts: the ouster of religion and its subsequent return to the fold. He then expands on the critical discussion concerning European secularism. See, for example, Casanova (2006, 2008).

[3] See, for example, the third part ("On Religion and Nationalism in Israel and the Nations") of Ben Yisrael (2004, 151–95). This matter comes up in an array of comparative studies on the question of religion and state.

has been challenged from various directions, in which many of the conventions commonly used for its description have been critically examined. As Talal Asad (2003, 1–2) has demonstrated in his groundbreaking analysis in the *Formations of the Secular*, "what is distinctive about 'secularism' is that it presupposes new concepts of 'religion,' 'ethics' and 'politics.'" Accordingly, fundamental dichotomies such as those between "science and religion" and "nationalism and religion" have been undermined, and the historical narratives on which they rested have been thoroughly dismantled.[4] It is widely accepted today that the perception of secularism as a universal doctrine of freedom of belief, pluralism, and so on cannot be taken as such and should be examined within the concrete discourses of modernity, with relation to concepts like ethnicity, culture, and race.

It should be clarified that the issue is not the principles of pluralism, freedom of belief, and so on that are often attributed to secularism, but whether historical Western secularism advances these principles or rather prevents their realization. In the words of Etienne Balibar (2004, 205), "the dominant form of European secularism (this is particularly the case with French laïcité) is also a form of resistance to real multiculturalism, since many cultures are deemed to be too 'religious' to become acceptable to the picture."[5] It may be wrong to reduce secularism to Orientalism and colonialism, but as Gil Anidjar (2007) has strongly demonstrated, the very attempt to analyze secularism as an autonomous domain is one of the ways in which secularism disguises its concrete attributes and represents itself as a universal doctrine of freedom of speech, without drawing attention to its implications on other people (see also King 1999).

Yet all these in and of themselves do not deny the unique aspects of Israel, being a state in which citizenship is determined on the basis of Orthodox Halachic (Jewish religious law) criteria, such that the Jewish state does not differentiate between nationalism and religion.[6] More important, the principal question with respect to Israel is not the relationship between religion and nationalism, but that between messianism (or to be more precise – the political interpretation of messianism) and nationalism. As I will argue briefly here, in this context, what is known as "secularization" (namely, the nationalization of Jewish consciousness) is the articulation of messianic imagination (which has merited a rich array of

---

[4] Even a proponent of secularization theory such as Peter Berger (1999, 7) now declares "that the assumption we live in a secularized world is false ... The world today is as furiously religious as it ever was."

[5] Cf. Charles Taylor (2007), who acknowledges the Christian origins of secularism and its colonial implications, but nevertheless insists that the model is still applicable to other contexts.

[6] Although we are veering off the topic at hand, it is only natural that we allude to this matter because it indicates the difficulty of labeling Israel a nation-state. The discourse on the "Law of Return" and citizenship is devoid of non-Halachic categories for determining "who is a Jew." This is clearly manifest in Israel's prolonged debate over conversion: the disagreement is not over whether rabbis should determine who is Jewish (a matter with obvious constitutional implications), but over which particular rabbis should be vested with this authority.

understandings and exegeses, spiritual or apocalyptic) as a political-national narrative in the modern sense of the word.

In practice, focusing the discussion on religion's place in Israel's public life (a topic that is important in its own right) presumes that Israel is (or strives to be) a secular nation-state. In consequence, the discussion overlooks the theological elements that stand at the very heart of the definition of Israel as a Jewish state. The attempt to separate the discussion of religion and state conceals earlier questions and ignores the apocalyptic dimension that inevitably accompanies Israel, and is determined from the so-called secularization of the idea of redemption by depicting it as a national myth. The centrality of the political theological aspect in the formation and definition of the State of Israel is undeniable, and consequently any attempt to separate religion from the state is impossible. Zionism is not simply a national identity based on religious elements, and it would be too simplistic to present Israel as a case study of a nation-state with a national "church."

Still, this aspect should also be examined in a wider context of Western secularization, namely, nationalism and colonialism: a notion of redemption and chosenness (inspired by biblical images) is to be found in many national identities and was also an important component of colonial consciousness that emerged simultaneously, mainly in England (Bhabha 1990; A. D. Smith 2004). As we shall see, what makes the Zionist theological perspective unique, however, is its direct relation to the Jewish-Christian messianic images and to the biblical images of Palestine. Furthermore, the exceptionality of Zionism is determined by the very attempt to "normalize" Jewish existence, to accommodate the Jewish notion of peoplehood to the model of territorial-ethnic nationalism. As I will argue in this chapter, in this context, secularization means the adoption of Jewish consciousness to a Christian, mainly Protestant, framework – which is central in Western colonial discourse. As such, while analyzing the exceptionality of Zionist narrative, we can also shed light on the model itself, namely, Western self-understanding and perceptions of secularism. Zionist discourse reminds us that it is impossible to distinguish the discussion of secularism from the discussion about Orientalism and colonialism.[7] In other words, the category of secularism disguises the real issue at stake – the colonial dimension of Zionism inherent in the notion of secularization and nationalization of the Jews. Moreover, all aspects recognized as "secular" in the Zionist discourse are particularly similar to other cases of settler colonialism (in the US, Australia, and elsewhere), where the Bible and the notion of mission had an important role. Accordingly, meaningful secularity should be associated to a process of decolonization. The sources for that shift cannot be found in the so-called secular, but perhaps in the religious terminology that had been denied (or rather disguised) by the secular – embodied mainly in the notion of exile.

---

[7] For understanding the linkage between colonialism and secularism I was deeply inspired by the scholarly discussion of India. See Chatterjee (1998); Nandy (1995, 1998); Yelle (2013).

A discussion on religion and nationalism in the Jewish context allows us to simultaneously explore the question of secularization from two different vantage points: the place of the Jewish question in the process of European secularization, and the meaning of the definition of the Jews as a territorial nation in the modern understanding of the term. Each of these perspectives reveals the difficulty of adapting the definition of the Jews to the modern language of nationalism, and consequently it demands the critical analysis of the very concepts of "secularism," "religion," and "nationalism."

RELIGION AND NATIONALISM IN THE SECULAR ORDER

First, we should realize that the very distinction between "religion" and "nationalism" is a cornerstone of the secular order. Secularism is not only an outlook on religion and nationalism but is also the process through which both terms were redefined as mutually exclusive terms, by the demand to privatize religion as part of the rise of the modern nation-state. Both religion and nationalism received their meanings in modern discourse at the same time as the former was being replaced with the latter. While it is widely accepted now that nationalism as a political term and as a demand for political sovereignty is a modern category, we should also emphasize that the notion of "religion" as we know it is also modern and is in fact a product of one of the main demonstrations of "the secular order."[8] The conventional understanding of the term religion – as a specific domain of human existence – is only possible when compared to a field that is considered as "non religious, as secular" (Asad 1993).[9] In opposition to the distinction between the sacred and the profane, which emerges from within "religion" and constitutes part of the "religious" framework (as an all-encompassing worldview), the religious-secular divide is determined from the specifically Protestant understanding of "religion" and the attempt to define "worldliness" that is allegedly "neutral."

The question of whether the Jews form a "religion" or a "nation" was one of the sites in which the definitions of these two terms, and the distinction between the privatized religion and the public, was established. The formative question of the Enlightenment discourse with respect to the Jews was mainly whether they are a religion (or "confession"), and thus capable of being integrated as citizens of the European nation-states, or a separate nation – an Oriental collective – whose culture is foreign and alien to that of the Occident. This question did not originate within

---

[8] This view is accepted by, inter alios, nationalism scholars who are identified with the "modernist" camp, as well as those like Anthony Smith who assumes that the roots of the nation go back further.

[9] Over the past few decades, much has been written on the dialectical direction of the attempts to characterize "religion" in the modern context. See, for example, Asad (1993); Dubuisson and Sayers (2007); Harrison (1990); Masuzawa (2005); McCutcheon (1997); C. Smith (1991); J. Z. Smith (1998); Stroumsa (2010).

the Jewish world but rather was directed against it and played a key role in the definition of the boundaries of national belonging in Europe. The Jews couldn't know how to answer the question of whether they formed a "nation" or "religion," as both terms were redefined at the moment that they were addressed toward and imposed on them. Jews saw themselves as a "people" (*Am*), the people of God, a people whose essence is the Revelation and the Torah, and as a "community," the autonomous-corporative body that defined Jewish premodern life, both of which identities were denied within the process of the rise of the nation-states in Europe.[10] The question of whether they formed a "nation" or a "religion" paralleled the question of whether the Orientalism of the Jews was essential and intrinsic, and thus in opposition to "secular" civility, or rather had developed as a result of the historic oppression directed against them.

The main Jewish discourse since the nineteenth century focused on various attempts to adapt Judaism to the new definition of "religion."[11] The internalization of the religious-national dichotomy was epitomized by the Jewish reform movement, whose explicit goal was to reinstitute Judaism as a *confession*, but as Batnizki (2011) convincingly argued, it reflect also the thinking of some Orthodox circles. In contrast, Zionism defined Judaism as a "nation," a Western nation. But both competing attitudes accepted the same distinction between nation and religion, and the desire to integrate the Jews as part of the West.

The second perspective to view secularism is provided by Zionism as a project of Westernization of the Jews, a process that in reality took place through an internalization of Christian perceptions of the Jews and their exile (Raz-Krakotzkin 2005, 2013). The secular Zionist, the figure that most represents the now fashionable "Judeo-Christian," has been constructed through a distinction from the East, from the Arab, and from the historical-exilic Jew. Zionism and the State of Israel provide an essential frame within which many aspects and perspectives that have been raised and studied during these ongoing debates can be observed in a most concentrated way: the theological sources of "secularization" – being a process embedded within Christian theology, as well as the obvious Orientalism inherent in the notion of the secular. Zionist thinkers accepted the definition of the Jews as a nation in the modern sense of the world – but a Western one, in opposition to the East.

---

[10] This question stands at the heart of the prolonged debate over the relevant developments in France. The very concepts for depicting this process differed in Germany, France, and England, for each state had a different outlook. That said, they all drew upon the same Protestant idea according to which religion is a private/individualistic affair. The general direction that is proposed herein basically follows in the footsteps of Arthur Hertzberg (1968) and Michael Marrus (1980). The revolution conferred a paradigmatic formulation; however, to understand it, we must also study its roots from the early modern era. See R. Schechter (2003).

[11] See Leora Batnizki's (2011) discussion of "How Judaism Became a Religion," who has recently proposed that Moses Mendelssohn should be viewed as the first thinker to define Judaism as a "religion" as per the unequivocally Protestant definition.

38 *Amnon Raz-Krakotzkin*

THEOLOGY AND THE NOTION OF THE SECULAR
IN ISRAELI DISCOURSE

More specifically, Zionism and the Jewish state are conceived as "the fulfillment of the "utopian return to Zion" after centuries of messianic longing, albeit by political rather than divine interference. The national-secular narrative (as expressed in the term "negation of exile") is based on the perception of Zionist settlement and sovereignty over Palestine as the return of the Jews to their homeland (regarded as empty), as the fulfillment of Jewish history, and the realization of Jewish prayers and messianic expectations. God was excluded from the discourse, yet biblical divine promise continued to direct political activity and to serve as a source of legitimacy. In that respect, Zionist national consciousness was not separate from the theological myth, but was rather a particular interpretation of that myth, considered to be the exclusive understanding of the Scriptures. Secularization in Zionism meant the nationalization of religious-messianic conceptions, not their replacement.[12] Accordingly, one can summarize the secular perception as follows: God does not exist, but he promised us the Land.

In spite of other important differences, this version was accepted by most Zionist trends in the twentieth century. We should not underestimate the role of the need for shelter for European Jews during crisis as an important argument in the early stages of Zionism – what might be seen as the secular dimension of the movement. Yet at least since the "Uganda Affair" (1903), when the idea of a Jewish settlement outside Palestine (in East Africa) was rejected by the Zionist movement, the priority of the idea of "return" over the need for shelter was repeatedly declared and confirmed.

In light of all of the above, the very distinction between the secular and the religious as the starting point in a discourse on Israeli society and Israeli nationalism is misleading and detracts from our understanding of "secularism" and its adherents in this context. In particular, it muddles the fact that the messianic-apocalyptic dimension of the Bible is not antithetical to but in fact intrinsic to the secular outlook. Moreover, this distinction prevents us from examining what stands behind the "secular" and, to a certain extent, from weighing the prospects of the seculariza-tion enterprise, namely, the creation of space between messianism and the outlook of the state and nationalism.

It should be emphasized that the very terms of the secular/religious debate in Israel define the borders of collectivity as exclusively Jewish and determine the exclusion of the Arab citizens of the state: on the various occasions in which the debate between "religious" and "secular" identities has been reproduced (in the academy, the media, etc.) – the participants are exclusively Jews. Palestinian citizens of Israel, even when they obviously hold "secular" attitudes, are not con-sidered as participants in the discussion about "secularism" because they are not

---

[12] Aspects of this process have been discussed by several scholars. See Almog (1998); Don Yehiya (1980); Shapira (1998).

considered as part of the public sphere. In Israel, being an Arab and being secular are considered to be mutually exclusive categories. This construction of the debate prevents the very possibility of secularity – that is to say, a space that includes all citizens and inhabitants.

The issue, therefore, is not "secularism" as such, but rather Jewish nationalism. In the Israeli context, the term "secular" does not refer to a civil vision (i.e., one that is inclusive of Jews, Arabs, and all other citizens) but explicitly and inexorably a Jewish one, and the debate is between two visions of a Jewish homogeneous collectivity. Rather than dividing the nation, as it is often assumed to do, this debate in fact creates and defines its boundaries through implicit inclusions and exclusions. By accepting that framework of discussion, the secular participants even strengthen and emphasize the ethnic boundaries. The exclusion of Palestinians is not done by "religion" but actually by the fundamental parameters of the secular. Hence the denial of "religion" is at the same time an act of exclusion of the Palestinians.

THE HEBREW BIBLE AND ZIONISM

This is not to say that Zionist consciousness directly follows or that it represents the Jewish "messianic tradition." In fact, it has been established on the explicit denial of Jewish postbiblical literature and tradition, and particularly in opposition to the existing Jewish community in Palestine, considered as "religious" and "traditional." It should be emphasized that unlike the Zionist "new" settlement, the "Old Yishuv" was not founded on a return to the Bible or on "negation of exile." On the contrary: As a response to Zionist ideas, leaders of the Old Yishuv's communities insisted on defining the present existence as "exile in the Holy Land" (Bartal 1984; Friedman 1977). Zionist thought was obviously inspired by many Jewish traditional sources. Besides, the desire for a national revival is definitely a prominent factor of Jewish exilic imagination.

However, the reformulation of the theological perception in modern "romantic" terminology of originality, authenticity, and return express a radical transition and means its accommodation into the Western perception of history, and particularly into Protestant theological imagination. The Zionist ideal of "return" to the ancient past was based on the fundamental Protestant ideal: The Zionist return was directed toward to the self-same image of the land as was the spiritual ideal of Protestantism – to the Holy Land of the Second Temple period, the age of Jesus, which is "as if" the origin of the "common culture" – what came to be known as the "Judeo-Christian." More importantly, the Zionist concept of return was articulated in the same terms and set of images that has been developed in Protestant literature. The image of the ancient Jewish community was the same image attributed to the early Church in Protestant thought, formulated in the same terms, and according to similar cultural images of a pious peasant community. The Jewish national ideal considered as secular followed the theological imagination of Protestantism. The Reformation should therefore be seen as the location of the shift from "traditional" to "national"

Jewish consciousness. In Protestant thought, the concepts of "chosen people," "promised land," and the very notion of history and redemption were reinterpreted in the way that prepared their role in the shaping of national and colonial discourses and the entire Western self-perception of superiority (Raz-Krakotzkin 2013). Zionism's return to the Bible, which is the core of what is considered to be secularism, is the return to this frame of interpretation.[13] This is the meaning of the articulation of Jews as the territorial nation. The so-called secularization is the interpretation of the biblical myth in European terms; it is the secularization of the Bible.

SECULARISM AND THE BIBLE

The Zionist enterprise is, in its poetic-historical imaginary, above all, a return to the Bible, especially to the books of Joshua and Judges and some of the prophets, which is also – at the same time – a "return to history" and to the "West." Biblical images were instrumental for the construction of the new culture. Until recently, they had a prominent role in the Israeli educational system and were instrumental to the self-perception of the new Jewish community. As Uriel Simon (1999) puts it, Zionism has transformed the Bible into a "national *midrash*" (exegesis) (see also Shapira 2005; Shavit and Eran 2007). The new Zionist culture saw in various biblical images a model for emulation. Accordingly, it viewed itself as the triumphal completion of a historical process.

The Bible to which the "return" is taking place is the Bible of the West. Recent scholarly attention given to the development of the Bible since the Reformation demonstrates its crucial role in what is considered as the modernization and secularization of Europe. The paradox is that what we have long recognized as the process of "secularization" in the West coincided with the growing role of the Hebrew Bible (the Old Testament) in the shaping of political thought, national identities, and colonial justifications (Hill 1993). Since the seventeenth century, the ancient Hebrews have become an object of reflection for many discussions on politics and religion. As Jonathan Sheehan has put it, the refutation of divine authority was part of the transformation of the Bible (and particularly the so-called Old Testament) and its reconceptualization as a fundamental "cultural" text (Sheehan 2005; see also Harrison 1998; Nelson 2010; Oz-Salzberger 2008; Sheehan 2009). The debate over various biblical models (the law of the Torah, the Judges, or the kingdoms of Judah and Israel) was at the core of the political discourse and the source of imagination of communal sovereignty both in Europe and in the colonies, in the various cases of settler nationalism.

---

[13] It is important to note here the ambivalent attitude toward Christianity in a variety of literary artifacts produced within Zionist culture, as the debate whether to include Jesus in the national canon.

Scholars also demonstrated the role of biblical models in the construction of national cultures and self-perceptions (Anderson 1991; Hastings 1997; Kohn 1955; Lehmann 1996; A. D. Smith 2004). The publication of vernacular translations of the Bible was fundamental to the construction of nineteenth-century European national identities and to various aspects of both popular and elite cultures throughout much of Europe (Weidner 2005). Furthermore, in Protestant thought, the concepts of "chosen people," "promised land," and the very notion of history and redemption were reinterpreted in a way that prepared their role as a source of imagination of communal sovereignty (Hutchison and Lehmann 1994; Lehmann 1996; A. D. Smith 2004). This provenance casts the entire question of "nationalism and religion" in a different light.[14] Concentrating on the Bible demonstrates the historical relationship between nationalism and colonialism, and between nation and empire, for all of these developed concomitantly on the basis of the same theological platform, with the same biblical imagery and justification. Parallel to its development as a source of nationalism in Europe, the Old Testament was instrumental in the justification of colonial expansion and colonial rule, and accordingly had a crucial role in the construction of settler-colonial settlement projects (Ilany 2012). The biblical consciousness, especially the notion of the chosen people, gave rise to the idea of national exceptionalism and at the same time to an absolute confidence of the superiority of the West. It served to justify the Occident's rule outside of Europe and the subjugation of other nations. Conquerors described their deeds as the conquest of Canaan by Joshua, and white Christian settlers imagined themselves in terms of the ancient Hebrew community, at the periods of Judges and the Kings. On the other hand, also the objection to these deeds was framed in biblical terms, emphasizing the cruelty of Joshua and the Israelites.

Obscuring the entanglement and complicity of nationalism with colonialism is among the underlying principles of the secular self-image, for talk of secularism as an ideology of liberation (both in the metropole and in the formerly colonized territories) is only plausible if secularism is detached from colonialism. This distinction is crucial for the depiction of modern European history as the history of secularization and democratization. Biblical discourse clarifies the distortion of this historical perception. The centrality of the Bible to modernity also demonstrates the link between theological Christian and Orientalist perspectives, as two complementary descriptions of the same phenomena. This link is obvious in the various images of Palestine, "the Holy Land," "the Land of Israel," and Palestine that became disseminated in the modern West. Etan Bar-Yosef described and analyzed the role of the image of Jerusalem both in the construction of English nationalism and in the shaping of the image of Palestine and dubbed it "vernacular orientalism" (Bar-Yosef 2005).

---

[14] The religious sources of nationalism were already examined many decades ago. See, for example, Baron ([1947] 1960); Pinson (1934).

Amnon Raz-Krakotzkin

This is the Bible to which the Zionist return is taking place and through whose images Zionism defined itself as both ancient and modern; the modern European completion of a historical process.

In Zionist discourse, like in other cases of settler colonialism, the biblical national and the biblical colonial narratives are completely integrated. The Zionist return to the biblical story was thus mediated by the Western Christian model, which evolved over the course of the secularization process.[15] Put differently, the return to the Hebrew Bible is essentially a return, albeit modified, to the Western, Christian (secularized) Bible, to the Old Testament. The ancient Hebrews were rendered a paradigm for Western-Christian imagination of the nation, and, in the end, the Jews are adjusting themselves to the Christian perception of themselves.[16]

We should notice that the first to describe the idea of political restoration of the Jews in modern political terms and as a Western vision were early modern Christian millenarians who regarded the return of the Jews to the Holy Land and the restoration of the Jewish polity as the precondition for the Second Coming. From the seventeenth century to the present, a vast quantity of literature has raised the idea of the return of the Jews to "the Holy Land" and the reestablishment of a Jewish state, and the restoration of the Temple, as a prominent issue in the messianic scenario. This literary activity produced a variety of images of the commonwealth. The idea of a Jewish state as a marker of the messianic age occupied many in the seventeenth century and had a continuous presence, albeit quite marginal, in English culture later on. The very term "state of Israel" first appeared in this context.[17] This is definitely the origin of the articulation of the idea of Israel as a state in the modern sense of the word in the language and imagery of European Christian culture. The term "state of Israel" appeared in the seventeenth century, the same period in which the general political concept of the state became a focus of philosophical discussion and the discussion of the ancient Hebrew polity dominated the European political and philosophical discourse. The state of Israel was an exceptional state, in fact: the state of exception; the marker of the apocalypse, the global war that will accompany the Second Coming – an exception that emerged as a concept during the establishment of the rule – centralist state and colonial conquest.

Zionist authors from Nahum Sokolof to Benjamin Netanyahu often turned to these millenarian treatises and relied upon them as a source of legitimacy for the

---

[15] It is worth noting that the attitude toward European Bible criticism was ambivalent and the subject of debate among Zionist scholars. According to the accepted outlook, the Hebrew Bible is an expression of the ancient nation's spirit, which will reemerge and be liberated upon connecting with the Hebrew Bible and detaching from "Jewish" culture.

[16] Nadia Abu El-Haj (2001) demonstrated, among other things, the ways in which Israeli archeology follows earlier European excavations, and accordingly showed the link between empire and nation inherent to Zionist discourse. Israeli archaeology is an obvious manifestation of the early Zionist biblical culture identified as secular.

[17] The literature on Christian Zionism is steadily expanding (Matar 1989). See also Lewis (2010); Masalha (2007); Matar (1987).

idea of a Jewish state.[18] By so doing, they indeed pointed to an influence that they sought to reclaim under the rubric of Jewish secularism: Christian millenarianism.[19] On another level, the idea of the restoration of the Jews in their land, in the Orient, has been raised as a solution to the existence of the Jews in European countries. Millenarianism (and also anti-millenarianism) was the context in which visions of redemption of the Jews were first presented as a political program, formulated in modern political concepts of state and sovereignty. The secularization – that is to say, nationalization – of Jewish consciousness meant its articulation according to the millenarian Christian language and its accommodation into the Christian perception of history. In other words, the nationalization of the Jews can be seen as the secularization (namely, realization) of the Christian millenarian perception. Secularization in that sense is realization of the theological.

In many versions of the idea of the restoration of Jewish settlement and sovereignty, the future conversion of the Jews into Christianity is an essential part of the vision. Zionism differed of course from millenarian doctrine. Nevertheless, we should remember that Zionism also desired the transformation of the Jew and the creation of "the New Jew," redeemed and different from the exilic rabbinic Jew, and imitating the ancient Hebrew. Moreover, we should emphasize again that the Zionist "return" to the Bible was accompanied by the renunciation of Jewish rabbinic tradition, the Talmudic literature, namely, the same corpus that was historically the target of Christian anti-Jewish polemics. As such, the reembracing of the Bible led to the creation of a shared Jewish-Christian field, from which the Jewish Talmudic (exilic) literature was removed. The Bible was secularized and identified as "national," and the Talmud (the fundamental Jewish postbiblical composition, considered as "the Oral Torah") as "religious."

In this fashion, Judaism was divided into two factions: a "nation" that signifies the memory-cum-imagination of the Bible commonly held by Jews and Christians; and a "religion" that was identified with the Talmud and Jewish law and was rejected by secular Zionism. Consequently, the Zionist attitude toward "religion" preserves and reproduces the Christian fundamental ambivalence toward traditional Judaism and, by extension, the Jews. This, then, is the context for Zionism's absolute identification with the West and contraposition to the East.

[18]   For example, Bentwich and Shaftesley (1966); Gelber and Koebler (1956). Later writers also lean on the Christian context as a source of legitimacy for Zionist demands. See, inter alia, Netanyahu (1993). Conversely, Nabil Matar (1989) argues that Zionist writers exaggerated the role of Christian Zionism and failed to mention the significant resistance to these streams.

[19]   As Nabil Matar (1989) pointed out, Zionists even overestimated the actual significance of these trends, and neglected the continuous opposition to the idea. Nevertheless, Matar himself showed the origins of Zionism in that context. See also Matar (1987). See also the studies of Eitan Bar-Yosef, which discuss the idea of the restoration within the general framework of English references to Jerusalem as a concept and as a place (Bar-Yosef 2005; Sharif 1983). Recently, the topic has been receiving more and more scholarly attention, as part of the growing interest in Christian Hebraism.

The nationalization of the myth, that is to say, the attempt to release it from theological binding, clarifies the obvious Orientalist dimension of the image of "return" – as a Western nation – defining itself as against the East, against the Arabs. Paradoxically, for Zionism, the exodus from Europe and the aspiration to create a distinctly Jewish political entity in the East has been always a means of joining the Christian West and an expression of identification with the latter's self-perceptions. "Return" was directed toward an imagined East – the proverbial cradle of Western (Judeo-Christian) civilization – imagined and constructed in opposition to the real Arab-Muslim world.

BETWEEN MESSIANISM AND "REDEMPTION"

It is not surprising that, within this framework and in the context of Jewish sovereignty and domination, Jewish traditional religious images and concepts reappeared in radical forms and generated radical nationalistic activities. But it should be emphasized that these interpretations became possible due to the visualization of the present, the creation and existence of a Jewish state, in redemptive terms, and the ambivalent and obscure attitude toward messianism in Zionist "secular" thought.

Zionist writers insisted on distinguishing Zionism from messianism, regarded as apocalyptic and irrational, on the one hand, and as an expression of the passivity attributed to exilic Jews, on the other. In contradistinction, Zionism emphasized the rational and realistic dimension of its own activity, as a political endeavor meant to establish a Jewish homeland in Palestine. At the same time, Zionist discourse remains grounded on an interpretation of the content of "messianism" as reflecting mainly a desire for national political redemption in the form of an independent state. Nevertheless, we should notice that despite the anti-messianic rhetoric, the so-called secular carries the notion of redemption.

This tension was remarkably revealed by Gershom Scholem, the noted scholar of Kabbalah and Jewish messianism. Scholem may be considered as one of those who participated in the construction of the Zionist meta-historical narrative, but at the same time he was also one of the most sensitive critiques of secular Zionism. In the conclusion of his famous article, "Toward an Understanding of the Messianic Idea," he declared:

> Little wonder that overtones of Messianism have accompanied the modern Jewish readiness for irrevocable action in the concrete realm, when it set out on the utopian return to Zion. This readiness no longer allows itself to be fed on hopes. Born out of the horror and destruction that was Jewish history in our own gener-ation, it is bound to history itself and not to meta-history; it has not given itself up totally to Messianism. Whether or not Jewish history will be able to endure this entry into the concrete realm without perishing in the crisis of the Messianic claim, which has virtually been conjured up – that is the question which out of his great

Religion and Nationalism in the Jewish and Zionist Contextt 45

and dangerous past the Jew of this age poses to his present and to his future. (Scholem 1971, 36–37)

The question posed by Scholem remains crucial also in Israel of today, when political-messianic fundamentalist movements are flourishing and receiving growing support. Scholem repeatedly and consistently warned against messianism. But what should be emphasized here is that his warnings were not directed against "messianic speculations" as such, or against "religion," but rather toward the interpretation it may gain in the context of "secular Zionism" – of "Jewish readiness for irrevocable action in the concrete realm," namely, the nationalization and so-called secularization of the Jewish messianic perceptions.[20] Even if the contents of the various images attributed to "messianism" are ancient, Scholem emphasizes that it is "the modern Jewish readiness for irrevocable action in the concrete realm," the secularization of messianism, that "conjured up" the messianic crisis. In this context, Scholem can only say that Zionism has not given itself up totally to messianism. Moreover, Scholem warns here against the dangers of the perception he himself formulates in this same paragraph: He describes Zionism, "the concrete realm," as "The Utopian Return to Zion" – namely, as messianism according to his own definitions of messianism. At the same time, he warned against messianism. He could say that the Jews came to establish a national homeland in Palestine, but he insisted on using the biblical phrase.

The distinction between the "utopian return to Zion" and messianism expresses Zionist ambivalence toward "messianism." Zionism rejected messianism for two reasons: On the one hand, messianism was seen as being merely a passive expectation for divine intervention, or for being apocalyptic, catastrophic, anti-rational, and unrealistic. In this sense, the distinction from messianism was crucial for the shaping of the new national Jewish self-image as that of a "productive," "realistic," and "rational-enlightened" community. On the other hand, messianism was interpreted as a national "secular" myth of return, and Zionism was perceived as its fulfillment – "the utopian return." Messianic figures were presented as national heroes and national leaders, and messianic texts were understood as political treatises (Werses 1988). Scholem contributed to that framework the most sophisticated description of an immanent dialectical process in which messianic content is crystallized and sublimed, until it receives its most sublimed form in the Zionist nationalization of the myth. In other words, Scholem warns against the result of the perception that he himself conveyed in the passage, which reflects the fundamental element of Zionism: the perception of the present as the utopian return to Zion; the understanding of the present in obvious messianic terms, while understanding messianism as national political sovereignty.

---

[20] As was noted by Moshe Idel (1998), the title of the article "The Messianic Idea in Israel" is problematic, as the notion of messianism and the Messiah is much more complicated.

When Scholem warned against "messianism," he was well aware of what he was talking about: the desire to restore the Temple – namely, to demolish the mosque, al-Haram al-Sharif. This demand and vision are still considered as an extremist political demand (though supported by more and more Israelis), but it is a logical conclusion from the Zionist so-called secular narrative. For the Jews, Zion was the Temple, to be restored (in one way or another) at the end of days. In many interpretations, the future Temple turns to be a spiritual vision; in others, it will be restored in the end of days, when all Gentiles will join the Jews. Sometimes, they imagined it according to the Muslim monuments on the Mount – mainly the Dome of the Rock. Most rabbis still prohibit the very entrance into the Mount, because of its holiness. It is the result of secularization – that is to say, the interpretation of redemption as a political vision.

But the main point is not to indicate the apocalyptic dimensions of secularization. The warning against messianism disguises the concrete attributes of the secular, of the "utopian return to Zion." The suppression of the "apocalyptic" and the warning against "religion" are actually the suppression of the concrete realm itself: between the catastrophe and the utopian return there is no place for the land, for its inhabitants, for its past, and present. The constructed tension between "redemption" and "messianism" designed an exclusively Jewish territorial space that denied the history of the land and determined the exclusion of its Arab inhabitants from the image of redemption, and consequently from the land. The national-theological perception begot a mythical perception of "The Land," regarded as the national motherland; "The Land" had no history outside its place in the Jewish-Christian theological myth and accordingly was imagined as the land of the Bible as depicted in conventional Orientalist imagery. Therefore, in Israel today, the history of Palestine since the Second Temple is absent from school curricula, both "secular" and "religious."[21] There is no "secular" history of the land, the history of its various inhabitants, communities, and rulers.

SECULARIZATION AND EXILE

Jewish attitude toward the Land of Israel is complex (and fundamental) in its own right, but it does not require such identification with the Christian perspective. However, Zionism defined itself on the explicit rejection of earlier Jewish perceptions of the Land of Israel and explicitly distinguished itself from the "Old Yishuv," the Jewish communities that existed in Palestine during the late Ottoman period (both Ashkenazi and Sephardi). This distinction was crucial for the construction of the "new" secular Jew in a way that follows

---

[21] On the denial of the land and its historical geography, see Benvenisti (2000). See also Piterberg (2001). On the suppression of the history of the land in Zionist historiography, see Barnai (1995). Barnai stressed the tendency to disregard the history of the country, and at the same time to make the presumed historical continuity of Jewish existence there the central theme of Zionist historiography.

Religion and Nationalism in the Jewish and Zionist Contextt

the Christian ambivalence toward the Jews and its relation to Orientalist discourse: the "New" that replaces the "Old" – the new rationalist and progressive community that replaces the stagnant and irrational Oriental and exilic community. The attitude toward the Old Yishuv is crucial for the concrete understanding of Zionism and its notion of the secular.

Unlike the Zionist "new" settlement, the Old Yishuv was not founded on a return to the Bible or on "negation of exile." On the contrary: as a response to Zionist ideas, leaders of the Old Yishuv's communities insisted on defining their present existence as "exile in the Holy Land" (Bartal 1984; Friedman 1977). Their messianic desire was not directed primarily toward political emancipation, but rather toward a spiritual process of *tikkun*, the Hebrew concept for repairing and transforming the broken world and achieving divine revelation through the practice of the *mitzvot*, the commandments, especially the commandments that can be observed only in the Land of Israel. They definitely desired the coming of the Messiah, but this belief did not mean necessarily, certainly not exclusively, political redemption in the form of a modern nation-state. Pre-Zionist settlement was not founded on an identification with the Christian West; consequently, its existence did not require the denial of the land. Certainly, this community emphasized, in its very existence, the crucial role of the land as the exclusive site of revelation. They believed in a coming redemption but did not reduce it to the idea of a national-colonial state.

Thus, in spite of the repeated insistence on the "continuous presence of Jews in Palestine," it is important to note Zionism's denial of important aspects of even the country's Jewish past. While the omission of the memories of the Arabs' existence on the land is quite obvious (and is a cornerstone in the construction of Israeli national perception of the territory), we should also notice the Jewish aspects that were rejected. The opposition to the Old Yishuv was a crucial aspect of Zionist self-definition, and one of the ways all these aspects are linked.

This aspect is clearly exemplified in the way that Zionism overlooked or even erased the sixteenth-century Jewish community in Safed from its conscious awareness. Safed of the sixteenth century, particularly after its conquest by the Ottomans, had been a center that gathered some of the most prominent personalities in Jewish history, figures who manifestly reshaped the Jewish world. Among them one should mention R. Yosef Karo, the author of the canonical *Set Table* (*Shulchan Arukh*), which became the standard book of codification, a composition that systematically organizes all the 614 commandments, and has remained so until the present; kabbalist writings, mainly of R. Issac Luria Ashkenazi, Ha-Ari, had a dramatic impact on Jewish thoughts and liturgy. In the words of Solomon Schechter:

> there can be little doubt that no place in Jewish history since the destruction of the
> Holy Temple could point to so brilliant a gathering of men, so great in their
> respective branches, so diversified in the objects of their study, and so united by

the dominant thought of religion, as were attracted to Safed during the greater part of the sixteenth century. (S. Schechter 1908, 232)

Despite Zionism's stated insistence on the "continuity of Jewish presence in Palestine," this significant moment was suppressed and excised from the national memory. And indeed, historical Safed provided an alternative model of Jewish settlement in Palestine. The context that attracted those who came to Safed in the sixteenth century was not the biblical: their outlook was that of the Tanaim, the sages who composed the *Mishna*, the foundation of the Jewish "Oral Torah" and of Talmudic literature. For them, the crucial moment in the history of the land dated to the first centuries after the destruction of the Second Temple, between the first and the fourth centuries. This extended period was conceived as the indispensable moment, and it was this moment – not the moment of sovereignty attributed to the Temple period – that they aimed to restore in order to bring about redemption and attain revelation. It was also considered to be the period in which the *Zohar*, the most important Kabbalistic composition, was revealed. While the consensus among scholars is that the *Zohar* was written in Spain in the thirteenth century, for the Safedian sages, the composition has been revealed to the sage R. Shimon Bar-Yochai, who lived in the second century AD (Scholem 1941, 156–204).

The great rabbis who came to Safed during that period expressed a desire for redemption, for "the end of days" (*Ha-Ketz*). But their understanding of messianism was different. In fact, they came to Safed because only in the land can one experience the state of exile, an experience that was seen as a precondition for revelation and redemption. Some of them had experienced as children the traumatic expulsion from Spain (1492) and Portugal (1497),[22] or were born to parents from Iberian origins who resettled in the Ottoman Empire. However, exile was a fundamental aspect not only of their life experience but also of their messianic perception. According to their approach, the exile of Israel is a manifestation of the state of exile of the world, a result of the crisis within divinity itself. The mission of the people of Israel is to repair this rupture through the practice of the commandments, prayer, and rituals. The goal of activity is the redemption of the Shekhina, a feminine manifestation of divinity identified with Israel, in order to bring her back into her place and to God, her husband. Messianism was not merely an expectation of the coming of the Messiah, but a permanent and active participation in the process of repair, to gather back the divine sparks that are scattered around the world (Idel 1998, 154–82; Scholem 1941, [1973] 2016).

---

[22] In 1492, the Jews were expelled from the newly united Spanish monarchy. Many Jews converted to Christianity, but many others preferred to leave the country and resettle in Italy and North Africa and were invited by the growing Ottoman Empire. In 1497, the Jews had to flee from Portugal, which had first offered shelter but then persecuted them. The Jews settled in many cities in the expanding Ottoman Empire, and established there new communities that joined the existing Arab-Jewish communities. On the background of the traumatic expulsion on the sages of Safed, see Scholem (1941).

The main aspect of the redemptive activity that directed Safed's sages was therefore cosmic, intended to repair the rupture found within the divine. Such activity can be conducted only in the Land of Israel. It is a national project, but the people of Israel are not the subject of redemption. Rather, they are its carriers. According to this perception, that is what distinguishes the Jewish people as a people.[23]

Accordingly, we can say that the understanding of the differences between Zionism and the legacy of Safed as one between a secular and religious approach is evidently wrong. These are two political theologies, each referring to a different period in ancient history: the Zionist to the Bible; Safed to the postbiblical, to Palestine after the Roman conquest and the destruction of the Temple. Focusing on the question of the Temple clarifies the essential contradiction of the so-called secular position and demonstrates that the Zionist secular perception is the apocalyptic among the two models: When redemption is conceived as the restoration and imitation of the biblical narrative, the growing desire to rebuild the Temple logically follows. It is impossible to expect a narrative of exodus, conquest, and settlement and to stop there – for the biblical story continues. Safed gives us a dramatically different perspective. The question of the Temple acquires a different function when the crucial moment is the moment *after* the destruction – when the reconstruction of the Temple cannot be seen as the conclusion of the process of redemption and liberation. The desire for the construction of the Temple is first of all the desire to bring about the resurgence of the Shekhina.

The legacy of Safed inspired during the centuries many future religious movements, like Hassidism in Europe and modern trends of Jews in the Muslim world. It also inspired, indirectly, non-Orthodox Jewish intellectuals, like Walter Benjamin, who elaborated on the notions of exile and rupture and employed those notions in contrast to Western perceptions of progress and secularity. The denial of its legacy in Zionist discourse clarifies the concrete attributes of the national. We should emphasize that the ambivalence toward the legacy of Safed is shared also by religious Zionists, who regard kabbalistic learning and rituals as Oriental superstitions. That is one significant difference between religious Zionism and other religious groups – many of the ultra-Orthodox, and particularly Mizrachi Jews, who considered themselves traditional and still preserve aspects of the Safedian culture.

Focusing on Safed teaches us about the notion of the secular in Zionist discourse, but may also propose alternative thinking of Jewish existence in Palestine. There is no

---

[23] See, for instance, the introduction of R. Yosef Karo (1551) to his monumental *Beit Yosef*: "in the name of God that created the world for the human kind, and chose his people to practice his Torah and its commandments." He then goes directly to the principles of codification. But we should notice his insistence to start the monumental composition that deals with internal Jewish law, with the declaration that the world was created for the entire humanity, and what distinguishes the Jews is their commitment to the Torah and the praxis of the commandments.

question that the Safedian project is "religious," but it can inspire also non-Orthodox thinking about the secularization of Jewish existence, namely, its decolonization. Later, non-Zionist Orthodox groups depicted their existence in the land as "exile in the Holy Land" and accordingly developed their approach toward the state, an approach ranging from their perception of Israel as a state like all states to the complete rejection of its existence. Although long before the beginning of Zionist settlement, ultra-Orthodox circles encouraged immigration to Palestine, they refused to see these efforts as a realization of redemption. They hoped that their deeds and praying in the Holy Land would advance the coming of redemption, but redemption was a matter of permanent practice, not a political vision. After the establishment of the State of Israel, they maintained what could be seen as a neutral attitude toward the state and rejected the sacred status attributed to it in secular thought (Ravitzki 1989, 5).

In giving attention to these Jewish views, I do not mean to claim that these tendencies have come up with a satisfactory alternative or indeed any comprehensive worldview to replace or challenge the present one. These attitudes cannot and should not be taken for themselves, but they definitely provide the only possible platform for the discussion of secularization in any meaningful sense: the existence of a Jewish political entity in *Eretz Israel* is a theological question that cannot be ignored, and this awareness is crucial for any genuine process of secularization. It clarifies that secularism cannot be addressed against religion, but can emerge only from the theological discourse. If the idea is to create a public sphere in which people who hold various beliefs (and nonbeliefs) can coexist, then secularism as such cannot provide the platform. In fact, it denies it.

Exile and exilic can be productive for thinking on the secularization of Israel. This is particularly important considering the fact that the result of the idea of "negation of exile" is the exile of the Palestinian people, the denial of its homeland in the name of the biblical promise as justification for the project of colonization. "An ancient time grants to this new time the keys of our doors," wrote Mahmoud Darwish, and this is the point of departure for the discussion of exile, and of Jewish existence. The voice that may generate the discussion on exile and renew sensitivities of previous generations is the Palestinian. After all, secularization is meaningless if not including its victims. The so-called secular-liberal Israeli approach prevents it.

REFERENCES

Abu El-Haj, Nadia. 2001. *Facts on the Ground: Practice and Territorial Self-fashioning in Israeli Society*. Chicago: University of Chicago Press.

Almog, Shmuel. 1998. "Religious Values in the Second Aliya." In *Zionism and Religion*, edited by Shmuel Almog, Yehouda Reinhartz, and Anita Shapira, 285–300. Hanover, MA: Brandeis University Press.

Anderson, Benedict. 1991. *Imagined Communities: Reflections on the Origin and Spread of Nationalism*. London: Verso.

Anidjar, Gil. 2007. *Semites: Race, Religion, Literature*. Stanford: Stanford University Press.

Asad, Talal. 1993. *Genealogies of Religion: Disciplines and Reasons of Power in Christianity and Islam*. Baltimore: Johns Hopkins University Press.

2003. *Formations of the Secular: Christianity, Islam, Modernity*. Cultural Memory in the Present. Stanford: Stanford University Press.

Balibar, Etienne. 2004. *We, the People of Europe: Reflections on Transnational Citizenship*. Translated by James Swanson. Princeton: Princeton University Press.

Barnai, Jacob. 1995. *Historiography and Nationhood: Trends in the Study of Eretz-Israel and Its Jewish Community, 634–1881* [in Hebrew]. Jerusalem: Magnes.

Baron, Salo W. (1947) 1960. *Modern Nationalism and Religion*. New York: Harper.

Bartal, Israel. 1984. *Exile in the Holy Land* [in Hebrew]. Jerusalem: Mossad Bialik and the Zionist Library.

Bar-Yosef, Etan. 2005. *The Holy Land in English Culture, 1799–1917: Palestine and the Question of Orientalism*. Oxford: Oxford University Press.

Batnizki, Leora. 2011. *How Judaism Became a Religion*. Princeton: Princeton University Press.

Bentwich, Norman, and John M. Shaftesley. 1966. "Forerunners of Zionism in the Victorian Era." In *Remember the Days: Essays on Anglo-Jewish History Presented to Cecil Roth*, edited by John M. Shaftesley, 207–39. London: The Jewish Historical Society of England.

Benvenisti, Meron. 2000. *Sacred Landscapes: The Buried History of the Holy Land Since 1948*. Berkeley: University of California Press.

Ben Yisrael, Hedvah. 2004. *The Nation: Essays and Articles on Nationalism and Zionism* [in Hebrew]. Beer Sheva: The Ben-Gurion Research Institute for the Study of Israel and the Ben-Gurion University Press.

Berger, Peter, ed. 1999. *The Desecularization of the World: Resurgent Religion and World Politics*. Washington, DC: William B. Eardmans Publishing.

Bhabha, Homi K., ed. 1990. *Nation and Narration*. London: Routledge.

Casanova, José. 1994. *Public Religions in the Modern World*. Chicago: University of Chicago Press.

2006. "Rethinking Secularization: A Global Comparative Perspective." *The Hedgehog Review* 8, no. 1–2: 7–22.

2008. "The Problem of Religion and the Anxieties of European Secular Democracy." In *Religion and Democracy in Contemporary Europe*, edited by Gabriel Motzkin and Yochi Fischer, 63–74. London: Alliance Publishing Trust.

Chatterjee, Partha. 1998. "Secularism and Tolerance." In *Secularism and Its Critics*, edited by Rajeev Bhargava, 345–79. New Delhi: Oxford University Press.

Don Yehiya, Eliezer. 1980. "Secularization, Negation and Integration of Elements of Traditional Judaism and Its Concepts in Socialist Zionism." [In Hebrew.] *Kivunim* 7: 29–46.

Dubuisson, Daniel, and William Sayers. 2007. *The Western Construction of Religion*. Baltimore: Johns Hopkins University Press.

Friedman, Menachem. 1977. *Society and Religion: The Non-Zionist Orthodox in Eretz-Israel, 1918–1936*. Jerusalem: Yad Ben Zvi.

Gelber, Nathan Michael, and Franz Koebler. 1956. *The Vision Was There: A History of the British Movement for the Restoration of the Jews to Palestine*. London: Lincolns-Prager.

Harrison, Peter. 1990. *"Religion" and the Religions in the English Enlightenment*. Cambridge: Cambridge University Press.

1998. *The Bible, Protestantism and the Rise of Natural Science.* Cambridge: Cambridge University Press.

Hastings, Adrian. 1997. *The Construction of Nationhood: Ethnicity, Religion and Nationalism.* Cambridge: Cambridge University Press.

Hertzberg, Arthur. 1968. *The French Enlightenment and the Jews.* New York: Columbia University Press.

Hill, Christopher. 1993. *The English Bible and the Seventeenth-Century Revolutions.* London: Allen Lane.

Hutchison, William R., and Helmut Lehmann, eds. 1994. *Many Are Chosen: Divine Election and Western Nationalism.* Minneapolis: Fortress Press.

Idel, Moshe. 1998. *Messianic Mystics.* New Haven, CT: Yale University Press.

Ilany, Ofri. 2012. "From Divine Commandment to Political Act: The Eighteenth-Century Polemic on the Extermination of the Canaanites." *Journal of the History of Ideas* 73, no. 3: 437–61.

Karo, Yosef. 1551. *Beit Yosef.* Edited by Yosef Karo. Vol. 1. Sabbioneta: Tobias Foa.

King, Richard. 1999. *Orientalism and Religion: Postcolonial Theory, India and "the Mystic East."* London: Routledge.

Kohn, Hans. 1955. *Nationalism: Its Meaning and History.* Princeton: Van Nostrand.

Lehmann, Hartmut. 1996. "The Germans as a Chosen People: Old Testament in German Nationalism." In *Religion und Religiosität in der Neuzeit: Historische Beiträge,* edited by Hartmut Lehmann, 205–58. Göttingen: Vandenhoeck und Ruprecht.

Lewis, Donald M. 2010. *The Origins of Christian Zionism: Lord Shaftesbury and Evangelical Support for a Jewish Homeland.* New York: Cambridge University Press.

Marrus, Michael. 1980. *The Politics of Assimilation: The French Jewish Community at the Time of the Dreyfus Affair.* Oxford: Clarendon Press.

Masalha, Nur. 2007. *Zionism and the Bible.* London: Zed Books.

Masuzawa, Tomoko. 2005. *The Invention of World Religions: Or, How European Universalism Was Preserved in the Language of Pluralism.* Chicago: University of Chicago Press.

Matar, Nabil I. 1987. "Milton and the Idea of the Restoration of the Jews." *Studies in English Literature* 27, no. 1: 109–24.

1989. "Protestantism, Zionism and Partisan Scholarship." *Journal of Palestine Studies* 18, no. 4: 52–70.

McCutcheon, Russell T. 1997. *Manufacturing Religion: The Discourse on Sui Generis Religion and the Politics of Nostalgia.* Oxford: Oxford University Press.

Nandy, Ashis. 1995. "An Anti-secularist Manifesto." *India International Quarterly* 22, no. 1: 35–64.

1998. "The Politics of Secularism and the Recovery of Religious Tolerance." In *Secularism and Its Critics,* edited by Rajeev Bhargava, 321–44. New Delhi: Oxford University Press.

Nelson, Eric. 2010. *The Hebrew Republic: Jewish Sources and the Transformation of European Political Thought.* Cambridge, MA: Harvard University Press.

Netanyahu, Benjamin. 1993. *A Place among Nations: Israel and the World.* New York: Bantam Books.

Oz-Slazberger, Fania. 2008. "The Political Thought of John Locke and the Significance of Political Hebraism: Then and Now." In *Political Hebraism: Judaic Sources in Early Modern Political Thought,* edited by Gordon Schochet, Fania Oz-Salzberger, and Meirav Jones, 231–56. Jerusalem: Shalem Press.

Pinson, Koppel S. 1934. *Pietism as a Factor in the Rise of German Nationalism.* New York: Columbia University Press.

Piterberg, Gabriel. 2001. "Erasures." *New Left Review* 10 (July–August): 31–46.

Ravitzki, Avi. 1989. "Exile in the Holy Land: The Dilemma of Haredi Jewry." *Studies in Contemporary Jewry* 5: 89–125.

Raz-Krakotzkin, Amnon. 2005. "Zionist Return to the West and the Mizrachi Jewish Perspective." In *Orientalism and the Jews*, edited by Ivan Kalmar and Derek Pensler, 162–81. Waltham, MA: Brandeis University Press.

2013. "Exile, History and the Nationalization of Jewish Memory: Some Reflections on the Zionist Notion of History and Return." *Journal of Levantine Studies* 3, no. 2: 37–70.

Schechter, Ronald. 2003. *Obstinate Hebrews: Representations of Jews in France 1715–1815*. Berkeley: University of California Press.

Schechter, Solomon. 1908. "Safed in the Sixteenth Century: A City of Legalists and Mystics." In *Studies in Judaism, Second Series*, edited by Solomon Schechter, 202–85. Philadelphia: Jewish Publication Society of America.

Scholem, Gershom. 1941. *Major Trends in Jewish Mysticism*. New York: Schocken Books.

1971. "Towards an Understanding of the Messianic Idea in Judaism." In *The Messianic Idea in Judaism and Other Essays on Jewish Spirituality*, edited by Gershom Scholem, 1–36. New York: Schocken Books.

(1973) 2016. *Sabbatai Ṣevi: The Mystical Messiah, 1626–1676*. Translated by R. J. Zwi Werblowsky. Princeton: Princeton University Press.

Shapira, Anita. 1998. "The Religious Motifs of the Labor Movement." In *Zionism and Religion*, edited by Shmuel Almog, Yehouda Reinhartz, and Anita Shapira, 251–72. Hanover, MA: Brandeis University Press.

2005. *The Bible and Israeli Identity* [in Hebrew]. Jerusalem: Magnes.

Sharif, Regina. 1983. *Non-Jewish Zionism: Its Roots in Western History*. London: Zed Books.

Shavit, Yaacov, and Mordechai Eran. 2007. *The Hebrew Bible Reborn: From Holy Scripture to the Book of Books*. Translated by Chaya Naor. Berlin: De Gruyter.

Sheehan, Jonathan. 2005. *The Enlightenment Bible*. Princeton and Oxford: Princeton University Press.

2009. "Sacrifice before the Secular." *Representations* 105, no. 1: 12–36.

Simon, Uriel. 1999. "The Place of the Bible in Israeli Society: From National Midrash to Existential Peshat." *Modern Judaism* 19, no. 3: 217–39.

Smith, Anthony D. 2004. *Chosen Peoples: Sacred Sources of National Identity*. Oxford: Oxford University Press.

Smith, Cantwell. 1991. *The Meaning and End of Religion*. Minneapolis: Fortress Press.

Smith, Jonathan Z. 1998. "Religion, Religions, Religious." In *Critical Terms for Religious Studies*, edited by Mark C. Taylor, 269–84. Chicago: University of Chicago Press.

Stroumsa, Guy G. 2010. *A New Science: The Discovery of Religion in the Age of Reason*. Cambridge: Cambridge University Press.

Taylor, Charles. 2007. *A Secular Age*. Cambridge, MA: Belknap.

van der Veer, Peter, and Helmut Lehman, eds. 1999. *Nation and Religion: Perspectives on Europe and Asia*. Princeton: Princeton University Press.

Weidner, Daniel. 2005. "Secularization, Scripture and the Theory of Reading: J. G. Herder and the Old Testament." *New German Critique* 94: 169–93.

Werses, Shmuel. 1988. *Haskalah and Sabbatianism: The Story of a Controversy* [in Hebrew]. Jerusalem: Zalman Shazar Center for Jewish History.

Yelle, Robert A. 2013. *The Language of Disenchantment: Protestant Literalism and Colonial Discourse in British India*. New York: Oxford University Press.

3

Religious Claims and Nationalism in Zionism

Obscuring Settler Colonialism

Nadim N. Rouhana

This chapter examines how nationalism, religious claims, and settler colonialism enmesh within Zionism, and demonstrates how their interaction played a major role for Israeli academia and politics in sidelining or obfuscating settler colonialism as an appropriate frame of analysis for Zionism's encounter with the Palestinians. The chapter will make three main arguments: first, that while settler colonialism is an obvious framework for analyzing and understanding the unfolding of the Zionist project in Palestine, the framework has been obscured by highlighting the connection between Jewish nationalism and religious claims; second, that the steady rise in religious encroachment into institutions and the public sphere in Israel is rooted in the need for legitimation (grounded in religious claims) in face of rising Palestinian resistance to the expansion of the settler-colonial project from Israel to the West Bank; and third, that while secularization was possible in other settler-colonial contexts such as South Africa, Northern Ireland, and North America, it is impossible to achieve secularization within a Zionist regime. Rather, for secularization and democratization to take place, Israel has to recognize the settler-colonial reality of the Zionist project, a recognition that will make it possible to free Israeli Jewish nationalism from religionism and work toward decolonization.

INTRODUCTION

On April 29, 2019, during a UN Security Council debate on the Middle East, Israeli Ambassador Danny Danon "defended the Jewish right to the Land of Israel, including the West Bank settlements" (Lazaroff 2019). That is, he defended the Jewish right to Palestine – all of it. During his speech, the secular ambassador covered his head with a black yarmulke, raised his right hand while holding the Hebrew Bible, and declared: "This is our deed to our land. ... God gave the land to the people of Israel in Genesis, when he made a covenant with Abraham" (Danon 2019). He then read from the Bible God's word to Abraham:

Religious Claims and Nationalism in Zionism

And I will establish My covenant between Me and you and your descendants after you throughout their generations for an everlasting covenant. And I will give to you, and to your descendants after you, all the land of Cana'an, for an everlasting possession. And I will be their God. (Danon 2019)[1]

Earlier that month, Israeli Prime Minister Benjamin Netanyahu "pledged to annex Jewish settlements in the occupied Palestinian territories and keep control of the whole territory if he [won] his country's election," which was due on April 9, 2019 (Holmes 2019). Thus, Ambassador Danon was presenting to the world body the justification for such a pledge. He was also responding to a question by the President of the Council, who asked him in an earlier session, in Danon's language, "to explain how Israel implements international law, specifically with regard to the Jewish communities of Judea and Samaria" (Danon 2019). Danon said that his answer starts with "four pillars that prove the case for Jewish ownership of the Land of Israel."[2] The first pillar was the Bible, as quoted above. Why did Danon start with the Bible? Let me first mention briefly the other three pillars, because the central point therein goes to the heart of this chapter's three main arguments. The second pillar was history, according to which a Jewish kingdom existed in *Eretz Yisrael*. "This was the kingdom over which King David and King Solomon ruled. It was the kingdom, with Jerusalem as its capital." Talking about 3,000 years ago,[3] Danon argues that when the Second Temple was destroyed by the Romans in the year 70 CE, "[e]ven the Romans themselves admitted the land was ours." The third pillar was international law, starting with the Balfour Declaration of 1917[4] in which Lord Balfour, the then British foreign secretary, wrote to Jewish leader Lord Rothschild that "His Majesty's Government views with favour the establishment in Palestine of a national home for the Jewish people, and will use their best endeavours to facilitate the achievement of this object" and ending with the UN General Assembly's Resolution 181 in November 1947 on the partition of Palestine into two states.[5] The fourth pillar is peace and security. The ambassador argued that the

---

[1]   For a video of the speech, see www.youtube.com/watch?v=vqgchSV2cn8. Lazaroff (2019) referred to the speech as "unusual."

[2]   For a full transcript of the speech, see Danon (2019).

[3]   According to Grant (2012), David became king in about 1000 BCE.

[4]   For the letter, see Laqueur and Schueftan (2016, 16).

[5]   Interestingly, Danon (2019) argues that these are not international borders, because the 1948 War with the Arab states ended with armistice lines. Thus, he states that "because these lines are not borders, the Jewish communities in Judea and Samaria, to this day, do not cross any international borders." It is true that the armistice agreements were not considered official borders. The agreement with Jordan, for example, included the phrase, in Article 2, paragraph 2, that "no provision of this Agreement shall in any way prejudice the rights, claims and positions of either Party hereto in the ultimate peaceful settlement of the Palestine question, the provisions of this Agreement being dictated exclusively by military considerations" (General Armistice Agreement, Isr.–Jordan 1949, art. 2, para. 2). This phrase was requested by the Arab states who signed the agreements, because Israel's borders at the time of signing had expanded much beyond the territory allocated to it by the UNGA resolution and also because the Arab states did not recognize the resolution.

Palestinians rejected opportunities to make peace, and that their leaders "refuse to acknowledge the right of the Jewish people to self-determination in the Land of Israel and insist on returning to the land in droves."

Danon starts with the Bible, a religious text, as the proof of the Jewish right to Palestine. This, as we will see, is not unusual for secular Zionist leaders. Danon's speech at the UN exemplifies the central three arguments I advance in this chapter, particularly the main argument about obscuring the settler-colonial dimension of Zionism (both from its followers and from the world body) by stressing the religious claims and consequently the connection between Jewish nationalism and religious claims.

In the following section, I discuss three components: settler colonialism, exclusively ethnic nationalism, and the religiously justified claims to Palestine. I then examine the complex interactions among these components, which occur in the context of relentless Palestinian resistance (and changing global dynamics) and try to show how these interactions were instrumental in masking the settler-colonial component in the academic and political discourse about the encounter between Zionism and the Palestinians, particularly in Israel. I conclude the chapter by addressing the questions of decolonization, secularization, and democratization.

ZIONISM: THE SETTLER-COLONIAL, THE NATIONAL, AND THE RELIGIOUSLY BASED CLAIMS

Whether Zionism is a settler-colonial project is not merely an academic question. The political and moral implications of this question are enormous to all involved, because settler-colonial regimes lack legitimacy given that they seek to exploit and/or replace native populations with people who come from outside the settler-colonial site, inevitably using violent means. Thus, at its core, the question is political too. Given the fundamental question of legitimacy that is integrally related to any settler-colonial project, the views about Zionism are sharply divided. This section examines Zionism as a settler-colonial project with national characteristics and vehement religiously based claims. I therefore refer to it as *settler-colonial nationalism* that is legitimized by religious claims.

Zionism as a Settler-Colonial Project

It is perhaps not surprising that to those who are on Zionism's receiving end – the Palestinians – the Zionist project has always been seen as a settler-colonial one. By and large and since the start of the encounter with Zionism in the late nineteenth century, Palestinians saw in it a project of people coming from Europe with the help of a colonial power, Great Britain, that sought to displace them and replace them in their homeland – *displacement and replacement*. The analysis and terminology from the start, as well as the modes of resistance (military and civil, as in the great revolt of

Religious Claims and Nationalism in Zionism   57

1936–39) and the political stances they took (including their rejection of the UN General Assembly Resolution 181 from November 1947 on the partition of Palestine to a Jewish state, an Arab state, and a special international regime for the city of Jerusalem) all represented an understanding of the conflict as, in what we would call in today's vernacular, a settler-colonial one.[6]

This view of Zionism has not changed, although a more complex understanding of Zionism might have evolved. After the PLO was established in 1964 among Palestinian refugees outside Palestine, its political program centered around "return and liberation" – that is, the return of Palestinians who were forced out of Palestine by the Jewish forces in the 1948 War and were not allowed to come back, and the liberation of Palestine from Zionist control – but without extensive discussion of what would govern the relationship between Arab and Jew.[7]

Academic theorizing of settler colonialism in Palestine (as opposed to its emergence in the popular and political consciousness) was initiated in the 1960s by Palestinians and others. Thus, the PLO Research Center in Beirut published Fayez Sayegh's (1965) book, *Zionist Colonialism in Palestine*, and other scholars engaged settler colonialism theoretically (see, e.g., Abu-Lughod and Abu-Laban 1974; Hilal 1976; Jabbour 1976; Rodinson 1973; Trabulsi 1969). As Salamanca et al. (2012, 2) observe, settler colonialism "once served as a primary ideological and political touchstone for the Palestinian national movement." Indeed, I have argued elsewhere (Rouhana 2014) that until the mid-1970s, the settler-colonial paradigm was the predominant paradigm among Palestinian scholars, guided much of their description and analysis, and informed Palestinian political thinking (albeit without the theoretical advancements that emerged in the last two or three decades). Settler-colonial understanding of the conflict permeated the Palestinian cultural sphere and public and political consciousness.

It was the PLO's shift toward the politics of statehood in the 1970s that expedited the emergence of the paradigm that the conflict between Zionism and the Palestinian national movement is a national conflict. The realpolitik of the international and Arab circumstances that arose after the 1973 War, which was opened by Egypt and Syria with the explicit goal of liberating Egyptian and Syrian lands Israel occupied in 1967 (and not Palestinian lands overtaken in 1948 or 1967), persuaded the dominant factions within the PLO to seek statehood in the territories occupied in 1967 (Gresh 1988). Starting with the PLO's "10-point program" in 1974 that called for the establishment of an independent national authority "over every part of Palestinian territory that is liberated" (Permanent Observer Mission of Palestine to the United Nations 1974) and continuing through the 1993 Oslo Accords, the PLO sought to achieve what is known as the "two-state solution" – a Palestinian state in

---

[6] See R. Khalidi (2020) and Said (1979).

[7] The 1968 "one secular democratic state" program advanced by the PLO envisioned Palestinians and Jews living equally in one state, but it did not offer details on the relationship or power-sharing arrangements it envisaged between the two communities. See Shaath (1977).

the West Bank and Gaza living alongside Israel on the basis of the 1967 borders. During this time frame, from the mid-1970s until recently, the *political* discourse on and the study of the settler-colonial paradigm has waned (Rouhana 2014). A new paradigm gradually emerged – that of conflict between two national movements, Zionism and the Palestinian national movement. It is important to notice that the national conflict paradigm that guided and still guides the Palestinian Authority's pursuance of the two-state solution and that is promoted by the Authority's political elites did not replace the settler-colonial paradigm in Palestinian consciousness (particularly among the cultural elites and in the public consciousness) but rather coexisted with it.

Recently there has been a vigorous return of the settler-colonial paradigm to the academic discourse on Palestine led not only by Palestinian but also international scholars. Whatever the factors that led to this return – the political conditions on the ground such as the failure of the national conflict paradigm to define the conflict and explain its dynamics; the increasing clarity of Israeli settler-colonial practices and structures; the persistence and resilience of Palestinian resistance; and the changing politics of knowledge production with the emergence of new generations of critical and native scholars and new areas of academic inquiry – the settler-colonial paradigm in studying Palestine has gradually become an indispensable framework making strides toward the mainstream discourse. This shift has occurred due to the work of many scholars who theorized and carried out comparative work with Palestine included (such as A. Bishara 2005, 2017; Busbridge 2018; Gordon and Ram 2016; Lloyd 2012; Mamdani 2015; Pappé 2008, 2012; Rouhana and Sabbagh-Khoury 2015; Shalhoub-Kevorkian 2014; Veracini 2006, 2019; Wolfe 2006, 2012; Zreik 2016) and a whole range of others who theorized and debated major issues within the paradigm as it relates to Zionism, and Israel.[8]

The hegemonic framing of Zionism within a settler-colonial paradigm in Palestinian political consciousness, cultural sphere, and academic discourse at least until the 1970s and its recent return stand in sharp contrast to the almost total absence of this paradigm on the Israeli side, including in academia, not even among what became known as the New Historians, a group of revisionist historians who mainly reexamined the dominant Zionist narrative of the 1948 War (Piterberg 2015).[9] Many Israeli scholars who refer to Israel's colonialism limit the scope of their inquiry to Israel's policies in the Palestinian territories occupied in 1967 (see, e.g., Shlaim 2009; Sternhell 1998). This view is also accepted politically by some in the "Zionist left" who consider Israel as the metropolis, and the Israeli settlers in the

---

[8] For a partial list, see the three special issues of *Settler Colonial Studies* from 2012 (vol. 2, no. 1), 2015 (vol. 5, no. 3), and 2019 (vol. 9, no. 1). See also the 2019 special issues of *Interventions: International Journal of Postcolonial Studies* (vol. 21, no. 4).

[9] Piterberg (2015) argues that at least two leading Israeli sociologists presented their work within a settler-colonial framework: Gershon Shafir and Baruch Kimmerling. For an alternative and nuanced reading of their work, see A. Bishara (2011).

West Bank as its emissaries. According to this view, the zero-point of the settler-colonial project in Palestine is the year 1967, when Israel occupied the West Bank and Gaza and started building settlements there right afterward, in 1968. The discourse focuses on *Israeli* settler colonialism and not necessarily on Zionism as a settler-colonial project, certainly not before the demarcating time line of 1967. Indeed, many people in what remains of the "Zionist left" parties view the Jewish settlers in these settlements as a major cause of the conflict and an impediment to resolution which can be achieved by their return (more accurately, the return of many of them) to the metropolis, Israel (within its pre-1967 boundaries). For them, Israel is a normal state – not the product of a settler-colonial project but a metropolis state that has started a settler-colonial project in the West Bank.[10]

These differing views notwithstanding, Zionism from its very start fits the frame-work of a settler-colonial project. It was conceived in the late nineteenth century in Europe by Europeans, in this case Jews,[11] who sought to establish an exclusive Jewish state in Palestine despite the fact that Palestine was inhabited by another nation[12] with a minority of Jews, between 8 and 9 percent at the turn of the twentieth century.[13] The Jews in Palestine at the time considered themselves, like other Jews in the Arab world, Arab Jews – Arabs of Jewish faith (Hayoun 2019; Shenhav 2006).

It is true that Zionism offered a mixture of historical and religious (and later other) justifications for settling Palestine and accordingly presenting the settlers as natives and denying this status to the Palestinian Arab indigenous population. I will discuss this justificatory system, particularly its religious component, in the next sections. But suffice it to say here that whatever the justificatory system, or the motivation of the fathers of the project or their global supporters, the project took the course of a settler-colonial undertaking. For that matter, neither the justifications nor the motivations were of major concern to the native Palestinians, whose continuous

---

[10] In the Israeli elections held on September 17, 2019, Meretz, the "Zionist left" party that holds these views, won 5 parliamentary seats out of 120.

[11] Although some argue that the roots of Zionist thinking go back to other Europeans – mainly Christian fundamentalists (e.g., Chapter 2 and Masalha 2007). As Masalha (2007, 30) among others (e.g., Goldman 2009; Rabkin 2012; Smith 2013) argues, the Bible's title deed to Palestine originated not in modern Zionism as "historically it was deeply rooted in the post-Reformation Protestant doctrine that Jewish restoration to Palestine would be to the fulfillment of biblical prophecy and the second coming of Christ." Gottlieb and Hagler (2019) describe Rev. John Hagee, the leader of Christians United for Israel, one of the largest pro-Israel lobbies in the US, as representing a "toxic blend of anti-Semitism, racism, homophobia, Islamophobia and sexism." This group believes that Israel's establishment fulfills a biblical prophecy and that when all Jews return to Israel and "rebuild a Jewish Temple in the Noble Sanctuary mosque complex in occupied East Jerusalem," Jews will convert to Christianity if they do not want to face death. Interestingly, the authors argue that this theology supported other (settler-)colonial projects and white supremacy (Gottlieb and Hagler 2019). Hagee offered a benediction at the opening of the US embassy in Jerusalem (Haag 2018).

[12] Whether the Arab inhabitants of Palestine have developed a national identity when the Zionist project started is, for this author, irrelevant for determining the settler-colonial character of Zionism. Yet, for an answer to this question, see al-Charif (1995) and R. Khalidi (1997).

[13] Rabinovich and Reinharz (2007, 571). This range reflects the Jewish population in Palestine between 1882 and 1918.

efforts to present what they considered as an unquestionably settler-colonial project[14] have not been well heard particularly in Western political, cultural, and academic circles.

A defining quality of the project is that in its goal of establishing a constitutionally exclusive Jewish state (Masri 2017; Rouhana 1997) was inherent the concept and practice of replacement of the native. Zionism came to build a *Jewish* homeland in Palestine. It is obvious that in practice, this could have only meant displacement and replacement, a major characteristic of many settler-colonial regimes. While displacement did not take the form of physical extermination as in other cases (nor was this one of the intended means to achieve displacement),[15] it did take the form of demographic elimination or demographic riddance – by using brute violence, as in various ways of ethnic cleansing that evacuated the part of Palestine on which Israel was established of the vast majority of its Palestinians – or legal means, such as citizenship laws that prevent Palestinian refugees from returning and open the gates to Jews to immigrate with particular ease. Displacement also included the geographic displacement or erasure by destroying more than 400 Palestinian towns inside the area of Israel (W. Khalidi 2006) and replacing them with hundreds of Jewish towns. It also included attempted cultural and historic erasure of Arab, particularly Palestinian, or Muslim presence and replacing it with Jewish history, employing and politicizing religious sites, archaeological projects (Abu El-Haj 2001; Herzog 2001; Whitelam 1996), the politics of museums and monuments building, and religious celebrations (Makdisi 2010; Shalhoub-Kevorkian 2017). Like other settler-colonial projects, the Zionist project employed toward the natives the psychological and epistemological justificatory systems of degradation, discrimination, disdain, racism, constructing as violent,[16] and establishing a system of colonial control with settler-colonial privileges that is anchored in law (Rouhana 2018).

[14] For how various Palestinian political parties viewed Zionism, see al-Charif (1995). The question of whether the Palestinians tried well enough to have their case presented to the world was often addressed in the cultural sphere. In Ghassan Kanafani's ([1963] 1999) foundational novel *Men in the Sun*, the truck driver – in whose tanker truck three Palestinians hid in the scorching heat of the desert sun to get to Kuwait from Iraq and who die after the driver stops for border customs – asks the Palestinians after he finds out about their death, "Why did you not knock on the walls of the tank?" This became a cultural metaphor for the Palestinian effort to present their case. A response came in Elias Khoury's (2019) *Children of the Ghetto: My Name Is Adam*, that the question is not so, but why the world doesn't want to hear the loud knocks.

[15] The many massacres of Palestinians by the Jewish forces during the 1948 War did not aim at physical extermination but rather at demographic elimination. They were enacted strategically to terrorize the native Palestinians into leaving their towns and their country. See, e.g., Jawad (2006, 2007). The massacres, which pose an embarrassment to the Zionist narrative (because a central theme of it is that Palestinians simply ran away – as if that matters in terms of the question of their return), are occasionally disclosed and fiercely debated. For the latest disclosure of previously undisclosed massacres and the debate over attempts Israeli archives to conceal the evidence, see Haaretz (2019a); Shezaf (2019).

[16] Israel's minister of public security said in a radio interview on October 7, 2019, referring to the Palestinian society in Israel, that "the Arab society is very, very and another one thousand times very violent. ... it is [their] cultural code." See Haaretz (2019b).

Religious Claims and Nationalism in Zionism

There are important characteristics of Zionism as a settler-colonial project that this chapter will not discuss; but two are particularly relevant to the main arguments I make – specifically the argument that Palestinian agency and resistance are closely tied to the rising power of the religious claims in modern Zionism by increasingly pressing Zionism to unveil its underlying core of religious legitimation. I therefore highlight these two features as laid out below.

First: The Zionist settler-colonial project over Palestine in its entirety (including Israel within its pre-1967 borders) has not ended. It has been aggressively using various means to achieve displacement and replacement (such as by relentless settlement of the West Bank; Judaization of Jerusalem; discriminatory immigration laws; and confiscation of Arab land inside Israel).[17] The project's final goal of establishing an exclusive Jewish state, although in terms of sovereign statehood on the ground has been achieved, is both aggressively continuing to expand (with no defined final borders), and at the same time, its future is not determined. Israel, as a state, is an ongoing project. One can say that many states are – in the sense that state identity, political system, demographic composition, international relations, and power constantly evolve. But Israel as an ongoing project has deeper meanings: Israel's borders remain undefined, and Israel itself declines to delineate its boundaries; its capital (itself with wholly undefined borders) is not recognized except by very few nations, which the UN considers null and void;[18] it occupies since 1967 a territory – the West Bank and Gaza (in addition to the Golan Heights) – not only with its control not recognized by even one state but with the Occupied Territories recognized by the UN General Assembly as a nonmember observer state; its Jewish settlements in the Occupied Territories are not recognized internationally and are considered to be illegal by the UN; its identity as a Jewish state is rapidly evolving with stronger national religious components; and its very legitimacy as a Jewish state is not accepted by its neighbors and is challenged by most of the people under its own control who are not Zionists – close to 50 percent of the population (citizens, residents, and occupied).[19] Most importantly, Israel's future – at least as what many Israelis call a "Jewish and democratic" state – is not seen by many of them as guaranteed. Under these circumstances, need for legitimacy is rising.

[17] For a survey of Israel's legal system toward the Arab citizens, see Sultany (2017).
[18] The US recognized Jerusalem as the capital of Israel on December 6, 2017. In light of this recognition, a UNGA resolution from December 19, 2017, "called upon all states to refrain from the establishment of diplomatic missions in the Holy City of Jerusalem pursuant to Security Council Resolution 470 (1980)." See UN News (2017).
[19] In 2019, Palestinian citizens in Israel comprised about 17 percent of the total number of citizens – about 1.56 million. Palestinians in occupied East Jerusalem – 362.3 thousand – which was annexed to Israel after its occupation in 1967, were granted residency but not citizenship rights; and Palestinians in the West Bank have no citizenship or residency rights. The total Arab population in Israel, according to the Israel Central Bureau of Statistics comprises about 20.9 percent of the Israeli population, (1,878,400 of a total of 8,967,600); this figure, however, includes Palestinians in occupied East Jerusalem (and Syrian Arabs in the occupied Golan Heights of about 26,200 residents). See CBS (2019a, 2019b).

Therefore, the project is in constant need of legitimation, both internally and internationally.[20] Furthermore, this need rises because the settler-colonial policies are constantly resisted by Palestinians in the West Bank, Gaza, and in Israel itself and are therefore more internationally visible.

Second: Zionism embarked on a settler-colonial venture at a time when settler-colonialism was waning. While after World War II, other settler-colonial projects were unwinding and the postwar era was more characterized by decolonization, Zionism continued in the opposite direction of history – first, within its 1948 borders and later, in the whole area of Palestine; furthermore, it faced and sought to subjugate a nation with a crystallized national identity and developed urban centers, cultural institutions, economic and political systems, and media centers – not much different from its neighbors. This timing of the project made the settler-colonial policies and the resistance to it more visible on the international stage like in South Africa, Zimbabwe, and Algiers.

Zionism as a National Movement

Zionism is also a national movement, yet not a national liberation movement. That is, Zionism did not seek to liberate a colonized, occupied, or controlled nation or homeland from a foreign power (or local dictatorship).[21] To the contrary, it required Europe's help – Britain specifically – to establish a Jewish homeland outside Europe. In this sense, Zionism is a *settler-colonial nationalism*, not liberation nationalism. It is true that Zionism sought to address the horrifying European treatment of Jews that peaked in the Holocaust; but the solution it sought was neither in Europe nor against the European regimes but in a faraway land: Palestine, Uganda, Argentina, and other far-flung places (Rovner 2014, 49–52).

Once Palestine was chosen, Zionism made it the object of nationalism and successfully created national consciousness among its followers. Long before Israel was established, the Zionist project started with forming national organizations including labor and military organizations, a land-acquisition fund, academic institutions, and media and cultural outlets. In this sense, a group of people was willing, determined, and successful in imagining and constructing themselves, or a part of them, as a nation. Challenging the authenticity of this perception, even if it

---

[20] Israel and its supporters in the US, for example, invest major efforts to "explain" Israeli policies through projects with leading academics, students in prominent schools, politicians, and media people. These major efforts (referred to in Hebrew as *hasbara*, or explanation) reflect deep anxiety about its policies and practices. The focus on the US is related to the fact that Zionism as a settler-colonial project has no one geographic motherland but it enjoyed political support of something akin to motherland by the British until 1948 and gradually by the US since then (W. Khalidi 1992). Thus, the public opinion in the powerful "political motherland" is fundamental for the project's ability to maintain political support.

[21] In the Zionist historical discourse, the concept of "liberation" is central. Thus, for example, the 1948 War is called "the Liberation War" – that is, liberating the land from its native inhabitants, the Palestinians. This is the war that established the settler-colonial sovereignty and political system.

is manipulated by elites and/or external powers, does not make it less genuine. After all, neither elites nor external powers can invent a nation if there are no basic elements for the success of such an invention – some basic cultural commonalities, grievance on the basis of collective identity, etc. But Zionism's fateful conflictual consequence is that the fulfillment of the national goal could have been achieved *only* by following a settler-colonial course, as described above. The fundamental issue here is that Zionism, as a national movement, could not have achieved the typical goal of national movements – that is, territorially based sovereignty and statehood – without being a settler-colonial project, whether implemented in Palestine or elsewhere. This is because it was forging a nation from a people who were scattered worldwide and not concentrated in any one territory.

Zionist nationalism is not only settler colonial and non-liberational, it also embodies an ideology of ethnic exclusivity rather than nationalism based on citizenship or that is conducive to become citizenship based.[22] It claims to represent the Jewish people, but the very definition of "who is a Jew," which has long occupied Israeli religious and political debates, centers around the role of *religious* definition of who is to be considered a Jew. Zionism is so exclusive that Israel, with about 25 percent of its citizens being non-Jews (CBS 2018), has not developed even the concept of "Israeli people" or "Israeli nation," because Israeli citizenry includes "non-Jews"; these terms do not exist in Hebrew.[23] In fact there is no "Israeli nationalism" in Israel, as determined by a ruling of the Supreme Court. On October 2, 2013, the Israeli Supreme Court rejected the appeal of twenty-one Israeli citizens (Jews and Arabs) to have their "nationality" defined as "Israeli" in the country's population registry. That is, they requested to change their nationality from either "Jew" or "Arab," nationalities that are currently used, to "Israeli" and were therefore seeking legal support for their claim that there is an "Israeli nation." The Supreme Court argued that "there was no proof of the existence of a uniquely 'Israeli people'" (Hovel 2013). The court reiterated arguments made forty years earlier in a similar case (see Gross 2013). One justice argued that "it has not been proven that, legally, there exists an 'Israeli nation' and it is not appropriate to encourage the creation of new fractions of a nation" (Hovel 2013). So, by law, Israel does not allow nationalism that can include Jews and Arabs (and others). The only recognized nationalism in Israel is Jewish nationalism,[24] and one can join

---

[22] For the difference between the two types of citizenship, see Brubaker (1998). See also Rouhana (1997) on Israel as a constitutionally exclusive Jewish state and A. Bishara (2017) on different types of citizenship.

[23] In Hebrew the word *a'am* translates to nation. The way it is combined with Israel is A'am Yisrael, which literally means "The Nation of Israel," a term used to refer to the Jewish people. It does not mean the Israeli nation or people as a nation of citizens like the French people, the American people, or the Lebanese people. The term that is closest to the "Israeli people" is "the citizens of Israel." When "Israelis" is used by itself in Hebrew, the implicit connotation often refers solely to Jewish Israelis.

[24] Although the Israeli identity card uses the terms "Arab" and "Jew" under the item of nationality, Israel doesn't recognize the Arabs as a national group, only the Jews.

Nadim N. Rouhana

this nation only through the religious route – i.e., conversion. The ethnic exclusivity of Zionism is demonstrated politically (based on constitutional law) (Masri 2017; Rouhana 1997). Palestinian citizens' claim for equal citizenship in a "state for its citizens" is considered extremism and can be used to deny political parties the right to run for the parliament (see Masri 2017; Rouhana 2014; Sultany 2017). The recent Nation-State Law re-constitutionalized Israel as the state of the Jews only, thus excluding about a quarter of its citizens (who are not Jewish) from claiming it as their state (Jabareen and Bishara 2019; Masri 2017)[25] or indeed as their home.

Zionism and the Fusion between Religion and Nationalism

As a national ideology (vs. political attitude as in Christian Zionism), Zionism represents an extreme case of fusion between religion and nationalism.[26] In order to understand the depth of this fusion, consider the total overlap between Jewish religion and Jewish nationalism: You are a Jew in nationality only if you are a Jew in religion and vice versa.[27] Thus, for example, immigrants from the former Soviet Union who are not Jewish in religion (but were accepted as citizens by Israel based on the Law of Return because of their relationship in a particular way to a Jew as the law stipulates) are not Jewish by nationality. They are Israeli citizens like other non-Jewish citizens, such as the Palestinian citizens, but because they are not Jewish themselves in *religious* terms (and therefore in national terms), there is a price to pay. As Kravel-Tovi writes,

> Israel has established a strong connection between the issues of conversion and matters of immigration, naturalization, and registration. . . . To the extent that one's status as a Jewish convert, for immigrants and citizens alike, defines how (or in fact, determines whether) she is granted civil recognition, financial benefits, and religious services (such as marriage and burial), this connection is quite strong. (Kravel-Tovi 2012, 373)

[25] In this sense, the fact that Zionism was both a settler-colonial project and an exclusively ethnic national movement constituted a double jeopardy for the Palestinians. The combination of a colonial project that did not seek an openly racial hierarchical system in which the natives could be incorporated and used for the benefit of the colonizers, with exclusive nationalism (claiming exclusive right over the homeland), favored the expulsion of the natives over their subjugation. For various reasons (related to the historical timing and other factors), Zionism did not seek to physically eliminate the native population.

[26] For comparative purposes, this volume addresses Serbian nationalism, the Hindutva movement, and Sinhalese nationalism. The Hindutva movement (Chapter 7) holds striking similarities in terms of the extent of this fusion.

[27] The Law of Return (1950) stipulates: "'Jew' means a person who was born of a Jewish mother or has become converted to Judaism and who is not a member of another religion." It knowingly accepts non-Jews if they are related to Jews according to the law. Specifically, it states that "[t]he rights of a Jew under this light and the rights of an *oleh* [Jewish immigrant to Israel] under the Nationality Law . . . are also vested in a child and a grandchild of a Jew, the spouse of a Jew, the spouse of a child of a Jews and the spouse of a grandchild of a Jew, except for a person who has been a Jew and has voluntarily changed his religion."

Kravel-Tovi describes how the hegemony of the Jewish religious orthodox rabbinical establishment shapes the official state conversion process. Converts can become Jewish by nationality only if they convert to Judaism according to Halachic Jewish law. Furthermore, the other way around also explains how the overlap is total. If a person leaves the Jewish religion, that person cannot by law claim to remain Jewish by nationality. That is, by law, a person cannot be Jewish by nationality while belonging to another faith (see Pap 2013, 144–49). Moreover, because Zionism regards all Jews as a nation and not only a religious group, it considers Jewish communities in countries other than Israel as members of the Jewish nation too, regardless of whether they agree.[28]

The political manifestations of Zionism's fusion with religious claims and therefore the manifestation of the religious claims in Zionism's sacralized politics are most evident in its claim that Palestine is the Jewish homeland, to which I turn in the following section. It is this particular claim, rather than seeking Uganda, for example, as the site of the settler-colonial project, that created the inextricable entanglement of nationalism and religion in Zionism and that made sacralized politics inevitable (as discussed below).

THE RELIGIOUS IN ZIONISM'S CLAIM OF PALESTINE

Religious metaphors and texts have been used in justificatory colonial discourses in many settler-colonial and colonial projects. Settler-colonial societies, to varying extents, invoked the Hebrew Bible in their projects, including in Northern America (Goldman 2004; Prior 1997; McSloy 1996), South Africa, and Northern Ireland (see Akenson 1992). But what sets Zionism aside as fundamentally different, indeed distinct, in terms of blending religious claims into the project, is that unlike other settler-colonial projects, the Jewish people have a cultural (with a strong religious component) and historical *connection* to Palestine. While other settler-colonial projects with different historical circumstances and political trajectories dropped the biblical claims and sought alternative sources of legitimacy, Zionists leaned in further and deeper on biblical justifications. The cultural connection to the land was crucial in this regard.

Originally, and paradoxically, it was secular Zionism that used religious claims to establish the entitlement to Palestine. The essence of Zionism as envisioned by its secular founders was to transform the cultural *connection* – zeroing in on the religious component – into political entitlement, that is, the Zionists' *exclusive* right of sovereignty over Palestine.[29] Masalha (2007) carefully demonstrates how, although Zionism started as a nonreligious movement whose founding fathers

---

[28] Thus, for example, even though the Jewish community in the US does not claim to be a national group, according to Zionism, its members are members of a national group.

[29] The point here is not only that Zionism claimed the right to Palestine, but that it claimed it exclusively for the Jewish people. The exclusive vision preceded the practice. If not for the exclusivity

were secular or atheists, the movement nonetheless used the biblical narrative to legitimize its claim to Palestine from the outset. This claim was based on the view that God, in the Bible, had given the land to the Jews. What Masalha calls the ethnocentric paradigm of "promised land – chosen people," according to which "the Bible provides for the Jews a sacrosanct 'title deed' to Palestine and beyond, signed by God" became the main legitimizing base for the establishment of a Jewish state in Palestine (Masalha 2007, 3). The secularist founder of the State of Israel and the leader of dominant "secular" Zionism at the time, David Ben-Gurion, told the British Royal Commission in 1937 that "the Bible is our Mandate" (Shapira 2015).[30] And on May 24, 2011, Benjamin Netanyahu, the contemporary leader of "secular" Zionism, addressed a joint session of the US Congress and presented the essence of Zionism's relationship to the West Bank (using the biblical name Judea and Samaria):

> In Judea and Samaria, the Jewish people are not foreign occupiers. We are not the British in India. We are not the Belgians in the Congo. This is the land of our forefathers, the Land of Israel, to which Abraham brought the idea of one God, where David set out to confront Goliath, and where Isaiah saw a vision of eternal peace. No distortion of history can deny the four thousand year old bond, between the Jewish people and the Jewish land.[31]

Thus, as Raz-Krakotzkin (Chapter 2) points out, for Zionism's founding fathers, God does not exist; yet he promised Palestine to the Jewish people. Therefore, when Israel's secular ambassador to the UN refers to the Bible as the Jewish people's "deed to the land" (as described above), he is following a solid secular Zionist tradition that, like a thread, connects the secular founders through the current secular leadership – to all branches of Zionism.

Invoking religion and religious claims to support the justificatory system of the colonial claim to Palestine augments the fusion, not only between religion and nationalism in Zionism, but also between religious claims and settler colonialism. In this particular case, as argued below, and because the settler-colonial project is ongoing at full pace while facing unrelenting resistance, the religious assertions become even more needed and accordingly more publicly articulated.

---

of the claimed right, some visions of sharing the land with the natives might have emerged in mainstream Zionism (as they did in marginal binational views within Zionism, such as Martin Buber's; see Mendes-Flohr 2005). The exclusive claim is consistent with and has been backed by God's promise to his chosen people.

[30] As Rick Richman (2017) observes, in that testimony Ben-Gurion made the important point that "The rights of the Jews in Palestine . . . were derived not from the Mandate and the Balfour Declaration but from the history chronicled in the Bible." Thus, Ben-Gurion told the Commission: "[T]he Bible is our Mandate . . . Our right is as old as the Jewish people. It was only the recognition of that right which was expressed in the Balfour Declaration and the Mandate. . . . [We are] re-establishing a thing which we had, which we held, and which was our own during the whole history of the Jewish people."

[31] For the full text, see Netanyahu (2011). Incidentally, Lis (2011) points out in *Haaretz* that the story of David and Goliath did not occur in the territory that Netanyahu specified.

Many scholars refer to the period from Israel's establishment until the early 1970s as the "secular period" in Israel's history (e.g., Peled and Peled 2018; Ram 2008). But as Azmi Bishara (2005, 31) points out about this period, "[a]t the height of its secularism, Zionism has never succeeded in creating a secular definition of Judaism that differs from the definition of the Jewish *halacha* for this affiliation, i.e., for religion. In the eyes of Zionism, a Jew in the national sense is also a Jew in the religious sense." While in comparison to what has recently been unfolding in Israel, one can say that politics during that period was less openly sacralized, its depiction as secular overlooks the underlying religious values, religious claims, and religious justifications in the most fundamental (secular) state-making components – *demographic control, land control, and exclusive state sovereignty* (as the political translation of the monopoly of the use of legitimate force). I discuss briefly the religious in each of these three components.

In terms of demographic control – from the ethnic cleansing of Palestinians in 1948 and thereafter to immigration and citizenship laws (many of which were in the service of demographic elimination), Israeli policies and laws are suffused with religious values, claims, or references. As Masalha (1992) argued, the concept of "transfer" itself – which is used in Zionist jargon as a euphemism for the ethnic cleansing of Palestinians and which historically occupied Zionist thinking pre-1948, when the destiny of the Palestinian population in the future Jewish state was discussed – is embedded in the same idea that Palestine belongs exclusively to the Jewish people on a biblical basis as their birthright.[32] This is why, in traditional Zionist discourse, Palestinians (the indigenous people) are considered to be strangers (or even invaders and infiltrators), and Jews (the recently arrived immigrants) are considered natives of Palestine – whatever their geographic origin. Immigration laws are based on the same biblical birthright conception (God's deed); therefore, Jewish immigrants "ascend" (in Hebrew *oleh*) to the country of God's promise, while those who emigrate descend from it (*yored*). For this reason, a Jewish immigrant is called an *oleh*. This term, however, is only applicable to an immigrant who is a Jew. These terms themselves are submerged with the deepest religious convictions. The citizenship of Arab and Jew itself is founded on God's promise, and thus citizenship has two different levels, one (more privileged) for a Jew and one (less privileged) for an Arab (A. Bishara 2017).

Beginning in the pre-state (secular) era, plans to take over Palestine through land acquisitions employed a mechanism infused with religious meaning called "land redemption," which literally means saving the land from its Arab owners and returning it to perpetual Jewish ownership. This "saving" was originally done by purchase – when the Zionist settlers did not have enough means to do it otherwise.

---

[32] According to Kimmerling (1999, 345), the Book of Joshua provided "the muscular and militaristic dimension of conquest of the land and the annihilation of the Canaanites and other ancient people that populated the 'Promised Land.'" Masalha (1992) shows how Ben-Gurion and Jabotinsky have often invoked the Book of Joshua in discussing views about the future of the Palestinian population.

Later it was done by force and by "legal" means. Land redemption (*geulat adama*) is a Halachic[33] concept that means returning the land to its original owner. For precisely this goal, the Jewish National Fund (JNF) was established in Basel, Switzerland, in 1901 – to save the land from its Arab owners (Wolfe 2012). Although this objective is completely consistent with the settler-colonial project, for the JNF to become "the custodian of the land for the Jewish people," the clause stipulates that the Jewish ownership should be permanent (Katz 2002), and that is why the JNF's land is not available for the Arab citizens in Israel.[34] This clause is based on the biblical injunction that "the land shall not be sold in perpetuity" (Leviticus 25:23; see Leon 2006, 115–21). The JNF's activities continue not only in Israel but also in the West Bank, to acquire Palestinian lands for future Jewish settlements, often through forgery and fraud (Peace Now 2017).

The political implications of encoding this exclusive ownership into state policies of urban planning and land distribution are immense. Israel took over the private and public property of the expelled Palestinians in the part of Palestine on which it was established – 78 percent of historic Palestine. The Palestinians who managed to stay in what became Israel owned private and public land of their own. But Israel started a series of land expropriation waves, all supported by laws it legislated, in order to transfer the majority of the Palestinian land to Jewish hands. Today, Israel controls 93 percent of the total land in the country; Arab citizens have no access to 80 percent of the state's land; and Arab municipalities control only 2.5 percent of the total land (Yiftachel 2002). The religious foundations of these political goals, which were all pursued prior to the state's founding during the so-called secular phase, are unmistakable.

The concept of exclusive sovereignty itself, the notion that the Jewish people have an exclusive right over the homeland, has its roots in the biblical promise. No other sovereignty is acceptable, even to be shared, as demonstrated in the recent Nation-State Law.[35] Thus, this sovereignty is not in the name of the Israeli people (which in any case does not exist, as discussed above); it is the sole monopoly not of Israeli citizens – a modern political term – but of the Jewish people *in their entirety throughout the world* – an across-boundaries ethno-religious term. Accordingly, the state symbols – the flag and the state symbol – are also ethno-religious (Fine 2016).

In its so-called secular phase of settler-colonial nationalism, Zionism, like any other nationalist movement, sought to invoke history, invent traditions, revive a language, and use archaeology – in the service of firming up the claim to Palestine. The Hebrew Bible and the religious foundations of the claim were evident, as discussed. Thus, in a major project, biblical names were used to rename the

---

[33] Of or pertaining to Jewish religious law.

[34] See S. Bishara (2018) and the debates over the Qaadan case in Jabareen (2002).

[35] The law stipulates: "The right to exercise national self-determination in the State of Israel is unique to the Jewish people." For an English translation, see www.timesofisrael.com/final-text-of-jewish-nation-state-bill-set-to-become-law/.

Palestinian landscape (Azaryahu and Golan 2001; Benvenisti 2002) while serving the settler-colonial purpose of erasure and replacement. A national effort focused on employing archaeological findings suffused with religious biblical meaning to legitimize exclusive Jewish sovereignty (Abu El-Haj 2001; Herzog 2001; Masalha 2007).

Many scholars showed how the Bible is treated as history in secular political Zionism. For example, Masalha (2007, 25) argues that the Bible is "reinvented as a nationalized and racialized sacred text central to the modern foundational myth of secular Zionism." Others argue:

> teaching the Bible as history to Israeli children creates the notion of continuity. It's Abraham ("the first Zionist," migrating to Palestine), Joshua and the conquest of Palestine (wiping out the Canaanites, just like today), King David's conquest of Jerusalem (just like 1967). (Beit-Hallahmi 1992, 119)

The secular Zionists' continual reference to the Bible as history was designed to achieve two goals: inventing modern Jewish nationalism internally for the Jewish public and making a case for taking over Palestine. In the process, however, Jewish nationalism became profoundly and inexplicably intertwined with religious claims.

Therefore, when we examine how religion is incorporated in Zionism, it is not sufficient to point to the rising strength of religious parties or to their power to achieve concessions from the secular. Scholars often refer to the agreement that Ben-Gurion famously reached in 1947, before Israel was established, with an ultra-Orthodox group (Barak-Erez 2009, 2495) as evidence that secular Zionism was forced to make concessions to the religious forces. Based on this document, which became known as "the status quo document," laws were passed and administrative arrangements reached that recognized marriage, divorce, conversion, and burial as the monopoly of the Orthodox Chief Rabbinate; thus state and religion are not separate. This status quo arrangement was the outcome of a bargain between the secular and the religious forces reflecting the political balance of power at the time. Yet, secular Zionism, which reached this arrangement with the religious forces, has itself been imbued with religious values and claims that were necessary to establish the legitimacy of the colonial project. The religious claims permeated the very fundamentals of the settler-colonial state-building and continue to penetrate and spread among the secular sector of society. This reality has far-reaching ramifications on how and why the religious are rising so powerfully in Israel, and not only the mere strength of the religious parties or national religious parties, as I discuss next.

THE STEADY RISE OF THE RELIGIOUS IN ZIONISM AND OBSCURING SETTLER COLONIALISM

My emphasis so far has been on the infusion of *secular* Zionism with religious claims, because this fusion is fundamental to our understanding of the gradual and

70   *Nadim N. Rouhana*

steady rise of religious nationalism in Israel since the 1970s and the aggressive expansion of the settler-colonial project both within Israel and in the West Bank. With this expansion, the discourse of religious legitimation and its penetration into the public sphere have been visibly rising.

Rarely does the discussion of religion's increasing presence in Israeli politics include the settler-colonial characteristic of the Zionist project. The discussion of sacralized politics in Israel often focuses on the increasing religionizing of Israeli society, how religion and nationalism interact, the increasing role of religious groups in politics, media, and the military, and so on. These discussions, including by leading Israeli scholars (e.g., Chapter 5; Peled and Peled 2018; Ram 2008; Shenhav 2007), do not see a place for settler colonialism. This is not surprising, because Israeli academia has by and large bypassed the discussion of Zionism and Israeli society within a settler-colonial framework. While in many cases of examining nationalism and religion, such as those referenced above, the analysis is valuable, its dead spot is overlooking or denying the settler-colonial context and its impact on why and how religious claims are being progressively employed as politics become more sacralized.

There is a consensus among scholars who study Israel that secular Zionism has gradually been weakened and that it has been giving way to religious Zionist trends (Davis and Coffman 2014). The gradual, yet steady, shift of religious discourse relating to politics and nationalism from the margin to the center has been well recorded (Scham 2018, 207–13). This includes exploration into why religious nationalism rose in power in Israel after 1967 (Bar-Tal and Salomon 2006, 26–27; Davis and Coffman 2014, 30–33; Tessler 2009, 411–12); the surge in the influence of Jewish religious parties in Israeli state institutions (Tessler 2009, 411–12); the penetration of Jewish religious values and discourse into the public sphere (Hasson 2015) and the military (Chapter 5). All these studies seem to focus on the immediate contact of the Jewish public with the Jewish religious sites in the West Bank after its occupation in 1967, as if that somehow caused a fundamental shift. After all, they argue that more Jewish religious sites exist in the part of Palestine that Israel occupied in 1967 (such as East Jerusalem, Hebron, Nablus, and the Bethlehem area) than inside Israel within its 1948 borders.

It is true that the shift started a few years after the occupation of the West Bank and coincided with the encounter with Jewish holy sites. Nevertheless, the fact that the settlement project in the West Bank was started immediately after the occupation,[36] by the Labor Party – the leader of "secular" Zionism at the time – and that East Jerusalem and several nearby Palestinian towns and villages were annexed to Israel within days of their occupation "in contravention of international law"[37] by the "secular" Zionist leadership illustrates that it

---

[36]   The first settlement was established in 1968. By the time Labor lost power to Likud in 1977, Israel had established over ninety settlements in the West Bank (Lesch 1977, 27; Tessler 2009, 466). See also Matar (1981).

[37]   See Erekat (2019).

Religious Claims and Nationalism in Zionism 71

was not an overt rise in the religious or national religious power and discourse that initially guided or spearheaded the settlement project. Furthermore, the settlement project gained considerable momentum under another secular leadership – that of the Likud Party – since it took the governing seat in 1977. Settlements continued to be supported under Rabin's and Barak's Labor Zionism's leadership later on when Labor managed to lead the government for limited periods. Secular Zionism – whether Labor, Likud, or otherwise – considers the West Bank to be an integral part of the Land of Israel (*Eretz Yisrael*), all of which was promised to the Jewish people; but this promise, as extended to the West Bank, had not developed into a full-fledged religious or even national claim before its occupation. Instead, the West Bank stayed in the background. Except for annexing East Jerusalem, the inward rationalization and outward legitimization for building settlements was grounded more in national security discourse than ethno-religious claims.

Ram (2008) points to the year 1977 in Israel as the year of explicit political crystallization of the fusion between religion and nationalism in Zionism. As part of his study on religious revivalism in Israel, he suggests a four-modules typology of political legitimacy based on the crosscutting of two axes: nationalism (strong/weak) and religion, or as he calls it religionism (strong/weak). Interestingly, even though he argues that nationalism and religion in Israel are fused, he places only the Israeli Jewish Bloc of the Faithful[38] in the category of strong nationalism and strong religionism to which he refers as religious nationalism – similar, he argues, to Hamas and Irish Catholicism.[39]

My argument in this chapter is not that no major political force of religious nationalism emerged in Israel that fits Ram's category. It did. My argument is that religionism has been an integral part of Zionism altogether, not only of religious nationalism, precisely because religion and nationalism are fused. Thus, while Ram rightly points out that the blend of nationalism and religionism in Zionism has shifted over history, he and many others underestimate the underlying fusion of religion and nationalism throughout all the various stages, including in the stage of what he calls "secular nationalism" in Israel that according to him peaked in the 1960s. The two missing links in such an argument are, first, the reluctance, often aversion, to seeing and analyzing Zionism as an ongoing settler-colonial project (with no completion goal or end in sight), driven by a continuous need to justify establishing an ethnically exclusive Jewish state in Palestine and a growing need to legitimize the unceasing settlement project; and second, Palestinian agency and resistance. I address each one separately next.

---

[38] The Orthodox Jewish fundamentalist movement that emerged after the 1967 War and spearheaded establishing Jewish settlements in the West Bank and the Gaza Strip. See Lustick (1988).

[39] For a different reading of Hamas and Irish Catholicism, see Chapters 12 and 14.

Religious Legitimation and Obscuring Settler Colonialism

The religious-national support for the settlement project is unquestionable. It has forceful roots in the openly religious Zionist discourse (Lustick 1988). But the direct or indirect blaming of religious nationalism or religious parties is, in my view, self-serving misplacement of responsibility from Zionism as a settler-colonial project. It is the convergence of the religious with the settler colonial and their interdependence that make both rise concurrently. Religious nationalism supports the settlement project and pushes toward expanding it; secular Zionism, in its settler-colonial project, increasingly needs the legitimation of the religious claims.

For further clarification of this point, let us imagine that Herzl's proposal to establish a Jewish homeland in Uganda (or for that matter, in Argentina or Australia as was discussed by the Sixth Zionist Congress in Basel on August 26, 1903) had been accepted (American-Israeli Cooperative Enterprise, n.d.; Gelvin 2014). What justification could the Zionist movement have used for such a project? Even if Zionism was a latecomer to settler-colonial projects, the movement might have opted to use the commonplace discourse of the settler-colonial civilizing mission or implicit (or explicit) messages of serving imperialist states (as indeed was the case in Palestine) (Thompson 2019). Alternatively, they could have argued that the long-term persecution of the Jews in Europe between 1880 and 1945, which culminated in the Holocaust, entitled the Jews to a state of their own (e.g., Gans 2008) to serve as a refuge secured by sovereignty. However, such argument(s) would have omitted the biblical foundational underpinning the legitimacy of Zionist claims to Palestine. We can safely assume, based on other settler-colonial projects in Africa, that Ugandans would have fought this project and that their resistance would escalate against privileging of settlers (Jews in this case) over natives and the processes of dispossession, exclusive Jewish settlements, exclusive sovereignty and self-determination that are all inherent in colonization. There is no reason to assume that their resistance would have been any less fierce than that of the Palestinians.[40]

---

[40] As it happens, an Israeli delegation headed by Prime Minister Benjamin Netanyahu visited Uganda on the fortieth anniversary of the Entebbe Operation (in which Israeli commandos stormed an Entebbe-bound airplane hijacked by a group of Palestinian and German guerrillas and rescued the passengers). The Ugandan president, Yoweri Kaguta Museveni, addressing the delegation on July 4, 2016, gave what media outlets reported as a bizarre speech in which he referred to Israel as Palestine several times. But the president said something of great importance, even if grounded in erroneous historical facts. He said that Balfour, as a foreign minister of the British Empire (he served as foreign minister between 1916 and 1919), suggested that Uganda be the homeland of the Jewish people. The president thanked the Jews for not accepting the idea and said to the Israeli delegation at the ceremony: "Fortunately, the Jews did not accept Balfour's idea – which was a good thing, otherwise we would have been fighting you now." See Danan (2016); Museveni (2016). This is indeed a simple but revealing statement made to an Israeli prime minister and his delegation point blank, showing that it is only natural to expect natives to resist Zionist settlement in their land. It was Herzl, the first president of the World Zionist Organization, who made this proposal in 1903. The proposal was voted down by the same organization in 1905, after Herzl's death. See Kornberg (1980). The Balfour Declaration issued in 1917 as a letter to Lord Rothschild was about Palestine, not Uganda. See note 4.

What would the state have used to legitimize – in the eyes of its Jewish settlers and the international community – its exclusive claim to land and Jewish supremacy over the native Ugandans? It could not invoke religion, God's promise, or the Bible in claiming that particular land. It would most probably have been exposed as a racist state like South Africa under apartheid, because the need for a refuge by itself could not justify Jewish supremacy over the native population. Furthermore, the Zionists could not have claimed to be natives (thereby denying the Ugandan natives this position) as they did in Palestine, because the claim of being natives to Palestine is also based on biblical justification. If one follows the South African example, one would expect that the settlers would seek to *become* natives. But this long process has its cost; it is called decolonization (Mamdani 2001; Rouhana 2018; Zreik 2016).

The stronger the challenge to the legitimacy of Israel's territorial claims and to Jewish supremacy, both in Israel itself and in the West Bank, the more the biblical promise and religious history are needed as legitimation. While in the Uganda scenario, the settler-colonial nature of the hypothetical state would be evident and resistance would make it even more so, in Palestine this was and continues to be obfuscated by the belief in the biblical claim internally, and the sympathy and support to it internationally.

Another case that can shed light on Zionism's increasing need to invoke religious claims for legitimation and thus contributing to the steady rise of religious forces and at the same time obscuring its settler-colonial character is the comparison between Armenia and Israel. Such invocations are valuable not only for the colonizers internally, but also to address their victims, and the international community. It also helps us understand why these invocations are likely to increase the more the settler-colonial character of the project is revealed – mainly through Palestinian resistance.

The Armenian and Jewish communities are ancient, both fusing religion and nationalism in some way. The Jewish religion played a major role in preserving Jewish communities in Europe (such as in ghettos) and Arab Jewish communities in the Middle East and North Africa.[41] In Armenia, Christianity was established as the country's religion in the early fourth century, leading to more than seventeen centuries of Christian history. The Armenian genocide during World War I and the Holocaust during World War II, as well as the earlier pogroms faced by both groups, became defining features of their modern history before and after achieving independent statehood. Yet there is a fundamental difference in state formation that impacts, among other things, the place of religion and religious claims in defining state identity and its legitimacy, democratic processes, and separation from the church. The difference is that Armenian state formation benefited from centuries

---

[41] As Arabs of Jewish religion (like Christian Arabs, for example). For how Zionist emissaries pre-1948 sought to transform Jewish religious communities in Arab countries into Zionists, see Shenhav (2006).

74   *Nadim N. Rouhana*

of Armenians continuously inhabiting their own land. This included conflict and cooperation with neighboring states and regional powers, leading to independence of the modern state of the Republic of Armenia in 1991 after the collapse of the Soviet Union.[42] But in their state formation in Armenia, Armenians did not come from other places in the world and did not displace and replace another nation that had inhabited the land for centuries before their arrival. By contrast, Israeli state formation was a settler-colonial project that Zionism, formed in Europe and formally proclaimed in 1897, established by taking over a land inhabited by the Palestinian nation, eliminating their physical presence by expelling hundreds of thousands, preventing their return, destroying hundreds of towns and villages, evacuating and taking over cities, and, in the process, conducting massacres and other atrocities in order to replace them. This rather bloody history required weighty justification. As argued above, the biblical claim rooted in ancient history was invoked to legitimize this project. Furthermore, as this project is still ongoing inside Israel itself and in the West Bank, including East Jerusalem, the justificatory system is needed now more than ever.

As in the Israeli case, religion seems to be a main component of Armenia's national culture and national identity.[43] However, the processes that are at work in great force in Israel, such as religionization of the public sphere, religious extremism, infiltration of religious doctrines and religious values into citizenship laws[44] and state institutions such as the military (see Chapter 5) and the education system, seem less vigorous in Armenia. This is so because there is no question of state legitimacy in Armenia, as the state itself was not established in another nation's homeland. Unlike Armenian nationalism, Zionism as settler colonialism faces continued challenges to its legitimacy, at least in the eyes of the native population of Palestine and the peoples of the Arab region, in addition to civil society organizations, and academic, cultural, and intellectual circles around the world; furthermore, there are countless UN resolutions criticizing Israel's policies.

The exercise of thinking about a Jewish state in Uganda and the comparison with Armenia can provide significant theoretical and political insights that I cannot fully

---

[42] Before becoming a republic within the Soviet Union in 1922, Armenia was independent between 1918 and 1922 (Encyclopaedia Britannica 2019).

[43] Article 18, paragraph 1, of the Constitution of the Republic of Armenia (1995) reads: "The Republic of Armenia shall recognise the exclusive mission of the Armenian Apostolic Holy Church, as a national church, in the spiritual life of the Armenian people, in the development of their national culture and preservation of their national identity." Article 18, paragraph 2, reads: "The relations between the Republic of Armenia and the Armenian Apostolic Holy Church may be regulated by law."

[44] Article 47, paragraph 3, of the Constitution of the Republic of Armenia (1995) states: "Armenians by national origin shall have the right to acquire citizenship of the Republic of Armenia upon settling in the territory of the Republic Armenia." Article 47, paragraph 4, states: "Armenians by national origin shall acquire citizenship of the Republic of Armenia through a simplified procedure prescribed by law."

address here.[45] Nonetheless, it is important to point out what the exercise reveals about the colonized. For whether the project was to be implemented in Uganda or Palestine, the question of the colonizers' motivation is irrelevant to the indigenous population, because the process of establishing an exclusive Jewish homeland (or white homeland) – despite the existence of native populations either in Uganda, South Africa, or Palestine – would inevitably follow policies and settler-colonial strategies, as the logic of the project's dynamics dictates. For the indigenous population, neither the historical arguments of having connection to the land (which by itself is undeniable in the case of Jews and Palestine) nor the religious claim based on biblical narrative or the search for refuge (in the form of exclusive sovereignty in another people's homeland) can obscure the nature of the project or dissuade them from vigorous resistance.[46]

Highlighting the motivation for a settler-colonial project is much more important to the colonizer's justification and the legitimation of their project for their constituency and their international audience. The issue of legitimation becomes particularly important in response to the natives' resistance – an issue that I address next.

Palestinian Resistance and Religious Legitimation

Another major determinant in the rise of the religious dimension of Zionism is Palestinian agency and resistance. I expand here upon a core concept in settler-colonial studies: A settler-colonial project based on the elimination of the native (in this case demographic and national elimination) is a *structure* rather than an *event* in Wolfean terminology (Wolfe 2006). This means that settler colonialism "erects a new colonial society on the expropriated land base," and because "settler colonizers come to stay: invasion is a structure not an event." As is clear from Israeli policies toward Palestinians, "elimination is an organizing principal of settler-colonial society rather than a one-off (and superseded) occurrence" (Wolfe 2006, 388). Wolfe provides numerous examples of strategies derived from this organizing

---

[45] It is worth thinking whether the rod of anti-Semitism could have been as easily used against people who criticized the colonial state had it been established in Uganda, or whether the framing of Zionism as a settler-colonial movement would have been more acceptable in this case.

[46] In a fascinating conversation as early as 1993 between two of the most prominent public intellectuals in the area – an Israeli and a Palestinian – the question of (settler) colonialism and Zionism was addressed. Azmi Bishara placed Zionism within the framework of settler colonialism. Yehoshua Leboweitz argued that Zionism is not a (settler-)colonial movement because "regarding this land that we call *Eretz Yisrael* and they call Palestine there are two peoples: each one of them has the deep awareness that this land is their home." He then adds that there is no colonial relationship because Zionism "doesn't have within it the aim to dominate another people" (although he argues that after 1967 domination became part of the conflict). Bishara's response was that the question of motivation is irrelevant to the indigenous population if the process of establishing the Jewish homeland in Palestine follows, by the logic of the project, settler-colonial paths. See Leibowitz (1993).

principle.[47] But missing in the analysis is the agency of the native and how the dynamics of settler strategies unfold in a *process* that can modify these strategies themselves through the settlers' interaction with the resistance of the colonized and other forces (such as global and regional forces and the international human rights assertions). These strategies can evolve in different directions and lead to different forms and policies – within the defining guidelines of the structure. I argue that while the *structure* refers to "organizing principles," the *process* – the interaction with the colonized and its various forms of resistance (that also are modified and accommodated in that process) – affect the internal dynamics within the settler society: the power relations between various factions; internal ideological variations; the emergence, weakening, or disappearances of ideological trends; resorting to new modes of legitimation; and the emergence of anti-colonial forces within the settlers' society – in our case anti-Zionist forces. Thus, as a structure, there is *currently* a consensus among all Zionist factions, religious and secular, on the erection of an exclusive Jewish state with Jewish privileges and on other fundamental issues (such as the denial of the right of return of Palestinian refugees to their homeland) but not on issues related to state and church relations, relations with the Palestinian citizens, the desirability of the two-state solution, or even the view within Zionist factions of whether the settlement project in the West Bank is a settler-colonial project or a "national" undertaking of return to the homeland – exactly as to the part of Palestine that was taken pre-1967.[48]

Applying this distinction between *structure* and *process* in the settler-colonial dynamics, the Zionist project as a structure of continual displacement-replacement did not need in the historical and global context of Israel's establishment (the so-called secular period) to resort as openly to religious legitimation as it has needed to do since the mid-1970s. The Palestinian national movement was defeated in the 1948 War and reemerged only in the mid-1960s. Israel, by contrast, was recognized by all major powers, including the Soviet Union (the first country to recognize Israel); it enjoyed the post-Holocaust European sympathy and guilt with some elements of deserved shame; and it claimed the legitimacy of the UN partition plan from 1947 (even though its borders exceeded by far the boundaries allocated to the Jewish state in the plan). The colonized were demographically dispersed outside their homeland, and only a weak group of about 150,000 Palestinians remained as Israeli citizens but were placed under military rule until 1966, absented from Jewish eyes, and subjected to the settler-colonial apparatus (Bäuml 2017; Robinson 2013; Rouhana and Sabbagh-Khoury 2015). *Security* was a main justificatory system of

---

[47] Examples include "officially encouraged miscegenation, the breaking-down of native title into alienable individual freeholds, native citizenship, child abduction, religious conversion, resocialization in total institutions such as missions or boarding schools, and a whole range of cognate biocultural assimilations." Most of these examples are not relevant to our case – Zionism.

[48] This difference does not exist among various Zionist factions in relation to Israel proper, which is seen by consensus as return to the homeland.

domination and continued colonization at the time (Rouhana 1997); the religious claims for overtaking Palestine used by the "secular" leadership was not as needed for legitimation, and thus the secular forces could shield against unnecessary religious discourse.

The gradual incorporation of the Palestinian territories occupied in 1967 into the settler-colonial project, and the continued policies toward the Palestinian community within Israel – a community that became stronger over the years – engendered different processes within the same structure. While the question of the legitimacy of Israel as a state was sidelined, particularly with the PLO recognition of Israel in the 1993 Oslo Accords, two major issues related to the question of legitimacy emerged. The first was how to legitimize the aggressive project of incorporating the West Bank or parts of it (including East Jerusalem), geographically, demographically, politically, and psychologically as an integral part of the Land of Israel (Lustick 1993). The second was Israel's demand that the Palestinians recognize it as a Jewish state (A. Bishara 2005; Ghanem 2014; Rouhana 2018).

The settlement project with its 131 settlements in the West Bank,[49] 110 settlement outposts, and estimated 623,000 settlers (as of the end of 2017)[50] lacks international legitimacy[51] and internal Israeli consensus. Most importantly, it faces massive Palestinian active resistance in different forms, supported by Palestinian consensus since the start of the occupation. Ongoing and unrelenting Palestinian resistance in the West Bank and Gaza since 1967 peaked in two major rebellions (civil and militarized), each lasting for a few years – the first starting in 1987 and the second in 2000. Palestinians in Israel challenge the legitimacy of a Jewish state; in Jerusalem they actively resist settler-colonial Judaization; in Gaza, they use various forms of resistance, most recently the popularly organized nonviolent weekly Marches of Return toward the borders of Israel; and internationally, the Boycott, Divestment,

---

[49] Not including occupied East Jerusalem and settlement enclaves in Hebron.

[50] See B'Tselem (2019).

[51] It is most relevant to observe that the only country that expressed views in support of recognizing annexation of parts of the West Bank has invoked religious considerations, at least as expressed by its ambassador to Israel. David M. Friedman, the US ambassador to Israel, declared: "Under certain circumstances Israel has the right to retain some, but unlikely all, of the West Bank." He added that Israel is certainly "entitled to retain some portion of it" (Halbfinger 2019a). Halbfinger reminds the reader that "[m]uch of the world considers Israeli settlements there illegal and would view annexation as compounding the crime." The fact that Mr. Friedman was "a major American supporter of the Israeli settlement enterprise before his appointment" adds an interesting dimension to his statement. As Landau (2019) argues, because under international law Israel has no right to these territories, the ambassador "was referring to historical or religious rights." This reading of the statement as referring to religious rights is reinforced by a previous Friedman statement: "Israel has one secret weapon that not too many countries have, Israel is on the side of God, and we don't underestimate that" (Halbfinger 2019b). Halbfinger reports in the same article that Hanan Ashrawi, a member of the PLO Executive Committee, noted that "the event at which Mr. Friedman had made the remark, with its echoes of religious warfare, was held in a hotel a stone's throw from the walls of the Old City, where Crusaders and Muslims had slaughtered one another for centuries." She added, "The last time we had people thinking that way in Palestine was in the Middle Ages, and look at what happened."

and Sanctions (BDS) movement has become a global force, pressing against Israel's policies mainly within international academic and cultural groups.

While settlement activities and related forms of violence can be seen as derived from the structure of settler colonialism, the unceasing resistance of the natives in their land including two intifadas, their international activism, and the increasing visibility of land theft in the eyes of many forces within the international community and even Israeli civil society are processes that drive the settler system to seek a different legitimization. Without legitimation, Israel and Zionism would be exposed as naked settler colonialism. The emerging legitimization is based on overtly religious claims. If Palestinians did not demonstrate intense resistance, the secularist would not have needed to resort to a religious-based system of legitimation, and the sharp rise in religious nationalism and sacralized politics would not have resonated with the need for legitimation.[52]

The second issue of legitimacy – demanding that Palestinians recognize Israel as the state of the *Jewish* people – is another example of a process dictated by the indigenous people's resistance to the settler-colonial structure. Israel has been engineered as the state of the Jewish people from the start of the Zionist project. It is this conceptually guiding structure that logically led to the ethnic cleansing of the Palestinians in 1948, preventing them from return and directing many of the ensuing policies. It was partly the process of defiance by Palestinian citizens within this structure that led to the Israeli demand for explicit recognition of Israel as the state of the Jewish people. The process started with demands of the Palestinian citizens for equality and culminated in a political platform calling for the transformation of Israel into a "state for all its citizens" as articulated by an Arab political party, the National Democratic Assembly, and its leader Azmi Bishara (Rouhana and Sabbagh-Khoury 2015). Israel's recently passed Nation-State Law defines Israel in terms of the Jewish people (rather than its citizens). It states that "[t]he State of Israel is the national home of the Jewish people, in which it fulfills its natural, cultural, religious and historical right to self-determination."[53] This law is seen as an upgraded response to the same demand for equality within a state for all its citizens (Jabareen and Bishara 2019). Notice that both the claim of Israel as the state of the Jewish people and the Nation-State Law are grounded in the religious legitimation of the settler-colonial project and that both were forcefully advanced by *secular* Zionist leaders. Israel basically wants Palestinians to recognize the Zionist settler-colonial project as legitimate and to accept the foundations of legitimacy suffused with Jewish religious claims as articulated by Israel's ambassador to the UN in the quote in the opening section above.

---

[52] Israel took advantage of the Islamophobic global trends, particularly after the 9/11 terrorist attacks in 2001 in the US. It tried to frame Palestinian resistance within such trends, but this was not sufficient to legitimize settler-colonial policies.

[53] For an English translation of the Nation-State Law, see Lis (2018).

INSTEAD OF A CONCLUSION: ON DECOLONIZATION

I argued in this chapter that in Zionism, the religious is fused with the national and both are integrated into the settler-colonial prerogatives. Thus, Zionism is national settler colonialism legitimized by religious claims. The three machineries of Zionism are so intertwined that it is hard to disentangle them. So far, the settler-colonial aspect was highlighted primarily by Zionism's victims and critical theorists, as well as by realities on the ground, while the centrality of religious claims to support mainstream secular Zionism has been downplayed. Instead, the religionism has been emphasized in the separated sphere of religious nationalist movements and in the creeping encroachment into the public sphere, but not as "inherent to Zionism." Yet, the original deployment of religious claims to legitimize the very raison d'être of Zionism and the rising invocation of these claims to legitimize the expansion of the settler colony to the occupied West Bank, including East Jerusalem, is crucial – I would say indispensable – for Zionism to avoid facing its settler-colonial actuality. Therefore, the questions of decolonization, secularization, and democracy are all intertwined in Israel.

Let us start with decolonization. For Zionism to face its settler-colonial actuality – an obvious prerequisite for decolonization – it will have to disentangle itself from the religious claim for the right to establish an exclusive Jewish state in Palestine. Thus, decolonization requires secularization in the sense of separating Jewish nationalism from the religious claims. For Jewish nationalism as defined by Zionism to face the settler colonial in it, the religious has to be neutralized. Religious claims stand in the face of the recognition of history; they facilitate doubling down and buttressing the claim on Palestine without recognizing its settler-colonial essence. As such, they open the door for further religious influence on the secular. Going back to the hypothetical example of Uganda, secularization of a Zionist settler-colonial project in Uganda would have been possible like in other settler-colonial contexts – South Africa, Northern Ireland, North America – because unlike Zionism in Palestine, the religious claims are not crucial to the claimed legitimacy of these cases.

Zionism has the inherent driving force for using religious claims to legitimize settler-colonial policies. Take, for example, the continued occupation of the West Bank and the aggressive settlement activities. If Zionism sees the West Bank as part of the Jewish homeland and Jerusalem as its heart, the religious cultural framing becomes the most relevant for such policies. This was precisely the logic that pushed the Serb elites under Milosevic to frame the conflict with Albanians in Kosovo in cultural religious terms. If Albanians were the majority (by about 90 percent in Kosovo), and they were seeking independence, the political realities would have made their political demands sensible. But if Kosovo were *religiously* the Serbs' Jerusalem, as Chapter 9 explains, then such demands would be framed as Orthodox Serb vs. Muslim Albanians and the demographic balance and geographic reality would be overlooked.

Unlike Serbian nationalism, the trap of Zionism is its indispensable need for religious claims for its legitimacy. While Serbian liberal intellectuals can warn against the destructive influence of the Kosovo myth (based on particular religious beliefs promoted by the Serbian Orthodox Church) on the Serbs' relationships with other ethnic groups, mainly Muslims in Kosovo and Bosnia, and can point to its recent revival in the service of Serbian nationalism (Chapter 9), Zionist intellectuals will be undermining the very legitimacy of the Zionist project if they point to similar myths, in particular the transformation of a religious concept such as "the promised land" to a settler-colonial project. They can seek such transformation only from *outside* Zionism.

Disentangling Zionism from the religious claim is as improbable as extricating capitalism from free market or capital, or communism from class struggle; it would be like extricating Hinduism from the Hindutva. But it is not improbable to disentangle Jewish nationalism in Israel from the religious claims, and consequently from settler colonialism, by transforming Israel itself into a state for its citizens in which Israeli Jewish nationalism and Palestinian nationalism are equally recognized. This again can be achieved outside of Zionism. That this opens the doors for a joint broader political future with the Palestinians is evident, but a full discussion is beyond the scope of this chapter. This idea was advanced in the 1990s by a Palestinian intellectual, Azmi Bishara,[54] but within Zionism, it is considered an extreme, even fanatical, political idea. Yet many who discuss the secularization of Israel seem to go back to the same idea (see, e.g., Ram 2008).

The religious claim is not only at the core of settler colonialism in Palestine, it is also at the heart of constitutional inequality in Israel. Only if Israel is designated as a Jewish state given by God (in whose existence we do not have to necessarily believe) exclusively to the Jewish people – the core claim of Zionism – can the calls for equality between Arab and Jew or transforming Israel into a state for all its citizens be labeled as "fanatic." Keep God and his promises out of it, and seek the kind of secularization mandated by decolonization as described above, and then equality and the civic state become the fundamentals of *democratization*. As the Serbian literary critic Miodrag Popović argued in the Serbian context, "if and when the mythical archaic thinking becomes a lasting mental attitude, collective mentality or national culture, institutionalized as a major national patriotic myth and a key collective identity component, it may become fatal to the people incapable of resisting its pseudohistorical spell" (quoted in Perica 2017). This fits our context too.

---

[54] Dr. Azmi Bishara was also the leader of a Palestinian political party that was represented in the Israeli Knesset (parliament) at the time and is still represented today. The party faced numerous legal challenges, because of its advocacy for equality in a "state for all its citizens." Bishara chose to resign from the Knesset and go into self-exile in 2005 after he was accused of security-related violations.

REFERENCES

Abu El-Haj, Nadia. 2001. *Facts on the Ground: Archaeological Practice and Territorial Self-fashioning in Israeli Society*. Chicago: University of Chicago Press.

Abu-Lughod, Ibrahim A. and Baha Abu-Laban, eds. 1974. *Settler Regimes in Africa and the Arab World*. Wilmette, IL: Medina University Press International.

Akenson, Donald H. 1992. *God's Peoples: Covenant and Land in South Africa, Israel, and Ulster*. Ithaca, NY: Cornell University Press.

American-Israeli Cooperative Enterprise. n.d. "Zionist Congress: The Uganda Proposal (August 26, 1903)." Jewish Virtual Library. https://jewishvirtuallibrary.org/the-uganda-proposal-1903.

Azaryahu, Maoz, and Arnon Golan. 2001. "(Re)naming the Landscape: The Formation of the Hebrew Map of Israel 1949–1960." *Journal of Historical Geography* 27, no. 2: 178–95.

Bar-Tal, Daniel, and Gavriel Salomon. 2006. "Israeli-Jewish Narratives of the Israeli-Palestinian Conflict: Evolution, Contents, Functions, and Consequences." In *Israeli and Palestinian Narratives of Conflict: History's Double Helix*, edited by R. I. Rotberg, 19–46. Bloomington: Indiana University Press.

Barak-Erez, Daphne. 2009. "Law and Religion under the Status Quo Model: Between Past Compromises and Constant Change." *Cardozo Law Review* 30, no. 6: 2495–507.

Bäuml, Yair. 2017. "Israel's Military Rule over Its Palestinian Citizens (1948–1968): Shaping the Israeli Segregation System." In *Israel and Its Palestinian Citizens: Ethnic Privileges in the Jewish State*, edited by Nadim N. Rouhana, 103–36. Cambridge: Cambridge University Press.

Beit-Hallahmi, Benjamin. 1992. *Original Sins: Reflections on the History of Zionism and Israel*. London: Pluto Press.

Benvenisti, Meron. 2002. *Sacred Landscape: The Buried History of the Holy Land since 1948*. Los Angeles: University of California Press.

Bishara, Azmi. 2005. *From the Jewish State to Sharon: A Study in the Contradictions of Israeli Democracy* [in Arabic]. Beirut: Dar al-Shorouk.

　　2011. "Israel Sociology and Baruch Kimmerling's Constribution." [In Arabic.] *Al-Mustaqbal al-'Arabi* 394 (December): 7–33.

　　2017. "Zionism and Equal Citizenship: Essential and Incidental Citizenship in the Jewish State." In *Israel and Its Palestinian Citizens: Ethnic Privileges in the Jewish State*, edited by Nadim N. Rouhana, 137–58. Cambridge: Cambridge University Press.

Bishara, Suhad. 2018. "The Jewish National Fund." In vol. 2 of *The Palestinians in Israel: Readings in History, Politics and Society*, edited by Nadim N. Rouhana and Areej Sabbagh-Khoury. Haifa, Israel: Mada al-Carmel.

Brubaker, Rogers. 1998. *Citizenship and Nationhood in France and Germany*. Cambridge, MA: Harvard University Press.

B'Tselem. 2019. "Statistics on Settlements and Settler Population." http://btselem.org/settlement/statistics.

Busbridge, Rachel. 2018. "Israel-Palestine and the Settler Colonial 'Turn': From Interpretation to Decolonization." *Theory, Culture, and Society* 35, no. 1: 91–115.

CBS (Central Bureau of Statistics). 2018. "Population of Israel on the Eve of 2019 – 9.0 Million." Press release no. 394/2018. December 31. www.cbs.gov.il/he/mediarelease/DocLib/2018/394/11_18_394e.pdf.

　　2019a. "Population, by Population Group." Statistical Abstract of Israel 2019 – No. 70. www.cbs.gov.il/en/publications/Pages/2019/Population-Statistical-Abstract-of-Israel-2019-No-70.aspx.

2019b. "Localities and Population, by Population Group, District, Sub-District and Natural Region." Statistical Abstract of Israel 2019 – No. 70. www.cbs.gov.il/en/publications/Pages/2019/Population-Statistical-Abstract-of-Israel-2019-No-70.aspx.

Al-Charif, Maher. 1995. *In Search of an Entity*. Nicosia, Cyprus: Center for Socialist Studies and Research in the Arab World.

Constitution of the Republic of Armenia. July 5, 1995.

Danan, Deborah. 2016. "Watch: Ugandan President's Gaffe-Filled Speech to Israeli Prime Minister Netanyahu." *Breitbart*, July 5, 2016. www.breitbart.com/middle-east/2016/07/05/watch-ugandan-presidents-hilarious-gaffe-filled-speech-israeli-prime-minister-netanyahu/.

Danon, Danny. 2019. "Jewish Ownership of the Land of Israel." Speech. United Nations Security Council. New York. April 29, 2019. https://embassies.gov.il/un/statements/security_council/Pages/stme-sc-danon-april-2019.aspx.

Davis, Walter T., and Pauline Coffman. 2014. "From 1967 to the Present: The Triumph of Revisionist Zionism." In *Zionism and the Quest for Justice in the Holy Land*, edited by Donald E. Wagner and Walter T. Davis, 28–62. Cambridge: Lutterworth Press.

Encyclopaedia Britannica. 2019. "Modern Armenia." www.britannica.com/place/Armenia/Modern-Armenia.

Erekat, Noura. 2019. *Justice for Some*. Stanford: Stanford University Press.

Fine, Steven. 2016. *The Menorah: From the Bible to Modern Israel*. Cambridge, MA: Harvard University Press.

Gans, Chaim. 2008. *A Just Zionism: On the Morality of the Jewish State*. Oxford: Oxford University Press.

Gelvin, James L. 2014. *The Israel-Palestine Conflict: One Hundred Years of War*. 3rd ed. New York: Cambridge University Press.

General Armistice Agreement, Isr.–Jordan. April 3, 1949. 656 U.N.T.S. 304.

Ghanem, Honaida, ed. 2014. *On Recognition of the "Jewish State."* Ramallah, Occupied Palestinian Territories: Madar.

Goldman, Shalom. 2004. *God's Sacred Tongue: Hebrew and the American Imagination*. Chapel Hill: University of North Carolina Press.

    2009. *Zeal for Zion: Christians, Jews, and the Idea of the Promised Land*. Chapel Hill: University of North Carolina Press.

Gordon, Neve, and Moriel Ram. 2016. "Ethnic Cleansing and the Formation of Settler Colonial Geographies." *Political Geography* 53: 20–29.

Gottlieb, Lynn, and Graylan Hagler. 2019. "Christian Zionist Lobby Is Built on Anti-Semitic Theology." *UPI*, July 9. www.upi.com/Top_News/Voices/2019/07/09/Christian-Zionist-lobby-is-built-on-anti-Semitic-theology/2621562674846/.

Grant, Michael. 2012. *The History of Ancient Israel*. London: Orion Books.

Gresh, Alain. 1988. *The PLO: The Struggle Within – Towards an Independent Palestinian State*. London: Zed Books.

Gross, Aeyal. 2013. "Court Rejection of Israeli Nationality Highlights Flaws of Jewish Democracy." Opinion. *Haaretz*, October 3. www.haaretz.com/opinion/.premium-is-israeli-a-nationality-1.5344174.

Haag, Matthew. 2018. "Robert Jeffress, Pastor Who Said Jews Are Going to Hell, Led Prayer at Jerusalem Embassy." *The New York Times*, May 14. www.nytimes.com/2018/05/14/world/middleeast/robert-jeffress-embassy-jerusalem-us.html.

Haaretz. 2019a. "Israel Didn't Aim to Distort History by Concealing Nakba Files, Former Defense Official Says." July 24. www.haaretz.com/israel-news/.premium-israel-didn-t-aim-to-distort-history-by-concealing-nakba-docs-ex-top-official-says-1.7570626.

Religious Claims and Nationalism in Zionism

2019b. "The Arab Society Is Very Violent." [In Hebrew.] October 7. www.haaretz.co.il /news/law/1.7950349.

Halbfinger, David M. 2019a. "US Ambassador Says Israel Has Right to Annex Parts of West Bank." *The New York Times,* June 8. www.nytimes.com/2019/06/08/world/middleeast/ israel-west-bank-david-friedman.html?searchResultPosition=1.

2019b. "US Ambassador Says Israel Is 'on the Side of God.'" *The New York Times,* May 14. www.nytimes.com/2019/05/14/world/middleeast/us-ambassador-israel-god.html? searchResultPosition=1.

Hasson, Shlomo. 2015. *State and Religion in Israel Possible Scenarios.* College Park, MD: The Joseph and Alma Gildenhorn Institute for Israel Studies.

Hayoun, Massoud. 2019. *When We Were Arabs: A Jewish Family's Forgotten History.* New York: The New Press.

Herzog, Ze'ev. 2001. "Deconstructing the Walls of Jericho: Biblical Myth and Archaeological Reality." *Prometheus* 4: 72–93.

Hilal, Jamil. 1976. "Imperialism and Settler-Colonialism: Israel and the Arab Palestinian Struggle." *UTAFITI: Journal of the Arts and Social Sciences* 1, no. 1: 51–69.

Holmes, Oliver. 2019. "Netanyahu Vows to Annex Jewish Settlements in Occupied West Bank." *The Guardian,* April 7. www.theguardian.com/world/2019/apr/07/netanyahu-vows-to-annexe-jewish-settlements-in-occupied-west-bank.

Hovel, Revital. 2013. "Supreme Court Rejects Citizenship Request to Change Nationality from 'Jewish' to "Israeli.'" *Haaretz,* October 3. www.haaretz.com/.premium-court-israeli-isn-t-ethnicity-1.5343897.

Jabareen, Hassan. 2002. "The Future of Arab Citizenship in Israel: Jewish-Zionist Time in a Place with No Palestinian Memory." In *Challenging Ethnic Citizenship: German and Israeli Perspectives on Immigration,* edited by Daniel Levy and Yfaat Weiss, 196–220. Oxford: Berghahn Books.

Jabareen, Hassan, and Suhad Bishara. 2019. "The Jewish Nation-State Law." *Journal of Palestine Studies* 48, no. 2: 43–57.

Jabbour, George. 1976. *Settler Colonialism in Southern Africa and the Middle East.* Khartoum: University of Khartoum.

Jawad, Saleh Abdel. 2006. "The Arab and Palestinian Narratives of the 1948 War." In *Israeli and Palestinian Narratives of Conflict: History's Double Helix,* edited by Robert I. Rotberg, 72–114. Indianapolis: Indiana University Press.

2007. "Zionist Massacres: The Creation of the Palestinian Refugee Problem in the 1948 War." In *Israel and the Palestinian Refugees,* edited by Eyal Benvenisti, Chaim Gans, and Sari Hanafi, 59–127. Beiträge zum ausländischen öffentlichen Recht und Völkerrecht, vol. 189. Berlin: Springer.

Kanafani, Ghassan. (1963) 1999. *Men in the Sun and Other Palestinian Stories.* Translated by Hilary Kilpatrick. Boulder, CO: Lynne Reiner Publishers.

Katz, Yossi. 2002. *And the Land Shall Never Be Sold: Heritage of the Jewish National Fund and Application of Its Principles in Israeli Legislation.* Ramat Gan: Jewish National Fund Research Institute, Cathedra for the Study of the History of the Jewish National Fund and Its Work, Bar-Ilan University.

Khalidi, Rashid. 1997. *Palestinian Identity: The Construction of Modern National Consciousness.* New York: Columbia University Press.

2020. *The Hundred Years' War on Palestine: A History of Settler Colonialism and Resistance, 1917–2017.* New York: Metropolitan Books.

Khalidi, Walid. 1992. *Palestine Reborn.* New York: I.B. Tauris.

Khalidi, Walid, ed. 2006. *All That Remains: The Palestinian Villages Occupied and Depopulated by Israel in 1948*. Beirut: Institute for Palestine Studies.

Khoury, Elias. 2019. *Children of the Ghetto: My Name Is Adam*. Translated by Humphrey Davies. Beirut: Archipelago.

Kimmerling, Baruch. 1999. "Religion, Nationalism and Democracy in Israel." *Constellations* 6, no. 3: 339–63.

Kornberg, Jacques. 1980. "Theodore Herzl: A Reevaluation." *The Journal of Modern History* 52, no. 2: 226–52.

Kravel-Tovi, Michal. 2012. "Rite of Passage: Bureaucratic Encounters, Dramaturgy, and Jewish Conversion in Israel." *American Ethnologist* 39, no. 2: 371–88.

Landau, Noa. 2019. "With One Word, Trump's Envoy Sets Stage for Israeli Annexation of West Bank." *Haaretz*, June 9. www.haaretz.com/israel-news/.premium-with-one-word-trump-s-envoy-sets-stage-for-israeli-annexation-of-west-bank-1.7344454.

Laqueur, Walter, and Dan Schueftans, eds. 2016. *The Israel-Arab Reader: A Documentary History of the Middle East Conflict*. 8th ed. New York: Penguin Books.

Law of Return. 1950. 5710 (as amended) (Isr.).

Lazaroff, Tovah. 2019. "Bible Is Jewish Deed to Land of Israel, Settlement Envoy Tells UNSC." *The Jerusalem Post*, April 30. www.jpost.com/arab-israeli-conflict/israel-defends-right-to-west-bank-settlements-at-unsc-watch-live-588178.

Leibowitz, Yehoshua. 1993. "Leibowitz in Conversation with Azmi Bishara." YouTube. Filmed June 2. www.youtube.com/watch?NR=1&feature=endscreen&v=SPazJTyNuYo.

Leon, Dan. 2006. "The Jewish National Fund: How the Land Was 'Redeemed.'" *Palestine-Israel Journal* 13: 115–23.

Lesch, Ann Mosely. 1977. "Israeli Settlements in the Occupied Territories, 1966–1977." *Journal of Palestine Studies* 7, no. 1: 26–47.

Lis, Jonathan. 2011. "The Facts and Fictions of Netanyahu's Address to Congress." *Haaretz*, May 26. www.haaretz.com/1.5016320.

2018. "Israel's Contentious Nation-State Law: Everything You Need to Know." *Haaretz*, July 19. www.haaretz.com/israel-news/.premium-israel-s-contentious-nation-state-law-everything-you-need-to-know-1.6292733.

Lloyd, David. 2012. "Settler Colonialism and the State of Exception: The Example of Palestine/Israel." *Settler Colonial Studies* 2, no. 1: 59–80.

Lustick, Ian. 1988. *For the Land and the Lord: Jewish Fundamentalism in Israel*. New York: Council on Foreign Relations.

1993. *Unsettled States/Disputed Lands: Britain and Ireland, France and Algeria, Israel and the West Bank–Gaza*. Ithaca, NY: Cornell University Press.

Makdisi, Saree. 2010. "The Architecture of Erasure." *Critical Inquiry* 36, no. 3: 519–59.

Mamdani, Mahmood. 2001. "Beyond Settler and Native as Political Identities: Overcoming the Political Legacy of Colonialism." *Comparative Studies in Society and History* 43, no. 4: 651–64.

2015. "Settler Colonialism: Then and Now." *Critical Inquiry* 41, no. 3: 596–614.

Masalha, Nur. 1992. *Expulsion of the Palestinians: The Concept of 'Transfer' Zionist Political Thought, 1882–1948*. Washington, DC: Institute for Palestine Studies.

2007. *The Bible and Zionism: Invented Traditions, Archaeology and Post-colonialism in Palestine-Israel*. London: Zed Books.

Masri, Mazen. 2017. *The Dynamics of Exclusionary Constitutionalism: Israel as a Jewish and Democratic State*. Oxford: Hart.

Matar, Ibrahim. 1981. "Israeli Settlements in the West Bank and Gaza Strip." *Journal of Palestine Studies* 11, no. 1: 93–110.

McSloy, Steven Paul. 1996. "'Because the Bible Tells Me So': Manifest Destiny and American Indians." *St. Thomas Law Review* 9, no. 1: 37–48.

Mendes-Flohr, Paul, ed. 2005. *A Land of Two Peoples: Martin Buber on Jews and Arabs.* Chicago: University of Chicago Press.

Museveni, Yoweri. 2016. "President Museveni Speech at Entebbe during Netanyahu's Visit Commemorating Entebbe Raid." NTV Uganda. Filmed July 4. YouTube video, 25:57. www.youtube.com/watch?v=rkM9xBkrwgQ&feature=youtu.be.

Netanyahu, Benjamin. 2011. "Speech to the US Congress." Speech. *Jerusalem Post*, May 24. www.jpost.com/Diplomacy-and-Politics/Text-of-PM-Binyamin-Netanyahus-speech-to-the -US-Congress.

Pap, András. 2013. "Overruling Murphy's Law on the Free Choice of Identity and the Racial-Ethnic-National Terminology-Triad: Notes on How the Legal and Political Conceptualization of Minority Communities and Membership Boundaries Is Induced by the Groups' Claims." In *The Interrelation between the Right to Identity of Minorities and Their Socio-economic Participation*, edited by Kristin Henrard, 115–58. Leiden: Martinus Nijhoff.

Pappé, Ilan. 2008. "Zionism as Colonialism: A Comparative View of Diluted Colonialism in Asia and Africa." *South Atlantic Quarterly* 107, no. 4: 611–33.

   2012. "Shtetl Colonialism: First and Last Impressions of Indigeneity by Colonised Colonisers." *Settler Colonial Studies* 2, no. 1: 39–58.

Peace Now. 2017. "Jewish National Fund Renews Land Purchases from Palestinians in the Occupied Territories." August 13. https://peacenow.org.il/en/jewish-national-fund-renews-land-purchases-palestinians-occupied-territories.

Peled, Yoav, and Horit Herman Peled. 2018. *The Religionization of Israeli Society*. New York: Routledge.

Perica, Vjekoslav. 2017. "Serbian Jerusalem: Religious Nationalism, Globalization and the Invention of a Holy Land in Europe's Periphery, 1985–2017." *Occasional Papers on Religion in Eastern Europe* 37, no. 6: 23–80.

Permanent Observer Mission of Palestine to the United Nations. 1974. "10 Point Program of the PLO (1974)." https://web.archive.org/web/20110805192136/http://www .un.int/wcm/content/site/palestine/cache/offonce/pid/12354;jsessionid=ED2AC7E70A8 2F5C7CCB42BC6357FCDEC.

Piterberg, Gabriel. 2015. "Israeli Sociology's Young Hegelian: Gershon Shafir and the Settler Colonial Framework." *Journal for Palestine Studies* 44, no. 3: 17–38.

Prior, Michael. 1997. *The Bible and Colonialism: A Moral Critique*. Sheffield, UK: Sheffield Academic Press.

Rabinovich, Itamar, and Jehuda Reinharz, eds. 2007. *Israel in the Middle East: Documents and Readings on Society, Politics, and Foreign Relations, Pre-1948 to the Present*. 2nd ed. Waltham, MA: Brandeis University Press.

Rabkin, Yakov. 2012. "Religious Roots of Political Ideology: Judaism and Christianity at the Cradle of Zionism." *Mediterranean Review* 5, no. 1: 75–100.

Ram, Uri. 2008. "Why Secularism Fails? Secular Nationalism and Religious Revivalism in Israel." *International Journal of Political Culture* 21, no. 1: 57–73.

Richman, Rick. 2017. "The 80th Anniversary of the Two-State Solution." *Mosaic*, October 2. https://mosaicmagazine.com/observation/israel-zionism/2017/10/the-80th-anniversary-of -the-two-state-solution/.

Robinson, Shira. 2013. *Citizen Strangers: Palestinians and the Birth of Israel's Liberal Settler State*. Stanford: Stanford University Press.

Rodinson, Maxime. 1973. *Israel: A Colonial-Settler State?* Translated by David Thorstad. London: Pathfinder Press.

Rouhana, Nadim. 1997. *Palestinian Citizens in an Ethnic Jewish State: Identities in Conflict.* New Haven, CT: Yale University Press.

2014. "The Palestinian National Project: Towards Restoring the Settler Colonial Paradigm." [In Arabic.] *Journal of Palestinian Studies* 19: 18–36.

2018. "Decolonization as Reconciliation: Rethinking the National Conflict Paradigm in the Israeli–Palestinian Conflict." *Ethnic and Racial Studies* 41, no. 4: 643–62.

Rouhana, Nadim, and Areej Sabbagh-Khoury. 2015. "Settler-Colonial Citizenship: Conceptualizing the Relationship between Israel and Its Palestinian Citizens." *Settler Colonial Studies* 5, no. 3: 205–25.

Rovner, Adam L. 2014. *In the Shadow of Zion: Promised Lands before Israel.* New York: New York University Press.

Said, Edward. 1979. "Zionism from the Standpoint of Its Victims." *Social Text* 1: 7–58.

Salamanca, Omar Jabary, Mezna Oato, Kareem Rabie, and Sobhi Samour. 2012. "Past Is Present: Settler Colonialism in Palestine." *Settler Colonial Studies* 2, no. 1: 1–8.

Sayegh, Fayez A. 1965. *Zionist Colonialism in Palestine.* Beirut: PLO Research Center.

Scham, Paul. 2018. "'A National That Dwells Alone': Israeli Religious Nationalism in the 21st Century." *Israel Studies* 23, no. 3: 207–15.

Shaath, Nabil. 1977. "The Democratic Solution to the Palestinian Issue." *Journal of Palestine Studies* 6, no. 2: 12–18.

Shalhoub-Kevorkian, Nadera. 2014. "Human Suffering in Colonial Contexts: Reflections from Palestine." *Settler Colonial Studies* 4, no. 3: 277–90.

2017. "The Occupation of the Senses: The Prosthetic and Aesthetic of State Terror." *British Journal of Criminology* 57, no. 6: 1279–300.

Shapira, Anita. 2015. *Ben-Gurion: Father of Modern Israel.* New Haven, CT: Yale University Press.

Shenhav, Yehouda. 2006. *The Arab Jews: A Postcolonial Reading of Nationalism, Religion, and Ethnicity.* Stanford: Stanford University Press.

2007. "Modernity and the Hybridization of Nationalism and Religion: Zionism and the Jews of the Middle East as a Heuristic Case." *Theory and Society* 36, no. 1: 1–30.

Shezaf, Hagar. 2019. "Burying the Nakba: How Israel Systematically Hides Evidence of 1948 Expulsion of Arabs." *Haaretz*, July 5. www.haaretz.com/israel-news/.premium.MAGAZINE -how-israel-systematically-hides-evidence-of-1948-expulsion-of-arabs-1.7435103.

Shlaim, Avi. 2009. *Israel and Palestine: Reappraisals, Revisions, Refutations.* London: Verso.

Smith, Robert. 2013. *More Desired than Our Own Salvation: The Roots of Christian Zionism.* Oxford: Oxford University Press.

Sternhell, Zeev. 1998. *The Founding Myths of Israel: Nationalism, Socialism, and the Making of the Jewish State.* Princeton: Princeton University Press.

Sultany, Nimer. 2017. "The Legal Structures of Subordination: The Palestinian Minority and Israeli Law." In *Israel and Its Palestinian Citizens: Ethnic Privileges in the Jewish State,* edited by Nadim N. Rouhana, 191–237. Cambridge: Cambridge University Press.

Tessler, Mark. 2009. *A History of the Israeli-Palestinian Conflict.* 2nd ed. Indian Series in Arab and Islamic Studies. Bloomington: Indiana University Press.

Thompson, Gardner. 2019. *Legacy of Empire: Britain, Zionism, and the Creation of Israel.* London: Saqi Books.

Trabulsi, Fawwaz. 1969. "The Palestine Problem: Zionism and Imperialism in the Middle East." *New Left Review* (September–October): 53–90.

UN News. 2017. "General Assembly Demands All States Comply with UN Resolutions Regarding Status of Jerusalem." December 21. https://news.un.org/en/story/2017/12/640152-general-assembly-demands-all-states-comply-un-resolutions-regarding-status.

Veracini, Lorenzo. 2006. *Israel and Settler Society*. London: Pluto Press.

2019. "Israel-Palestine through a Settler-Colonial Studies Lens." *Interventions* 21, no. 4: 568–81.

Whitelam, Keith. 1996. *The Invention of Ancient Israel: The Silencing of Palestinian History*. New York: Routledge.

Wolfe, Patrick. 2006. "Settler Colonialism and the Elimination of the Native." *Journal of Genocide Research* 8, no. 4: 387–409.

2012. "Purchase by Other Means: The Palestine Nakba and Zionism's Conquest of Economics." *Settler Colonial Studies* 2, no. 1: 133–71.

Yiftachel, Oren. 2002. "'Ethnocracy': The Politics of Judaizing Israel/Palestine." *Constellations* 6, no. 3: 363–90.

Zreik, Raef. 2016. "When Does a Settler Become a Native? (With Apologies to Mamdani)." *Constellations* 23, no. 3: 351–64.

4

On the Uses and Abuses of Tradition

Zionist Theopolitics and Jewish Tradition

Yaacov Yadgar

INTRODUCTION

One of the intriguing curiosities of the human sciences – especially social sciences – is the persistence of the religious-secular binary. Although this conceptual dualism has been critically deconstructed and shown to be misleading, the discourse it produces endures. Critical studies of the history, politics, epistemology, and ontology of the religious-secular dichotomy have convincingly proven that "religion," "secular," "politics," and other categories adjoining this dichotomy are far from universal, ahistorical, neutral facts of humanity. Rather, they are all historical constructs, their meaning shaped by changing configurations of power. Critiques of secular normativity assert that "religion" and other categories are *not* neutral descriptive and analytical terms but are, on the contrary, prescriptive and normative. They are "rhetorical constructions" (Fitzgerald 2007, 24). Yet, these categories are widely used as though they are objective and factual, and thus conceal their origins. Indeed, Timothy Fitzgerald, in his critique of the wider field of religious studies, argues that:

> Despite the appearance of common sense, a term such as "religion" does not tell us what is in the world, but what we collectively think ought to be in the world. It is a classificatory device, a function of Euro-American world making, but it has acquired an appearance of being immutably in the nature of things. (Fitzgerald 2007, 24)

Mainstream academic discourse on religion and politics tends to "embed these categorical structures into the nature of things and render them difficult to see for what they are: collective affirmations about what kind of world we want to experience" (Fitzgerald 2007, 25). This ultimately culminates in a distortion of our comprehension of reality, as we force on it concepts and categories that may be foreign to the specific historical and sociocultural contexts we may be studying. To put this differently, the "religion/religious vs. the secular" duality, which has been used in various fields of the study of humanity as a universal, ahistorical, "objective" tool to identify and analyze the supposed social *facts* that correspond to these terms, perpetuates, by this continuing use, a certain distribution of power, which by definition, is far from "objective." This distribution or configuration of power endows the modern, so-called secular nation-state with dominance, designating it as the rational arbitrator of public matters (as opposed to what is now seen as the irrational-by-definition religious realm). As a result, important features of the reality built around the nation-state, such as the state's use of violence – features that clearly do not correspond to the essence of secularity that I will explore below as the "theopolitics" of the nation-state – are hidden behind a smoke screen fed by our use of the dominant terminology (Cavanaugh 2009).

Yet the use of the religious-secular dichotomy persists. It is still heavily influential in academic and public and political discourses. Critical studies of the religious-secular dichotomy – for the sake of simplicity, let us call them "post-secular" – have thus refocused their attention on the motives behind the enduring presence of this duality. And they tend to focus our attention on the interests of the nation-state:

> [T]he attempt to say that there is a transhistorical and transcultural concept of religion that is separable from secular phenomena is itself part of a particular configuration of power, that of the modern, liberal nation-state as it developed in the West. In this context, religion is constructed as transhistorical, transcultural, essentially interior, and essentially distinct from public, secular rationality. To construe Christianity as a religion, therefore, helps to separate loyalty to God from one's public loyalty to the nation-state. (Cavanaugh 2009, 59)

Cavanaugh directs our attention to the ways in which the construction of the state as secular works to legitimize state violence. The secular(ist) discourse constructs the power – and violence – of the Western, modern, liberal nation-state as rational and legitimate by positing it as the opposite of "religious violence" (which is, by this categorical definition, irrational and illegitimate). By "purifying" state violence the duality of the secular and the religious enables the secular to preserve its self-image as enlightened as opposed to the benighted religious. Viewed more broadly, this normalization of the secular entails the legitimation of a whole array of sociopolitical practices that would otherwise be deemed inferior, illegitimate, and unethical.

This chapter discusses some of the ways in which the secular-religious duality – while being constantly constructed and deconstructed and affirmed and violated – enables the nation-state (the State of Israel, in the case discussed here) to act on racial logic while preserving its self-image as enlightened, secular, and liberal.

I do not directly examine the use of state violence; instead I interrogate the application of race and racial distinction for the organization of the public/political sphere in relation to civil and human rights. I argue that the admittedly murky yet persistent sense of a fundamental distinction between matters that are secular and of-the-state's and matters that are religious and not-of-the-state's, which dominates the political (and, to a large degree also the social-scientific) discourse in Israel, allows the state to act on a racial logic of belonging and otherness, while celebrating itself as democratic, liberal, and enlightened (as is "naturally expected" from a secular, or at least "not-religious" entity). This is enabled by a division of labor that puts the "burden" of maintaining and applying the racially logical criteria of inclusion and exclusion – which is vital for the state's ability to uphold its very raison d'être – on the "religious" (people, institutions, parties, etc.). Furthermore, this division of labor is justified as a "compromise" between the two sides (the secular and the religious), in which the secular is allegedly (so the narrative would have us believe) forced to concede to the demands of the religious. These concessions entail the secular's supposed endurance of the suspension of its enlightened, liberal-democratic principles (that would, of course, delegitimize the application of a racially driven inclusion and exclusion). Yet, this racially logical principle of inclusion and exclusion stands at the core of the allegedly *secular* ideology upon which the nation-state is established and in the name of which it exercises its sovereignty. Thus, relying on the rhetoric of "forced" concessions to religious demands, it is secular ideology itself that facilitates the implementation of racial inclusion and exclusion.

ON THE THEOPOLITICS OF THE NATION-STATE

This view of sociopolitical reality comes to the fore when we look carefully at what seems to be, even to the uncritical observer, a "complicated" relationship between the theopolitics of the sovereign, modern nation-state and communal traditions that preceded its establishment and continue to live alongside the newly invented national traditions. By theopolitics I mean to highlight (following Cavanaugh 2003, from whom I borrow the use of the term) that "[f]ar from being 'secular' institutions and process," the state, civil society, and globalization are "ways of imagining [that] organize bodies around stories of human nature and human destiny which have deep theological analogies. In other words, supposedly 'secular' political theory is really theology in disguise" (Cavanaugh 2003, 2). As Carl Schmitt (2006, 36) famously put it, "All significant concepts of the modern theory of the state are secularized theological concepts." Crucially, theopolitics signals the fact that "the modern state is built upon a soteriology of rescue from violence," a foundational "myth of the State as Saviour" (Cavanaugh 2003, 2), the basis of the modern (Hobbesian) concept of sovereignty. In order to establish itself, the sovereign nation-state also "imagines" collectives (Anderson 1998) and "invents" traditions (Hobsbawm and Ranger 1992) that narrate theopolitics and sustain the state's existence.

The term theopolitics, then, helps us in overcoming the debilitating predominance of the secular vs. religious dualism. Informed by a post-secular critique, theopolitics is a discursive tool that enables us to both see the theological aspects of the supposedly secular nation-state, and to devise a meaningful discourse on how the state uses so-called religious traditions in the process of constructing an imagination of the nation and the sovereign state as secular.

In the Israeli case, the relationship between the state's theopolitics and communal traditions that precede the state – yet continue to live alongside and within it – opens up space to explore several ongoing foundational tensions, among them:

1. The ways that Israeli nationalist theopolitics makes use of or manipulates preceding communal (Jewish) traditions, which in themselves constitute the fabric of communities that the nation-state wishes to include as part of the larger, imagined "nation." (This inclusion is often done through dissolving these communities' particular collective identities, in effect dismantling these very communities; national unity tends to be intolerant to their persistence.)
2. The ways that this theopolitics handles the immanent contradictions and conflicts between the sovereign nation-state's self-justifying claims and preceding traditions, which do not subscribe to the same modern nation-statist notion of sovereignty (in addition to the replacing of God as Sovereign with the political body of the state, we may also keep in mind the historically perpetual Jewish insistence that the lack of self-rule is exactly what the divine wills), and which the state nevertheless wishes to mobilize to promote its own interests.
3. The ways that traditions that preceded the theopolitics of the Israeli nation-state react to processes of appropriation, negation, rewriting, etc. that the sovereign nation-state imposes on them.

In order to consider these issues, we must first liberate our thinking from the hold of the largely debunked, yet still-dominant epistemology of secularism (Asad 1993, 2003; Cavanaugh 2009; Dubuisson 2007; Fitzgerald 2007). Secularism assumes, narrates, and reifies a set of mutually enhancing binaries, such as modern versus traditional, the secular versus religion, and enlightened versus benighted. It views these binaries as the "neutral" building blocks of human reality (Jakobsen and Pellegrini 2008). This view has encouraged the misconception of the nation-state as a secular realm of the rational conducting of public affairs, namely, politics, as opposed to the private, spiritual, and apolitical business of religion. This premise, built on an ahistorical and acultural (mis)understanding of both religion and politics, legitimizes the modern, Western, sovereign nation-state's monopolistic use of violence and delegitimizes competing demands for fatal loyalty and uses of force (such as those posed by the Church in Western, Christian contexts). Prevalent and convenient as it may be (as in providing us with a prism through which to judge reality, allowing us to "clearly see" that "religious" violence is irrational, unjustified, and bad, while the violence inflicted by the "secular" nation-state is rationally justified and ultimately works for the greater good), this epistemology has time and again failed to account for the obviously theological – or rather "theopolitical" (see above) – cores of the nation-state's claim to sovereignty and use of power.[1] Thus, to give one obvious example, which is making big headlines at the time of writing, we are witnessing the specter of liberal secularists struggling to explain to us that while a governmental decree forcing women to cover parts of their bodies in order to conform to an Islamic sense of modesty is an expression of a benighted religious coercion and the result of a dangerous mixing of religion and politics, other similar-in-essence decrees that force women to expose parts of their bodies so as to comply with a "modern," Western sense of "secular liberation" are an expression of rational, enlightened politics.[2]

ZIONIST THEOPOLITICS BEYOND THE SECULARIST FALLACY

I shall address the abovementioned issues by examining the history and the socio-politics of the attitude of Zionist and Israeli theopolitics. I evaluate Zionist and Israeli attitudes toward Jewish histories that preceded the Zionist imagining of the Jews as a political nation and the culmination of this project in the establishment of the sovereign nation-state of the Jews.[3] More specifically, my discussion focuses on the Zionist and Israeli construction and definition – or, in effect, the lack of a positively meaningful definition – of Jewish identity. Historically, most of the vigor of political Zionist thought and practice has been focused on the articulation of a "rebellious" stance vis-à-vis Jewish traditions from which the Zionist ideologues emerged. Theirs was primarily a project of reimagining Jewish identity as "secular" and "national," driven by a revolutionary sense of rebellion against the "religious" past. These historical ideological roots culminated in the constitution of a nation-state of Jews as the ultimate expression of the (re-)politicization (and supposed secularization) of Judaism/Jewishness. Yet Zionist ideology and Israeli political culture have devoted only scarce resources to the question of the positive (*Jewish*) meaning of this self-proclaimed "new" Jewish (or "Hebrew") identity; they have failed to answer the fundamental question of what makes this project or state *Jewish*. While most of the Zionist impetus has been historically aimed against "old" Jewish traditions, Zionism, and the State of Israel following its cue, have not bothered to

---

[1] Carl Schmitt (2006) is usually identified as the foremost (modern) voice on the theological core of the nation-state; recent works have expanded the discussion on the matter, and it would be futile to try and give a comprehensive review of the literature here. For a review, see Scott and Cavanaugh (2008).

[2] I am referring here primarily to the various iterations of the burkini ban, a series of bylaws passed mainly in France during 2016, by which certain clothing and swimwear that are deemed disrespectful of secularism are legally prohibited. The news reports of the time were teeming with images of policemen enforcing the laws on the beaches of France, ostensibly forcing women to undress so as to comply with secular normativity. See Quinn (2016).

[3] My discussion here is largely based on a work I more fully present in a recently published book (Yadgar 2017). For the sake of brevity and clarity, I will leave most citations out of this chapter; the reader interested in a fuller exploration of my epistemological and empirical arguments can refer to the abovementioned book, especially chapters 1–3.

Zionist Theopolitics and Jewish Tradition

construct an alternative meaning-instilling structure (an invented tradition, we might say), national or otherwise, for Jewish identity.

Yet Zionism has never given up on its claim to be the national movement *of Jews*; and the State of Israel self-identifies as the state of the Jewish nation (and not as the state of the Israeli nation; the state has consistently denied the viability of this term). This means that the Zionist movement and the state it has established are essentially, existentially dependent upon an a priori, or external (in relation to Zionist ideology's mainstream claims), definition of Jewish identity. As Israeli political history has shown, the nation-state of the Jews has been fundamentally dependent upon the "demographic," racial-at-root composition of its population. As long as those the state counts as Jews constitute a majority of its population, the state can view itself as upholding its raison d'être, that is, its "identity" as the nation-state of the Jews. The state's theopolitics, its "soteriology of rescue from violence" (Cavanaugh 2003, 2) – meaning, in this case, its status as guarantor of the very existence of the Jewish people – is dependent on it maintaining a majority of "Jews" under its immediate sovereignty and actively marking them as the subjects on behalf of whom the state exercises its sovereignty. The state must classify the majority of its citizenry as Jews, most of all to distinguish them from the national Other – the non-Jewish Palestinian Arabs.

Yet the state itself, following its foundational Zionist ideology, does not offer a meaningfully positive definition of Jewish identity. It does not explicitly articulate what makes someone or something Jewish. It does not outline, for example, a "secular" (as in nonreligious or non-rabbinical) demarcation of Jews from non-Jews. This may come as a surprise to someone viewing Israel through a liberal-democratic framework. However, the simple fact is that Israel does not offer a political/civil/secular path for joining the nation in the name of which it exercises its sovereignty. Similarly, scarce attention is given to the question of what makes the state's administration of public/political affairs Jewish. (What is Jewish about the way Israel handles its budget, its military, its diplomacy, etc.?) Zionist ideologues have left this issue vague, referring time and again to a mythological notion of an undefined "Jewish spirit." The state, whose own logic demands that it differentiates Jews from non-Jews, relies on the services of Orthodox rabbinical gatekeepers for adjudicating this crucial task. This, it must be reiterated, is a political, *nation-statist* practice of drawing, redrawing, and maintaining inclusion and exclusion, belonging and otherness, majority and minority. As I noted above, these matters are of crucial importance for the state's raison d'être, as dictated by its own propagated nationalist ideology. Yet at the same time, rabbinical gatekeepers operate mechanisms of distinction, inclusion, and exclusion that the state itself, through the "secular" worldview it propagates, views as "religious" (often perceived in pejorative terms), and thus inconsistent with the principles of Western liberal democracy.

This entanglement is enabled by the fact that Israeli political culture preserves a division of labor in which "the religious" (synonymized with "Orthodox" in this political-cultural context) are endowed with the claim to traditional Jewish authenticity, while "the secular" Zionist/Jewish Israelis are seen as defining the meaning of a modern, rational politics of sovereignty. This division of labor is serviced by political myths (primarily, but not exclusively, narratives titled as the "status quo"[4] and the "religious coercion" that accompanies it) that enable the masking of this political reality by depicting it as an outcome of compromise or even extortion, in which the enlightened secular subject must forego the realization of some of its central values due to practical considerations of coalitional rule.

What I am arguing here directly contradicts the "commonsensical" view of Israeli sociopolitics on matters that are usually called "religion and politics" in Israel. Instead, I see the reliance on a narrow, "religious" reading of Jewish identity as inherent to the intellectual/ideological and political history of Zionism and the State of Israel. The binary distinction between the religious and the secular is used as a self-purifying mechanism that allows the state to proclaim its liberal and democratic self-image and explain the politics it practices, while in effect relying essentially on mechanisms of distinction, inclusion, and exclusion that are, at root, racial.

Given that Zionism has been clearly triumphant in positioning the sovereign nation-state as the gravitational core of the discourse on modern Jewish identity, functioning as a horizon to which Zionists, anti-Zionists, and non-Zionists alike repeatedly address themselves in their discussion of modern Jewish identity,[5] and given that this triumph reflects directly upon the ways in which various Jewish traditions have been understood and practiced, this chapter sheds light on the wider study of modern Jewish identity. Considering this volume's topic more generally, the Zionist and Israeli case study in theopolitics highlights the urgency of transcending a simplistic secularist epistemology in considering an alleged "fusion" between religion, nationalism, and the violence that ensues.

---

[4] The "status quo" (or, in a longer form, "the secular-religious status quo," and even "the status quo on matters of religion and politics") is the name commonly assigned to various arrangements, laws, practices, and political-cultural norms that touch upon the "unique" and controversial "combination" of "religion and politics" or even of "secularity and religiosity" practiced in Israel. See Barak-Erez (2008); Don-Yehiya (1999); G. Levy (2011); Yadgar (2017, 187–210).

[5] This may indeed seem to be a definition of Jewish identity offered by the state (contrary to what I argued above), yet the fact that Israel has managed to come to dominate the discourse on Jewish identity does not amount to it offering an alternative, meaningful construction of Jewish identity. Needless to say, there are those who would claim that the "statist" Judaism manifested in political Zionism and the State of Israel is the real, superior definition of Jewishness. The Israeli author and essayist A. B. Yehoshua is probably the most vocal of contemporary advocates of this idea, relying, in turn, on David Ben-Gurion's notion of Jewish nationalism in Israel. Yet it is quite clear (as Yehoshua himself laments in many of his essays) that this political view of Jewish identity has not gained traction among Israelis and Jews, mainly because it renders the Jewishness (if not very humanity) of non-Israeli Jews "missing" and "partial" by definition. For an exposition of Yehoshua's view, and the controversy it instigates, see Yehoshua et al. (2006). For a critique of his ideas, see Yadgar (2017, 187–210).

ON THE "CURIOUS" NATURE OF NATIONALIST POLITICS IN ISRAEL

In what follows, I will present several "riddles" from contemporary Israeli politics. These have all to do with what may be (mistakenly, I would insist) seen as a curiously Zionist/Israeli mixture, or "fusion" between religious claims, ideas, worldview, laws, and so on, and what modern Western political thought designates as the "secular" politics of the sovereign nation-state. These issues, I argue, all illuminate the urgency of narrating an alternative interpretation of the alleged "fusion" or "confusion" of religion and politics in Israel.

As we shall see, the Israeli case shows how the secularist epistemology has enabled the theopolitics of the nation-state to hide behind a smoke screen of accusations against "the religious" for allegedly not allowing the state to be loyal to its own liberal-democratic ideals (such that would dictate "civil," or "nationally secular" criteria for political membership[6]) and to practice – as a matter of state ("secular") policy – a racial logic of inclusion, exclusion, and preference, and to constitute and perpetuate a hierarchy of identities that dictate the application and denial of civil and human rights. Zionism's and Israel's failure (or lack of interest/refusal thereof) to formulate a viable national identity that is independent of what the self-proclaimed secularist Zionist ideology itself has viewed (largely negatively) as Jewish *religion* renders the state's definition of Jewish politics a matter of racial exclusionary logic.[7]

Zionism entails a transition from the understanding of Jewish identity through a dialogue with diverse traditions to a racial/ethnic definition of this identity.[8] By doing so, the predominant Zionist and Israeli understanding of "Jewish politics"

---

[6] An early formulation of such an alternative framework of inclusion and exclusion can be found in the debate on the practical interpretation of the Law of Return, which grants Jews almost immediate citizenship rights in the State of Israel. As law professor Ruth Gavison (2010) explains,

> On March 10th, 1958, Israel Bar-Yehudah (Ahdut ha-Avodah), who was at the time the Minister of the Interior, issued a directive which stated that: "An individual who in good faith declares that he is a Jew, will be registered as a Jew, and no additional proof will be required." These directives were based, in part, on the opinion of Haim Cohn (2010, 62), who was at that time the Attorney General and wrote, on February 20th, 1958: "It is inevitable that at times the religious determination will be different in content and nature from the secular determination. The fact that an individual is considered by the Jewish law to be a non-Jew, does not prevent or preclude the same individual from being considered a Jew for the purposes of implementation of the law, and vice versa."

[7] It would be futile to try and formulate here a potential alternative framework for national identity. Furthermore, such a formulation would by definition be part of a national *ideological* framework, which this chapter does not pretend to be. The history of modern Jewish political movements offers several potential alternatives to the Zionist framework of Jewish politics (see Pianko 2010). In the context of Israeli history, the New Hebrews (aka Canaanites) presented a challenging ideological rebuke to what they saw as a Zionist entrapment in a Jewish religious framework. See Kurzweil (1953); Porath (1989); Shavit (1987). Most recently, an appeal to the Israeli Supreme Court in which the state was demanded to recognize "Israeli" as a viable designator of nationality brought into sharp relief some critical aspects of the matter at hand.

[8] Alcalay (1992) offers a comprehensive consideration of the implications of this transformation and its historical Levantine alternatives.

in effect conditions the viability of this politics on the existence of a racial/ethnic Jewish majority; the state can be considered as embodying the notion of a political Jewish body only as long as its population is overwhelmingly Jewish. Compounded by Zionism's notion of an inherent antinomy between Jewishness and Arabness, this nationalist-racial logic marks Israel's non-Jewish Palestinian citizens a threat to the very existence of the state and renders both Palestinian-Israeli and Jewish-Arab identities precarious anomalies.[9] Moreover, while this exclusionary nationalist logic has very little of substance to do with traditional understandings of Jewish identity, it nevertheless carries one critical "religiously" traditional implication, as it leaves the nation-state inherently dependent upon Orthodox interpreters of Jewish ("religious") law for the definition and preservation of the state's Jewish identity.

While this chapter does not aim to offer an alternative ideological understanding of "Jewish politics," we can imagine that such alternative understandings would or could identify certain values, ideas, practices, epistemologies, and so on as manifesting a certain "Jewish essence," which must be embodied in the state's (or other political bodies"[10]) constitutive framework in order for them to be considered "Jewish." Theoretically at least, these would mean that the state or whatever relevant alternate formations of political organization would remain "Jewish" as long as their constitutive framework is observed, regardless of the ethnic or racial makeup of its population. I would encourage readers to engage in their own thought experiment of figuring out the details of such a framework. Prominent scholarly, moral, and philosophical discussions on the topic would suggest that this alternative framework could be based on foundational notions of Jewish "ethics" or law. In any event, a dominant Zionist ideological reading insists against such essentialism (which, it suspects, must end up in the imposition of religious law as the designated constitutive framework) and prefers instead to view Israel as the nation-state of the Jews – and not as a "Jewish state" – in order to avoid assigning any essential Jewish element to its politics.

Let us consider, then, even if only superficially, three major, recent political controversies that have dominated public debate in Israel: (1) the political debate on religious conversion; (2) the Basic Law: Israel – the Nation-State of the Jewish People, passed in 2018; and (3) the Israeli court's 2013 ruling denying the viability of Israeli national identity. I use these examples as windows through which to appreciate the larger picture of the alleged fusion or confusion of religion and politics in Israel. I must note that while these are seemingly mainly intra-Jewish Israeli controversies or debates, they in effect deal not only with the Jewishness of Israel, but also, often primarily, with its non- and anti-Arabness, marking a racially logical distinction between these identities. They thus carry far-reaching

---

[9] The literature on the role of the Arab Other in Israeli national identity is quite extensive. For a comprehensive consideration, see Bar-Tal and Teichman (2005).

[10] It must be noted that a politics that is Jewish does not have to be dictated by the logic of the modern sovereign nation-state.

Zionist Theopolitics and Jewish Tradition 97

implications for the image and status of non-Jewish Palestinian Arabs in Israel, the viability and legitimacy of Jewish Arab identity, and Israel's relation to the wider Middle East.

The convoluted application and denial of both the racial logic of inclusion and exclusion and the distinction between the secular and the religious (and the corresponding duality of religion versus politics) is revealed in what must be understood as the *political* controversy over *religious* conversion in Israel.[11] An observer unfamiliar with the Zionist politics of Jewish identity may indeed be perplexed when confronted with the spectacle of this ongoing controversy over conversions. Why is the political sphere in its entirety so preoccupied with the intricacies of the Orthodox interpretation of what is collectively seen as a *religious* act of conversion into Judaism (which the official institution overseeing the conversions – the Orthodox Rabbinate – clearly views as synonymous with conversion into Jewish religion, as in accepting and observing the dictates of religious law in its Orthodox interpretation)? Why does the state – whose law, if not essence, is deemed secular, and for which "Hebrew" law (the common codename for Jewish, "religious" law) functions merely as a source of "inspiration" – devote so many resources and so much attention to the rabbinical (Orthodox) interpretation and practice of religious conversion? Why would a non-theocratic state that often celebrates itself as "the only democracy in the Middle East" designate certain organs of the statist machinery[12] as agents responsible for the (religious) education and successful conversion of non-Jewish citizens – excluding (one is tempted to add "of course"; but this taken-for-granted sense of exclusion must not evade our critical gaze) Palestinian Arab citizens of the Israeli democracy? Furthermore, why is it that of all state organs capable of this task, it is the military that plays a dominant role in the preparation of young Israeli citizens (recently drafted to the army regardless of their religious identity, as the "secular" law of the nation-state demands) for the process of religious conversion?[13] This already baffling practice becomes even more staggering if we take into account the fact that the act of conversion itself is overseen

[11]   As can be deduced from my previous comments, I find the use of these terms as if they entail distinct universal categories to be misleading. My use of these terms echoes their prevalent presence in the Israeli political/public sphere, which, as I have already noted, maintains this distinction while constantly annulling its main sense.

[12]   The Israeli government has declared the conversion of non-Jewish immigrants from the former Soviet Union a "national mission." They have established a "Conversion Administration," currently located in the Prime Minister's Office, which is the main governmental body involved in preparing candidates to convert via the Rabbinical Court for Conversion. The various bodies and initiatives run and overseen by this administration are too numerous to outline here. For a detailed overview, see Goodman (2008, 2009) and Kravel-Tovi (2017).

[13]   The Israeli army plays a central role in the preparation of newly drafted non-Jewish citizens, the vast majority of whom were either born in the former USSR or are decedents of these immigrants. These individuals were awarded almost immediate Israeli citizenship by application of the Law of Return. (The law grants this right to "return" to both Jews and children or grandchildren of Jews, as well as to their spouses.) This preparation process includes primarily an intensive study program (based on the Orthodox interpretation of Jewish law and view of the meaning of Jewish identity) that culminates, if

and carried out by an Orthodox rabbinical establishment whose members for the most part belong to a community of ultra-Orthodox Jews who are largely exempt from the draft, regarding the military as an ethically and religiously corrupting institution[14] (Goodman 2008, 2009; Kravel-Tovi 2017). Lastly, and most importantly, what alternative, if any, national-political (and not religious) path to joining the nation does the (so-called secular, or at least nonreligious) nation-state of the Jews offer those who are interested in conversion? (The answer to all of the above questions is that the state does not offer such an alternative path.)

Or take, as another example of the alleged "enigma" at hand, the controversial Basic Law: Israel – the Nation-State of the Jewish People,[15] which seeks to constitutionally enshrine and ensure the State of Israel's "Jewish identity." What is the purpose of this law in the first place? Is it not the case that the constitutive logic of the State of Israel dictates that it is the nation-state of Jews? And why does the Basic Law assert Israel's identity as the nation-state of the Jewish people by negating and excluding recognition of other peoples' (read: Palestinians') similar claims for nationhood? Does a declarative-constitutional Jewishness of the state necessarily amount to an explicit commitment of the state to prefer Jews and their interests over (Palestinian Arab) non-Jews? Such preference, or rather discrimination, can be quite clearly deduced from the bill's decree that the state shall encourage immigration of Jews, encourage and support the settlement of Jews, and will strengthen the affinity between the State of Israel and Jewish communities outside of the state. Earlier versions of the law also included a clause that would allow the establishment of "Jews only" settlements; this was ultimately dropped from the text of the law. And why does the bill demote Arabic from the status of official language, thus excluding the language of not only Israel's Palestinian Arab citizens but also of many Israeli Jews who originate from Arabic-speaking countries, a language in which many foundational Jewish texts were written?[16] Does the law imply that Israel's wish to be "both" Jewish and democratic is unachievable, as it makes the state's Jewish identity – or Judaism – superior to its commitment to democracy? And lastly, and perhaps most importantly, how has it come to be that the law, originally proposed

---

successful, in the examination and conversion of the candidates by the Rabbinate. On Jewish conversion in Israel, see Kravel-Tovi (2012).

[14] The roots of this Orthodox animosity to service in the Israeli army are deep. Generally, the Orthodox authorities fear that serving in the army would expose the young men and women to what these authorities view as immoral, irreligious, and the wrong behavior, values, and beliefs. Historically, as well, the Orthodox establishment has been quite suspicious of the Zionist movement.

[15] For the English full text of the Basic Law, which cleared the final legal hurdles in late July 2018, see www.jpost.com/Israel-News/Read-the-full-Jewish-Nation-State-Law-562923. Simon Rabinovitch has been curating and editing a forum on Marginalia, published in the Los Angeles Review of Books (http://marginalia.lareviewofbooks.org/defining-israel-forum-recent-attempts-determine-israels-char acter/), on the law during almost a decade of debate over it, in which he offers both updated versions of the relevant legal documents and an ongoing discussion on the proposed bill.

[16] Needless to say, like other parts of the law, this specific decree is aimed primarily at excluding the Palestinian Arab citizens; yet, its consequential denial of Jewish Arabness should not be overlooked.

Zionist Theopolitics and Jewish Tradition

and advanced by so-called secular members of Israel's parliament (most of whom adhere to a secularist Zionist discourse), relies on Jewish tradition and "heritage" – what is commonly referred to by the same secularist discourse as Jewish religion – for the preservation and maintenance of the (Jewish) identity of the supposedly secular nation-state of the Jews?

As a last example, consider the declarative rulings by the Israeli Supreme Court – a celebrated champion of liberal (secularist) Zionism – that explicitly and rather vehemently deny the viability of an Israeli national identity (Agranat 1972; Solberg 2008; Vogelman 2013). This has come to light more than once (both in the early 1970s and as late as 2013), as appellants requested that the court order the state (through the Interior Ministry) to register them as "Israeli" under the category designating their nationality (*le'om*, as distinct from their registered religion, *dat*, and citizenship, *ezrahut*) in the state's population registry. The court has viewed this request as threatening the very core of the Zionist project's claim to Jewish nationhood and as a denial of the unity of the entire Jewish people. Crucially, it has determined that the very existence of an Israeli nation has not been proven; that, empirically speaking, such a nation does not exist at all. We may wonder: What motivated the court to address this obviously ideological matter in the first place, and why did it view the possibility of acknowledging an Israeli national identity as a threat to Zionism? And how does this ruling reflect upon the status of non-Jewish Israelis and on Israel's position in the larger Middle East?[17]

RELIGION AND POLITICS IN ISRAEL: BEYOND THE SECULARIST DISCOURSE

Contradictions around conversion, the Basic Law, and the dismissal of an Israeli nationality all point to the foundational tension at the core of the Zionist construction of Jewish nationalism. To understand this tension, we may consider for a moment the source of the apparent confusion that these cases, and similar others, tend to bring about: All turn on a fundamental contradiction between, on the one hand, a secularist discourse and conceptual framework that designates secular/rational politics and religion into separate realms of human life and, on the other, a reality that does not obey this framework's expectations and requirements. It is commonly assumed, whether implicitly or explicitly, that "Jewish religion" and "Israeli politics" are two separate, distinguishable realms that, for historical and political reasons, are entangled and confused. Commentators often assume that Israeli society and politics are essentially dictated by the (secularist) epistemological tension between religion and politics and by the sociocultural cleavage between secular and religious Jews in Israel, commonly identifying the former as committed to liberal-democratic (secular) values and the latter as an antidemocratic, theocracy-

---

[17] For a review and discussion of this case history, see Yadgar (2017, 163–86).

100   *Yaacov Yadgar*

craving conservative minority (Ben-Porat 2013; Cohen and Susser 2000; Liebman and Don-Yehiya 1983, 1984).

Needless to say, this premise regarding an essential, categorical distinction between "religion" and "politics" reflects a broader worldview that dominates corresponding discussions on similar issues outside of Israel (often dubbed matters of church and state). In other words, this discourse on Israel echoes a (historically situated, European, Protestant) secularist discourse; it imports and implants this discourse – and its epistemological and ontological assumptions – on its particular roots and history, transferring its logics into the Jewish, Zionist, and Israeli cases.

Yet, as I noted above, a growing body of "post-secular" literature has convincingly established that this dominant, secularist discourse on religion and politics (outside of Israel and the Jewish case) is fallacious.[18] Applied as a universal conceptualization of human development, secularist normalization misleads and distorts more than it enlightens.[19] It assumes its main concepts (iterations of the categories of religion and the secular) to be ahistorical and universal while they – or the way we commonly understand them today – are in effect the products of a specific, historically situated configuration of power (which they, in turn, serve).

The application of this conceptual scheme of distinct religious and secular categories to the Jewish-Israeli case is doubly misleading. It both perpetuates the interests hiding behind its dominance (i.e., the worldview of the modern, sovereign nation-state) and ties the histories of Jews (and their Judaisms) into the conceptual parameters of Western, Protestant, colonial modernity. Following this epistemology's dictates, the debate on religion and politics in Israel perpetuates the mythology that Zionism has been an essentially secular project. It is a myth that assumes that Israel is a secular, liberal, and democratic nation-state, which for one reason or another – primarily, the representational and coalitional structure of the Israeli regime, which allegedly endows the "religious" parties with the ability to "extort" compromises and concessions from the "secular" majority – is forced or coerced to pass and implement laws that impose Jewish religion on the public sphere and on the private lives of Israeli citizens.

This, after all, is the idea encapsulated in one of the foundational myths of Israeli politics, namely, the (in)famous "status quo." According to the narrative, the status quo is a kind of armistice, a historic and dynamic compromise between two contested parties: the "secular camp" (which is committed to establishing an enlightened, secular, liberal, and democratic regime, in which religion is excluded

---

[18] For example, see Asad (1993, 2003); Cavanaugh (2003); Connolly (1999); Dubuisson (2007); Fitzgerald (2007); Jakobsen and Pellegrini (2008); Masuzawa (2005); J. Z. Smith (1982, 1998); W. C. Smith (1963).

[19] It would be a futile attempt to reference all of the major works in this field. Cavanaugh (2009, especially 57–122) offers a comprehensive review of this field's critical arguments. See also Asad (1993); Dubuisson (2007); Masuzawa (2005); J. Z. Smith (1982); W. C. Smith (1963). In a previous work (Yadgar 2012), I have elaborated the argument regarding the irrelevance of this discourse to the Zionist Israeli case.

from public matters) and the "religious camp" (which is committed to the enforcement and coercion of Jewish law onto the state and the private lives of its citizens). This (mis)understanding of the status quo fails to appreciate both the ways in which and the degree to which the supposedly secular state relies on what it views as religious traditions (and on an Orthodox establishment it has endowed with the role of determining the practical meaning of this tradition) for preserving its "Jewish character," and thus the state's sovereignty as the nation-state of the Jews, or even as a Jewish nation-state. This narrative fails, in other words, to appreciate the reliance of the theopolitics of the ("secular") state on ("religious") theology.

The religious-secular dichotomy generates consequential misunderstandings that prevent us from carefully assessing the unresolved nature of the relationship between Zionism, followed by the nation-state it has established, and what mainstream Zionist ideology itself has viewed (following the cue of contemporaneous Jewish European thought) as "Jewish religion," seen as distinguishable from "Jewish nationality." This distinction between the religious and the political/secular, it should be reiterated, is an idea born out of the coercion of Jewish traditions into the splint of the essentially European, Christian, historically situated categories of "religion" and "nationalism." As such, this discussion hides several important foundational facts regarding the meaning of Jewish and Israeli identity. It thus encourages a misunderstanding of some of the foundational characteristics of Israeli politics and their implication to the politics of the Middle East.

THE POLITICS OF TRADITION

One of the more fruitful ways to transcend this discourse's narrow horizon and to engage in an examination – a construction, even – of its alternatives, is to identify the matters at hand not as a problem of "religion and politics" in Israel, but rather as a (quintessentially political) matter of our (i.e., humans') relations with our traditions. In other words, I propose that we engage in a critical Jewish reading of the unresolved, problematical, often manipulative nature of the State of Israel's approach to the numerous histories of Jewish communities, histories that are manifested in the Jewish traditions that preceded the Zionist project and its culmination in the State of Israel.

Thus we come to face the central issue to be addressed: How does the Israeli nation-state's theopolitics – constituted, as it is (symbolically, at least), on an "invented" national tradition – approach Jewish traditions that preceded it and continue to live alongside it? The "problem" with those Jewish traditions is that they do not fit easily, if ever, into commonly used categorical frameworks such as "nation," "ethnicity," "race," and, perhaps most importantly, "religion," which originate in modern Western discourse. Let us ignore for a moment, even if only for the sake of argument, the tendency to view these categories, born as they are from a specific European Christian history, as if they were a universal language of human

102   *Yaacov Yadgar*

life, which is necessarily also applicable to the histories of (all) Jewish communities. What is critical to note is that in many meaningful senses "Judaism"[20] answers each and every one of these terms/categories *and* none of them. This is because Jewish traditions are comprehensive ways of life that touch upon various dimensions of human experience, which are variously labeled under one or the other of the abovementioned categories at different times.

Bearing this in mind, I offer a short assessment of three critical issues that are seen in a new light once one foregoes the misleading secularist epistemology and discourse on "religion and politics." These deal with the role of Jewish traditions in (a) the shaping of the Zionist project; (b) the shaping of the Israeli public sphere; and (c) the formation and development of Jewish identities in Israel. The explication of these matters reveals new insights about the "enigmas" of Israeli politics described above.

ZIONISM AND THE INVENTION OF JEWISH "RELIGION"

One of the more fruitful ways to understand Zionism is *not* to identify it as an attempt at secularizing Judaism (or Jewish traditions) through the invention of a national tradition. Predominant as such a description is, it nevertheless suffers from some acute deficiencies, not least of which is its lack of clarity as to the meaning of "secularization."[21] Instead, Zionism would be better understood if viewed as a counterreaction to another act of invention that preceded Zionism: the transformation of Judaism into a "religion" (or the "invention" of Jewish religion). This has to do with the modern ideological innovation and practical transformation that originated in Europe, mostly in Germany, from the eighteenth century onward, which sought to reinterpret Jewish traditions so as to render them applicable to the allegedly universal (and, again, essentially European Protestant) category of religion, in itself a contemporaneous invention.

Zionism emerged as a forceful argument against the idea that Judaism is in essence a religion, that is: a system of belief, a "faith," an essentially personal and apolitical matter of spirituality. The original formulation of the idea that Judaism *is* a religion – exactly that which is labeled under this title and nothing beyond it – is usually accredited to Moses Mendelssohn. Its further development and articulation (mostly by other German Jewish philosophers) brought about the formation of Reform Judaism, encouraged the shaping of the Historical Positivist school (better known today as Conservative Judaism), and, ultimately, facilitated the shaping of modern Orthodoxy and ultra-Orthodoxy as counterreactions to the Reform interpretation of the implications of this idea (Batnitzky 2011).

---

[20] For the sake of being concise, I am avoiding here the obviously relevant critical assessment of the very term "Judaism." On this, see Neusner (2003); Satlow (2006); J. Z. Smith (1982).

[21] For influential formulations of viewing Zionism as secularization of Judaism, see Avineri (1981) and Shimoni (1995). For a comprehensive critique of this view, see Yadgar (2017, 67–83).

Zionist Theopolitics and Jewish Tradition   103

A central argument implied by the idea that Judaism should be understood as a religion (indeed, this argument is the main motivation behind the invention of Judaism as a religion) is that Judaism is not a nationality, at least in the prevalent contemporaneous European nation-state oriented, *political* sense of this term. By making Judaism a religion, European Jews had allegedly solved the potential tension in their identification as members of an alien, foreign nation living among host nationalities. It enabled Jews, as the famous term or phrase states, to become "German (or French, or otherwise) nationals of the Mosaic faith" – loyal citizens and subjects of the nation-state who differ from the majority only in the limited, politically inconsequential realm of religious faith.

Zionism sought to negate this argument and the whole project of political and cultural assimilation it entailed. The driving ideological force of the Zionist movement has been fundamentally based on a competing argument, which also used the contemporaneous European political discourse: Judaism, so argues the Zionist idea on its various formulations, is a nationality – it is about *national* (i.e., political, "secular") identity.[22] Political Zionism, the ultimately triumphant stream of Zionist ideology, would further argue that this Jewish nationalism must be expressed and realized in the political framework of a nation-state, in which the true meaning of Judaism as a nationality will be reincarnated.

This nationalism – which many Zionist thinkers preferred to label "Hebrew," not Jewish (this terminological issue encapsulates Zionism's uneasy relationship with its own Jewish histories and traditions) – was thus presented by its ideologues as a broader frame of meaning, which incorporates in it "Jewish religion" but is surely neither dictated by this religion nor identical to it.[23] This understanding of Jewish identity also stands at the very ideological, politico-cultural foundation of the State of Israel, the nation-state of Jews.

As in other cases of emerging nationalist movements, the Zionist project has also involved a wide-ranging endeavor of inventing a national tradition. Zionism was required to instil the notion of a national Jewish identity with a positive meaning, and Zionist ideologues were required to rewrite "Jewish history," that is: to reinterpret Jewish meaning and subjects throughout history so as to render these consistent with the nationalist meta-narrative of a collective identity and to generate a political conflation between territory and identity (whether ethnic, national, linguistic, etc.).

Needless to say, Zionism has found the building blocks for this rewriting in the histories of Jews, specifically in and from Jewish traditions. But it arrived at this move as it was already deeply immersed in the context, or discourse, of the "secularization" of Judaism (a move that originated in the movement of Jewish Enlightenment, the *haskala*). This project of a national rewriting of traditions was, from the outset,

---

[22] For a comprehensive presentation and analysis of Zionist ideology, see Avineri (1981); Hertzberg (1970); Shimoni (1995).

[23] This, indeed, is a claim presented in some formulation by practically all major ideologues of political Zionism. See Avineri (1981); Hertzberg (1970); Shimoni (1995).

based upon the false distinction between Jewish religion and other, essentially secular, dimensions (political, national, cultural, linguistic, etc.) of Judaism. Moreover, prevalent streams in Zionist ideology tended to view this same religion (in their own terms) as oppressing the national vitality and as being the root cause of what they viewed as the decline of the Jewish people in exile, that is, the state of lacking political sovereignty.

How, then, has Zionism constructed its position vis-à-vis Jewish traditions that had preceded it (and were, so the mainstream Zionist argument has claimed, besmirched by the stain of "religiosity")? Several Zionist thinkers – including, to the embarrassment of many, Theodore Herzl – chose largely to ignore this question, focusing instead on the notion of Jewish political power by way of imagining the "Jews' State" as a sort of European nation-state – indeed, a German-speaking state, at that[24] – that is ruled by Europeans of Jewish decent. Other ideologues were fiercely critical of this neglect. Foremost among them was, of course, Aḥad Haʿam (1902), who wondered aloud what exactly is *Jewish* about Herzl's *Judenstaat*? These ideologues viewed the Zionist project as primarily obligated to "secularize" Judaism, that is, to reinterpret Jewish traditions so as to make them consistent with a rationalist, modernist, utilitarian worldview, which will be (in the mainstream political reading of Zionism) the basis of the (secular) nation-state of the Jews.

This notion of reinterpretation fed the self-image of those socialist Zionist ideologues who arrived in Palestine with the declared aim of rewriting the meaning of their Jewish (or "Hebrew") identity. These ideologically motivated immigrants, most of whom had received a traditional Jewish education and were driven by a sense of rebellion against the authority of the way of life into which they were born, had an intimate, unmediated familiarity with certain Jewish traditions (mostly East European ones), and they sought to reinterpret parts of these traditions. They did so from a confrontational, aggressive position. Thus, to give but one of the most familiar examples, they rewrote the traditional Jewish ritual of the Passover *seder* and *haggadah* so as to render these consistent with their ideology and worldview (see Liebman and Don-Yehiya 1983).

It should be noted that this aggressive confrontation with tradition ultimately manifests a certain dialogue with tradition, nourished by an intimate knowledge of at least some central parts of this tradition. A rebellion against authority is also an acknowledgment of it, and it is surely informed by a familiarity with it. But once the ideological enthusiasm had ebbed, and the unmediated familiarity with tradition was lost, the sons and daughters of these ideological pioneers were left with a sour residue of resentment against "tradition'" and "religion," although they were largely ignorant of the content of these objects of their derision. These Zionist, Israeli successors have, of course, continued to be identified as Jewish. But the positive meaning of this identity (that is, the question of what makes their political project a

---

[24] As can be referred from the Herzlian utopia in Aḥad Haʿam (1902).

Zionist Theopolitics and Jewish Tradition

Jewish project[25]), beyond the fact that they have been committed to the establishment of a Jewish nation-state (Zionism, ultimately, has chosen Herzl's vision over Aḥad Ha'am's), became increasingly vague. The dialogue between them and their Jewish tradition gradually fell silent.

THE POLITICS OF JEWISH IDENTITY IN THE STATE OF THE JEWS

The establishment of the State of Israel did not resolve this dilemma of Zionist, *Jewish* nationalism. In the end, the state seems to have chosen to focus primarily on the constitution of a Jewish majority – a matter of "demography" – as the principal condition for its existence as the state of the Jewish people. The Zionist movement allocated relatively few resources to answering the questions of how to converse with, and reinterpret, the Jewish traditions of the communities that constitute this majority. In the famous contest between two possible translations of Herzl's *Judenstaat*, Zionists chose to focus on the establishment of a state of Jews, not necessarily on the constitution of a Jewish state. Indeed, this seems to be the core understanding of the meaning of Israel as a Jewish nation-state among liberal, secularist Zionist circles, who vehemently oppose the aforementioned proposed Basic Law,[26] as well as other attempts by the Israeli government to bolster Israel's "Jewish identity." As put, for example, by a *Haaretz* editorial opposing the Ministry of Religious Services' designation of a "Jewish identity administration" as an act of "religious coercion:"

> Zionism dreamed of a state for the Jews, not a Jewish state: a refuge for members of the Jewish people, not a state with an official religion like Muslim Saudi Arabia. The Balfour Declaration promised a national home, not a religious one. On Israeli identity cards, "Jewish" describes a nationality. (Haaretz 2013b)

But even such a limited understanding of Jewish politics – this, simply, is politics run by people of Jewish origins – must address certain issues of Jewish identity in order to govern a nation-state that identifies as the state of the Jews. Critically, the state is required to decide who counts as a Jew and who does not – to outline, in other words, the contours and definition of the "nation" in the name of which it functions. The solution devised by the allegedly secular state was to rely on the "official representatives" of "Jewish religion" (rabbis and politicians who adhere to a conservative, Orthodox interpretation of Jewish tradition) to operate as the nation's gatekeepers – whether by assigning them with the responsibility to decide "who is a Jew?"

---

[25] Aḥad Ha'am has dedicated his thought to this question, arriving at what other ideologues critically viewed as the essentialism of Jewish tradition, to which they objected. See Shimoni (1995).

[26] In one furious editorial in the Israeli Hebrew daily newspaper *Haaretz*, for example, the proposed Basic Law: Israel – the Nation-State of the Jewish People was referred to as the "Basic Law: Apartheid in Israel" (Haaretz 2013a).

or by giving them the monopolistic authority to manage Jewish citizens' personal matters (marriage and divorce), greatly inhibiting marriages between Jews and non-Jews, and thus preserving the distinction between these two constitutive groups.

It is worth noting here that the State of Israel has never attempted to build an Israeli national identity that would be liberated, so to speak, from Jewish "religion" and would naturally include the non-Jewish citizens of the state. Instead, the state has focused on the construction of a Jewish national identity that is distinct in one critical respect: It is a national identity reserved for Jews only. In addition, the state has viewed the diversity of Jewish traditions as a threat to national unity and devoted its resources and attention to the abusive project of the "melting pot," which, as its name suggests, treats these traditions as practices that should be dissolved.

Of course, the state still espouses a notion of a distinction between Jewish religion and nationality, but as has been demonstrated by the political and legal debates surrounding the "paradoxes" this distinction creates, the state, as well as the culture it has engendered, remain loyal to the notion that these two categories are essentially identical. This idea stands at the core of the national school curriculum, and it feeds a series of laws that enforce a notoriously narrow interpretation of Jewish tradition (mainly, if not solely, in terms of practice, or rather the prohibition of certain practices) on the public sphere.

This, then, is the key to understanding the Israeli status quo on matters of religion and politics. It is not a matter of a compromise and a submission of the "secular majority" to the whims of the "religious minority"; rather, it is an expression – an obviously unwieldy one at that – of the state's reliance (a state, it should be stressed, that is ruled by representatives of that same "secular majority") on a narrow, "religious" interpretation of the meaning of Jewish traditions for the purpose of regulating the public sphere and administrating national politics.

The "secular majority" needs this "religious coercion" more than any other party in this relationship. This coercion is what secures the maintenance and preservation of this majority's Jewish identity in a nation-state that identifies as the state of the Jews. Being a Jew in Israel means belonging to the majority, which enjoys a privileged position in every aspect of life; whoever is Jewish enjoys a political, symbolic, and cultural capital that is reserved for Jews only. And were it not for the state's enforcement of its narrow interpretation of "Judaism" in the public sphere, most members of this majority would be lacking the possibility to positively understand the meaning of their Jewish identity. The state, in other words, enforces "religion" in the public sphere and thus guarantees the distinction between Jews and non-Jews, as well as the privileging of the former over the latter.

JEWISH IDENTITIES IN ISRAEL

A focus on our (humanity's) attitudes about tradition also sheds new light on the matter of Israeli Jews' Jewish identity. Examining tradition exposes the negative and distorting influence of the "cleavage discourse," which tends to view the binary distinction between "secular" and "religious" as the constitutive axis of Jewish identities in Israel. Take, for example, the "secular majority." The positive meaning of its "secularity" is so enigmatic that the surveyors of the most comprehensive poll on Jewish beliefs, observance, and costumes among Israeli Jews replaced the label "secular" in their questionnaires with the negative designation "not religious" (Arian and Keissar-Sugarmen 2011; S. Levy, Levinsohn, and Katz 2002). Needless to say, the source of this terminological problem is the religious-secular cleavage discourse, which gives birth to such baseless polar images (e.g., "religious" is someone who observes, Orthodoxly so, each and every small tag of the 613 *mitzvot* (religious precepts), while "secular" is someone who is completely indifferent to Jewish observance). Instead, it would be more useful to adopt a "traditionist" point of view (Yadgar 2015), one that raises the question of Jewish Israelis' attitudes to their Jewish traditions.

I have already outlined the formation of Jewish Israeli secularity – or at least revealed the Jewish identity of most of those who identify as secular as a matter of designating a "default" option in terms of their Jewishness, not as a matter of identifying with an explicit secularist ideology – as an outcome of the waning dialogue between the individual and his/her reference group and their traditions. These "secular by default" (Liebman and Yadgar 2009, 159) Israeli Jews have assigned (mostly passively so) the state and its institutions with the role of maintaining their Jewish identity: The state's institutions educate their children to know certain aspects of Jewish history as their history, they force on them the Jewish (or "Hebrew") calendar, they compel them to recognize the Jewish Sabbath as their day of rest, and they make it difficult for them to marry non-Jews (to mention a few of the facets of this "religious coercion").

The key to understanding Jewish Israeli secularism, then, is its inability to conduct a meaningful dialogue with the Jewish traditions from which it has emerged. This absence has been acknowledged by an important minority of intellectuals and elite circles, and it is the driving force behind what is sometimes dubbed the "Jewish renaissance," which revolves around a mostly textual (at least for the time being) endeavor to get reacquainted with the "raw materials" of these traditions.[27]

Secular Israeli Jews are not the only group lacking dialogue with their Jewish traditions. A negation of such a dialogue has also become the founding ideology of Jewish ultra-Orthodoxy, which prefers to view its relation with tradition as a dictation or blind obedience, but surely not as a conversation. Tradition, so the ultra-

---

[27] For a review of this Israeli "Jewish renaissance," see Sheleg (2010).

Orthodox argument goes, is set and sealed, and we must obey it. This stance is of course riddled with self-denial. It denies the dynamic nature of tradition and ignores the fact that even the staunchest of conservatives is forced to continuously and incessantly interpret the meaning of tradition's dictation, consequently updating the meaning of this tradition.

Religious Zionism, which views itself as committed to a reinterpretation of its Jewish tradition, conducts this reinterpretation under the heavy shadow of its commitment to a foreign European tradition (nationalism) and to synthesizing two alien organs (Jewish theology and the theopolitics of the nation-state). Religious Zionism tends to view the nation-state, or its political theology, in the colors of "religious" theology, in a move that stains the latter more than it promotes the former.

There are some Jewish Israelis who do not acquiesce to the rigid boundaries of the secular-religious opposition. People who maintain a *masorti* stance,[28] for example, are mostly Mizrahim (Israeli Jews who trace their origins to Arab and Muslim lands) and tend not to accept the dichotomous distinction of either secular or religious as the constitutive axis of their Jewish identity. This position allows the *masortim* to engage in what might be the most challenging dialogue about their Jewish traditions. But they do so without proper institutional support, and are constantly, harshly criticized for what both "religious" and "secular" Israeli Jews depict as the inconsistent nature of the *masorti* way of life. *Masortim* present rather immediate, constantly developing possibilities of fruitful dialogue with tradition and still remain active, participating actors in modern life (which, it must be admitted, remains largely defined by Zionist politics for lack of an authentically Jewish alternative). It is not hard to see how they become threatening to both of those opponents, the "religious" and the "secular," who build their identity as mutual opposites, assuming as they do that modernity leaves us with only a limited choice: either we abandon tradition, or we blindly obey its dictates.

Given the proper institutional backing, *masortiness* could have developed into a full-fledged alternative to the dichotomous construction of modern Jewish national identity along the "religious vs. secular" binary. The understanding embodied by *masortim* holds some key components of such an alternative: an Arab Jewish history, an emphasis of intra-Jewish ethnic identities and histories, and the overall rejection of a narrative of rupture between the past and the present that is so crucial to the secularist narrative of the enlightenment. Yet, is seems that *masortiyut* has failed to develop into such an alternative and is instead being incorporated into a Zionist nationalism.

---

[28] *Masorti* was originally conceptualized as a residual category of those neither secular nor religious. It has later been positively instilled with meaning to designate an attempt to transcend the dichotomy at hand. See Yadgar (2015).

CONCLUSION

Israel's claim to a Jewish identity brings to life a specifically charged tension, if not an outright paradox of political, nation-statist Zionism. Here, we can borrow Wael Hallaq's (2012) critique[29] to illustrate this point. Claiming that there is an imminent, unsolvable tension at the very core of the idea of a modern sovereign nation-state (a concept born out of European, Protestant history) that is at the same time *Islamic* (i.e., adheres to the traditionally Islamic understanding of governance), Hallaq dubs this idea "the impossible state." In a similar vein, we may identify the Zionist project, which wishes to harness Jewish traditions that have preceded it into the splint of modern sovereignty, as arguing for what is, at its core, an "impossible state." There is an especially deep gap between, on the one hand, traditional Jewish understandings of Jewish identity and concepts of government, sovereignty, and theopolitics and, on the other, the Zionist, modern understanding of these same concepts, which is shaped by European, Christian (specifically Protestant) conceptions.

I have discussed here only a few dimensions of the intellectual history of Zionism, the cultural and political practice of the pre-sovereignty Zionist movement and its relation to the Jewish traditions from which Zionist proponents have emerged, and certain controversial issues in the recent history of Israeli politics that expose the fault lines of the Zionist state's attitude toward Jewish traditions that have preceded it. These all point to the Zionist and Israeli failure to instill a political, so-called secular Israeli identity with a positively meaningful understanding of Jewish identity. While most of the vigor of political Zionist thought has been focused on rebelling against Jewish traditions from which the Zionist ideologues emerged (i.e., a project of reimagining Jewish identity, which is driven by a revolutionary sense of disavowing the past), and on the constitution of a nation-state of Jews as the ultimate expression of a politicization of Jewishness, Zionist ideology has devoted only scarce resources to the question of the positive (Jewish) meaning of its self-proclaimed "new" Jewish (or "Hebrew") identity. In other words, while most of the Zionist impetus was aimed against "old" Jewish traditions, Zionism, and the State of Israel following its cue, have not bothered to construct an alternative meaning-instilling structure (an invented tradition, if we wish), national or otherwise, for *Jewish* identity.

Yet Zionism has never given up its claim to be the national movement *of Jews*, and the State of Israel self-identifies as the Jews' state (and not, for example, as the Israelis' state). The movement and the state it has established are essentially, existentially dependent upon an a priori assumed definition of Jewish identity. The nation-state of the Jews is thus fatally dependent upon the demographic, racial-at-root (according to the state's own interpretation and practice) datum of the proportion of "Jews" in its population. As long as Jews constitute a majority of its population, the state can view itself as upholding its very raison d'être, that is, its

---

[29] Hallaq borrows MacIntyer's (1984, 1988, 1991) conceptualization of tradition.

110 *Yaacov Yadgar*

identity as the nation-state of the Jews. However, because the "secular" state itself does not offer a meaningfully positive definition of Jewish identity, it relies on the services of Orthodox, rabbinical gatekeepers, who handle for the state the task of differentiating Jews from non-Jews. These gatekeepers operate mechanisms of distinction, inclusion, and exclusion that the state itself, on the "secular" worldview it propagates, views as "religious," benighted, and inconsistent with the very principles of Western democracy.

REFERENCES

Agranat, Shimon. 1972. CA 630/70 Tamarin v. State of Israel.

Alcalay, Ammiel. 1992. *After Jews and Arabs: Remaking Levantine Culture*. Minneapolis: University of Minnesota Press.

Anderson, Benedict. 1998. *Imagined Communities: Reflections on the Origin and Spread of Nationalism*. New York: Verso.

Arian, Asher, and Ayala Keissar-Sugarmen. 2011. *A Portrait of Israeli Jews: Beliefs, Observance, and Values of Israeli Jews, 2009*. Jerusalem: Israel Democracy Institute.

Asad, Talal. 1993. *Genealogies of Religion: Discipline and Reasons of Power in Christianity and Islam*. Baltimore: Johns Hopkins University Press.

    2003. *Formations of the Secular: Christianity, Islam, Modernity*. Stanford: Stanford University Press.

Avineri, Shlomo. 1981. *The Making of Modern Zionism: Intellectual Origins of the Jewish State*. New York: Basic Books.

Barak-Erez, Daphne. 2008. "Law and Religion under the Status Quo Model: Between Past Compromises and Constant Change." *Cardozo Law Review* 30: 2495–508.

Bar-Tal, Daniel, and Yona Teichman. 2005. *Stereotypes and Prejudice in Conflict: Representations of Arabs in Israeli Jewish Society*. New York: Cambridge University Press.

Basic Law. 2018. Basic Law: Israel – The Nation State of the Jewish People (Isr.).

Batnitzky, Leora Faye. 2011. *How Judaism Became a Religion: An Introduction to Modern Jewish Thought*. Princeton: Princeton University Press.

Ben-Porat, Guy. 2013. *Between State and Synagogue*. Cambridge: Cambridge University Press.

Cavanaugh, William T. 2003. *Theopolitical Imagination: Christian Practices of Space and Time*. London: Bloomsbury T&T Clark.

    2009. *The Myth of Religious Violence: Secular Ideology and the Roots of Modern Conflict*. New York: Oxford University Press.

Cohen, Asher, and Bernard Susser. 2000. *Israel and the Politics of Jewish Identity: The Secular-Religious Impasse*. Baltimore: Johns Hopkins University Press.

Connolly, William E. 1999. *Why I Am Not a Secularist*. Minneapolis: University of Minnesota Press.

Don-Yehiya, Eliezer. 1999. *Religion and Political Accommodation in Israel*. Translated by Deborah Lemmer. Jerusalem: The Floersheimer Institute for Policy Studies.

Dubuisson, Daniel. 2007. *The Western Construction of Religion: Myths, Knowledge, and Ideology*. Baltimore: Johns Hopkins University Press.

Fitzgerald, Timothy. 2007. *Discourse on Civility and Barbarity*. New York: Oxford University Press.

Gavison, Ruth. 2010. "The Law of Return at Sixty Years: History, Ideology, Justification." Jerusalem: The Metzilah Center for Zionist, Jewish, Liberal and Humanist Thought.

Goodman, Yehuda. 2008. "Citizenship, Modernity and Belief in the Nation-State: Racialization and De-racialization in the Conversion of Russian Immigrants and Ethiopian Immigrants in Israel." In *Racism in Israel*, edited by Yehouda Shenhav and Yossi Yonah, 381–415. Jerusalem: The Van Leer Jerusalem Institute.

———. 2009. "Converting Immigrants: Citizenship, Governmentality and Religionization in Israel during the 2000s." In *Citizenship Gaps: Migration, Fertility, and Identity in Israel*, edited by Yossi Yonah and Adriana Kemp, 207–38. Jerusalem: The Van Leer Jerusalem Institute and Kibbutz Hamehuhad.

Haʿam, Ahad (Asher Ginzburg). 1902. "Altneuland." *Hashiloah* 10, no. 6. https://goo.gl/tNPAic.

Haaretz. 2013a. "Basic Law: Apartheid in Israel." Editorial. May 30. https://goo.gl/x9SGk1.

———. 2013b. "The Jewish Coercion Administration." Editorial. May 22. www.haaretz.com/opinion/the-jewish-coercion-administration-1.525281.

Hallaq, Wael B. 2012. *The Impossible State: Islam, Politics, and Modernity's Moral Predicament*. Reprint edition. New York: Columbia University Press.

Hertzberg, Arthur. 1970. *The Zionist Idea: A Historical Analysis and Reader*. Westport, CT: Greenwood Press.

Hobsbawm, Eric J., and Terence O. Ranger. 1992. *The Invention of Tradition*. Cambridge: Cambridge University Press.

Jakobsen, Janet, and Ann Pellegrini. 2008. "Times Like This." In *Secularisms*, edited by Janet Jakobsen and Ann Pellegrini, 1–35. Durham, NC: Duke University Press.

Kravel-Tovi, Michal. 2012. "'National Mission': Biopolitics, Non-Jewish Immigration and Jewish Conversion Policy in Contemporary Israel." *Ethnic and Racial Studies* 35, no. 4: 737–56.

———. 2017. *When the State Winks: The Performance of Jewish Conversion in Israel*. New York: Columbia University Press.

Kurzweil, Baruch. 1953. "The New Canaanites in Israel." *Judaism* 2: 3–15.

Levy, Gal. 2011. "Secularism, Religion and the Status Quo." In *Religion and the State: A Comparative Sociology*, edited by Jack Barbalet, Adam Possamai, and Bryan S. Turner, 93–119. London: Anthem Press.

Levy, Shlomit, Hanna Levinsohn, and Elihu Katz. 2002. *A Portrait of Israeli Jews: Beliefs, Observance, and Values of Israeli Jews, 2000*. Jerusalem: The Israel Democracy Institute.

Liebman, Charles S., and Eliezer Don-Yehiya. 1983. *Civil Religion in Israel: Traditional Judaism and Political Culture in the Jewish State*. Berkeley: University of California Press.

———. 1984. *Religion and Politics in Israel*. Jewish Political and Social Studies. Bloomington: Indiana University Press.

Liebman, Charles S., and Yaacov Yadgar. 2009. "Secular-Jewish Identity and the Condition of Secular Judaism in Israel." In *Religion or Ethnicity? Jewish Identities in Evolution*, edited by Zvi Gitelman, 149–70. New Brunswick, NJ: Rutgers University Press.

MacIntyre, Alasdair. 1984. *After Virtue: A Study in Moral Theory*. 2nd ed. Notre Dame, IN: University of Notre Dame Press.

———. 1988. *Whose Justice? Which Rationality?* Notre Dame, IN: University of Notre Dame Press.

———. 1991. *Three Rival Versions of Moral Enquiry: Encyclopaedia, Genealogy, and Tradition*. Notre Dame, IN: University of Notre Dame Press.

Masuzawa, Tomoko. 2005. *The Invention of World Religions: Or, How European Universalism Was Preserved in the Language of Pluralism*. Chicago: University of Chicago Press.

Neusner, Jacob. 2003. *The Way of Torah: An Introduction to Judaism*. 7th ed. Belmont, CA: Cengage Learning.

Pianko, Noam. 2010. *Zionism and the Roads Not Taken: Rawidowicz, Kaplan, Kohn.* Bloomington, IN: Indiana University Press.

Porath, Yehoshua. 1989. *The Life of Uriel Shelah.* Tel-Aviv: Maḥbarot Lesifrut.

Quinn, Ben. 2016. "French Police Make Woman Remove Clothing on Nice Beach Following Burkini Ban." *The Guardian,* August 23. www.theguardian.com/world/2016/aug/24/french-police-make-woman-remove-burkini-on-nice-beach.

Satlow, Michael L. 2006. "Defining Judaism: Accounting for 'Religions' in the Study of Religion." *Journal of the American Academy of Religion* 74, no. 4: 837–60.

Schmitt, Carl. 2006. *Political Theology: Four Chapters on the Concept of Sovereignty.* Translated and edited by George Schwab. Chicago: University of Chicago Press.

Scott, Peter, and William T. Cavanaugh. 2008. *The Blackwell Companion to Political Theology.* Malden, MA: Blackwell Publishing.

Shavit, Jacob. 1987. *The New Hebrew Nation: A Study in Israeli Heresy and Fantasy.* London: Frank Cass.

Sheleg, Yair. 2010. *The Jewish Renaissance in Israeli Society: The Emergence of a New Jew.* Jerusalem: Israel Democracy Institute.

Shimoni, Gideon. 1995. *The Zionist Ideology.* London: Brandeis University Press.

Smith, Jonathan Z. 1982. *Imagining Religion: From Babylon to Jonestown.* Chicago: University of Chicago Press.

   1998. "Religion, Religions, Religious." In *Critical Terms for Religious Studies,* edited by Mark C. Taylor, 269–84. Chicago: University of Chicago Press.

Smith, Wilfred Cantwell. 1963. *The Meaning and End of Religion: A New Approach to the Religious Traditions of Mankind.* New York: Macmillan.

Solberg, Noam. 2008. HP (Jerusalem) 6092/07 Ornan, et al. v. Interior Ministry (Isr.).

Vogelman, Uzi. 2013. CA 8573/08 Ornan, et al. v. Interior Ministry (Isr.).

Yadgar, Yaacov. 2012. *Beyond Secularization: Traditionists and the Critique of Israeli Secularism.* Jerusalem: The Van Leer Jerusalem Institute/Hakibutz Hameuchad Publishing House.

   2015. "Traditionism." *Cogent Social Sciences* 1 (1061734): 1–17. https://goo.gl/epMpQo.

   2017. *Sovereign Jews: Israel, Zionism, and Judaism.* Albany: SUNY Press.

Yehoshua, Avraham B., et al. 2006. *The A. B. Yehoshua Controversy: An Israel-Diaspora Dialogue on Jewishness, Israeliness, and Identity.* New York: Dorothy and Julius Koppelman Institute on American Jewish-Israeli Relations, American Jewish Committee.

5

The Relations between the Nationalization of Israel's Politics and the Religionization of Its Military, 1948–2016

Yagil Levy

INTRODUCTION AND THEORETICAL FRAMEWORK

Scholars who study relations between the military and religion in Israel largely agree that since its inception, the military has become increasingly "religionized" following the growing presence of religious conscripts in the army. Religionization of the military is a process in which there is a strengthening of religious elements in the military's culture, symbols, ethics, and conduct, resulting in an expanding religious influence (see, e.g., Drory 2015; Gal and Libel 2012; Levy 2016; Libel and Gal 2015). This process has occurred in tandem with the broader religionization of Israeli politics through the religionization of nationalism, or, as sociologist Uri Ram (2008, 69) puts it, Jewishness "has been transposed entirely from a 'religion of a nation' to a 'national religion.'" I accept both arguments here as a point of departure.

Studies of the religionization of the Israeli military have attributed this process to the demographic changes in the military's social composition. The growth of religious conscripts led to increasing engagement of extra-military religious authorities in managing military affairs and to the religionization of Israeli military culture. Nevertheless, studies have not questioned the correlation between the religionization of the Israel Defense Forces (IDF) and a politics in which nationalism was imputed with religiosity, as Ram implied, nor have they asked how the level of the nationalization of politics impacts the internal military culture of the IDF. This chapter engages with this neglected correlation.

Israel is among very few democracies in which military conscription survives. Conscription applies to both males and females with the exception of Palestinian citizens, ultra-Orthodox Jews (Haredim, religious observants who reject the modern secular culture and are partly exempted from the military), and Jewish religious women (of all denominations). No less important, Israel lacks separation between church and state, thus facing an enduring tension between democracy and Torah-based religion, which, by definition, is nondemocratic (Ben-Yehuda 2010, 7). Considering this uniqueness, we may expect to find a broad correlation between the political-cultural trends taking place in Israeli society and those within the military.

Theoretically, according to conventional wisdom, militaries reflect the societies within which they operate, particularly in a democratic society, and especially in countries that maintain conscription (Hassner 2014, 5; Patterson 2014). Therefore, it is reasonable to conclude that the religionization of society would be reflected in various degrees in the military. Nevertheless, even as religious values filter into military culture, we should consider variations in the effects of religious influence, particularly when the military bears less resemblance to the general society in three situations. First, the military as such is the major tool for promoting nationalist sentiments, because it is tasked with the defense of national sovereignty. Therefore, the way it socializes its soldiers to be ready to sacrifice for the nation may be imbued with nationalist attitudes, especially when defense is perceived as national survival itself. When nationalist sentiments are fused with religious values, militaries can use religious ideology to recruit, mobilize, and motivate soldiers (Hassner 2014, 5), and thus religious symbols may be more conspicuous in the military than in society.

Second, and more complicated, to the extent that since the eighteenth century, military service has come to be acknowledged as socially valuable and thereby affecting the social status of the groups who participate in it, military service also has become a crucial arena of intercultural contentions over the identity and values of the larger political community (Krebs 2005). Therefore, different inflections of religionization in a society may yield contradictory outcomes for the military: Denationalization (i.e., the decline in the salience of national values and symbols), secularization, liberalization, and demilitarization of politics (in the sense that military values, symbols, and mindset play a less impactful role in politics and culture) may encourage religious groups to improve their position within the military. This encouragement assumes that as a conservative organization, the military can be more attentive than civilian sectors to religious and nationalist values. Thereby, empowerment within the military may compensate religious groups for their declining status in a society that is experiencing the trends mentioned above. In this context, for example, we can understand the evangelization of the US military in the post-Vietnam era, when American society became more religiously diversified and secular (Loveland 2014, 17–19). At the same time, social groups often legitimize their claims for improving their intra-military status by invoking the dominant themes of the political discourse, such as capitalizing on republicanism to justify their claims for rights in return for military sacrifices (Krebs 2006). It follows that religionization in society empowers groups associated with religious and nationalist values, thus encouraging and legitimizing these groups' attempts to religionize the ranks further by amplifying nationalist and religious socialization within the military.

Notwithstanding these intra-military struggles over power, theories of collective action offer us another option. Military sacrifice in the modern era is built upon the exchange of sacrifice for rewards, mainly symbolic ones, with social and political rights that groups obtain from their military service at the center. When a social group feels that it is under-rewarded for its military contribution, actually or potentially, the group's status in the military (or the belief that this status can potentially be reinforced) plays a major part in shaping the nature, scope, and strategy of its collective actions aimed at repairing this unbalanced exchange of sacrifice for rewards. Therefore, the group can struggle to improve its position in the military or work to take advantage of its already-attained military status to convert it into social rewards. Alternatively, it can also work to create an extra-military upward mobility track (see Levy 2008). Similar considerations may guide religious groups in their efforts to reinforce their social status.

With these general, theoretical insights in mind, we can better understand how the religionization of politics affects the religionization of the military in Israel in particular. It is argued that we can identify four main stages of the relationship between the religionization of military and politics, each signifying variations in the convergence of Israel's military and its society. During the first stage, which was the formative period of the state and the military (1950s–60s), the partial religionization of the military reflected similar processes in the general society. In the second stage, following the 1967 War, the responses to the war's aftermath strengthened ethno-national religionization. However, ethno-national religionization prompted the proponents of this process – the national-religious sector – to develop an extra-military avenue for upward mobility in the form of the settlement enterprise in the Occupied Territories, instead of competing within the military where their status was marginal. The third stage (1980s–90s) was characterized by the denationalization of Israeli politics with the Oslo Accords (by which the Israeli and the Palestinian leaderships committed themselves to the process of conciliation), at its center. During this stage, the national-religious sector increased its strongholds in the military by leveraging new opportunities created by the partial retreat of secular groups from the military as an avenue of upward social mobility. The fruits of this move were felt in the fourth stage (2000s), when the religionization of the military occurred in tandem with, and was bolstered by, the religionization of politics. These four main stages are discussed below.

STAGE 1: PARTIAL RELIGIONIZATION OF THE ISRAELI MILITARY AND POLITICS

With the creation of the Israel Defense Forces (IDF) in 1948, struggles emerged over the shape of its internal culture. The founders of the military and the early state builders (associated with the secular Zionist labor movement) sought to shape the IDF as a secular organization in the spirit of the premilitary, underground militias on which the newly established state's military was drawn. But the religious minority had its own agenda. This minority had two main components: (1) the Orthodox Jews, particularly national-religious communities who link religion with a vision of the national mission, and (2) the ultra-Orthodox Jews. Together, both comprised about 10 percent of the Jewish population during this period. Blocking proposals to create separate units for religious soldiers, the mainstream, national religious Zionists demanded and successfully achieved the integration of religious soldiers within mixed units, thereby imposing dietary laws and observance of the Jewish Sabbath and holy days on all units (Kampinsky 2009).

Equally as important, Prime Minister and Defense Minister David Ben-Gurion allowed the establishment of the Chief Military Rabbinate, whose authority extended over all soldiers regardless of whether or not they were observant. As part of this authorization, military chaplains were tasked with communicating the principles of Jewish rituals and teachings to all Jewish personnel, influencing the culture of the entire institution in which secular individuals constituted the majority (S. A. Cohen, Kampinsky, and Rosman-Stollman 2016). This was the first move toward the religionization of the IDF inasmuch as the foundations were laid for religious influence within the ranks, led by the Chief Military Rabbinate.

This move can be seen as part of a broader series of politically motivated compromises negotiated between Ben-Gurion and the religious parties affecting all of Israeli Jewish society (Kampinsky 2009, 433–34). Among these compromises, the state law system established the monopoly of Jewish religious law regulating marriage and divorce of Jewish citizens and institutionalized the autonomous status of religious elementary schools (Barak-Erez 2008). However, if we push this explanation further, beyond serving political interests, the religionization of the military was part of the early, partial religionization of politics of the young state.

Originally, Zionist ideology was an endeavor to reinvent Jewish nationhood as a new secular identity. However, as Shafir and Peled (2002) argue, for Zionism, "the need to rely on primordial factors for legitimation and mobilization was particularly acute, since there was no modern culture common to all Jews." Among other things, this dictated "the use of a whole array of Jewish religious symbols and other cultural constructs" (Shafir and Peled 2002, 149). Israel, moreover, adopted a Jewish nationality as a way to secure the boundaries and membership of the nation while precluding the formation of an Israeli nation that might have included the Arab minority – those Palestinians who stayed in what became Israel following the 1948 War. In this Zionist nation-building context, religion served as the ideological equivalent to ethnicity (Ram 2008, 61).

In this spirit, Ohana (2012, 362–63) maintained that Ben-Gurion was the architect of "a historical experiment in nationalizing religious concepts and metamorphosing them into the secular sphere ... Ben-Gurion's act of nationalization in many spheres of life, was a broad, comprehensive, and multifaceted secular ideology which took hold of religious myths and harnessed them to a project of statehood." The use of biblical symbols was part of this cultural and political project (Ram 2008, 65). However, religious permeation into the civilian sphere also weakened secularism. Indicatively, in 1955 a Jewish Consciousness Program was implemented in the secular education system, largely associating this consciousness with Orthodox worship (Shapiro 1998). A year later, following Israel's temporary occupation of the Sinai Peninsula in Egypt (during the 1956 Suez War), Ben-Gurion promised that Israel would annex the Strait of Tiran (the sea passage from the Red Sea to Israel). He declared, "Yotvat, also known as Tiran, will once again be part of the Third Kingdom of Israel," thus conferring biblical significance on this security move (cited in Gluska 2011).

The religionization of the IDF thus reflected the early, partial religionization of Israeli political culture. To the extent that Jewish religious symbols were harnessed to legitimize the new state, the IDF, its main symbol (as any military might be in a young state), could not be shaped as a purely secular institution. Nevertheless, the IDF's intra-military culture was essentially secular, and the military remained a secular stronghold and symbol during the early years of state formation. Religious recruits usually did not seek prestigious positions within the IDF, particularly in combat, because of fears of coming into close contact with secular conscripts, which might have a negative effect on the religious soldiers' observance and beliefs. This anxiety led many religious soldiers into auxiliary roles and away from the possibility of a military career and was accompanied by sentiments of alienation from the secular IDF and of social marginality (Levy 2015, 53–59). The turning point emerged following Israel's military victory in the 1967 War, giving rise to further religionization of Israel's politics.

STAGE 2: ETHNO-NATIONAL RELIGIONIZATION OF ISRAELI POLITICS

Ethno-national religionization strengthened in the aftermath of the 1967 War, as the Israeli Jewish community experienced a renewed encounter with historically venerated sites that were previously inaccessible but now came under Israeli military occupation, such as the Old City of Jerusalem and the city of Hebron in the West Bank. For religious and rightist groups, the occupation facilitated the reassertion of their identification with Jewish tradition. These sentiments were accompanied by the revival of the historical, religious concept of *Eretz Israel* (Land of Israel), rather than *Medinat Israel* (State of Israel), the term prevalent in the statist rhetoric of *mamlachtiyut* (statism), the state ideology, until the 1970s (Kimmerling 1985).

For many, traditional Judaism, which invoked primordial symbols in the building of the Israeli Jewish community, became a crucial factor in redefining the boundaries of Israeli society. Compared to the republican spirit that had governed Israeli political culture since 1948 and was reflected in *mamlachtiyut*, the ethno-national ethos saw the state as an embodiment of the Jewish community, not as an instrumental entity separate from it. Therefore, citizenship was not conceived around individual rights or duties derived from the citizen's formal belonging to the state. Instead, citizenship status was expected to be attained merely by belonging to the Jewish collective and was no longer seen as dependent on historical or contemporary contributions – military or otherwise – as the secular, statist, republican discourse had previously asserted. This new public discourse sharpened the distinction between Jews and Arabs, seeing them as primordial identities. This distinction created an ethnic hierarchy defined by ascriptive belonging and advocated an aggressive stance toward the surrounding Arab states, rooted in a theological or nationalist rationale (Shafir and Peled 2002, 87–94). Ethno-national religionization appealed to many Mizrachi immigrants (the wave of Jewish immigration to Israel from predominantly Arab countries during the 1950s), for whom the *mamlachtiyut* criteria denied them first-class citizenship vis-à-vis the preferred status of the Ashkenazi (Jewish immigrants from European backgrounds) nation-builders (Shafir and Peled 2002, 91–95).

For the national-religious communities, with the renewal of Jewish religious symbols across Israeli society, military service gained a new value as conscripts began to be cast in playing the role of protectors of the "Greater Land of Israel." More than just protecting national territory, now soldiers could imagine themselves defending a sacred land. Furthermore, in light of the IDF's decisive military victory and conquest of the Occupied Territories in the 1967 War, Israeli political culture was further militarized when public figures and politicians applied military strategy to political aims, such as resisting the exchange of a full withdrawal from the Occupied Territories for peace. Military policies and political rhetoric gradually erased the "Green Line" that separated Israel and its new territories from both physical and cognitive maps (Lustick 1993, 275–76).

This combination of ethno-national religionization and militarization encouraged the national-religious young generation to improve its position within the IDF. To the extent that the military became a crucial institution by which the "common good" of the Israeli community was defined, national-religious communities could not accept their marginalization within the military. Efforts were therefore made by both the religious leadership and the IDF to establish special programs that encouraged the recruitment of religious youth into combat units without risking their religious identity. A particularly effective program illustrating these efforts was the *yeshivot hesder* (literally "arrangement academies"), which combined Torah study in a *yeshiva* with a shorter military service in an all-religious company or platoon. While the *hesder* program began in 1965, it expanded significantly after the 1967 War as the favored track for the religious elite.

Following the 1973 War, in which Israel was surprised by an Egyptian-Syrian attack, *hesder* soldiers became the role model for many religious youth and gained the admiration of the IDF command. The *hesder* combatants were idealized for their mental stamina and fighting skills in this extremely challenging war, dispelling the myth of the secular warrior's military omnipotence. The rabbis who headed the *yeshivot* leveraged this new image of the powerful *hesder* soldier in order to make demands that enhanced the status of the *hesder yeshiva* (Levy 2015, 94–98).

Nationalization and the Military's Religionization in Israel

Notwithstanding this effort, the main strategic move of the national-religious communities was the establishment of Gush Emunim ("Bloc of the Faithful") in 1974, an uprising of the young generation of religious Ashkenazim. They protested against their marginal cultural and political status and their exclusion from equal participation in shaping notions of the "common good" of the Zionist project. This movement also signified a rebellion of the young generation against the politics of their parents' generation, whom it accused of being marginalized by the secular labor movement, and of making pragmatic compromises in the "rearguard battle" over the religious character of Israeli society. Gush Emunim activities thus demonstrated its members' disappointment, not only with the perceived weakness of their parents' generation, but also with their semi-peripheral status in the army (Levy 2015, 82–92).

With the refutation of the myth of the secular warrior following the 1973 War, the Gush put forward the idea of Jewish settlement in the Occupied Territories as an alternative to the symbols of Israeli military service (see Levy and Peled 1994, 221–23). Therefore, the movement's main agenda was to establish Jewish settlements in populated areas of the West Bank. Gush activists thereby challenged the secular militarist rationale, such as that of "balance of forces," which had heretofore governed decisions about military actions. Instead, the Gush offered religious criteria (such as the sanctity of the land) as a justification for deploying military force (see Kimmerling 1993). This agenda often contradicted government policies and sometimes led to violent clashes with the army, which reluctantly tried to block the Gush's efforts to settle in the West Bank. It is safe to assume that if the 1973 War had not undermined the myth of the secular soldier, the Gush could not have challenged the IDF in such an unprecedented manner. To a large extent, the settlement project, imbued with religious meaning, brought religious Zionism in from the margins of society and turned it into a central political and cultural stream.

In cultural terms, the Gush and the *hesder* gave rise to a new stream within the national-religious communities, the national ultra-Orthodox wing (Hardal), advocating strictness in religious practices and propagating nationalistic and messianic theology (see Leon 2010). Paradoxically, however, the combination of these two strategies (*hesder* and Gush) did not affect the IDF's internal culture until the 1980s. The national-religious community's energy was channeled into extra-military efforts, most notably the project to settle the Occupied Territories, which became the main track through which this community left its imprint. As predicted by the theory of collective action (as elaborated upon in the introduction), the Gush opted for a collective action that challenged military service rather than struggling over the status of Jewish religious conscripts in the IDF, which had excluded or alienated religious youth up to that point. Rather than competing for status within the military, where it had been culturally marginalized, the Gush developed an extra-military avenue for upward social mobility through the settlement enterprise. At the same time, the increasing presence of *hesder* conscripts did not have any impact on the

120   Yagil Levy

military culture, because these conscripts served in all-religious units and in relatively small numbers (about a few hundred [Warhaftig 1988, 238]). Only in the late
1980s did new opportunities in the army emerge for religious Israelis.

STAGE 3: DENATIONALIZATION OPENS
UP NEW OPPORTUNITIES

During the 1980s, following the rise to power of the nationalist Likud Party in
1977, Gush Emunim underwent a gradual process of institutionalization by setting
up state-funded municipal regional councils and the "Council of Settlements in
Judea, Samaria, and Gaza" to manage the settlement project (Newman 2005).
Concurrently, after the peace process with Egypt (1978), the Israeli government
limited the construction of new settlements. The settlements that were approved by
the government were often seen as an attempt to offer Israelis opportunities to
improve their quality of life, rather than motivated by religious ideology (Levy
2015, 125–27). In 1982, moreover, when Israel withdrew from the militarily occupied
Sinai Peninsula and returned it to Egypt for the peace agreement, the Gush failed to
stop Israel's withdrawal. Finally, for the Gush activists, the First Intifada of 1987 – the
Palestinians' uprising against Israel's rule in the Occupied Territories – signified the
demise of the "Greater Land of Israel" as a viable political idea (Lustick 1993, 20–22).

Consequently, with institutionalization, political failures, and ideological
demise, the Gush lost much of its appeal as the route through which young religious
Jews could influence Israeli society. Gradually, some of its leaders even acknowledged that the Gush had not "settled in the hearts" of the Israelis, and thus did not
successfully mobilize the majority of Jewish citizens for its cause (Feige 2009, 4). At
the same time, the *hesder* program offered limited opportunities for the upward
mobility of religious soldiers in the military because of the short term of service that
impeded their advancement to officers' training courses. Hence, this track caused
frustration among the national-religious young generation (B. Cohen 2012, 335–38).

At the same time that mobility through the settlement project narrowed, new
opportunities opened up for national-religious youth. Beginning in the 1980s, the
Israeli military experienced a cultural transition, similar to processes that unfolded
in other Western countries, the most important of which was the decline in the
motivation of the young, secular middle class, the historical backbone of the IDF, to
sacrifice in the military. The IDF's prestige diminished as well, beginning with
military deficiencies in the 1973 War. Over the 1980s to 1990s, political disputes over
the use and necessity of military force increased (such as the conditions under which
the state would initiate a war). And between 1982 and 2000, Israel waged an
indecisive war of attrition with Hezbollah militias in Lebanon. As the republican
ethos weakened in Israeli society, moreover, the country gradually transformed into
a liberal market society. The Israeli public began to place less value on protecting
the country as they perceived decreasing external threats, especially following the

Nationalization and the Military's Religionization in Israel

peace treaty with Egypt in 1978. At the same time, the internal culture of the IDF was liberalized, by, for example, lifting some barriers to the full integration of homosexuals and women and increasing the intervention of parents of soldiers in decisions that had heretofore been the province of military professionals, such as the placement and terms of service of their sons and daughters (Levy 2007, 58–70).

These trends were symptomatic of broader social processes, driven by the globalization of Israeli society. Globalization strengthened the ethos of the market economy with its characteristic liberal discourse, at least among the secular middle and upper classes, and weakened national values such as solidarity, patriotism, and localism. Prominent in this emergent liberal discourse were values such as individualism, privatization, competition, achievement, efficiency, consumerism, democratization, sensitivity to civil rights, and casualty sensitivity, which has played a pivotal role in restraining Israel's military policies since the first Lebanon War in 1982. This new agenda gave rise to the demilitarization of Israeli political culture in the sense that the IDF's status and the importance ascribed to military power declined. This process facilitated and gained traction from the withdrawals from Lebanon (in the years 1985 and 2000), and the Oslo Accords with the Palestinians in 1993–95 (Levy 2007, 92–97). Furthermore, globalization and the empowerment of the market economy together with mass immigration from the former Soviet Union (from the late 1980s to early 1990s, including the naturalization of many non-Jews) reinforced secular trends. They were mainly noticeable in areas such as the enactment of civil marriage and civil burial, the sale of (nonkosher) pork, and the opening of shopping areas on the Jewish Sabbath (Ben-Porat 2013). With globalization, demilitarization, and secularization, denationalization of politics was at work in the sense that national values and symbols declined.

As predicted by the theory about the linkage between extra-military and intra-military processes (presented in the introduction), the denationalization of politics may paradoxically lead to the religionization of the military. The effects of demilitarization on the military opened up new opportunities for religious youth to improve their position in the IDF by taking advantage of the partial loss of interest in the military of their secular peers. These opportunities were reinforced with the outbreak of the First Intifada in 1987, inviting religious soldiers to defend Israel's contested control over what these soldiers perceived as the holy West Bank. Against this background, an alternative, new social mobility track appeared.

In 1988, the first premilitary Torah academy (*mechina*) was established and headed by rabbis belonging to the national ultra-Orthodox wing. The premilitary academy allowed many of the religious conscripts to defer their enlistment to study for twelve to eighteen months for "spiritual fortification," in an effort to reduce the probability that religious soldiers would be secularized during their military service (S. A. Cohen 1999, 2004). Major General Amram Mitzna, the (secular) Commander of the Central Command, played a pivotal role in persuading prominent rabbis to establish the premilitary academy during the First Intifada in order to encourage religious youth to serve their full military service and advance to officers' training courses. Manpower shortfalls drove the IDF to attract the religious youth. The premilitary academy program gained momentum, as tens of new religious academies were founded, dominated by the national ultra-Orthodox wing. They have gradually become the main driving force behind the increasing presence of religious conscripts in the combat units and the command echelon (Rosman-Stollman 2014, 104–6). In the beginning of the 2010s, the graduates of the religious premilitary academies and *hesder yeshivot* constituted about 10 percent of the army's combat force, while the overall proportion of religious soldiers in regular combat units was about 25 to 30 percent, mainly concentrated in the ground forces (Levy 2016, 308).

As new avenues of military mobility opened up, the religious young generation of the 1990s strengthened its hold on the combat units from which the older generation of religious soldiers had been culturally marginalized in the past. For religious youth, increased recruitment into the army formed a complementary layer to the activity of the older generation led by Gush Emunim.

Furthermore, the religious leadership's rhetoric revealed a new version of fusion between religion and nationalism: First, most of the religious academies and many *hesder yeshivot* are located in the West Bank, symbolically demonstrating both the connection between Jewish settlement and military service and that the recent religious generation follows in the footstep of Gush Emunim. The institutions' location reinforces this link by settling not only in the territories but also in the center of power of Israeli society, the IDF. Second, the leaders of the *hesder yeshivot* and premilitary academies affirmed this linkage in their speeches and writing. For example, Rabbi Eli Sadan, the founder of the religious premilitary academies, explained to his students, that the Oslo Accords

> resulted in hundreds of dead Jews, thousands injured, bereaved families and permanent damage ... all the problems that Israel is facing, internationally and militarily, against Hamas and Hizbullah – all of it began with the Oslo Accords which were the most terrible crime ever committed by an Israeli government against the people. (Cited in Benari 2011)

Another leader, the head of the West Bank Nokdim premilitary academy, Rabbi Itamar Cohen (2005), said that there is no such thing as a Palestinian people who is entitled to rights. Another premilitary academy, Yeshiva Ateret Yerushalayim (n.d.), defined its mission as follows: "We strengthen the Jewish hold in the Old City of Jerusalem, especially in the so-called 'Muslim' Quarter (i.e., the Renewed Jewish Quarter)."

With their increasing presence in the military as an identity group, the religious soldiers were imbued with the pride of being the new service elite, supplanting the old, supposedly "evading" secular elites and thus curbing the liberal trends that had allegedly infected the military (Lebel 2013). Leading rabbis even called on religious youth to assume responsibility of the future of the nation unlike older generations and to be trained as the new elite by adopting an approach of a new avant-garde. Rather than being assimilated within the secular sector, the rabbis formulated the goal of healing the "infection" of this sector (Lebel 2016, 3). No wonder that religious conscripts saw themselves as "shouldering the state on their back" (Horowitz 2009).

Consequently, intra-military hierarchies were reestablished, through which soldiers invoked Judaism as the core element in their construction of solidarity and identity in the IDF. As a result, even secular soldiers considered their religious peers as the ones who preserved the ideas constitutive of the collective identity within the IDF (Røislien 2013). Nevertheless, as denationalization opened up new opportunities for the national-religious sector, it also posed new threats to it.

STAGE 4: RELIGIONIZATION OF NATIONALISM

During the early to mid-1990s, the Oslo Accords threatened to demolish the Jewish settlement project. In 2005, the disengagement from the Gaza Strip nearly turned this threat into a reality when Israel evicted about 8,000 settlers from the Strip, along with four settlements in the northern West Bank. It was the IDF that carried out this evacuation. For the national-religious sector, the main symbolic gain in exchange for its military participation was carrying out the mission of renewing Jewish control over what they perceived as the Holy Land. Serving in the IDF to promote this mission helped forge an alternative autonomous identity to that of the dominant secular Zionist by taking part in promoting the newly defined "common good" of the Israeli community. However, the potential destruction of the settlement enterprise threatened to return religious Zionism to the status of just another sector in society rather than being the sector leading a major national project supported by successive Israeli governments, while also undermining the self-identity of a considerable number of conscripts as bearers of a national mission (Sheleg 2004, 76). This was especially so because following the disengagement from Gaza, the focus shifted to the West Bank as the defining arena of critical decision-making that could resolve the Israeli-Palestinian conflict. This was evidenced by Prime Minister Ehud Olmert's proposal, over which he negotiated with the Palestinians during 2007–8, to evacuate about 20 percent of the settlements in the West Bank (Zanany 2015).

Mindful of these threats, the rabbis who headed the *hesder yeshivot* and the premilitary academies developed an agenda of increasing the critical mass of religious soldiers in order to limit the military's deployment of troops to dismantle settlements (Levy 2015, 208–19). For example, Rabbi Sadan called upon religious youth to join the military ranks, the secret service, and the police to develop the infrastructure for the "ideal state" (Sadan 2008, 42). Rabbi Yitzhak Nissim, the head of the premilitary academy Elisha in the West Bank, testified that since the withdrawal from Gaza he has put more emphasis on finding students with the potential to become military leaders to help Israel fulfill what he saw as its true nature (Gorenberg 2009). Indeed, the number of students enrolling in the premilitary academies grew in the years 2005–12 (the period reflecting the national-religious community's reaction to the Gaza disengagement) by 30 percent,[1] while the number of religious graduates in the infantry officers' course rose by about 20 percent (B 2010, 53).

This increasing presence of religious conscripts in military units and military leadership positions has borne fruit since the beginning of the 2000s, even before the disengagement. A critical mass of religious soldiers translated into an increase in the bargaining power of rabbis (heads of the national ultra-Orthodox-dominated *hesder yeshivot* and premilitary academies) vis-à-vis the military. At the minimum, the rabbis' expectation was to impose strict cultural arrangements that would enable religious youth to serve in the military without compromising their religious beliefs and observance. Beyond respecting dietary laws and observing the Jewish Sabbath, the rabbis escalated their demands to reshape military culture toward religionization. Pressure for changes in this direction came not only from the "top down" but also from the "bottom up": The ex-students, particularly from the *hesder yeshivot* and premilitary academies, frequently turned to the rabbis who educated them for spiritual guidance in resolving conflicts between religious and professional issues, such as functioning on the Sabbath or serving with women (S. A. Cohen 2007, 115; Rosman-Stollman 2014, 170–71).

From the perspective of the IDF command, since the late 1990s, they operated on the assumption that the military was dependent on the national-religious sector to provide the high-quality, dedicated personnel needed to fill combat units. Therefore, the IDF leadership has encouraged religious diversity. Yet, the more the national-religious sector's power has been translated into demands seeking to reshape the military's culture and policies toward religionization, the more the military has compromised its freedom of action in order to guarantee an uninterrupted flow of manpower from religious communities (Levy 2015, 184–356).

In the escalating religionization of the IDF, two contradictory social, extra-military processes played a role. First, denationalization had counter effects. The IDF command used religiosity to inspire sacrifice when the IDF leadership acknowledged the need to deal with the decline in military motivation of the secular middle class, which was aggravated by denationalization and liberalization during the 1990s. The outbreak of the Second Intifada in 2000, resulting in renewed hostilities between Israelis and Palestinians, was particularly significant. It not only required new sacrifices but also legitimized the command's attempts to curb the post-Oslo liberal trends and their apparent negative impact on motivation by instilling religious values.

---

[1] Supervisor responsible for implementing the Freedom of Information Law, Israeli Ministry of Education, letter to author, July 7, 2013 (Hebrew).

Therefore, in the wake of the Second Intifada, the Military Rabbinate was empowered and the role of military chaplains grew from their traditional position of providing Jewish religious services to the religious socialization of secular soldiers (Kampinsky 2009, 447–88). The military command unprecedentedly formalized the rabbinate's new task to instill a Jewish consciousness in the soldiers and commanders in order to "reinforce their fighting spirit" (State Comptroller 2011, 1621). As the IDF's Chief Rabbi indicated in 2006, secular Zionism was in crisis, and therefore: "Part of my job as the Chief Military Rabbi, perhaps the central part, is to reconnect the soldiers with the values of Judaism" (cited in Ringel-Hoffman 2006). To this end, the rabbis also increased their presence in the field units, functioning as "priest[s] anointed for war," whose role was to inspire the troops and ensure that they were prepared physically and spiritually for combat (Kampinsky 2010, 167–69). The rabbinate's expanded roles dismantled the monopoly of the relatively liberal Education Corps over educational activity in the IDF (State Comptroller 2011, 1620–23).

Looking for solutions to instill motivation among its conscripts, rabbis offered the military a ready-made toolkit for educating soldiers while from the military's perspective, secular institutions could be viewed as being identified with the post-Oslo liberal trends. Furthermore, commanders acknowledged the association between "good" soldiering and Jewishness, reflected in the statement by the former Israeli chief of staff that, "Soldiers must have deep roots to know what they are fighting for" (Sorek 2006, 2). This insight helps to explain why religious values seemed more attractive than secular, patriotic, or nationalist ones.

Against this background, in 2002, the military took the unprecedented step of drafting a document entitled *Identity and Purpose*, defining its collective identity as the military of the Jewish democratic state. To this end, the Chief of the General Staff recruited Beit Morasha, a center for Judaic studies headed by Rabbi Benjamin Ish-Shalom, to assist the IDF Education Corps in strengthening Jewish identity and enhancing the connection of commanders and soldiers to their land, values, heritage, and people, with the intention of filling a vacuum apparently identified in the secular school system (Sorek 2006).

Consequently, the IDF created the infrastructure to privilege the status of religion within the military and solidify the influence of rabbis, both from the military and those heading the *hesder yeshivot* and the premilitary academies (Lebel 2013). When this general process intersected with the definition of the state as a Jewish and democratic one, codified in the Basic Laws passed in 1992, the status of religion in the military was elevated, evidenced by the empowerment of the Military Rabbinate (Meltzer 2012, 355, 362–63). In other words, the national-religious sector's claim of reshaping military culture could gain legitimacy.

A clear manifestation of the new rabbinate authority appeared during Operation Cast Lead in 2009 against the Hamas-controlled Gaza Strip, when rabbis joined troops in the field and worked to "spiritually elevate" the soldiers by circulating theological propaganda. Rabbis directed the appropriate code of conduct in the field by declaring, "When you show mercy to a cruel enemy, you are being cruel to pure and honest soldiers. This is terribly immoral" (cited in A. Harel 2009). As one of the soldiers testified about rabbis who addressed the troops: "Often … analogies are made, equating the Palestinians with the Amalekites, for example. The Palestinians are the enemy, whether they are Israeli citizens or subjects of the Palestinian Authority makes no difference. This covers everyone" (Breaking the Silence 2009, 41). Amalek was the first tribe that attacked Israel after the exodus from Egypt. For this sin, God commanded that Amalek and his name be absolutely wiped out, without sparing women and children. By equating the Palestinians with the Amalekites, they were dehumanized and the military could enhance the legitimacy of targeting Gaza's civilians. Far from being an exception, this rhetoric represented other rabbis' opinions and the guidance they gave to their students when they were called up to the military (Rotenberg 2010).

After Operation Cast Lead, Israel Harel, an intellectual settler leader, described the struggle between the conflicting values of the relatively secular-liberal Education Corps against the rabbinate as follows:

> The struggle is not between the Education Corps and the Chief Military Rabbinate, but between two spiritual streams: one is represented by those attacking the Chief Rabbi, leading the IDF to ambivalence and undermining its full faith in its cause, resulting in impairment of the IDF's operational capabilities. The counter stream, whose roots were discovered in Operation Cast Lead, is based on full identification with the Zionist and national, not necessarily religious, roots of the State of Israel. (I. Harel 2009)

In other words, Harel clarified the "right" way to educate the soldiers. Within the context of this clash between the Education Corps and the Military Rabbinate, a senior officer released a statement lamenting that, "The army is deciding for you what kind of Jew you will be: a national-religious [Orthodox] Jew" (A. Harel 2011).

In the war that Israel launched in the summer of 2014 against the Hamas-controlled Gaza Strip (Operation Protective Edge) religionization was further elevated. A brigade commander, Colonel Ofer Winter, a graduate of a premilitary academy in the West Bank settlement of Eli, dispatched a "battle order," telling his troops they were going to war "to wipe out an enemy" who "curses, blasphemes and scorns the God of Israel" (cited in Sharon 2014). He thus presented the battle against the Palestinians not only as the extension of a war rooted in the Bible against Amalek, as the rabbis had previously done, and not only as a state defense against an enemy, but also as a religious war aimed at protecting the reputation of God. It was the first time that a senior commander publicly provided religious legitimacy for the use of force. While in the past commanders had invoked the Bible, it was as a historical reference rather than a source of divine guidance. In practice, the colonel appropriated the function of the "priest anointed for war" from the rabbinate's monopoly.

Confirming that the colonel echoed the socialization to which he had been exposed at the premilitary academy, Rabbi Eli Sadan, the Eli academy's head, went even further. Preaching to his students (and future combatants) in the midst of the operation, he described the mission as an attempt to topple the "Gates of Gaza," like the feat of Samson, the biblical hero. This would pave the way for realizing Sadan's ideal, the reestablishment of a Davidic kingdom in Hebron (dating back to about 1000 BC). Much as other rabbis had done, he equated the Palestinians to the ancient Philistines. After founding the kingdom, "you would not find any more Philistines," said the Rabbi (Sadan 2014). Therefore, for Colonel Winter and Rabbi Sadan, the campaign in Gaza was regarded as a part of a religious war that could not conclude before a decisive victory, and victory, as Sadan implied, may require ethnic cleansing.

Only in 2016 did IDF Chief of Staff Gadi Eisenkot recognize that religious authorities had gained too much power within the military and took steps to reduce the power of the Military Rabbinate and resolve conflicts between the rabbinate and the Education Corps (A. Harel 2016). At the time of writing, the effectiveness of this effort has not yet been measured, but it seems that they were instrumental in institutionalizing religionization rather than weakening it (Levy 2018).

As for the second process, as militarization rose again, religious values in the social sphere permeated into the military. The failure to resolve the Israeli-Palestinian conflict and the outbreak of the Second Intifada, which was increasingly viewed by large segments of Israeli society as a struggle between Jews and non-Jews, reinforced Jewish identification in Israeli society, leading to the strengthening of a religious, or at least a non-secular, identity (Yadgar 2012). Jewishness was transmuted into a nationalist territorial cult, legitimizing the settlement project and demarcating firmer boundaries between the Jewish majority and the Palestinian minority. These boundaries had been partially blurred following the Oslo process a decade earlier, partly because the agreement empowered the Palestinian citizens of Israel. Yet in the early 2000s, Jewishness came to surveil the boundaries between Jews and Palestinians, not only within the "Green Line" but also between Jews and Palestinians in the West Bank. US Secretary of State John Kerry warned that the demise of the Oslo Accords, reoccupation of the West Bank, and the entrenchment of the settlement project "offer a glimpse into a reality of one state for two peoples" (cited in Ravid 2015). While the marker for this monitoring of boundaries is religious, argues Ram, the purpose is national (Ram 2008, 71).

To indicate the extent to which politics has been religionized, while only about 10 percent of the total Jewish population in Israel is categorized as "religious" (Orthodox) there is a sizeable Israeli Jewish population, about 22 percent, that identifies itself as belonging to the national-religious camp, though it does not necessarily define itself as just "religious" (Hermann et al. 2014, 9–10). Politically, this process of post-Second Intifada religionization generated massive electoral support (particularly in the 2013 elections) for the national-religious party Ha-Bayit

Ha-Yehudi (The Jewish Home), moving the national-religious camp from the margins to the sociopolitical center stage (Hermann et al. 2014, 4).

The nationalization of politics during the Second Intifada occurred alongside remilitarization, evident in the IDF's aggressive reaction to the Palestinian hostilities. It culminated with Operation Defensive Shield in 2002, a large-scale military operation during which Israel recaptured the main Palestinian cities in the West Bank. Later, following the disengagement, in the years 2008–14, Israel launched four large operations against the Hamas-controlled Gaza Strip. As a result, hundreds of Gazan civilians were killed (see Levy 2017), with religious socialization playing a more prominent role as described above.

Nationalization-cum-militarization has reached new heights since the fall of 2015, when the so-called Third Intifada erupted, mainly in the form of lone-wolf attacks on Israeli civilians and soldiers carried out by young Palestinians from the West Bank. While the IDF generals seemed to restrain their response to these individual attacks, right-wing politicians called for harsher military actions. Rules of engagement and the use of force against suspected attackers became a disputed issue. For example, unprecedented protests were launched by right-wing Israelis against the IDF's decision to jail a soldier (Elor Azarya) serving in Hebron, who in March 2015 fatally shot a Palestinian attacker (Abd al-Fattah Yusri al-Sharif), even though al-Sharif had been disarmed and seriously injured and lay on the ground, immobilized. In October 2015, polls showed that 53 percent of Jewish interviewees agreed with the statement that, "Any Palestinian who has perpetrated a terror attack against Jews should be killed on the spot, even if he has been apprehended and no longer poses a threat" (Peace Index 2015). No wonder divisions emerged between Israel's civilian and military leaders. In July 2016, polls showed that among the "hard" right, about half do not see alignment between values of the IDF's senior command and those of the general public (Peace Index 2016).

In sum, this combination of nationalization, militarization, and religionization of Israeli politics could provide a revived tailwind to intra-military attempts to religionize the troops. At this stage, moreover, religionization and nationalization have been mutually reinforcing within the military domain. Religiosity has bolstered nationalism by wrapping it in religious symbols, portraying warfare between Israel and the Palestinians as a necessary religious war, a "commandment war." In this new formula of religious nationalism, sacrifice has not been demanded for the protection of land, economic resources, or even state security, but for the very identity of the fighting nation and its God-commanded moral beliefs. Hence also, the fighting enhanced the status of those bearing the burden of such a sacrifice. This recent religious inflection has empowered rabbis to claim authority to decide or advise on theological issues that affect the military, such as setting ethical standards for waging the "commandment war." Thereby, as Stuart Cohen (2013, 143–67) notes, religious authorities extended Jewish theological writing on the rules of war to new areas. At the same time, nationalism reinforced religiosity by relocating the latter from the practice of learning and belief (that traditionally typified, and also marginalized, religious groups) to the practice of the fulfillment of religious commandments, by which the Israeli military becomes holy inasmuch as it is committed to fighting a commandment war. In this spirit "the practice of Torah [in the military] is greater than its study," coined one of the premilitary academy academies, citing the Jewish sages to praise the track of the premilitary academies, through which military service comes at the expense of full dedication to Torah study (Levy 2015, 157–58).

CONCLUSION

This chapter analyzed the relations between the nationalization, denationalization, and renationalization of politics and the religionization of the military in Israel. Table 5.1 depicts the four main stages identified in the chapter: partial religionization, ethno-national religionization, denationalization, and the religionization of nationalism.

During the formative period of the Israeli state and the military, the partial religionization of the military reflected similar processes in the wider society of which the military was a part. In the second stage, after the 1967 War, the ethno-national religionization of politics prompted the bearers of this process, the national-religious sector, to develop an extra-military social mobility track in the form of the settlement enterprise to compensate for its inferior status within the military. In this stage, the military partly insulated itself from the emerging cultural trends in society. In the third stage, the denationalization of Israeli politics during the 1980s and 1990s (with the Oslo process at the center) created new opportunities for the national-religious sector, for which military service became a site of social mobility. Again, the military only partly reflected the trends in the general society, because the increasing presence of religious soldiers signified the deep currents hidden beneath

TABLE 5.1 *Four stages of nationalization and religionization of Israel's politics and military*

Time period	Nationalization of politics	Religionization of the military
1948–1967	Partial religionization	Partial religionization
1970s–mid-1980s	Ethno-national religionization	Limited impact Gush Emunim as an extra-military avenue for upward mobility
Mid-1980s–late 1990s	Denationalization	Liberalization of the military and society paradoxically opened up new opportunities for national-religious conscripts
2000s	Religionization of nationalism	Religionization of the military

the surface of the denationalization of politics. However, these currents surfaced in the beginning of the 2000s. Then, the fruits of the national-religious sector's strategic moves were realized when the religionization of the military developed in tandem with the religionization of nationalism. In this stage, the military reflected general trends taking place in the surrounding society. With the renewal of hostilities and the renationalization that it inspired, the national-religious groups held resources necessary for the military, namely, religious socialization, by which they legitimated their claim to reshape the military's culture.

Theoretically, examining these interactions between religion, nationalism, and the military in Israel has enriched our understanding about the extent to which militaries culturally mirror their ambient societies and the variations in this reflection. Although over time militaries cannot be deeply religionized unless they reflect larger social processes, there are variations in the level of this diffusion of values from society into the military, as the case of Israel shows. A comparative effort may set the agenda for future research.

REFERENCES

B [Anonymous IDF senior officer]. 2010. "The Place of Religious in the Tactical Command of the IDF." [In Hebrew.] *Ma'arachot* 432: 50–57.

Barak-Erez, Daphne. 2008. "Law and Religion under the Status Quo Model: Between Past Compromises and Constant Change." *Cardozo Law Review* 30, no. 6: 2495–507.

Ben-Porat, Guy. 2013. *Between State and Synagogue: The Secularization of Contemporary Israel*. New York: Cambridge University Press.

Benari, Elad. 2011. "Rabin had Virtues But Was a Poor Leader." *Arutz Sheva*, November 16, 2011. www.israelnationalnews.com/News/News.aspx/149789.

Ben-Yehuda, Nachman. 2010. *Theocratic Democracy: The Social Construction of Religious and Secular Extremism*. New York: Oxford University Press.

Breaking the Silence. 2009. *Soldiers' Testimonies from Operation Cast Lead, Gaza 2009*. Jerusalem: Breaking the Silence.

Cohen, Boaz. 2012. "Army Uniform as a Religious Commandment: The Zionist-Religious Public and the Army." [In Hebrew.] *Iyunim Bitkumat Israel* 22: 325–58.

Cohen, Itamar. 2005. *See Faith: Land of Israel to the People of Israel* [in Hebrew]. www.mnokdim.org/shiurim.asp?page=2.

Cohen, Stuart A. 1999. "From Integration to Segregation: The Role of Religion in the IDF." *Armed Forces and Society* 25, no. 3: 387–405.

  2004. "Dilemmas of Military Service in Israel: The Religious Dimension." *The Torah u-Madda Journal* 12: 1–23.

  2007. "Tensions between Military Service and Jewish Orthodoxy in Israel: Implications Imagined and Real." *Israel Studies* 12, no. 1: 103–26.

  2013. *Divine Service? Judaism and Israel's Armed Forces*. Farnham, UK: Ashgate.

Cohen, Stuart A., Aaron Kampinsky, and Elisheva Rosman-Stollman. 2016. "Swimming against the Tide: The Changing Functions and Status of Chaplains in the Israel Defense Forces." *Religion, State and Society* 44, no. 1: 1–10.

Drory, Ze'ev. 2015. "The 'Religionizing' of the Israel Defence Force: Its Impact on Military Culture and Professionalism." *Res Militaris: European Journal of Military Studies* 5, no. 1: 1–21.

Feige, Michael. 2009. *Settling in the Hearts: Jewish Fundamentalism in the Occupied Territories*. Detroit: Wayne State University Press.

Gal, Reuven, and Tamir Libel, eds. 2012. *Between the Yarmulke and the Beret: Religion, Politics and the Military in Israel* [in Hebrew]. Tel Aviv: Modan Publishing House.

Gluska, Ami. 2011. "What Turned Ben-Gurion from Hawk into a Dove?" *Haaretz*, June 3. www.haaretz.com/1.5019113.

Gorenberg, Gershom. 2009. "Settling for Radicalism." *The American Prospect*, May 20. https://prospect.org/features/settling-radicalism/.

Harel, Amos. 2009. "IDF Rabbinate Publication during Gaza War: We Will Show No Mercy on the Cruel." *Haaretz*, January 26. www.haaretz.com/1.5067403.

2011. "Is the IDF Becoming an Orthodox Army?" *Haaretz*, July 22. www.haaretz.com/1.5032934.

2016. "Just One More Battle in War between IDF and Rebel Rabbis." *Haaretz*, July 24. www.haaretz.com/israel-news/.premium-just-one-more-battle-in-bitter-war-between-idf-and-rebel-rabbis-1.5414506.

Harel, Israel. 2009. "The Struggle between the Chief Education Officer and the Chief Military Rabbi." [In Hebrew.] *Haaretz*, January 19. https://news.walla.co.il/item/1426101.

Hassner, Ron E. 2014. "Introduction: Religion in the Military Worldwide – Challenges and Opportunities." In *Religion in the Military Worldwide*, edited by Ron E. Hassner, 1–19. New York: Cambridge University Press.

Hermann, Tamar, Gilad Be'ery, Ella Heller et al. 2014. *The National-Religious Sector in Israel 2014*. Jerusalem: The Israel Democracy Institute.

Horowitz, N. 2009. "Halacha, Society and Politics: Service of Male Religious Soldiers in the IDF." [In Hebrew.] Paper presented at the Symposium-Religion and Gender in the Military. Raanana, Israel. November 11.

Kampinsky, Aaron. 2009. "Support and Reservations: Ben-Gurion's Attitude towards the Institutionalization of Religion in the IDF." [In Hebrew.] *Iyunim Bitkumat Israel* 19: 447–48.

2010. "The Military Rabbinate and Its Dual Loyalty." [In Hebrew.] In *The Beret and the Kippa*, edited by Moshe Rachimi, 309–35. Elkana: Orot College Press.

Kimmerling, Baruch. 1985. "The Reopening of the Frontiers, 1967–1982." In vol. 3 of *Politics and Society in Israel*, edited by Ernest Krausz, 81–116. Studies in Israeli Society. New Brunswick, NJ: Transaction Books.

1993. "Patterns of Militarism in Israel." *European Journal of Sociology* 34, no. 2: 196–223.

Krebs, Ronald R. 2005. "One Nation under Arms? Military Participation Policy and the Politics of Identity." *Security Studies* 14, no. 3: 529–64.

2006. *Fighting for Rights: Military Service and the Politics of Citizenship*. Ithaca, NY: Cornell University Press.

Lebel, Udi. 2013. "Postmodern or Conservative? Competing Security Communities over Military Doctrine: Israeli National-Religious Soldiers as Counter [Strategic] Culture Agents." *Political and Military Sociology: An Annual Review* 40: 23–57.

2016. "The 'Immunized Integration' of Religious-Zionists within Israeli Society: The Pre-military Academy as an Institutional Model." *Social Identities* 22, no. 6: 642–60.

Leon, Nissim. 2010. "The Transformation of Israel's Religious-Zionist Middle Class." *The Journal of Israeli History* 29, no. 1: 61–78.

Levy, Yagil. 2007. *Israel's Materialist Militarism*. Madison, WI: Rowman and Littlefield/Lexington Books.

2008. "Israel's Violated Republican Equation." *Citizenship Studies* 12, no. 3: 249–64.

2015. *The Divine Commander: The Theocratization of the Israeli Military* [in Hebrew]. Tel Aviv: Am Oved and Sapir Academic College.

2016. "Religious Authorities in the Military and Civilian Control: The Case of the Israeli Defense Forces." *Politics and Society* 44, no. 2: 305–32.

2017. "The Gaza Fighting: Did Israel Shift Risk from Its Soldiers to Civilians?" *Middle East Policy* 24, no. 3: 117–32.

2018. "This Is How Eisenkot Institutionalized the Religionization in the IDF." [In Hebrew.] *Haaretz*, January 17. www.haaretz.co.il/magazine/the-edge/.premium-1.5743689.

Levy, Yagil, and Yoav Peled. 1994. "The Utopian Crisis of the Israeli State." In vol. 3 of *Critical Essays on Israeli Social Issues and Scholarship*, edited by Russell A. Stone and Walter P. Zenner, 201–26. Books on Israel. Albany: SUNY Press.

Libel, Tamir, and Reuven Gal. 2015. "Between Military–Society and Religion–Military Relations: Different Aspects of the Growing Religiosity in the Israeli Defense Forces." *Defense & Security Analysis* 31, no. 3: 213–17.

Loveland, Anne C. 2014. *Change and Conflict in the U.S. Army Chaplain Corps since 1945*. Knoxville: University of Tennessee Press.

Lustick, Ian S. 1993. *Unsettled States, Disputed Lands: Britain and Ireland, France and Algeria, Israel and the West Bank-Gaza*. Ithaca, NY: Cornell University Press.

Meltzer, Hanan. 2012. "The IDF as the Military of the Jewish and Democratic State." [In Hebrew.] *Law and Business Journal* 14: 347–94.

Newman, David. 2005. "From Hitnachalut to Hitnatkut: The Impact of Gush Emunim and the Settlement Movement on Israeli Politics and Society." *Israel Studies* 10, no. 3: 192–224.

Ohana, David. 2012. "The Politics of Political Despair: The Case of Political Theology in Israel." In *By the People, For the People, Without the People? The Emergence of (Anti) Political Sentiment in Western Democracies and in Israel*, edited by Tamar S. Hermann, 356–78. Jerusalem: The Israel Democracy Institute.

Patterson, Eric. 2014. "Conclusion: Promising Themes, Future Approaches." In *Religion in the Military Worldwide*, edited by Ron E. Hassner, 227–40. New York: Cambridge University Press.

Peace Index. 2015. "The Peace Index: October 2015." www.peaceindex.org/indexMonthEng .aspx?num=298&monthname=October.

2016. "The Peace Index: July 2016." www.peaceindex.org/indexMonthEng.aspx? num=307&monthname=July.

Ram, Uri. 2008. "Why Secularism Fails? Secular Nationalism and Religious Revivalism in Israel." *International Journal of Politics, Culture, and Society* 21, no. 1: 57–73.

Ravid, Barak. 2015. "Kerry Warns: Escalation in Israeli-Palestinian Violence Illustrates One-State Reality." *Haaretz*, October 28. www.haaretz.com/israel-news/kerry-israeli-palestine -escalation-illustrates-one-state-reality-1.5414652.

Ringel-Hoffman, Ariela. 2006. "IDF Chief Rabbi: Not Sure Secular Zionism Exists." *Ynetnews*, October 17. www.ynetnews.com/articles/0,7340,L-3316079,00.html.

Røislien, Hanne Eggen. 2013. "Religion and Military Conscription: The Case of the Israel Defense Forces (IDF)." *Armed Forces and Society* 39, no. 2: 213–32.

Rosman-Stollman, Elisheva. 2014. *For God and Country? Religious Student-Soldiers in the Israel Defense Forces*. Austin: University of Texas Press.

Rotenberg, Hagit. 2010. "Caution, Lawyers behind You." [In Hebrew.] *Arutz Sheva*, October 28.

Sadan, Eli. 2008. *Call to Religious Zionism* [in Hebrew]. Eli: Bnei David.

2014. "Protective Edge: Carrying the Gates of Gaza to the Sleepers in Hebron – The Action of Unity and the Kingdom of Israel." [In Hebrew.] July 27. Video, 45:55. https://bit.ly/3jQA5cP.

Shafir, Gershon, and Yoav Peled. 2002. *Being Israeli: The Dynamics of Multiple Citizenship*. Cambridge: Cambridge University Press.

Shapiro, Yonathan. 1998. "The Secular Politicians and the Status of Religion in the State of Israel." [In Hebrew.] In *Multiculturalism in a Democratic and Jewish State*, edited by M. Mautner, A. Sagi, and R. Shamir, 663–74. Tel Aviv: Ramot.

Sharon, Jeremy. 2014. "Religious Overtones in Letter from IDF Commanders to His Soldiers Draws Criticism, Support." *The Jerusalem Post*, July 14. www.jpost.com/Jewish-World /Jewish-News/Religious-overtones-in-letter-from-IDF-commander-to-his-soldiers-draws -criticism-support-362673.

Sheleg, Yair. 2004. *The Political and Social Ramifications of Evacuating Settlements in Judea, Samaria and the Gaza Strip* [in Hebrew]. Jerusalem: The Israel Democracy Institute.

Sorek, Yoav. 2006. "Building Jewish Identity." [In Hebrew.] *Makor Rishon Dyokan Magazine*, October 13.

State Comptroller. 2011. *Report No. 62* [in Hebrew]. Jerusalem: The State Comptroller of Israel.

Warhaftig, Zerach. 1988. *A Constitution for Israel: Religion and State* [in Hebrew]. Jerusalem: Mesilot.

Yadgar, Yaacov. 2012. "The Need for an Epistemological Turn." *Israel Studies Review* 27, no. 1: 27–30.

Yeshiva Ateret Yerushalayim. n.d. "The Mechina's Mission." www.ateret.org.il/english/ mechina/goals.asp.

Zanany, Omer. 2015. *The Annapolis Process: Negotiations and Its Discontents*. Tel Aviv: The Tami Steinmetz Center for Peace Research and Molad.

6

Sacralized Politics

The Case of Occupied East Jerusalem

Nadera Shalhoub-Kevorkian

INTRODUCTION

Eid al-Adha 2019, one of the holiest holidays of the year for Muslims, was received by Palestinian Muslim worshippers in Jerusalem, with the raid of their mosque, al-Aqsa, by more than 1,700 police-backed religious Israeli settlers (Barghoti 2019). Later, heavily armed military personnel invaded the mosque and began attacking the tens of thousands of worshippers, families, and children who had come to al-Aqsa to worship on their holy day. The army assaulted them using physical violence, gas canisters, and rubber bullets. Sixty-one Palestinians were injured. For the settlers, this day was *Tisha Ba'av*, a Jewish holiday, but their violent festivities were not the mark of traditional rites related to that holiday. A few days following this incident, two Palestinian boys, one from East and one from South Jerusalem, were shot near the al-Aqsa Mosque after an alleged stabbing of an Israeli soldier. One of them, fourteen-year-old Nassim Abu Roumi, subsequently died; Hammouda Khader Sheikh, aged sixteen, was severely injured and is now in prison (IMEMC 2019).

The invasion of spaces of worship, the desecrating settlers' violence, the killing of Nassim Abu Roumi, and the wounding of Hammouda Khader Sheikh[1] are all typical of events that routinely recur in today's Jerusalem. The combination of the invasion of sacred places on religious holidays and daily police/military violence prompts me to examine the Jewish settlers' acts of violence in light of sacralized politics – that is, an ideological religio-nationalist worldview that instigates the settlers' regime of governance informing, shaping, and stirring legal, cultural, economic, spatial, and securitized interventions to control Palestinians in Jerusalem.

Governance, as Foucault (1977, [1980] 2008) has explained, is located in a variety of different sites and practices, and in governmental and nongovernmental authorities. Governance at a distance, as Foucault's genealogical approach reveals, allows us to critically and historically examine governmental power, expanding the net of

---

[1] See the full video of this event: www.youtube.com/watch?time_continue=12&v=nqouctNyw6Y; see also ACRI (2012).

social control, and set out a new problematic for the analysis of "power beyond the state" (Garland 1997, 182). Furthermore, "the social" is an additional realm of government that includes hospitals, schools, churches, experts, professions, dissolving the rigid line of demarcation between the "public" and the "private" (Garland 1997). In the social realm, "governing does not rely upon sovereign force, nor even upon discipline. Instead it rests upon a multiplicity of expert authorities and upon the willingness of individuals – whether as family members, or workers, or citizens – to exercise a 'responsibilitized' autonomy and to pursue their interests and desires in ways that are socially approved and legally sanctioned" (Garland 1997, 180). Borrowing from Foucauldian theorization, I look closely at sacralized governance in the settler colony as an economy of power that is not confined solely to the state authority, but rather extends to its institutionalized and noninstitutionalized apparatus including its cultural, social, religious, and legal structures, military operations, public administrations, and politically motivated and organized individuals; all set on the production and reproduction of settler-colonial state formations.

By focusing on the context of the 2014–19 intensification of violence in Jerusalem following the burning alive of sixteen-year-old Mohammad Abu Khdeir (Ihmoud 2015) and examining the nationalist-religious violence perpetrated against Palestinians, this chapter will analyze the settler state and its modalities of violence operating in the interlocking dynamics between Israel's settler-colonial governance and the Zionist religious and nationalist ideologies. The close examination of the operationalization of Israel's modalities of violence and the ways it forms and informs the state's policy can help us understand Israel's sacralization of politics in the context of Israeli-occupied East Jerusalem (oEJ). These modalities of violence demarcate the difference between the colonizer and the colonized. They also manifest themselves in a religio-nationalist discourse and practices that position the act of violating the native's rights, desecrating and excluding the native "Other" – his/her body and communal spaces – as part of religious ethics. Sacralized politics, as I will demonstrate, draw the lines of what is sacred and profane in correspondence with the settler-colonial social formations that divide people based on a racialized discourse that determines who must be "destroyed" in order to be "replaced" (Wolfe 2006).

To further our understanding of the sacralized politics underlying the Israeli state's modalities of governance, it is important to reveal the operationalization of violence in light of the global regimes of tolerance that not only contribute to, but also enhance, the eviction of the native and the indigenization of the settler. These global forces are epitomized by the Trump administration's unquestioning backing of Israel and his reiteration of the Israeli religious claims over Jerusalem in his presidential announcement proclaiming Jerusalem – including Nassim and Hamouda's place of worship – as "the capital of the Jewish people established in ancient times" (Trump 2018). In my understanding, the various modalities of racialized violence that circulate globally and locally in the colonial order mark the difference between the colonizer and the colonized and make it possible to produce sacralized governing rationalities against Palestinians as disposable Others.

The chapter attempts to share the political significance of such fusion, examining inscriptions of power over three colonized sites and moments within the colonized space of oEJ: (1) law and legal practices pertaining to residency, citizenship, and property rights; (2) a specific type of vigilante attack, violence, or vandalism known in Israel as "Price Tag" (*Tag Mehir* in Hebrew)[2] that is perpetrated by organized religious Jewish settlers mostly attacking Palestinians; and (3) the "occupation of the senses," which refers to the state-sponsored incursion into the sensory experience of the native community in their places of residence (Shalhoub-Kevorkian 2017). The chapter analyzes the authorization of state and non-state violence as a form of *sacralized politics* that produces the displacement, dispossession, and desecration of the native community and its spaces while advancing and consecrating the Judaization of the land. The chapter demonstrates how these sacralized politics are essential in the violent governance of the Palestinian body and space and thereby to the maintenance and reproduction of Zionist and settler-colonial politics.

THE DUAL STRUCTURE OF SETTLER COLONIALISM

The spaces and bodies of colonized peoples are a central focus in settler-colonial governance and its dual structure of destroy to replace. While Patrick Wolfe (2006, 388) argues that "[t]erritoriality is settler colonialism's specific, irreducible element," the colonization of space is frequently manifested through colonial power becoming marked on the bodies of colonized subjects that inhabit the space (Shalhoub-Kevorkian 2019). Colonial justificatory frameworks of racialized hierarchies between fully human colonists and subhuman indigenous populations often find their imaginary basis in the human flesh – that is, in differentiating and rendering colonized subjects through a racialized discourse (Weheliye 2014). In our case, Israeli settler-colonial political legitimation is generated through rendering the spaces and bodies of the colonized as disposable (Perera and Razack 2014) and using religio-nationalist rationalizations to turn the colonized civilian population, its infrastructure, and the spaces it inhabits into threatening targets to be feared, in life and in death (Graham 2004a; Shalhoub-Kevorkian 2015). The governance of the native through casting out civilians, their neighborhoods, and their cities and placing them "beyond the privileges and protections of law so that their lives (and death) [are] rendered of no account" (Gregory 2003, 311) requires the production of particular modalities of violence wrought upon the Palestinian human body and communal space. How do such modalities of

---

[2] These practices are distinguished by the scrawling of the words *Tag Mehir* in Hebrew at the site of each attack.

violence, embedded in the settler's logic of destroy to replace, come about once the religious claims resting at the heart of the nationalist ambitions of the settler colony operate?

Take, for example, the centrality of Israel's plan to cast Palestinians out of Jerusalem via demographic biopolitics and spatial policies (i.e., statistical knowledge and its demographic projections, building walls, cutting Palestinian neighborhoods, demolishing homes, and confiscating land), and "unify" the city using religious and nationalist justificatory claims (Abu Baker 2000; Samman 2017). Demographic and spatial politics are embedded in biblico-nationalist claims that insist on the need to Judaize Jerusalem and its religious shrines, including the Old City's holy places, while reducing the number of Palestinian residents and cutting them from their community members who happen to reside outside state-asserted demarcation lines (Shargai 2010). In his book, *City of Stone*, Meron Benvenisti, the former deputy mayor of Jerusalem, situates the need for Judaization and the violent conflict in Jerusalem, mainly over the holy places, within an extremist shift in Jewish religious thinking advanced by Rabbi Yisrael Ariel (Benvenisti 1996). Ariel is the founder and head of the Temple Institute, which is an Israeli nonprofit educational and religious organization in the Jewish quarter of Jerusalem's Old City "dedicated to every aspect of the 'Biblical Commandment' to build the Holy Temple of G-d on Mount Moriah in Jerusalem" (Temple Institute n.d.). Ariel's ideological trajectory affirms that the Third Temple might indeed be rebuilt with human hands as opposed to waiting for the Messiah to rebuild it (Benvenisti 1996, 70).

In general, the settler-colonial state's ideology, in tandem with its political mechanisms of destroying native spaces (Wolfe 2006), produces a particular spatial imaginary that marks Palestinians and their spaces (e.g., cities, religious shrines, neighborhoods) as inferior and dangerous. Abujidi and Verschure (2006) suggest that state military operations against Palestinian cities such as Nablus are clear examples of what they call "urbicide." As they write, urbicide is a "process and coordination of different elements and stages of control, planning and implementation of design by destruction or construction" (Abujidi and Verschure 2006, 218). Scholars (e.g., Abujidi and Verschure 2006; Graham 2003, 2004a, 2004b; Weizman 2004) have explained how the Israeli military occupation of the Palestinian city has functioned to demonize and dehumanize Palestinian inhabitants and render their spaces as dangerous. This demonization/dehumanization is associated with the Zionist imaginary in which the Palestinians and the city/land they inhabit are construed as primitive, dangerous, irrational, and rabid entities that should be cleansed through embodied acts of orchestrated destruction (Graham 2004a).

Defining Palestinian urban spaces such as Nablus, Jenin, Hebron, Gaza, and Jerusalem and their inhabitants as "an urban cancer," "dangerous places," and "terrorist nests" (Abujidi and Verschure 2006) frames Palestinians and their living spaces as hostile targets that can be destroyed without compunction (Graham 2003,

2004a, 2004b; Weizman 2003, 2004). In the case of Palestine and oEJ in particular, as the work of Samman (2017) and Saifi and Samman (2019) demonstrates, religious, cultural, and national meanings and their spatial dynamics manifest themselves in extreme acts of violence through systems designed to exert spatial control over the colonized. In discussing lived space under Israeli colonial rule, when talking about oEJ, Samman showed how Israeli governance of the space furthers the buildings of new Jewish settlements to Judaize the space and minimize the number of Palestinians in Jerusalem. Samman reveals how the state uses its laws to "legally" settle Jewish Israeli settlers, demolish Palestinian houses, and prevent Palestinian urban expansion. She explains:

> Housing permits for Arab Palestinians are rarely issued. They need a very expensive and long procedure, with limited areas permitted for building. Building permits for Israelis reach 1,500 per year, while for Palestinians an average of 100 building permits are issued annually. This number, however, is decreasing by the year. Houses are demolished if built without building permits. Jerusalemites are left in small crowded housing units, with a shortage of more than 25,000 housing units. (Samman 2017, 145)

The spatial eviction of the colonized from Jerusalem, I argue, has little to do with law and legality and more to do with the settler state's governance embedded in deeply ideological processes through which Israel understands itself as being an exclusively Jewish state. Understanding the complex way of governance, in which systems of oppression (Jewish supremacy based on biblico-national entitlement to Jerusalem) operate on the psychic as well as the daily lives of the native, can help reveal the multi-scaled effect of Israel's sacralized policies and their "legalities."

SACRALIZED LEGALITIES: CASTING OUT THE NATIVE

Amir, a Palestinian man from oEJ, was finishing his engineering degree abroad as he learned about the sudden death of his mother, aged forty-two, who suffered from an aggressive form of cancer. Amir insisted on leaving his studies, postponing his exams, and returning home to mourn with his family. As he arrived at the Israeli airport, Amir was told that he would not be allowed to enter the country or proceed to his hometown, and that his Jerusalem residency had been revoked. In an interview, he told me:

> Think about me, a young man in pain, who had just lost his mother ... standing in front of various officers, needing to deal with their [Israeli] racist laws and policies .... They want us [Palestinians] out of Jerusalem, and [meanwhile they] are bringing all those "birthright" people, young Jewish men and women from around the world. They were with me in the airport singing and chanting and I was in pain. Well, they crossed [into Israel], and I was banned from even paying the last farewell to my mother. (Interview with the author, October 2017)

Another story is that of Marwa, whose family home, which was constructed on land legally owned by her father, was demolished due to lack of a building permit. She explained,

> We applied to get building permits, but, as they always do with Palestinians, they kept on postponing, for over seventeen years, promising us that we will get approved, and now, look around you, they demolished the house. All you can see now is rubble ... (silence). They turned our lives into rubble .... *Radem* [rubble] ... *Kulha radem* [it is all rubble]. (Marwa, Jerusalem)

In Jerusalem, as Amir and Marwa explained, Palestinians' belonging to their own hometowns and homes are constantly targeted. While state legality sanctions the contentious and inflammatory further settlement of Jewish residents deeper into Arab East Jerusalem notwithstanding international law, the same legal framework sanctions Amir and Marwa's uprooting. In examining the violent governance of the state, this section will examine how Zionist religious-nationalist claims entrenched racialized hierarchies of rights into the politico-legal structure of Israel, consecrating the settlers and settlement, while occupying the native's senses, desecrating their spaces, and furthering the dispossession and elimination of the local population.

First, what role do nationalistic religious claims play in the structuring of the backbone of the Israeli legal system? I argue that the discussed legalized modes of exclusion and dispossession reflect the infrastructural settler-colonial modus operandi. Citizenship and residency laws, as well as housing, zoning, and planning laws govern the relationship between the native and the settler such as to produce the Palestinian as perpetually unwanted (Samman 2017; Shalhoub-Kevorkian 2015). The illegality and indeed violent governmentality of such practices as home demolitions, as Marwa intimated to me, are irrelevant, since Israel's state criminality is backed by what appears to be unconditional US support. "They steal together," she said, "as Trump further stole Jerusalem and gave it to them." Looking closely at Israeli laws and regulations that govern residency status, housing, zoning, and planning in oEJ reveal the violence of laws against the native as violence operating to produce and reproduce the imagined superiority of the "sacred." For example, after the establishment of the State of Israel in 1948, an anxiety took hold that the masses of Palestinians expelled and absented from their land would return and assert their citizenship rights as held under international law (Jefferis 2012). Therefore, the first Knesset enacted the Absentee Property Law of 1950, which defined "persons who were expelled, fled, or who left the country after 29 November 1947, mainly due to the war, as well as their movable and immovable property (mainly land, houses and bank accounts etc.), as 'absentee'" (Adalah n.d.). This definition, in other words, ratified the legal definition of Palestinians outside the country, as "absentees" who have no right of ownership over their homes and their homeland, no citizenship or status, and hence, no right to return. Palestinians who remained in their homeland,

and following the enactment of the Israeli Citizenship Law, acquired the Israeli citizenship by residence (for more details, see Jefferis 2012). These laws insured that the demographic engineering and citizenry infrastructure of Israel was set so that it includes and excludes populations based on the ethnicity of the residents, affirming the ethno-nationalist impetus of the settler-colonial nation-state (Tawil-Souri 2011; Zureik, Lyon, and Abu-Laban 2010).

When looking closely at Israeli laws and the ways in which they were applied in oEJ, as explained in my other works, one can detect how the settler state responds to its deep demographic anxiety (Y. Jabareen 2017; Samman 2017; Shalhoub-Kevorkian 2012, 2015). In 1967, following the occupation of East Jerusalem, the Israeli Knesset unilaterally annexed the neighborhoods of East Jerusalem, an act that was immediately condemned by the UN and is considered illegal under international law (Jefferis 2012). Israel then confiscated over 70,000 dunams (1 dunam = 1,000 sq. meters) of land to the municipal boundaries of Jerusalem and applied Israeli law, in breach of international law (Y. Jabareen 2017, 9). The new municipal boundaries were primarily motivated by Israel's "demographic concerns," mainly to ensure a Jewish majority in Jerusalem (Benvenisti 1996; Y. Jabareen 2017). The expansion of Jerusalem's municipal boundaries created major demographic and "security" concerns mainly due to the spatial closeness of various Palestinian neighborhoods to Palestinian cities and communities in the West Bank. These concerns were related to the potential for a strong urban continuity to emerge, a demographic increase of the Palestinian population in the newly occupied areas that the Israelis defined as the "annexed" area of East Jerusalem – prospects that were and continue to be perceived as threatening the legitimacy of Israeli settler supremacy and political claims over the land. The various demographic managements and Judaization of spaces in oEJ are clear technologies of racial violence against the Palestinians. Jabareen asserts:

> Israel's territorial tools were geared toward building a Jewish nation-state with "United Jerusalem" as its "eternal capital." In accordance with this principle, in June 1967, immediately following the occupation of East Jerusalem, David Ben-Gurion, Israel's first prime minister (who was out of office by this time but was still an influential political figure), advised a number of Israeli cabinet ministers that "Jews must be brought to East Jerusalem at all costs." (Y. Jabareen 2017, 10)

Since the occupation of East Jerusalem, the Israeli government, the municipality of Jerusalem, and the local and national planning institutions have employed a policy of "demographic dispersion" of Jews in the occupied Palestinian Territories (oPT), which has been based on the demographic ideology that "Jerusalem in general and East Jerusalem (which until 1967 was completely inhabited by Palestinians) in particular should be populated by a distinctly Jewish majority" (Y. Jabareen 2017, 6, 10).

Israel, furthermore, held a census in 1967 in the occupied Jerusalem area, and Palestinians who happened to be outside the municipal area at that precise time lost their right to return. Those who were present were given the status of "permanent residents."[3] Under Israeli law this status can be revoked on various grounds, as happened to Amir. The legal creation of tracks of citizenship (Braverman 2007; Y. T. Jabareen 2007) is essentially based on a system of classification that gives every Jew in the world a sacred, religiously based "birthright" to acquire Israeli citizenship, while erasing the rights of those who were born in the homeland. As Adalah (2012) commented in its press release at the time, "The Supreme Court approved a law the likes of which do not exist in any democratic state in the world, depriving citizens from maintaining a family life in Israel only on the basis of the ethnicity or national belonging of their spouse."

Israel's "techniques of illegality" (Braverman 2007) and its "bureaucracies of occupation" (Barda 2012), in addition to various technologies used by the Jewish state to evict the native (Khamaisi and Nasrallah 2003), intensify – by law – state forces governing the native. These practices aim at increasing the number of Jewish settlements and decreasing – through outcasting – Palestinian presence in their land through state-run operations, including the demolitions of their homes in Jerusalem. One clear example is apparent in Braverman's observation when referring to a proposed plan by the Jerusalem municipality for the demolition of eighty-eight "illegal" houses in Silwan for the purpose of creating a National Garden in what it calls the King's Valley. In an emergency meeting held on June 19, 2005, the then-head of the Israeli Knesset Committee for Internal Affairs and Environment stated:

> This is sheer madness. Does someone really think that they could recreate an imaginary vision from thousands of years back? ... they say it used to be a garden, and that King [David] walked in this garden ... Do they think they are playing chess?! ... They are playing with real people, destroying real families! (Quoted in Braverman 2007, 367–68)

Building on Marwa and Amir's voices and learning from Ilham Siyam's[4] case, we learn how the natives are regarded as being outside the boundaries of the law. Because of their status and their ethnicity, their eviction is deemed legitimate. Likewise, Amir is prevented from participating in his mother's funeral and forced to lose his "permanent" residency. Jews from around the world, meanwhile, in the name of supposed "birthrights," are welcomed to enter the country with ease and speedily receive Israeli citizenship.

---

[3] "Palestinians in Jerusalem are not citizens, but rather permanent residents; in 2014, the residency status of 107 Palestinian residents of Jerusalem was revoked" (ACRI 2015).

[4] Ilham Siyam lost her legal battle after twenty-five years in the Israeli courts. The Jerusalem District Court ruled on June 12, 2019, in favor of Elad settler organization's claim to ownership of the majority of Siyam's family home (Hasson 2019).

The religio-nationalist imaginations that govern the Zionist state, its racialized ethnocratic nature apparent and applied by its laws (ACRI 2012; Bollens 2000; Braverman 2007; Halper 2015; Y. Jabareen 2017; H. Jabareen and Zaher 2012; Jefferis 2012), suggest that religion and religious affiliations are not only the base of all governing laws but are the powers enabling the Israeli legal system to maintain a preferential discriminatory system.

GLOBALIZED SACRALIZATION

These ethno-religious exclusivist claims embodied in the laws of Israel also constitute a violation of Israel's obligations under international law. They deviate from Israel's duties as a state signatory to the International Covenant on Civil and Political Rights (ICCPR) and the Convention on the Elimination of All Forms of Racial Discrimination (CERD) (Nikfar 2005). The governing laws violate the ICCPR's Article 17 (protection against arbitrary or unlawful interference with one's privacy, family, home, or correspondence) and Article 23 (protection of an individual's right to marry and raise a family), as well as the CERD's Article 26 (protection against discrimination and guarantee of equal protection under domestic law) (Nikfar 2005). In order to understand Israel's blatant disregard of international law, we must scrutinize the geopolitical configuration of power that sanctions Israel's behaviors. Here I refer to the unconditional endorsement of the State of Israel by the dominant superpower in international politics, the US government; particularly here, embodied by the Trump administration.

The remarks of the US ambassador to Israel, David Friedman (who is known for his staunch backing of the Jewish settler state and its illegal settlement project in the West Bank and Jerusalem), regarding Israel's historic right to Jerusalem illustrate how the sacralization of politics (consecrating Jewish settlement and the uprooting of Palestinians) operates on a global scale. Friedman's remarks concerning the "altar" and "holy" connection to Israel and his message that Israel "is on the side of God" powerfully portray US reproduction of religious discourse so as to further the settler-colonial project. As he explained Trump's move of the US embassy to Jerusalem, Friedman stated:

> The move of the embassy was a validation by the strongest nation in the world, not just strong militarily, strong economically, but strong morally, strong ethically, with a bedrock of Judeo-Christian values that govern every citizen's attachment to this country. That country recognized the unbreakable, historical truthful connection between the Jewish people and the city of Jerusalem. (TV7 Israel News 2019)

Not only does Friedman demonstrate his belief in "historic" claims of Jewish connection to the land and thereby the dispossession of the Palestinians; he enshrines his discourse in a "Judeo-Christian" ethos, tying Zionist religious claims with Western Christianity. The Zionist political agenda is validated by a global order, which, in the eyes of Friedman, is defined by a Judeo-Christian character that bounds it to see Israel's behavior as divinely sanctioned. A year later, in 2019, Friedman reiterated the historical religious significance of the US embassy move to those in attendance at the annual AIPAC conference:

> The move of the embassy was the culmination of a 2,000-year-old quest of the Jewish people to return to Zion, a synonym for Jerusalem. It was a recognition by the most powerful nation on earth of the validity, the authenticity, and the morality of this ancient journey coming to fruition in our times. (Friedman 2019)

For Friedman, it seems, the moral role of the US in international politics is to validate the religious-political underpinnings of the exclusivist Zionist claims to Jerusalem and Palestine.

Indeed, Friedman's predisposition in US politics is not unfamiliar in terms of its employment of messianic beliefs so as to sanction Israeli nationalist claims over the land. Other than having intersecting economic-political interests in the region, American and Israeli politics are both influenced by religious traditions that justify Israel's claims over Palestinian land. Friedman comes from a long line of American, Christian, and Jewish, pro-Zionist neoconservative politicians and lobbyists. Israel is backed by American neoconservatives who see the "Return of the Jews to their national home" and the building of a Jewish sovereign state as imperative to the fulfillment of the Christian biblical prophecy that in their view will bring about the end times, Judgment Day, and salvation (Finney 2016). This Christian Zionism has a long history in the US. Powerful proponents of this right-wing Christian-political stream made sure to entrench the theological and political convictions that they share with Zionism at the center of US foreign policy, which dominates the international order (e.g., pressuring leaders not to "restrain" Israel in times of its use of excessive violence against Palestinians) (Finney 2016). Trump's administration is filled with such ideologues, including his secretary of state. Evangelical citizens who are most inclined to these doctrines comprise a significant portion of Trump's voter base. The American political system is thus influenced by a religious worldview that sees illegal settlement as a positive development in light of a divinely ordained sanctioning and a messianic trajectory; arguably, Trump's main motive to recognize Jerusalem as the capital of Israel was to strengthen his evangelical base (Kirk 2019). This is now added to by his latest announcement on January 28, 2020, of the so-called Deal of the Century, which fully embraces the Jewish biblical narrative (Bar'el 2020). In this way, the US, which has a dominating influence on the global order, participates in the sacralization of Jewish supremacy and sovereignty.

The adoption of a Zionist religious narrative regarding the history of the land in Friedman's concluding remarks is presupposed by the historical uprootedness of the Palestinians and the denial of their historical roots and collective rights:

We're part of a 4,000-year-old continuum, a 4,000-year-old history. Most of those 4,000 years were very difficult years, very unpleasant years, for Jewish people and for non-Jewish people ... Israel has grown, flourished, bloomed in ways that no one could have expected. ... We need to keep moving forward, keep moving up the ramp, and I think if we keep doing that we can bring the relationship between the United States and Israel to greater and greater heights. (Friedman 2019)

The outspoken, unqualified backing of Israel's moves in Jerusalem and provocations of US officials has led to increased anger among Palestinians both in the city and outside it. In fact, it caused rising upheaval in the city and the commencement of the March of Return in the Gaza Strip on March 30, 2018. On the first day, while Friedman's embassy was being officially opened in Jerusalem with prominent US and Israeli politicians, millionaires, and religious leaders in attendance, in Gaza, Palestinians who marched in protest near the walls that enclose the Strip demanding their right of return were indiscriminately shot at by Israeli military snipers, resulting in 60 Palestinians dead and 2,771 injured in one day (Dabashi 2018). This staunch backing of the US position led, as I see it, to a sense of omnipotence for Israel and justified the increase of repression on the state's part, as well as the acceleration of its settlement process, its Judaization of Jerusalem, and its codifying of ever more racist laws. What we realize here is how the sacralization of politics and its global and local governance clearly operates within, and is sustained by, a theologized and securitized regime (Shalhoub-Kevorkian 2015). For beyond being a regime of impunity, this regime reproduces the religious claims of Zionism and reaffirms and solidifies the disposability of the native Palestinians (Makdisi 2020).

GOVERNANCE AT A DISTANCE: "PRICE-TAG" (*TAG-MEHIR*) ATTACKS

In addition to spatial governance, Palestinians in oEJ are subjected to "governance at a distance" that consists of a form of sacralized politics that appears to derive authorization from extra-state sources but is, in fact, tacitly supported and encouraged by the state. I argue that this governance at a distance, facilitated by chains of actors who translate the power of the settler state in other means, where knowledge can be accumulated and governance can be orchestrated (Garland 1997), constitutes state crime (Shalhoub-Kevorkian and David 2016). In this section, I examine specifically non-state political violence embodied by the so-called Price-Tag phenomenon, which exemplifies a sacralized political violence that aims at "purifying" the land of its Palestinians in the name of preserving its Jewishness – an openly racist motto (Shalhoub-Kevorkian and David 2016). The concept of Price Tag refers to the "retaliatory"[5] violence predominantly carried out against

---

[5] As I have described elsewhere (Shalhoub-Kevorkian and David 2016), the Israeli media, various politicians, and activists present this violence as mostly retaliatory, although it is not always clear

Palestinians by Israeli Jewish settlers. In addition to being used to describe the various acts of violence committed against Palestinians, Price Tag also refers to a religious-nationalist Jewish movement whose members use violence against Palestinians as part of a political strategy to work toward attaining Jewish "purity." Perpetrators of Price-Tag attacks include students and graduates from extremist religious *yeshivas* (Orthodox Jewish colleges or seminaries), rabbis, and "hilltop youth" (a term used to describe young radical Jewish settlers living in unauthorized outposts in the Occupied Territories) (Eiran and Krause 2016). The Price-Tag movement typically commits the following types of crimes: painting racist graffiti; burning and uprooting Palestinian olive trees; destroying crops; attacking Palestinian Muslim and Christian religious sites; damaging property; and committing physical violence against individuals. The movement draws its ideological inspiration from the extremist (outlawed) Kach political party and its leader, the late Rabbi Meir Kahane, who viewed the forcible expulsion of non-Jews from the "Land of Israel" as a religious duty.

Perpetrators of Price-Tag attacks draw on the text *Torat ha-Melekh* (*The King's Torah*), written in 2010 by two prominent settler rabbis, which provides quasi-religious justification for committing violence against non-Jews (The Forward and Estrin 2010). The year it was published, *The King's Torah* was described in an article in the Israeli daily *Haaretz* as a "rabbinic instruction manual outlining acceptable scenarios for killing non-Jewish babies, children and adults" (The Forward and Estrin 2010). The article relates that,

> The prohibition "Thou Shalt Not Murder" applies only "to a Jew who kills a Jew" ... Non-Jews are "uncompassionate by nature" and attacks on them "curb their evil inclination," while babies and children of Israel's enemies may be killed since "it is clear that they will grow to harm us." (The Forward and Estrin 2010)

While sometimes portrayed as a fringe movement of extremists whose interests clash with those of the Israeli government on the basis that they harm its international image, in logic, the Price-Tag movement can be seen functioning alongside the state apparatus in that it achieves the same shared objectives of uprooting the natives. The movement's "sporadic" acts of violence are not dissimilar to the means that pre-state Jewish militias and terror groups used during the original Nakba era in the late 1940s to displace a majority of Palestine's indigenous population (Robinson 2003; Sa'di and Abu-Lughod 2007). In the same way today, the Price-Tag practices facilitate settler colonization in that they advance the Judaization of land and the delegitimization of the natives' presence on their land (Shalhoub-Kevorkian and David 2016), leading to their ultimate dispossession. Furthermore, Price-Tag vigilantes often act with impunity and rarely incur Israeli government condemnation for their actions (Eiran and Krause 2016).

against whom retaliation is directed and for what reason. Framing it as retaliatory is problematic insofar as it carries the connotation that it might somehow be justified, which it is not.

The trademark Price-Tag graffiti, often left at the site of an attack on persons or property by its perpetrators, relays a wide range of messaging, including justifications for violence, dehumanizing statements toward Palestinians and non-Jews, religious symbolism, and calls for eviction and ethnic cleansing. This graffiti often deals with what can be seen as biopolitical and necropolitical themes, with messages such as "Jewish blood is not for the taking" and "Kahane lives, death to Arabs," evoking the Price-Tag movement's outlook on the rightfulness to life and death based on a religiously justified racialized hierarchy. In other instances, the graffiti calls for the eviction of non-Jews from a targeted geographical location (i.e., "Arabs out" ["*Aravim Hahutza*"]) (Shalhoub-Kevorkian and David 2016, 6). Such graffiti is left at sites of symbolic, religious, or personal importance to Palestinians, with the deliberate intent of violating the sanctity and intimacy of colonized spaces (Shalhoub-Kevorkian and David 2016, 5). The performative nature of Zionist settler-colonial violence becomes apparent through such graffiti; it can be read as a necropolitical declaration asserting the legitimacy of the domination of the Jewish people over the colonized Palestinians and symbolic designation of which group is worthy of life and which of death (Mbembe 2003).

Beyond graffiti, the Price-Tag movement also commits actions intended to strip Palestinians of their means of economic self-sufficiency and independence (Hanieh 2016; Roy 2001; Turner and Shweiki 2014). Frequently, this is committed through burning and uprooting Palestinian olive trees and other crops, which are not only immensely symbolically significant in Palestinian culture, but, given the historic importance of agriculture in the Palestinian economy, they are also an important means of financial sustainability. The World Bank estimates that 100,000 Palestinian families in the oPT (West Bank) depend to some extent on olive-tree cultivation for their livelihoods (World Bank 2006). Between January 2009 and November 2014, more than 50,000 trees belonging to Palestinian farmers in the occupied West Bank were destroyed by Jewish settlers[6] (UN OCHA 2014). This further reveals the violent trajectory of the Price-Tag movement, which views even the Palestinian community's means of sustainability as targets to be desecrated and destroyed.

The Price-Tag movement frequently commits acts of desecration and arson toward non-Jewish religious sites. According to the head of *Tag Meir* ("Spreading the Light Tag" – a wordplay on *Tag Mehir*), a forum established to oppose the movement's actions in all locations within the Israeli borders, in oEJ, and in the oPT, between 2006 and August 2013, 24 Muslim and Christian religious sites were burned by perpetrators, who, after committing their arson acts, left inscriptions identifying their actions as being part of the Price-Tag movement (Tag Meir

---

[6] Note that most data presented in this section relate to the entirety of the occupied Palestinian Territories (oPT), not only oEJ, because that is how it is locally tracked and compiled. It is very difficult to get data on Price-Tag attacks for oEJ only. Furthermore, the very definition of what is and is not oEJ is highly problematic and disputed given the location of the Separation Wall on lines that are not contiguous with the Israeli-declared municipal border.

Conference 2013). An even higher number is reported by Israeli journalist Avi Ashkenazi: between 2010 and 2015, the group committed 44 attacks on Muslim and Christian sites (Ashkenazi 2015). The Price-Tag movement also targets Palestinian homes, private spaces, and property. Based on data from UN OCHA (2014), from 2011 to 2014 alone, over 1,500 settler-related incidents resulted in Palestinian property damage or casualties. The Price-Tag movement is most well-known for its direct acts of physical violence toward Palestinians, often portrayed as "retaliatory" or part of a "cycle of violence" in media narratives, which falsely indicate parity between colonizer and colonized. While the most well-known manifestations of the movement's colonial violence are the lethal burnings of Palestinian teenager Mohammad Abu Khdeir in oEJ in July 2014 and the Dawabshe family in the village of Duma near the occupied West Bank city of Nablus in July 2015, these represent merely two instances of a broader phenomenon of settler-colonial attacks on Palestinian life. In 2014 alone, 329 Palestinians were injured and 1 Palestinian was killed in attacks committed by Israeli settlers in the oPT (UN OCHA 2014). These published statistics do not include unreported events and everyday incidents of verbal abuse and harassment (Shalhoub-Kevorkian and David 2016).

The Price-Tag movement, while publicly considered extremist by some state officials, mimics the tactics of the Israeli state forces, which are notorious for attacking Palestinian urban spaces (Abujidi and Verschure 2006; Graham 2003, 2004a; Weizman 2003). The experience of feeling physically threatened and unwelcome is not singular to attacks on agriculture, but is seen repeatedly as the outcome of other activities by state authorities. For example, home demolitions, justified by state officials as a means of population control, urban planning, and discipline, serve to punish the collective population along with the affected family, for whom the compounded financial, physical, and psychological trauma can be devastating (see Shalhoub-Kevorkian and David 2016). The Price-Tag movement deploys similar tactics designed and intended to inflict harm and incite fear. A major difference between the two is that the state action is done "legally" thus within the confines of the law, but Price-Tag violence is committed without the need for the justificatory "legal" process.

The settlers responsible for these actions are rarely held accountable for their crimes (Yesh Din 2015). Although official Israeli reporting shows an increase in prosecution rate (Ministry of Justice n.d.), Israeli scholars Eiran and Krause (2016, 639), who studied the effect of Price-Tag attacks both in Jerusalem and the West Bank, found that: "Despite the tough talk and the significant impact on the daily lives of Palestinians and Israelis in the West Bank, only 5% of Price-Tag incidents have resulted in arrests of suspects." In 2010, Israeli Channel 2 News reported that, according to police, ninety-seven Price-Tag attacks occurred over the previous five years without a single individual prosecuted (Hamo 2010). Further, organizations and media outlets have documented evidence of systematic delays and failure to investigate cases brought to the District Police Department involving attacks on Palestinians and legal violations by the Price-Tag movement (see Yesh Din 2014). Reports state that soldiers serving in the occupied West Bank are reluctant to become involved in tamping down confrontations, either siding with the settlers or hardly interceding (see B'Tselem 2012, 2014; Yesh Din 2006, 2014). The culmination of racist graffiti, torching of olive trees, property damage, physical violence, and the lack of convictions for the perpetrators, therefore, must be seen as part of a systematic strategy of eviction and expulsion carried out by an unofficial, yet tacitly state-sanctioned, apparatus of the settler-colonial process.

Price-Tag activities sear the consciousness of Palestinians with perpetual existential fear. Perhaps the most striking feature of the Price-Tag movement's activity is the parallel between the marking of Palestinian spaces with anti-Arab threats and religious Jewish imagery and the more literal marking of Palestinian bodies through acts of physical violence. The two forms of violence – the symbolic and the real – maintain a mutually productive relationship. The constant interplay is central to the logic of the Price-Tag movement's purification project. Without condemnation or repercussion, these symbolic acts transition fluidly to realities of loss and death. The Price-Tag threats, slogans, and destruction of property are themselves a reminder to Palestinians of the enduring possibility of death and eradication from the land. These actions reinforce the limitations placed on Palestinians within oEJ, regulating Palestinians to spaces or uninhabitable zones, where they constantly fear for their lives. The palpable sense of terror is not limited to adults; children also experience it, as I have discovered by visiting schools and collecting letters from Palestinian schoolchildren in Jerusalem about their lives. For example, as one schoolgirl whom I met during a visit to her school explained to me:

> their constant [Price-Tag] attacks on my home and against my siblings reminds me of the Dawabsheh family … I dream that my home was turned into a graveyard because they burned us all, as they burned the Dawabshehs …. I always feel suffocated and afraid, and no one can stop them, no one. (Interview with the author, June 2018)

The deep sense of horror, fear of being attacked by Price-Tag settlers, reading graffiti such as that stating "Death to Arabs," and added to the burning alive of a 16-year-old school-boy, Mohammad Abu Khdeir, was repeatedly mentioned in over 500 letters that I have collected from Palestinian schoolchildren living in Jerusalem.

Furthermore, Price-Tag attacks in oEJ are ominously on the rise. UN OCHA's May 2019 biweekly report stated: "Since the beginning of 2019, the biweekly average of settler attacks resulting in Palestinian casualties or property damage has witnessed a 40 and 133 percent increase, compared to the biweekly average[s] of 2018 and 2017" (UN OCHA 2019). The violent politics of Price Tag – which sanctify the dispossession and killing of the "Other" while adopting supremacist theological doctrines – augment the state's negligent politics that fail to hold criminals accountable and refrain from engaging with intra-Israeli conflicts between extremist settler groups, religious-nationalist parties, and other governmental entities. As such, the Price-Tag movement furthers the reproduction of sacralized colonial politics. That is, as a political practice, these activities, while taking a non-state form, are nonetheless part and parcel of the state's Zionist ethno-religious, exclusivist apparatus, which postulates casting out the Arab, desecrating his or her spaces, positioning the Palestinian in a state of constant fear for his or her life, and killing the Arab – all as a Jewish religious duty.

SACRALIZING GOVERNANCE THROUGH SENSES: "THE OCCUPATION OF THE SENSES"

The convergence between the settler colonial and the religious maintains and performs racial supremacy, producing and reproducing itself through management of the native's sensory experience. The graffiti and violence of the Price-Tag movement forms part of a larger sensory power regime that operates in oEJ. Elsewhere, I have described this aesthetic of violence, enacted by the Israeli state over the colonized, as the "occupation of the senses" (Shalhoub-Kevorkian 2017). "Occupation of the senses" is a strategy generated by the technologies that manage language, sight, sound, time, space, and human bodies and is operated by a religio-national discourse legitimizing in its turn the dispossession of the colonized. This concerns the ways in which the settler colony manages sensory stimuli as a means of violence with the aim of invading and reshaping the experience of the colonized. This includes the sensory and material acts that invade colonized spaces and bodies, generating a performance of colonial domination. Drawing on a settler-colonial framework, I attempt to reveal the colonizer's everyday regime of imagery and symbols, smells, and sounds and show the way in which they demarcate between the sacred and the profane through the fabrication and imposition of new images and stereotypes while employing religious and nationalist symbols.

I choose to view the sensory and material stimuli circulated by the settler colony as a form of aesthetic/cultural violence that marks distinctions and renders exclusivity, producing and reproducing religious, national hierarchies that project colonial state power. In this sense, the aesthetics of violence performed in the settler colony are critical sites of inquiry to understand how state mechanisms employing religio-nationalist symbols are deployed, "at a distance," through the occupation of the senses to further produce the prominence and exclusivity of the colonizer's regime of violence/power. I use the term "occupation of the senses" to signify the control over the sensory and lived experiences of those who live under occupation – the smells, sights, and sounds, and sensations imposed on the colonized subject. I argue that the colonizer exerts its control through both seemingly mundane "cultural" or "artistic" forms of sensory imposition and more overtly violent means of marking bodies and spaces. I propose that both of these phenomena – the sensory and the violent – operate under the same colonial logic, serving to reinforce Israeli domination over Palestinian space in all aspects, including the sensory, thus ultimately advancing its material and structural domination over the settler colony in the process.

Some forms of spatial colonization are presented as benign cultural or artistic displays, lacking overt political content. For instance, Israel's annual Jerusalem Light Festival, which was initiated by various Israeli governmental bodies (the Ministry of Jerusalem and Heritage, the Jerusalem Municipality, and the Jerusalem Development Authority) and involves the projection of colorful imagery onto the walls of the Old City, appears at first sight to be little more than an enjoyable, festive spectacle of light. However, for Palestinians and other non-Jews living in the Old City, the whimsical illuminated displays turn the space into a celebratory, overwhelmingly Jewish atmospheric venue for raucous tourists from outside the Old City while whitewashing the harsh political realities faced by Palestinians who live there. Jewish holidays are another occasion when such dominating light displays occur. During the 2015 Hanukkah celebrations in Jerusalem, for example, images of dreidels, menorahs, and other traditional Jewish symbols were projected onto the Old City's walls. Here, the more explicit use of Jewish religious imagery serves as a means of declaring exclusive ownership over the space through sensorial hegemony. Naturally, no similar visual displays occur during holy days for Muslims, Christians, or any other religion. Nor are local non-Jewish residents of oEJ involved in the programming of such festivals in any respect. Rather, these events are aggressively imposed upon them, and there is no avenue for them to complain, protest, or even register their opinions about such events. In fact, the festivals are staged for one public only – the wider Jewish public – and the Old City is even closed to entry for residents' vehicles during the festival, giving the explicit message that residents, the majority of whom are not Jews, are not its intended audience.

A more overt and violent manifestation of the occupation of the senses occurs during marches and parades by right-wing political and Jewish religious groups throughout the Palestinian neighborhoods in oEJ. These events invade colonized spaces with visual and auditory stimuli intended to restructure the daily sensory stimuli that the indigenous Palestinian residents experience. For example, on "Jerusalem Day," an annual Israeli national holiday celebrating the "reunification" of Jerusalem – i.e., the military occupation of the eastern part of the city on that day in 1967 – large Zionist parades are held in the Old City. The parades penetrate Palestinian spaces and neighborhoods, flaunting a sea of Israeli flags and other Jewish nationalist symbols. During these marches, Israeli Jews seize and dominate the streets, loudly, aggressively, and disruptively transforming Palestinian neighborhoods and marketplaces to demonstrate control, intimidate Palestinian residents, and incite fear designed to motivate Palestinians to stay put in silence and remain invisible.

Moreover, a Jewish religious-nationalist movement known as *Sivuv Shearim* (Encircling the Gates) organizes monthly public marches around the walls of the Old City. On these marches, crowds of religious Jews who support rebuilding the "Third Jewish Temple" in place of the al-Aqsa Mosque and the Dome of the Rock, two of the holiest major sites in Islam, wave flags depicting the Temple and recite Hebrew songs calling for its reconstruction. The sensory colonization of Palestinian space that takes place during these events mirrors the marchers' ultimate goal of Judaizing the Old City entirely (see Shargai 2010). These marches are conspicuous and loud, crowding every corner of the Old City. Marchers use foghorns and chant offensive pronouncements in Hebrew, such as "Muhammad [the prophet in Islam] is dead" and "David is the king of Israel." The ability of Israeli Jews to walk throughout the Old City, singing songs of domination, eviction, and hate, contrasts starkly with the draconian restrictions the state places on public expression by Palestinians in oEJ, such as the Knesset's ban on singing the Palestinian anthem, even in schools or community centers.[7]

As a result of the state's domination over Palestinian sensory experiences in oEJ, aesthetic violence against Palestinians becomes an active colonial theater replete with religious and nationalist symbols. Rancière (2013) makes evident that the state itself controls the distribution of sensory stimuli. In settler-colonial regimes, the distribution of sensory experiences enables states to further the policing, control, and the remanufacturing of the colonized spaces and thereby Palestinians' daily sensual experience within them. Furthermore, this aesthetic of racialized separation, as Rockhill (2013, xiii) explained, "presupposes a prior aesthetic division between the visible and the invisible, the audible and the inaudible, the sayable and the unsayable." Through the performative/theatrical characteristic of Jewish religious-nationalist parades in the Old City, this division is made even clearer. On parade days, Palestinians are obliged to remain invisibly confined – or perhaps more accurately imprisoned – by closing their stores and staying locked inside their homes. The overwhelming outpouring of sensory stimuli that invade dispossessed Palestinian spaces flood and deaden the senses of the colonized.

The noise, language, and other modes of sonic theatrical violence function as psychological warfare – a technique of torture. These parades are overwhelming by design: They attempt to break Palestinians down, forcing them to succumb to the colonizer's Zionist projection of reality, where the Palestinian has no place. Just as prison guards use sound, light, and smell against the incarcerated to force confession and self-incrimination (Abujidi and Verschure 2006; Graham 2003, 2004a; Weizman 2003, 2004), these public demonstrations of power simultaneously occupy Palestinians' spaces and their senses to produce new spaces solely available to the colonizer in an effort to push the Palestinian community out, even of the

---

[7] For instance, the interior minister has proposed a draft bill that proposes to proscribe and penalize activities organized in East Jerusalem that are associated in any way with the Palestinian Authority (MEMO 2019).

imagination. Under such conditions, Palestinians are obliged to reduce their visibility, as the people dominating the streets are calling for their death. Unlike what Rancière describes as silent speech (*la parole muette*), these marches do not need an interpreter to reveal their inner truths, nor will the settler colonialists allow their voices to sink into irretrievable silence (Rockhill and Watts 2009, 199). Instead, these marches serve as an aggressive reminder to Palestinians that the settler colony is entitled to their land and then, by extension, to allocate their sensory experiences, disrupt the orientation of their bodies, and exhibit its power via procedures where violence and aggression are performed as part of the logic of domination.

A vicious illustration of the Israeli police's "redistribution of the sensible" (Rancière 1999) can be found in the brutal murder of a young Palestinian boy by a group of settlers. In July 2014, three religio-nationalist settler Israeli youths kidnapped sixteen-year-old Mohammad Abu Khdeir from in front of his family home (in the Shu'afat neighborhood of oEJ) during the early dawn hours as he was awaiting the dawn prayers. They took him in their car, beat and tortured him, and burned him alive in a forest in West Jerusalem (Khoury 2014). Such extreme forms of corporeal violence, directed toward a child next to his home, can be viewed as the logical culmination of the repeated public demonstrations calling for the expulsion of Palestinians. In addition to invading the senses and the public and private spheres, the state's approval of such violent marches reproduces and reifies the structures of Jewish supremacy, which serve, in turn, to rationalize such cruelty. Through the distribution of the sensible (Rancière 1999), the state governs the colonized by building a system of facts and indeed, sensations, intended to define and construct the social hierarchy of those within it and outside of it.

In the context of oEJ, then, public ceremonies, marches, parades, and festivities become key vehicles for maintaining Jewish supremacy. By these means, the colonizers' religious claims, race, language, culture, symbols, holidays, and governance are imposed on the city space where the colonized reside. The usurpation of territory, history, and bodies by colonial authorities reifies the exclusiveness of Jewish power and control. The performative aesthetics of events like the annual Jerusalem Festival of Lights, with its imagery designed to appeal to and resonate with Jewish citizens only, and the annual commemoration of "Jerusalem Day," with its interplay between historical, religious, and contemporary Zionist dispossessions, are projected over the same space where Palestinian children are frequently arrested, Palestinian families are evicted on flimsy legal pretexts, and Palestinian homes are routinely demolished for being built without permits (Y. Jabareen 2017). Such practices are embedded in the settler colony's eliminatory logic. Each aesthetic and political act contributes, in its own way, to strengthening the structure of settler colonialism, or the power of the colonizer to control all aspects of the existence of the colonized. Critically analyzing Israeli policies reveals a specific trajectory of domination. Settler-colonial institutions produce and reproduce the sacralization of Jewishness, Jewish exclusivity, and Palestinian dispossession not only on the level of land, body, and life, but also on the level of the senses, which constitute much of lived experience. The compounded and various invasions of the senses, on a daily or even hourly basis, relentlessly broadcast the colonizer's force and systems of power being imposed on, interpreted by, internalized by, and resisted by the colonized.

CONCLUSION: GEOPOLITICS AND SACRALIZED COLONIALISM

Occupied East Jerusalem tells the story of Israeli violence against Palestinian bodies, lives, land, and senses as a colonial story while fusing the religious and the national. Colonial laws, Price-Tag attacks, and the occupation of the senses discussed in this chapter have revealed how sacralized governance anchored in the unending violent attempts to "destroy" the native community and "replace" it with Jewish settlement and Judaization in the settler colony is an economy of power not confined solely to the state authority. The Judaization of Jerusalem, which plays a fundamental role in state governance, is, at base, a structured ideology that gives rise to distinctive sacralized technologies for managing the colonized. The sacralization of the regime that controls oEJ has produced racialized structures of differentiation apparent in laws and politics.

I opened this chapter with the recent invasion of the al-Aqsa Mosque by Jewish settlers, which was followed by the extrajudicial killing of fourteen-year-old Palestinian Nassim Abu Roumi; these moments compact the principles of the sacralized political violence and strongly reveal the supremacist and eliminatory impetus of the settler state.

The various modalities of sacralized violence governing the Palestinians in oEJ embody settler performances of ownership of land and life and cast out Palestinians, rendering them disposable. These racialized differences, as scholars have pointed out (Makdisi 2018; Zureik, Lyon, and Abu-Laban 2010), reaffirm the ongoing settler-colonial arrangements of power and are apparent in the colonizer's practices and performances of power, in law, economy, culture, and entitlement to the land (e.g., Povinelli 2002; Rifkin 2009; Razack 2011). They render Palestinians disposable in order to justify their eviction (Roy 2001; Shalhoub-Kevorkian 2015; Turner and Shweiki 2014). The racialized difference entrenched on both the local and global scale produces – in terms of how Fanon's analysis informs us in *The Wretched of the Earth* – a colonial world that is a "world cut in two," divided by "lines of force, and, inhabited by 'two different species'" (Fanon 2004; Bergland 2000).

As the statement made by US President Donald Trump and his ambassador recognizing the historical right of Jews over Jerusalem shows: Israel's colonial practices in the city are not only abetted by the violent ideological projection of a "unified" Jewish Jerusalem. Rather, the statement does not even see Palestinians as a part of the land, or as legitimate owners with a just cause. The US Christian biblically embedded unconditional support furthers settler colonization and its geopolitical racialized violence. It creates a one-sided blind affirmation of the religious claims over Jerusalem by a global superpower that actually has no direct experience of the place. The power of global politics, local settler-colonial politics, and national laws, far from being neutral or abstract, are embedded in a biopolitical regime rooted in the subordination of the colonized. The continuation of a globally supported settler-colonial violence that claims the exclusivity of Jewish rights in the "promised land," sacralizes politics, and leads to a Jewish state whose oppression, discrimination, exploitation, and cruelty against the Palestinians and the killing of children like Nassim Abu Roumi are necessary to stabilize and maintain its nationhood and domination. Nassim's unheard voice of resistance unveiled the binaries apparent in Israel's sacralized arrangements and governance of privilege in oEJ. His story, as the story of oEJ, demonstrates that only by violent governance embedded in religio-nationalist and sacralized rationalities can the settler state uphold its governance.

REFERENCES

Abu Baker, Amin. 2000. *The Greater Jerusalem Project 1967–2020* [in Arabic]. PLO: The Christian-Islamic Committee for the Support of Jerusalem.

Abujidi, Nurhan, and Han Verschure. 2006. "Military Occupation as Urbicide by 'Construction and Destruction': The Case of Nablus, Palestine." *The Arab World Geographer* 9, no. 2: 126–54.

ACRI (Association for Civil Rights in Israel). 2012. "The High Court Failed to Uphold Basic Human Rights." https://law.acri.org.il/en/2012/01/12/citizenship-law-petitions-rejected/.

2015. "East Jerusalem 2015 – Facts and Figures." http://law.acri.org.il/en/2015/05/12/ej2015/.

Adalah. n.d. "Absentee's Property Law." Discriminatory Laws in Israel. www.adalah.org/en/law/view/538.

2012. "Israeli Supreme Court Upholds Ban on Family Unification." Press Release. January 12. www.adalah.org/en/content/view/7185.

Ashkenazi, Eli. 2015. "Tens of Attacks, Zero Charges: Does the State Not Have a Solution Against 'Price Tag'?" [In Hebrew.] *Walla News*, June 19. http://news.walla.co.il/item/2865121.

Barda, Yael. 2012. *The Bureaucracy of the Occupation* [in Hebrew]. Tel Aviv: Hakibutz Hameuchad and the Van-Leer Institute.

Bar'el, Zvi. 2020. "Trump's Plan Embraces the Jewish Biblical Narrative. History Is Only Getting in the Way." *Haaretz*, February 1. www.haaretz.com/israel-news/.premium-trump-s-vision-is-based-the-bible-while-ignoring-palestinians-historical-right-1.8474417.

Barghoti, Aness Suhail. 2019. "Over 1,700 Settlers Storm Al-Aqsa Mosque." *Anadolu Agency*, August 11. www.aa.com.tr/en/middle-east/over-1-700-settlers-storm-al-aqsa-mosque/1555098.

Benvenisti, Meron. 1996. *City of Stone: The Hidden History of Jerusalem*. Translated by Maxine Kaufman Nunn. Berkeley: University of California Press.

Bergland, Renée L. 2000. *The National Uncanny: Indian Ghosts and American Subjects*. London: University Press of New England.

Bollens, Scott A. 2000. *On Narrow Ground: Urban Policy and Ethnic Conflict in Jerusalem and Belfast*. Albany: SUNY Press.

Braverman, Irus. 2007. "'Powers of Illegality': House Demolitions and Resistance in East Jerusalem." *Law and Social Inquiry* 32, no. 2: 333–72.

B'Tselem. 2012. "B'Tselem 2011 Annual Report on Human Rights in the Occupied Territories." March 12. www.btselem.org/press_releases/20120321_2011_annual_report.

2014. "Soldiers Secure Stone-throwing Settlers, 'Urif, 2014.'" January 10. Video, 7:20. www.btselem.org/video/139121.

Dabashi, Hamid. 2018. "Palestine after the May 14 Massacre." Opinion. *Haaretz*, May 22. www.aljazeera.com/indepth/opinion/palestine-14-massacre-180521110715978.html.

Eiran, Ehud, and Peter Krause. 2016. "Old (Molotov) Cocktails in New Bottles? 'Price-Tag' and Settler Violence in Israel and the West Bank." *Terrorism and Political Violence* 30, no. 4: 637–57.

Fanon, Frantz. 2004. *The Wretched of the Earth*. Translated by Richard Philcox. New York: Grove Press.

Finney, Mark T. 2016. "Christian Zionism, the US, and the Middle East: A Sketch and Brief Analysis." In *The Bible, Zionism and Palestine: The Bible's Role in Conflict and Liberation in Israel-Palestine*, edited by Michael J. Sanford, 20–31. Vol. 1 of *Bible In Effect*. Dunedin, New Zealand: Relegere Academic Press.

Foucault, Michel. 1977. *Discipline and Punish: The Birth of the Prison*. New York: Vintage Books.

(1980) 2008. *Power, Knowledge: Selected Interviews and Other Writings 1972–1977*. Harlow, UK: Longman.

Friedman, David M. 2019. "Remarks at the 2019 AIPAC Policy Conference." Speech. Washington, DC. March 26. US Embassy in Israel. https://il.usembassy.gov/u-s-ambassador-to-israel-david-m-friedman-delivers-remarks-at-the-2019-aipac-policy-conference/.

Garland, David. 1997. "'Governmentality' and the Problem of Crime: Foucault, Criminology, Sociology." *Theoretical Criminology* 1, no. 2: 173–214.

Graham, Stephen. 2003. "Lessons in Urbicide." *New Left Review* 19: 53–78.

2004a. "Introduction: Cities, Warfare and States of Emergency." In *Cities, War, and Terrorism: Towards an Urban Geopolitics*, edited by Stephen Graham, 1–26. Oxford: Blackwell.

2004b. "Constructing Urbicide by Bulldozer in the Occupied Territories." In *Cities, War, and Terrorism: Towards an Urban Geopolitics*, edited by Stephen Graham, 192–213. Oxford: Blackwell.

Gregory, Derek. 2003. "Defiled Cities." *Singapore Journal of Tropical Geography* 24, no. 3: 307–26.

Halper, Jeff. 2015. *War against the People: Israel, the Palestinians and Global Pacification*. London: Pluto Press.

Hamo, O. 2010. "'Price Tag' Activities: 97 Investigations – 0 Prosecutions." [In Hebrew.] *Mako*, October 20. www.mako.co.il/news-military/security/Article-0ea1ca723aacb21004.htm.

Hanieh, Adam. 2016. "Development as Struggle: Confronting the Reality of Power in Palestine." *Journal of Palestine Studies* 45, no. 4: 32–47.

Hasson, Nir. 2019. "Family from East Jerusalem Home, Lets Settlers Take Over." *Haaretz*, June 19. www.haaretz.com/israel-news/.premium-israeli-court-evicts-palestinian-family-from-e-j-lem-home-lets-settlers-take-over-1.7392845.

Ihmoud, Sarah. 2015. "Mohammed Abu-Khdeir and the Politics of Racial Terror in Occupied Jerusalem." *Borderlands* 14, no. 1: 1–28.

IMEMC (International Middle East Media Center). 2019. "One Child Killed, One Seriously Injured by Israeli Police Following Alleged Stabbing in Jerusalem." August 16. https://imemc.org/article/israeli-troops-open-fire-on-jerusalem-crowd-after-alleged-stabbing-of-police-officer/.

Jabareen, Hassan, and Sawsan Zaher. 2012. "Israeli Citizenship Laws Are Unconstitutional." *Jurist*, February 10. http://jurist.org/hotline/2012/02/jabareen-zaher-israel-citizenship.php.

Jabareen, Yosef. 2017. "The Right to Space Production and the Right to Necessity: Insurgent versus Legal Rights of Palestinians in Jerusalem." *Planning Theory* 16, no. 1: 6–31.

Jabareen, Yousef T. 2007. "An Equal Constitution for All? On a Constitution and Collective Rights for Arab Citizens in Israel." Position Paper. May. Mossawa Center: Haifa, Israel. www.mossawa.org/eng/Public/file/02007%20An%20Equal%20Constitution%20For%20All%20(1).pdf.

Jefferis, Danielle C. 2012. "Institutionalizing Statelessness: The Revocation of Residency Rights of Palestinians in East Jerusalem." *International Journal of Refugee Law* 24, no. 2: 202–30.

Khamaisi, Rassem, and Rami Nasrallah, eds. 2003. *Envisioning the Future of Jerusalem.* Jerusalem: The International Peace and Cooperation Center.

Khoury, Jack. 2014. "Palestinian Kidnap Victim Was Alive When Burned, PA Says." *Haaretz*, July 5. www.haaretz.com/palestinian-victim-was-alive-when-burned-1.5254502.

Kirk, Mimi. 2019. "Countering Christian Zionism in the Age of Trump." *Middle East Report Online*, August 8. https://merip.org/2019/08/countering-christian-zionism-in-the-age-of-trump/.

Makdisi, Saree. 2018. "Apartheid/Apartheid/[]." *Critical Inquiry* 44, no. 2: 304–30.

2020. "What's New about Trump's Mideast 'Peace' Plan? Only the Blunt Crudity of Its Racism." *The Nation*, January 30. www.thenation.com/article/world/israel-palestine-trump-netanyahu/.

Mbembe, Achille. 2003. "Necropolitics." Translated by Libby Meintjes. *Public Culture* 15, no. 1: 11–40.

MEMO (Middle East Monitor). 2019. "Israel Minister's Draft Bill: 3 Years Jailtime for Supporting PA Activity in Jerusalem." June 18. www.middleeastmonitor.com/20190618-israel-ministers-draft-bill-3-years-jailtime-for-supporting-pa-activity-in-jerusalem/.

Ministry of Justice. n.d. "Israel's Investigation and Prosecution of Ideologically Motivated Offences against Palestinians in the West Bank." State of Israel. https://mfa.gov.il/ProtectiveEdge/Documents/IdeologicalOffencesAgainstPalestinians.pdf.

Nikfar, Bethany M. 2005. "Families Divided: An Analysis of Israel's Citizenship and Entry into Israel Law." *Northwestern Journal of International Human Rights* 3, no. 1.

Perera, Suvendrini, and Sherene H. Razack, eds. 2014. *At the Limits of Justice: Women of Colour on Terror.* Toronto: University of Toronto Press.

Povinelli, Elizabeth A. 2002. *The Cunning of Recognition: Indigenous Alterities and the Making of Australian Multiculturalism.* Durham, NC: Duke University Press.

Rancière, Jacques. 1999. *Disagreement: Politics and Philosophy.* Translated by Julie Rose. Minneapolis: University of Minnesota Press.

2013. *The Politics of Aesthetics: The Distribution of the Sensible.* Translated by Gabriel Rockhill. London: Continuum.

Razack, Sherene H. 2011. "The Space of Difference in Law: Inquests into Aboriginal Deaths in Custody." *Somatechnics* 1, no. 1: 87–123.

Rifkin, Mark. 2009. *Manifesting America: The Imperial Construction of US National Space.* New York: Oxford University Press.

Robinson, Shira. 2003. "Local Struggle, National Struggle: Palestinian Responses to the Kafr Qasim Massacre and Its Aftermath, 1956–1977." *International Journal of Middle East Studies* 35, no. 3: 393–416.

Rockhill, Gabriel. 2013. "Introduction." In *The Politics of Aesthetics: The Distribution of the Sensible*, by Jacques Rancière, vii–x. Translated by Gabriel Rockhill. London: Continuum.

Rockhill, Gabriel, and Philip Watts, eds. 2009. *Jacques Rancière: History, Politics, Aesthetics.* Durham, NC: Duke University Press.

Roy, Sara. 2001. *The Gaza Strip: The Political Economy of De-development.* Washington, DC: Institute for Palestine Studies.

Sa'di, Ahmad H., and Lila Abu-Lughod, eds. 2007. *Nakba: Palestine, 1948, and the Claims of Memory.* New York: Columbia University Press.

Saifi, Yara, and Maha Samman. 2019. "Housing in Jerusalem: From a Flourishing Hope to Slow 'Urbicide.'" *Open House International* 44, no. 2: 27–35.

Samman, Maha. 2017. *Trans-colonial Urban Space in Jerusalem: Politics and Development.* New York: Routledge.

Shalhoub-Kevorkian, Nadera. 2012. *Birthing in Occupied East Jerusalem: Palestinian Women's Experience of Pregnancy and Delivery.* Jerusalem: YWCA.

  2015. *Security Theology, Surveillance and the Politics of Fear.* Cambridge: Cambridge University Press.

  2017. "The Occupation of the Senses: The Prosthetic and Aesthetic of State Terror." *British Journal of Criminology* 57, no. 6: 1279–300.

  2019. *Incarcerated Childhood and the Politics of Unchilding.* Cambridge: Cambridge University Press.

Shalhoub-Kevorkian, Nadera, and Yossi David. 2016. "Is the Violence of *Tag Mehir* a State Crime?" *British Journal of Criminology* 56, no. 5: 835–56.

Shargai, Nadav. 2010. *Demography, Geopolitics, and the Future of Israel's Capital: Jerusalem's Proposed Master Plan.* Jerusalem: Jerusalem Center for Public Affairs.

Tag Meir Conference. 2013. Tel Aviv University. September 16.

Tawil-Souri, Helga. 2011. "Colored Identity: The Politics and Materiality of ID Cards in Palestine/Israel." *Social Text* 29, no. 2: 67–97.

Temple Institute. n.d. "About the Temple Institute." https://templeinstitute.org/about-us/.

The Forward and Estrin. 2010. "The King's Torah: A Rabbinic Text or a Call to Terror?" *Haaretz*, January 22. www.haaretz.com/1.5088576.

Trump, Donald. 2018. "Speech on the Opening of the US Embassy in Jerusalem." Speech. Jerusalem. *Politico*, May 14. www.politico.com/story/2018/05/14/text-trump-on-opening-of-us-embassy-in-jerusalem-transcript-584452.

Turner, Mandy, and Omar Shweiki. 2014. *Decolonizing Palestinian Political Economy: De-development and Beyond.* New York: Palgrave Macmillan.

TV7 Israel News. 2019. "US–Israel Celebrate Anniversary of Embassy's Jerusalem Inauguration." May 15. www.tv7israelnews.com/u-s-israel-celebrate-anniversary-of-embassys-jerusalem-inauguration/.

UN OCHA (United Nations Office for the Coordination of Humanitarian Affairs). 2014. "Protection of Civilians: Reporting Period: 23–29 December 2014." Protection of Civilians Weekly Report. https://unispal.un.org/pdfs/WBN587.pdf.

  2019. "Protection of Civilians Report: 23 April – 6 May 2019." Protection of Civilians Report. www.ochaopt.org/poc/23-april-6-may-2019.

Weheliye, Alexander G. 2014. *Habeas Viscus: Racializing Assemblages, Biopolitics, and Black Feminist Theories of the Human.* Durham, NC: Duke University Press.

Weizman, Eyal. 2003. "Politics of Verticality." In *Territories, Islands, Camps and Other States of Utopia*, edited by Eyal Weizman and Rafi Segal, 65–112. Cologne: Verlag der Buchhandlung Walther König.

——— 2004. "Builders and Warriors: Military Operations as Urban Planning." Wooloo.org. www.wooloo.org/Terror/weizman.html.

Wolfe, Patrick. 2006. "Settler Colonialism and the Elimination of the Native." *Journal of Genocide Research* 8, no. 4: 387–409.

World Bank. 2006. "Brief Overview of the Olive and Olive Oil Sector in the Palestinian Territories." United Nations. www.un.org/unispal/document/auto-insert-203052/.

Yesh Din. 2006. "A Semblance of Law: Law Enforcement upon Israeli Civilians in the West Bank." January 1. www.yesh-din.org/en/a-semblance-of-law-law-enforcement-on-israeli-civilians-in-the-west-bank/.

——— 2014. "Law Enforcement on Israeli Civilians in the West Bank." Yesh Din Monitoring Update Data Sheet. November. https://go.aws/2UntNot.

——— 2015. "Data Sheet May 2015: Prosecution of Israeli Civilians Suspected of Harming Palestinians in the West Bank." May 17. www.yesh-din.org/en/data-sheet-may-2015-prosecution-of-israeli-civilians-suspected-of-harming-palestinians-in-the-west-bank/.

Zureik, Elia, David Lyon, and Yasmeen Abu-Laban. 2010. "Colonialism, Surveillance, and Population Control: Israel/Palestine." In *Surveillance and Control in Israel/Palestine: Population, Territory and Power*, edited by Elia Zureik, David Lyon, and Yasmeen Abu-Laban, 3–46. London: Routledge.

PART II

India

7

Hindutva

The Dominant Face of Religious Nationalism in India

Tanika Sarkar[*]

FAITH AND NATION IN HINDUTVA

Religious nationalism, in any form or context, must fuse faith and nation into a single, indivisible whole. This involves investing faith with a modern political ideology, as well as reconfiguring the nation as an object of ardent religious worship, significantly changing both in the process. However, the ways in which this doubled movement is achieved, and the purposes that such a construct serves, differ, even within the same country. In this chapter, I try to identify some critical aspects of the belief structure that Hindu religious nationalism propagates and acts upon in contemporary India.

Hansen (1999, 10) perceptively points out: "Hindu nationalism has indeed successfully recruited and subsumed religious sentiments and public rituals into a larger discourse of national culture." Its actual objectives, however, go far beyond religious purposes and "are centrally concerned with notions of national honour," stability, and global power (Hansen 1999, 177–214). Such a transmutation is, indeed, the first step in Hindu nationalist strategy. But the ideology is so deeply mortgaged to religious symbolism, emotionalism, and vocabulary that faith and politics actually circle each other endlessly, their distinctions blurring after a point.

Faith and nationalism may, in any case, share certain generic affinities. Opinions differ on what belief and ritual do for believers. Max Weber said that while early religious systems offered meanings for a largely incomprehensible world and its mysterious ways, the bureaucratic state and modern science have made those functions largely redundant, leading to a general decline in faith (Whimster 2004, 214). Others contest Weber's thesis of a disenchanted, faithless world, arguing that even in fully modernized countries, faith has not really waned; rather, it has sought out fresh pastures. Indian modernity was thinly secularized, whether at state or at societal levels. The work of religion, therefore, remains paramount and relevant, though in an altered form.[1]

---

[*] A different version of this article is scheduled to appear in a forthcoming collection on Hindutva from Hurst Publishers, UK.

[1] For the limited spheres of secularization in India, see Vanaik (2017, 95–164).

162 Tanika Sarkar

I argue that for growing numbers of contemporary Hindus, religious nationalism has come to interpret the world they inhabit. In other words, it has usurped some of the functions that traditional faith performed – albeit, in the name of faith itself.

We may trace the roots of this religious nationalism from the rapid growth of cultural nationalism from the late nineteenth century. In colonized India, cultural nationalism, both Hindu and Muslim, sought to insulate faith and ritual from an early nineteenth-century cosmopolitan liberal culture that had stimulated a measure of self-reflexivity and self-reform. By contrast, it insisted that religious norms should be preserved intact in order to maintain selfhood and identity against colonial cultural onslaughts. This requires, more than ever before, an absolute faith in one's own culture and an absolute conviction in others' inferiority: self-pride and hatred, mingling in equal measure (T.Sarkar 2001).

Inevitably, this also implied an unequivocal defense of traditional caste and gender inequalities, which are embedded in holy texts. After decolonization, however, as India entered an era of democratic politics with full adult suffrage, their open defense became risky, given the new need to strike roots in mass political constituencies that now included women and people from the "low castes" in large numbers. Those realities forced subtle doublespeak and convoluted discursive strategies on Hindu nationalism later.

From the early twentieth century, moreover, a parallel and powerful ideological sphere had developed: that of anti-colonial political nationalism, with its liberal vision of a sovereign nation, freed from colonial tutelage by popular resistance. Its immense emotional power drew much from a strikingly religious appeal, whether for Gandhian nationalism or for the Muslim League's Pakistan demand. From its birth, then, Indian political nationalism remained tied to matters of faith, much as cultural nationalism had been, though with vastly different aims and methods. Hindu religious nationalism, on the other hand, never shared this history of anti-colonial movements or its relatively liberal, inclusive politics. Instead, it took the theme of foreign conquest and Indian resistance into an imagined medieval past where Hindus were apparently enslaved by tyrannical Muslim rulers. So, despite a common appeal to faith, anti-colonial nationalist politics and Hindu religious nationalism had fundamental mutual differences.

Yet, all nationalisms do possess certain characteristics that closely resemble faith. They work, not so much as parallel fields, but rather as overlapping, symbiotic ones. Often cast as essentially a religious duty, nationalisms – cultural and political – bind disparate peoples and places together through the imaginary of the homogeneous time and space of the affective nation. Both borrow terms from religious morality like good and evil, struggle and sacrifice: be it for decolonized India, for *Ram Rajya*, or for Pakistan.[2] With

---

[2] In the early twentieth century, M. K. Gandhi, soon to emerge as undisputed leader of anti-colonial mass movements, inspired Hindus with a vision of independent India that would recover the glorious reign of Ram, a divine incarnation, and an epic hero. In 1940, M. A. Jinnah, leader of the Muslim

rare exceptions,[3] the nationalist community imagines the nation as perennial, organic, based on a singular ethnic substance: and also as perpetually threatened by its Other/s. (These various imaginaries are not identical, but they share strong affinities.) In several ways, then, the nationalist community resembles the community of faith.[4]

Nationalism, like faith, also shows a way out of the human predicament of finite time and mortality by positing an image of the everlasting nation that renders the mortal individual deathless: just as faith promises the devout an immortal soul and eternal salvation.[5] Civic or exclusively political nationalism, therefore, found relatively little purchase in modern India, and nationalism and faith did not bifurcate completely. This created a particularly hospitable space for Hindu religious nationalism in our times.

THE SANGH: ORGANIZATION AND IDEOLOGY

A specific Hindu version of religious nationalism has now come to dominate the entire Indian political scene. It is best exemplified by a federated structure of Hindu extremist politics that is equipped with multiple wings, commonly known as the Sangh Parivar or the "family" of the Rashtriya Swayam Sevak Sangh (RSS) (T.Basu et al. 1993; Jaffrelot 2005a). In 2014, the Bharatiya Janata Party (BJP), the electoral wing of the RSS (A.Basu 2015) that professes the ideology of "Hindutva,"[6] captured state power in India and won an absolute majority of parliamentary seats.[7] What sets the BJP apart from all other Indian political parties is the excess it uniquely enjoys over its electoral organization and agenda, for behind it lies the gigantic cadre base supplied by the RSS and its numerous auxiliaries – the Vishwa Hindu Parishad

---

    League, demanded the separation of Muslim-majority parts of the country to constitute Pakistan of the Muslim Holy Land. This led to the partition of the subcontinent in 1947.

[3] Jawaharlal Nehru, who went on to become the first prime minister of independent India, used a more modern, secular-democratic vocabulary to describe the nation without, however, developing a critique of religious nationalism, unless it turned violent. Far more radical imaginaries came from Dalit or untouchable caste leaders like B. R. Ambedkar or E. V. Ramaswamy Naicker, who produced systematic critiques of Hindu faith and preached either atheism or rational Buddhism.

[4] Gandhi imagined an inclusive nation and, indeed, he was assassinated in 1948 by Hindutva fanatic Godse for his commitment to that ideal. Yet, his vocabulary and religious understanding was anchored in Brahmanical social ideology and theological texts like the *Gita*. See Hansen (1999); van der Veer (1994, 94–99).

[5] For elaborations of these views of nationalism, see Anderson (1961); Bauman (1992); Breuilly (1996); Smith (1998); and Taylor (1999), among others.

[6] Hindutva, their self-designation, is a term coined by V. D. Savarkar in 1923, who claimed that it referred to the cultural essence of Indian nationhood (Savarkar [1923] 1969). We will discuss this later. It is different from Hinduism as religious faith and embodies an authoritarian nationalism that claims to represent the community of Hindus as the only authentic Indians.

[7] There has earlier been another BJP-led coalition government at the center between 1998 and 2004. The BJP has ruled over several regional states as well, and their numbers are steadily growing. However, the scale of victory in 2014 was staggering, giving Prime Minister Modi almost unlimited power. About 30 percent of Hindus voted for Modi as a large bloc.

(VHP) being the best known among them.[8] These cadres work tirelessly among numerous regions and social groups, biting deep into the everyday of vast segments of Hindu society and forming affiliates and sub-affiliates for women's, students', and teachers' organizations, trade unions, schools, temples and religious sects, entertainment business, and leisure industries. Their reach extends among Adivasi/tribals, slum dwellers and nonresident Indians, in the army and the media. The BJP reaps a rich electoral harvest from their labor.[9] Its huge electoral success in 2014 indicates Hindutva's coming of age.

All Sangh branches are held together by a striking unity of beliefs, going back nearly a century, when V. D. Savarkar, ideological guru of the Sangh, provided the full ideological apparatus in his seminal tract of 1923: *Hindutva: Who Is a Hindu?* Savarkar made Hindu and Indian synonymous, each forming a monolithic unit. He described the land of India as marked by rivers and mountains that have been mentioned in ancient Hindu holy texts. Dotted with Hindu pilgrimages, it is territory made sacred through its association with Hindu cosmogony and mythology. India, he said, therefore belongs to those Indians whose religions originated within this land: thus tying up territory and belief with a double knot. The rest – Indian Christians and Muslims – are not truly Indians, however long their ancestors may have lived in this land. Their religion dooms them to be stranded in their own country as perpetual foreigners. Even though he began his discourse with a division between Hinduism as faith and Hindutva as the cultural essence of Indian people, he soon came to the point: "Hindutva, that is Hindudharma ... that was being fought out on the hundred fields of battle."

National identity is, above all, an act of exclusion.

> We Hindus are bound together not only by the tie of the love that we bear to a common fatherland and the common blood that courses through our veins, but also by the common homage we pay to ... our Hindu culture ... We are one because we are a nation, a race and own a common Sanskrit ... in the case of our Mohammedan or Christian countrymen ... Though Hindustan to them is Fatherland ... yet it is not their Holyland too. Their mythology and Godmen ... are not the children of this soil ... their names and their outlook smack of a foreign origin. (Savarkar [1923] 1969, 91–92)

Muslims were dangerous outsiders, carrying a sinister history and purpose. Whereas earlier invaders came with the mission of conquest alone, Muslims

---

[8] Among the best known are the BJP (its electoral front); Vishwa Hindu Parishad (its religious front); Bharatiya Mazdoor Sangh (its trade union front); and Akhil Bharatiya Chhatra Parishad (the student wing). But there are numerous such fronts, some of them working in obscurity, others entirely unknown as yet, and each spawning numerous sub-affiliates of their own.

[9] In February 2018, for instance, there was an election slated for the eastern state of Tripura. For a whole year, 50,000 workers from the Rahtriya Swyamsevak Sangh, the mother organization that calibrates all Hindutva fronts, has been working in many sectors in this state where the BJP never had a significant presence. Many of them work full time (Roy 2018). For the many fronts in which they work, see T.Basu et al. (1993); Hansen (1999); Jaffrelot (2005a).

Religious Nationalism in India

invaded to destroy the Hindu faith. Their fanaticism was also driven by immoderate greed:

> Religion is a mighty motive force. So is rapine. But when religion is goaded by rapine and rapine serves as the handmaiden to religion, the propelling force that is generated by these together is only equaled by the profundity of human misery and devastation they leave behind . . . . Day after, day, decade after decade, century after century, the ghastly conflict continued and India single-handed kept up the fight morally and militarily. (Savarkar [1923] 1969, 44)

In 1939, Golwalkar, second supremo of the Sangh and its real architect, found an appropriate model to look up to:

> To keep up the purity of the nation and its culture, Germany shocked the world by her purging the country of the semitic races . . . Race pride at its highest has been manifested here . . . all the constituents of the Nation idea have been boldly vindicated in modern Germany and that, too, in the actual present, when we can for ourselves see and study them . . . a good lesson for us in Hindustan to learn and profit by . . . The Nazi lesson for India was "they (non-Hindus) may stay in the country wholly subordinated to the Hindu nation, claiming nothing, deserving no privileges . . . not even citizen's rights." (Golwalkar 1939, 76–93)

The Sangh has very recently expunged this segment from a text that otherwise remains canonical. It is viscerally opposed to Western ideas, be they liberalism, socialism, feminism, or social justice. Fascism, however, is the only Western ideology to which it has acknowledged a lasting debt.

The words of Savarkar and Golwalkar provide the basis for the Sangh's ideological apparatus, to this day. They are simplified and refracted through daily teachings at its training centers and among its myriad affiliates. Savarkar spoke exceptionally strong words. Bereft of even a single substantiation for his assertions, he made them carry conviction by sheer rhetorical passion, his language weaving together love for the Hindu nation and hatred for its imagined enemy. Savarkar's love, however, has a fleeting presence and purpose: it exists simply to stoke anger. His was, from beginning to end, a mysticism of hate.

Since then, Hindutva has repeatedly organized great violence against religious minorities.[10] But the puzzle is that it does so even while staying within a formal democratic framework, revealing a significant gap between constitutional-democratic norms and actual practices of democratic politics in India.[11] Its ideological and organizational apparatus, moreover, is strongly anchored in a long historical process that began as far back as the nineteenth century and matured in the early twentieth. It has had plenty of time to insert itself into the popular common sense among large segments of Hindus. The Indian National Congress, chief

---

[10] For an especially brutal pogrom in Gujarat in 2002, see Ayyub (2016).

[11] This reflects on the practice of Indian democracy in interesting ways. I am indebted to A.Sarkar (2018) for this important distinction.

166 *Tanika Sarkar*

architect of anti-colonial movements and comfortably in power from the time India became independent in 1947 until the 1970s, on the other hand, had no corresponding charismatic rhetoric or agenda for mass mobilization, once the purpose of anti-colonialism had been achieved and the new nation-state steered through its formative years.

SITES OF VIOLENT RELIGIOUS PRACTICES

Let us now identify the primary ingredients of Hindutva's ideological apparatus. Hindu historical romances, from the late nineteenth century onward, as well as recent Hindutva historical constructions, have persistently focused on four alleged cardinal Muslim sins: demolishing Hindu temples; killing the cow, which is sacred to Hindus; forced conversions to Islam; and abduction and rape of Hindu women. Each individual issue speaks of injuries done to sacred Hindu bodies – human, animal, or non-corporeal. Each issue leaches into the others to compose a thick and sensational narrative of systematic Muslim attacks. Among them, supposed acts of conversion and abduction of women smoothly fold into each other. Conversion reduces the population of the abandoned community and augments numbers for the new community; abduction of women, however, will not only add to enemy numbers but will also produce future progeny for abductors.[12] The allegations were, therefore, strategically chosen for their emotional evocativeness.

Yet another implicit link unifies the two. Hindu nationalists reconfigure inter-community love as abduction or seduction by Muslim men. They prohibit it with determined violence, just as they similarly oppose conversions away from Hinduism on the grounds that it is always the result of force or fraud. The individual's right to choose her faith and love – though legally sanctioned – stands, in practice, as forbidden acts. This was made most evident in the infamous "Hadiya" case. A twenty-four-year-old Hindu girl, Akhila, converted to Islam and married a Muslim. Her parents alleged fraud and force, and the Kerala High Court agreed with them. Akhila (renamed Hadiya) was steadfast in her resolve, and the Supreme Court took a very long time to confirm the validity of her marriage (Krishnan 2017). Blocking the right to love or to convert diminishes individual liberties and auton-omy, keeps adults perpetually under parental discipline, and shores up Hindu endogamous marriage norms. It ensures the production of docile citizens who do not question the powers that be – familial, caste, community, and state – and, therefore, has a broader purpose that goes beyond instigating communal hatred. The holy cow and the sacred temple, on the other hand, allegedly under attack from

---

[12] After independence, the state abolished Hindu polygamy. Muslims, by contrast, are still allowed an upper limit of four wives. Hindutva derives a faux arithmetic from this difference, widely claiming that each Muslim marriage produces twenty children and Hindu numbers stand imperiled; overlooking the simple fact that a woman can only bear one child at a time, irrespective of whether four are married to a single man or one. Polygamy does not make a difference to the overall population.

Muslims since medieval times, function in this discourse as concrete, visible, and wounded bodies of faith itself.

Disseminated systematically and continuously through innumerable grassroots institutions over ninety-two years,[13] each individual issue whips up a fresh storm of conflicts – until an older one is retrieved after a gap, engorged now on memories of other issues which had held the stage in the meantime. The theme of abduction has been in use from the 1920s, while cow slaughter riots go back to the late nineteenth century in some parts of the country. Temple destruction has always been a common topic in Hindu nationalist historical propaganda, and it provoked the "revenge demolition" of a sixteenth-century mosque in the North Indian town of Ayodhya in 1992, amidst years of huge violence against Muslims. Allegations of forced conversions to Islam and Christianity have fomented aggressive counter-conversion campaigns, especially against Indian Christians (Gopal 1992; Gupta 2001; Pandey 1983; S.Sarkar 1999).

Hindutva discourses use a marvelous narrative strategy. Highly distorted and manufactured "historical" memories of Muslim aggression are produced in a manner wherein the first offence is invariably attributed to them in whatever remote past. Hindu aggression in the present, thereafter, is always presented and justified as retaliatory, defensive, retrospective. Spectacular aggression is thereby made to appear as necessary defensive action, mere survival strategy – not aggression at all.

HINDUTVA AND DEMOGRAPHY

By the early twentieth century, a mix of cultural pride and hatred had acquired a coherent political form and content, embodied in the RSS, which was capable of fomenting and stabilizing continuous intercommunity hostility and conflict. A new demographic imperative emerged in the 1920s that systematically prepared the ground for suspicion against non-Hindus. Colonial constitutional reforms opened up a limited electoral arena within provincial legislatures from the early twentieth century. That introduced an unprecedented emphasis on the relative numbers of different communities (since electorates were defined in religious terms), their precise enumeration enabled by decennial censuses from the late nineteenth century.

This provoked a game of competitive numbers, leading to sharp Hindu anxieties about future electoral prospects and about the fate of the numerical majority that they enjoyed vis-à-vis other Indian religious communities. Hindu ideologues translated these worries into campaigns against conversions to non-Hindu faiths and allegations that Muslims habitually abduct Hindu women to convert, marry, and impregnate them. Accusations were further strengthened with manufactured

---

[13] The Rashtriya Swayamsevak Sangh (RSS) was founded in 1925.

"historical memories": of medieval Muslim royal figures stealing Hindu queens and engaging in forced conversions. Savarkar wrote:

> It was a religious duty of every Muslim to kidnap and force into their own religion non Muslim women. This incited their sensuality and lust for carnage and while it increased their number, it affected the Hindu population in an inverse proportion. ... Muslims ... considered it their highly religious duty to carry away forcibly the women of the enemy side as if they were commonplace property, to ravish them, to pollute them, and to distribute them to all and sundry ... and to absorb them completely in their fold ... which increased their number. (Savarkar 1970, 174–75)

Savarkar's notion of innate and exuberant Muslim lust for Hindu women has proved remarkably tenacious, providing, to this day, pretexts for vicious attacks on Muslims who are suspected of seducing Hindu women to convert and marry them and then to traffic them to Islamic countries, or to Pakistan. Intercommunity love and marriage are now renamed as "love *jihad*" planned by Muslim terrorists: love being a Muslim ruse for political conspiracy and terror. Narratives of alleged and imagined terror produce and justify actual terror, forced separations, and deaths (Dixit 2014).

Muslims do not share the Hindu prohibition on beef eating – indeed, cow sacrifice is an annual ritual event for many – so it is easy to brand them as habitual cow killers and eaters, even when they are not doing either. By definition, then, they become enemies of faith, literally killing and eating the religion of Hindus. Cow slaughter allegations had long led to conflicts. In 1966, shortly after the VHP was founded in 1964 to coordinate temples, sects, and ascetics, bands of Hindu holy men rioted in many northern and central Indian towns, demanding a complete ban on cow slaughter (T.Basu et al. 1993, 1–12). After the BJP's victory in 2014, cow-centered violence has become rampant and brutal, and Muslim consumption of any kind of meat, or their cattle trade, are now suspect activities. Vigilante mobs roam around at will, attacking, lynching, and murdering suspects. The toll between 2015 and 2017 amounted to twenty-four incidents involving thirty-four murders, two rapes, and numerous floggings. Culprits are soon freed on bail and penalties, if any, are token ones (Citizens Against Hate 2017).

All four pretexts roll onto one another. Together, they produce such toxic hatred that, in the present, no pretexts are needed for brutalities. All Muslim bodies can become an open stage upon which the wrath of Hindus may be freely inscribed. In December 2017, Afrazul, a young Bengali Muslim migrant laborer working in the North Indian town of Rajsamand in Rajasthan, was hacked to death, and the murder was happily filmed by a fourteen-year-old Hindu boy. It went viral among Hindus. The killer brought no charges of misdeed against Afrazul; it sufficed that he was a Muslim (Mander, Dayal, and Shrivastava 2017).

HINDUTVA AND ITS OTHERS

To resume our brief historical sketch: A problem emerged when, at Gandhi's insistence, the Indian National Congress decided to join hands with the Khalifatist movement for the restoration of the Turkish khalifa to his former status after the Great War. The prospect of joint Hindu-Muslim anti-colonial struggles deeply worried communal leaders. The founder of the RSS, Dr. Hedgewar, wrote:

> As a result of the Non Cooperation Movement for Mahatma Gandhi, evils in social life that the movement generated, were raising their head. The *yavana* (Muslim) snakes, reared on the milk of Non Cooperation, were provoking riots in the nation with their poisonous hissing. (Bhishikar 1979)

Unity between Hindus and Muslims concerned him, since ceaseless conflict was the aim.

The nationalist right-wing Hindu Mahasabha was active from 1919, and the RSS was formed in 1925 – the former to uphold Hindu upper-caste electoral interests; the latter to organize and educate an upper-caste Hindu social leadership in combative militancy. Though they were born in colonial times, neither ever opposed the state nor ever faced any state repression. The RSS now runs thousands of daily sessions (*shakhas*) all over the country to train its members in combat skills and Hindutva ideology.[14] Leaders of all affiliates come out of their ranks, thus imparting a common disposition to multifarious fronts. Prime Minister Modi used to be a full-time RSS preacher, and he is still an RSS member. Almost all of the important BJP and VHP leaders come out of RSS ranks.

Most disturbing for the combine was the simultaneous growth of "low caste" and untouchable/Dalit political critiques and protests against Brahmanical Hinduism, especially in southern and western India, under formidable leaders like E. V. Ramaswamy Naicker and B. R. Ambedkar. The Sangh could not name caste as a problem for itself. Caste taboos rendered the myth of an organic, unified, and seamless Hindu *volk* fragile, even untenable, exposing bitter fault lines among Hindus. Dalits/untouchables and "low" castes are, indeed, Hinduism's inner demons: unmentionable as such, but persistent thorns in their side. The problem cannot be resolved within their framework of unified Hinduism, based on ancient scripture, for Hindu canonical texts unanimously prescribe caste inequalities and untouchability.

The religious affiliation of "low castes" does, indeed, make them a part of the Hindu community, and Hindu electoral and demographic interests combine to retain them there and prevent their conversion to other faiths. At the same time, without radical social-ideological transformations in caste-based purity-pollution norms and in production relations where caste and class exploitation are intertwined, "low caste" protests could not be stemmed. Upper- and dominant-caste

---

[14] By the latest count, 56,859 *shakhas* operated daily in India in 2016 (Joshi 2017).

social guardians, on the other hand, were not prepared to consider egalitarian changes: due to their long-standing and tenacious religious and ritual habits and prejudices, as well as their material self-interests, because these subordinated and stigmatized groups are doomed to provide captive labor power to the privileged.

Hindutva was written at a time when southern and western India were rocked by "lower" caste protests and challenges to Brahmanical power. Savarkar had to refer to caste divisions among Hindus. He claimed that such divisions have long been superseded by miscegenation and mixing of blood among castes. All Hindus, high and low, share primeval family ties based on common blood. "No people in the world can more justly claim to get recognized as a racial unit than the Hindus and perhaps the Jews" (Savarkar [1923] 1969, 90). Interestingly, Savarkar used the term "race" and invoked the Jews as the perfect example of racial unity, while Golwalkar did the same with the Nazis. Despite the seeming gulf between the similes, an affinity can perhaps be seen between the Nazism of yesteryear and present-day Israeli Zionism.

But even the metaphor of blood was not enough to forge Hindu unity. So Savarkar invoked the Muslim. "Nothing makes Self conscious of itself so much as a conflict with non-self. Nothing can weld people into a nation and nations into a state as the pressure of a common foe. Hatred separates as well as unites" (Savarkar [1923] 1969, 42–43). A Hindu nation that wants to mask power lines internal to Hindu society needs an external threat to actualize unity. Hatred is, therefore, foundational. In the same measure, in the very act of invoking and then immediately dissolving the specter of caste inequality, exploitation, and stigmatization, Savarkar actually provided both a cover and a subtle justification for them. In order to mask gross internal inequalities, the Hindu nation must rely upon the enemy figure. In other words, the real discursive purpose of the non-Hindu was to provide an alibi for Hindu caste exploitation.

So, caste foisted a curiously doubled discourse upon Hindutva. Unlike its open calls for violence against Muslims and Christians, Hindutva pays much lip service to Ambedkar,[15] in order to co-opt Dalit masses to its cause[16] – but it reveres him as the author of the Indian Constitution, not as the ferocious critic of Hindu faith that Ambedkar certainly was. On the other hand, Hindutva chooses to ignore – or covertly support rather than publicly defend – atrocities against Dalits that are

---

[15] B. R. Ambedkar is the iconic leader of "low" or Dalit castes who brilliantly refuted all arguments on behalf of caste and who uncovered the deep relationship between all forms of Hinduism and caste. He led massive Dalit movements in western India between the 1920s and 1950s. He converted to Buddhism in 1956. As the first law minister of independent India, he radically reformed Hindu gender laws.

[16] The RSS-BJP also try to mobilize the Dalit masses' loyalty to the Hindutva cause by offering them a transient egalitarianism, even exaltation in moments of communal violence. The RSS-BJP try to substitute demands for real change and citizenship rights with the vision of the Hindu nation whose glory would also cover them.

rampant across the country.[17] Often Hindutva actively colludes with upper and dominant castes in stamping down Dalit protests. At Una in the western state of Gujarat, now ruled by the BJP for three successive terms, seven Dalit youths were beaten up with iron rods in July 2016 for supposedly skinning a dead cow. They were then paraded half-naked in public and beaten all the way to the police station.[18] This led to a massive upsurge of Dalit anger that has created something like a caste war in many parts of the country today.[19] The fear of Dalit rights carries over into the Hindutva diaspora. Vishwa Hindu Parishad (VHP) has agitated quite success-fully to block the incorporation of caste issues within the anti-racist legal rubric in Britain (see Waughrey 2018).

To return to our brief historical sketch: As vast popular anti-colonial movements in the first half of the twentieth century eventually made Independence imminent, mutual hostility turned into a bloodbath as community leaders competed for future political ascendancy. Even though the Indian National Congress – the chief anti-colonial platform – promised a secular-democratic constitution, the aggressive stance of Hindu extremist organizations, claiming to represent the majority com-munity, led the Muslim League to call for a partition of the subcontinent. Consequently, Muslim-majority states in the western and the eastern regions came together to form Pakistan. India was partitioned in 1947 amidst terrible violence, mass displacements, an unprecedented refugee crisis, and a persistent legacy of mutual hatred between the two new nation states (S.Sarkar 1983).

A new and a most efficacious grievance now entered Hindutva discourses. In the late nineteenth century, Hindu literature had invented a new goddess of the motherland/nation – Bharat Mata – who immediately outstripped the conventional divine cosmogony (T.Sarkar 2009, 192–229). Later, towering temples were dedicated to her in most pilgrimages, and she is worshipped with immense adoration (McKean 1996). Imagined as a Hindu goddess, she is a deity who cannot be worshipped by Muslims and Christians (S.Bhattacharya 2003). Hindu nationalists immediately translated the religious objection of Muslims and Christians to the Hindu divinity personification of the country as hostility to the nation.

Partition added fresh ballast. Most Hindus blamed the Muslim League exclu-sively for it, without reckoning with the enormous complexities in communal relationships that led the League – only from 1940 – to demand a separate Muslim nation state (Jalal 1985). Hindutva chose to shift a political-territorial division onto a metaphorical register, redescribing partition as "mutilation of the nation." It was as

---

[17] Recently, it remained silent and refused, for several critical days, to petition the Supreme Court, which has mandated a watering down of a law meant to check atrocities against Dalits. Faced, however, with massive protest marches and an all-India shutdown of services on April 3, 2018, it finally did ask the Court, under severe duress, to reconsider its mandate. See Wani and Lal (2020).

[18] An excellent study is Citizens Against Hate (2017).

[19] See Indian Express (2018, 9). See also Jha (2016) for statistics on cases registered for atrocities against Dalits and Adivasi/tribals, their non-resolution, and the widespread ignorance among Dalits about their basic constitutional rights.

172   *Tanika Sarkar*

if Muslims had abducted portions of the divine feminine body to form their Pakistan. From now on, this became the supreme sign of Muslim sinfulness, the culmination of a centuries-long assault on nation and faith – beginning with Muslim invasions and now climaxing with a physical vivisection. The RSS worships the map of undivided Bharat – India – and refuses to accept the reality of partition (T.Sarkar 2001). M. S. Golwalkar, the most important architect of the RSS, called partition the "rape" of the motherland (Andersen and Damle 2005, 29).

Though both sides were equally combative in 1946–47, Hindutva has steadfastly maintained that Hindus were the sole victims of partition violence.[20] Since then, several wars with Pakistan, conflicts over the possession of the erstwhile independent kingdom of Kashmir (which, along with the northeastern states, remains under virtual army rule), and, more recently, terror attacks[21] have further strengthened the older narrative of Islamophobia, wherein ordinary Indian Muslims of our times are made to stand in for partition rioters as well as for contemporary terrorists. Interestingly, those very Indian Muslims who did not migrate to Pakistan and chose to stay on in India even as a small and beleaguered minority are the very people who are branded as global terrorists – a covert fifth column of invading enemies.

Each Indian Muslim also stands in for medieval Muslim imperial dynasties and for representing demons of Hindu mythology. Hindutva "history" thus erases the borders between history and myths, belief and reality. In 1992, when the Babri Mosque was demolished to make room for a temple for Lord Ram – divine incarnation and epic hero – the Muslim was metaphorically merged with the demons whom Ram had vanquished.[22] All these substitutions partly explain the ease with which Muslims are brutalized these days. Lynch mobs can always tell themselves that they are "killing demons."

As large numbers of Muslims migrated to Pakistan after 1947, Indian Muslims were reduced to a small numerical minority without a national-level party,[23] and they had marked social, educational, and economic disadvantages.[24] Despite their

---

[20] In Punjab, in the north, for instance, by March 1948, 6 million Muslims and 4.5 million Hindus and Sikhs had become refugees; the Muslims outnumbered the others considerably (S.Sarkar 1983, 434).

[21] The last large-scale attack was in 2008, at Mumbai. Interestingly, Pakistan faces far more numerous and continuous terror attacks by "Islamicist" forces.

[22] Hindutva organizations propagated the spurious argument that the sixteenth-century Babri Mosque in the North Indian city of Ayodhya was built by the Mughal emperor Babur by demolishing an ancient temple that commemorated the birthplace of the divine incarnation of Ram, a demon-slaying royal figure in a Hindu epic. From 1986, they built up mass campaigns for the demolition of the mosque, which was ultimately accomplished, amidst great violence against Muslims, in 1992. The Ramjanambhumi movement exemplified the triumphant merging of historical, mythological, and contemporary figures. See N.Bhattacharya (1991).

[23] According to the 2011 census, Hindus constitute an overwhelming 79.8 percent of the total population of India; Muslims 14.23 percent; and Christians 2.3 percent (Ministry of Home Affairs 2011).

[24] This is abundantly demonstrated by the 2011 Sachar Committee Report on the status of the minorities (Prime Minister's High-Level Committee 2006).

profound vulnerabilities, Hindutva history continues to represent them, with ever-strengthening emphasis, as perpetual aggressors, invaders, and agents of terror. The more they become helpless in the face of the supreme electoral power and clout that the BJP now exercises against them, the more we hear of their eternal wrongdoing.

Hindutva invests Indian Christians with a different image. Although Christianity struck roots in parts of India from ancient times, the Sangh insists on equating Indian Christianity with British imperialism and European missionaries; in other words, Indian Christians are made to signify Western cultural conquest of Hindu faith. Missionaries often educated segments of marginalized Adivasi/tribal communities in remote regions, as well as "low" and untouchable castes, thus breaching, to an extent, the control of upper-caste Hindus over these deprived communities. They represented, therefore, a particularly grave danger to Hindu social leaders. After independence, conversions away from Hinduism were viewed with the deepest suspicion, and several Indian states passed laws to constrain them. On the other hand, Hindutva evangelists are encouraged to promote conversions from other faiths (Chatterji 2009). In order to wean Adivasi – too often brutally dispossessed of land and forest rights in the interests of corporate capital investment – from Christian influence, Hindutva runs projects to merge their traditional belief and worship systems with a Hindu theogony (Thomas 2019). In the hill state of Himachal Pradesh, at Kulu, RSS ideologues join hands with local subaltern traditional prophets and ex-kings to reinterpret divine messages and align them to a Hindu divine order (Berti 2006). Annexation of tribal deities and beliefs into a Hindu belief structure substitutes for transformation of their real material deprivations.

The distinctive politics of Hindutva combines older Hindu orthodox traits of caste and gender discipline, though cleverly camouflaged, and a pronounced authoritarian imperative in a world now dominated by multinational capital. Communalism, parading as defense of faith and traditional values, provides the moral cement that binds the two together, enabling Hindutva's simultaneous success among ordinary Hindus and among corporate capital (see also Hansen 1998).

Hindutva's women's organizations – Rashtrasevika Samiti (T.Sarkar 2005, 178–93) or Durga Vahini (Paheja 2012) – do allow women a public identity in shared communal politics. But that is framed within a systematic inculcation of domesticity, chastity, obedience, and piety.

At the same time, conventional womanly religious duties are transvalued. Golwalkar asked women to produce and train children in Sangh values. He invested Hindu motherhood with political functions and aims (Golwalkar 1996). Savarkar found women at their most beautiful when they nurse their babies at their breast. But, she must feed her infants, he said, like the lioness who sits on the mangled remains of her kill and nurtures her cubs on that bloody site: so that they learn the need for violence at their earliest infancy and defend their holy nation when they grow up. Maternalism, in Hindutva discourses, is a nationalist-religious activity, born and bred in anger, for the purpose of instilling the killer instinct in the infant (Agarwal 1995).

HINDUTVA'S THEOLOGY

Does Hindutva have its distinctive religious vision and interpretation of Hindu theology? The RSS prides itself on its liberalism toward all religions (T.Basu et al. 1993, 56–111). But if we look more closely at its oral and written texts, we find that the vaunted openness is actually and exclusively restricted to an accommodation of Hindu religious diversity alone (T.Basu et al. 1993, 12–55). If the Ram cult, with its firm base in North India, has been the dominant inspiration behind recent violent campaigns, the sacrality of other deities – Ganesh, Shiva, Kali, or Durga, for instance – is also fully acknowledged and kept in reserve for possible violent use. Hindutva is not partisan so far as Hindu sects and cults are concerned. It takes no particular stand on the multiplicity of Hindu doctrinal debates, ranging from image worship to monism and spanning innumerable divisions among Hindu sects. The vast Hindu cosmogony and diverse liturgical-ritual practices are treated with perfect neutrality; the validity of none is denied.

Such internal liberalism has a peculiar effect, which goes largely unnoticed. Hinduism has been, from early times, a contested world, divided among many sects, beliefs, practices, and gods. (In fact, what became known from the nineteenth century as Hinduism had been, in premodern times, a conglomeration of sects, cults, and extremely heterogeneous beliefs and practices, loosely bound by certain sacred texts and by the pervasive practice of caste hierarchies (Sen 2005).) Hindutva's accommodation of all on equal terms actually amounts to an elimination of older, intense preoccupation with metaphysical-philosophical-doctrinal as well as with sectarian concerns. Its "history" now overshadows religious doctrine.[25] Such over-fullness of Hindu diversity actually is another name for emptiness. Religious thought becomes a vast and empty shell, with no swell or flow of life running through it. As we will see, however, the formal unification of Hindu multifariousness still insidiously restores the primacy of certain ritual and mythological preferences that shore up the authority of Brahmanical myths and priesthood.

Walter K. Andersen and Shridhar D. Damle (1987) have tried to endow the RSS with a spiritual vision and a definite theological perspective, associated with the most abstract and rationalist of Hindu philosophical systems: that of Advaita monism, or the principle of non-division between the souls of the Creator and the created, between divinity and devotee.[26] They offer a most eclectic and a rather confused lineage for Hindutva, from the *Upanishads* to the *Gita* and thence to medieval devotional Bhakti streams of thought, which posited a direct, unmediated relation-

---

[25] In 2008–9, I visited RSS bookshops in Delhi and found not a single religious text there, either in Sanskrit or in Hindi vernacular. When I asked priests at a VHP temple at Ramakrishnapuram in Delhi about the significance of idols there and about their mythological referents, they proved extremely vague and uncaring.

[26] For an elaboration of these terms, see, for instance, Hildebeitel (2011) or Olivelle (2009).

Religious Nationalism in India

ship between God and devotee. There is little evidence, however, that any RSS ideologue ever reflected seriously or publicly on such questions. Even Golwalkar, who had briefly joined the Advaita-oriented Ramakrishna Mission briefly in his youth, never discussed monism.

Andersen and Damle base their notion of an Advaitist affiliation because of Hindutva's evocation of the concept of *chiti*, or a single, all-encompassing soul. What they choose to overlook, however, is that *chiti* does not indicate a non-divided cosmic soul or universal principle.[27] Golwalkar refers to a single soul that animates the entire Hindu *nation*. "The same philosophy of life, the same goal, the same supremacy of the inner spirit over the outer gross things of matter, the same faith in rebirth,[28] the same adoration of certain qualities like *brahmacharya*, *satya* etc,[29] the same holy *samskaras*[30] – in short, the same life blood flowed through all the limbs of our society" (Golwalkar 1966, 102). So *chiti* actually implies a monolithic nation. Golwalkar goes on to say that sages should interpret laws and act as custodians of the "national soul" (Golwalkar 1966, 102). Sages were, by definition, Brahmans, the "purest" caste. Implicitly, then, this acknowledges the monopoly of Brahmans over sacred truth. He also privileges celibacy as well as *samaskaras*, which refer actually to Hindu life cycle rites, thus restoring the conventional ritual order as well as caste and gender-based differences, since the rites are differentiated along caste and gender axes.

"We want a 'living' God," said Golwalkar. He called the nation that god. The ideal RSS man must free himself from all other attachments and dedicate himself to the cause of the divine mother or nation (Golwalkar 1966, 29). Durkheim had argued that each religious community casts God in the image of the social form that it inhabits: "It reflects all of its aspects, even the most vulgar and the most repulsive" (Durkheim 1965, 415–47). The nation god of Hindutva is the community or the society of Hindus.

Golwalkar repeatedly warned about enemies who threaten the indivisible unity of the holy substance or who contaminate *chiti* with alien religious doctrines. The ideal Hindu has to be a disciplined warrior, ever ready to confront and vanquish them (Golwalkar 1996, 19). War against Muslims, or non-Hindus in general, is thereby inscribed into Hindutva as its central mode of worship. Pogroms constitute the new ritual (Andersen and Damle 2005, 29).

Andersen and Damle describe the RSS as egalitarian in its social principles. They cite from Golwalkar:

[27] The concept was elaborated by Deen Dayal Upadhyay, founder of Bharatiya Jana Sangh, a precursor of the BJP (Upadhyay 1968, 52).

[28] This is the unique Hindu philosophy of the cycle of rebirths wherein one's station in this life is decided by the nature of one's actions in the past birth and will, in turn, decide one's situation in the next birth. The principle has always been a theodicy to explain caste inequality.

[29] Purity and truth, both being associated with Brahmanical virtues.

[30] *Samskara* is a ritual order that is focused on essential life cycle rites.

The feeling of inequality, of high and low, which has crept into the Varna system[31] is comparatively of recent origin ... But in its original form, the distinctions in social order did not imply any discrimination of big or small, high or low ... On the other hand, the Gita tells us that the individual who does his assigned duties in life in a spirit of selfless service only worships God through such performance. (Andersen and Damle 1996, 81)

At first sight, then, caste is depicted as nondiscriminatory. But is that a recipe for egalitarianism, or is it a strategy that cloaks real material, social, and moral stigma and deprivation under imagined harmony – not canceling inequality but rather making it appear unimportant and thereby, giving it new life? Golwalkar immediately goes on to hide inequality under a common mission that should unite all Hindus, even as it leaves their blatant divisions intact: all castes, the beggar (obviously the Shudra untouchable) and the great scholar (by definition, the Brahman), can come together on the basis of their great love for the "Nation-God" (Golwalkar 1966, 107). Nation worship takes care of the caste problem.

THE VHP AND HINDUTVA'S RITUAL PRACTICES

If the RSS neither interpreted nor reformed religion but left its orthodox principles implicitly unchallenged, what about the Vishwa Hindu Parishad, or the VHP, which was founded in 1964 as the ecclesiastical wing of the Sangh (T.Basu et al. 1993, 56–111; Jaffrelot 2005b, 319–40)? It originally aimed at replacing Christian missionary activism in the northeastern states where Christianity is widespread, and which have seen insurrectionary movements for secession from India. It was born, therefore, with intertwined political and religious ambitions that encompass the entire global Hindu diaspora. Swami Chinmayananda, an ascetic and founder of the VHP, came up with elaborate plans for counter-conversions of Christians to Hinduism. These were immediately blessed and incorporated into the RSS agenda. S. S. Apte, RSS *pracharak*, became the main architect of counter-conversion plans henceforth, naming them as Ghar Wapsi or homecoming – on the assumption that becoming a Hindu is the natural state of being for all Indians. At its first World Hindu Conference at the pilgrim city of Allahabad in 1966, 25,000 delegates from as many sects were brought together under its overarching rubric. Even the Ramakrishna Mission, a highly respected global Advaitist monastic organization famed for philanthropic and intellectual activities – and not in the least associated with any form of mob violence – cooperated with VHP projects in Nagaland and in

---

[31] *Varna* refers to the ancient Hindu hierarchical principle by which the entire society was seen as a single body, created from God's body. From his head came the purest of all, the Brahmans; from his arms were born the warrior Kshatriyas; from his thighs came Vaishyas or traders; and from his feet, the Shudras or manual workers. Thus was social precedence, the order of high and low, decided, according to the most ancient holy texts. The untouchables were beyond the fourfold order, too polluted to count within it. Later the *varnas* fragmented into multiple *jatis*, or subcastes, who were carefully placed within the broad caste hierarchy.

Religious Nationalism in India

Arunachal Pradesh in the northeast (Kanungo 2012, 134–37; Thomas 2019). From the outset, then, the VHP's religion was combative and confrontational.

Female ascetics have been star activists and mass mobilizers for violent VHP campaigns (T.Sarkar 2001, 412–32). In an audiocassette released shortly before October 30, 1990, in tandem with the peaking of the Ramjanambhoomi movement for the demolition of the Babri Mosque and broadcast repeatedly from temples in North India, Saddhi Rithambhara, a VHP woman ascetic, issued a clarion call to violence against Muslims: *Khoon kharapa hona hai to ekbaar ho jaane do* ("If there must be bloodshed, then let it happen here and now"). A chief speaker at a VHP rally at India Gate on April 4, 1991, when the VHP and BJP publicly expressed mutual support for demolition, her harsh and long speech, seemingly cracking under the strain of a terrible emergency, called mothers to see themselves as wombs that will give birth to anger and revenge. It also called upon men to make themselves into a clenched fist, fixed in furious resolve. In her eyes, men, women, and children are but embodied anger and hatred. The speech was played from temple loudspeakers when all else failed to bring forth riots in places that had never witnessed communal violence. Temples also played recorded simulated riot sounds between 1990 and 1992 with female voices apparently crying out for help against Muslim attacks on them. This, too, incited much violence. Videocassettes like *Bhaye Prakat Kripala* and *Pran Jaye Par Vachan Na Jay* were widely circulated by Jain Studios to bolster the appeal for demolishing the Babri Mosque. They showed Ram as a homeless baby – irresistibly delightful, and heartbreakingly appealing, pleading with devotees to grant him a temple home by destroying the mosque (T.Basu et al. 1993). Media technology was skillfully used to create a virtual reality, to stimulate passionate emotional-devotional responses that could instantly turn manufactured fears into aggression. Contemporary social media, with its huge possibilities for circulating fake audiovisual news, now steps in to form instant aggressive communities, bound together by an infinitely elastic, global dis/information circuit.

The VHP organizes annual conclaves of ascetics and sect leaders who formally bless its violent projects. The 1979 VHP conference was attended by 100,000 Hindu leaders, and it has steadily grown in strength since then. It has its own branches like the Durga Vahini, the women's wing, and the Bajrang Dal, the youth wing. It trains temple as well as domestic priests, gaining a foothold in public and private worship, implicating them deeply in its agenda. In 2002, shortly after the huge anti-Muslim carnage in Gujarat, I saw a Delhi temple advertising "self-defense" combat training to Hindu youths. Bajrang Dal cadres told us that their function is to organize violence – what they called "tit for tat" (T.Basu et al. 1993). The Delhi VHP leader, B. L. Sharma Prem, told us in 1990 that the outfit exists to prepare Hindus in violence against Muslims.[32] Durga Vahini trains young girls in

---

[32] This was when we were researching material for T.Basu et al. (1993).

178 *Tanika Sarkar*

gun fight and instills deep communal hatred and fears at regular camp sessions.[33] The largest chain of temples in North India, Sanatan Dharm temples, proclaimed their allegiance to the Sangh Parivar and applauded VHP campaigns against Muslims and Christians (T.Basu et al. 1993). The VHP, therefore, unifies a highly diverse world of global Hindu institutions on the basis of communal hatred: bringing together orthodox, image-worshipping Sanatan Dharm bodies with the reformist and monotheistic Arya Samaj. It has also formed cells among Sikh institutions.

The VHP organizes a violent Hindu will by mobilizing its guardian angels – accredited and respected sectarian heads and priests. It also penetrates everyday household practices, providing a minimum code of conduct for all Hindus: sun worship, twice a day; making the traditional auspicious om symbol highly visible and ubiquitous in public places, among households and on personal wear; daily worship of the central sacred text *Gita* for every Hindu household, and of the sacred *tulsi* plant: frequent pilgrimages and a domestic shrine in each home (Jaffrelot 2005b, 319–40). By recombining traditional Hindu ritual practices in a slightly different order, it plugs into the comfort zone of devotional familiarity but, at the same time, it leaves its own small icons all over this well-known world: pictures of the Ram temple, which should be built on the site of the demolished mosque; pictures of the baby Ram and of the warrior Ram (T.Basu et al. 1993, 56–111).

The RSS observes six annual religious-nationalistic festivals: Navaratri-Vijaya Dashami in autumn, when the divine incarnation Ram was enthroned; Makar Sankranti in January, to celebrate "integral nationalism"; Varsh Pratipada in April, when Yudhisthira, an epic monarch, and King Vikramaditya supposedly inaugurated the Hindu calendar; Hindu Samrajya Diwas, to celebrate the sixteenth-century Maratha warrior hero Shivaji; Rakshabandhan in August, to remind the RSS of its duty to sacrifice life and to protect the honor of Hindu society; and Vyas Puja in September, when the RSS saffron flag is worshipped and donations are collected (T.Basu et al. 1993; Jaffrelot 2005b, 319–40; Mathur 2008, 1–49; Tyagi 2016).

Though some are added and subtracted from time to time, the purpose and the format of this rather strange medley of traditional ritual events and RSS political commemorations remain constant. The first occasion is strictly a major public traditional worship. The second is a traditional religious ritual that now goes under the name of an important RSS political treatise. The third is a freshly minted event, meant to publicize a Hindu temporality within an epic-mythological cast. The fourth celebrates Shivaji, who fought the Mughals, as a Hindu empire builder. His historical feat is recast as a religious occasion. The fifth is a widespread Hindu ritual event when brothers tie a band on the wrists of their sisters. It is sometimes associated with a Rajput custom, dating from Mughal times, when queens of embattled Hindu kingdoms appealed to other royal clans for protection. The

---

[33] See actual footage of camp activities in Paheja (2012).

latter pledged help by tying a *rakhi* or silken band on their wrists as a sign of fictive kinship between brother and sister. The RSS remaking of this traditional event is a reminder of how Hindu women's honor is supposedly threatened by Muslims and how the RSS is replicating the honorable duties of Rajput kings. The sixth is a purely practical RSS fundraising event that gains sacrality by its incorporation into the new ritual calendar.

This curious amalgamation of the religious, the ritualistic, and the political-communal actually represents the reconstituted Hindu world in the microcosm of public religious festivals. By displaying as well as hiding its own indelible, yet small footprint within a larger and familiar Hindu universe of festivities, it develops a rather unusual strategy of appropriation and self-publicization: of "steadfastly refusing claims to originality and innovation" and also "dispersing its own agenda among as widely spread out network as possible of Hindu institutions" (T.Basu et al. 1993, 59) – to present its own work as the Hindu general will, which is always already there.

HINDUTVA'S SELF-REPRESENTATION

Hindutva has a strange relationship with religion that has gone through several historical twists and turns. Since Savarkar, who defined Hindutva as national culture rather than faith and then immediately described the national in religious terms, Hindu extremists have persisted in this uneasy relationship with faith: partly sliding away from it, yet, insistently returning to claim its beliefs, rituals, sacred spaces, and times. Last year, the head of the powerful Gorakhnath sect, Yogi Adityanath, was made the chief minister of Uttar Pradesh, leaving none in doubt of a theocratic bent in the BJP, which otherwise claims a modernized self-image under Modi.

And yet, there are always traces of the early reserve and distance. Such a guerrilla tactic was necessary, because India has always been a land of many cultures and faiths. Because Hindutva wants to represent Hinduism as well as the Indian nation, it has to show its ownership of a multifaceted country and also to declare its possession of a particular faith, until such time as it manages to close the gap between the two entirely.

Savarkar moved restlessly from the faith and ritual of Hindus to an essential cultural core that would, hopefully, be common to all Indian patriots. He wanted to marginalize philosophical-mystical-devotional resources of Hinduism, its quietistic and intellectual aspects, as no more than individual quirks that were of little importance to the people as a whole. With what would he replace them? He initiated a two-way process. India becomes the sacred geography of Hindus, while the Hindu faith is overwritten by Indian nationalism. In a penultimate move, he defined both Hindutva and Indianness as an inherited affiliation to the land, a patrimonial inheritance: land of our fathers, land of our action – *pitribhu*, *karmabhu*. This, however, would render Hindutva wide open to all who have lived and worked in India. In a final masterstroke, he avoided that peril by making it the land of our gods – *punyabhu* – and, consequently, of those alone whose places of worship are restricted within its territorial boundaries.

As we saw, hatred of the enemy kept the national structure intact, torn as it is between religious particularities and national wholeness. How is hatred produced, especially toward people who are not aliens or invaders and who are far more vulnerable and disempowered than Hindus (at least than upper-caste and upper-class leaders)? In place of doctrine, dogma, and theology, Savarkar defined the Hindu community through "history" – history that produces a single-minded Hindu will to violence. The RSS continues with that. This history is told in its daily sessions, at devotional congregations, in children's literature, on websites, in RSS school textbooks, in government-sponsored textbooks in BJP-ruled states. Drawing its elements from a diffused popular common sense, it builds on it, tweaking around some of the points, altering and modifying others, combining separate elements to produce a new bricolage out of familiar stories. Because the constituent elements are already familiar, the new assemblage easily gains traction in popular conviction. Its sources are historical fiction and fictionalized histories, discrete fragments from myths and legends, political gossip, rumors, fake news. All histories reiterate the same story: unprovoked Muslim attacks and necessary Hindu reprisals.

From faith to community, from community to nation, from Indian nation to Hindu nation – in this transvaluation of Hindu faith, protagonists of Hindu Rashtra actually take on an impossibility: Hindutva has to appear as the general will of *both* faith and nation, of Hindus and India, since both, ultimately, are one in their vision. The universality of the claim must annihilate and disavow that which disrupts or questions its completion, its absolute fullness.

So, Hindu India is haunted by two separate orders of particularities: (1) the "low caste," the poor, the non-communalized Hindu, whose existence reveals the class-caste-ideological particularities of Hindutva that its Hindu universality tries to conceal; and (2) by Indian Christians and Muslims, whose presence contradicts Hindutva's claim to Indian universality. Hindutva tries to defend the twin particularities by the theory of miscegenation among Hindus and with the image of the threat of Others, who reside in the nation only in order to demolish it.

This is a difficult claim to sustain, as it is contradicted by the lived experiences of so many Hindus who have vivid memories and experiences of struggles, work, and culture that they have shared with other communities. Hindus also have equally vivid memories of oppression, exploitation, and humiliation received from the hands of other Hindus. Hindus must necessarily inhabit what Gramsci has described as contradictory consciousness, which sets limits against Hindutva's hegemony over Hindus.

That, however, may not demolish their strength as many secularists like to imagine. In a tortuous manner, the very multifariousness of subjectivities,

Religious Nationalism in India

identities, and locations may lead to a terror about fragmented selves and strengthen an identity politics whose violence is necessary to stabilize a centered selfhood.[34] So, on one hand, the Hindu/Indian self is perpetually stained by particularities of both Hindus and Indians, and Hindu Rashtra's self-image is doomed to be haunted by what it tries to abolish. On the other hand, the staining lends itself to a shrill paranoia, feeding from doubled sources. Its impossible claim constitutes, in the same move, the strength and the limits of Hindutva.

REFERENCES

Agarwal, Purushottam. 1995. "Surat, Savarkar and Draupadi: Legitimising Rape as a Political Weapon." In *Women and the Hindu Right*, edited by Tanika Sarkar and Urvashi Butalia, 29–57. Delhi: Kali for Women.

Andersen, Walter K., and Shridhar D. Damle. 1987. *The Brotherhood in Saffron: The Rashtriya Swayamsevak Sangh and Hindu Revivalism.* Boulder, CO: Westview Press.

1996. *The Brotherhood in Saffron: The Rashtriya Swayamsevak Sangh and Hindu Revivalism.* Reprint. Delhi: Penguin Books.

2005. "RSS: Ideology, Organization, and Training." In *The Sangh Parivar: A Reader – Critical Issues in Indian Politics*, edited by Christophe Jaffrelot, 23–55. Delhi: Oxford University Press.

Anderson, Benedict. 1961. *Imagined Communities.* London: Verso.

Ayyub, Rana. 2016. *Gujarat Files: Anatomy of a Cover Up.* CreateSpace. Kindle.

Basu, Amrita. 2015. *Violent Conjunctures in Democratic India.* New York: Cambridge University Press.

Basu, Tapan, Pradip Datta, Sumit Sarkar, Tanika Sarkar, and Sambuddha Sen. 1993. *Khaki Shorts, Saffron Flags: A Critique of the Hindu Right.* Delhi: Orient Longman.

Bauman, Zygmunt. 1992. *Mortality, Immortality and Other Life Strategies.* Stanford: Stanford University Press.

Berti, Daniela. 2006. "The Memory of Gods: From a Secret Autobiography to a Nationalist Project." *Indian Folklife* 24: 15–18.

Bhattacharya, Neeladri. 1991. "Myth, History and the Politics of Ramjanambhoomi." In *Anatomy of a Confrontation: The Babri-Masjid-Ram Janambhumi Movement*, edited by S. Gopal, 122–40. Delhi: Penguin Books.

Bhattacharya, Sabyasachi. 2003. *Vande Mataram: Biography of a Song.* Delhi: Penguin Books.

Bhishikar, C. P. 1979. *Keshav: Sangh Nirmata.* New Delhi: Suruchi Sahitya Prakashan.

Breuilly, John. 1996. "Approaches to Nationalism." In *Mapping the Nation*, edited by G. Balakrishnan, 146–74. London: Verso.

Chatterji, Angana. 2009. *Violent Gods: Hindu Nationalism in India's Present.* Delhi: Three Essays Collective.

Citizens Against Hate. 2017. *Lynching without End: Fact Finding Investigation into Religiously Motivated Vigilante Violence in India.* September 2017 Report. Delhi: Citizens Against Hate.

Dixit, Neha. 2014. "Love Jihad: War on Romance in India." *Al Jazeera*, October 14. www.aljazeera.com/indepth/features/2014.

---

[34] On the fear of dissolving identity boundaries, see S.Sarkar (1999).

Durkheim, Emile. 1965. *The Elementary Forms of Religious Life: A Study in Religious Society.* London: Allen and Unwin.

Golwalkar, Madhav Sadashiv. 1939. *We or Our Nationhood Defined.* Nagpur: Bharat Prakashan.

1966. *Bunch of Thoughts.* Bangalore: Vikrama Prakashan.

1996. *Bunch of Thoughts.* 3rd ed. Bangalore: Sahitya Sindhu Prakashan.

Gopal, Sarvepalli, ed. 1992. *Anatomy of A Confrontation: Ayodhya and the Rise of Communal Politics in India.* London: Zed Books.

Gupta, Charu. 2001. *Sexuality, Obscenity, Community: Women, Muslims and the Hindu Public Sphere in Colonial India.* Delhi: Permanent Black.

Hansen, Thomas Blom. 1998. "The Ethics of Hindutva and the Spirit of Capitalism." In *The BJP and the Compulsions of Politics in India,* edited by Thomas B. Hansen and Christophe Jaffrelot, 291–314. Delhi: Oxford University Press.

1999. *The Saffron Wave: Democracy and Hindu Nationalism in Modern India.* Princeton: Princeton University Press.

Hildebeitel, Alf. 2011. *Dharma: Its Early History in Law, Religion and Narrative.* New York: Oxford University Press.

Indian Express. 2018. "Dalit Protests: BSP Leader among 100 Held for Inciting Hapur Protests" [Delhi edition]. April 7.

Jaffrelot, Christophe. 2005b. "The Vishva Hindu Parishad: Structures and Strategies." In *The Sangh Parivar: A Reader – Critical Issues in Indian Politics,* edited by Christophe Jaffrelot, 318–34. Delhi: Oxford University Press.

Jaffrelot, Christophe, ed. 2005a. *The Sangh Parivar: A Reader – Critical Issues in Indian Politics.* Delhi: Oxford University Press.

Jalal, Ayesh. 1985. *The Sole Spokesman: Jinnah, Muslim League and the Demand for Partition.* New York: Cambridge University Press.

Jha, Satish. 2016. "Village of Una Attack Accused, Upper Castes Angry, Dalits Afraid." Report of September 8. Reproduced in *The Indian Express* [Online edition], December 4, 2020.

Joshi, Suresh. 2017. *RSS Annual Report.* Coimbatore.

Kanungo, Pralay. 2012. "Fusing the Ideals of the Math with the Ideology of the Sangh." In *Public Hinduisms,* edited by J. Zavos, P. Kanungo, D. Reddy, M. Warrior, and R. B. Williams, 119–40. Delhi: Sage.

Krishnan, Kavitha. 2017. "Hadiya's Choices." *The Indian Express* [Delhi edition], November 30.

Mander, Harsh, John Dayal, and Kavita Shrivastava. 2017. "Rajasthan Hate Murder: The Other Tragedy in Afrazul's Killing is a Famine of Compassion, Outrage." Scroll.in, December 18. https://scroll.in/article/861826/rajasthan-hate-murder-the-other-tragedy-in-afrazul-khans-murder-is-a-famine-of-compassion-outrage.

Mathur, Shubh. 2008. *The Everyday Life of Hindu Nationalism: An Ethnographic Account.* Delhi: Three Essays Collective.

McKean, Lise. 1996. *Divine Enterprise: Gurus and the Hindu Nationalist Movement.* Chicago: University of Chicago Press.

Ministry of Home Affairs. 2011. "Population Enumeration Data: Final Population." Government of India. www.censusindia.gov.in/2011census/population_enumeration.html.

Olivelle, Patric. 2009. *Dharma: Studies in Its Semantic, Cultural and Legal History.* Delhi: Motilal Banarasidas.

Paheja, Nisha, dir. 2012. *The World Before Her.* Toronto: Kino Smith.

Pandey, Gyan. 1983. "Rallying Round the Cow Sectarian Strife in the Bhojpuri Region, c. 1888–1917." In vol. 2 of *Subaltern Studies: Writings on South Asian History and Society,* edited by R. Guha, 60–129. Delhi: Oxford University Press.

Prime Minister's High-Level Committee. 2006. *Social, Economic and Educational Status of the Muslim Community of India*. Government of India. www.minorityaffairs.gov.in/sites/default/files/sachar_comm.pdf.

Roy, Esha. 2018. "In Run-Up to Polls, How BJP Built Its Army for Battle against Left." *The Indian Express* [Delhi edition], February 11. http://epaper.indianexpress.com/1539665/Jaipur/February-11,-2018.

Sarkar, Adity. 2018. "The Authoritarian Handbook." Paper presented at the University of Edinburgh, Scotland. February.

Sarkar, Sumit. 1983. *Modern India*. London: Macmillan.

1999. "Conversions and the Politics of the Hindu Right." *Economic and Political Weekly* 34, no. 26. www.epw.in/journal/1999/26/special-articles/conversions-and-politics-hindu-right.html.

Sarkar, Tanika. 2001. "Aspects of Contemporary Hindutva Theology: The Voice of Saddhvi Rithambhara." In *Charisma and Canon: Essays on the Religious History of the Indian Subcontinent*, edited by Vasudha Dalmia, Angelika Malinar, and Martin Christof, 412–32. Delhi: Oxford University Press.

2005. "The Gender Predicament of the Hindu Right." In *The Sangh Parivar: A Reader – Critical Issues in Indian Politics*, edited by Christopher Jaffrelot, 178–93. Delhi: Oxford University Press.

2009. *Rebels, Wives, Saints: Designing Selves and Nations in Colonial Times*. Ranikhet, India: Permanent Black.

Savarkar, Vinayak Damodar. (1923) 1969. *Hindutva: Who Is a Hindu?* 5th ed. Bombay: Veer Savarkar Prakashan. https://archive.org/details/hindutva-vinayak-damodar-savarkar-pdf/.

1970. *Six Glorious Epochs of Indian History*. Delhi: Rajdhani Granthagar.

Sen, Amartya. 2005. *The Argumentative Indian*. New York: Farrar, Straus, and Giroux.

Smith, Anthony D. 1998. *Nationalism and Modernism: A Critical Survey of Recent Theories of Nations and Nationalisms*. London: Routledge.

Taylor, Charles. 1999. "Nationalism and Modernity." In *Theorizing Nationalism*, edited by Ronald Beiner, 219–45. Albany: SUNY Press.

Thomas, John. 2019. "From Sacred Rocks to Temple: Recasting Religious Identity in North Eastern India." In *Landscape, Culture and Belonging: Writing the History of Northeast India*, edited by Neeladri Bhattacharya and Joy Pachuau, 314–32. Delhi: Cambridge University Press.

Tyagi, Aastha. 2016. "Sadhana Karte Chalein." MPhil diss., Department of Sociology, University of Delhi.

Upadhyay, Deen Dayal. 1968. *Integral Humanism*. Delhi: Navchetan Press.

Vanaik, Achin. 2017. *Hindutva Rising: Secular Claims, Communal Realities*. Delhi: Tulika Books.

van der Veer, Peter. 1994. *Religious Nationalism: Hindus and Muslims in India*. Berkeley: University of California Press.

Waughrey, Annapurna. 2018. "Caste in Britain: Public Consultation on Caste and Equality Law." *Economic and Political Weekly*, March 10.

Wani, Javed Iqbal, and L. David Lal. 2020. "The Precarity of Dalit Lives in India." *The Indian Express* [Online edition], October 27.

Whimster, Sam, ed. 2004. *The Essential Weber: A Reader*. London: Routledge.

PART III

Sri Lanka

8

The Genesis, Consolidation, and Consequences of Sinhalese Buddhist Nationalism

Neil DeVotta

There was much reason for optimism in 1948 when Sri Lanka, then called Ceylon, achieved independence. Notwithstanding some prior tensions between the majority Sinhalese and minority Tamils rooted in political representation, elites from both communities joined hands to ensure power transferred from the British to locals. That this transition took place peacefully, without the ruckus and violence associated with British India's independence, also bode well for the island. As the political scientist and future American ambassador to Sri Lanka, William Howard Wriggins (1961, 314), noted, "Of all the new Asian countries, Ceylon seemed to have the best chance of making a successful transition to modern statehood. It began its independence most auspiciously with seasoned leadership drawn from nearly all ethnic groups." Additionally, 60 percent of its people were literate at independence; the country had practiced universal suffrage starting in 1931; and "per capita GNP was higher than in any other country in the area apart from Japan" (Wriggins 1961, 314).

By the time Wriggins wrote this, however, Sri Lanka had passed a bill that made the majority community's Sinhala language the island's only official language, experienced two anti-Tamil riots in 1956 and 1958 related to linguistic nationalism, and stationed the military in the predominantly Tamil northeast to counter Tamils protesting against an increasingly ethnocentric state. Those events and attempts by successive governments to promote Sinhalese Buddhist interests at the expense of especially Tamils' aspirations led to a civil war between the government and Tamil rebels dominated by the Liberation Tigers of Tamil Eelam (LTTE) that lasted nearly three decades, killed over 100,000 people, and displaced thousands more (DeVotta 2019a, 167). The civil war ended in brutal fashion in May 2009 with the LTTE using Tamil civilians as human shields and government forces indiscriminately bombing Tamil areas without differentiating between civilians and rebels (DeVotta 2009). Notwithstanding the alleged war crimes committed by both sides, the expectation was that the end of the conflict would enable the government to deal meaningfully with Tamils' grievances. But not only have Sinhalese Buddhist nationalists opposed accommodating legitimate Tamil concerns, they have since targeted the country's Muslims, leading to scores of mosques, businesses, and homes being destroyed. Why did this island that appeared to have the capacity to make a successful transition to modern statehood squander that promise and become a reference point for ethno-religious carnage?

In seeking to explain nationalist movements and ethnic conflicts, scholars resort to constructivist, rational choice, and institutional reasoning. One could use each framework to argue why Sri Lanka regressed on the ethnic front and experienced a brutal civil war (DeVotta 2004; Horowitz 1985; Rabushka and Shepsle 1972). Every theoretical prism, however, must confront the Sinhalese Buddhist nationalist ideology and explain when, how, and why it contributed to the island's sad saga, because this ideology justifies the logic, tactics, and aspirations associated with Sinhalese Buddhist nationalists. This chapter incorporates strands of constructivist, rational choice, and institutionalist reasoning to explain the genesis, consolidation, and consequences of the Sinhalese Buddhist nationalist ideology. It argues that while this nationalist ideology has triumphed, it has done so by poisoning interethnic and interreligious relations, promoting institutional decay, and, consequently, undermining democracy and the rule of law. Sri Lanka is thus an example of how ethno-religious nationalism can triumph even as it represents well the debacle stemming from such triumphs.

THE GENESIS OF SINHALESE BUDDHIST NATIONALISM

The Portuguese, Dutch, and British had together colonized Sri Lanka for nearly 450 years when the island gained independence in 1948. Today the country's population approximates 21 million, and the following statistics speak to its complex multiethnic and multireligious character. Ethnically, the Sinhalese are 74.9 percent of the population, while Sri Lankan Tamils, Indian Tamils, and Muslims are 11.2 percent, 4.1 percent, and 9.3 percent, respectively. From a religion standpoint, Buddhists are 70.1 percent, while Hindus, Christians, and Muslims are 12.6 percent, 7.6 percent, and 9.7 percent, respectively (Department of Census and Statistics 2011). Most Sinhalese are Buddhist and speak the Sinhala language, while most Tamils are Hindu and speak Tamil. While the Sri Lankan Tamils have most likely inhabited the island since time immemorial, the British recruited Indian Tamils as indentured laborers starting around the 1830s, and they continue to be among the most marginalized communities in the country socioeconomically. The Tamil language is also the Muslims' primary language, although most Muslims under forty now speak Sinhala (DeVotta 2018, 288). But the Muslims, who are mainly of South Indian heritage, use Islam as their primary identity since doing so effectively differentiates them from the Tamil communities. The island's Christians consist of Sinhalese, Tamils, and Burghers (the latter a diminishing Eurasian demographic), with Catholics being the largest group.

THE *MAHAVAMSA* AND SINHALESE BUDDHIST IDENTITY

Scholars of ethnicity point to how ethnic identity is inherently constructed, and claims pertaining to Sinhalese origins prove the point. The Sinhalese origin myth is located in a historical text called the *Mahavamsa* (*Great Chronicle*), which documents events starting in 543 BCE, although scholars claim Buddhist monks started putting together the text only around the sixth century AD. The story of the Sinhalese in this text takes place in an area called Vanga, which gets located around the Indian state of West Bengal and Bangladesh. It revolves around the king's daughter who, as prophesied, was abducted by a lion and cohabited with it. Their son eventually killed his leonine father, returned with his mother and sister to Vanga, took over the kingdom from his grandfather, and married his sister. As one scholar has noted, this is an origin myth rooted in bestiality, parricide, and incest (Obeyesekere 1970, 45). The oldest of the twin sons resulting from the incestuous relationship is Vijaya, whose deplorable behavior causes his family to force him and his followers out of Vanga.

The *Mahavamsa* says that Vijaya landed in a Sri Lanka inhabited by demons the day Buddha died, and the dying Buddha predicted Vijaya would promote his teachings. Vijaya consorts with a demon queen and thereafter destroys the other demons on the island. He and his follows are called Sihala, in line with Vijaya's leonine origins, and become the progenitors of the Sinhalese. All this in turn led to notions of *sihadipa* (island of the Sinhalese) and *dhammadipa* (the island ennobled to preserve and propagate Buddhism).

Sri Lanka is about 22 miles from South India. Consequently, the notion that coastal South Indians, who have used catamarans for centuries to navigate the ocean, were unaware of the island or did not care to settle there until some group came from northern India approximately 2,500 years ago, is altogether implausible. Indeed, economic relations between Sri Lanka and South India even before the *Mahavamsa* was composed suggest trade likely played an important role in populating the island (C. R.De Silva 1997, 12). Accounts put together by Chinese pilgrims around the time the *Mahavamsa* was composed even claim Vijaya was of South Indian origin (Wijeyeratne 2014, 18). Thus while the *Mahavamsa* seeks to attribute a North Indian ancestry to the Sinhalese – because that geographically connects the group to Buddha – today's Sinhalese, like the Tamils, are mainly the progeny of South Indians who over time developed a unique identity after Buddhism spread and the Sinhala language (which is derived mainly from the Buddhist Pali scriptures) evolved. Over time, this new ethnicity emphasized its basic features – religion and language originating in North India – to differentiate itself from others in the region (Ponnambalam 1983; Tambiah 1986). From this standpoint, the "constructed" Sinhalese ethnicity is a more fantastic version of the invented identities one encounters around the world.

Sinhalese Buddhist nationalists have branded themselves variously when mobilizing – i.e., Bauddha Jatika Balavegaya (Buddhist National Force),

Mavbima Surakime Vyaparaya (Movement to Protect the Motherland), Sinhala Urumaya (Sinhala Heritage), Sinhala Veera Vidhana (Sinhala Heroism), and Sinhala Arakshaka Sanvidhanaya (Sinhalese Organization for Self-defense). While emphasizing different issues (i.e., Sri Lanka's status as a unitary state, threats emanating from a hegemonic India, neocolonial proclivities of Western countries, Tamil separatism) and targeting different communities (Catholics, evangelical Christians, Tamils, and Muslims), they have consistently utilized the nationalist ideology rooted in *sihadipa* and *dhammadipa*. The beliefs are so ingrained that even Buddhist monks who promote ethno-religious tolerance (Dewasiri 2016) embrace Sri Lanka's *sihadipa* and *dhammadipa* status and remain sympathetic toward the Sinhalese Buddhist nationalist ideology.

THE NATIONALIST IDEOLOGY

This nationalist ideology claims Sri Lanka is the island of the Sinhalese and chosen repository of Buddhism; Sinhalese Buddhists have been ennobled to preserve and propagate Buddhism; minorities live there thanks to Sinhalese Buddhist sufferance and must hence respect the majoritarian ethos (DeVotta 2007; DeVotta and Stone 2008; Tambiah 1992). Thus a prominent monk of the extremist Bodu Bela Sena (Buddhist Power Force, or BBS) could say:

> This is a Sinhala Buddhist country. Can you go to England or the US and say that they are a multi-religious country? Of course there are other communities in those countries, but they are Christian countries. It's the same here. Other communities have been living here, but this is a Sinhala Buddhist country. You call a coconut plantation a coconut plantation. We don't identify it by the other small plants that have grown there. (Jayasuriya 2013)

And Sarath Fonseka, who ran for the presidency and is a current member of parliament, could similarly claim (when he was commander of the army) that the "country belongs to the Sinhalese but there are minority communities and we treat them like our people . . .. They can live in the country with us. But they must not try to, under the pretext of being a minority, demand undue things" (LankaNewspapers. com 2008). Likewise, Galagoda Aththe Gnanasara, a controversial monk with the BBS, has argued: "This is a Sinhala Buddhist country. We have a Sinhala Buddhist culture. This is not Saudi Arabia. But you must accept the culture and behave in a manner that doesn't harm it" (The Economist 2013, 35).

The Sinhalese Buddhist nationalist ideology further argues that all those who challenge the hegemonic Sinhalese Buddhist position seek to diminish the pre-eminence of Buddhism and Sinhalese Buddhist predominance and are, therefore, traitors (Daily Mirror 2006; Mahindapala 2006). Those branded traitors may include minorities, nongovernmental organizations, civil society associations, journalists, and media that speak out on minorities' rights. Foreign governments that criticize human rights abuses or activities that threaten or marginalize ethnic and religious minorities also get accused of seeking to undermine the island and Buddhism. This patriot-traitor narrative ends up portraying non-Sinhalese and non-Buddhists a threat to the state. The rhetoric associated with the patriot-traitor narrative reached new heights when the Mahinda Rajapaksa government waged the no-holds-barred war against the Tamil rebels. With military personnel branded *ranawiruwo* (war heroes), all those who portrayed the military in a negative fashion were automatically branded traitors (Fernando 2005; Hewamanne 2009). This narrative continues postwar, especially when nationalists defend certain politicians and military personnel who now stand accused of sanctioning and committing war crimes.

FUSING LANGUAGE AND RELIGION

It is important to recognize that Sri Lanka's civil war was mainly ethnic, and not religion, based. It was the ginning up of linguistic nationalism by Sinhalese ethnic entrepreneurs that propelled the island toward war. From a religion standpoint, Hindu practices and beliefs have seeped into Buddhism, and the resulting syncretism prevents viscerally anti-Hindu attitudes taking root among Sri Lankan Buddhists. Similarly, while the vast majority of LTTE cadres were Hindu, the group was a strictly secular organization and its leader, Velupillai Prabhakaran, often criticized the caste divisions and gender discrimination that Hinduism influenced. The fact that many Christians, including Catholic clergy, supported the LTTE and its quest for *eelam* (a separate state) may have also conditioned its secular character.

Buddhism and monks have played important roles in galvanizing and legitimating the majority community's quest for ethnic domination. For instance, monks played a crucial role in securing sole official status for the Sinhala language in 1956 (see below), and some Buddhist clergy even sought to use the religion to promote a just-war ideology during the ethnic conflict (Bartholomeusz 2002). This was easier to do after the LTTE attacked Buddhist monks and the famous Temple of the Tooth in Kandy in 1998 as part of its terrorist activities.

Language and religion can combine in potent ways to fan nationalism. This is certainly the case when it comes to the Sinhalese, because the Sinhala language is inextricably linked to Buddhism. For it was Buddhist monks who recorded, preserved, and propagated the Buddhist scriptures in Pali; and the transformation of Pali over the centuries is what gradually gave birth to modern Sinhala. Buddhism is therefore central to Sinhala, since one could argue: no Buddhism, no Sinhala. Thus, Sinhalese Buddhist nationalism fuses religion and language, with nationalists using one or the other as primary and secondary identities depending on the situation. In this regard, Buddhism is now the primary marker, with the Sinhala language, which was the main marker of nationalism in the 1950s, taking on secondary status (DeVotta 2001).

Indeed, many Sinhalese Buddhists see country, language, and religion coalescing to create their ethnic identity, and the *Mahavamsa* has played a leading role in propagating the notion that it is the historical destiny of Sinhalese Buddhists to strengthen "the land, the race, and the faith" (Wilson 1988, 60). As the Sri Lankan historian K. M.De Silva (1981, 512) has noted, in Sinhala "the words for *nation, race* and *people* are practically synonymous" and the idea of society being multiracial or multi-communal is a "meaningless abstraction," which causes the island's Buddhists to equate Sinhalese nationalism with Sri Lankan nationalism.

The *Mahavamsa* is primarily a text designed to document and cement Buddhist origins in Sri Lanka and was also written to legitimize the rule of certain kings, but nationalists treat its contents as indisputable ethno-religious history. The origin myths stemming from the text's mythohistories now get taught in many schools as historical fact and are invoked in Buddhist sermons and political speeches. As Ernest Renan (1996, 52) noted, "Of all cults, that of the ancestors is the most legitimate, for the ancestors have made us what we are. A heroic past, great men, glory ... this is the social capital upon which one bases a national idea." The Vijaya myth, mentioned above, provides the necessary ingredients in this regard. Renan, in pointing out how ethnic identities are constructed, also noted, "getting its history wrong is part of being a nation" (Hobsbawm [1990] 1992, 12). The fictitious narratives may evolve inadvertently; but elites seeking political gain often manipulate them deliberately, and this has been the case in Sri Lanka.

IMPETUS FOR NATIONALISM

One account in the *Mahavamsa* embellished and dissembled for nationalistic purposes pertains to the second-century BCE king Duthagamani. The son of a southern ruler, he was terribly upset by the Cholas from South India usurping power in the island's then capital of Anuradhapura. The young Duthagamani, accompanied by 500 monks and with a Buddha relic attached to his spear, went to war with the much older Chola king Elara and killed him. The *Mahavamsa* says Elara was among 32 rulers Duthagamani waged battle against and that many Buddhists supported Elara. The battle may thus have been a regional affair. It is also possible that the scholar-monk Mahanama, who initiated the *Mahavamsa*, exaggerated the Duthagamani-Elara episode to overcome "sectarian struggles" within the Buddhist clergy and privilege his order at a time when it was being marginalized (Kulke 2000, 134). Whatever the reasons, nineteenth- and twentieth-century Sinhalese Buddhist nationalists emphasized the Sinhalese and Tamil identities of Duthagamani and Elara, respectively, and claimed the two groups were enemies over two millennia. And as noted below, this particular episode also provided activist Buddhist monks with fodder when justifying violence against non-Buddhist enemies.

There is no gainsaying that the mythohistorical *Mahavamsa* has provided Sri Lanka and the Sinhalese a unique identity; but the claim that the Sinhalese and Tamils were enemies in the island over two millennia is fallacious. This is because the identity the Sinhalese built over time privileged Buddhism even as it accommodated other religions and nationalities. It is telling that the kings who ruled the Kandyan Kingdom from 1739 to 1815 were South Indians who used Sinhala and Tamil as official languages and worshipped at both Hindu and Buddhist shrines. Sinhalese nobility, in the main, had no issues with Tamil sovereigns, provided they protected Buddhism. Most among them also had no problem transferring their loyalty to the British when they too promised to protect and foster Buddhism. This is not to suggest that Buddhists failed to differentiate between themselves and Tamils, Hindus, Christians, Muslims, and the British. It instead signifies that Buddhists were relatively tolerant of other ethnicities and nationalities, provided Buddhism's status in the island was undiminished. This was partly evident when the Sinhalese Buddhist kingdom of Kandy provided Muslims territory to settle in when the Portuguese and Dutch persecuted them (Dewaraja 1994). It was further evident when some Buddhist monks provided space within their temples for Christian missionaries to preach their message (Malalgoda 1976).

Yet the rise in Christian missionary activities, especially after the British unified the island in 1815, changed the extant milieu of religious tolerance. Buddhism depends on subventions from the state and alms from the laity, and historically Buddhist orders were closely associated with the ruling court. Buddhism legitimated the court, which in turn facilitated Buddhism's centrality by appointing monks to advisory roles, maintaining and building temples, and protecting Buddhist temporalities in general (DeVotta 2001, 76). The 1815 convention that led to total British rule over the island promised to sustain Buddhism, but the authorities soon reneged on their pledge. Additionally, Christian missionaries began proselytizing throughout the island, and Christian converts were provided favorable economic and civil benefits (Malalgoda 1976, 207). This took place even as colonial authorities and missionaries belittled and ridiculed Buddhism and the monks. Related to this was the buildup of Christian schools that catered mainly to Christian converts and British divide-and-rule practices that privileged Christians and Tamils within the colonial bureaucracy. All this asserted "the superiority of Christianity over other religions, and a general contempt for Oriental religions and cultures" (K. M.De Silva 1986, 7). When the monks and Buddhist scholars hit back, they used the same tactics (debates with Christian missionaries and printed materials) that the proselytizers had hitherto used. In so doing, they propagated an anti-colonial nationalism that fused Buddhism with patriotism (DeVotta 2001, 77).

Among the laity leading the assault was the Buddhist scholar Anagarike Dharmapala, who deftly crafted a religious nationalism steeped in Buddhism's virtues that enabled Sinhalese Buddhists to differentiate themselves from the British, Tamils, and Muslims and even Sinhalese Christians whose "Christian cultural markers ... [were considered] alien" (Obeyesekere 1997, 381). In this way, Dharmapala praised Buddhism and Buddhist Sinhalese, blamed the British and ethno-religious minorities, suggested Buddhism in Sri Lanka may become extinct, and hoped for a Sinhalese Buddhist ascendency. The following typified his rhetoric:

> This bright, beautiful island was made into a Paradise by the Aryan Sinhalese before its destruction was brought about by the barbaric vandals. Its people did not know irreligion .... Christianity and polytheism [Hinduism] are responsible for the vulgar practices of killing animals, stealing, prostitution, licentiousness, lying and drunkenness .... This ancient, historic, refined people, under the diabolism of vicious paganism, introduced by the British administrators, are now declining and slowly dying away. (Quoted in Guruge 1965, 482)

Dharmapala claimed that Sri Lanka flourished thanks to Buddha's influence, and Buddhist kings built all manner of infrastructure that benefitted people and brought fame to the island (quoted in Guruge 1965, 481). But non-Buddhists and colonialism compromised Buddhism and the Sinhalese, causing "the sweet, tender, gentle Aryan children of an ancient, historic race ... [to be] sacrificed at the alter of the whiskey-drinking, beef-eating, belly-god of heathenism" (quoted in Guruge 1965, 484). The so-called Buddhist revival was well under way by the time Dharmapala came along, but he was prominent in laying the groundwork for the reactive nationalism Sinhalese Buddhist activists adopted (Kemper 2015).

In addition to proselytization and the Buddhist revival, demands for local representation, often within a communal context, helped promote ethno-religious divisions – an outcome to which the British, who were maestros of dividing and ruling, were not averse. While Tamils were numerically a minority, the community viewed itself as a dominant entity, and Tamil politicians, anticipating independence, called for a 50–50 formula whereby the Sinhalese, who were nearly 65 percent of the population, would have 50 percent of representatives while the minorities shared the rest (DeVotta 2004, 36). The scheme was scuttled, and thanks to the relative confidence Tamils reposed in D. S. Senanayake, the island's first prime minister, independence was achieved seamlessly. But Senanayake died a few years following independence. In any case, the constitution the British designed prior to granting independence did not include minority guarantees, and this allowed Sinhalese Buddhist nationalists to use the "one person, one vote" principle in a parliamentary system to arrogate gains in ways that catapulted the country toward an ethnocracy and eventual civil war (DeVotta 2004; Tambiah 1986; Wilson 2000).

THE CONSOLIDATION OF SINHALESE BUDDHIST NATIONALISM

The first major riots in Sri Lanka occurred in 1883, when a noisy Buddhists' festival organized on Easter Sunday passed by the Roman Catholic cathedral in Kotahena, Colombo. A rumor that Buddhists were carrying "a cross with a monkey nailed to it and a statue resembling the Virgin Mary" no doubt fueled the violence between Buddhists and Catholics (Tambiah 1996, 51). With Catholics constituting Sinhalese and Tamils, the violence was rooted in religious divisions as opposed to ethnic rivalries. Indeed, this was mainly a riot between Sinhalese Catholics and Sinhalese Buddhists, which evidences that interreligious tensions were more acute at this point (Bartholomeusz 1995). The next major riots were between Sinhalese and Muslims in 1915 and stemmed from Muslims protesting against a Buddhist procession that bypassed their mosque. On this occasion, leading Tamil politicians were at the forefront defending their Sinhalese counterparts the British had imprisoned for alleged involvement in the rioting. Thus while the island's communities had clashed, it was not along ethnic lines and not between Sinhalese and Tamils. This changed soon after independence when Sinhalese sought to make their Sinhala language the country's only official language.

English continued to serve as the island's only official language postindependence, despite the fact only around 10 percent of the population was proficient in it. The Sinhala and Tamil languages could have replaced English, but S. W. R. D. Bandaranaike, leader of the newly formed Sri Lanka Freedom Party (SLFP), decided to ally with nationalists clamoring for a "Sinhala Only" policy as part of his quest to become prime minister (Dharmadasa 1992; Kearney 1967). The governing United National Party (UNP) had stood for linguistic parity, but when it realized how potent the "Sinhala Only" issue was, it too embraced pro-Sinhalese Buddhist policies. Both the SLFP and UNP thereafter resorted to a process of ethnic outbidding that sought to promote the interests of Sinhalese, especially at the expense of Tamils (DeVotta 2004). Bandaranaike became prime minister and passed the "Sinhala Only" Act of 1956, which made Sinhala the only official language. The first riots between Tamils and Sinhalese began as parliament debated the bill.

The "Sinhala Only" Act was the second major state-sponsored discriminatory policy geared toward ensuring Sinhalese Buddhist supremacy. The first appeared soon after independence, when the government refused to naturalize Indian Tamils, many from families who had worked for generations in the island's coffee and tea plantations. The conservative UNP and British tea-estate owners feared that citizenship and enfranchisement would cause Tamil laborers to support leftist parties demanding labor reforms, and this was a major reason they opposed naturalizing Indian Tamils. Caste considerations also influenced the upper-caste Sri Lankan Tamil elites against granting the lower-caste Indian Tamils citizenship. The rhetoric used, however, suggests that the foremost consideration was Sinhalese Buddhist concerns that a large Tamil population would vitiate their political influence (Bass 2013; Nayak 2014). This led to discussions with India to force Indian Tamils to settle there, and the efforts generated an agreement between the two countries that saw the Indian Tamil population go from 11.73 percent in 1946 to 5.52 percent in 1981 (Department of Census and Statistics 1996).

British policies led to Sri Lankan Tamils being disproportionately overrepresented in the bureaucracy, armed forces, and universities, and Sinhalese now sought to use the "Sinhala Only" Act to expand their presence in these sectors. Indeed, Bandaranaike's embrace of "Sinhala Only," the SLFP and UNP's embrace of ethnic outbidding, and the Sinhalese embrace of ethnocentrism are easily explained using rational choice theorizing. The Sinhalese support for the "Sinhala Only" policy was rational, as they stood to gain from it. Tamil opposition was likewise rational, as they stood to lose from it economically and feared "Sinhala Only" would adversely affect Tamil culture. And this is what quickly happened, with the percentage of Tamils in the bureaucracy plummeting from 30 in 1956 to 5 in 1970, and the percentage of Tamils in the armed forces from 40 in 1956 to 1 in 1970 (The Economist 2016, 31).

But the absence of any ironclad constitutional guarantees for minorities allows for an institutionalist explanation as well, because it was the institutional architecture that enabled parties and opportunistic politicians to more easily manipulate ethno-nationalist sentiment. Many in Sri Lanka like to claim majoritarianism and ethnocentrism would have been eschewed had the island's first prime minister lived longer, but there is no reason to assume this at all; because faced with demands for "Sinhala Only," the extant political structure would have forced Senanayake to embrace the same outbidding tactics his UNP colleagues did. In any case, the anti-Tamil rioting that took place in 1956 was the beginning of the Sinhalese-Tamil divide.

The Federal Party, headed by S. J. V. Chelvanayakam, was at the forefront in representing Tamils at this time. Seeking to minimize the burgeoning interethnic animus, Bandaranaike and Chelvanayakam agreed on a pact that would recognize Tamil as a minority language. The so-called B-C Pact could well have solved the language dispute between Sinhalese and Tamils, but the UNP and Sinhalese Buddhist nationalists, headed by Buddhist monks, rabidly opposed the pact. Such opposition took place even as Bandaranaike's government sent buses into the predominantly Tamil north with the Sinhala letter "sri" imprinted on their vehicle license plates. The Tamil protests that ensued led to additional rioting. These 1958 riots were more intense than the riots of 1956 (Vittachi 1958), and the mayhem contributed to Bandaranaike tearing up a copy of the pact in front of protesting monks who cheered in joy (Swamy 1994, 12). A subsequent UNP government sought to mollify Tamils with the District Councils Bill of 1968, which would have privileged Tamils by developing and allocating state lands in the predominantly Tamil northeast, but this time around the SLFP, together with other political parties and Buddhist clergy, vehemently opposed the agreement. The opposition to the B-C Pact and the District Councils Bill by the UNP and SLFP, respectively, highlights the extent to which ethnic entrepreneurs were eager to outbid each other for partisan gain at the expense of what was best for the country. The prominent role Buddhist clergy played in goading them against the agreements, on the other hand, evidences the extent to which Sinhalese Buddhist nationalism encompasses notions of "the land, the race, and the faith" referenced above.

A disgruntled Buddhist monk assassinated Bandaranaike in 1959 and, following some confusion within the SLFP, his wife, Sirimavo, succeeded him. Some Tamil radicals had called for creating a separate Tamil state, but the anti-Tamil policies Mrs. Bandaranaike's two governments (1960–65 and 1970–77) pursued justified the Tamil quest for separatism in the eyes of most Tamils.

TOWARD SINHALESE BUDDHIST SUPREMACY

Under Mrs. Bandaranaike, the courts system saw "Sinhala Only" instituted even in the northeast, where the vast majority of Tamils spoke and understood no Sinhala. Tamil civil servants were forced to learn Sinhala when seeking promotions. The government avoided hiring Tamils into the bureaucracy in subsequent years. Sinhalese civil servants who spoke no Tamil were stationed in Tamil areas to ensure linguistic hegemony. Quotas were introduced to increase the number of rural Sinhalese students in the university system (which also negatively impacted urban Sinhalese, although the main target were Tamils). Tamil students were required to score higher in order to enter the universities (with some in government making the dubious claim that Tamils scored high on exams only because Tamil examiners inflated grades). The government avoided developing Tamil areas (in especially irrigation), even when international aid was earmarked for these areas, and in some instances used the aid to develop Sinhalese areas. The government aggressively pursued ethnic flooding of the predominantly Tamil Eastern Province by sponsoring Sinhalese colonization. Tamil literature and entertainment entering the island from the neighboring Indian state of Tamil Nadu were banned or controlled (C. R.De Silva 1978; Peebles 1990; Shastri 1990; Tiruchelvam 1984). Additionally, in 1961 the military was stationed in the Northern Province in response to peaceful Tamil protests and the army soon came to be seen as an occupation force. Indeed, much of this was taking place even as some Sinhalese bureaucrats sought to set up military camps that surrounded the Northern Province so as to keep the Tamils subdued (Jayaweera 2008).

Postindependence, many nationalists considered the Catholic education system and the disproportionate presence of Catholics within various sectors of the economy to be antithetical to a predominantly Buddhist Sri Lankan milieu, and they began agitating against the Catholic Church's supposed influence with the island's elites. Catholics were accused of undermining Buddhism and conspiring "to bring Ceylon under the suzerainty of the Vatican" (Bauddha Jatika Balavegaya 1963, 117). This led to Mrs. Bandaranaike's first government taking over numerous Catholic schools. What used to be Catholic private schools became government-run schools, except for the few permitted to remain private provided they levied no fees. Associated with this was the policy to abolish the English-language stream in schools, which led to students only being able to study in either Sinhala or Tamil. With the government mainly hiring Sinhalese into the bureaucracy and armed forces, the policy allowed non-English speaking Sinhalese Buddhists to benefit and strengthened the Sinhalese Buddhist character of the state. Doing so became easier after 1962, when Catholics in the army attempted a coup that failed, because nationalists claimed the coup had been organized in response to the government taking over the Catholic schools.

Mrs. Bandaranaike's second government also promulgated a new constitution in 1972 that further strengthened the Sinhalese Buddhist character of the state. Moderate Tamils opposed to separatism had long called for a federal political structure, whereas Sinhalese Buddhist nationalists claimed federalism was the first step toward separatism, and the island therefore had to have a unitary state structure (i.e., a strong central government that determined policies for the whole island with provinces provided little or no autonomy). The 1972 constitution thus declared Sri Lanka a unitary state even as it made the state responsible to "protect and foster Buddhism" (The Constitution of Sri Lanka (Ceylon) 1972, 4).

When a new government under the UNP introduced the island's current constitution in 1978, it made Tamil an official language and tweaked the section dealing with Buddhism to say the state will "protect and foster the Buddha Sasana." In Pali, Buddhasasana refers to "the universal Buddhist church," although in Sri Lanka the majority community appropriated the term to claim the destiny of the sasana rested with the Sinhalese Buddhists (Obeyesekere 1997, 356). Since the term was added to the 1978 constitution, the courts have rendered judicial interpretations that go beyond protecting the Buddhist religion; Buddhasasana has now come to mean Buddha's complete legacy, including "properties, shrines, statutes, temples, other material objects, and geographic spaces" (Schonthal 2016, 1992). The geographic spaces may refer to all of Sri Lanka or Sinhalese villages. This means Sinhalese Buddhists must oppose devolution in any form, since only a unitary state wherein Sinhalese Buddhists are a majority in all nine provinces can protect Buddha's complete legacy. It also means predominantly Buddhist areas must not tolerate churches and mosques in their midst, lest Buddhist culture and demographics be diminished. That Sri Lanka could, within two centuries, go from a country that tolerated Tamil kings ruling a Buddhist kingdom to a one where even non-Buddhist places of worship in predominantly Buddhist villages are opposed highlights the extent to which Sinhalese Buddhist nationalism has won out.

Numerous individuals played prominent roles helping to consolidate Sinhalese Buddhist supremacy, and Anagarika Dharmapala, referenced above, was among them. It is important to recognize that the manner in which colonial malpractices adversely affected Buddhism was what primarily fired up Dharmapala, but his racist

The Consolidations of Sinhalese Buddhist Nationalism

rhetoric goaded many nationalists toward Sinhalese Buddhist majoritarianism. Another individual who played a prominent role consolidating Sinhalese Buddhist supremacy was the scholar-monk Walpola Rahula. He was most responsible for legitimizing monks' involvement in politics as an extension of their social service (Seneviratne 1999). He also legitimized a just-war ideology involving monks, provided the fight was to save nation and religion (Bartholomeusz 2002). Rahula did so by pointing to the Duthagamani story that said monks had accompanied the king's army to the battlefield. As per Rahula,

> From this time the patriotism and the religion of the Sinhalese become inseparably linked ... and assumed such overpowering proportions that both *bhikkhus* [monks] and laymen considered that even killing people in order to liberate the religion and the country was not a heinous crime." (Rahula 1974, 21)

Rahula and his ilk thus promoted a political Buddhism that legitimated ethnocentrism, majoritarianism, and militarism (Tambiah 1992).

It is important to recognize that while Buddhism promotes nonviolence, the religion "was, almost from the start, profoundly political at its very core" (Shulman 2018, 30). In that sense, the political Buddhism one sees in Sri Lanka, where elites and clergy disregard Buddhist values when seeking to restructure society using mythohistory and majoritarian violence, is hardly surprising. The notion that Buddhist societies were always peaceful is also not rooted in history, because "a peaceful state never existed in South Asia" (Singh 2017, 245). Indeed, violence is an important and effective part of the nationalists' toolkit when ensuring Sinhalese Buddhist domination. Consequently, when the LTTE and other rebel groups threatened secession beginning in the mid-1970s, nationalists were easily able to combine Buddhism and violence to counter them.

The LTTE threat to the island's Buddhist heritage only added to extant Buddhist insecurities stemming from long-standing transformations related to textual, popular, and ideological strands coexisting and competing with each other (Uyangoda 2007). There is, for instance, no unified Buddhism or Buddhist hierarchy, which makes it easy for Buddhists to consider themselves divided even as others view the religion in monolithic terms. The forces of modernization and materialism have also corrupted monks, leading some to run business enterprises and abandon temple life after receiving an education. Given the pivotal role monks have played maintaining and promoting Buddhism in Sri Lanka for over two millennia, this understandably creates angst among nationalists. Furthermore, Buddhist nationalists harbor a siege mentality when they compare their numbers to the over 70 million Tamils in Tamil Nadu, over 1 billion Hindus in India and South Asia, and the billion-plus Muslims and Christians in the world. Their angst stems from the sense that while Sri Lanka's Tamils, Christians, and Muslims can look to religio-civilizational homes outside the country, the Sinhalese Buddhists only have Sri Lanka. Thus Rahula could argue:

Sri Lanka is a Buddhist Sinhala country. Let no one make a mistake. Seventy percent of the country consists of Buddhists and Sinhala people. Also ... Sri Lanka is the only Buddhist Sinhala country in the world. If we don't live here, are the LTTE and some of the Tamil parties asking us to jump in to the sea? (Quoted in Peiris 1996)

THE CIVIL WAR

If Sinhalese Buddhist nationalism was due to real and manufactured slights and threats, Tamil nationalism was a reaction to the anti-Tamil policies successive Sri Lankan governments pursued (Wilson 2000). For it was the government's systematic marginalization of Tamils using multiple mechanisms that pushed Tamil youth to fight for a separate state beginning in the early 1970s. Some seasoned Tamil politicians believed they could use the youth unrest to pressure the Sri Lankan government to achieve some of their goals. But the young Tamil rebels only turned more radical and soon marginalized Tamil elder statesmen (Swamy 1994).

The new Sri Lankan government, headed by J. R. Jayewardene, that came to power in 1977 enjoyed a five-sixths majority in parliament and was in a solid position to nip the burgeoning Tamil rebellion in the bud by promoting devolution. However, it refused to do so despite Tamil youth having formed numerous groups to fight for separatism and targeting government institutions in the predominantly Tamil northeast. When the LTTE attacked an army convoy and killed thirteen soldiers in July 1983, anti-Tamil riots erupted throughout the island. Hundreds of Tamils were killed with impunity, with some parliamentarians and police and security personnel encouraging rioters. Many Tamils fled the island, leading to a Tamil diaspora that soon mobilized in host countries to support *eelam* (a separate Tamil state). The year 1983 is thus considered to mark the beginning of Sri Lanka's civil war.

Jayewardene had jettisoned the previous government's policies rooted in autarky and dirigisme and instead collaborated with the International Monetary Fund (IMF), the World Bank, and Western powers to pursue structural adjustment reforms. His government was pro-West at a time when India experienced tense relations with especially the United States. The fear that Sri Lanka was interacting with the United States and other Western powers in ways that disregarded Indian security considerations caused India to arm and train Tamil youth determined to secede from Sri Lanka. India never intended to sunder Sri Lanka. It hoped to use the Tamil rebellion to leverage its security interests in the region. But it too miscalculated and paid a heavy price for its involvement in the Tamil quest for *eelam*. Both Indian involvement and the Tamil diaspora's politicking internationalized Sri Lanka's civil war in ways that justified an even more strident Buddhist nationalism.

Sinhalese Buddhist nationalists have not forgiven India for supporting Tamil rebels early on and superimposing the 1987 Indo-Sri Lanka Peace Accord, which partly led to an Indian Peace Keeping Force (IPKF) stationed in Sri Lanka's northeast. The IPKF was supposed to halt the conflict between Tamil rebels and the Sri Lankan government, but it ended up fighting India's longest war against the LTTE. By the time the Indian troops retreated, the LTTE was in a position to dominate all other rebel groups and claim to be the sole representative of Sri Lanka's Tamils.

The LTTE combined discipline, creativity, and savagery as part of its modus operandi. It murdered Tamil detractors and eliminated or co-opted other rebel groups so it could lead the Tamil liberation struggle. Its suicide cadres killed Sri Lankan political and military leaders and former Indian Prime Minister Rajiv Gandhi. The group manipulated successive ceasefires to retrain and rearm, because its leader Velupillai Prabhakaran was determined to secure *eelam* militarily. It demanded that every Tamil family living in the territories it controlled give up one child to fight for Tamil *eelam* and dragooned children into its armed forces. Eventually over thirty foreign governments proscribed the group for forcibly recruiting child soldiers and resorting to terrorism. The consensus among foreign and local military strategists was that the LTTE could not be militarily defeated. But Sinhalese Buddhist nationalists and their political acolytes kept demanding a military solution to the ethnic conflict (DeVotta 2007, 28).

This happened in May 2009, when the Sri Lankan government under President Mahinda Rajapaksa brutally defeated the LTTE. Being surrounded by Sri Lanka's military, the LTTE forced over 300,000 Tamil civilians to stay with it and used them as human shields, while the military indiscriminately bombed areas and may have killed nearly 40,000 civilians during the latter stages of the war (UNSG 2011). The Sri Lankan government disputes this figure, but as per Rayappu Joseph, the former Catholic Bishop of Mannar, as many as 147,000 Tamils are unaccounted for in the northeast (The Economist 2017, 39). This could mean that Tamil deaths from the conflict are much higher than assumed.

Tamil activists have claimed that what transpired in Sri Lanka was a genocide. While government forces refused to differentiate between LTTE cadres and innocent civilians and deliberately shelled self-declared "no-fire zones," over 300,000 Tamils from LTTE-controlled areas ultimately sought refuge in government-controlled areas, and the state also eventually rehabilitated over 11,000 LTTE cadres (Ferdinando 2018). This is hardly how a government bent on genocide acts. That said, Sinhalese Buddhist nationalists want to see the Northern and Eastern Provinces have majority Buddhist populations and hence approve of a reduced-minority population. The term "rolling genocide" has been used to refer to violence designed to control, subjugate, and weaken minorities over an extended period so as to make the group irrelevant eventually (Kingsbury 2012), and some among Sri Lanka's politicians and military personnel may have acted with such a mindset. While the military fears that Tamil separatism may be revived, the manner in which the Rajapaksa government instituted surveillance systems throughout the northeast postwar, the additional buildup of military camps, and the attempts to marginalize Tamils socioeconomically lend credence to this notion. The international community now pressures the Sri Lankan government to account for the innocent Tamils killed, but emboldened Sinhalese Buddhist nationalists oppose any such accounting.

Sri Lanka's grotesque war shows what can happen when a government discriminates against and represses a territorialized minority community. As per the postwar Lessons Learned and Reconciliation Commission, "the root cause of the ethnic conflict in Sri Lanka lies in the failure of successive Governments to address the genuine grievances of the Tamil people" (Commission of Inquiry on Lessons Learnt and Reconciliation 2011, 291). Many dared to think that with the LTTE defeated and the separatist threat eliminated, a more consensus politics would take root. Instead, the triumphalist Rajapaksa government sought to extend Sinhalese Buddhist hegemony by cavalierly neglecting Tamils and fanning Islamophobia.

THE CONSEQUENCES OF SINHALESE BUDDHIST NATIONALISM

Sinhalese Buddhist nationalism has triumphed to the point where nearly all of the major aims of the nationalists have now been achieved. For instance, thanks to the Sinhala language operating as the only official language until 1978 and its continued privileged status, Sinhalese Buddhists now dominate the military and other state sectors. It is a fair estimate that today Buddhists comprise over 97 percent of the Sri Lankan military and over 92 percent of the state bureaucracy.[1] As noted above, Buddhism has also been prominently privileged and clearly occupies a hegemonic position in religious affairs. Furthermore, the country remains a unitary state with no meaningful autonomy provided for Tamils, and nationalists consider any political structure hinting of federalism to be anathema. Additionally, the LTTE was militarily defeated, just as nationalists insisted, and the Tamils were marginalized and weakened. Indeed, the civil war led to the militarization of the northeast and postwar the military presence has expanded, with soldiers now operating farms and hotels among other business activities throughout that region. Finally, thanks to the discriminatory policies against Indian Tamils and prolonged ethnic conflict, which besides killing thousands forced tens of thousands of Tamils to flee abroad, the respective demographic percentages of Sinhalese and Buddhists have risen from 66.1 and 60 in 1911 to 74.9 and 70.2 today (Denham 1912, 196, 245; Department of Census and Statistics 2011).

---

[1] It does not appear that government service representation based on ethnicity and religion gets tabulated. These numbers are estimates based on interviews with politicians, civil society activists, and government servants.

The Consolidations of Sinhalese Buddhist Nationalism

These gains have hardly satisfied Sinhalese Buddhist nationalists. Many among them want to see the Buddhist population further increased, and some have therefore called for Sinhalese women to have more children. Politicians seeking popular support have sometimes felt pressure to speak to the issue. Thus a provincial chief minister recently said "each and every Sinhala mother should deliver at least five children" because "increasing the Sinhala race is the only means to safeguard Buddhism, language and our nation" (Samarakoon 2017). This obsession with demography is also behind the nationalists' expressing concern over the fact that the demographic percentage of Muslims on the island has risen from 7.55 in 1981 to 9.7 today (Department of Census and Statistics 2011).

As noted above, Sinhalese Buddhist nationalists want to make Northern Province and Eastern Province into majority-Sinhalese provinces. After the war, assisted by the military and certain politicians, various groups are systematically introducing Sinhalese into Tamil and Muslim areas of the northeast (Kannangara and Wickrematunge 2013; Watchdog 2013). Often Sinhalese names are provided for hitherto Tamil villages. Moreover, bo trees (*ficus religiosa*, sacred to Buddhists) and Buddha statues are planted in Muslim and Tamil areas where Buddhists have never lived (Balachandran 2016; Watchdog 2013). Once a sacred bo tree is planted or Buddha statue erected, typically on state-owned land, government officials, including police and military personnel, prevent them being removed until the courts can rule on the matter. With court cases proceeding slowly and government officials sympathizing with Buddhist agitators, a vocal movement may develop against removing the sacred tree or statue. In many instances, the tree or statue is barricaded and Buddhist flags hung around it. In some instances, military personnel are stationed to protect trees and statues. Tamils and Muslims oppose such colonization and Sinhalization of their traditional lands, but can do little against zealous Buddhist activists who believe they must sacralize all space to propagate Buddha's legacy. All this takes place even as monuments commemorating military battles and victories against the LTTE have been erected, especially in the Northern Province.

ANTI-MUSLIM AGITPROP

With the LTTE separatist threat extirpated and Tamils utterly weakened and marginalized (Sri Lanka Campaign for Peace and Justice 2014), the triumphant Sinhalese Buddhist nationalism now targets the Muslim community. As noted above, the mainly Tamil-speaking Muslims have long used their religious identity as their primary identity marker. They not only opposed the LTTE's quest to create a separate state, their political leaders lobbied predominantly Muslim countries to support Sri Lanka at various global forums, and Muslims familiar with northeast terrain helped the military gather intelligence. The Muslims' opposition to Tamil *eelam* caused the LTTE to evict more than 60,000 Muslims from the Northern

Province in 1990, and the group went so far as to murder Muslims while they prayed in mosques (DeVotta 2018, 288).

While there has long been an eddy of anti-Muslim sentiment among all communities, the extent of it among especially Sinhalese Buddhists was masked thanks to the civil war. Thus, while periodic clashes between Muslims and Buddhists took place, they were localized. But post-civil war triumphalism and the Islamophobia trending globally have allowed Sinhalese Buddhist nationalists to target Muslims more widely. The nationalists need to conjure up a threat against Sinhalese Buddhist society to stay relevant. The Muslims' relative insularity and self-segregation, their livelihoods rooted in business and trading, slight rise in population, and conspicuous piety that is now manifested through Arab attire like the burqa[2] and *thobe*[3] and the proliferation of mosques have especially allowed nationalists to portray Muslims as a challenge to Sinhalese Buddhist civilization and dominance.

The recent calibrated attacks against Muslims began in late 2011 when a Sinhalese mob destroyed a nearly 300-year-old Sufi shrine. Since then, more than 650 attacks against mosques, businesses, and homes have taken place throughout the island, with a number of newly formed groups leading the fray (DeVotta 2018, 282). The BBS, which first carried out a campaign against halal[4] products being marketed (Haniffa 2017), has been the most prominent in this regard. The group thereafter agitated against women wearing the burqa and niqab,[5] Sinhalese women being employed in Muslim establishments, new mosques being built using Middle Eastern funds, and the slaughter and sale of beef (in which primarily Muslims engage). Its tub-thumping leaders claimed Muslim men sexually targeted Buddhist women so as to convert them, Muslim employers forced Buddhists to work on Buddhist holidays, and Muslim businesses sold undergarments with Buddha's image and also marketed a unique female underwear that caused Sinhalese women to become sterile (DeVotta 2016, 157–58; Silva 2016). Conveniently overlooking the fact that some within Sri Lanka's parliament were accused of dealing with illegal drugs, the group claimed Muslims were at the forefront of the narcotics business. The worst anti-Muslim violence the BBS inspired took place in June 2014 in Aluthgama, a town located about 40 miles south of Colombo. The violence saw scores of Muslim shops and homes demolished and damaged, with residents claiming that some security personnel assisted the rioters.

The Rajapaksa government's connivance emboldened the BBS to orchestrate Islamophobic hate speech and anti-Muslim violence. While Sri Lanka's minorities

[2]   A burqa is an enveloping outer garment worn by women in some Islamic traditions to cover themselves in public, which covers the body and the face.
[3]   A *thobe* is an ankle-length, long-sleeved, gownlike garment worn chiefly by men of the Arabian Peninsula.
[4]   Halal denotes meat prepared as prescribed by Muslim law.
[5]   A niqab is a garment of clothing like a face veil that covers the face, worn by a small minority of Muslim women as a part of a particular interpretation of hijab (literally, "modesty").

vote mainly for their ethnic parties during parliamentary elections, they usually overwhelmingly support the UNP candidate during presidential elections. Rajapaksa belongs to the SLFP, although he and his supporters now seek political domination through a new party called the Sri Lanka Podujana Peramuna (SLPP). In a fit of postwar hubris, he decided he could win elections by relying solely on the Sinhalese Buddhists. Violence that diminished Muslim turnout at elections thus suited Rajapaksa and the SLFP. With Tamils now subjugated, playing up the Muslim threat was perhaps also designed to mask the country's economic challenges and authoritarianism that Rajapaksa and his family were attempting to institute.

Such collusion led to BBS rallies that vilified Muslims being televised on especially state-owned television channels even as security personnel were apparently instructed not to interfere when BBS monks egged on mobs to vandalize certain prominent Muslim businesses. A search on YouTube will show some of these events unfolding with the police looking on nonchalantly. The BBS has been relatively quiet over the past two years, although other groups have taken over the anti-Muslim activities it spearheaded. The expectation was that the government that dethroned Rajapaksa in January 2015, which Muslims helped pull off with their high-voter turnout, would crack down on anti-Muslim acts. Yet, anti-Muslim violence flared up again in November 2017 in Gintota, in the Southern Province, and in March 2018 in the Kandy district (Taub and Fisher 2018).

While the extent to which such agitprop and violence have radicalized Sri Lanka's Muslims is debatable, there is no gainsaying that the Islamophobia some Sinhalese Buddhist nationalists have promoted was partly responsible for the 2019 Easter Sunday suicide bombings that killed over 250 people (DeVotta 2019b). Wahhabi and Salafi ideology and the extremism promoted by the Islamic State clearly influenced the leaders of the Easter Sunday attacks, but the siege mentality foisted on Muslims no doubt helped the architects of the bombings attract recruits. Most of those killed by the ISIS-inspired bombers were Christians at Easter Sunday church services, and this makes it easier for both Sinhalese Buddhists and Christians to combine forces against the island's Muslims down the road.[6]

Ethno-religious violence takes place because individuals and parties profit from such mayhem. For instance, zealous nationalist elites may promote such violence to ensure ethno-religious supremacy; politicians may promote it because doing so mobilizes their base and helps them stay in power; businessmen may support ethno-religious violence because it dislocates and eradicates competitors; run-of-the-mill individuals may do so to settle scores or arrogate land and homes; hoodlums may participate in ethno-religious violence because of the opportunity to loot; and depraved and predatory individuals may do so because it allows for sexual violence

---

[6] Thanks to Muslims supplying authorities with information, the bombers' accomplices were arrested within a few days. Indeed, Muslims had alerted authorities to the extremist nature of the National Tawheed Jamaat, which orchestrated the suicide attacks, but the information was not dealt with seriously.

with impunity. In short, people resort to ethno-religious violence for various reasons. By recasting the perpetrators of violence as "defenders of the nation," a nationalist ideology helps justify their acts within a narrative the community at large sympathizes with. This is the case with the Sinhalese Buddhist nationalist ideology, which necessitated a civil war and now legitimates Islamophobia.

POLITICAL DECAY

But civil war and Islamophobia are not the only deleterious consequences stemming from this ideology. The political decay that has befallen Sri Lanka and the breakdown in the rule of law also stem to a great degree from the ethnocentrism that Sinhalese Buddhist nationalism promoted. Political decay is "a process marked by the erosion and breakdown of previously accepted and observed rules and norms governing organizational behavior" (Barany 2008, 585). Typically such decay ensues when the institutions effectuating politics "fail to adjust to changing circumstances" (Fukuyama 2011, 7). But it is important to recognize that elites who desire to monopolize power can deliberately undermine institutions and thereby engender political decay (DeVotta 2014). This is what happened in Sri Lanka starting in the mid-1950s when successive governments pursued policies designed to satisfy the majority Sinhalese Buddhists. The ensuing majoritarianism inevitably eroded secularism, pluralism, and liberal democracy. Indeed, if Sri Lanka was a burgeoning liberal democracy postindependence, it has since gradually regressed into a veritable ethnocracy, because today being part of the politically and culturally dominant Sinhalese Buddhist nation ranks above being Sri Lankan.

The determination to privilege Buddhists not only led to discriminatory policies that targeted minorities, it also forced the government to scrap professionally functioning institutions thought to hamper Sinhalese Buddhist hegemony. Thus the Ceylon Civil Service (CCS) was disbanded in 1963 and replaced with the Ceylon Administrative Service (SAS) because the former was insufficiently sensitive "to the spirit of the new times" (Weerakoon 2004, 127). The forced retirements from the CCS enabled the government to hire mainly Sinhalese to the SAS. Similarly, the 1972 constitution replaced the impartial Public Service Commission with the State Services Advisory Board and State Services Disciplinary Board and placed their personnel under the purview of cabinet ministers who privileged Sinhalese Buddhists when hiring. This may have helped rectify the overrepresentation of especially Tamils in government service, but it also led to substandard hires that vitiated the professionalism and quality of state institutions and gradually contributed to the rule of law being weakened.

Majoritarianism inevitably impacts the rule of law, because a state that blatantly discriminates against its minorities prevents the rule of law from operating impartially. Tamils began experiencing this especially under Mrs. Bandaranaike's governments, but the situation was exacerbated when civil war erupted. Exceptional

The Consolidations of Sinhalese Buddhist Nationalism 207

periods of crisis, such as civil wars, allow governments to disregard rules, norms, and laws because the most important goal becomes ensuring security and sovereignty. During such exceptional periods, practices that established social orders would typically oppose are tolerated. Thus the more radical and potent the LTTE became, the more Sri Lankans tolerated lengthy periods of emergency rule, draconian anti-terrorism legislation, illegal detentions, torture, disappearances, and murder (DeVotta 2015). With most Tamils thought to support separatism, it was the Tamils who typically were the victims of such practices. But the civil war also militarized the island and Sinhalese Buddhist society (De Mel 2007; Hewamanne 2009) and contributed to a culture of impunity that further undermined institutions. This was especially the case under President Rajapaksa and his grasping family who went out of their way to deinstitutionalize the state while trying to create a political dynasty. Ultimately, while nationalists have indeed secured hegemonic status for Sinhalese and Buddhism, this has come at a steep price for all Sri Lankans.

CONCLUSION

It is tempting to imagine what postindependence Sri Lanka could have been had the island avoided an ethnocentric trajectory and instead embraced inclusive politics undergirded by a multiethnic and multi-confessional agenda. Scoring relatively high on the human development index and with professional institutions, including well-functioning schools and universities, the country could have avoided the carnage the civil war unleashed and positioned itself well to compete globally. The failure to do so, however, suits Sinhalese Buddhist nationalists who prefer ethno-religious superiority above all else.

Ethno-religious nationalists seek to dominate; they hardly support structures that promote tolerance and pluralism. In this regard, the Sinhalese Buddhist quest for majority superordination and minority subordination has succeeded spectacularly. From making Sinhala the only official language from 1956 to 1978 – which provided Sinhalese Buddhists ample time to arrogate positions within the state, military, and educational sectors – to ensuring hegemonic status for Buddhism, nationalists' preferences have been achieved. The military defeat of the LTTE was another nationalist aspiration that succeeded, and the ongoing militarization and systematic Sinhalese colonization of the northeast amidst the diminution of Tamils will likely see the Northern and Eastern Provinces have mainly Sinhalese Buddhist populations in a few decades. Disregarding periods when multiple kingdoms existed on the island, nationalists have insisted that Sri Lanka must be a unitary state in order to ensure the legacy of *sinhadipa* and *dhammadipa*. Notwithstanding Tamil demands for a more devolved political structure, this status too is now secure.

Many Sri Lankans recognize that the quest for Sinhalese Buddhist hegemony was partly, if not mainly, responsible for the ethnic conflict, but they do not associate this quest with the institutional decay, culture of impunity, and breakdown in the rule of law with which the island now grapples. They fail to see how the extrajudicial and extraconstitutional practices necessitated by the civil war undermined democracy and good governance. This also means they fail to realize how the civil war enabled authoritarianism under Mahinda Rajapaksa, because many of the draconian practices the Rajapaksa regime embraced were justified within the context of the war.

The former president remains a Sinhalese Buddhist icon, with his promoters portraying him as a modern-day Duthagamani. The Sinhalese Buddhist nationalist narrative is that Duthagamani defeated the Tamil king Elara and thereby consolidated the land for Buddhism. By militarily defeating the LTTE and securing the island's territorial integrity, Rajapaksa is said to have done likewise. Linking Rajapaksa with heroes in the *Mahavamsa* evidences the extent to which the presence of the past sacralizes the Sinhalese Buddhist zeitgeist.

Rajapaksa's ouster in January 2015 stymied the authoritarian project, but he and his family have now made a spectacular political comeback. Younger brother and former defense secretary Gotabaya Rajapaksa was elected president in November 2019, which saw Mahinda Rajapaksa becoming prime minister. Ethnocentrism and militarism have since undergirded the government's policies, with numerous serving and retired military personnel (many of whom have been accused of perpetrating war crimes) overseeing hitherto civilian-led affairs. The COVID-19 pandemic has further accelerated militarization. Given the new president's predilection for authoritarianism, Sri Lanka now appears headed toward an autocratic and militarized ethnocracy (DeVotta 2021).

During the civil war, Sinhalese Buddhist nationalists claimed that the country did not have an ethnic problem; it merely had a terrorist problem. It was a convenient way to overlook the ethnocentric policies that spawned the civil war and instead emphasize the LTTE's depredations. But were terrorism the main problem, its demise ought to have led to a tolerant milieu. Instead, postwar ethno-religious triumphalism has inspired attacks against the island's Muslims even as legitimate Tamil aspirations get suppressed. The upshot is that Sinhalese Buddhist nationalism is more potent today than at any point in the past. Triumphant nationalism undergirded by religious beliefs and empowered by military victory does not lead to tolerance; it instead leads to more dominance. This does not bode well for Sri Lanka's minorities. Ultimately, in the long term, it will not bode well for the Sinhalese Buddhists either.

REFERENCES

Balachandran, P. K. 2016. "North Sri Lankan Governor Defends Building Buddhist Temples." *The Indian Express*, August 18. www.newindianexpress.com/world/2016/aug/18/North-Sri-Lankan-Governor-defends-building-Buddhist-temples-1510667.html.

The Consolidations of Sinhalese Buddhist Nationalism

Barany, Zoltan. 2008. "Civil-Military Relations and Institutional Decay: Explaining Russian Military Politics." *Europe-Asia Studies* 60, no. 4: 581–604.

Bartholomeusz, Tessa. 1995. "Catholics, Buddhists, and the Church of England: The 1883 Sri Lankan Riots." *Buddhist-Christian Studies* 15: 89–103.

2002. *In Defense of Dharma: Just-War Ideology in Buddhist Sri Lanka*. London: Routledge.

Bass, Daniel. 2013. *Everyday Ethnicity in Sri Lanka: Up-country Tamil Identity Politics*. London: Routledge.

Bauddha Jatika Balavegaya. 1963. *Catholic Action: A Menace to Peace and Goodwill*. Colombo: The Bauddha Pracharaka Press.

Commission of Inquiry on Lessons Learnt and Reconciliation. 2011. *Report of the Commission of Inquiry on Lessons Learnt and Reconciliation*. Colombo: Government of Sri Lanka. www.priu.gov.lk/news_update/Current_Affairs/ca201112/FINAL%20LLRC%20REPORT.pdf.

Daily Mirror. 2006. "People Requesting Surrender of a Part of the Country Are Traitors: Ven. Medananda Thera." September 13.

De Mel, Neloufer. 2007. *Militarizing Sri Lanka: Popular Culture, Memory and Narrative in the Armed Conflict*. New Delhi: Sage Publications.

Denham, E. B. 1912. *Ceylon at the Census of 1911*. Colombo: Government Printer.

Department of Census and Statistics. 1996. *Statistical Pocket Book of the Democratic Socialist Republic of Sri Lanka*. Colombo: Department of Census and Statistics.

2011. "Sri Lanka Census of Population and Housing 2011." www.statistics.gov.lk /PopHouSat/CPH2011/index.php?fileName=pop43&gp=Activities&tpl=3.

De Silva, Chandra Richard. 1978. "The Politics of University Admissions: A Review of Some Aspects of the Admission Policy in Sri Lanka, 1971–1978." *Sri Lanka Journal of Social Sciences* 4, no. 2: 85–123.

1997. *Sri Lanka: A History*. 2nd ed. New Delhi: Vikas.

De Silva, K. M. 1981. *A History of Sri Lanka*. Delhi: Oxford University Press.

1986. *Religion, Nationalism and the State in Modern Sri Lanka*. USF Monographs in Religion and Public Policy, no. 1. Tampa: University of South Florida.

DeVotta, Neil. 2001. "The Utilisation of Religio-Linguistic Identities by the Sinhalese and Bengalis: Towards a General Explanation." *Commonwealth and Comparative Politics* 39, no. 1: 66–95.

2004. *Blowback: Linguistic Nationalism, Institutional Decay, and Ethnic Conflict in Sri Lanka*. Stanford: Stanford University Press.

2007. *Sinhalese Buddhist Nationalist Ideology: Implications for Politics and Conflict Resolution in Sri Lanka*. Policy Studies, no. 40. Washington, DC: East-West Center.

2009. "Liberation Tigers of Tamil Eelam and the Lost Quest for Separatism in Sri Lanka." *Asian Survey* 49, no. 6: 1021–51.

2014. "Parties, Political Decay, and Democratic Regression in Sri Lanka." *Commonwealth and Comparative Politics* 52, no. 1 (January): 139–65.

2015. "From Counterterrorism to Soft-Authoritarianism: The Case of Sri Lanka." In *Critical Perspectives on Counter-Terrorism*, edited by Lee Jarvis and Michael Lister, 210–30. London: Routledge.

2016. "A Win for Democracy in Sri Lanka." *Journal of Democracy* 27, no. 1: 152–66.

2018. "Religious Intolerance in Post-Civil War Si Lanka." *Asian Affairs* 49, no. 2: 278–300.

2019a. "Island of Violence: Sinhalese Buddhist Majoritarianism and Ethno-religious Conflict in Sri Lanka." In *Political Violence in South Asia*, edited by Ali Riaz, Zobaida Nasreen, and Fahmida Zaman, 167–81. London: Routledge.

2019b. "Sri Lanka's Christian and Muslims Weren't Enemies." *Foreign Policy*, April 25. https://foreignpolicy.com/2019/04/25/sri-lankas-christians-and-muslims-werent-enemies/.

2021. "Sri Lanka: The Return to Ethnocracy." *Journal of Democracy* 32, no. 1: 96–110.

DeVotta, Neil, and Jason Stone. 2008. "Jathika Hela Urumaya and Ethno-Religious Politics in Sri Lanka." *Pacific Affairs* 81, no. 1: 31–51.

Dewaraja, Lorna. 1994. *The Muslims of Sri Lanka: One Thousand Years of Ethnic Harmony, 900–1915*. Colombo: The Lanka Islamic Foundation.

Dewasiri, Nirmal Ranjith. 2016. *New Buddhist Extremism and the Challenges to Ethno-religious Coexistence in Sri Lanka*. Colombo: International Center for Ethnic Studies.

Dharmadasa, K. N. O. 1992. *Language, Religion, and Ethnic Assertiveness: The Growth of Sinhalese Nationalism in Sri Lanka*. Ann Arbor: University of Michigan Press.

Ferdinando, Shamindra. 2018. "Rehabilitated Tigers Strike in the Wake of Political Chaos." *The Island*, December 8. http://island.lk/index.php?page_cat=article-details&page=article-details&code_title=195530.

Fernando, Susitha R. 2005. "Filmmaking on War: Traitors and Patriots." *Sunday Times*, October 9. www.sundaytimes.lk/051009/tv/4.html.

Fukuyama, Francis. 2011. *The Origins of Political Order: From Prehumen Times to the French Revolution*. New York: Farrar, Straus, and Giroux.

Guruge, Ananda. 1965. *Return to Righteousness: A Collection of Speeches, Essays and Letters of the Anagarike Dharmapala*. Colombo: Ministry of Education and Cultural Affairs.

Haniffa, Farzana. 2017. "Merit Economies in Neoliberal Times: Halal Troubles in Contemporary Sri Lanka." In *Religion and the Morality of the Market*, edited by Daromir Rudnyckyj and Filippo Osella, 116–37. Cambridge: Cambridge University Press.

Hewamanne, Sandya. 2009. "Duty Bound? Militarization, Romances and New Spaces of Violence among Sri Lanka's Free Trade Zone Garment Factory Workers." *Cultural Dynamics* 21, no. 2: 153–84.

Hobsbawm, E. J. (1990) 1992. *Nations and Nationalism since 1780: Programme, Myth, Reality*. 2nd ed. Cambridge: Cambridge University Press.

Horowitz, Donald. 1985. *Ethnic Groups in Conflict*. Berkeley: University of California Press.

Jayasuriya, Ranga. 2013. "'We Are Not Extremists' – Kirima Wimalajothi Thera." *Ceylon Today*, June 24.

Jayaweera, Neville. 2008. "Into the Turbulence of Jaffna." *The Island*, October 5. www.island.lk/2008/10/05/features2.html.

Kannangara, Nirmala, and Raisa Wickrematunge. 2013. "Systematic Sinhalisation of the North." *The Sunday Leader*, April 28. www.thesundayleader.lk/2013/04/28/systematic-sinhalisation-in-the-north/.

Kearney, Robert N. 1967. *Communalism and Language in the Politics of Ceylon*. Durham, NC: Duke University Press.

Kemper, Steven. 2015. *Rescued from the Nation: Anagarike Dharmapala and the Buddhist World*. Chicago: University of Chicago Press.

Kingsbury, Damien. 2012. *Sri Lanka and the Responsibility to Protect: Politics, Ethnicity and Genocide*. New York: Routledge.

Kulke, Hermann. 2000. "Sectarian Politics and Historiography in Early Sri Lanka: Wilhelm Geiger's Studies of the Chronicles of Sri Lanka in the Light of Recent Research." In *Wilhelm Geiger and the Study of the History and Culture of Sri Lanka*, edited by Ulrich Everding and Asanga Tilakaratne, 112–36. Colombo: Goethe Institute and Post-Graduate Institute of Pali and Buddhist Studies.

LankaNewspapers.com. 2008. "Country Belongs to the Sinhalese, Minorities Cannot Demand Says Sarath Fonseka." September 26. www.lankanewspapers.com/news/2008/9/32834_space.html.

Mahindapala, H. L. D. 2006. "Intellectual Crimes against the Sri Lankan People." *Daily News*, January 16. http://archives.dailynews.lk/2006/01/16/fea03.htm.

Malalgoda, Kitsiri. 1976. *Buddhism in Sinhalese Society, 1750–1900: A Study of Religious Revival and Change*. Berkeley: University of California Press.

Nayak, Sharada. 2014. *The Raj Agent in Ceylon 1936–40*. New Delhi: Educational Resources Center Trust.

Obeyesekere, Gananath. 1970. "Religious Symbolism and Political Change in Ceylon." *Modern Ceylon Studies* 1: 43–63.

———. 1997. "The Vicissitudes of the Sinhala-Buddhist Identity through Time and Change." In vol. 1 of *Sri Lanka: Collective Identities Revisited*, edited by Michael Roberts, 355–84. Colombo: Marga Institute.

Peebles, Patrick. 1990. "Colonization and Ethnic Conflict in the Dry Zone of Sri Lanka." *Journal of Asian Studies* 49, no. 1: 30–55.

Peiris, Roshan. 1996. "Rahula Hits Back." *Sunday Times*, May 5. www.sundaytimes.lk/970921/news2.html.

Ponnambalam, Satchi. 1983. *Sri Lanka: The National Question and the Tamil Liberation Struggle*. Thornton Heath, Surrey: Tamil Information Center.

Rabushka, Alvin, and Kenneth A. Shepsle. 1972. *Politics in Plural Societies: A Theory of Democratic Instability*. Columbus, OH: Charles E. Merrill.

Rahula, Walpola. 1974. *The Heritage of the Bhikkhu: A Short History of the Bhikkhu in Educational, Cultural, Social and Political Life*. New York: Grove Press.

Renan, Ernest. 1996. "What Is a Nation?" In *Becoming National: A Reader*, edited by Geoff Eley and Ronald Grigor Suny, 42–55. New York: Oxford University Press.

Samarakoon, Pradeep Prasanna. 2017. "CM Isura Calls on Sinhala Mothers to Produce More Children." *The Island*, July 2. www.island.lk/index.php?page_cat=article-details&page=article-details&code_title=167653.

Schonthal, Benjamin. 2016. "Securing the Sasana through Law: Buddhist Constitutionalism and Buddhist-Interest Litigation in Sri Lanka." *Modern Asian Studies* 50, no. 6: 1966–2008.

Seneviratne, H. L. 1999. *The Work of Kings: The New Buddhism in Sri Lanka*. Chicago: University of Chicago Press.

Shastri, Amita. 1990. "The Material Bases for Separatism: The Tamil Eelam Movement in Sri Lanka." *Journal of Asian Studies* 49, no. 1: 56–77.

Shulman, David. 2018. "Review of *Political Violence in Ancient India*, by Upinder Singh." *The New York Review of Books*, April 5, 30–32.

Silva, Kalinga Tudor. 2016. "Gossip, Rumor, and Propaganda in Anti-Muslim Campaigns of the Bodu Bala Sena." In *Buddhist Extremists and Muslim Minorities: Religious Conflict in Contemporary Sri Lanka*, edited by John Clifford Holt, 119–39. New York: Oxford University Press.

Singh, Upinder. 2017. *Political Violence in Ancient India*. Cambridge, MA: Harvard University Press.

Sri Lanka Campaign for Peace and Justice. 2014. "Crimes against Humanity in Sri Lanka's Northern Province: A Legal Analysis of Post-war Human Rights Violations." https://cja.org/downloads/Crimes%20Against%20Humanity%20in%20Sri%20Lanka_s%20Northern%20Province.pdf.

Swamy, M. R. Narayan. 1994. *Tigers of Lanka: From Boys to Guerrillas*. Delhi: Konark.

Tambiah, Stanley J. 1986. *Sri Lanka: Ethnic Fratricide and the Dismantling of Democracy*. Chicago: University of Chicago Press.

1992. *Buddhism Betrayed? Religion, Politics, and Violence in Sri Lanka*. Chicago: University of Chicago Press.

1996. *Leveling Crowds: Ethnonationalist Conflicts and Collective Violence in South Asia*. Berkeley: University of California Press.

Taub, Amanda, and Max Fisher. 2018. "Where Countries Are Tinderboxes and Facebook Is a Match." *The New York Times*, April 21. www.nytimes.com/2018/04/21/world/asia/face book-sri-lanka-riots.html.

The Constitution of Sri Lanka (Ceylon). 1972. https://bit.ly/36psJ9Q.

The Economist. 2013. "Fears of a New Religious Strife." July 27, 35.

2016. "Crossed in Translation." March 4, 30–31.

2017. "No Closure." March 18, 39.

Tiruchelvam, Neelan. 1984. "Ethnicity and Resource Allocation." In *From Independence to Statehood: Managing Ethnic Conflict in Five African and Asian States*, edited by Robert B. Goldman and A. Jeyaratnam Wilson, 185–95. New York: St. Martin's Press.

UNSG (United Nations Secretary-General). 2011. "Report of the Secretary-General's Panel of Experts on Accountability in Sri Lanka." March 31. www.refworld.org/docid/4db7b23e2 .html.

Uyangoda, Jayadeva. 2007. "Paradoxes of Buddhism." In *Religion in Context: Buddhism and Socio-political Change in Sri Lanka*, edited by Jayadeva Uyangoda, 1–5. Colombo: Social Scientists' Association.

Vittachi, Tarzie. 1958. *Emergency '58: The Story of the Ceylon Race Riots*. London: Andre Deutsch.

Watchdog. 2013. "State Facilitated Colonization of Northern Sri Lanka–2013." *Groundviews*, September 19. https://groundviews.org/2013/09/19/state-facilitated-colonization-of-northern-sri-lanka-2013/.

Weerakoon, Bradman. 2004. *Rendering unto Caesar: A Fascinating Story of One Man's Tenure under Nine Prime Ministers and Presidents of Sri Lanka*. Colombo: Vijitha Yapa Publications.

Wijeyeratne, Roshan de Silva. 2014. *Nation, Constitutionalism and Buddhism in Sri Lanka*. London: Routledge.

Wilson, A. Jeyaratnam. 1988. *The Break-up of Sri Lanka: The Sinhalese-Tamil Conflict*. London: C. Hurst.

2000. *Sri Lankan Tamil Nationalism: Its Origins and Development in the Nineteenth and Twentieth Centuries*. Vancouver: University of British Columbia Press.

Wriggins, Howard. 1961. "Impediments to Unity in New Nations: The Case of Ceylon." *American Political Science Review* 55, no. 2: 313–20.

PART IV

Serbia

9

Serbian Jerusalem

Inventing a Holy Land in Europe's Periphery, 1982–2019

Vjekoslav Perica[*]

INTRODUCTION

The southeastern periphery of Europe, known today in international relations literature as the Western Balkans, was the focus of world public opinion during the breakup of Yugoslavia and the series of globally televised wars that followed in the 1990s. The military stage of the conflict, which started in 1991 and concluded with a massive NATO bombing of Serbia in 1999, aimed at ending a Serb-Albanian war in the Kosovo province that later became an independent nation. It was during the NATO intervention that the West heard about the Serbian nationalist perspective that Kosovo was the "Serbian Jerusalem," drawing parallels between the conflicts in the Balkans and the Middle East. The crisis leading to the breakup of Yugoslavia began in the early 1980s with nationalist disputes over Kosovo, then an autonomous province of Tito's Yugoslavia. The post-Yugoslav wars started in Croatia in 1991, spread to Bosnia and Herzegovina, and ended where the conflict began – in Kosovo.[1] In the wider region that has been unstable ever since, the war over Kosovo never actually ended.

The costs of the Balkan Wars of the 1990s include about 150,000 lives and several million people forcibly resettled.[2] The United Nations International Criminal Tribunal for the former Yugoslavia (ICTY) in The Hague, the Netherlands, prosecuted the cases of genocide, war crimes, and crimes against humanity committed by all warring factions, but among those sentenced, Serb military and political leaders were the most numerous (Bowcott 2017).

[*] I would like to thank Nadim Rouhana and Nadera Shalhoub-Kevorkian for the opportunity to contribute to this important volume. Thereby I also completed a long-developing project previously presented in fragments or in lectures. I am grateful to the following colleagues who read and commented on some versions of the text or invited me for presentations: Marie-Janine Calic, Paul Mojzes, and Mila Dragojević. My very special thanks go out to Kate Rouhana and Stephanie Williams for their help with editing the text in the final stage of writing and publication.

[1] There is voluminous, international literature on Yugoslav disintegration, the Balkan Wars of the 1990s, and the Kosovo controversy. See, for example, Popov and Gojković (2000); Ramet (2005); Rathfelder (2010).

[2] See Tabeau (2009).

216   *Vjekoslav Perica*

The Balkan conflict is the result of competition among several nationalist ideologies and state-building projects developing from the nineteenth through the twentieth centuries. These follow the ethnic-civic dichotomy, yet in this case, ethnic nationalism is fused with religious nationalism. Ethnic nationalisms pursued a type of homogenous ethnic nationhood in which the majority group's ethnic and religious identities merged, redrawing boundaries to separate the neighboring groups regardless of a shared language. Thus, religion would become the key differentiating factor separating the common language-speaking Serbs, Croats, and Bosniaks into the Orthodox Christians (Serbs), Roman Catholics (Croats), and Muslims (Bosnians who converted to Islam under the Ottoman Turkish rule). By contrast, ideologies of pan-Slavic integration that were influential from the mid-nineteenth century until the breakup of Yugoslavia in the 1990s held that a lasting peace and modernization for this backward region of Europe would be possible only through an interethnic alliance within a larger common state. Contrary to ethno-nationalist myths of the current regimes in the Western Balkans that see themselves as "traditional" and "natural" in contrast to purportedly "artificial" multiethnic projects, the ideology of the pan-Slavic and South-Slav multiethnic and interconfessional integration is much older and involves far more prominent intellectuals, secular as well as religious, who, as pointed out by leading students of nationalism, play key roles in nationalist movements and the formation of national-states in Europe (Hobsbawm 1992; Hroch 1985). The intellectual effort in the Yugoslav case was a gigantic and in many respects utopian venture, seeking both interethnic integration and cooperation among religions as well as modernization. The ethnic nationalist projects, by contrast, relied mainly on inventing tribal rivalries, sectarian feuds, mythmaking, ethnic cleansing, and genocide, which regularly accompanied the projects of making ethnically homogenous states from the First Balkan War of 1912, during World War II, and on to the recent Balkan Wars of the 1990s (International Commission 1914; Mojzes 2011). In a longer historical perspective, ethno-confessional nationalisms in the Western Balkans are largely a twentieth-century product, in contrast to the ideologies of multiethnic integration and interfaith cooperation, which originated as early as the sixteenth century and increased in influence in the nineteenth and through most of the twentieth centuries (Perica 2002, 3–42, 89–108).

Although the main historical events of the "Serbian Jerusalem" discourse – namely, the Battle at the Kosovo Field and the downfall of the Serbian Empire – occurred in the fourteenth century, the phrase "Serbian Jerusalem" in reference to Kosovo as a "holy land" for the Serbs is a recent invention with contemporary connotations. Serbian Jerusalem as a concept, discourse, and strategy in a nationalist mass movement has been a product of recent history and a wider context than the local imperial conquest, Balkan ethnic relations, folklore, and the Serbian Church's saintly cults. Even the claim that the Balkan province of Kosovo is the central theme in the history of the Serbs and the "national cradle" or "holy land" of Serbia equivalent to Jerusalem in the Israeli-Palestinian conflict is, as argued most recently by Belgrade anthropologist Ivan Čolović, among other anti-nationalist Serb scholars, a modern invention. Though it involves some folklore, myth, and legend, its contemporary ideas, forms, and discourses are largely invented traditions (Hobsbawm and Ranger 1983). Notably, the idea of Kosovo as the "nation's cradle" and "holy martyred land" is a recent construct replacing the previous emphasis on the modern Serbian state founded in the nineteenth century in the Catholic Habsburg lands of Central Europe, which comprise today's Croatia, Hungary, and northern Serbia. As pointed out by Čolović, the Kosovo myth as a founding myth of the nation and the keystone of Serbia's national ideology is a construction of the Serbian state and its elites that originated in the last decades of the nineteenth century and the first decade of the twentieth century and has been revised many times since as national regimes and international alliances changed (Čolović 2016, 127). In this chapter, I will show how the discourse on "Serbian Jerusalem" emerged in the early 1980s amidst the crisis leading to the collapse of Tito's Yugoslavia and the restructuring of nations in this part of southeastern Europe. I consider "the making of Serbian Jerusalem" a major part of the ethnic nationalist movement undoing Yugoslavia to Balkanize it into several states separated along ethno-confessional boundaries. This movement and its rivals have been influenced by the three major religions and religio-nationalist claims. The new "religious" nationalism or, in the Balkan case, more appropriately called ethno-religious, is usually described as the fusion of religious and national identities. More specifically, "religious nationalism relies on religious identities and myths to define the nation and its goals" (Grzymala-Busse 2019, 2).

The phrase "Serbian Jerusalem" has become a hallmark of the new sacralized public discourse developed into a major nationalist strategy in Serbia during the last decade of Tito's Yugoslavia. Inaugurated by the ethno-religious nationalist zealots of the Serbian Orthodox Church, the parallel between the historic monuments in holy places has since expanded into a comparison of the historic fates of Serbs and Jews.

In order to explain the origins, connotations, and influence of these sacralized politics, I will first critically examine the idea of a Kosovo-centered Serb history and the influence of myth that I see as yet another recent invention of the globally advancing ethno-religious nationalism. I will also explore how the comparisons between the historical fates of the Serbs and the Jews and the Kosovo-Jerusalem analogy resonated in Israel. Finally, I will outline an epilogue, or a short concluding section, to indicate the effects and consequences of the uses of "Serbian Jerusalem" and related concepts in the religious-nationalist strife for land, state power, and religious-nationalist revival.

THE RISE OF RELIGIOUS NATIONALISM AND THE DOWNFALL OF YUGOSLAVIA

Writing in the spring of 1999 as NATO bombs fell on Belgrade to intervene in the Serb-Albanian war over Kosovo, British businessman Alexander Karađorđević, who had returned to postcommunist Serbia in hope of inheriting the last Yugoslav king's throne, penned an open letter to Western leaders. In order to explain the significance of the contested Kosovo province from the Serbian perspective, Karađorđević compared it to Jerusalem:

> France, the United Kingdom and the United States have been traditional allies of Serbia in the West. That makes me wonder whether the use of NATO air strikes against Serbia has been the only appropriate response to the failure of diplomatic negotiations . . . [I]t should not be forgotten that Kosovo is a Serbian Jerusalem and a cradle of the Serbian state. The greatest sacred monuments, part of the Serbian heritage, are located in Kosovo . . . Kosovo is an inalienable part of Serbia and Serbs have the right to defend what is theirs. (Telegraf Online 2016)

At the same time, a Belgrade-based organization called the Serb-Jewish Friendship Society took special care of arguing Serbia's position on the Kosovo controversy in the United States. At a rally in Chicago, using similar analogies, the Society's representative alleged:

> As you know, Serbs compare Kosovo to Jerusalem. Yet, to the Serbs, Kosovo means even more than Jerusalem to the Jews. Kosovo is also the Serb Masada. There was a battle at Kosovo in 1389 [the Battle of Kosovo], the Serbian kingdom's last stand against the Ottoman Empire in which many thousands of Serbs – every Serbian soldier in the battle – were killed. In many ways . . . the Balkans are like the Middle East, when neighbor is fighting neighbor. (Yearwood 1999)

The discourse on Kosovo as a "Serbian Jerusalem" served foreign policy agenda in Serbia during the 1999 NATO intervention and afterward. The idea of a "Serbian Jerusalem," however, had originated earlier, in the 1980s, during the crisis leading to the collapse of Tito's Yugoslavia and the Balkan wars of the 1990s. The decade that followed longtime Yugoslav leader Tito's death in 1980 saw upsurges of separatist ethnic nationalisms accompanied by a religious revival in which ethnic nationalism was championed through religious organizations, commemorations, and jubilees. A massive ethno-religious nationalist movement emerging in the largest Yugoslav ethnic nation of Christian Orthodox Serbia upset the country's interethnic and interconfessional relations by turning Serbs against the founding Yugoslav ethnic nations (Catholic Croats and Slovenes), while also disturbing regions with large Muslim populations such as Bosnia and Herzegovina and Kosovo. The Serb nationalist movement began in Kosovo, the medieval seat of Serbian Church and state, a Balkan province now predominantly populated by ethnic Albanians, mostly Muslims.[3] The Serbian movement's symbolic beginning invoked the medieval religious heritage of Kosovo allegedly endangered by the hostile faith and ethnicity.

---

[3] In 2017, Kosovo had an estimated population of 1.895 million. Ethnic Albanians were the majority (92.9 percent). The 75,000 remaining Serbs (down from the 200,000 in the 1980s) lived mostly in North Kosovo. Albanians have had a relative majority in Kosovo at least since the 1690 great migrations of Serbs. See World Population Review (2019) and World Factbook (2018).

Serbian Jerusalem

On Good Friday in 1982, a group of Serb Orthodox clerics led by the outspoken zealot theologian Atanasije Jevtić, later Bishop in Kosovo, released a document entitled "Appeal for the Protection of the Serbian Population and Their Sacred Monuments in Kosovo" (also known as the Appeal of Twenty-One Serbian Priests).

> "The Kosovo issue," says the appeal, is the issue of the spiritual, cultural, and historical identity of the Serbian people. ... [L]ike the Jewish people who return to their Jerusalem in order to survive, the Serbian people are fighting once again the very same battle of Kosovo that our ancestors began to fight in 1389 at the Kosovo field. ... And when it seemed that the battle has been won once and for all, Kosovo is being taken away from us and we are no longer what we are! ... Without an exaggeration, it could be said that a planned genocide has been carried out against the Serbian people in Kosovo. The Albanian quest for an ethnically homogenous Albanian Kosovo free of Serbs is the evidence of genocide. (Perica 2002, 134)

Exaggerating ethnic tensions and dramatizing the situation, Serb nationalism rose by appealing to the most emotionally sensitive aspect of Serb national identity – the memory of a medieval empire under Serb ethnic rulers destroyed by Ottoman Turkish invasions of the Balkans. The Serbian Orthodox Church and nationalist intelligentsia in Serbia's capital, Belgrade, urged Serbs to mobilize against Albanian separatist nationalism in Kosovo. Serbian nationalism called for abolishing Kosovo's autonomy granted under Tito's federalism in favor of the province's direct rule from the capital, Belgrade.

While the Serb-Albanian feud over Kosovo alone could not ruin Yugoslavia, it aggravated Serbo-Croat relations that have been crucial for the country's stability ever since its foundation. By 1986–89, the Serb nationalist movement pressured the Yugoslav founding groups of Croats and Slovenes to accept a more centralized Serb-dominated federation or negotiate breakup and territorial partitions.

Serbian nationalism perceived the Serbs as eventual collective victims, although they had been the liberators of South Slavs and enablers of Yugoslavia. The Serbian Church developed a politics of commemorating Serb suffering under the Muslim and Catholic regimes including Ottoman Turkey, Austria, and – most tragically – the Croat fascist regime of the pro-Axis Independent State of Croatia that incorporated Croatia and Bosnia and Herzegovina in World War II.

The Serbian Orthodox Church – which had been not just a religion but also a national institution representing Serbs and Serbia ever since the medieval kingdom – viewed Serb conflicts with Albanians, Croats, and Bosniaks as religious in character, unveiling a purported perennial religious strife and clash of empires and civilizations in the Balkans. The Church backed nationalist territorial claims by emphasizing the historic sacred monuments as markers of historic and future state borders.[4]

---

[4] See the details on these struggles in Perica (2002, 123–64).

The Serb territorial claims and the Kosovo-centered mythical perspectives on history, memory, and the role of religion in the formation of nationhood aggravated the disputes with Kosovo Albanians, Croats, and Bosnian Muslims. Each responded with its own nationalist mobilization. From the political changes of 1989 to 1991, the rival nationalist movements became warring factions with paramilitary wings of the ethnic parties. Their leaders publicly debated yet failed to agree on any peaceful post-Yugoslav territorial arrangement. They spoke about exchanges of territories and population transfers in order to create ethno-religiously homogenous states. Following the breakup of Yugoslavia, an increasingly pro-Serb Yugoslav army provoked a wider war by attempting to impose the Greater Serbian project and secure its imagined borders in Croatia and Bosnia and Herzegovina. The wars in Croatia and Bosnia and Herzegovina ended with the Dayton Agreement in 1995; the Serb-Albania war in Kosovo ended with the NATO bombing of Serbia in 1999.

NATO forced Serbia to capitulate, withdraw its military, and grant the majority-Albanian, mostly Muslim, population the right to national self-determination even though Serbia has thus far not diplomatically recognized Kosovo's independence. The Serb nationalist project has been defeated in Croatia and Kosovo and partly won in Bosnia thanks to the Dayton Accords provision for a Serbian republic created via ethnic cleansing. In postwar Kosovo, only a small Serb population and scattered monastic communities of the Serbian Church have remained in an emerging Albanian state. Serbia was facing a catastrophe on a territory it had designated as a Serbian holy land comparable to Jerusalem.

Serbia has continued the struggle for Kosovo through diplomacy and the Serbian Orthodox Church. Serbian representatives focused on presenting to the West the Serb side of the story in which Serbs were victims. Diplomacy and the Church used the parallel between Kosovo and Jerusalem to illustrate the importance of Kosovo to the Serbs and to justify the use of force against Kosovar Albanian separatists whom Serb representatives likened to the Palestinians while comparing the Serbs to the Israelis. In a 2011 speech at an evangelical Christian college in the US, Serbia's Foreign Minister Vuk Jeremić remarked:

> We Serbs have an unbreakable bond with Kosovo … It is the wellspring of the Serbian spiritual tradition, and of our statehood; the heart and soul of our nation – indivisible and essential … Kosovo is our Valley Forge and Yorktown, our Alamo and Gettysburg, our Pearl Harbor and Iwo Jima – all rolled into one. It is in our dreams at night, and in our prayers in church. It is the "apple of our eye." It is our Jerusalem. (Jeremić 2011)

The Belgrade government was aided by the Church, traditionally both a national institution and a marker of national identity. Church leaders emphasized the historic sacred monuments and art from the medieval seat of the Church and state in Kosovo to support Serbian claims to the region and delegitimize those of the Albanians who did not preserve such material evidence of their own. To underscore this point, the Church reissued an encyclopedia followed by several similar monographs showing its well-preserved cultural heritage, including several hundred churches and monasteries in Kosovo (Mileusnić 2001). Since then, the Church has also insisted on the older historic name for the province as "Kosovo and Metohija," the latter word being of Greek origin and meaning "land and property owned or administered by monasteries."

Church leaders kept monastic land under the Belgrade patriarchate's canonical jurisdiction with the intention of remaining part of the Serbian state. The leader of the Serbian Orthodox Church, Patriarch Irenei (Gavrilović), once said:

> An Albanian government or any non-Christian authority, cannot be trusted with taking care of the Serbian sacred heritage and monuments of Kosovo. Kosovo Albanians only want to destroy it, they do not even know what history is and how spiritual legacies are preserved. (Andrejić 2017)

The statement echoes and expands to the Kosovo conflict the earlier theses about "wars of religions" and the "clash of civilizations" used by Serbian ethnic and church leaders to explain the war in Bosnia-Herzegovina, 1992–95. This war, however, was caused not by the religious differences or the clash between Islam and Christianity but primarily by the Serb nationalist aggression to facilitate the destruction of Tito's Yugoslavia, ethnic cleansing, and the making of a Greater Serbia (Sells 1998). Moreover, until the war in Bosnia-Herzegovina, Islam in the former Yugoslavia was relatively less religious-nationalistic and less militant than Serbian Orthodoxy and Croat Catholicism (Perica 2002, 74–88, 133–64).

In 2006, following several waves of Albanian nationalists' attacks on Serbian Church property, UNESCO placed four Serb historic monuments in Kosovo on its "List of World Heritage in Danger" (UNESCO 2006). Subsequently, Serbian Church and government officials further internationalized the Kosovo controversy via cultural diplomacy in Western Europe and the US by staging exhibits and lectures about Kosovo's sacred medieval monuments such as at Columbia University and Library of Congress in 2015.

In 2009, US Vice President Joseph Biden visited Kosovo's Dečani Monastery to hear the familiar message from the Serb abbot: "Kosovo is our holy land, the Serbian Jerusalem" (Janjić 2008).

In the eyes of the Serbian Church, the military loss of Kosovo following the NATO intervention has been a tragedy comparable to the 1389 Battle of Kosovo. Ever since then Serbian nationalism has further emphasized the collective victimhood narrative. In a 2013 statement, Patriarch Irenei found hope in the comparison between the historical fates of the Serbs and the Jews:

> If the ruthless world powers took away our Jerusalem from us, we have the example of the Jewish people who waited for 2,000 years to bring their Jerusalem back into

the Jewish state. And they survived to see that day coming! (Quoted in Zečević and Radulović 2013)

Accordingly, since the early 1980s, the Church has inaugurated and itself adopted the phrase "Serbian Jerusalem" as a hallmark of the new sacralized public discourse that eventually developed into a major nationalist strategy.

INVENTING A HOLY LAND IN EUROPE'S PERIPHERY

Although mentioning the word "Jerusalem" (let alone its parallels and metaphors) implies a long history, I will argue that the phrase "Serbian Jerusalem" and the related discourses comparing Serbs and Jews are recent phenomena. Such discourses have been introduced by the Serbian nationalist movement since it began developing in the 1980s. The key role of the Church and the use of sacred sites and historic monuments as the evidence to sustain territorial claims were first introduced by the modern Serbian state in the early twentieth century and were then revived at the end of it. To begin with, a Kosovo-centered Serb history is, among other things, an example for the nationalist practices that Hobsbawm and Ranger call "the invention of tradition."[5] Furthermore, the strong showing of religion in nationalist movements is not a revival of an ancient religion but the late modern and postmodern desecularizing of all three monotheistic religions – Christianity, Judaism, and Islam – that has been resurgent worldwide since approximately the 1970s (Huntington 1996; Kepel 1994).

Some legends about the 1389 Battle of Kosovo are of premodern origin, but the use of the narrative as a nation-building myth is modern. The memory of the 1389 Battle of Kosovo, preserved in Serb folklore and through the saintly cults of the Serbian Orthodox Church, became a political myth and part of nation-building ideology sanctioned by the Serbian state in the late nineteenth and early twentieth centuries. The Serbian state in the same period also recognized the Serbian Orthodox Church as a national institution and the Memorial Day of the Kosovo battle (also the day of the saintly Prince Lazar, the martyr of Kosovo) as national holidays. From the 1890s to the Balkan Wars of 1912–13, Serbian nationalism for the first time used the medieval sacred monuments, sites of memory, churches, and monasteries as evidence in support of Serb territorial claims and potential state boundary markers. In about the same period, Orthodox Churches in Serbia and Montenegro called for revenge against Turks and other Balkan Muslims while the liberation of Kosovo as Old Serbia (to be reunited with the new modern one) became the foreign policy priority of the modern Serbian state (Čolović 2016, 234).

---

[5] The invention of tradition involves "modern nationalist practices of using ancient materials to construct invented tradition of a novel type for quite novel purposes ... the new traditions use old materials, invent new language or devices, extend the old symbolic vocabulary beyond established limits" (Hobsbawm and Ranger 1983, 6–7).

Serbian Jerusalem 223

In the First Balkan War of 1912, Serbian armies defeated Ottoman Turks and occupied Kosovo. The war aims, as Serbian diplomacy explained to Britain and other Western powers meditating in the conflict, included the liberation of local Christian communities from oppressive Muslim rule and the protection of Serbian medieval monuments and the Serbian Church's property. In a book published in the 1980s, Serbian church historian Dimitrije Bogdanović cites a document by which Serbia claims Kosovo as follows:

> It was rightly said (in the Serbian Memorandum to the ambassadors of the European Powers in London in 1913) that this territory is a kind of "Holy Land" for the Serbian people ... In the negotiations about territories and borders in Kosovo and Metohija at the 1913 conference in London, Serbia prioritized the historic, ethnographic, cultural and moral criteria. These include the continuity of the Serb statehood and culture in Kosovo.[6]

While it is clear that Kosovo symbolizes an important phase in Serb history and its preserved historic monuments matter, the idea of Kosovo as the holiest of all historically relevant places for the Serbs was not spontaneous and "traditional" but rather a politically and strategically calculated addition to the discourse of Serbian nationalism. In the late nineteenth and the early twentieth centuries, as the young Serbian nation-state developed a blueprint for territorial expansion, Kosovo became the most sacred space or "holy land" to be liberated first (Čolović 2016, 234). The irredentist claims focused on Kosovo and Macedonia, aka "Old Serbia," as "unredeemed historic lands" because the modern Serbian state had succeeded by the late nineteenth century to incorporate both the territory where the early medieval Serbia originated and modern Serbia was founded.

The earliest Serbian state and a self-governing Eastern Christian Church originated between 1217 and 1219 at church councils and royal coronations at monasteries and churches located in central Serbia's Rascia (Raška) province.[7] The founder of the Church and the state and the first canonized native Serb saint, Archbishop Sava the "Enlightener" (Rastko Nemanjić), lived and governed in Serbia outside Kosovo and retired to a monastery in Greece more than 100 years before the Kosovo battle. Under Sava's successors of the Nemanjic dynasty, who were governing an expanding state and an independent Church, Kosovo would become the center of a large regional empire and a Church elevated to the highest authority of the patriarchate. The king of Serbia, Stefan Uroš IV Dušan (1331–46), ruled as "Emperor of the Serbs, Bulgars, Romanians, Greeks, and Albanians" (1346–55). He established the imperial

---

[6] "Therefore, Serbia emphasizes that the land on which stand the historic monasteries and shrines such as the Patriarchate of Peć, the Dečani monastery and the Orthodox cathedral at Đakovica, have always been a holy land for all Serbs. Hence, no Serb or Montenegrin government would cede the holy land of the Serbs to the Albanians or anyone else. On that point, the Serbian people will not make any concessions, transactions or compromise" (Bogdanović 1986, 34).

[7] Studenica monastery stands near the town of Kraljevo in the historic Raška district. UNESCO posted Studenica on its World Heritage List in 1986. See also UNESCO (2013).

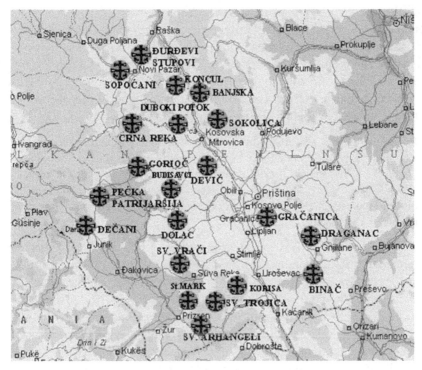

MAP 9.1 Historic Serbian monasteries in Kosovo

seat in the Kosovo town of Prizren and relocated the patriarchate to the Kosovo town of Peć (Pejë, Ipek; see Map 9.1). The Archbishop of Peć is honored with the title "Serbian Patriarch." Patriarchs actually co-rule with kings and emperors, and in absence of a functioning government, may even adopt the government's powers. The legend about the 1389 battle at the Kosovo field was preserved, not merely as folklore, but even more importantly in Church liturgy and saintly cults. The Church commemorated the loss of independent statehood and encouraged the struggle for its renewal. The Church canonized Prince Lazar, the leader of the Christian army at Kosovo. He is portrayed as a devout Christian who rejects vassalage to a non-Christian authority and possible conversion to Islam. He chooses death instead or, in religious discourse, he opts for a "heavenly empire" (*carstvo nebesko*, i.e., "empire in heaven," not kingdom, as it is commonly translated in English texts on this topic). The story's moral suggests that it is better to dream about empire in the domains of memory, myth, and religion than it is to live in an actual earthly state under a foreign non-Christian authority.

The stories of Kosovo energized Serbian liberation wars in the nineteenth century and the renewal of statehood in 1878. As noted earlier, the first territorial expansion of modern Serbia was the deliverance of Kosovo as a "holy land" in 1912. Following a pattern similar to that seen in the First Balkan War of 1912, amidst the Yugoslav crisis of the 1980s, Serb nationalism effectively awakened the Serb emotional attachment to Kosovo. The last US ambassador to Yugoslavia, Warren Zimmermann, keenly observed the prewar crisis in Yugoslavia not only as a professional diplomat but also as a Yale- and Cambridge-trained student of history and humanities. He noticed the rise of the militant spirit of Kosovo through a series of processions dedicated to the martyred Prince Lazar. The Church had the decapitated saint's relics carried around through territories claimed by Serbia in a possible conflict including Kosovo, Serbia proper, and Bosnia. The Lazar's tour was one of the Serbian nationalist movement's preparatory practices of mass mobilization leading to the gathering in 1989 of some 2 million Serbs at the historic Kosovo battlefield to mark the 600th anniversary of the Kosovo battle. Zimmermann argued that Lazar's processions and the rally were nationalistic parades under religious symbols, a provocative show of force against all the potential enemies of the emerging greater Serbia. Zimmermann (1996, 206–7) saw this religious-nationalist movement as a prelude to the breakup of Yugoslavia and to the Balkan Wars of the 1990s.

Amidst the Yugoslav collapse and wars, religion moved to the public sphere and merged with ethnic nationalist movements. In ethnic mass movements, religious organizations and ethnic parties merged, fusing the ideology of ethnically homogenous states with majority religions seeking a monopoly in the religious sphere. The retreat of moderates and the rise of zealots occurred through the churches' involvement in the historical controversies and ethnic elites disputes about how to restructure the country (Perica 2002, 43–73, 133–64). During the Croatian and Bosnian wars of 1991–95, the Kosovo conflict paused thanks to moderate Albanian leaders. When militants rose provoking the Milosevic regime, the Serbo-Albanian war broke out in 1998 and ended with NATO's intervention in 1999. The Serb-Albanian conflict over Kosovo continued after the cessation of armed struggle as well as the Serb-Croat and Serb-Bosnian Muslim conflicts following the wars in Croatia and Bosnia-Herzegovina, from 1991 to 1995.

The following two symbolic discourses have dominated the narrative of the Balkan conflict since the 1980s: (1) the discourse on Kosovo, now called "Serbian Jerusalem," including the analogy between the historical fates of the Serbs and the Jews and between present-day Serbia and the State of Israel; and (2) the discourse on the Croat genocide against the Serbs in the pro-Nazi Croat wartime state, notably in the concentration camp of Jasenovac. Run by the Croat fascist Ustašes, Jasenovac was the largest death camp in the Balkans. The brutal regime carried out genocidal persecution of Serbs, Jews, and Roma, as well as massive war crimes and reprisals against members of the anti-fascist resistance of various nationalities (I.Goldstein 2018; I.Goldstein and Goldstein 2016; Tomasevich 2001).

THE BALKANS-MIDEAST CONNECTION

Some discursive references and symbolic links between Kosovo and Jerusalem can be found in Balkan legend and folklore, notably the story of divine messages sent from Jerusalem to Kosovo on the eve of the 1389 battle or the description of the Kosovo defeat of 1389 and the ensuing downfall of the Serbian kingdom as "Serbian Golgotha." The legend about the 1389 battle on the Kosovo field, first mentioned in Western literature in the sixteenth century (Čolović 2016), narrates that Prince Lazar received a message from the Holy Mother of God carried by prophet Elijah (as a grey falcon) flying from "Jerusalem the Holy" to land in the Christian camp on the battlefield. The holy message commanded Lazar not to surrender to Muslim authority but rather make a Christ-like sacrifice.[8] Similarly, the Serbian Church would later describe the 1389 defeat of the Christian army on the Kosovo battlefield as "Serbian Golgotha," after the hill in Jerusalem where Jesus was crucified (Emmert 1990). However, the specific phrase "Serbian Jerusalem" is contemporary and can be properly understood only in the present context that draws parallels between some aspects of the conflicts in the Balkans and the Middle East. Serbian nationalism introduced the phrase as a catchy slogan to rally mass mobilization of Serbs in support of the breakup of Yugoslavia and the making of a Greater Serbia on its ruins. Despite the seductive slogans and discourses of this nationalist movement, the politics carried out under the "Serbian Jerusalem" slogan has been far more pragmatic than poetic. The phrase "Serbian Jerusalem" used in political discourse was probably first published in the 1930s and revived in the 1980s. Since then, it has been reused and revised to fit in the new sociohistorical context of the fall of Yugoslavia, the post-Yugoslav civil wars in the Balkans in the 1990s, and Serbia's extended struggle for Kosovo afterward. These recent uses of the discourse and its context are crucial for understanding the contemporary Balkan conflict and Serbian nationalism as its major driving force.

Beginning as a catchy slogan in the mid-1980s, "Serbian Jerusalem" expanded into a nationalist concept applied to contesting territorial claims in Kosovo and Bosnia and Herzegovina. Serb novelist Vuk Drašković (2013) stated on a television show at the time: "As you know, I was the one who invented that metaphor Serbian Jerusalem about Kosovo." Drašković was one of the communist leaders who had converted to the "new religion" of ethnic nationalism to lead the new post-Yugoslav ethno-religious states, like Serbia's Slobodan Milošević and Dobrica Ćosić, or the Croat President Franjo Tudjman. Drašković claimed that he invented the "Serbian Jerusalem" metaphor in his 1985 letter that he, as chairman of the Serbian national writers' association, published and sent to the Israeli national writers' association.

---

[8] "There flies, a grey bird, a falcon, From Jerusalem, the holy; And in his beak, he bears a swallow. That is no falcon, no grey bird; But it is the Saint Elijah. He carries no swallow; But a book from the Mother of God. He comes to the Tsar at Kosovo, He lays the book on the Tsar's knees" (quoted in West 2007, 909–11).

The discourse, of course, neither emerged out of the blue nor was it solely the product of Drašković's genius. As noted earlier, the Serbian government portrayed Kosovo as the "holy land of the Serbs" to justify the territorial acquisitions in the First Balkan War of 1912. Apparently, Drašković was not even the first Serb nationalist leader who published the phrase "Serbian Jerusalem" in reference to Kosovo. As quoted by Belgrade anthropologist Ivan Čolović (2016, 317) in his recent study about the Kosovo myth, General Milan Nedić, the chief Nazi collaborator in occupied Serbia during World War II, used the phrase "Serbian Jerusalem" in reference to Kosovo. Thus, on the occasion of the 550th anniversary of the Battle of Kosovo in June 1939, Nedić wrote in a Belgrade newspaper: "Serbs are again seeking spiritual renewal and new energy by returning to Kosovo – Serbian Jerusalem" (quoted in Čolović 2016, 317). Nedić regularly spoke of the heroic spirit of Kosovo as he led Serbia's collaboration with the Nazis that resulted in massive crimes including the Serb contribution to the Holocaust by which the Nedić regime had cleansed Serbia of its Jewish population by August 1942.[9] The great Kosovo myth, according to Nedić regime's propaganda, was the remedy that healed and protected Serbia from the "Jewish-Freemasonic-Bolshevik internationalist disease" (Čolović 2016, 327).

Drašković probably borrowed the phrase from Nedić, whom Serb nationalists today consider a patriot and victim of communism. Another potential source may be the leading Serb theologian, later canonized saint, Bishop Nikolai Velimirović (1881–1956). In 1939, as the co-organizer of the 550th jubilee of the Battle of Kosovo, Velimirović delivered patriotic homilies representing the Church while, on the same occasion, General Nedić was the keynote speaker on the 1389 battlefield. Also in speeches during the 1930s, Velimirović compared Hitler to Saint Sava and Serb to German nationalism as mutually inspiring and having a lot in common (Byford 2004).

THE MAKING OF SERBIAN JERUSALEM

Following the release of the earlier-quoted Appeal of Twenty-One (Serbian Orthodox) Priests in 1982 containing analogies between Kosovo and Jerusalem and the parallels between historical fates of Serbs and Jews, the chief ideologue of new Serbian nationalism, the novelist Dobrica Ćosić, stated in a 1983 interview: "The Serb is the new Jew at the end of the twentieth century" (quoted in Perica 2002, 124). Ćosić was probably the first among prominent Yugoslav political figures who proposed partitioning Kosovo into two segregated, ethnically homogenous enclaves, a Serbian and an Albanian one (Spahiu 1999). Drawing from Ćosić (and possibly from Velimirović and Nedić) the self-proclaimed inventor of "Serbian Jerusalem,"

---

[9] The Semlin concentration camp (also known by its Serbian name Sajmište) was one of the main sites of the Holocaust in Nazi-occupied Serbia. Between March and May 1942, approximately 7,000 Jewish women, children, and elderly (almost half of the total Jewish population of Nazi-occupied Serbia) were systematically murdered there by the use of a mobile gas van. See Byford (2011).

228 *Vjekoslav Perica*

Vuk Drašković, then as chairman of the Serbian national writers' association, wrote to Israeli writers to make them aware of similarities between the Serbs and the Jews as perennial, heroic, and suffering nations. The preserved Serb and Jewish historic monuments, places of worship, and archeological sites in Kosovo and in Israel, Drašković wrote, sustain territorial claims against the Muslims who occupy these lands today. Kosovo is therefore "Serbian Jerusalem," a holy land and ancestral homeland from which Serbs, like Jerusalem's Jews, were forced into exile but to which they will always return. According to Drašković, Yugoslavian Serbs and Jews were the major victims of the Croat fascist genocide in World War II. This memory, as well as the contemporary conflict with militant Islam in both Kosovo and Palestine, brings Serbs and Jews together as allies.[10]

The Serbian Orthodox Church advanced Bishop Velimirović's idea from the 1950s about the collective victimhood of Serbs being comparable only to the fate of the Jews in the Holocaust. Žarko Gavrilović, a senior Orthodox cleric from Belgrade, wrote in 1987 that "the Serbs are the greatest martyrs of humankind . . . no other people in the world, except the Jews, have suffered so much for their faith and nation" (quoted in Perica 2002, 124–25). Interestingly, Enriko Josif, then the cochairman of the Yugoslav Jewish federation, was first to use a parallel between Auschwitz and the Ustaše-run Jasenovac concentration camp in northern Croatia.[11] Historian Vladimir Dedijer (1992) later borrowed the Auschwitz analogy for the title of his book on the Ustaše genocide focusing on the role of the Vatican as the alleged chief foreign sponsor of the Ustaše state.[12]

After Tito's death, Serb nationalism revised the Tito-era patriotic myths emphasizing interethnic cooperation in the struggle against foreign imperialism. The new perspective viewed Serbo-Croat relations as a centuries-long conflict driven by religious hatred and tribal envy. Serbian nationalism accused the Catholic Church in Croatia of being an accomplice in Ustaše crimes, for Catholicism was a state religion in wartime Croatia and many priests sided with the Ustaše Croat Catholicism. The latter itself turned increasingly nationalistic, vehemently denied

---

[10] The letter is quoted in detail in Zivkovic (2000).

[11] The Ustaše (Insurgents) was a Croatian fascist and ultranationalist organization founded in 1929 to resist a royal dictatorship by Serb King Alexander. The Ustaše assassinated Alexander in 1934 in retaliation for Serb nationalists' killing of Croat parliamentary deputies in 1928. The self-appointed Ustaše "fuhrer," Ante Pavelić, was initially sponsored by Mussolini but moved close to Hitler after the foundation of a pro-Axis satellite state named the Independent State of Croatia (NDH in Croatian), in which the Ustaše passed the Nazi-like racial laws. The Ustaše fought for a Greater Croatia to encompass today's Croatia and Bosnia and Herzegovina (yet not the Dalmatian coast that was ceded to Italy). The territory was to be cleansed from ethnic Serbs while Muslims were considered ethnic Croats and allies. The Ustaše imitated Nazis to run concentration camps in which hundreds of thousands of Serbs, Jews, Romani (Gypsy), and anti-fascist resistance fighters were killed. In 1945, a multiethnic, predominantly Serbo-Croat anti-fascist Partisan army led by the communist Marshal Tito, and backed by Soviet Russia, defeated the Ustaše and other ethnic nationalist factions including the Serb Chetniks.

[12] Josif's statements are quoted in Perica (2002, 124–25).

allegations of genocide, minimized Ustaše crimes, and even made martyrs of a number of pro-Ustaše priests executed by the communists. As a slap in the face of the Serbian Orthodox Church, the Croatian episcopate lobbied for the beatification of Cardinal Alojzije Stepinac (1899–1960) who led the Church during World War II, and was imprisoned by the communists for allegedly supporting the Ustaše movement.

BORROWING FROM CONTEMPORARY ISRAELI NATIONALISM

The meanings and uses of "Serbian Jerusalem" in the Balkan conflict can be properly understood in the contemporary context that draws parallels between the conflicts in the Balkans and the Israeli-Palestinian conflict. For contemporary Serbian nationalism (and also some other currents, such as Russian and Croatian, for example), Israel appears as a role model to follow in the nationalist struggles for land. Founded by the victims of racism, chauvinism, and ethnic cleansing, the State of Israel has anyhow become a world authority on the ideas and practices used to torment the Jews for centuries. In his 2006 collection of essays, French philosopher Alain Badiou (2006, 62–72), comparing the Balkans and the Middle East in recent history, notes that in the Balkan Wars of the 1990s, Serbian ethnic nationalist militias carried out "ethnic cleansing" aimed at "clearing their enemies out of the territories they coveted" and thereby emulating "the techniques masterfully utilized by the Israelis in Palestine since 1947."

In a cynical statement, Russian President Vladimir Putin justified the 2014 Russian annexation of the Crimean Peninsula in these words: "The Crimea has a sacred meaning for Russia. Like the Temple Mount for Jews and Muslims, the Crimea is the spiritual source of the formation of the multifaceted but monolithic Russian nation . . . . It was on this spiritual soil that our ancestors first and forever recognized their nationhood" (Coyer 2015). In a similar vein, Serbia's main Balkan rivals, the Croats, invoked Israel as a role model in the struggle for territory with Serbs and Muslims in Croatia and Bosnia-Herzegovina. A Croat right-wing nationalist leader stated as follows: "We in Croatia are like Israel. Croatia lives in a strange environment . . . there is danger of new wars with Serbia . . . we need to invest in rearmament . . . . Let us now make another Israel out of Croatia here in the Balkans" (Jutarnji.hr 2016).

Contemporary Serbian nationalism imitates Israel in the following ideas and practices:

1. The use of Jerusalem as the key metaphor of a symbolic discourse to justify land claims by history, myth, and religion – i.e., "sacralizing" the contested territory claimed by several different ethnicities and religions
2. Developing a military force like the Israeli army as a model army for managing holy lands and waging holy wars

3. Using settlements and expanding settler communities across disputed territories planned for annexation
4. Advancing the myth of a collective martyrdom (in the world's contest among nations for a greatest martyr nation)
5. Seeking international alliance and special relationship with the State of Israel.

To begin with the last point about the diplomatic alliance with Israel, during the 1990s and afterward, the new discourses and the international media focus on the Yugoslav wars prompted a dynamic, unprecedented communication between Israel and the Balkans. Slobodan Milošević's regime tried to influence Israeli public opinion through the Jewish federation of Yugoslavia and the Serb-Jewish Friendship Society. Meanwhile, many prominent Yugoslav Jews (such as Danilo Kiš, Filip David, Oskar Davičo, and Laslo Sekelj) joined Serbia's anti-Milošević opposition (Sekelj 1997). When the US encouraged Kosovo's independence, Israel did not recognize Kosovo and condemned its unilateral secession lest it embolden Palestinian Arab separatism. According to an Israeli journal's correspondent from the Balkans, "Kosovo is not just a part of Serbia but also 'the cradle of its nationalism and culture.' If the 'Serbian Jerusalem' is taken away from it, why should 'al-Quds' not be taken from us in the future and become the capital of the independent Palestine?" (Primor 2007).

After the wars of the 1990s, a number of prominent Israeli representatives visited Serbia and the neighboring Balkan states. Michael Freund, a New York-born Israeli journalist and founder of the Israeli-Serbian Friendship Society, visited Serbia in March 2014. Serb media portrayed him as a highly educated man, knowledgeable of Serb history and culture. Freund said in an interview that he understood well the meaning of Kosovo to the Serbs, explicitly making the comparison: "Jerusalem is our Kosovo" (Intermagazin 2014).

That same year, Israeli Prime Minister Benjamin Netanyahu was also in Belgrade. To this day, historians debate whether Netanyahu was joking when he stated at a press conference that Jews and Serbs have been friends since the time of the Roman Republic; that is, since the fourth century BCE, even though the first written record mentioning the Serbs, Croats, and other barbarian Slavic tribes invading the Roman Empire is in a Byzantine document from the tenth century CE. In Belgrade, Netanyahu also voiced the Serb revisionist perspective on history, reducing the complexity of World War II in the Balkans to "the joint suffering of Jews and Serbs at hands of Nazis and their collaborators" (Bulatović 2014; see also Israel Ministry of Foreign Affairs 2014).

In the meantime, the rock icon Bob Dylan, who lives in Israel and the US, caused a scandal in the Balkans when he spoke in a 2012 interview about hatred and distrust among various peoples worldwide. Dylan used as an example the Serbo-Croat conflict, on which he adopted the Serb nationalist perspective. "Just like Jews can sense Nazi blood and the Serbs can sense Croatian blood," Dylan stated. The

Croatians promptly objected, "complaining that his comment smears all Croatians, past and present" (S.Goldstein 2013a). In a separate response, Slavko Goldstein, the prominent Croatian publisher and leader of the local Jewish community, wrote an op-ed in *The New York Times* criticizing Dylan for ignorance about the joint Serbo-Croat anti-fascist resistance that defended Serbs and Jews from genocide and militarily defeated the Croat pro-Nazi Ustaše regime (S.Goldstein 2013b).

In November 2017, former Israeli senior official Yaakov Kedmi allegedly stated in an interview for Serbian and Russian audiences that Israel has always stood by Serbia and would never forgive Croatia's Ustaše crimes. He added, "Kosovo Albanians attempt to eradicate the historic memory of [the] Serbian and Christian past in Kosovo, and it is known that Kosovo was one of the centers of the Serbian nation ... Likewise, in Israel, the Palestinian leaders do not recognize Israeli sacred heritage and historic monuments, ancient temples, they say all is Zionist fabrication; [the] Palestinian movement is trying to destroy all traces of the 3,000 years of Jewish history" (Novosti Online 2017).

Finally, in July 2018, Israeli President Reuven Rivlin ventured on a Balkan tour. Standing with the Croatian president at the site of the World War II concentration camp Jasenovac, Rivlin succeeded in getting the first-ever explicit condemnation of Croat Ustaše genocidal crimes from a leader of the long-ruling Croat nationalist party (AFP 2018). Then, President Rivlin visited Serbia. Among other activities there, he attended a ceremony in Belgrade's Zemun suburb (formerly in Austria) where a street was to be named after the Zemun-native Theodor Herzl, the founder of the Zionist movement. Actually, ancestors of ethnic Albanians from Kosovo and Albania probably settled in the Balkans more than 2,000 years ago, even before Jews and for sure before the arrival of the Serbs and other South Slavs (Malcolm 1999; Vickers 1998).

In the meantime, it has been revealed that Israel negotiated a massive transfer of military technology to both Serbia and Croatia. While Croatia's attempt to acquire Israeli warplanes has eventually failed due to a US veto, Serbia succeeded in acquiring new military helicopters and fighter jets from Russia, thus influencing the regional balance of power. Israeli historian Efraim Zuroff of the Simon Wiesenthal Center criticized his government's meddling in the Balkan conflict and regional rivalries in southeastern Europe where Israel has no particular interest to protect or advance.[13]

At any rate, Balkan states, as noted above, have been particularly impressed with the Israeli army. In an article published in the Belgrade press in 1986, the Serbian army's role in the holy land of Kosovo is compared to the Israeli army's mission to defend the historic lands and sacred places in the Holy Land:

---

[13] Israeli historian Efraim Zuroff said in an interview: "Why would Israel take sides in Balkan wars? Honoring a victory that led to the expulsion of hundreds of thousands of Serbs, is not a good idea – it does not make any sense" (Keinon and Ahronheim 2018).

The Jews ... who have been banned for nearly 2000 years by European states from serving in the military and choosing military professions, today have one of the best organized and best armed, also perfectly trained and most combat-ready military forces in the world. The Israeli army's superiority has been successfully tested in wars it has won against much larger enemy armies. This is the kind of military force Serbia needs today in order to protect Kosovo Serb and Orthodox Christian shrines from the Muslim threat. (Klarin and Tajtelbaum 1986, 10)

The next point to elaborate is the imitation of the Israeli army. The authors of this text had also anticipated an increasing collaboration between the Serbian Orthodox Church and the Serbian national armed forces, referring again to Israel as a role model. Similarly, according to an analyst for *Peščanik*, a leading Serbian anti-nationalist journal, since the 1990s, a "Serb Christian-Orthodox nationalism" has become the new official ideology of Serbia's armed forces (Veljković 2016). Serb Orthodox clerics are appointed as military chaplains working alongside the career military officers. Group visits to the historic Serbian monasteries by military academy cadets have become a routine part of the new military schools' curriculum and training. According to Veljković (2016), a publication entitled *Handbook for the Serb Orthodox Soldier* issued in 2012 by a monastery in Serbia and adopted by the Army of Serbia (Vojska Srbije) for its troops' training and service summarizes the Serb soldier's duties as follows:

Duties of the Serb Orthodox soldier serving in the National Army of Serbia include: protection of the Church, the Christian Orthodox Faith, Saint Sava's teachings, and Serbian popular and religious customs. The Serb Orthodox soldier will safeguard and protect Serbian places of worship and establish stable conditions under which the Orthodox priest can celebrate the bloodless sacrifice to the Glory of our Lord for the sins of the people and his own.[14]

In July 2017, representatives of the Serbian Ministry of Defense visited Jerusalem. Upon their return to Belgrade, Defense Minister Aleksandar Vulin (2017) reported the following about signing a military cooperation treaty with Israel to Serbian state television: "We have a lot to learn from Israel, in particular how to be effective in a turbulent territory – it requires both military firmness and diplomatic skill." Yet, Serbian ultranationalists, traditionally pro-Russian, are uncomfortable with the government pro-Israeli rhetoric. A Serb populist leader has recently stated: "Russia should become to Serbia the same as America [is] to Israel ... Russia is our only sincere friend protecting us like America protects Israel" (Danas Online 2017).

Regarding the expansion of settlements as the method for land grab in disputed territories, the Israeli influence on Serbian nationalism has become obvious since

---

[14] According to Veljković (2016), which cites the publication *Priručnik za Pravoslavnog Vojnika* (*Handbook for the Serb Orthodox Soldier*), issued by the Serbian army for internal use but published by the Serbian Orthodox Church Monastery Rukumija at Lapovo, Serbia, 2012. The authors are monks and military officers.

2016. In addition to imitating the Israeli army, Serbia has introduced in Kosovo a new practice reminiscent of the Israeli settlers' movement. In March 2016, the government of Serbia started construction of new settlements in northern Serb-populated enclaves of Kosovo and also in the heavily Albanian-populated south. The first new Serb settlement, "Sunny Valley," broke ground to mark the seventeenth anniversary of the 1999 Serb exodus from Kosovo. The settlement includes a residential complex with 300 housing units and other buildings designed, according to the Belgrade government, as "a project of love for our own nation, aimed at alleviating the consequences of ethnic cleansing, bloody expulsions and extermination of Serbs in Kosovo" (Tanjug 2016). The Kosovar Albanian government declared the construction of Serb settlements to be illegal and politically dangerous, foreshadowing a territorial partition of Kosovo (Krstić 2016).

The imitation of the myths concerning Jerusalem as a historic sacred center and therefore the contemporary national capital is evident from the recent strategy of the Serbian Orthodox Church regarding an "update" to the role of the historic ecclesiastical authority in Kosovo and Metohija. In March 2018, the Serbian Orthodox Church adopted a new name, "The Serbian Orthodox Church – the Patriarchate of Peć," to make Kosovo one of the Church's active headquarters. This new policy is outlined in a 2003 document entitled "Memorandum of the Serbian Orthodox Church on the Situation in Kosovo and Metohija" in which the Church declared:

> Kosovo is Serbian Jerusalem, the center of spiritual, cultural, national and human identity of the Serb people, where Serbs became the mature historic people, and no state or any other authority can surrender Kosovo and Metohija to a non-Serb authority. (Đorđević 2003)

Patriarch Irenei explained the new Church's name:

> Kosovo is not just a geographic space but a holy land without which Serbia cannot exist … Kosovo is at present an occupied Serbian land. It cannot be traded, partitioned or recognized as a foreign land but only liberated and returned to Serbia. (Beta 2012)

At the same time, by canonizing three new Serb saints martyred in Kosovo under Ottoman rule, the Church further strengthened the religious and psychological connection between Serbia and Kosovo while pointing at Islam as the enemy. The new national saints canonized in May 2018 were all Kosovo-born Serb Christians martyred for refusing conversion to Islam under Ottoman rule. These canonizations and their subsequent liturgical commemorations provide detailed graphic descriptions of the torture and suffering that Kosovo Serbs had suffered at hands of the Muslim enemy. The purpose is to trigger traumatic responses among the faithful while stoking a collective sentiment of endangerment and fear of the historic torture and suffering being repeated.

Finally, the ideas of collective martyrdom and eternal victimization have become a hallmark of contemporary Serbian nationalism with church leaders' frequent references to Israel. Following parliamentary resolutions on the Armenian genocide from the Vatican, Germany, France, and eleven other EU member countries, the Serbian Church added the Armenian genocide to the parallels with the Holocaust to the discourse on the collective suffering and eternal victimization of the Serbs (Smale and Eddy 2016). At a commemoration in August 2016, Patriarch Irenei spoke about the Serb suffering in World War II and concluded: "Only Jews and Armenians, besides Serbs, have seen such a Golgotha" (Al Jazeera Balkans 2016). On several occasions since then, church leaders have referred back to this analogy between Serbs and Armenians, sometimes also mentioning the comparison between Serbs and Jews. In October 2017, at a commemoration in Bosnia, Patriarch Irenei said: "The twentieth century was so glorious yet tragic for the Serbs, that human history never recorded such a grave suffering of a people. It seems that the suffering of the Serbs exceeded the gravity of the calamities of Jewish and Armenian peoples" (Al Jazeera Balkans 2017).

Serbia's anti-nationalist opposition has successfully explained the nationalist ideology yet remained weak to halt its advancement through the state, the Church, the state-controlled media, and nationalistic or populist parties. Explaining the Serb nationalists' victimization theme, the Serbian historian Dubravka Stojanović refers to contemporary Israeli author Amos Oz. According to Stojanović:

> In the words of Amos Oz, we are witnessing a world championship tournament for a greatest collective victim. Because the prestigious position of the "greatest victim" brings moral advantage and provides a permanent weapon against the perpetrators who are constantly reminded how they did not pay their real and symbolic debts. Furthermore, current or future violence by the "victims" may be justified in the name of past suffering. The victim has absolution for all present and future deeds. (Stojanović 2013)

Similarly, political scientist Jasna Dragović-Soso points out that "Kosovo allowed the Serb nationalist intelligentsia . . . to adopt the role of guardians of both national and universal values – the vision of Kosovo as the 'Serbian Jerusalem,' a holy land of an inestimable importance to national identity" (Dragović-Soso 2002). Historian Radmila Radić (2007, 293) questions the historical foundations of the nationalist discourse about Kosovo as the "cradle" of Serbia. Filip Ejdus and Jelena Subotić analyze the nationalist politics of "sacralization of territories" and the invention of "holy land" in Kosovo during the Balkan crisis from the 1990s to the 2000s (Ejdus and Subotić 2014). Social anthropologist Marko Živković writes specifically about what he calls a "Jewish trope, " as "one of the most important of . . . the elements of Serbian national narratives, linking the central Serbian myth of Kosovo to the more recent cycle of narratives that focus on the Ustaše genocide against Serbs during the Second World War" (quoted in Zivkovic 2000, 69).

However, the nationalist government of Serbia ignored the opposition as weak and isolated. Today the regime has consolidated the Kosovo-centered Serb identity, in which the Kosovo-Jerusalem parallel is one of the key concepts. Radical nationalist circles would go even further by expanding massive pilgrimages to Kosovo beyond Saint Vitus Day and religious-national holidays as daily practices to develop into folk customs. In a Saint Vitus Day 2019 interview, Ivica Todorović, a senior researcher affiliated with the Serbian academy of sciences and arts, says that his "scientific research" in history and ethnology has proved that "Serbia is a 'New Israel' founded on a sacred 'Kosovo covenant,'" which makes the Serbs "ancient people of noble origin with the idea of a divine election, mission and specific role in global historical processes," to conclude that identity of the Serbs "is built on very strict patterns that ever since Saint Sava has become unchangeable" (Todorović 2019a). Todorović calls for a national revival in which the state and the Church will ask every individual Serb, every family, and every community to make Kosovo pilgrimages a part of their lives – the new sacred duty of spiritual journeys and frequent visits to the shrines and historic sites of Kosovo and Metohija. According to Todorović:

> New Israel is real and will come to life before his very eyes (says the Bible). . . . Precisely in this meaning, spiritual journeys and indeed every visit to Kosovo will be for every Serb like a pilgrimage in which the traditional codes of meaning serve as the initiation into nationhood and reinforcement of identity. The pilgrimage to the heartland of our Holy Land will be like a tribute within the initiation process by which the sacralization of the entire collective and individual life is being achieved. (Todorović, 2019b)

EPILOGUE: A JERUSALEM BALKANIZED

From various religious and mythical narratives to artistic masterpieces such as Verdi's opera *Nabucco* and William Blake's unofficial hymn of England, Jerusalem has been one of the most worldwide influential symbols and metaphors. Yet, like in religion, when sacralized politics and religious nationalism use Jerusalem, that involves both inclusion and exclusion – that is, integration and separation. Jerusalem can symbolize an indivisible cultural property sacred to several religions, cultures, and nationalities that must be shared despite their differences (Barkan and Barkey 2015). At the same time, separatist-nationalistic politics and sectarian appropriations of land create bitter and long-standing conflicts. Such examples can be found in Palestine, Kosovo, Bosnia and Herzegovina, in India, and elsewhere (Barkan and Barkey 2015; Juergensmeyer 2003; Perica 2002; van der Veer 1994). A 2019 study by Frank J. Korom compares religious nationalism in India and Serbia. Korom argues as follows:

> In both places, the golden age is connected to a sacred place, so that Ayodhya takes on cosmic meaning for Hindus and Kosovo does the same for Serbs. In both

instances, medieval events triggered a long period of fomentation that resulted in the revival of militant nationalism in the pre- and modern period, especially in postcolonial times ... Regional narratives that became national myths developed over several centuries, but they were then appropriated and revived in the 1990s. Contemporary politicians used the same heroic narratives of Ram and Lazar respectively to rally militants based on misguided religious sentiment. In both cases, the revitalization of national myths concerning sacred ground, tinged with ideas about "chosen people," led to the demonization of religious others. In the final analysis, it cannot be denied that it was religion that served as a purportedly unifying principle. (Korom 2019)

The discourses on myth and religion helped the transfer of power from the old disintegrating multiethnic Yugoslavia to the new regimes of ethnically and religiously homogenous states. These also needed international support and used the discourses of myth and religion for approaching coreligionists (Huntington 1996). The Serb nationalist propaganda resonating worldwide during the wars in Bosnia and Kosovo emphasized the idea of a heroic self-sacrificing Serbia defending Christian Europe against the Muslim danger today as it used to do in the Kosovo battle of 1389. When the wars in Iraq and Syria brought a new wave of Islamist terror to Europe, militant Christian responders found in Serbia an inspiring example. Thus, in March 2019, the mass murderer who attacked mosques in New Zealand killing the worshippers included in his manifesto references to the Balkan Wars and admired the major war criminal charged with genocide in Bosnia. Also, he was allegedly familiar with the Kosovo myth and engraved in his weapons the names of the heroes of the Kosovo epic. According to an international research network, "[the] gunman who killed 49 people in a terror attack on two mosques in Christchurch in New Zealand is believed to be an admirer of Balkan nationalists and historical figures, and he played a song honoring Radovan Karadzic before opening fire" (Zivanovic 2019).

The rival states of Serbia and Kosovo, like the rest of ex-Yugoslav space destroyed by ethno-religious nationalism, today believe in Balkanization as the solution for their contesting perspectives on history, religion, culture, and politics. The dominant ideology of the ethno-religious nationalism imagines the past, present, and future in separated, irreconcilable communities organized as sovereign states and nations, mutually hostile and constantly feuding neighbors. These peoples have been separated by the mental walls of myth, as well as physical barriers with numerous checkpoints crisscrossing the space that has been integrated for many centuries. Each successor state of the former Yugoslavia is now ethnically and religiously homogenous. Their regimes discriminate against minorities and are ready to restart wars with neighboring states trying to protect their coreligionists and ethnic relatives. Bosnia and Herzegovina, once the most diverse part of the Balkans and probably more similar to Jerusalem and the Middle East than Kosovo, has been particularly tragically affected by partitions and

Serbian Jerusalem

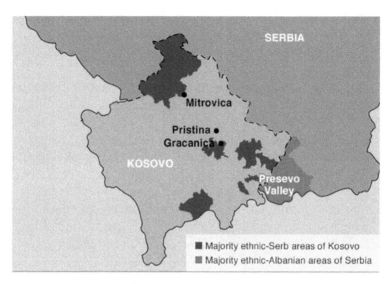

MAP 9.2 Proposed territory swap between Serbia and Kosovo

creations of separate ethno-religious enclaves. Bosnia, the Balkan country that once took pride in the landscape adorned by mosques and churches standing peacefully side by side amidst dynamic multiethnic communities, has by now lost nearly half of its prewar population and never recovered. Remembering Sarajevo's fate, Pope Francis appealed in a 2014 interview that several European countries struggling with ethnic separatism must avert "the tragedy of Balkanization" (Johnson 2014).

In 2018, the states of Serbia and Kosovo announced a possible deal to manage the Kosovo conflict by exchanging territories and transferring populations in northern Kosovo and southwestern Serbia. Under the agreement, the territories populated by the remaining Kosovo Serbs (except the key monastery compounds seeking a special status) would adjoin Serbia and the Albanian-majority enclaves along the Kosovo-Serbia border would merge with the Republic of Kosovo (see Map 9.2).

Three former UN High Representatives for Bosnia and Herzegovina, fearing risks of a new Bosnian war if the Kosovo partition set a dangerous precedent, warned in an open letter to EU member states: "Sustainable peace can only come when we learn to live in multiethnic communities, rather than redrawing borders to create monoethnic ones" (Lakic 2018). While Germany and the EU temporized, the Kosovo partition plans devised by the two equally hard-line nationalistic regimes in Belgrade and Priština have received a green light from both Russia and the US (Bassuener and Vogel 2019; Morina 2018; Rudic 2018). In September 2020 in Washington, Serbia and Kosovo signed a US-sponsored agreement on political normalization and economic ties. In his election campaign, President

Donald Trump took credit for ending the Kosovo war, as he put it repeatedly. In reality, the agreement changed little in the Balkans but Trump did a political favor for the Netanyahu government in Israel by urging Serbia to relocate its embassy from Tel Aviv to Jerusalem, which Kosovo would also follow.

In the meantime, the numbers of the few remaining ethnic Serbs in Kosovo are shrinking due to migrations to northern Serbia and abroad, such that the Serbian Orthodox Church's monks and nuns may soon become the sole onsite residing successors of the medieval Serb empire (Visoki Decani Monastery n.d.). Meanwhile, Serbia proper has also suffered a demographic catastrophe. A Belgrade daily reports: "Serbs flee the country and will never return: Serbia second in the world by the brain drain" (Telegraf Online 2015). Interestingly enough, the Albanians of Kosovo opt for migrations to the West instead of the new nation building. "Kosovars who fought for land are now eager to leave," *The New York Times* reported from Kosovo in 2015 (Smale 2015). Since then, the situation has only worsened. Thus, the number of migrants from the Balkans (mostly South Slavs and Kosovo Albanians) in Germany alone reached 2.6 million by 2018 (Dimitrov 2018).

To conclude, the invention of "Serbian Jerusalem" has been a problematic idea from the beginning and a flawed project in the end. The analogy itself is problematic in many respects. Modern Serbia was created in southeastern Europe by an anti-Turkish liberation movement backed by Russia and Western Europe. Although Serbia was traditionally pro-Russian, the Western-leaning elites dominated nation-building strategies first in a smaller ethnic kingdom and then within larger Yugoslav states (Perović 2006). By contrast, the anti-Western ethno-religious nationalists have been responsible for Serbia's unnecessary, failed, and costly attempts to "return" to "Old Serbia" (Kosovo and Macedonia), as well as the pursuit of the restoration of Tsar Dušan's empire. Specifically, the sacralization of Kosovo as the "cradle of Serbia" is an invented tradition, as well as a religious-nationalistic myth, which worked only for the conservative clerical-nationalistic elites while they were ruining Serbia and exporting the disaster to the neighboring countries. Finally, Kosovo is not analogous to Jerusalem, and sacred historic monuments do not possess mystical power for mobilizing the masses without a political party, movement, or state that pursues a political agenda while manipulating historical memories and symbolic discourses. If a place in the Balkans were to be the most analogous to Jerusalem, that would be Sarajevo, as it used to be before the recent conflict. Once an integrated culturally diverse urban center with a multiethnic and religiously pluralistic community of Christian and Muslim South Slavs, Jews, and others, Sarajevo is now a devastated, Balkanized space. Sarajevo today is an almost ethnically monolithic, decaying town in the neglected periphery of Europe within a partitioned and Balkanized country. Jerusalem itself can only learn from Sarajevo to avoid Balkanization driven by a similar kind of sacralized nationalism.

Serbian Jerusalem 239

REFERENCES

Al Jazeera Balkans. 2016. "Vučić: Oluja više neće biti." August 4. http://balkans.aljazeera.net /vijesti/vucic-oluja-vise-nece-biti.

———. 2017. "Islamska zajednica BiH osuđuje izjave patrijarha Irineja." October 25. http://balkans .aljazeera.net/vijesti/islamska-zajednica-bih-osuduje-izjave-patrijarha-irineja.

Andrejić, Božidar. 2017. "Treba li dijalog o Kosovu biti tabu za crkve" [Should dialogue on Kosovo be a taboo for churches?]. *Al Jazeera Balkans*, September 27. http://balkans .aljazeera.net/vijesti/treba-li-dijalog-o-kosovu-biti-tabu-za-crkve.

AFP (Associated Foreign Press). 2018. "Rivlin Tells Croatia to 'Deal' with Its Fascist Past." *The Times of Israel*, July 26. www.timesofisrael.com/rivlin-tells-croatia-to-deal-with-its-fascist-past/amp/.

Badiou, Alain. 2006. *Polemics*. London: Verso.

Barkan, Elazar, and Karen Barkey. 2015. *Choreographies of Shared Sacred Sites: Religion and Conflict Resolution*. New York: Columbia University Press.

Bassuener, Kurt, and Toby Vogel. 2019. "Germany Must Stop Dangerous Drive to Partition." *Balkan Insight*, March 13. https://balkaninsight.com/2019/03/13/germany-must-stop-dangerous-drive-to-partition-kosovo.

Beta. 2012. "Patrijarh: Kosovo nije geografski prostor, nego sveta zemlja." *Blic*, July 11. www.blic.rs/vesti/politika/patrijarh-kosovo-nije...nego.../et9slho.

Bogdanović, Dimitrije. 1986. *Knjiga o Kosovu*. Beograd: Srpska akademija nauka i umetnosti.

Bowcott, Owen. 2017. "Yugoslavia Tribunal Closes, Leaving a Powerful Legacy of War Crimes Justice." *The Guardian*, December 20. www.theguardian.com/law/2017/dec/20/former-yugoslavia-war-crimes-tribunal-leaves-powerful-legacy-milosevic-karadzic-mladic.

Bulatović, N. 2014. "Netanjahu Potvrdio Deretića: 'Srbi i Jevreji su prijatelji hiljadama godina, još od Starog Rima!'" [Netanyahu confirms Deretić: "Serbs and Jews have been friends for thousands of years, since ancient Rome!"]. *Srbija Danas*, December 1. www.srbijadanas.com/clanak/netanijahu-potvrdio-deretica-srbi-i-jevreji-su-prijatelji-hiljadama-godina-jos-od-starog-rima.

Byford, Jovan. 2004. "From 'Traitor' to 'Saint': Bishop Nikolaj Velimirović in Serbian Public Memory." Analysis of Current Trends in Antisemitism, no. 22. Jerusalem: Vidal Sassoon International Center for the Study of Antisemitism, The Hebrew University of Jerusalem.

———. 2011. *Staro Sajmište: Mesto sećanja, zaborava i sporenja* [Staro Sajmište: A site remembered, forgotten, contested]. Belgrade: Helsinki Center for Human Rights.

Čolović, Ivan. 2016. *Smrt na Kosovu Polju: Istorija kosovskog mita* [The death on the Kosovo field: History of the Kosovo myth]. Belgrade: Biblioteka XX vek.

Coyer, Paul. 2015. "Putin's Holy War and the Disintegration of the 'Russian World.'" *Forbes*, June 4. www.forbes.com/sites/paulcoyer/2015/06/04/putins-holy-war-and-the-disintegration-of-the-russian-world/#6e0a9e8e285b.

Danas Online. 2017. "Što je Amerika Izraelu da Rusija postane Srbiji" [Russia should become to Serbia what America is to Israel]. December 27. www.danas.rs/dijalog/licni-stavovi/sto-je-amerika-izraelu-da-rusija-postane-srbiji/.

Dedijer, Vladimir. 1992. *Yugoslav Auschwitz and the Vatican: The Croatian Massacre of the Serbs During World War Two*. Translated by Harvey L. Kendall. Buffalo, NY: Prometheus Books.

Dimitrov, Martin. 2018. "Balkan Migrants in Germany Number 2.6 Million." *Balkan Insight*, August 3. https://balkaninsight.com/2018/08/03/at-least-2–6-million-immigrants-from-the -balkans-live-in-germany-08–03-2018/.

Đorđević, Mirko. 2003. "Crkva i njeno odlučno 'ne' državi" [The Church said "no" to the state]. *Republika*, no. 316–17: 1–30. www.republika.co.rs/316–317/09.html.

Dragović-Soso, Jasna. 2002. *Saviors of the Nation? Serbia's Intellectual Opposition and the Revival of Nationalism*. London: Hurst and Co.

Drašković, Vuk. 2013. *Ćirilica*. BN Television. April 1.

Ejdus, Filip, and Jelena Subotić. 2014. "Kosovo as Serbia's Sacred Space: Governmentality, Pastoral Power, and Sacralization of Territories." In *Politicization of Religion, the Power of Symbolism: The Case of Former Yugoslavia and Its Successor States*, edited by Gorana Ognjenović and Jasna Jozelić, 159–84. Palgrave Studies in Religion, Politics, and Policy. New York: Palgrave Macmillan.

Emmert, Thomas A. 1990. *Serbian Golgotha: Kosovo, 1389*. East European Monographs. New York: Columbia University Press.

Goldstein, Ivo. 2018. *Jasenovac*. Zagreb: Fraktura.

Goldstein, Ivo, and Slavko Goldstein. 2016. *The Holocaust in Croatia*. Pittsburgh: University of Pittsburgh Press.

Goldstein, Slavko. 2013a. "Bob Dylan's Croatian Error." *The New York Times*, December 15. www.nytimes.com/2013/12/16/opinion/bob-dylans-croatian-error.html.

2013b. *1941: The Year That Keeps Returning*. Translated by Michael Gable. New York: New York Review of Books.

Grzymala-Busse, Anna. 2019. "Religious Nationalism and Religious Influence." In Oxford Research Encyclopedia, Politics. March 26. https://doi.org/10.1093/acrefore/9780190228637.013.813.

Hobsbawm, Eric J. 1992. *Nations and Nationalism since 1780: Programme, Myth, Reality*. Cambridge: Cambridge University Press.

Hobsbawm, Eric J., and Terence Ranger. 1983. *The Invention of Tradition*. Cambridge: Cambridge University Press.

Hroch, Miroslav. 1985. *Social Preconditions of National Revival in Europe: A Comparative Analysis of the Social Composition of Patriotic Groups among the Smaller European Nations*. Translated by Ben Fowkes. New York: Cambridge University Press.

Huntington, Samuel P. 1996. *The Clash of Civilizations and the Remaking of World Order*. New York: Simon and Schuster.

Intermagazin. 2014. "Majkl Frojnd: Srbi i Jevreji su braća po žalosti i sdbini, i zato Izrael nece priznati nezavisnost Kosova" [Michael Freund: Serbs and Jews are brothers by the tragic fate and sorrow and because of that Israel will not recognize Kosovo's independence]. March 20. www.intermagazin.rs/majkl-frojnd-srbi-i-jevreji-su-braca-po-zalosti-i-sudbini-i-zato-izrael-nece-priznati-nezavisnost-kosova/.

International Commission to Inquire into the Causes and Conduct of the Balkan War. 1914. *Report of the International Commission to Inquire into the Causes and Conduct of the Balkan Wars*. Washington, DC: Carnegie Endowment for International Peace.

Israel Ministry of Foreign Affairs. 2014. "PM Netanyahu Meets with Serbian PM Vučić in Jerusalem." December 1. https://mfa.gov.il/MFA/PressRoom/2014/Pages/PM-Netanyahu-meets-with-Serbian-PM-Vucic-1-December-2014.aspx.

Janjić, Sava. 2008. "Father Sava Janjic: Kosovo Is Serbian Jerusalem." Interview. YouTube video, 2:35. April 7. https://youtu.be/MUWcU1m-GCI. [The video featuring Biden and Father Sava has been removed as of June 2, 2020. Father Sava makes a similar comment to the quoted text in this video.]

Jeremić, Vuk. 2011. "Identity, Reconciliation, and the Struggle over Kosovo." Address at the J. Dennis Hastert Center for Economics, Government and Public Policy at Wheaton College, Wheaton, IL. March 17. https://bit.ly/35lTHj8.

Johnson, Simon. 2014. "Pope Voices Fears over Scottish Independence." *The Telegraph*, June 13. www.telegraph.co.uk/news/uknews/scottish-independence/10897888/Pope-voices-fears-over-Scottish-independence.html.

Juergensmeyer, Mark. 2003. *Terror in the Mind of God: The Global Rise of Religious Violence*. Berkeley: University of California Press.

Jutarnji.hr. 2016. "Mi smo kao Izrael, u čudnom okruženju" [We are like Israel in the strange encirclement]. *Jutarnji List*, February 24. https://bit.ly/2It9eVO.

Keinon, Herb, and Anna Ahronheim. 2018. "Israeli F-16s Get in Middle of Bitter Serbian-Croatian Dispute." *Jerusalem Post*, August 5. www.jpost.com/Israel-News/Israeli-F-16s-get-in-middle-of-bitter-Serbian-Croatian-dispute-564204.

Kepel, Gilles. 1994. *The Revenge of God: The Resurgence of Islam, Christianity, and Judaism in the Modern World*. Translated by Alan Braley. University Park, PA: Pennsylvania State University Press.

Klarin, Mirko, and Raul Tajtelbaum. 1986. *Israel in a Verbal Civil War*. Belgrade: Partizanska knjiga.

Korom, Frank J. 2019. "Folklore and Nationalism in India and Serbia: A Comparative Exploration." *Annual Papers of the Anthropological Institute* 9: 87–100.

Krstić, Branislav. 2016. "Kosovo Vows to Halt Serb Refugee Settlement." *Balkan Insight*, July 1. https://balkaninsight.com/2016/07/01/pristina-vows-to-halt-kosovo-serb-refugee-settlement-06-30-2016/.

Lakic, Mladen. 2018. "Former Bosnia Governors Condemn Kosovo-Serbia Land Swap." *Balkan Insight*, August 29. www.balkaninsight.com/en/article/former-high-representatives-call-eu-to-abandon-plans-on-swapping-territory-08-29-2018.

Malcolm, Noel. 1999. *Kosovo: A Short History*. New York: Harper Perennial.

Mileusnić, Slobodan. 2001. *The Monasteries of Kosovo and Metohija*. 2nd ed. Novi Sad: Pravoslavna reč.

Mojzes, Paul. 2011. *Balkan Genocides: Holocaust and Ethnic Cleansing in the Twentieth Century*. Lanham, MD: Rowman and Littlefield.

Morina, Die. 2018. "Putin Will Back Kosovo-Serbia Deal, Thaci Insists." *Balkan Insight*, November 12. https://balkaninsight.com/2018/11/12/kosovo-s-thaci-putin-supports-an-agreement-between-kosovo-and-serbia-11-12-2018/.

Novosti Online. 2017. "Izraelski obaveštajac: Bili smo uz Srbiju, za Hrvate nema oproštaja" [Israel intelligence: Israel stood by Serbia, will never forgive Croats]. Новости, November 5. www.novosti.rs/vesti/naslovna/drustvo/aktuelno.290.html:694331-Izraelski-obavestajac-Bili-smo-uz-Srbiju-za-Hrvate-nema-oprostaja.

Perica, Vjekoslav. 2002. *Balkan Idols: Religion and Nationalism in Yugoslav States*. New York: Oxford University Press.

Perović, Latinka. 2006. *Srbija u modernizacijskim procesima XIX i XX veka* [Serbia in the modernization processes of the nineteenth and twentieth centuries]. Belgrade: Helsinški odbor za ljudska prava u Srbiji.

Popov, Nebojša, and Drinka Gojković, eds. 2000. *The Road to War in Serbia: Trauma and Catharsis*. Translated by Central European University Press. Budapest: Central European University Press.

Primor, Adar. 2007. "Kosovo, in Israeli Eyes." *Haaretz*, December 19. www.haaretz.com/1.4967806.

Radić, Radmila. 2007. "Relations between Catholic and Orthodox Churches during the Disintegration of Yugoslavia." In *Pisati istoriju Jugoslavije: Viđenje srpskog faktora*, edited by Mile Bjelajac. 283–301. Belgrade: Institut za noviju istoriju Srbije.

242 *Vjekoslav Perica*

Ramet, Sabrina P. 2005. *Thinking about Yugoslavia: Scholarly Debates about the Yugoslav Breakup and the Wars in Bosnia and Kosovo.* Cambridge: Cambridge University Press.

Rathfelder, Erich. 2010. *Kosovo: Geschichte eines Konflikts* [Kosovo: History of a Conflict]. Berlin: Suhrkamp.

Rudic, Filip. 2018. "US Won't Oppose Serbia-Kosovo Border Changes – Bolton." *Balkan Insight,* August 24. https://balkaninsight.com/2018/08/24/us-will-not-weigh-in-on-serbia-kosovo-partition-08-24-2018/.

Sekelj, Laslo. 1997. "Anti-Semitism and Jewish Identity in Serbia after the 1991 Collapse of the Yugoslav State." *Analysis of Current Trends in Antisemitism,* no. 12. Jerusalem: Vidal Sassoon International Center for the Study of Antisemitism, The Hebrew University of Jerusalem.

Sells, Michael A. 1998. *The Bridge Betrayed: Religion and Genocide in Bosnia.* Berkeley: University of California Press.

Smale, Allison. 2015. "Kosovars Who Fought for Land Are Now Eager to Leave." *The New York Times,* March 7. www.nytimes.com/2015/03/08/world/europe/kosovars-who-fought-for-land-are-now-eager-to-leave-it.html.

Smale, Allison, and Melissa Eddy. 2016. "German Parliament Recognizes Armenian Genocide, Angering Turkey." *The New York Times,* July 2. www.nytimes.com/2016/06/03/world/europe/armenian-genocide-germany-turkey.html?_r=1.

Spahiu, Nexhmedin. 1999. "Serb Proposals for Partitioning Kosova." *Transitions Online,* June 28. www.tol.org/client/article/13214-serb-proposals-for-partitioning-kosova.html.

Stojanović, Dubravka. 2013. "A Role Play: Perpetrators and Victims in Serbian History Textbooks." *Peščanik,* September 22. https://pescanik.net/a-role-play-perpetrators-and-victims-in-serbian-history-textbooks/.

Tabeau, Ewa, ed. 2009. *Conflict in Numbers: Casualties of the 1990s Wars in the Former Yugoslavia (1991–1999).* Testimonies, vol. 33. Belgrade: Helsinki Committee for Human Rights in Serbia. www.helsinki.org.rs/doc/testimonies33.pdf.

Tanjug. 2016. "Cornerstone Laid for Returnees Residential Complex in Kosovo." *Glas Jovnosti,* June 9. www.glas-javnosti.rs/aktuelne-vesti/2016–06-09/cornerstone-laid-returnee-residential-complex-kosovo.

Telegraf Online. 2015. "Serbs Flee the Country and Will Never Return: Serbia Second in the World by the Brain Drain. Here's Who's Worse than Her!" April 28. https://bit.ly/36y1wSc.

2016. "Kosovo je naša kolevka i srpski Jerusalim! Ovo je Kralj Srbije poručio Klintonu Bleru i Širaku tokom bombardovanja Srbije" [Kosovo is our cradle and Serbian Jerusalem! This is what the king of Serbia ordered from Clinton, Blair, and Shirak during the bombing of Serbia]. March 24. https://bit.ly/35n2f9n.

Todorović, Ivica. 2019a. "Da li se Srbi spremaju za veliku pobedu? (1. део)" [Are the Serbs getting ready for a great victory? (Part 1).] *Pečat,* June 28. www.pecat.co.rs/2019/06/dr-ivica-todorovic-da-li-se-srbi-spremaju-za-veliku-pobedu-1-deo/.

2019b. "'Srpska ideja' jasno je suprotstavljena ideji savremenog globalizma" [The "Serbian idea" clearly confronts contemporary globalism]. *Pečat,* July 4. www.pecat.co.rs/2019/07/dr-ivica-todorovic-srpska-ideja-jasno-je-suprotstavljena-ideji-savremenog-globalizma-2-deo/.

Tomasevich, Jozo. 2001. *War and Revolution in Yugoslavia, 1941–1945: Occupation and Collaboration.* Stanford: Stanford University Press.

UNESCO. 2006. "World Heritage Committee Puts Medieval Monuments in Kosovo on Danger List and Extends Site in Andorra, Ending This Year's Inscriptions." July 13. http://whc.unesco.org/en/news/268.

2013. "Medieval Monuments in Kosovo (UNESCO/NHK)." YouTube video, 2:56. www.youtube.com/watch?v=5Q6DzpisSOM&feature=youtu.be.

van der Veer, Peter. 1994. *Religious Nationalism: Hindus and Muslims in India.* Berkeley: University of California Press.

Veljković, Vladimir. 2016. "Pravoslavni nacionalizam u Vojsci Srbije" [Orthodox nationalism in the army of Serbia]. *Peščanik*, January 20. https://pescanik.net/pravoslavni-nacionalizam-u-vojsci-srbije/print/.

Vickers, Miranda. 1998. *Between Serb and Albanian: A History of Kosovo.* New York: Columbia University Press.

Visoki Decani Monastery. n.d. "Visoki Decani Serbian Orthodox Monastery: Kosovo and Metohia." www.kosovo.net/edecani.html.

Vulin, Aleksandar. 2017. "Vulin: We Have a Lot to Learn from Israel." Interview. Radio Television of Serbia Evening News. YouTube video, 2:05. July 25. https://youtu.be /2YHH2HaoM-E.

West, Rebecca. 2007. *Black Lamb and Grey Falcon: A Journey through Yugoslavia.* New York: Penguin Books.

World Factbook. 2018. "Kosovo." Central Intelligence Agency. www.cia.gov/library/publica tions/the-world-factbook/geos/print_kv.html.

World Population Review. 2019. "Kosovo Population 2019." http://worldpopulationreview .com/countries/kosovo-population/.

Yearwood, Pauline Dubkin. 1999. "Another Side to the Store of Kosovo." *Jewish World Review*, April 19. www.jewishworldreview.com/0499/serb.jews1.asp.

Zečević, D., and I. Radulović. 2013. "Patrijarh Irinej: Kosovo – naš Jerusalim" [Patriarch Irinej: Kosovo – Our Jerusalem]/ Новости, March 17. www.novosti.rs/vesti/naslovna/ drustvo/aktuelno.290.html:424821-Patrijarh-Irinej-Kosovo–nas-Jerusalim.

Zimmerman, Warren. 1996. *Origins of a Catastrophe: Yugoslavia and Its Destroyers – America's Last Ambassador Tells What Happened and Why.* New York: Times Books.

Zivanovic, Maja. 2019. "New Zealand Mosque Gunman 'Inspired by Balkan Nationalists.'" *Balkan Insight*, March 15. https://balkaninsight.com/2019/03/15/new-zealand-mosque-gunman-inspired-by-balkan-nationalists/.

Zivkovic, Marko. 2000. "The Wish to be a Jew: The Power of the Jewish Trope in the Yugoslav Conflict." *Cahiers de l'Urmis* 6: 69–84. https://journals.openedition.org/urmis/ 323?file=1.

PART V

Iran

10

The Crossing Paths of Religion and Nationalism in Contemporary Iran

Ali Banuazizi

Religion and nationalism have served as two powerful ideological bases for political mobilization and state legitimacy in Iran over the past century. The relationship between the two has varied over time, not only in response to changing historical contexts and political circumstances, but also as a function of how their advocates – political leaders, cultural elites, the clergy, and public intellectuals – have utilized religious or nationalist claims in pursuit of their broader political objectives. Thus, for example, depending on whether the clergy held a "quietist" interpretation of Shi'i Islam – i.e., one that eschews direct involvement in politics and state affairs – or a politically assertive one, their relationship with the country's nationalist movements has varied significantly from one period to another. Similarly, on the nationalist side, the more that nationalists sought to limit the role of the clergy and to keep religion out of the political arena, the more adversarial became their relationship with religiously based groups and movements.

In this chapter, I explore the relationship between religion and nationalism in Iranian politics in two distinctly different periods in the country's recent history. In the first period, under the autocratic rule of the two Pahlavi monarchs, Reza Shah (1925–41) and Mohammad Reza Shah (1941–79), a state-centered, secular nationalism served as the dominant ideology in promoting Iran's national sovereignty, political integration, modernization, and socioeconomic development. At the same time, the Pahlavi monarchs' secularization policies sharply limited the influence of the clergy in Iranian politics and society, especially in such realms as education, the judiciary, and social welfare. In the second period, beginning with the fall of the Pahlavi monarchy and the triumph of the Islamic Revolution in 1979 and continuing to the present, a theocratic political Islam has served as the hegemonic ideology of the clerically dominated state. The postrevolutionary leaders' stance toward nationalism, however, has not been entirely consistent or coherent. In the immediate aftermath of the revolution, they tended to condemn nationalism as being contrary to the Islamic ideal of unity among all believers (the Muslim *umma*). However, soon thereafter, when faced with internal resistance for abandoning popular national symbols and rituals or when in need of recruiting hundreds of

248 Ali Banuazizi

thousands of young men to fight in a bloody eight-year war (1980–88) with Iraq, they adopted nationalist slogans to rally mass support for the war.

For each of the above periods, I show how the prevailing domestic and international circumstances, combined with ideas, selective historical narratives, and traditional cultural symbols and rituals, have been used to foster nationalism, political Islam, or an amalgam of the two as hegemonic state ideologies.

NATIONAL IDENTITY, NATIONALISM, AND POLITICAL ISLAM

Before examining the relationship between Islam and nationalism in the Iranian context, a brief explanation of my use of these terms is in order. Following Anthony Smith (2010), I use the term "nationalism" to refer to a *political ideology* that seeks to unite and mobilize a people, usually within the bounds of a contiguous territory or an internationally recognized state, in their pursuit of sovereignty, self-determination, and perceived collective interests.[1] As such, nationalism can be distinguished from the related concept of "national identity," which is based on a people's real or imagined historical experiences, cultural traditions, collective memories, and shared values. National identity, as Smith points out, "relates to *cultural* issues that other ideologies neglect – and every nationalism pursues the goal of national identity in varying degrees" (Smith 2010, 10; emphasis added). Not all aspects of a nation's identity are fully or equally shared by every segment of its population, particularly when the nation is ethnically, linguistically, or religiously heterogeneous. And parts of a nation's cultural identity may be shared with groups beyond its borders with which it has had long-standing ties, including its diaspora communities.

While "nationalism" and "national identity" are closely related concepts, they function differently in the political arena. The cultural strands that make up a people's national identity tend to be diffuse and politically dormant. To be turned into nationalist ideologies, they need to be stirred up, emotionally charged, and crafted in ways that could foster group loyalty and a proclivity toward political action. This is often achieved by identifying or creating near and distant "others" who can be blamed for not abiding by the nation's cherished values, challenging its interests, or, in the extreme, threatening its security and survival.

In the case of Iran, at least four sets of elements have contributed to the formation of a distinctive Iranian national identity. These include: (1) *a long pre-Islamic historical legacy* that stretches from the establishment of the Sasanian Empire (224 CE) – if not even earlier from the reign of Cyrus the Great and the founding of the first Persian Empire, the Achaemenids (550–330 BCE) – to the Arab conquest of

---

[1] Smith (2010, 9) considers autonomy, unity, and identity as three core elements that are critical for a nation's survival, thus defining nationalism as "[a]n ideological movement for attaining and maintaining autonomy, unity, and identity for a population that some of its members deem to constitute an actual or potential 'nation.'"

Persia in 651 CE (see, for example, Gnoli 1989; Yarshater 1998; Zarrinkoub 2017); (2) *Islam or, more specifically, Shi'ism*, the country's officially declared religion since the formation of the Safavid Empire in 1501 and the faith of some 90 percent of its present-day inhabitants (see, for example, Motahhari 1349 Sh./1970); (3) *the Persian language*, the mother-tongue of some 55 percent of Iran's current population and long the literary and "court" language in parts of South Asia and a trans-regional lingua franca in several parts of Central Asia – the so-called Persianate world (see Amanat and Ashraf 2018; Fragner 1999; Meskoob 1992; Perry 2018); and finally (4) *the diffuse cultural bonds*, fictive or real, among a people who, despite their ethnic, linguistic, or religious differences and intermixing with various foreign conquerors and outsiders, have inhabited roughly the same geographic territory, with the same name, for over two millennia.

The above conception of Iranian national identity and its constitutive elements has not been without its critics in the burgeoning scholarly literature on the topic.[2] Some authors have challenged the very idea that there exists a singular, unique, and enduring Iranian national identity, particularly one whose roots can be traced back to the early pre-Islamic period. For them, the notion of a continuous Iranian identity is an invented or "imagined" idea that was constructed in the late nineteenth and early twentieth centuries (see, for example, Vaziri 1993). Other critics have questioned whether and to what extent ethnolinguistic minorities, comprising nearly half of the country's population, share in a Persian-speaking national identity (Elling 2013; Zia-Ebrahimi 2016). Still others have argued that a sense of "territorial identity," rather than the cultural bonds based on shared language or religion, has been the more tenacious and enduring basis for an Iranian identity. They point to the fact that the territory called Persia or Iran (*Iranshahr* or *Iranzamin*), with roughly the same or more expansive boundaries as present-day Iran, has existed for over two millennia, initially as an ancient empire and later as a series of sovereign states. A coherent sense of an Iranian national identity or "Iranianness," they argue, was reinforced in the latter part of the nineteenth century with the use of territorial demarcations, international boundaries, and "closed frontiers" to mark a distinctive "nation-state" (see, for example, Kashani-Sabet 2002, 163; Kashani-Sabet 1999). In an extensive review of the competing approaches to Iranian national identity, Ahmad Ashraf seeks to go beyond what he refers to as "romantic" and "modernist" approaches to national identity. Instead, he proposes a "historicizing" approach that distinguishes between an Iranian identity (*Iraniyat*) as a historical entity and an "Iranian *national* identity," which he regards as a modern construct that cannot

---

[2] For recent overviews of Iranian national identity and/or nationalism, see Adib-Moghaddam (2018); Aghaie and Marashi (2014); Ahmadi (1378 Sh./1999); Amanat and Vejdani (2012); Ansari (2012); Ashraf (1395 Sh./2016); Boroujerdi (1998); Elling (2013); Kashani-Sabet (1999); Litvak (2017a); Marashi (2008); Schirazi (1396 Sh./2017); Sharifi (2013); Siavoshi (1990); Tavakoli-Targhi (2001); Vaziri (1993); Zia-Ebrahimi (2016).

be applied retrospectively to earlier historical periods. While the modern conceptions of an Iranian national identity were constructed subjectively from ancient myths, symbols, and collective memories, they are based on verifiable ethnolinguistic and territorial ties (Ashraf 2006).

What I mean by "religion" – in the present case, Islam – may also need some clarification. I begin with the premise that the once-popular notion in the social sciences that modernity will necessarily lead to a decline of religiosity, the so-called secularization paradigm, is no longer tenable. In the words of a leading sociologist of religion, Peter Berger (1999, 9), "The world today is massively religious, is *anything but* the secularized world that had been predicted (whether joyfully or despondently) by so many analysts of modernity [including Berger himself in his earlier writings]." Furthermore, it seems clear that this worldwide resurgence of religion has not been the result of a rise in individual religiosity, but rather is due to the increasing presence of religion in the public sphere and its instrumental use in politics. Hence, in exploring the relationship between nationalism and religion in the aforementioned periods of Iranian history, my focus will be on the public aspects of religion and its ideological uses, rather than its spiritual or theological dimensions. In the postrevolutionary period and the formation of the "Islamic Republic," I discuss the role of religion in recasting Iran's national identity as a revolutionary Islamic state, shaping its political institutions, and serving – along with nationalism – as a pillar of state legitimacy.

THE RISE OF NATIONALIST SENTIMENTS IN LATE NINETEENTH-CENTURY IRAN

The idea of the "nation" and expressions of nationalist sentiments appeared for the first time in Iran in the closing decades of the nineteenth century in the writings of a small group of intellectuals and literati. The word *mellat*, which in Persian as in Arabic and Turkish had referred traditionally to a religious community, came to be used in the Western sense of the term to designate a "nation" or "nation-state." In their attempt to define a new identity for their countrymen as a nation, these "enlightened thinkers" aggrandized the country's pre-Islamic past and placed much of the blame for its fall from grace and continued backwardness on the seventh-century Arab conquest of Persia and blind adherence to age-old Islamic traditions. Inspired by Western liberal ideas of popular sovereignty, the rule of law, and individual rights, they demanded an end to the arbitrary and despotic rule of the Qajar dynasty (1796–1925) and the country's increasing dependence on foreign powers (mainly Great Britain and Russia). The growing voices of these largely secular intellectuals coincided with strong condemnations of the Qajar rulers for their deviations from Islamic norms of justice and subservience to foreign powers by several prominent religious leaders (mujtahids). By the early 1900s, yet another segment of the population – the bazaar community of merchants, shopkeepers,

Religion and Nationalism in Contemporary Iran

artisans, and guild members – joined the opposition to the Qajar rule. The merchants, for their part, accused the government officials of imposing unfair price controls in the face of a rapid inflationary cycle and offering lucrative concessions to foreigners.

With added support from progressive members of the political elite, sympathetic tribal leaders, and thousands of ordinary urban dwellers, the different opposition groups formed a common front against the despotic Qajar state. An earlier, modest call for a "house of justice" (*edalatkhaneh*) was turned into a novel and more radical demand for a popularly elected national assembly and a constitution. The movement scored a major victory on August 5, 1906, when the Qajar monarch Mozaffar al-Din Shah (r. 1896–1907) capitulated to its principal demand and signed a decree authorizing the formation of a National Consultative Assembly (Majles-e shora-ye melli). Soon thereafter, a hastily elected assembly drafted a constitution (referred to as the "Fundamental Law"), modeled largely after the Belgian constitution, under which the Qajar state was to be transformed into a constitutional monarchy. It declared Shi'ism as Iran's official religion, but it also stipulated that the monarch's sovereign power was granted to him by the people rather than bestowed on him by God. The new constitution was approved by the ailing monarch on December 31, 1906, a few days before he died. Less than a year later, the Majles passed a "Supplementary Fundamental Law" that, inter alia, offered explicit guarantees for the protection of the basic rights and liberties of all citizens.

The alliance between the clerical and the secular deputies in the Majles, however, was short-lived. Barely a few months after the convening of the new parliament, the question of whether constitutional law should replace Islamic law (Shari'a) and the passage of several laws that sought to limit the authority and privileges of the clergy in educational, judicial, and charitable realms created a major rift between the traditionalist clergy and the secularist deputies. The clerics, with a few notable exceptions, demanded close adherence to Shari'a laws and accused the secularists of adopting ideas and practices that were alien, if not contrary, to Islam and its sacred traditions.

The new king, Mohammad Ali Shah (r. 1907–9), displayed a hostile attitude toward the newly elected Majles and resented the limits that the new constitution had placed on his authority. Following months of subterfuge and opposition against the elected assembly, he made a pivotal assault on the nascent constitutional regime by declaring martial law and ordering the Russian-led Cossack Brigade (the only disciplined and professionally organized military force in the country at the time) to bombard the parliament building in June 1908. The attack, supported by the reactionary elements within the clergy, was followed by the arrest of a number of deputies and their supporters, several of whom were subsequently put to death or exiled. The king's brazen action, however, failed to break the resolve of the constitutionalists and proved to be only a temporary setback for the movement. The center of resistance shifted from the capital, Tehran, to the country's largest city, Tabriz, where the constitutionalists and local militias formed a powerful front against the royal court. By July 1909, with the backing of several leading clerics, tribal leaders, and liberal political figures, the pro-constitution forces made a successful attack on the royalist contingents in the capital, forcing Mohammad Ali Shah to step down and seek refuge in Russia. His eleven-year-old son, Ahmad (1898–1930), was declared his successor to the Qajar throne as a "constitutional monarch."

In its second session, the parliament passed several pieces of legislation to broaden its own electoral base, guarantee near-universal male suffrage, and allow for representation by religious minorities. But soon, ideological battles, dissensions, and factionalism among the deputies, as well as escalating tensions between the parliament and the court, made it impossible for the fledgling legislative body to manage the country's financial affairs and prevent its slide toward bankruptcy. The political crisis was intensified by rebellions in several parts of the country, foreign interventions (including the invasion of two northern provinces by the Russian government), and the gathering storm of the Great War. The outcome was the closure of the parliament and an end, at least temporarily, to constitutional rule.

Despite the above setbacks, the Constitutional Revolution had a profound and lasting impact on Iran's political culture and institutions by "incorporating such modern concepts as nationalism, the rule of law, limits to state power, individual rights, and people's representation" (Amanat 2017, 317). For the following seven decades, the constitution served – in theory, if not always in practice – as the legal foundation for successive Iranian governments, as well as the basis for opposition against autocratic rule and denial of fundamental political rights.

SECULAR NATIONALISM IN THE PAHLAVI PERIOD

The outbreak of World War I (1914–18) marked the beginning of one of the most turbulent periods in Iran's modern history. Despite Iran's declaration of neutrality, the warring powers, including Britain, Russia, Germany, and the Ottomans, invaded the country in pursuit of their own broader and often conflicting interests (see Atabaki 2006; Lenczowski 1983). The ravages of the war, including large-scale destruction of farmlands, severe famines, and epidemics of cholera, typhus, and influenza, claimed the lives of as many as two million Iranians between 1914 and 1920. In the meantime, separatist movements and tribal uprisings in several provinces severely undermined the authority of the government and threatened the country's territorial integrity. The young Qajar monarch, Ahmad Shah (r. 1909–25), was too inexperienced and weak-willed to manage the spiraling crisis and save the country from economic bankruptcy and political disintegration. These chaotic conditions led many reformist politicians and influential intellectuals to conclude that only a strong and decisive leader could save the country from virtual disintegration, protect its independence, and restore its national unity. The man

Religion and Nationalism in Contemporary Iran 253

who, by virtue of his military background, forthright character, and proven ability to lead, seemed most fit to play such a role was Colonel Reza Khan, the commander of the Cossack Brigade.

In February 1921, Reza Khan with 2,500 Cossack Brigade soldiers under his command and accompanied by a pro-British journalist-politician, Seyyed Zia Tabataba'i, staged what turned out to be a nearly bloodless coup against the incumbent government. The objective of the coup, Reza Khan claimed, was not to overthrow the Qajar monarchy but to strengthen the authority of the central government. Following the coup, he launched a military campaign to subdue the secessionist movements in several provinces and to disarm the rebellious tribes. His success in achieving a measure of security and political stability for the country catapulted him up the ladder of power and authority from the commander of the armed forces to prime minister in a short span of four years. By 1925, Reza Khan and his supporters in the parliament felt confident enough to put forward a plan to abolish the Qajar dynasty and declare him the new monarch. The plan was approved by a hastily formed constituent assembly and, on April 25, 1926, he crowned himself as Reza Shah Pahlavi, the founder of the new Pahlavi dynasty.

As M. Reza Ghods (1991, 35) has pointed out, "Reza Khan's transformation from Cossack colonel to Shah of Iran was fostered primarily by Iranian nationalism, which sought a strong centralized government to replace the administrative chaos in the aftermath of the Constitutional Revolution and World War I." Reza Shah's state-centered nationalist agenda over the relatively short course of his reign (1925–41) had several distinctive features. First, much like Atatürk in neighboring Turkey, his nationalism was not a mere ideological crusade, but rather an unfaltering effort to build a modern nation-state.[3] To do so, he established a modern military and an administrative bureaucracy; created a system of public education open to both sexes; made major improvements in the country's infrastructure, transportation, and communication systems; and expanded the public sector of the economy by starting several state-run industries – all without reliance on foreign loans or concessions.

Second, to foster a sense of patriotism (*mihan-parasti*), national unity (*vahdat-e melli*), and national independence (*esteqlal-e melli*), particularly among the youth, he had these values placed at the core of the curriculum in the nation's newly created public schools (see Menashri 1992, 94). Furthermore, he took several measures to anchor Iran's national identity in its pre-Islamic cultural traditions. The Islamic lunar calendar was replaced with a Persian solar one, using old Persian names for months instead of Arabic-derived names. Classical Persian poets were celebrated by building monuments in their names. Foreign governments were asked to use "Iran" (the name that Iranians themselves had used for centuries to refer to

---

[3] For a comparison between Reza Shah and Atatürk, see Atabaki and Zürcher (2004); Keyman and Yilmaz (2006); White (2013).

their country) rather than "Persia" (the name by which Westerners since the time of the Greeks had referred to the country) in their official communications. The use of Persian language – to the exclusion of minority languages – was enforced in schools, the media, governmental institutions, and official communications. A special academy was created in order to "purify" the Persian language by replacing loanwords (mostly Arabic) with their Persian equivalents or newly coined words derived from Persian roots.

Third, he introduced a variety of measures to curtail the manifold roles of the clergy in the judicial, educational, and philanthropic spheres. These included enacting secular civil, criminal, and commercial legal codes modeled after those in the West to replace Shari'a-based laws, abolishing the religious courts, and appointing secular judges in the newly established judicial system; establishing a secular elementary and secondary system of public education open to both sexes; founding the coeducational University of Tehran and teachers' education colleges; and placing the administration of charitable endowments (*awqaf*) under state authority. To make Iranians more "modern" in their appearance, he imposed a Western-style dress code for men (trousers, short jackets, and a European-style hat instead of the traditional robe and headgear) and, more controversially, a ban on women wearing the traditional Islamic hijab (*chador*) in public (Chehabi 1993). These moves, as well as his other initiatives to promote women's participation in public life, were praised by the intelligentsia and welcomed by the emerging modern middle class. They were denounced, on the other hand, by the clerical hierarchy for being contrary to Islamic values and resisted strongly by the more traditional social strata.

Reza Shah's reign ended abruptly in the summer of 1941, when the Allied Powers, concerned about his pro-German leanings, occupied Iran and demanded his abdication in favor of his twenty-one-year-old son, Mohammad Reza Shah (r. 1941–79). Shortly thereafter, Reza Shah was forced into exile, first in the British island of Mauritius, and later in Johannesburg, where he died in 1944.

The end of Reza Shah's autocratic rule and his son's initially tenuous grip on power created a relatively free – and at times chaotic – environment for political parties, the press, labor unions, and civil society groups to flourish. Chief among these were the communist Tudeh Party, several Islamist groups, and a loose coalition of political parties and individuals with a liberal, nationalist ideology that came to be known as the "National Front." The latter was led by Mohammad Mosaddeq, initially as a prominent member of the Majles and later as the prime minister (1951–53). The highly popular cause around which Mosaddeq rallied his followers, and eventually most of the nation, was the nationalization of Iran's oil industry, the lifeblood of the nation's economy. Since its inception in the early twentieth century, the oil industry had been owned and operated by the Anglo-Iranian Oil Company (AIOC), a British firm in which the British government was the majority shareholder. Mosaddeq turned the oil dispute with Britain into

Religion and Nationalism in Contemporary Iran

a popular nationalist cause against a foreign power with a long history of interference in Iran's domestic affairs. The British, on their part, considered the nationalization move to be an illegal expropriation of their property and organized an international embargo against the marketing of Iranian oil with crippling consequences for the country's economy. After exhausting all options to regain control over the AIOC or reach a compromise with Mosaddeq, they persuaded the Eisenhower administration to organize and finance a jointly sponsored coup to topple Mosaddeq's government. The military coup – the first such venture in "regime change" by the United States in the post-World War II era – was planned months in advance by the Central Intelligence Agency (CIA) and the British foreign intelligence (MI6). It was staged successfully on August 19, 1953, by military officers loyal to the shah and the support of several key members of Mosaddeq's earlier coalition, including some notable religious leaders, tens of thousands of pro-shah supporters, and street toughs paid by the coup-makers.[4]

The overthrow of the democratically elected Mosaddeq ended an intense and tumultuous period of nationalism in Iran's modern history. Mosaddeq himself was charged with attempting to overthrow the monarchy by sparking an uprising, tried and convicted by a military tribunal, imprisoned for three years, and placed under surveillance in his country estate until his death in 1967. In the eyes of the majority of his countrymen he became not only a national hero who stood against an imperialist power in defense of Iran's national interests but a leader who created a democratic, civic, and inclusive form of nationalism that transcended ethnic, regional, and class boundaries. To place the blame for Mosaddeq's overthrow entirely on the coup's foreign sponsors, however, ignores the fact that his own unbending stance throughout the crisis and the consequent worsening of the country's economic conditions had turned some of his earlier allies and supporters against him. As Homa Katouzian, a generally sympathetic observer of the nationalist movement, puts it,

> the coup was the product of the close collaboration of Mosaddeq's domestic and foreign opponents, even though the role of the two foreign powers, especially the United States, in organizing and financing it was all but indispensable .... [T]he foreign powers could not possibly have brought down Mosaddeq by a coup without the cooperation of his domestic opponents. (Katouzian 2004, 16–17)

For many Iranians, the coup rekindled memories of earlier interventions by Britain and Russia, though this time it was the US that was seen as the malevolent power. It changed the image of the US from a distant, noninterventionist country to yet another imperialist power prepared to meddle in Iran's internal affairs in much the same way that Britain and Russia had done over the previous century and a half. More generally, coming at the end of a do-or-die national struggle against the

---

[4] For an all-encompassing, meticulously researched, and balanced account of the 1953 coup, see Rahnema (2015); see also Abrahamian (2013); Bayandor (2010); Kinzer (2008).

country's old imperial nemesis, the coup reinforced the exaggerated preoccupation with foreign intrigues and malice in the Iranian nationalist thinking. As Ali Ansari has argued, the "uncomfortable reality" of the coup led to

> the construction of a pervasive and pernicious myth of anti-imperialism, a myth that sought to exculpate Iranians of any guilt and any responsibility in this particular act of nationalist martyrdom .... No longer primarily a constructive exercise, it was increasingly defined through a confrontational posture against the other, and this exclusivity was as much against internal as external foes. (Ansari 2012, 140)

In the decade following the 1953 coup, Mohammad Reza Shah secured his hold on power by safeguarding the loyalty of the military, suppressing political opposition, and creating a national security organization (SAVAK) that over time became a ruthless and much feared tool of the regime for crushing all forms of dissent. The shah's stance toward the religious establishment was for a time more conciliatory than his father's, which helped to win him the backing of the top clerics in the aftermath of the coup. He displayed his own religiosity by making the obligatory pilgrimage to Mecca (the hajj), occasional visits to Muslim shrines in Iran itself, and claiming that he had at times received divine inspiration.

In the early 1960s, the shah initiated a set of progressive socioeconomic reforms under the banner of the "White Revolution." The key parts of the program included the redistribution of the large landlords' holdings to landless peasants; granting voting rights to women for the first time; requiring companies to share profits with their workers; and sending educated young men to the countryside to teach reading and writing to villagers as members of "literacy corps" as an alternative to military service. The reform program received overwhelming support in a national referendum in January 1963, but soon it was denounced by a number of clerics and seminarians who objected, in particular, to two of its provisions: allowing women to vote and implementing the land distribution program. With regard to the latter, aside from the claim that the program was in violation of private property rights in Islam, the clerics were concerned that the program's potential extension to charitable estates (*awqaf*) under their custodianship would deprive them of one of the main sources of their income. In the ensuing protests and riots that broke out in June 1963 in Qum and several other cities, scores of rioters were killed by the security forces. The person whose words and sermons had helped to instigate these riots was Ayatollah Ruhollah Khomeini, a prominent senior cleric in Qum who was not yet well known nationally. He was jailed briefly and put under house arrest for several months for instigating the uprisings. Shortly after his release in 1964, he made yet another inflammatory speech from the pulpit in which he lambasted the shah for enacting a law that granted immunity from prosecution in Iranian courts to American military and technical personnel working in Iran. He was arrested and exiled to Turkey and later to Iraq, where he spent the next fourteen years. Forced to leave Iraq in 1978, he moved to a suburb of Paris, where he stayed until his return to Iran days before the collapse of the Pahlavi regime and the triumph of the Islamic Revolution.

Mohammad Reza Shah followed his father's path of placing the institution of monarchy at the center of the Iranian national identity by linking his reign to the ancient, pre-Islamic tradition of Persian kingship. In an extravagant celebration of the 2,500th anniversary of the founding of the Achaemenid dynasty held at the ancient ruins of Persepolis (the Achaemenids' ceremonial capital), he declared himself to be heir to the founder of the dynasty, Cyrus the Great. In his emotion-laden speech before scores of invited heads of states and other dignitaries, he said:

> Cyrus, great king, king of kings, Achaemenian king, king of the land of Iran, from me, king of kings of Iran and from my nation, I send greetings ... you, the eternal hero of Iranian history, the founder of the oldest monarchy in the world, the great freedom giver of the world, the worthy son of mankind, we send greetings! ... Cyrus, we have gathered here today at your eternal tomb to tell you: sleep in peace because we are awake and we will always be awake to look after our proud inherit-ance. (Translated from the Persian and cited by Ansari 2019, 278)

A few years later, in his continuing attempt to associate the nation's identity with its ancient past, he changed Iran's official calendar year from 1355 to 2535, i.e., from the traditional Islamic calendar that marked the number of (solar) years past since the Prophet's migration from Mecca to Medina in 622 CE, to one dating back to the founding of the Achaemenid dynasty by Cyrus. (The calendar change was scrapped with the coming of the 1979 Revolution.)

The decade and a half following the socioeconomic reforms of the early 1960s marked a period of impressive economic growth, rapid urbanization, expansion of educational opportunities, and increasing participation by women in all spheres of public life. As noted by Esfahani and Pesaran,

> Between 1963 and 1976, GDP per capita grew at unprecedented rates that aver-aged 8.0 percent per year .... Iran's per capita income moved well above the average for developing countries and was quickly closing its gap with the average income levels in Western Europe. At its peak in 1976, per capita income in Iran had reached about 64 percent of the average for 12 Western European countries. (Esfahani and Pesaran 2009, 189)

The driving engine for the country's economic growth was the dramatic increases in oil revenues, which jumped from $300 million in 1963, to $5 billion in 1973, and to $24 billion in 1977 – an 80-fold increase over a period of 14 years. As is often the case in the early stages of rapidly growing economies, not all segments of the population benefitted equally from the country's new prosperity. There were glaring disparities among different provinces, ethnic groups, the ratio of top-to-bottom income deciles, social classes, and most notably between the fast-growing cities and the relatively stagnant rural areas. Over the same period, with a significant expansion of its military and huge purchases of American arms and modern weapons systems, Iran became the dominant power in the Persian Gulf region. In addition to its strategic alliance with the US, the shah was able to maintain friendly relations with most Arab states, Israel, Western Europe, the Soviet Union, China, and other socialist-bloc countries.

Buoyed by the high performance of the economy, prospects of the continuing flow of oil income, and Iran's relatively favorable international standing, the shah turned his focus from Iran's past to what he touted as its bright future. In various speeches and in a book entitled *Toward the Great Civilization* (*Be su-ye tamaddon-e bozorg*) (Pahlavi [1355 Sh./1976] 1994), he declared that Iran was on the cusp of a new era in its history, one that would enable it to put an end to poverty, exploitation, corruption, ignorance, and other ills that had long plagued the nation. Iranian identity and nationalism, he argued, must now be based on the country's bright future as a "great civilization." What was missing in this utopian vision of the country's future was a recognition that without opportunities for genuine political participation, especially for the rising middle classes and the better-educated younger generation, material prosperity alone could not guarantee political stability and support for the monarchy.

Opposition to the Pahlavi regime in its final two decades was not limited to those demanding free elections, political freedoms, or an end to its human rights violations. It included, in addition, militant clerics and their allies in the bazaar community, poverty-stricken rural migrants in major cities, and radical Marxist-Leninist and Islamic-Marxist groups that engaged in occasional acts of violence and terror against the regime and were in turn brutally repressed. Dissident intellectuals, too, played a key role in creating an atmosphere of discontent among the intelligentsia, especially on university campuses. They criticized the country's pursuit of modernity and indiscriminate adoption of Western cultural values and practices, likening it to a disease on the body of the nation that they branded as *gharbzadegi* (Westoxification) (Al-e Ahmad 1982).[5] For many of them, the nativist call for a "return to the self" and "cultural authenticity" led to an embrace of political Islam akin to a "theology of liberation" that promised to bring independence, cultural autonomy, and social justice to the nation.

As a broadly based social movement that unfolded over a period of one and a half years from the autumn of 1977 to February of 1979, the Islamic Revolution included numerous groups and segments of the population. Its long- and short-term causes, ideological orientations, leadership, the role and extent of participation of different social classes, and patterns of mobilization are the subjects of a vast corpus of scholarly literature (see Arjomand 1998; Bakhash 1990; Dabashi 1993; Kurzman

---

[5] For an extensive discussion of the nativist turn in the discourse of Iranian intellectuals in the 1960s and 1970s, see Boroujerdi (1996); see also Nabavi (2003).

Religion and Nationalism in Contemporary Iran 259

2004; Milani 1994; Moaddel 1993; Mottahedeh 1985; Parsa 1989). As the revolution approached its climactic end, the shah left the country on January 16, 1979, for what turned out to be a precarious and short life in exile. He died in Egypt on July 27, 1980. Less than two weeks after the shah's departure, Ayatollah Khomeini returned to Tehran, where he was received with jubilation by millions of people from all ranks of society as the undisputed leader of the revolution. His first stop upon his return to the country was a symbolic visit to the capital's major cemetery (Behesht-e Zahra) to pay homage to the fallen martyrs of the revolution. Shortly thereafter, he appointed Mehdi Bazargan, a moderate religious-nationalist polit-ician, as prime minister of a provisional revolutionary government in a direct challenge to the existing government headed by Shapur Bakhtiar, a prominent opposition figure and former member of the National Front who had been appointed as prime minister by the shah before his departure weeks earlier. The revolution reached its triumphant peak with the collapse of the Bakhtiar government and marking the end of the Pahlavi monarchy on February 11, 1979.

THE ISLAMIC REVOLUTION, SACRALIZATION OF THE STATE, AND RISE OF RELIGIOUS NATIONALISM

While the idea of an "Islamic Republic," along with "independence" and "free-dom," became a favorite slogan of the revolutionary crowds in the final stages of the 1979 Revolution, few Iranians had any notion of what an Islamic Republic meant as a system of government. Nearly a decade earlier in 1970, Ayatollah Khomeini (1378 Sh./1999), still living in exile in Najaf, Iraq, had put forward the concept of "Islamic government" (*hokumat-e eslami*) or "governance of the jurist" (*velayat-e faqih*) in a series of lectures to his immediate followers. He had argued that, after the death of the Prophet in 632 CE and the subsequent regency of the twelve Shi'i imams, the primary responsibility for the guardianship (*velayat*) of the Muslim community was passed on to high-ranking jurists (the *fuqaha*) who had expert knowledge of Shari'a and Islamic jurisprudence. This responsibility has continued since the disappearance and occultation of the twelfth imam in 874 CE,[6] and it will remain in effect until his return: "the same governance that was exercised by the Most Noble Messenger (upon whom and his family be peace and blessings), and by the imams (upon whom be peace) is also the prerogative of the *fuqaha*" (Khomeini 1981, 124). Furthermore, he argued, the responsibilities of the jurist (or jurists) go beyond guiding the faithful in their spiritual and personal affairs, but must include the legislative, judicial, and executive matters related to the governance of the

---

[6] According to the Shi'i Muslims' eschatological creed, the twelfth successor (imam) to the Prophet, named Muhammad al-Mahdi, disappeared as a child in 874 CE and will remain under occultation until the end of time. Referred to as the "hidden imam," he is expected to return before the Day of Judgment with his chosen companions to restore justice, end all evil, and rule over the Muslim community.

260   *Ali Banuazizi*

Muslim community. Contrasting his position on the "breadth and the focus" of the jurists' role to the more traditional views of Muslim scholars (mujtahids) of his time, he stated:

> The Qur'an and the books of hadith [Prophetic traditions], which represent the sources for the commands and ordinances of Islam, are completely different from the treatises written by the mujtahids [religious scholars] of the present age both in breadth of scope and in the effect that they are capable of exerting on the life of society. The ratio of the Qur'anic verses concerned with the affairs of society to those concerned with ritual worship is greater than a hundred to one. Of the approximately fifty sections of the corpus of hadith containing all the ordinances of Islam, not more than three or four sections relate to matters of ritual worship and the duties of man toward his Creator and Sustainer. (Khomeini 1981, 29)

At the time, Khomeini's advocacy of a direct executive role for the *fuqaha* did not receive any visible support from the high-ranking Shi'i authorities in Iran or Iraq, and few people expected that Khomeini himself would assume such a role in a future Iranian state.[7]

After the revolution's victory in February 1979, a hastily arranged referendum provided overwhelming support for an "Islamic Republic" as the country's new form of government, though again there was no clear sense of what such an "Islamic Republic" would be like. Shortly after the referendum, a preliminary draft of a new constitution, which had been prepared at Khomeini's direction while he was still in Paris, provided a framework for a future Islamic government. It proposed the formation of a republic based on Islamic laws, but one that would uphold the principles of popular sovereignty, separation of powers, and the protection of the citizens' basic rights. There was no mention of an executive role for a supreme jurist (*faqih*) in the proposed draft. After a contentious debate within Khomeini's inner circle, it was decided that the draft constitution be reviewed, and where needed revised, by a yet-to-be-elected Assembly of Experts (Majles-e Khobregan). In the subsequent election campaign for that assembly, thanks to the concerted efforts of a clerically dominated Islamic Republic Party (IRP), fifty-five of the seventy-three seats went to the staunchly pro-Khomeini clerics. And much to the consternation of a handful of its secular and liberal members, the assembly drafted a new constitution that fully incorporated Khomeini's doctrine of "governance of the jurist" (*velayat-e faqih*). The new constitution was ratified in a speedily arranged national referendum in December 1979.[8] It placed the legal foundation of the Islamic Republic on

---

[7] For an analysis of the evolution of Ayatollah Khomeini's views on the role of the guardian jurist, see Rahnema (2014); for a critique of Khomeini's concept of governance of the jurist by a leading scholar of Shi'i thought, see Kadivar (1379 Sh./2001, 1380 Sh./2002).

[8] For a detailed analysis of the political process that led to the adoption of the constitution, see Arjomand (2011) and Schirazi (1997, especially 22–58). For the text of the constitution in translation, see Algar (1980); for a more recent translation, including amendments that were adopted in 1989, see Papan-Matin (2014).

Shari'a laws as interpreted, in practice, by a "supreme jurist" (later referred to as the "Supreme Leader") and an unelected twelve-member "Council of Guardians":

> Article 4. All civil, penal, financial, economic, administrative, cultural, military, political, and other laws and regulations must be based on Islamic criteria. This principle applies absolutely and generally to all articles of the Constitution as well as to all laws and regulations, and the *fuqaha* [jurists] on the Council of Guardians have the duty of supervising its implementation.

The constitution described the position of the *faqih* in specifically Shi'i eschatological terms as follows:

> Article 5. During the Occultation of the Lord of the Age [the twelfth imam] (May God hasten his renewed manifestation!), the governance and will devolve upon the just and pious *faqih* [jurist] who is acquainted with the circumstances of his age; courageous, resourceful, and possessed of administrative ability; and recognized and accepted as leader by the majority of the people.

As expected, the new constitution (Article 110) named Ayatollah Khomeini as the Islamic Republic's first Supreme Leader. It granted him the ultimate authority to set the broad directions for the country's domestic and foreign policies, to serve as the commander-in-chief of the armed forces, and to appoint the chief of the judiciary as well as half the twelve-member Council Guardians (with the other half to be chosen by the head of the judiciary, who is himself appointed by the Supreme Leader). The principal functions of the Council of Guardians are to review legislations passed by the parliament (Majles) to ensure that they are compatible with Islamic principles and to vet candidates for election to the parliament and the presidency.

As had been the case with the 1906 constitution, the new constitution declared Twelver Shi'ism as Iran's official religion (Article 12) and granted recognition to Zoroastrianism, Judaism, and Christianity as legitimate minority religions (Article 13). This left out Iran's largest religious minority, the Baha'is, who have been deprived of their basic civil rights and subjected to various forms of official and unofficial discrimination, intimidation, and frequent attacks on their lives, places of business, and burial sites since the establishment of the Islamic Republic. The constitution also declared Persian as the country's official language (Article 15), thus continuing the Pahlavi regime's policy of recognizing Persian as the sole national language in all official, educational, and cultural spheres and the public media.

Less than a decade after the ratification of the constitution, in an abrupt move to bolster the authority of the Islamic state and, by implication that of the ruling *faqih*, Khomeini issued a new and binding directive in January 1988 that placed the interests and preservation of the Islamic state above all ordinances of Islam. "The state," he declared, "which constitutes a part of Prophet Mohammad's *Velayat-e Motlaqeh* [Absolute Rule], is one of the primary ordinances of Islam and has precedence over all the secondary ordinances, and even prayer, fasting, and pilgrimage" (translated and cited by Tabaar 2018, 189). Shortly thereafter, he ordered the establishment of a new deliberative body, the Expediency Discernment Assembly of the State (Majma'-e tashkhis-e maslaehat-e nezam) to help the Supreme Leader discern the interests of the state and to serve as the final arbiter between the Majles and the Guardian Council. The issuance and subsequent incorporation of this decree into the amended version of the constitution in 1989 was a further decisive step toward the "sacralization of the state," albeit in the form of a theocratic *republic* with a democratically elected parliament and president.

In the early years of the Islamic Republic, nationalism was viewed as an alien and secular ideology incompatible with Islam and its emphasis on Islamic unity beyond national or ethnic boundaries. Khomeini (1981, 302) himself saw nationalism as "contrary to the Noble Qur'an and the order of the Noblest Messenger ... [and] a stratagem concocted by foreigners who are disturbed by the spread of Islam." The Islamic Republic often prided itself for being a model of progressive Islam to be emulated by all Muslims in their struggles against their oppressive and corrupt rulers, as well as arrogant foreign powers. Within Iran itself, high government officials and prominent religious leaders tried to downplay or in some cases to stamp out pre-Islamic symbols, rituals, and cultural practices, including the ancient celebration of Nowruz (the start of the Persian New Year on the first day of spring). Most such efforts, however, were quietly abandoned due to public resistance.

The eight-year Iran-Iraq War (1980–88) – the most devastating conflict in Iran's modern history with staggering human casualties and destruction of towns and villages in both countries – put to a test the relative symbolic power of nationalism versus Islam as tools for political mobilization. In the early stages of the war, Ayatollah Khomeini and other revolutionary leaders used highly charged religious rhetoric to mobilize the nation for combat (Gieling 1999). They cast the war as a conflict between Islam and blasphemy and characterized Iran's response to the Iraqi aggression as a *"sacred defense"* by a "martyr-producing nation" (*mellat-e shaid-parvar*). Tens of thousands of young men with little or no military training who were "carrying plastic keys that purported to deliver the holder to heaven in the event of his death were pushed into 'human wave' charges through the Iraqi minefields" (Litvak 2017b, 118; Samuel 2017). But as the war dragged on and the Iraqi side presented the conflict in ethnic terms (Arabs versus Persians) and received support from other Arab countries (with the exception of Syria), the regime's religious rhetoric of sacrifice and martyrdom lost some of its persuasive power. It was combined with, and replaced largely by, nationalist propaganda that portrayed the war as a *patriotic* duty to defend the Islamic homeland against a Ba'athist Arab aggressor.

The use of Islam and nationalism as two complementary elements of Iranian identity continued beyond the war years. The reformist President Mohammad Khatami (1997–2005) often emphasized this dual basis of Iranian national identity in his writings and speeches. He considered "both *Iraniyat* (Iran's pre-Islamic culture) and *Islamiyat* (its Islamic culture) as integral and authentic to Iranian national identity . . . . Islam is Iranianised and furthermore the framework for the political apparatus is not simply politicised Islam, but rather *Iranian* political Islam" (Holliday 2010, 4). His successor, the populist President Mahmoud Ahmadinejad (2005–13), went further in his emphasis on pre-Islamic roots of the Iranian identity. He and his son-in-law and chief of staff, Esfandiar Rahim Masha'i, spoke of an "Iranian school of Islam" that combines Iran's pre-Islamic and humanistic ideals with the core teachings of Islam. In a symbolic move to foster this viewpoint, Ahmadinejad arranged for the Cyrus Cylinder (a sixth-century BCE text that exhibits Cyrus's religious tolerance toward his new subjects after his conquest of Babylon and his emancipation of the Jews from their Babylonian captivity) to be brought and displayed in Tehran on loan from the British Museum. At a ceremony in September 2010, he praised Cyrus as the "king of the ancient world" and the cylinder as "the standard by which 'all rulers and kings in the history of humankind' must be measured" (Chenar 2010). His placing Iran's pre-Islamic heritage alongside of Islam in defining Iranian identity – without explicitly acknowledging Islam's supremacy – provoked the ire of the conservative clerical establishment, who chastised the president harshly and called Masha'i an apostate (*kafir*).

In its foreign relations, the Islamic Republic has moved considerably beyond its earlier zealous support for Islamic movements in other parts of the world to a more pragmatic focus on its own national interests. Its alliances with the Lebanese Hezbollah, the various Shi'i factions in Iraq, and the Bashar al-Assad regime in Syria, which may have been based initially on sectarian ties and ideological commitments, represent Iran's own strategic interests and foreign policy priorities, including its long-standing objective of creating an "axis of resistance" across Iraq, Syria, and Lebanon against Israel. Similarly, the Islamic Republic's support for the Houthis in Yemen's civil war has been driven more by its long-standing hegemonic rivalry with Saudi Arabia in the Persian Gulf than by sectarian affinities toward the followers of a nonorthodox Shi'i sect. In numerous other cases, economic and political exigencies have outweighed the regime's professed commitment of support for oppressed fellow Muslims in other countries. A recent case in point was Iran's joining a number of other governments in July 2019 to sign a letter to the president of the United Nations Human Rights Council lauding China for its "remarkable achievements in the field of human rights" and for restoring peace and security through "counterterrorism measures and vocational training" (New York Times 2019). The object of the statement's unqualified praise was China's mass detention, torture, and mistreatment of over one million of its Muslim Uighur minority in Xinjiang region (Human Rights Watch 2018).

In more recent years, as the anthropologist Narges Bajoghli (2019) has noted, there has been a concerted effort by some elements within the powerful Islamic Revolutionary Guard Corps (IRGC) to rebrand the Guards as the defender of the

Iranian nation and homeland rather than the Islamic Revolution and regime. In her extensive fieldwork in Iran with members of the media production teams of the IRGC and the paramilitary militia (Basij), she found that they "appeal to notions of nationalism as a unifying force beyond political ideology, especially in the face of growing sectarianism in the region, proxy wars with Saudi Arabia, and a realization that Iran's youth is no longer motivated by political Islam" (Bajoghli 2019, 117). She cites the blunt words of an IRGC commander to his colleagues: "People are tired of us only showing them images of pious men who fought for this country . . .. Young people no longer respond to it, so we have to find another way" (Bajoghli 2017, 1).

Both nationalism and religion have played a key role, also, in how Iran has justified its nuclear ambitions, an issue that has dominated the country's adversarial relationship with the US and other world powers for the past two decades. Iran has long maintained that, as a sovereign nation, it has the right to develop its nuclear technology and produce enriched uranium to fuel its nuclear power plants and, at a higher level of enrichment, for use in its nuclear medicine reactors. It has rejected the charge that a further goal of its program is to develop a nuclear-weapons capability by pointing out that Iran is a signatory to the 1968 Non-Proliferation Treaty (NPT) and has complied consistently with intrusive inspections carried out by the International Atomic Energy Agency (IAEA). Furthermore, it has claimed that any use of weapons of mass destruction, including nuclear weapons, has been proscribed since 2003 in several statements and edicts (fatwas) by the Supreme Leader Ayatollah Ali Khamenei as being contrary to Islamic principles:

> The Islamic Republic of Iran considers the use of nuclear, chemical and similar weapons as a great and unforgivable sin. We proposed the idea of "Middle East free of nuclear weapons" and we are committed to it. This does not mean forgoing our right to peaceful use of nuclear power and production of nuclear fuel. (Khamenei 2012)

The degree to which such statements or fatwas can be taken as trustworthy or binding commitments on the part of the Iranian government is far from certain. Shi'i jurisprudence allows for a subsequent fatwa by a "Supreme Leader" – or one by another high-ranking ayatollah (or a "source of emulation") – to revise or supersede an existing one. As Eisenstadt and Khalaji have pointed out,

> fatwas are issues in response to specific circumstances and can be altered in response to changing conditions. Ayatollah Khomeini modified his position on a number of issues during his lifetime – for instance, on taxes, military conscription, women's suffrage, and monarchy as a form of government. Thus nothing would prevent Khamenei from modifying or supplanting his nuclear fatwa should circumstances dictate a change in policy. (Eisenstadt and Khalaji 2011, ix)

It should be noted, however, that despite the fact that nearly all the skepticism regarding compliance with the NPT and the terms of the 2015 nuclear agreement between Iran and the five permanent members of the UN Security Council plus Germany (formally called the Joint Comprehensive Plan of Action or "JCPOA") was directed against Iran, it was the US that unilaterally withdrew from the agreement under President Trump in 2018. The American withdrawal from an international agreement that had been reached after two years of intense negotiations and subsequently ratified by the UN Security Council gave credence to the hard-liners' position within the Iranian regime who had warned all along that the US should not be trusted to keep its word and adhere to the terms of a negotiated nuclear agreement.[9]

CONCLUSION

Although ideas of the "nation-state" and nationalism did not enter Iran's political discourse until the last decades of the nineteenth century, they were readily embraced by a number of Iranian intellectuals, the reform-minded members of the political elite, several prominent religious leaders, and, within a matter of few years, by a broad segment of the urban population. Over the past century, as the foregoing analysis has shown, Iranian nationalism has appeared in different forms and guises. As part of the ideology that steered the 1905–11 Constitutional Revolution, nationalism championed the idea that a country's population, despite its diversity, makes up a "nation" to be governed by the rule of law and whose members, as *citizens* rather than *subjects* of a "royal domain," have the right to hold accountable those who rule over them. In the Pahlavi era (1925–79), a top-down monarchical form of nationalism served as the official ideology of an autocratic state that promoted modernity and secularism for nearly six decades, while denying genuine political participation and basic political freedoms to its people. The Pahlavi period included an interlude (in the late 1940s and early 1950s) in which a populist, inclusive, and largely democratic form of nationalism roused the nation in an uphill struggle to end an unfair monopoly over the country's economic lifeline by a foreign power. And finally, over the past four decades, nationalism has been interlaced with Islamism in the form of "religious nationalism" as the legitimizing ideology of the quasi-theocratic Islamic Republic.[10]

Two aspects of Iranian nationalism and its vicissitudes are especially noteworthy. The first is a pervasive belief on the part of many Iranians that their country's misfortunes and perils have all been the results of the ill intents and machinations of foreign powers. This belief is based on such distant and recent memories as the

---

[9] For a detailed overview of the 2015 nuclear agreement (JCPOA), see Samore (2015); for the reactions by the Islamic Revolutionary Guard Corps (IRGC) to the Trump administration's withdrawal from JCPOA and the subsequent "maximum pressure" policy toward Iran, see Hecher (2019).

[10] For an analysis of Islamic-Iranian nationalism, see Aghaie (2014); on the worldwide resurgence of religious nationalism, see Brubaker (2011); Juergensmeyer (2006); Omer and Springs (2013); Zubaida (2011).

Russian and British interventions in Iran during the nineteenth and early twentieth centuries; occupation of the country by the Allied Powers during World War II, which forced the ruling monarch, Reza Shah, to abdicate; Russian and later Soviet support for secessionist movements in Iran's outlying provinces; the US-sponsored coup in 1953 that overthrew a popular government; and finally Western support of Saddam Hussein in the Iran-Iraq War. These historical memories have led to far-fetched conspiracy theories (see Ashraf 1992; Abrahamian 1993) and a sense of victimhood that makes Iranians overly suspicious and unforgiving in their perceptions and dealings with foreign powers.

A second notable feature of Iranian nationalism has been its conflation with religion. Given the prominence of religion in the private and public lives of the vast majority of Iranians, strictly secular nationalist ideologies have never had much popular appeal. Thus, for example, while the secularizing efforts of the Pahlavi period (1925–79) reduced the clergy's role in the country's educational, legal, and charitable institutions, they could hardly diminish the influence of religion in the daily lives of the vast majority of the people. The public role of religion and its relationship with nationalism changed dramatically, of course, with the 1979 Revolution and the establishment of the Islamic Republic. In the immediate aftermath of the revolution, Islam served not only the legal foundation for the new regime but also as the official state ideology that shaped the political, social, and cultural spheres of the nation's life. Nationalism was rejected initially as a secular, alien, and divisive ideology that had been perpetrated by the West and adopted by the Pahlavi rulers to undermine people's faith and promote subservience to Western values and interests. But, in response to increasing public resistance to the regime's suppression of nationalist symbols and rituals and the utility of nationalist slogans for mobilizing vast numbers of young people in the war against Iraq – a fellow Muslim country with a majority Shi'i population – the regime adopted its own nationalist claims and propaganda. What emerged was a form of "religious nationalism," which Mark Juergensmeyer has labeled as "ideological religious nationalism" and describes in the following terms:

> It *religionizes* politics. It puts political issues and struggles within a sacred context. Compatability [*sic*] with religious goals becomes the criterion for an acceptable political platform. The Islamic revolution in Iran, for instance, was a classic example of ideological religious nationalism that turned ordinary politics upside down. Instead of the western ideal of a nonreligious political order providing space for religious activities, in Iran a religious authority has set the context for politics. (Juergensmeyer 1996, 5)

Juergensmeyer (1996, 4) contrasts this form of religious nationalism with what he calls "ethnic religious nationalism" – as in the paradigmatic cases of Catholics and Protestants in Northern Ireland or Serbs, Croats, and Muslims in former

Religion and Nationalism in Contemporary Iran

Yugoslavia – in which religion is *politicized* and is fused with a culture of domination or liberation. One may place the prevalent Jewish nationalism in Israel, too, under this latter type of religious nationalism.

In postrevolutionary Iranian politics, both nationalism and religious nationalism have had their impact primarily on the country's foreign relations. Domestically, it has been religion that has served as the guiding ideology of the Islamic Republic over the past four decades, allowing the theocratic state and the clerical hierarchy to claim divine authority over all state institutions, the economy, the educational system, and cultural and philanthropic organizations. Its decades-long record of placing severe restrictions on personal and political freedoms of its citizens, denial of the basic rights of members of religious minorities, and use of repressive and often brutal measures against all forms of dissent and organized political opposition bears testimony to the fact that religionization of politics – if it leads to an instrumental use of religion to sacralize politics and claim divine provenance for a modern state – can lead to the arbitrary use of power, corruption, intolerance, and tyranny just as easily as secular authoritarian ideologies.

REFERENCES

Abrahamian, Ervand. 1993. "The Paranoid Style in Iranian Politics." In *Khomeinism: Essays on the Islamic Republic*, edited by Ervand Abhrahamian, 111–31. Berkeley: University of California Press.

2013. *The Coup: 1953, the CIA, and the Roots of Modern U.S.–Iran Relations*. New York: The New Press.

Adib-Moghaddam, Arshin. 2018. *Psycho-nationalism: Global Thought, Iranian Imaginations*. New York: Cambridge University Press.

Aghaie, Kamran Scot. 2014. "Islamic-Iranian Nationalism and Its Implications for the Study of Political Islam and Religious Nationalism." In *Rethinking Iranian Nationalism and Modernity*, edited by Kamran Scot Aghaie and Afshin Marashi, 181–203. Austin: University of Texas Press.

Aghaie, Kamran Scot, and Afshin Marashi, eds. 2014. *Rethinking Iranian Nationalism and Modernity*. Austin: University of Texas Press.

Ahmadi, Hamid. 1378 Sh./1999. *Qowmiyat va qowmgara'i dar Iran: Afsaneh va vaqe'iyat* [Ethnicity and ethnic loyalty in Iran: Myth and realities]. Tehran: Nashr-e Ney.

Al-e Ahmad, Jalal. 1982. *Plagued by the West (Gharbzadegi)*. Translated by Paul Sprachman. Delmar, NY: Caravan Books.

Algar, Hamid, trans. 1980. *Constitution of the Islamic Republic of Iran*. Berkeley, CA: Mizan Press.

Amanat, Abbas. 2017. *Iran: A Modern History*. New Haven, CT: Yale University Press.

Amanat, Abbas, and Assef Ashraf, eds. 2018. *The Persianate World: Rethinking a Shared Sphere*. Leiden: Brill.

Amanat, Abbas, and Farzin Vejdani, eds. 2012. *Iran Facing Other: Identity Boundaries in a Historical Perspective*. New York: Palgrave Macmillan.

Ansari, Ali M. 2012. *The Politics of Nationalism in Modern Iran*. New York: Cambridge University Press.

2019. *Modern Iran since 1797: Reform and Revolution*. 3rd ed. New York: Routledge.

Arjomand, Said Amir. 1998. *The Turban for the Crown: The Islamic Revolution in Iran.* New York: Oxford University Press.

2011. "Constitution of the Islamic Republic." In Encyclopaedia Iranica. www.iranicaonline.org/articles/constitution-of-the-islamic-republic.

Ashraf, Ahmad. 1992. "Conspiracy Theories." In Encyclopaedia Iranica. www.iranicaonline.org/articles/conspiracy-theories.

2006. "Iranian Identity i. Perspectives." In Encyclopaedia Iranica. www.iranicaonline.org/articles/iranian-identity-i-perspectives.

1395 Sh./2016. *Hoviyat-e Irani: Az dowran-e bastan to payan-e Pahlavi* [Iranian identity: From ancient times to the end of Pahlavis]. Translated and edited by Hamid Ahmadi. Tehran: Nashr-e Ney.

Atabaki, Touraj, ed. 2006. *Iran and the First World War: Battleground of the Great Powers.* London: I.B. Tauris.

Atabaki, Touraj, and Erik J. Zürcher. 2004. *Men of Order: Authoritarian Modernization under Atatürk and Reza Shah.* London: I.B. Tauris.

Bajoghli, Narges. 2017. "The Genesis of a New Iranian Nationalism." *Al-Monitor,* December 14. www.al-monitor.com/pulse/originals/2017/12/iran-new-nationalism-religion-politics-trump-saudi-isis.html.

2019. *Iran Re-framed: Anxieties of Power in the Islamic Republic.* Stanford: Stanford University Press.

Bakhash, Shaul. 1990. *The Reign of the Ayatollahs: Iran and the Islamic Revolution.* Rev. ed. New York: Basic Books.

Bayandor, Darioush. 2010. *Iran and the CIA: The Fall of Mosaddeq Revisited.* New York: Palgrave Macmillan.

Berger, Peter L. 1999. "The Desecularization of the World: A Global Overview." In *The Desecularization of the World: Resurgent Religion and World Politics,* edited by Peter L. Berger, 1–18. Grand Rapids, MI: William B. Eerdmans Publishing Co.

Boroujerdi, Mehrzad. 1996. *Iranian Intellectuals and the West: The Tormented Triumph of Nativism.* Syracuse: Syracuse University Press.

1998. "Contesting Nationalist Constructions of Iranian Identity." *Critique: Journal for Critical Studies of the Middle East* 12: 43–56.

Brubaker, Rogers. 2011. "Religion and Nationalism: Four Approaches." *Nations and Nationalism* 18, no. 1: 2–20.

Chehabi, Houchang E. 1993. "Staging the Emperor's New Clothes: Dress Codes and Nation-Building under Reza Shah." *Iranian Studies* 26, no. 3–4: 209–29.

Chenar, Ali. 2010. "'Hail Cyrus': An Extravagant Cry Echoes with Irony." *Frontline.* www.pbs.org/wgbh/pages/frontline/tehranbureau/2010/09/hail-cyrus.html.

Dabashi, Hamid. 1993. *Theology of Discontent: The Ideological Foundation of Islamic Revolution in Iran.* New York: New York University Press.

Eisenstadt, Michael, and Mehdi Khalaji. 2011. "Nuclear Fatwa: Religion and Politics in Iran's Proliferation Strategy." Policy Focus 115. Washington, DC: Washington Institute for Near East Policy. https://bit.ly/38Cer8k.

Elling, Rasmus Christian. 2013. *Minorities in Iran: Nationalism and Ethnicity after Khomeini.* New York: Palgrave Macmillan.

Esfahani, Hadi Salehi, and M. Hashem Pesaran. 2009. "Iranian Economy in the Twentieth Century: A Global Perspective." *Iranian Studies* 42, no. 2: 177–211.

Fragner, Bert G. 1999. *Die Persophonie: Regionalität, Identität und Sprachkontakt in der Geschichte Asiens* [Persophonia: Regionalism, identity, and language contacts in Asian history]. Berlin: Das Arabische Buch.

Ghods, M. Reza. 1991. "Iranian Nationalism and Reza Shah." *Middle Eastern Studies* 27, no. 1: 35–45.

Gieling, Saskia. 1999. *Religion and War in Revolutionary Iran*. New York: I.B. Tauris.

Gnoli, Gherardo. 1989. *The Idea of Iran: An Essay on Its Origin*. Rome: Instituto Italiano per il Medio ed Estremo Oriente.

Hecher, Pia. 2019. "'Maximum Pressure' Campaign Is Bolstering Iran's Revolutionary Guards." *Atlantic Council*. https://bit.ly/3lrAthE.

Holliday, Shabnam. 2010. "Khatami's Islamist-Iranian Discourse of National Identity: A Discourse of Resistance." *British Journal of Middle Eastern Studies* 37, no. 1: 1–13.

Human Rights Watch. 2018. "'Eradicating Ideological Viruses': China's Campaign of Repression against Xinjiang's Muslims." www.hrw.org/report/2018/09/09/eradicating-ideological-viruses/chinas-campaign-repression-against-xinjiangs.

Juergensmeyer, Mark. 1996. "The Worldwide Rise of Religious Nationalism." *Journal of International Affairs* 50, no. 1: 1–20.

2006. "Nationalism and Religion." In *The Sage Handbook of Nations and Nationalism*, edited by Gerard Delanty and Krishan Kumar, 182–91. London: Sage Publications.

Kadivar, Mohsen. 1379 Sh./2001. *Daghdagheha-ye hokumat-e dini* [Concern over religious governance]. Tehran: Nashr-e Ney.

1380 Sh./2002. *Hokumat-e velayi* [Juridical governance]. 2nd ed. Tehran: Nashr-e Ney.

Kashani-Sabet, Firoozeh. 1999. *Frontier Fictions: Shaping the Iranian Nation, 1804–1946*. Princeton: Princeton University Press.

2002. "Cultures of Iranianness: The Evolving Polemic of Iranian Nationalism." In *Iran and the Surrounding World: Interactions in Culture and Cultural Politics*, edited by Nikki R. Keddie and Rudi Matthee, 162–81. Seattle: University of Washington Press.

Katouzian, Homa. 2004. "Mosaddeq's Government in Iranian History: Arbitrary Rule, Democracy, and the 1953 Coup." In *Mohammad Mosaddeq and the 1953 Coup in Iran*, edited by Mark J. Gasiorowski and Malcolm Byrne, 1–26. Syracuse: Syracuse University Press.

Keyman, E., and Suhnaz Yilmaz. 2006. "Modernity and Nationalism: Turkey and Iran in Comparative Perspective." In *The Sage Handbook of Nations and Nationalism*, edited by Gerard Delanty and Krishan Kumar, 425–37. London: Sage Publications.

Khamenei, Ali. 2012. "Nuclear Weapon Is Haraam; Nuclear Energy Is a Right." *Khamenei.ir*. http://english.khamenei.ir/news/2270/Nuclear-weapon-is-Haraam-Nuclear-energy-is-a-right.

Khomeini, Ruhollah. 1981. *Islam and Revolution: Writings and Declarations of Imam Khomeini*. Translated and edited by Hamid Algar. Berkeley: Mizan Press.

1378Sh./1999. *Velayat-e faqih* [Mandate of the jurist]. Tehran: Moassesse-ye Chap va Nashr-e Asar-e Emam Khomeini.

Kinzer, Stephen. 2008. *All the Shah's Men: An American Coup and the Roots of Middle East Terror*. New York: John Wiley.

Kurzman, Charles. 2004. *The Unthinkable Revolution*. Cambridge, MA: Harvard University Press.

Lenczowski, George. 1983. "Foreign Powers' Intervention in Iran during World War I." In *Qajar Iran: Political, Social and Cultural Change, 1800–1925*, edited by Edmund Bosworth and Carole Hillenbrand, 76–92. Edinburgh: Edinburgh University Press.

Litvak, Meir, ed. 2017a. *Constructing Nationalism in Iran: From the Qajars to the Islamic Republic*. New York: Routledge.

Litvak, Meir. 2017b. "Martyrdom Is Bliss: The Iranian Concept of Martyrdom during the War with Iraq, 1981–88." In *Martyrdom and Sacrifice in Islam: Theological, Political and Social Contexts*, edited by Meir Hatina and Meir Litvak, 116–30. London: I.B. Tauris.

Marashi, Afshin. 2008. *Nationalizing Iran: Culture, Power, and the State, 1870–1940*. Seattle: University of Washington Press.

Menashri, David. 1992. *Education and the Making of Modern Iran*. Ithaca: Cornell University Press.

Meskoob, Shahrokh. 1992. *Iranian Nationality and the Persian Language, 900–1900*. Translated by Michael C. Hillmann. Washington, DC: Mage Publishers.

Milani, Mohsen M. 1994. *The Making of Iran's Islamic Revolution: From Monarchy to Islamic Republic*. 2nd ed. Boulder, CO: Westview Press.

Moaddel, Mansoor. 1993. *Class, Politics, and Ideology in the Iranian Revolution*. New York: Columbia University Press.

Motahhari, Morteza. 1349 Sh./1970. *Khadamat-e moteqabel-e Iran va Islam* [The reciprocal contributions of Iran and Islam]. Tehran: Sherkat-e Enteshar.

Mottahedeh, Roy. 1985. *The Mantle of the Prophet: Religion and Politics in Iran*. New York: Simon and Schuster.

Nabavi, Negin. 2003. *Intellectuals and the State in Iran: Politics, Discourse, and the Dilemma of Authenticity*. Gainesville: University Press of Florida.

New York Times. 2019. "Beijing's Response to Rebuke: Russian and Saudi Praise." July 13. www.nytimes.com/2019/07/12/world/asia/china-human-rights-united-nations.html?module=inline.

Omer, Atalia, and Jason A. Springs. 2013. *Religious Nationalism: A Reference Handbook*. Santa Barbara, CA: ABC-CLIO.

Pahlavi, Mohammad Reza. (1355 Sh./1976) 1994. *Toward the Great Civilization*. London: Satrap Publishing.

Papan-Matin, Firoozeh, trans. 2014. "The Constitution of the Islamic Republic of Iran (1989 Edition)." *Iranian Studies* 47, no. 1: 159–200.

Parsa, Misagh. 1989. *Social Origins of the Iranian Revolution*. New Brunswick, NJ: Rutgers University Press.

Perry, John R., ed. 2018. *Persian Literature from Outside Iran: The Indian Subcontinent, Anatolia, Central Asia, and in Judeo-Persian*. London: I.B. Tauris.

Rahnema, Ali. 2014. "Ayatollah Khomeini's Rule of the Guardian Jurist: From Theory to Practice." In *A Critical Introduction to Khomeini*, edited by Arshin Adib-Moghaddam, 88–114. New York: Cambridge University Press.

   2015. *Behind the 1953 Coup in Iran: Thugs, Turncoats, Soldiers, and Spooks*. New York: Cambridge University Press.

Samore, Gary. 2015. *The Iran Nuclear Deal: A Definitive Guide*. Cambridge, MA: Belfer Center for Science and International Affairs.

Samuel, Annie Tracy. 2017. "Guarding the Nation: The Iranian Revolutionary Guards, Nationalism and the Iran-Iraq War." In *Constructing Nationalism in Iran: From the Qajars to the Islamic Republic*, edited by Meir Litvak, 248–62. London: Routledge.

Schirazi, Asghar. 1997. *The Constitution of Iran: Politics and the State in the Islamic Republic*. London: I.B. Tauris.

   1396 Sh./2017. *Iraniyat, melliyat, qowmiyat* [Iranianness, nationality, ethnicity]. Tehran: Jahan Ketab.

Sharifi, Majid. 2013. *Imagining Iran: The Tragedy of Subaltern Nationalism*. Lanham, MD: Lexington Books.

Siavoshi, Sussan. 1990. *Liberal Nationalism in Iran: The Failure of a Movement*. Boulder, CO: Westview Press.

Smith, Anthony D. 2010. *Nationalism: Theory, Ideology, History*. 2nd ed. Cambridge: Polity Press.

Tabaar, Mohammad Ayatollahi. 2018. *Religious Statecraft: The Politics of Islam in Iran*. New York: Columbia University Press.

Tavakoli-Targhi, Mohamad. 2001. *Refashioning Iran: Orientalism, Occidentalism, and Historiography*. New York: Palgrave Macmillan.

Vaziri, Mostafa. 1993. *Iran as Imagined Nation: The Construction of National Identity*. New York: Marlowe and Company.

White, Jenny. 2013. *Muslim Nationalism and the New Turks*. Princeton: Princeton University Press.

Yarshater, Ehsan. 1998. "The Persian Presence in the Islamic World." In *The Persian Presence in the Islamic World*, edited by Richard G. Hovannisian and George Sabagh, 4–125. Cambridge: Cambridge University Press.

Zarrinkoub, Abdolhossein. 2017. *Two Centuries of Silence: An Account of Events and Conditions in Iran [Persia] during the First Two Hundred Years of Islam, from the Arab Invasion to the Rise of the Tahirid Dynasty*. Translated and edited by Paul Sprachman. Costa Mesa, CA: Mazda Publishers.

Zia-Ebrahimi, Reza. 2016. *The Emergence of Iranian Nationalism: Race and the Politics of Dislocation*. New York: Columbia University Press.

Zubaida, Sami. 2011. "Islam and Nationalism: Continuities and Contradictions." In *Beyond Islam: A New Understanding of the Middle East*, edited by Sami Zubaida, 175–99. London: I.B. Tauris.

PART VI

Saudi Arabia and Wahhabism

11

Saudi Nationalism, Wahhabi *Daʿwā*, and Western Power

*Michael A. Sells**

INTRODUCTION

Saudi Crown Prince Muḥammad bin Salmān was among the first state visitors to the White House in the aftermath of Donald Trump's inauguration as President of the United States. Not long after, Trump was a guest of honor in Riyadh where he, Saudi King Salmān ibn ʿAbd al-ʿAzīz, and Egyptian President ʿAbd al Fattāḥ al-Sīsī extended their hands over a glowing orb in a ceremony inaugurating the Saudi-based Global Center for Combating Extremist Ideology.[1]

The seemingly incongruous phenomenon of a Saudi regime opening a center to counter extremism, a form of which it has spent decades promoting worldwide, occurred during a time of aggressive nationalist rhetoric in Saudi Arabia and around the world. Nationalism, long overshadowed or contained by Cold War bipolar geopolitics and the rise of commercial and NGO globalization, reasserted itself with Brexit, the 2016 US elections, attacks on transnational security alliances and multilateral trade pacts, and ethno-populist nationalist movements coming to power across Europe and Asia.

Muḥammad bin Salmān (known journalistically as MbS), the de facto ruler of Saudi Arabia, seems to fit the emerging model of the populist nationalism. He has adopted the profile of the swaggering populist, plunged Saudi Arabia and its Gulf

---

[*] I have used the formal transliteration system of the *International Journal of Middle Eastern Studies* for Arabic names and terms, except in quotations using different naming protocols or referring to authors who, although their names may be Arabic in origin, spell them with different transliterations. Words that are most commonly Anglicized such as madrasa, fatwa, Sufi, Salafi, Hanbali, and Wahhabi appear without italics or transliterations. I owe particular gratitude to Erin Atwell for her invaluable help in editing drafts of this chapter; to Jamel Velji and the Claremont McKenna University community for inviting me to present a talk on "'Wahhabism' and Global Conflict" on March 22, 2016; and to the Fletcher School of Law and Diplomacy at Tufts University and organizers of the conference on "The Fusion of Religion and Nationalism in Comparative Perspective" on March 31, 2016, at which I presented the paper that forms the basis for this chapter.

[1] See Arab News (2017) for a photo and a sympathetic write-up of the event. For a reflection of recent Saudi efforts to disassociate itself from responsibility for extremist movements, see Ansary (2018). The Arabia Foundation played a particularly high-profile role in the US as an aggressive advocate of the policies of Saudi Arabia and its de facto ruler, Prince Muḥammad bin Salmān, from 2017 to 2019. (A notice still posted as of August 26, 2019, on www.arabiafoundation.org states that the Foundation discontinued operations as of July, 2019.)

276 Michael A. Sells

allies into a war in Yemen, boycotted Saudi Arabia's Gulf-state rival Qatar, and organized the kidnapping and detention of Lebanese Prime Minister Saad Hariri in order to attempt to force Lebanon into supporting his regional agenda. He also launched a public relations campaign in the US that included everything from sophisticated lobbies with American academic advisors to *The New York Times* to a glossy magazine special edition put out by the publishers of *The National Enquirer*, the leading American gossip and conspiracy tabloid. At the same time, he has used social media both to track opponents and manipulate public opinion.

The authenticity and sustainability of MbS's vision remain in question. Saudi Arabia and its Gulf allies are, in varying degrees, deeply enmeshed in Wahhabism, which since the 1960s has projected a vehement anti-nationalist ideology and demonstrated profound ambivalence over the nation-state as an institution.

ORIGINS OF WAHHABISM

I use the term "Wahhabism" to refer first and foremost to the teachings and the movement of the eighteenth-century Arabian preacher and activist Muḥammad ibn ʿAbd al-Wahhāb, who in 1744 entered into a fateful agreement with a local chief named Muḥammad ibn Saʿūd. The agreement, as it evolved over time, set the model for subsequent Saudi-Wahhabi rule: The clerics (ʿulamā') – Ibn ʿAbd al-Wahhāb and his successors – would decide what is and is not proper Islam, while the rulers (umarā') – Muḥammad ibn Saʿūd and his descendants – would enforce the clerics' interpretation of Islam, take and control territory, and administer the state.[2] The clerical elite is known as Āl al-Shaykh (i.e., the progeny of Ibn ʿAbd al-Wahhāb), although high clerical positions can be exercised by those without such genealogical pedigree, who have demonstrated their ground in and loyalty to Wahhabi teachings. The royals are known as Āl Saʿūd, the progeny of Muḥammad ibn Saʿūd.

In the early twentieth century, ʿAbd al-ʿAzīz Āl Saʿūd, known in Western historiography as Ibn Saʿūd, revived the Saudi-Wahhabi alliance, conquered much of the Arabian Peninsula, and ushered in the Kingdom of Saudi Arabia as an internationally recognized nation-state – a project that required skillful (and sometimes violent) negotiation of tensions between the Wahhabi zeal of the tribal forces that had served as his major military force, on the one side, and his nation-state interests: defined border, modern communication technologies, and security cooperation with the non-Muslim US and European powers, on the other.[3] After his death in 1953, nationalist, republican, and royalist forces competed to shape the kingdom, with Fayṣal ibn ʿAbd al-ʿAzīz emerging as de facto ruler in the early 1960s. During the Arab Cold War, which broke out in the 1960s, Fayṣal instrumentalized Wahhabi

---

[2] For a thorough study of Ibn ʿAbd al-Wahhāb, his movement, and his early critics, see A. S. al-ʿUthaymīn (2009). For a general overview of early Wahhabism, see Peskes (2016a). For a meticulous historical overview of Wahhabi doctrinal and legal developments, see al-Fahad (2016).

[3] See Commins (2009, 71–93); Lacroix (2011, 12); al-Rasheed (2002, 14–38, 41–71).

Saudi Nationalism, Wahhabi Da'wā, and Western Power

doctrines in order to advance a pan-Islamic ideology (da'wā) that would serve to counter the Arab nationalist movement led by Egyptian President Jamāl 'Abd al-Nāṣir and his emulators and rivals in the Arab world and to quash liberal, socialist, and Marxist currents within Arab and Islamic societies more widely.

Below I elaborate on Wahhabi doctrine and modern Wahhabi ideology. At the same time, it is important to note that there are few Wahhabi individuals in the world: Very few Muslims identify themselves as Wahhabis or acquiesce to being identified in that way. Many of those influenced by and governing their lives through the principles taught by Ibn 'Abd al-Wahhāb prefer to identify themselves as "Salafis," hearkening to what they believe is the Islam taught and practiced by the Prophet and his early followers, who are known as the *salaf* ("the select" or "authentic ones"). Many historians trace modern Salafism to late nineteenth-century reformers like Muḥammad 'Abduh of Egypt. In the wake of World War I and the resurgence of Saudi Wahhabism, many early Salafis adopted Wahhabi teachings, including 'Abduh's follower and long-time collaborator, Rashīd al-Riḍā, who published an influential early print edition of the collected works of Ibn 'Abd al-Wahhāb (Ibn 'Abd al-Wahhāb et al. 1926). Since the 1960s, Saudi Arabia has used its wealth, power, and geography to propagate Wahhabi teachings under the guise of Salafism, and by doing so, transformed Wahhabism into a global ideology. Over the past six decades, Saudi-sponsored scholarship, preaching, philanthropy, social activism, and jihadist movements have propagated Wahhabi teachings among Muslims worldwide by presenting Wahhabism's understanding of the first generations of Islam as a matter of fact and have trained generations of scholars in methodologies that would vindicate Wahhabi doctrines. At the same time, however, many Salafis, led by Nāṣir al-Dīn al-Albānī (d. 1999), focus as much or more on sustained study of *ḥadīth* accounts of the Prophet and his companions than they do Wahhabi doctrine.[4]

The principle followed by most academic approaches to the study of religion regarding signifiers of religious identity is simple: If a group self-identifies or accepts being identified by a particular term – Muslim, Christian, Hindu, or Buddhist – or subcategory, such as Salafi, Catholic, or Baptist, the appellation is to be taken at face value. Yet despite that principle and despite the complexity of the Wahhabism-Salafism distinction, there is a disingenuous note in the protests of Saudi rulers and Saudi clerics against the word "Wahhabi" on the grounds that they are simply

---

[4] Although Wahhabism has been associated with the attack on following (*taqlīd*) one of the four traditional schools of Sunni law and a core principle of the Albānī tendency within Salafism, I find no evidence in the works of Ibn 'Abd al-Wahhāb and his early followers that *taqlīd* was a major issue for them. In later periods, however, Saudi religious scholars have influenced and been influenced by South Asian religious scholars associated with the Ahl-e Ḥadīth in developing an intellectually and institutionally robust anti-*taqlīd* or *lā madhhab* (no legal school) stance, according to which Muslim *'ulamā'* and, in some cases, Muslims more generally, should engage the *ḥadīth* corpus directly, in all its complexity, rather than relying on what one of the Hanafi, Maliki, Shafi'i, or Hanbali *schools* have propounded. See Commins (2009, 144–45, 248n65). On this point, see Lacroix (2009) for a discussion of Nāṣir al-Dīn al-Albānī and Abou Zahab (2009) on the interconnections between the Islamic University of Medina and the Ahl-e Ḥadīth groups in Pakistan.

278 *Michael A. Sells*

reaffirming the original, authentic Islam of the first three generations of Muslims.[5] Many if not most Muslims have viewed themselves as following the faith of Muḥammad and his early followers. Yet Wahhabi scholars from the time of Ibn ʿAbd al-Wahhāb to the present assert that since the second century of Islam, most Muslims abandoned the essential teachings of the Prophet and his followers. So yes, Saudi royals and clerics may genuinely view themselves as Sunni Muslims loyal to the Prophet, his companions, and followers. But they also maintain that the authentic Islam those early generations taught and practiced was precisely in line with the core teachings of Ibn ʿAbd al-Wahhāb and one that only a select few have actually followed.

THE WAHHABI DOCTRINE OF *TAWḤĪD*

Classical Wahhabism distinguished itself primarily through its highly distinctive position on *tawḥīd*, that is, the affirmation that there is "no god but God" (*lā ilāha illa Allāh*). That affirmation makes up the first half of the testimony of Muslim faith and is repeatedly emphasized throughout the Qurʾān. Ibn ʿAbd al-Wahhāb taught that the vast majority of Muslims living in his time were in fact practitioners of idolatrous polytheism (*shirk*), as had been the majority of Muslims since the eighth century CE.[6] Such idolatry was not only pervasive among Muslims, he wrote, it was also worse in kind than the *shirk* of the *jāhiliyya* (or age of idolatrous ignorance before the advent of Islam).[7] It is not enough for Muslims to carry out the daily prayers, fast during Ramadan, give alms, attempt to make the pilgrimage to Mecca, and affirm that "there is no god but God" in order to avoid the charge of idolatrous polytheism: they must also renounce all beliefs and practices that negate – implicitly or explicitly – the oneness of God. Whoever denies, doubts, or wavers in affirming the idolatrous nature of such beliefs and practices is himself an apostate.[8] *Takfīr* is the Arabic word for anathematization, the declaration of such of beliefs and practices of fellow Muslims as contrary to Islam and the branding of those who practice them as apostates. Wahhabi teachings on *tawḥīd* are marked by a distinctive understanding of and concern with *takfīr*.

Ibn ʿAbd al-Wahhāb considered a wide array of practices to be idolatrous or conducive to idolatry: building mausoleums or even simple grave markers that rise

---

[5]　See, for example, the 2014 op-ed column coauthored by Nawaf Obaid, a former advisor to Saudi Prince Turkī al-Fayṣal (Obaid and al-Sarhan 2014), or the statement on the subject by the Saudi religious scholar Ṣāliḥ al-Fawzān (n.d.), which appears under the title "The Obligation to Ascribe to the Salafiyya."

[6]　See, for example, the remarks on this point in his treatise *Mufīd al-mustafīd fī kufr tārik al-tawḥīd* in Ibn ʿAbd al-Wahhāb (2010a, 1:123).

[7]　Ibn ʿAbd al-Wahhāb (1979, 44); Ibn ʿAbd al-Wahhāb (2010b, 1:56–57), the latter reference being from Ibn ʿAbd al-Wahhāb's treatise *Kitāb al-Shubuhāt*.

[8]　Whoever fails to anathematize the idolaters or has doubts about their apostasy or holds their *madhhab* to be correct is himself an apostate, according to consensus: Ibn ʿAbd al-Wahhāb (2010b, 1:148) (the third of the *nawāqid* or nullifiers of Islam).

Saudi Nationalism, Wahhabi Da'wā, and Western Power

more than a few inches from the ground; visiting shrines of saints or Shi'ite imams in order to obtain a blessing; making or displaying images; and making or wearing talismans, strings, or other items believed to be propitious and which are popular throughout many Islamic cultures. He also condemned the enactment of any law that is not God's law as taught by the Prophet Muḥammad; any sign of disrespect for Islam or Muḥammad; and aiding non-Muslims against Muslims. In order to root out apostasy, he insisted, it was necessary to eliminate tombs, shrines, and images along with the apostates who value them, or else such structures and art works might serve as an expedient (*dharī'a*) toward *shirk*. Wahhabi scholars have defined the prohibited images to include all sculptures, bas-relief works, paintings, or drawings that represent human beings or animals. The most influential modern Wahhabi clerics have included photographs of human beings or animals within the list of prohibited images.[9]

This more subtle form of *shirk* pervades the world and has led the vast majority, with the exception of those in the first three generations of Islam, into apostasy, Wahhabi scholars wrote. At the end of the introductory chapters of his most widely known book, *Kitāb al-Tawḥīd*, Ibn 'Abd al-Wahhāb makes the radical implication of his doctrine of *tawḥīd* and *takfīr* explicit. He begins by quoting a *ḥadīth* (a saying attributed to the Prophet or one of his companions), according to which Muḥammad said, "Whoever says 'there is no God but God' (*lā ilāha illa Allāh*) and disbelieves in what is worshipped other than Allah – his property and blood is protected." Ibn 'Abd al-Wahhāb then writes, as if he were stating the self-evident meaning of the *ḥadīth* in question:

This is the weightiest of the statements that make clear the meaning of *lā ilāha illa Allāh*. It does not make the oral declaration of *lā ilāha illa Allāh* sufficient to protect one's property and blood; nor the oral declaration when made along with an understanding of its meaning; nor the repetition of it; nor accompanying it with

---

9 The Saudi Shaykh Muḥammad Ṣāliḥ al-'Uthaymīn was one of several religious scholars who argued that because photography was a purely mechanical process and did not involve human creative activity, it was not forbidden. As 'Uthaymīn put it, the photographer does not actually draw or shape the figure of the sentient being. For a discussion of the question of photography and *shirk*, and a list of scholars on either side of the debate; see al-Dubaykhī and Ibn 'Abd al-Wahhāb (2011–12, 775n8). Noteworthy here is that the preponderance of opinions has been that photographs of sentient beings do constitute *shirk*, and that the Saudi Permanent Committee on Fatwas has so ruled (al-Dubaykhī and Ibn 'Abd al-Wahhāb (2011–12, 775n8). As Nāṣir al-Dīn al-Albānī pointed out, photography is a human artistic enterprise rather than an automatic, neutral technology, and the photography shapes the photograph through positing, focus, and other means. For an anti-photograph argument, see the opinion published by Saudi Shaykh Ṣāliḥ al-Munajjid (IslamQA 1998) on his widely viewed website "Islam Question and Answer": "Taking pictures with a camera involves human actions such as focusing, pressing the shutter, developing, printing, and so on. We cannot call it anything other than 'picture-making' or *tasweer* [*taṣwīr*, the term for the action performed by the image-makers or *muṣawwarīn* that were rebuked in the *ḥadīth* reports cited in the chapter on the image-makers in *Kitāb al-Tawḥīd*], which is the expression used by all Arabic-speakers to describe this action." Photographs of sentient beings are widely shown in the kingdom, and photographic portraits of the present king, Salmān ibn 'Abd al-'Azīz Āl Sa'ūd al-Shaykh, are widely posted.

the affirmation that "none other than Allah who has no partner or associate (*sharīk*) should be called upon." No one's property and blood is protected until he adds to all of that the declaration of disbelief in everything worshipped besides Allah, and if he hesitates or has doubts about any of this, then his property and blood are unprotected. (Ibn 'Abd al-Wahhāb 2010b, 1:14)[10]

In view of what will follow during the rest of *Kitāb al-Tawhīd*, the conclusion is stark. The remaining chapters of *Kitāb al-Tawhīd* are for the most part given over to naming, enumerating, and defining the beliefs and practices that are prohibited and, of those, the ones that constitute the capital offense of apostasy. Any Muslim who does not denounce everything that Ibn 'Abd al-Wahhāb denounced as *shirk* is himself an apostate; and as such his wealth and blood are not protected – that is, he can and should be killed. As Ahmad Dallal (2016, 38) wrote, "The concept of *tawhīd* is thus linked in the thought of Ibn 'Abd al-Wahhāb to an act of repudiation, which functions as a rite of initiation in Wahhabism. The uninitiated remains guilty of *shirk*."

In addition to the detailed discussions on the practices and beliefs that turn a Muslim into an apostate that he presented in *Kitāb al-Tawhīd*, Ibn 'Abd al-Wahhāb also wrote a short, sweeping epistle on the subject of *takfīr*. Although the epistle, titled *The Nullifiers [Nawāqid] of Islam*, consists of fewer than 600 words, it continues to exercise wide influence over Islamic communities through both scholarly productions and popular transmission via the Internet. I translate here the basic list of nullifiers – that is, those practices and beliefs that nullify a Muslim's faith and turn him into an apostate.[11]

1. Idolatrous polytheism (*shirk*) in the worship of Allah. This category includes those who sacrifice to the Jinn or to a grave.

---

[10] *Kitāb al-Tawhīd* is divided into approximately sixty-six chapters (the chapter numbering can vary slightly depending on the edition). The first five chapters cover a wide array of questions on proper belief; on the virtue of *tawhīd*; on how *tawhīd* covers over the sins of the believer, thus sparing the believer from punishment in the afterlife; and on the necessity of the believer's cultivation of a fear of *shirk*, on the grounds that such polytheistic idolatry takes subtle forms and poses a pervasive, enduring, and constant threat. These opening chapters outline as well a division of *tawhīd* into three categories: the *tawhīd* of lordship (*tawhīd al-rubūbiyya*), which is the affirmation of the one God as creator and ruler of the universe; that of divinity (*ilāhiyya*), which is also known as the *tawhīd* of worship (*tawhīd al-ilāhiyya*); and that regarding the divine names, which entails accepting all and only the names and attributes attributed by the Qur'ān to God, without any attempt to interpret them in metaphorical or symbolic fashion or in a variety of other manners that Wahhabism has rejected. It is in the area of the *tawhīd* of divinity or worship that Ibn 'Abd al-Wahhāb made his historic intervention.

[11] I have omitted here the Qur'ānic quotations and some short parenthetical comments. For the complete text, see Ibn 'Abd al-Wahhāb (2010b, 1:148). The list concludes with the following declaration: "In regard to each of these nullifiers, there is no difference between the one who is acting in jest, in all seriousness, or in fear, except for one who acts under compulsion. They are all of the gravest importance and most likely to occur. The Muslim must be on guard against them and must fear lest he fall under them."

Saudi Nationalism, Wahhabi Daʿwā, and Western Power

2. Placing intermediaries between oneself and Allah, calling out to them, asking them for intercession, or relying upon them.

3. Refusing to declare the polytheists to be infidels, expressing doubt that they are infidels, or approving of the path they are on.

4. Holding anyone's guidance or judgment to be better than that of the Messenger of God (Muḥammad) – like those who prefer the ruling of ṭawāghīt (idols, idolatrous religions) to his judgment.

5. Hating anything that the Messenger enjoined, even if one acts in accordance with it.

6. Making light of any aspect of the religion of the Messenger or its punishment or reward.

7. Sorcery, which includes spells that repel (ṣarf) or that attract (ʿaṭf).

8. Supporting and assisting the polytheists against the Muslims.

9. Believing that certain people may receive exemption from the sharīʿa of Muḥammad.

10. Avoiding the religion of Allah by neglecting to learn it or carry it out.

Most chapters of Kitāb al-Tawḥīd consist largely of quotations from the Qurʾān and ḥadīth. The quotations begin with broad principles and each quotation narrows the focus, giving the last one capital importance. The chapter on the "image-makers" (al-muṣawwirīn) exemplifies this method, even as it proclaims the radical iconoclasm that is a particularly distinctive characteristic of Wahhabi doctrine. To that effect, Ibn ʿAbd al-Wahhāb begins with a ḥadīth qudsī, that is, a ḥadīth reporting a message given to the Prophet Muḥammad outside of the Qurʾān, followed by four more ḥadīth reports. The reports make the following points:

1. God has rebuked those who attempt to create something like his creation (or create as he created), saying "let them create one mote or one grain of wheat or one grain of barley."

2. The worst punishment on the Day of Resurrection will be reserved for those who attempted to rival God in the act of creating.

3. Image-makers will be tormented eternally in hell; and for each image that a person made on earth, that person will be given an extra soul to be tormented, thereby compounding the wretch's torment many times over.

4. Whoever creates an image in the world will be required in the afterworld to breathe into it the spirit of life, but will be unable to do so.

5. ʿAlī, Muḥammad's cousin, son-in-law, and the fourth caliph in the Sunni tradition, said that Muḥammad had sent him out with the instruction to "leave no image without obliterating it and no raised tomb without leveling it." (Ibn ʿAbd al-Wahhāb 2010b, 1:43–44)[12]

---

[12] The first, attributed to the prolific ḥadīth narrator Abū Hurayra, states that Muḥammad had recited the Qurʾānic verse, "Who is more transgressive (aẓlama) than those who set out to create the like of my creation (yakhluku ka-khalqiya): let them create one mote or one grain of wheat or one grain of sand."

282   Michael A. Sells

The fifth is considered to be the conclusive *ḥadīth*.

After the listing of the reports, Ibn 'Abd al-Wahhāb presents a list of summary issues, the last of which states simply: "The command to obliterate such images and tombs wherever they are found."[13]

FROM WAHHABI DOCTRINE TO PAN-ISLAMIC IDEOLOGY

By the early 1960s, Fayṣal was organizing a transnational propagation campaign, *da 'wā*, meant to revitalize the teachings of Wahhabi Islam within the kingdom and to create Saudi centers of Islamic education that would train Islamic scholars from around the world. Prior to Fayṣal, Wahhabi doctrine had exerted influence beyond the Arabian Peninsula, but that influence had spread largely through private channels and had never come to dominate other Islamic communities.[14] That equation

---

It is followed by a *ḥadīth* attributed to 'Ā'isha, Muḥammad's wife and important *ḥadīth* narrator, in which Muḥammad is quoted as saying that "those who will suffer the worst punishment on the Day of Resurrection are those who attempt to rival (*yuḍāhi 'ūna*) God in the act of creating." That *ḥadīth* is followed by a third, which is attributed to Ibn 'Abbās, a companion of the Prophet: "I heard the Prophet of God say: 'Each image-maker (*muṣawwir*) will be in the fire, where for each of the images he formed (*ṣawwara*), he will be given a soul that will be tormented in hell.'" The fourth *ḥadīth*, also by Ibn 'Abbās, states that Muḥammad said that whoever makes an image in the world is required to breathe into it the spirit of life and will not be able to do so. There follows the concluding and conclusive *ḥadīth*, narrated by Abū Hayyāj (al-Asadī), a much less-known figure than the other named *ḥadīth* narrators. The *ḥadīth* states that 'Ali ibn Abī Ṭālib (Muḥammad's cousin, son-in-law, and the fourth caliph in Sunni tradition) said: "Do I not send you [Abū Hayyāj] with the same instructions that the Messenger of God sent me with: to leave no image (*ṣūra* or, in another versions of the *ḥadīth*, *tamthīl*) without obliterating it and no raised tomb without leveling it?" Ibn 'Abd al-Wahhāb's doctrinal writings as well as those of his immediate successors are driven by the fear that tombs as well as other structures, such as the homes of the Prophet's companions or other people held to be righteous by tradition, could and, inevitably would, entice believers into worshipping the dead. Turning toward the dead for succor, wrote the Shaykh's son 'Abdullāh ibn Muḥammad ibn 'Abd al-Wahhāb al-Tamīmī, is the "root of idolatrous polytheism in the world." See Ibn Muḥammad (1996, 27).

13   The Wahhabi position on iconoclasm was viewed both by its proponents and its opponents as a position that had not been affirmed or practiced by most Muslims, but there was nothing inherently strange about the theological premise upon which it was based. In the substance and the vehemence of its critique of shrines, images, and practices associated with them, the Wahhabi movement bears strong similarities with similar movements in other religious traditions such as, to mention just one example, the Protestant iconoclasm of the Reformation period, with its denunciations of what it considered Catholic art, rituals, saint-devotion, indulgences, and alleged apostasy. Once its exegetical and theological premises are accepted, Wahhabi doctrine is neither irrational nor arbitrary.

14   See, for example, *The Strengthening of the Faith (Taqwiyat-ul-Iman)* (Shaheed 1995) composed in Urdu by Shah Ismail Shaheed (d. 1831), a grandson of the famous scholar Shah Waliallah of Delhi. Shah Ismail composed it after his return from his three-pilgrimage journey to Saudi Arabia. The book bears remarkable similarities to *Kitāb al-Tawhīd* in its treatment of *tawhīd* and its focus on the various forms of *shirk* in regard to the *tawhīd* of worship. Unlike *Kitāb al-Tawhīd*, however, it does not call explicitly for *takfīr*, nor does it call for the physical destruction of all raised graves. The English translation was produced by Dar-us-Salam Publications (1995), which is also the main publisher and distributer of English renditions of Wahhabi Arabic scholarship from Ibn 'Abd al-Wahhāb through Ibn Bāz down to the present.

Saudi Nationalism, Wahhabi Da'wā, and Western Power 283

was to be decisively altered. In 1962, Saudi Arabia led the establishment of the Muslim World League, which served to fund mosques and Islamic centers worldwide and, by doing so, to construct a transnational infrastructure for the propagation of Wahhabi or Wahhabi-consonant doctrines. The *da'wā* campaign led by Fayṣal targeted communism, socialism, and modernism as anti-Islamic and folded its criticism of such modern ideologies into Ibn 'Abd al-Wahhāb's attack on *shirk*. Equally significant was the establishment, from 1969 to 1971 under Saudi auspices, of the Organization of the Islamic Conference (OIC) in order to construct the pan-Islamic bloc sought by Fayṣal and to assure Saudi Arabia a dominant role within it.

Fayṣal used the teachings of Saudi clerics to assist in his campaign to crush those favoring popular elections as well as socialists and Nasserites within the royal family, and used the rapidly expanding Saudi oil revenues to finance the international dissemination of Wahhabi rhetoric. He also backed factions in Yemen that tied down the forces of Egyptian President Jamāl 'Abd al-Nāṣir (commonly known as Nasser in the West). During his de facto rule as crown prince and later under his direct rule, he enabled radicalized members of the Muslim Brotherhood as well as followers of the Pakistani Islamist Abū A'lā Mawdūdī to achieve new stature and security within Saudi Arabia.[15]

Noteworthy in this regard is the case of Muḥammad Quṭb, the brother of Sayyid Quṭb, the leader of the Egyptian Muslim Brotherhood who was executed in 1969. After his brother's death, Muḥammad Quṭb received a faculty position at King 'Abd al-'Azīz University in Mecca. In his own writings, Muḥammad Quṭb launched an attack against the modern *jāhiliyya* as unremitting as that of his brother, although he made some allowances that seemed to persuade his Saudi sponsors that he was not attacking the monarchy as an instrument of the *jāhiliyya*. He also published a new edition of his brother's final work, *Milestones*, a book that served to galvanize revolutionary Islamist circles bent on overthrowing Muslim regimes they viewed as failing to support the true Islam. Also joining the faculty of King 'Abd al-'Azīz University was the Palestinian-born, Muslim Brotherhood-associated scholar and activist 'Abdullāh 'Azzām, who would become one of the ideological and activist founders of the global jihadist movement. Osama bin Laden, who studied at King 'Abd al-'Azīz University, was influenced by both men. Quṭb was also the mentor and dissertation advisor of Safar al-Ḥawālī, who would rise to prominence in the 1990s as a leader of the Saudi Sahwa movement that would openly object to the presence of American troops in the kingdom and walk a fine line between dissent and open rebellion against the Saudi monarchy.[16]

---

[15] For the interactions between the Egyptian Muslim Brothers and Wahhabis over the past decades, see International Crisis Group (2004); Lauzière (2016); Zaman (2007, 160–70). On the Saudi connections with Mawdūdī, see Commins (2009, 145–47).

[16] On Fayṣal and the development of a pan-Islamic Saudi *da'wā*, see Commins (2009, 150–54); al-Rasheed (2002, 117–43). On political Islamism in Saudi Arabia, see Dekmejian (2016). On Muḥammad Quṭb and 'Abdullāh 'Azzām at King 'Abd al-'Azīz University in Saudi Arabia, see Commins (2009, 174–75, 186). The adulatory biography of Fayṣal by Kéchichian (2008) ignores almost

284   *Michael A. Sells*

Yet it was the establishment Wahhabi clerics rather than Islamist intellectuals like Muḥammad Quṭb that came to exert a more long-lasting influence within the international *da'wā*. 'Abd al-'Azīz ibn Bāz (d. 2000), the most important Saudi cleric of recent history, took a leading role in the production and dissemination of neo-Wahhabi ideology. At one time or another, Ibn Bāz was President of the Senior Scholars Committee of Saudi Arabia; President of the Saudi Standing Committee for Islamic Research and the Issuance of Fatwas; a member of the Saudi Supreme Committee for Islamic Propagation; President of the Islamic Jurisprudence Assembly of Mecca; Chancellor of the Islamic University of Medina; Grand Mufti of Saudi Arabia; Chairman of the Founding Committee of the Muslim World League; and Chairman of the World Supreme Council for Mosques.

Ibn Bāz and the other Saudi clerics of his generation oversaw a major program to revive, explain, and disseminate the writings of Ibn 'Abd al-Wahhāb on *takfīr* and to interpret them in a maximalist manner. "Apostasy from Islam is a grievous crime punishable by death," wrote Saudi scholar 'Abd al-Raḥmān ibn Ḥammād al-'Umar in a 1991 book published with the official seal of the Saudi Supreme Head Office for Religious Researches, Religious Pronouncements, *Da'wā*, and Guidance. "Anyone who commits apostasy from Islam rejects truth after he had known it, thus, he does not deserve life and loses the raison d'être of his existence," he added.[17]

In the collected commentary of Ibn Bāz on Ibn 'Abd al-Wahhāb's *Nullifiers of Islam*, Ibn Bāz (2011, 98, 107) vigorously reasserted the claim that the majority of Muslims are, in fact, apostates. He affirmed that even a non-scholar can carry out *takfīr*; and when concerns were brought to him about the potentially damaging effects on the Islamic community if individuals with little or no religious training are allowed to issue declarations of apostasy, he responded by dismissing such concerns as *jahl* (idolatrous ignorance) and added that "if there exists a valid reason for something to be declared apostasy, it should be declared" (Ibn Bāz 2011, 98–107, 276). On the question of whether or not Jews and Christians were infidels (*kāfirūn*), a question of considerable subtlety and complexity within the Qur'ān, Ibn Bāz had little patience: Any Muslim who refused to denounce the *kufr* (idolatrous infidelity) of Jews and Christians or had doubts about it was himself a *kāfir*, an apostate deserving of death (Ibn Bāz 2011, 105–6). There is a well-known *ḥadīth* that quotes the Prophet Muḥammad as warning that if a man calls his brother a *kāfir*, then either the accuser or the accused must be one, a *ḥadīth* that has been cited by Muslims as a warning that the resort to *takfīr* risks leading the Islamic community into self-destructive interior strife, or *fitna*. Ibn Bāz responded to that concern with the assurance that the *ḥadīth* only applied to those who falsely charge others with apostasy (Ibn Bāz 2011, 106–7). When a Sudanese reformist, Maḥmūd Muḥammad Ṭāhā, presented an interpretation of the Qur'ān that Ibn Bāz disagreed

---

completely Fayṣal's martialing of Wahhabi clerics and teachings toward the goal of creating a global ideology and allied state powers to defeat liberal, socialist, and anti-monarchical trends in Islam.

[17] Ibn Ḥammād al-'Umar (1991, 118) followed by his version of the *Nullifiers* (118–21).

Saudi Nationalism, Wahhabi Daʿwā, and Western Power

with, Ibn Bāz declared him an apostate deserving of death (Ibn Bāz 2011, 276–77). After Sudan's ruler, Jaʿfar al-Numeiri, had the seventy-six-year-old Ṭāhā arrested, tried, and executed, Ibn Bāz sent Numeiri a letter of congratulation (Ibn Bāz 2011, 296–97).[18] Those making the charge of apostasy seldom had to defend it, and many of those accused of apostasy found that even if they were able to escape jail or execution, their careers along with their future financial and physical safety continued to be at risk.

Ibn ʿAbd al-Wahhāb and his immediate successors had shown relatively little concern for non-Muslims generally or for European inroads into the Middle East in particular. For them, Muslim apostates were the problem. But for Ibn Bāz and the other major Wahhabi clerics of his generation, Jews and Christians had become an existential threat. Ibn Bāz claimed that Jews and Christians were engaged in an ideological attack against Islam that operated through education, financial aid, interreligious dialogue, human rights and gender equality discourse, and seductive media images to penetrate Islam and destroy it from within (Ibn Bāz 1999, 35–52).

It was under Ibn Bāz's supervision that there emerged a fiercely polemical English rendition of the Qurʾān: *The Interpretation of the Meanings of the Noble Qurʾān in the English Language* (hereafter: *NQEL*) by Muḥammad Taqī al-Dīn al-Hilālī and Muḥammad Muḥsin Khān (Hilālī and Khan 1996, 1999).[19] *NQEL* renders the last verses of the Fātiḥa, the Qurʾān's opening passage that is also the most important liturgical text in Islam, as follows: "Guide us to the Straight Way. The Way of those on whom You have bestowed Your Grace, not (the way) of those who earned Your Anger (such as the Jews), nor of those who went astray (such as the Christians)." Their interpretation of the verse as referring to Jews and Christians and those like them was not new: the fourteenth-century commentator Ibn Kathīr featured it as the most likely possibility for "those with anger upon them" and "those who have gone astray," and it was given as the default interpretation in the fifteenth-century digest of Qurʾānic exegesis known as the *Tafsīr al-Jalalayn*, a work widely consulted among Sunni Muslims today. Hilālī and Khān's innovation was to insert such interpretations into their English version of the Qurʾānic text, thereby weakening, even collapsing, the distinction between the Qurʾānic verses as rendered into English and specific interpretations of those verses. But their interpolations into the Fātiḥa were just the beginning. For the Qurʾānic verse regarding the Day of Judgment that

[18] See also Abū Samra (2009, 281–88); An-Naʾim (1986).

[19] The first edition that I have found dates from 1985. Since that time, dozens of editions have been printed, with occasional slight modifications to the text and with some modifications as well to introductory or explanatory material. The 1996 and 1999 editions are quoted in this chapter. The official online edition of *NQEL* can be found at the website for the King Fahd Complex for Printing the Holy Qurʾān, www.qurancomplex.gov.sa/?Lan=en. Note that in the recent electronic version, the interpolation of Jews and Christians has been removed from the Fātiḥa, but not from the many other verses in the Qurʾān in which Hilālī and Khān inserted it. The electronic version is otherwise identical to the print version, and the small change to the Fātiḥa does not alter the overall message of the translation regarding Jews and Christians, which is rigorously reinforced through parentheses throughout the work. For a study of the career of Muḥammad Taqī al-Dīn al-Hilālī, one of the two translators, see Lauzière (2016).

states "Some faces that Day will be downcast," NQEL reads "Some faces that day will be humiliated (in the Hell fire, i.e., the faces of all disbelievers, Jews, and Christians)."[20] The Arabic word *al-yahūd* (Jew) appears only 11 times in the traditional text of the Qur'ān, and the word *al-naṣārā* (Christians) only 14 times.[21] Moreover, the Qur'ānic position concerning Jews and Christians abounds with complexities. It is by no means an easy task to extract a simple message in this regard from the text of the Qur'ān. In NQEL, however, the Qur'ānic references to them are made out to be far more numerous – with more than 100 instances of "the Jews" and, according to the glossary entry for the 1996 printed edition, as many as 600 instances of "the Christians."[22] NQEL thereby trains the eyes, ears, and minds of readers and Internet searchers, Muslim and non-Muslim alike, to perceive "Jews" and "Christians" as targeted for opprobrium in a wide variety of passages where they are never mentioned. And by portraying all Christians and Jews as deceitful by nature, the translators signal to Muslim readers that anything they might hear or learn from Jews and Christians about what specific adherents practice and believe, beyond the generalizations on Christianity and Judaism presented in NQEL, might be a falsehood meant to undermine Islam.[23]

The translators also interpolate Wahhabi terminology regarding *tawḥīd* directly into their English rendition of the Qur'ān.[24] An appendix to the volume, with subheadings such as *"Tawḥīd* – (Islamic Monotheism),"* is an organized summary of the principles of Ibn 'Abd al-Wahhāb's *Kitāb al-Tawḥīd*, although it does not acknowledge itself as such (Hilālī and Khān 1996, 825–45; 1999, 854–68). Indeed, in the 1999 edition of NQEL, any connection to Wahhabi doctrine is disavowed explicitly in a bilingual facing page notice (*i 'lān*) placed at the end of the volume (Hilālī and Khān 1999, 925–26). The notice states that NQEL is "the explanation of the meanings and interpretations of the Glorious Qur'ān based on the creed of *Ahlu-Sunnah wal-Jama 'ah*" and emphasizes that its interpretations are taken from the Qur'anic commentaries al-Ṭabarī, al-Qurṭubī, and Ibn Kathīr, and from *ḥadīth* sayings recorded in the collection of al-Bukhārī. It concludes:

> Then how can one say that this translation of Noble Qur'ān done by Dr. Taqī al-Din al-Hilālī and Dr. Muḥammad Muḥsin Khān is taken from Muḥammad ibn 'Abd al-Wahhāb who died in the year 1206 AH, as there are hundreds of years (400–1000) between him and al-Qurṭubī, Ibn Kathīr and al-Bukhārī. For general information, it

[20] Q 88:2 as rendered by Hilālī and Khān (1996, 787).

[21] See Böwering (2008, 81–82). The Qur'ān also refers in one instance to the "People of the Gospel."

[22] The index of in the 1996 edition of NQEL states under the entry "Christians" that "this word appears more than 600 times in the Qur'ān" so frequently that it would require an entry too long to fit within the glossary. Of course the word "Christians" only appears so many times in NQEL because it has been interpolated into the text (Hilālī and Khān 1996, 866). The index of the 1999 edition omits the entry "Christian" without explanation, although the systematic interpolation of the word "Christian" into the text of NQEL remains identical to that of previous editions.

[23] An earlier version of this discussion of NQEL can be found in Sells (2006).

[24] See, for example, NQEL's rendition of Q 9:10–11.

is being clarified that there is no book called *"Tafsīr al-Qur'ān"* done by Muḥammad ibn 'Abd al-Wahhāb. (Hilālī and Khān 1999, 927)[25]

NQEL includes another appendix as well, titled "The Call to Jihad," by Shaykh 'Abdullah ibn Muḥammad ibn Ḥumayd, the chief justice of Saudi Arabia (Ibn Ḥumayd 1995).[26] In it, Ibn Ḥumayd propounds the Wahhabi view that the vast majority of Muslims fell into apostasy after the first three generations of Islam, and that their idolatry is worse than that fought by the Prophet Muḥammad (Hilālī and Khān 1996, 883–904).

NQEL bears the official seal of 'Abd al-'Azīz ibn Bāz as well as 'Umar Muḥammad Fallātah, then general secretary of the Islamic University of Medina.[27] The King Fahd Center for the Printing of the Qur'ān sponsored the distribution of NQEL in print and electronic formats and has posted the entire work online. When participants in classes at mosques or Islamic study centers in the Anglophone world wished to obtain English-language translations, Saudi institutions provided this edition without charge. The Khān and Hilālī Qur'ān thus became a default choice for Qur'ānic study for millions around the English-speaking world. Internet searches for "Jews, Qur'ān" and "Christians, Qur'ān" prioritize the Khān and Hilālī version of the text, which, because of its massive insertions of the words "Jews" and "Christians" into the text, contains far more instances of the search terms than other renditions of the Qur'ān into English.[28]

---

[25] I have altered the transliteration style in the text quoted here, which is the style preferred by many Wahhabi and Salafi writers, for the sake of editorial consistency in this chapter. The importance of the seriousness of the Saudi-Wahhabi *da'wā* has been largely dismissed by the Western news media, but it has also been underestimated among scholars. For example, in his criticism of what he perceived was the mistaken tendency to see Wahhabism as more important and globally influential than he believed it was, Devji (2008, 289) wrote that, "Even [Saudi] material is sometimes taken from non-Wahhabi sources, for instance an English translation of the Qur'ān by the Indian Shi'ite 'Abdullāh Yūsuf 'Alī, whose objectionable passages and footnotes the Saudis simply expurgated after purchasing its copyright." It was indeed true that for many years Saudi Arabia preferred an adapted version of the 'Abdullāh Yūsuf 'Alī translation, but before Saudi Arabia sponsored, and Ibn Bāz supervised, NQEL. By the time Devji's article appeared, NQEL had long replaced the rendition of 'Abdullāh Yūsuf 'Alī as the Saudi-approved and sponsored English translation of the Qur'ān.

[26] For a discussion of Ibn Ḥumayd's background, his relationship to the networks of *'ulamā'* in Saudi Arabia, his rise to the highest levels of the clerical elite, and the possibility that, as his son has himself risen to high positions, the Ibn Ḥumayd family may have developed into a scholastic dynasty within the kingdom, see Mouline (2016, especially 208–9).

[27] Ibn Bāz's approval was in his capacity as President of the Department of Scholarly Research, Legal Opinion, Propagation, and Guidance. He dated his approval Dhū al-Qa'da 21, 1404H (May 2, 1994).

[28] NQEL has been influential in shaping the views of both Muslims and non-Muslims concerning Qur'ānic teaching regarding Jews and Christians. For those presenting Islam as inherently and violently intolerant, the Hilālī and Khān Qur'ān has become a proof text. In *Islam: Religion of Peace?*, Gregory Davis (2006, 31) wrote that he had used Hilālī and Khān for all Qur'ānic quotations, because it "is much clearer to the non-Arabic reader than other translations." He then explains why he finds this particular English rendition to be clearer than the others: Hilālī and Khān, he explains, "frequently use Arabic terms [sic], which they explain parenthetically as opposed to confining themselves to a single 'best' word. This approach helps the reader grasp the meaning of the original

THE 1979 REVOLT AND THE RADICALIZATION
OF THE SAUDI *DAʿWĀ*

On the first day of the year 1400 of Islam (November 20, 1979), a group of religion students and former students led by Juhaymān al-ʿUtaybī seized the Grand Mosque in Mecca and called on Muslims to prepare for battle. ʿUtaybī's group grew out of mid-1960s formations of self-appointed religious police. In an incident known as the "Breaking of the Images," the vigilantes set about destroying representations of living beings, including pictures, photographs, and window fashion displays that utilized mannequins. When the attack on commercial property resulted in arrests and short jail terms, members of the group sought support from ʿAbd al-ʿAzīz ibn Bāz, who recommended they be released and agreed to serve as the group's *murshid* or authoritative guide. Under the influence of Nāṣir al-Dīn al-Albānī, the Syrian Salafi scholar who had been invited, with Ibn Bāz's support, to teach at the University of Medina, the group also rejected any practice, such as praying before a prayer-niche, that they could not find clearly attested in a sound *ḥadīth*. After some of the group's leaders decided to move toward a less confrontational way of activism, ʿUtaybī led the more zealous members in storming the Grand Mosque. His grievances included the placing of an image of the king of Saudi Arabia on coins and the requirement that students at the University of Medina provide a photograph of themselves in order to enroll; the kingdom's acceptance of the support of non-Muslims, Christians in particular; and, in one of many echoes with the early revolt by the Wahhabi fighting forces known as the Ikhwān, the failure of the Saudi leaders to promote jihad (religious warfare) beyond the borders of the nation-state. Saudi authorities faced a dilemma. If they launched a frontal assault, they would violate the prohibition against fighting in the sacred area (*ḥaram*); on the other hand, if they held back, their authority would have eroded. Ultimately Ibn Bāz and other senior clerics provided a fatwa (judgment made by an Islamic jurist) authorizing an assault on the Grand Mosque, but the Saudi and Pakistani soldiers who were sent to crush the revolt were unable to uproot the rebels from their carefully prepared sanctuaries beneath the mosque. Saudi rulers once more accepted Western support, this time in the form of French commandos. After the rebellion was crushed, the Saudi government moved to placate the Wahhabi religious establishment, which shared many of the rebels' grievances, by turning over sectors of social and educational policy to it.

term in a general sense rather than relying on a single word chosen according to the personal preference of the translator." Hilālī and Khān do not in fact "use Arabic terms" in constructing most of their parentheses, but the work is composed in such a way that it might give the impression of having presented Arabic terms or transliterations of them (since readers who do not know Arabic would not be able to decode the Arabic terms in the original script). Thus, *NQEL* is indeed "clearer" for an anti-Islamic author like Davis than the other major translations of the Qurʾān in English and other languages. It is also clearer than the original Arabic Qurʾān in bringing out an interpretation more consonant with the militantly intolerant Islam expounded by Ibn Bāz.

Saudi Nationalism, Wahhabi Da'wā, and Western Power

At the same time, the Soviet invasion of Afghanistan provided a timely opportunity for the kingdom to promote jihad outside the Arabian Peninsula. Ibn Bāz declared jihad in Afghanistan to be a general obligation for Muslims, and the US eagerly supported the Afghan jihad and readily acquiesced in the internationalist jihadist ideology advanced, with different inflections, by 'Abdullāh 'Aẓẓām and Osama bin Laden.[29]

The year 1979 saw a tectonic shift in political and geopolitical alignments across the Middle East and Asia. Islamic revolution in Iran unleashed a wave of Islamist, anti-monarchical enthusiasm that, combined with its hostility toward Shi'ism, inflamed the already vigorous Saudi-Wahhabi *da'wā*, led the Saudi kingdom and its Gulf allies to support Iraqi President Saddam Hussein in the Iraqi invasion of Iran and to finance Iraqi's ten-year war with Iran – a war that was also supported with American financial, industrial, and security aid. That same year saw an Islamist general, Muhammad Zia ul-Haqq, seize power from the constitutionally elected president in Pakistan, imprison and then execute his predecessor, and launch a systematic program to Islamicize Pakistan that was backed by Saudi financial might and the expertise of Saudi religious scholars. As well, the Soviet Union militarily intervened in Afghanistan to support the Marxist Afghan regime against Afghan Muslim resistance, and the US responded with massive financial and military support to the jihadists fighting the Soviets and their local allies – and for Zia ul-Haqq's Islamicist regime in Pakistan. The US also acquiesced to Pakistan's nuclear weapons program and its sale of nuclear weapons technology abroad, and it turned a blind eye to the Pakistani military's sponsorship of Sunni Muslim terrorist organizations as a tool in border disputes with India and Afghanistan. Also in 1979, Israel and Egypt signed a peace treaty; Israel followed its return of the Sinai Peninsula to Egypt with an explosive escalation of its settlement of the disputed West Bank; and reaction began against President Sadat in Egypt that would culminate with his publicly staged assassination and the development of Islamist and Wahhabi cells that would destabilize the Egyptian government and economy over the next decades and inspire Ayman al-Zawahiri, the future cofounder of al-Qaeda, as well as many of al-Qaeda's high military and operational commanders.

In the decades that followed, the Saudi *da'wā* ideology expanded its global reach even as the US expanded its military and security presence within the Saudi kingdom. Then, in 1991, after Saddam Hussein turned on his Gulf Arab sponsors by invading Kuwait, King Fahd of Saudi Arabia welcomed American troops onto Saudi soil to deter a future Iraqi attack and to stage Operation Desert Storm against Iraq. The American presence was met with a wave of protest by Wahhabi clerics and members of the Saudi intelligentsia. Many of them, including al-Qaeda founder Osama bin Laden, identified with the Sahwa (Awakening) movement, which had

---

[29] See Benjamin and Simon (2002, 88–91); Commins (2009, 163–71); Hegghammer and Lacroix (2007); Kéchichian (1986, 1990); Trofimov (2007).

developed during the 1980s and combined traditional Wahhabi Salafism with Sayyid Quṭb's revolutionary call for social justice.[30]

In the wake of public criticism, the kingdom repressed its most outspoken critics while again appeasing Wahhabi clerics by ceding to them ever more control of Saudi education and society.[31] Saudi rulers and clerics also encouraged those who might otherwise have criticized Saudi rulers for not enforcing Wahhabi teachings within the kingdom to fight outside of it against other Muslim-led governments, militias, or parties – a policy that has been described as one of "obedience at home and rebellion abroad" (al-Rasheed 2008a). In turn, the Wahhabi clerical establishment emphasized that it was not generally permissible to declare a Muslim ruler to be an apostate, thereby repudiating the position of Sayyid Quṭb and other radical Islamists that it had once embraced as long as the Muslim rulers in question were not Saudi. But their reasoning was a cold form of reassurance for the House of Sa'ūd. A Muslim ruler could only be declared an apostate if he deliberately enacted laws that were not God's law, Saudi clerics explained. If he allowed *shirk* and other activities that violate God's law to flourish under his rule out of ignorance or moral depravity, he should continue to be upheld as the legitimate ruler while being counseled in private.[32] After a 1990 fatwa by Ibn Bāz and other senior clerics justifying King Fahd's request for American forces to set up bases in the kingdom to protect it from Iraq, the Sahwa leader Safar al-Ḥawālī pointed out that it was Ibn Bāz himself who years earlier had rebuked Egyptian President Jamāl 'Abd al-Nāṣir for calling for the aid of Soviet advisors, a contradiction that was widely noted within Saudi clerical and intellectual circles (Lacroix 2011, 160–61).[33] When American forces entered Afghanistan in 2001 in order to attack al-Qaeda bases and bring down the Taliban emirate in which they were located, the Saudi cleric Nāṣir al-Fahad issued a treatise titled "Revealing the Apostasy of Those Who Help the Americans" (*al-Tibyān fī kufr man a'ān al-Amrikān*). In it, he portrays the US as a degenerate society along the lines of Muḥammad Quṭb's generalized anti-Western polemics and praises Taliban rule as one of the first modern efforts to establish a society based on the rule of Islam. Muslims who aid non-Muslims in their conflict with Muslims were in violation of one of Ibn 'Abd al-Wahhāb's *Nullifiers of Islam*,

[30] For the Sahwa movement in Saudi Arabia, see Lacroix (2009, 2011). On Wahhabism in Saudi Arabia during and after the Gulf War, see Commins (2009, 171–204).

[31] Along with the political and religious fields, dominated respectively by the royal family and the Wahhabi clerics, an intellectual field had taken on a significant role in Saudi society, but both political and religious leaders have kept that field within limits. See Hegghammer (2010); Lacroix (2011).

[32] See, for example, Ibn Bāz's discussion of the fourth nullifier: Ibn Bāz (2011, 108–31). For Ibn Bāz's position on private counseling, see al-Atawneh (2016, 278–79).

[33] In his rebuke of Jamāl 'Abd al-Nāṣir, Ibn Bāz wrote: "If there was a higher interest in making alliance with infidels, Arab or not, or in calling on their help, then God would have authorized it and allowed his creatures to do so. But since God knows the considerable evils and the disastrous consequences that would bring about, he has forbidden it and condemned anyone who indulges in it." Translated by Lacroix (2011, 317n46) from Ibn Bāz's 1988 treatise *Naqd al-qawmiyya al-'Arabiyya*.

Saudi Nationalism, Wahhabi Da'wā, and Western Power 291

he pointed out, even as he surveyed the historical sweep of Wahhabi scholarship supporting his argument and explained that "helping" the non-Muslims against Muslims includes various kinds of support, from physical combat to verbal support or written opinion. All Muslims who engaged in any such form of support for the American effort in Afghanistan were apostates, he concluded.[34] Fahad's *takfīr* was arguably directly in line with the doctrine of Ibn 'Abd al-Wahhāb and his followers, despite the complication that the American forces were fighting alongside the *mujāhidīn* of the Northern Alliance.

Saudi religious scholars supported Taliban edicts and actions: bans on common pastimes such as chess and on kite-flying; strict prohibition on shaving beards; a ban on musical performances; destruction of musical instruments; a ban on videocassettes, televisions, and cameras; destruction of pre-Islamic art and heritage; efface-ment of paintings of human beings and animals; attempted destruction of the national film archive of Afghanistan; and dictates prohibiting women's education and access to male doctors until proper conditions for it could be established. The latter ruling caused serious harm to women's health in war-torn Afghanistan. The same positions had been propounded by the most authoritative Saudi clerics of the late twentieth century and distributed worldwide by Saudi officials and nonprofit organizations as part of the *da'wā*.[35] Although the Taliban emerged from Afghans who were studying in Pakistan madrasas of the South Asian Deobandi movement that had emerged in the wake of British occupation of India, the madrasas in which they studied and the Deobandi circles had been strongly affected by the Saudi *da'wā* through the financing of madrasas and the provision of Saudi-trained instructors. Nāṣir al-Fahad's view, then – that the Taliban emirate was the closest thing to a true Islamic state in the modern world – would have been of little surprise to students of Saudi Wahhabi teachings. After decades of increasing Saudi ties to the West and tolerance within the kingdom for videos, music (almost all forms of which have been condemned by Saudi-Wahhabi scholars, with the exception of hymns [*anāshīd*], songs sung by males without musical accompaniment), photographs, the voice of women in public or even on television, and of course, the intimate economic, military, and security alliances between Saudi Arabia and the *kāfir* nations of the West, important Wahhabi scholars, such as Abū Muḥammad al-Maqdisī, were led to declare Saudi Arabia an apostate state.[36]

---

[34] On Fahad's positions in this regard and the support he reserved from religious scholars and Sahwa movement members within the kingdom, see the detailed discussion of al-Rasheed (2007, 139–47).

[35] See the rulings of 'Abd al-'Azīz Ibn Bāz, Muḥammad Sāliḥ al-'Uthaymīn, and 'Abdullāh ibn Jibrīn (1988, especially 3:184–85, 296–308, 356–72). The volume was collected, published, and disseminated by the Saudi Permanent Committee on Fatwas.

[36] Abū Muḥammad al-Maqdisī, who resides in Jordan, is a Palestinian-born scholar who spent much of his youth in Kuwait and ultimately discovered in Saudi Arabia the teachings and resources that, by his own account, made him a "real Salafi," and who cited the multivolume collection of Wahhabi scholarship from the time of Ibn 'Abd al-Wahhāb through the early part of the twentieth century, known as *al-Durar al-saniyya* (Ibn Qāsim 1997) as exerting a transformative influence upon him. See

THE *DA'WĀ*, ITS SPONSORS, AND TRANSNATIONAL SALAFISM

In what follows, I review the methods and operations of the transnational Wahhabi *da'wā*. Before proceeding, some important caveats are in order. First, state sponsors of the *da'wā* ideology – Saudi Arabia (as well as Qatar, and in a less formal but no less significant way, Kuwait) – are not in active control of Salafis who have studied in the *da'wā*-sponsoring states or have been influenced by publications and media produced in them. Indeed, for the leading intellectuals of the *da'wā* and for at least some of their sponsors, the *da'wā* is an end in itself rather than a means to any particular political goal. Second, the flow of Muslim guest workers and students from around the world to Saudi Arabia and their circulation back to their home countries does not affect individuals in a uniform manner, and the influences range across a wide spectrum in both substance and intensity. Third, although the transnational flow of Sunni Muslims to and back from the Wahhabi states of the Gulf affects the Gulf Arab societies and teachings even as it is affected by them, the dominant direction of influence has flowed from the Arab Gulf outward. Fourth, not everyone who has been exposed to the *da'wā* through one or more of the channels mentioned below has embraced it as a whole. Indeed, many may have reacted against it or remained indifferent to it, but, as was the case with both Western and Soviet ideological outreach during the Cold War, with time, a massive sustained propagation effort can have a strong overall effect.[37] Fifth, although Wahhabi doctrine in regard to *takfīr*, the prohibition of images of living beings, and the obligation to such images and graves has to my knowledge been rejected by few

in particular Wagemakers (2012, 32–37). An influential work of Maqdisī is his *Religion of Abraham* (*Millat Ibrāhīm*), which, like many of his works, is primarily distributed online in undated form (al-Maqdisī n.d.), but is also available in a 1994 English translation (al-Maqdisī 1994). For detailed studies of Maqdisī, see Wagemakers (2009, 2012, 2015).

[37] The Wahhabi movement and Salafism have generated a strong scholarly literature in recent years. For studies focused on Saudi Arabia and its global role in propagating Wahhabi perspectives, see Basbous (2002); Farquhar (2015, 2016); al-Rasheed (2005a, 2008a). For a recent perspective on Salafi militancy in the West, see Egerton (2011). For studies with a national focus, the following are particularly germane to the argument presented here: on France, Adraoui (2009); on Germany, Damir-Geilsdorf and Menzfeld (2016), Nordbruch, Müller, and Ünlü (2014), Schneiders (2014); on Jordan, Wiktorowicz (2001); on Indonesia, Hasan (2007, 2008, 2009, 2010); on Lebanon, Pall (2014), Rabil (2014); on the Netherlands, de Koning (2009); on Palestine, Hroub (2009); on Pakistan, Abou Zahab (2009); on the UK, Birt (2005), Hamid (2009), al-Rasheed (2005b); on the US, Doumato (2008); and on Yemen, Bonnefoy (2009). These works have drawn attention to the various channels through which the Wahhabi or Salafi *da'wā* is propagated; the local conditions of the various regions and nations in which it has to one degree or another taken root; and the appeal of the *da'wā* for those who adopt its positions. The studies vary in emphasis and approach, a variation due to the difference in actual situations studied as well as the different disciplines and perspectives of the authors. In my own earlier studies, I take up the case of American activist Ali al-Tamimi. In Sells (2006), I probe the role of Ibn Bāz and his circles in al-Tamimi's personal transformation. In Sells (2013), I take up the relationship between al-Tamimi's apocalypticism and that of Safar al-Ḥawālī, which was revealed in a court case after the appearance of my 2006 essay. Heffelfinger (2011) also discusses the case of al-Tamimi along with his general overview of militancy in the US. For Wahhabi positions on Shi'ites, see Hasson (2006).

Salafi leaders or groups, it is impossible to state (without a massive social-scientific research program) the urgency and intensity of such doctrines and the requirement to act upon them among all Salafi individuals or groups.

Since the founding of the Muslim World League in 1962, Saudi Arabia has pursued the Wahhabi *da'wā* through a variety of interconnected channels. Some channels, such as the immense financial resources of the Gulf rentier states, are hard to measure, though it is clear that a request for monetary or other types of support from the financial elite in the Gulf may be facilitated by behavior, dress, or discourse that indicate receptivity to Salafism. Below is a brief survey of several of the more measurable *da'wā* channels that are clearly intertwined with one another, but which are placed in a list form here for the purpose of summary.

(A) The financial and political dominance of Saudi Arabia and its Gulf allies within intergovernmental organizations such as the fifty-one-nation Organization of the Islamic Community (OIC) exerts ideological soft power on the member states that have come to rely on the financial support of the wealthy Gulf Arab states.[38]

(B) Since the oil boom of the 1970s, millions of Sunni Muslims have moved to Saudi Arabia and other Gulf nations. Engineers and other technicians from countries such as Egypt and Pakistan could settle in the kingdom, receive a salary at multiples of anything they could have hoped for at home, and send remittances to their families. Many return home after years working in the Gulf with a new economic status.[39] Those who were influenced by Wahhabi teachings would then be able to fund local Islamic communities or institutions aligned with their own beliefs and influence others.

(C) Wahhabi ideology is propagated to international visitors and guests through several related channels. Saudi control of the Islamic holy sites of Mecca and Medina and of the *ḥajj* and *i'timār* pilgrimages has resulted in close control over various aspects of the pilgrimage, particularly those concerning the mixing of genders or the question of women's dress – items that are not doctrinal matters but have become a core concern of Saudi clerics – as well as the discouragement of visits to graves of the family members and companions of the Prophet.[40] The use of the pilgrimages to reinforce Wahhabism occurs as well through the manuals distributed internationally to those considering or about to make a pilgrimage.[41] The enlargement of the holy mosques in Mecca and Medina has occurred in concert with the

---

[38] Shehabi (2008, 188) notes that by its own account, the kingdom donated more than 100 billion dollars to OIC countries during one 17-year period.

[39] For a glimpse into the magnitude of the guest worker presence in Saudi Arabia, see De Bel Air (2014).

[40] See Piscatori (2016, 158–59) on 'Uthaymīn's and Ibn Bāz's roles in the development of new gender segregation and dress codes for the pilgrimage. For a discussion of Iranian disputes with Saudi Arabia over pilgrimage control, see also Kramer (1990).

[41] On this point, see al-Rasheed (2007, 126–29), and the quotes therein from the pilgrimage manuals written by Ibn Jibrīn and Ibn Bāz.

destruction of much of the historical architectural heritage of the Hijaz and its replacement with apartment towers, hotels, and shopping centers that according to critics has proceeded with little or no attempt to reflect the traditions of Saudi urban spaces and architecture. Protests over the destruction by Muslims lamenting the loss of heritage have been in vain. As Ibn Bāz explained, reaffirming traditional Wahhabi teachings, attachment to historical monuments can lead to *shirk*.[42] Hence, from the time of Ibn 'Abd al-Wahhāb's destruction of the home of one of the Prophet's companions to the present, Saudi rulers have been working to destroy buildings or remains of buildings associated with the Prophet's family and companions as well as raised tombs with the exception of that of the Prophet himself.[43] The annual *hajj* sermon delivered by the Saudi king offers yet another channel for connecting the holy sites (*haramayn*) to the Saudi-Wahhabi enterprise.

(D) Each year a number of pilgrims take advantage of the opportunity to extend their stay in Saudi Arabia to study with Saudi clerics. The kingdom makes a significant effort to attract international students to its schools, universities, and study circles. The Islamic University of Medina has been the high-prestige focus of Wahhabi outreach to non-Saudis. It has brought in non-Saudi faculty to teach at the university and has offered generous scholarships, living stipends, and annual round trip tickets home to large numbers of young men from around the world who master Wahhabi doctrine and immerse themselves in classical Islamic texts, which they learn through the filter of that doctrine. They are then prepared to return home as teachers in madrasas, as imams, or as founders of their own study circles.

With their knowledge of classical Arabic and their ability to cite chapter and verse from classical texts to defend any item of Wahhabi doctrine, young men educated in Saudi Arabia, particularly those who have graduated from the Islamic University of Medina, return home with elevated status and prestige. They can also attract and inspire those who find themselves drawn toward the vision of immersing themselves in classical Arabic, spoken and written, and in learning the sophisticated methods of *hadīth* study. At the same time, it is the Wahhabi position about that early world, such as the Abū Hayyāj al-Asadī *hadīth* on image and grave destruction, that is embedded at the heart of *hadīth* study programs taught by Saudi or other Wahhabi shaykhs, and students are trained to use their mastery of classical Arabic and *hadīth* traditions to defend and promote such positions. Relatively few who have followed the rulings of one of the four classical Sunni schools of law (particularly in areas where the level of Arabic has declined, as in the former Soviet republics) would be

---

[42] On dismay over Saudi destruction of shrines and heritage and the claims that the expansion of the mosques in Mecca and Medina was not needed, see Piscatori (2016, 147–48); Sardar (2014). On Ibn Bāz's comments on heritage preservation and *shirk*, see Ende (2016, 240–42).

[43] Given that a key source for Wahhabi doctrine on graves is the abovementioned *hadīth* of Abū Hayyāj stating that the Prophet himself had instructed 'Alī to destroy all the raised graves he found, Wahhabi clerics have developed complex explanations for acquiescing in the Saudi kingdom's refusal to authorize the destruction of the Prophet's own tomb in Medina.

Saudi Nationalism, Wahhabi Daʿwā, and Western Power

ready to respond to the chapter-and-verse arguments of Wahhabi or Saudi-trained Salafi challengers.

(E) Saudi outreach programs have included the Muslim World League, the World Assembly of Muslim Youth, Saudi embassy programs, the Ḥaramayn Foundation, and the International Islamic Relief Organization. The Kuwait-based Revival of Islamic Heritage Society (RIHS), along with Saudi organizations and individuals, played key roles in the Wahhabi *daʿwā* program to finance mosques worldwide. Such mosques often come with an Islamic center, library, or school, and their generous funding can allow services for the local community, from lower tuition to the provision of books, that local Islamic communities find difficult to match. Other philanthropic organizations, such as the Saudi Relief Committee for Bosnia and the Saudi Joint Relief Committee for Albania and Chechnya, can work in concert with mosque funding but are able to leverage their financial clout by providing a particularly wide array of services in societies that have been devastated by war. In war-shattered or impoverished areas like Bosnia and Kosovo, Saudi mosque funding and philanthropy brought with it a campaign to destroy graves, shrines, and even centuries-old Ottoman-period mosques that had survived the Croat and Serb nationalist efforts to annihilate Muslim heritage in the region. As of August 2004, Saudi Arabia had established 200 Islamic colleges, 2,010 Islamic centers, 1,500 mosques, and 2,000 schools for Muslim children in non-Islamic countries, according to King Fahd's personal website.

Wahhabi publishing and media networks are among the most advanced in the Islamic world. Many of the radical Salafi movements in Arab countries, such as that in Jordan, have been given detailed attention by scholarship and have been treated as largely homegrown movements. There may indeed be a homegrown element in the growth of such movements, but the books to which many young Salafis have devoted such intense study are composed by Saudi Wahhabi scholars or by scholars supported by Wahhabi networks in the Gulf. The books are supplied or funded through the same sources. Their teachers have often studied in Kuwait and Saudi Arabia, and the students who gather around them can reasonably aspire to receive scholarships to study at prestigious institutions or in highly regarded teaching circles within those nations.

(F) Wahhabi scholars have also worked meticulously to ground Ibn ʿAbd al-Wahhāb's doctrine in the *ḥadīth*, the writings of the classical jurists (of all four major Sunni schools), and early Sunni commentaries on the Qurʾān – and to further advance the long-standing effort to prove that the writings of Ibn Taymiyya and Ibn Qayyim al-Jawziyya support Wahhabi positions on *shirk* and *takfīr*.[44] This effort has produced ever more extensive and polished annotated editions of Ibn ʿAbd al-Wahhāb's works

---

[44] For one example of a sophisticated, well-funded, and deeply scholarly Saudi production of Wahhabi perspectives on *takfīr*, see Abū al-ʿUlā (2004).

on *tawḥīd*, as well the early Islamic sources that are viewed as the basis for Ibn ʿAbd al-Wahhāb's teaching. One goal of the Wahhabi self-disavowal mentioned at the beginning of this chapter is to provide carefully produced, selected sets of early Islamic sources that will allow Ibn ʿAbd al-Wahhāb's doctrine to be taught without any appeal to his authority or even, in many cases, mentioning his name. Saudi-trained teachers and *daʿwā* practitioners can now propagate the ideas found in *Kitāb al-Tawḥīd* and the *Nullifiers of Islam* by quoting earlier sources, citing chapter and verse, often with a command of classical Arabic and a facility in argument and debate that years of training with Wahhabi scholars or Wahhabi-trained scholars can offer.

(G) *Daʿwā* publishing and dissemination through other media, such as audiocassettes and audio-video files of sermons and lectures and highly sophisticated Internet and social media channels, is not limited to Arabic.[45] Many of the advanced web platforms have menus across a range of languages, and other works, rather than being translations of Arabic materials, are composed with the non-Arabic reader or listener in mind. In 1994, King Fahd established a $130 million printing plant in Medina devoted to producing Saudi-approved translations of the Qurʾān, most notably the Hilālī and Khān English rendition. By 2000, the kingdom had distributed 138 million copies worldwide. The Saudi Qurʾān Complex website now features Saudi-approved translations in numerous languages. The major works of Ibn ʿAbd al-Wahhāb and his foremost modern Saudi expositors such as Ibn Bāz and Muḥammad Ṣāliḥ al-ʿUthaymīn (d. 1999) (M. S. al-ʿUthaymīn 2010) have also been translated into a variety of languages. Of particular importance for the *daʿwā* within Russia and the post-Soviet republics has been the translation of such material into Russian. More recently, the *daʿwā* translation effort has moved on to the various Turkic and Persian vernaculars within Russia and the post-Soviet region.[46]

[45]   For a self-description of Dar-us-Salam publishers, see (Dar-us-Salam Publications n.d.): "Darussalam is a Multilingual International Islamic Publishing House, headquartered in Riyadh, Kingdom of Saudi Arabia, and branches and agents in major cities around the world. The foremost obligation of Darussalam is to publish authentic Islamic books in the light of the Qurʾān and the *Sahih Ahâdith* [canonical *ḥadīth* collections] in all major international languages. To impart and impel the above mentioned sacred obligation, Darussalam has been engaged, from inception, in producing books on Islam in Arabic, English, Urdu, Spanish, French, Hindi, Persian, Malayalam, Turkish, Indonesian, Russian, Albanian and Bangla languages. The main theme of these books is to present to the reader the fundamentals of Islam as explained by the most recognized Islamic Scholars in the Muslim world."

[46]   A 2008 report of the International Crisis Group on Azerbaijan offers a glimpse into one particular case of multi-channeled *daʿwā* operations. It reports that, according to interviews with a Salafi scholar, the Salafi movement in Azerbaijan began with Azeri students who had studied in Saudi Arabia and pilgrims returning from the *ḥajj*. The emergent Salafi movement received significant support from the Kuwait-based RIHS, which – by the time it was closed in 2001 in Azerbaijan after its branches in Pakistan and Afghanistan were accused of links to al-Qaeda – had financed the construction of the Abu Bakr Mosque in Baku, which became the center for Wahhabi-Salafi teaching, as well as the reconstruction of sixty-two other mosques in the country. The Saudi-based International Islamic Relief Organization, which had been providing aid to refugees in the country, had its presence reduced after one of its members was arrested in Canada on terrorism-related charges after a flight

SAUDI ARABIA AND EXTREMIST IDEOLOGY

Despite the denials by Saudi rulers, Wahhabi doctrine has inspired and driven militant movements from al-Qaeda to al-Qaeda-in-Iraq to the Islamic State (widely known as ISIS). Indeed, ISIS made Ibn ʿAbd al-Wahhāb's *Kitāb al-Tawḥīd* a core requirement for middle school students throughout its territories (ages 12–15), and the importance attached to that particular work shows through clearly in an ISIS-required curriculum in the Syrian town of Mayadin: *Kitāb al-Tawḥīd* (179 pages); Mathematics (64 pages); Biology (37 pages); Arabic Language (30 pages); English Language (30 pages); and Physics and Chemistry (25 pages) (Syrian Observatory for Human Rights 2015).[47]

In the wake of the 2011 Arab Spring, tombs and Sufi shrines were desecrated or destroyed in Tunisia, Libya, Mali, and other areas of Africa where there was a vacuum of power. Wahhabi Salafi militias carried out much of the destruction; in other cases, local individuals or groups influenced by Wahhabi preachers may have taken it upon themselves to damage or desecrate a shrine. The systematic destruction of religious and cultural heritage carries a human toll as well. Sufis, Shiʿites, artists, architects, archaeologists, and others who resist the destruction can face death or persecution.

ISIS-controlled Syria and Iraq endured a more systematic application of Wahhabi iconoclasm. The second issue of the ISIS magazine, *Dabiq*, features "A Photo Report on the Destruction of *Shirk* [idolatry or polytheism]" (Islamic State 2014). The captions on the photographs from that issue reveal clearly ISIS's rationale for destroying Islamic heritage in the Iraqi province of Nineveh: "Blowing Up the 'Husayniyyat ul-Qubbah' Temple in Mosul" (14); "A Soldier of the Islamic State Clarifies to the People the Obligation to Demolish the Tombs" (15); "Demolishing the 'Grave of the Girl' in Mosul" (15); "Demolishing the Shrine and Tomb of Ahmad ar-Rifaʿi in the District of al-Mahlabiyya" (16); and "Blowing up the 'Husayniyyat Jawwad' Temple in Tal ʿAfar" (17). ISIS acted with equal fervor against pre-Islamic artistic and architectural heritage from Nineveh in Iraq to Palmyra in Syria.

At the time that ISIS was engaged in this campaign of tomb, shrine, and heritage destruction, influential Wahhabi websites in Saudi Arabia and Qatar were promoting fatwas celebrating the Taliban for destroying the monumental Buddha statues at Bamiyan and then smashing other artwork across

---

from Baku. Another Kuwait-based organization, the Asian Muslims Committee, combined refugee relief work in Baku with the distribution of *daʿwā* material, a glimpse of which was provided by a report that, in 2005, it sent fourteen tons of allegedly Wahhabi materials, in Arabic and Russian, to the Caucuses Board of Muslims in Azerbaijan. Books in Kazakh and Uzbek were also alleged to have been dispatched along with humanitarian assistance. See International Crisis Group (2008, 5–6). For more on the RIHS, its reputed support for al-Qaeda and other terrorist organizations, and the more than ninety-five committees and national chapters through which it has operated, see US Department of Treasury (2008).

[47] On ISIS educational policy and *Kitāb al-Tawḥīd*, see al-Jablawi (2016).

Taliban-ruled Afghanistan in 2001. The fatwas also urged Muslims to destroy such idols and tombs wherever they could do so; made particular mention of the areas of Syria, Iraq, and Egypt; and specifically singled out the "idol" of the sphinx and the tombs of the pyramids for destruction. When challenged by those who asked why the first four caliphs and their military commanders had not destroyed the tombs and idols in such areas, they argued that they destroyed everything they could in that regard but that many such objects were buried or otherwise inaccessible at the time. With widespread visibility of such objects in museums and in archaeological sites today, there is no such excuse for the Wahhabism-inspired believer today, although some Wahhabi clerics have written that a believer is not required to destroy such idols immediately if there is a serious, practical impediment to doing so.

The most high-profile platform for militant Wahhabism, IslamQA.info (Islam Question and Answer), is the project of Saudi-based Shaykh Muḥammad Ṣāliḥ al-Munajjid, a former protégé of Ibn Bāz. The Alexa ranking of religious websites, based on the number of digital visitors, lists it among the top sites in the world, along with or exceeding, for example, the official website of the Vatican. Indeed, I have found that google Arabic searches for *ḥadīth* phrases on any topic often show an IslamQA result at or near the top of hundreds of results, even though the IslamQA link shown will often have little information on the phrase beyond a quotation in some secondary context. (Other website managers might envy him getting IslamQA to rise to a Wikipedia-like default top of the list in searches, as least in areas like *ḥadīth* reports, one of the most important aspects of Muslim religious life.) The Saudi government does not allow Munajjid to promote his site *within* Saudi Arabia, because he is not part of the official Saudi commission on fatwas, but it has given him a powerful base from which to project his rulings abroad and, although he does not label them as fatwas, they take the exact form of official fatwa reports. Another high-profile platform is IslamWeb, the official site of Qatar's Ministry of Religious Endowments. It offers the same rulings on images and grave destruction as IslamQA, and, like IslamQA, it makes its rulings available in both Arabic and English.[48]

IslamQA addresses other core questions as well. "Must all apostates be killed?" Yes, states IslamQA unequivocally and IslamWeb with near certainty.[49] And then there are the questions regarding sex with one's slave. As ISIS began expanding its conquests in Iraq and Syria and opening up a slave market for young women and boys captured by ISIS fighters, such

---

[48] See IslamQA (2002, 2003a, 2003b, 2015); IslamWeb (2002, 2004, 2011, 2012).

[49] See IslamQA (2003a, 2003b, 2010); IslamWeb (2005, 2008, 2015). IslamWeb (2005) offers a glimpse into a particular kind of Wahhabi casuistry. It states that it is impermissible to kill an apostate without a ruler's permission, but then adds a twist: In the case of an unauthorized killing, the killer is relieved of being subject to retribution because the life of an apostate is not inviolable under Islamic law.

a question would have taken on a contemporary relevancy. A man in ISIS territory might well wish to check on whether having sex with the slave he purchased was permissible under religious law. IslamQA's response was emphatic. In a post entitled "Ruling on Having Intercourse with a Slave Woman When One Has a Wife," it ruled that not only is intercourse with a slave permitted, but that the slave-purchaser's wife "has no cause to complain." The IslamWeb fatwas on the topic take a similar position, although their tone tends to be less one of celebration of such a "right" than of resignation to the divine plan and hopes that other idolatrous peoples might accept Islam before undergoing such a fate.[50]

Since Fayṣal ibn ʿAbd al-ʿAzīz began the transformation of Wahhabism into a global ideology that could compete with liberal capitalism and its socialist rivals in the mid-1960s, the kingdom has played, with striking success, what its critics have long claimed was a double game: accepting its status as ally to the non-Muslim West, on the one hand, and proclaiming a Wahhabi ideology that anathematizes Muslims who aid non-Muslims and demonizes Jews and Christians, on the other. It refuses to enforce Wahhabi doctrines at home but exports them, in increasingly militant forms, abroad. It rails against Western ideology and the crimes committed by the West, while providing lucrative arms purchases and the cheap oil supply needed (at least until recently) by the US and its allies to carry out the very policies, wars, and protection of Israel that Wahhabi ideologues use to enhance the urgency of their message.

In any event, the US and Saudi Arabia have continued to proclaim a symbiotic economic and security relationship. In 2005, the US took a step back from its consistent adherence to and backing for Saudi policies when it concluded a nuclear power agreement with Iran, infuriating the leaders of Saudi Arabia, its Gulf allies, and Israel, but the Obama administration had achieved acceptance of the US-Iran agreement only in the face of deep resistance in Congress, and the election of Donald Trump, who had promised to "tear up" the agreement, signaled its demise. During the same visit, which saw Trump and the Saudi monarch inaugurating the Global Center for Combating Extremist Ideology, the two nations announced potential US arms sales and infrastructure sales to Saudi Arabia of $110 billion (Wilts 2017). And the following year, the Trump administration unilaterally renounced the nuclear agreement with Iran (see Table 11.1).

---

[50] The IslamQA page titled "Ruling on Having Intercourse with a Slave Woman When One Has a Wife" was taken down, but it can still be accessed on the Internet archive: see IslamQA (n.d.). A similar position is propounded in the fatwa, "Ruling on Sexual Intercourse with One's Polytheistic Slave-Woman" (IslamWeb 2014).

300 Michael A. Sells

TABLE 11.1 *Saudi-Wahhabi chronology*

Pact between Ibn ʿAbd al-Wahhāb and Muḥammad ibn Saʿūd	1744
Death of Ibn ʿAbd al-Wahhāb	1792
Saudi forces conquer Taif, Karbala, Mecca, and Medina	1801–6
Egyptian-Turkish army conquers and razes Wahhabi center at Dirʿiyya	1818
ʿAbd al-ʿAzīz Āl Saʿūd (Ibn Saʿūd) captures Riyadh	1902
ʿAbd al-ʿAzīz becomes king of Najd and king of Hijaz	1926–27
Ikhwān revolt against ʿAbd al-ʿAzīz is crushed with the support of Britain	1929
ʿAbd al-ʿAzīz establishes the Kingdom of Saudi Arabia	1932
Commercially significant oil discovered in Saudi Arabia	1938
Death of ʿAbd al-ʿAzīz Āl Saʿūd, succeeded by Saʿūd ibn ʿAbd al-ʿAzīz	1953
Founding of the Islamic University of Medina	1961
Founding of the Muslim World League	1962
Fayṣal ibn ʿAbd al-ʿAzīz replaces Saʿūd as king	1964
Founding of the World Assembly of Muslim Youth (WAMY)	1962
King Fayṣal assassinated	1975
Juhaymān al-ʿUtaybī assault on Grand Mosque in Mecca	1979
Sahwa protests in Saudi Arabia	1991–92
Ibn Bāz designated as grand mufti	1993
Death of Ibn Bāz and al-Albānī	1999
ʿAbdullāh ibn ʿAbd al-ʿAzīz becomes king	2005
Salmān ibn ʿAbd al-ʿAzīz becomes king	2015
Saudi Arabia and regional allies intervene militarily in Yemen	2015
Global Center for Combating Extremist Ideology is established in Riyadh	2017
US renounces its nuclear agreement with Iran	2018

REFERENCES

Abou Zahab, Mariam. 2009. "Salafism in Pakistan: The Ahl-e Hadith Movement." In *Global Salafism: Islam's New Religious Movement*, edited by Roel Meijer, 126–42. New York: Columbia University Press.

Abū al-ʿŪlā, Rāshid. 2004. *Ḍawābit takfīr al-muaʿyyan ʿinda shaykhay al-islām Ibn Taymiyya wa Ibn ʿAbd al-Wahhāb wa-ʿulamāʾ al-daʿwat al-iṣlāḥiyya*. Edited by Ṣāliḥ Ibn Fawzān. Riyadh: Maktabat al-Rushd.

Abū Samra, Muhammad. 2009. "Liberal Critics, ʿUlamaʾ and the Debate on Islam in the Contemporary Arab World." In *Guardians of Faith in Modern Times: ʿUlamaʾ in the Middle East*, edited by Meir Hatina, 265–89. Leiden: Brill.

Adraoui, Mohamed-Ali. 2009. "Salafism in France: Ideology, Practices and Contradictions." In *Global Salafism: Islam's New Religious Movement*, edited by Roel Meijer, 364–73. New York: Columbia University Press.

An-Naʾim, Abdullahi Ahmed. 1986. "The Islamic Law of Apostasy and Its Modern Applicability: A Case from the Sudan." *Religion* 16: 197–224.

Ansary, Abdullah F. 2018. "Combating Extremism: A Brief Overview of Saudi Arabia's Approach." *Middle East Policy* 15, no. 2: 433–54.

Atawneh, Muhammad al-. 2016. "Is Saudi Arabia a Theocracy? Religion and Governance in Contemporary Saudi Arabia." In vol. 2 of *Wahhabism: Doctrine and Development*, edited by Esther Peskes, 271–88. Berlin: Gerlach Press.

Arab News. 2017. "Arab-Islamic-American Summit Fosters Global Peace, Stability." May 22. www.arabnews.com/node/1103126/saudi-arabia.

Basbous, Antoine. 2002. *L'Arabie Saoudite en Question: du Wahhabisme à Bin Laden, aux Origines de la Tourmente*. Paris: Perrin.

Benjamin, Daniel, and Steven Simon. 2002. *The Age of Sacred Terror*. New York: Random House.

Birt, Jonathan. 2005. "Wahhabism in the United Kingdom: Manifestations and Reactions." In *Transnational Connections and the Arab Gulf*, edited by Madawi al-Rasheed, 168–84. London: Routledge.

Bonnefoy, Laurent. 2009. "How Transnational Is Salafism in Yemen." In *Global Salafism: Islam's New Religious Movement*, edited by Roel Meijer, 321–41. New York: Columbia University Press.

Böwering, Gerhard. 2008. "Reconstructing the Qur'an." In *The Qur'an in Its Historical Context*, edited by Gabriel Reynolds, 70–87. New York: Routledge.

Commins, David. 2009. *The Wahhabi Mission and Saudi Arabia*. Ithaca: I.B. Tauris.

Dallal, Ahmad S. 2016. "The Origins and Early Development of Islamic Reform." In vol. 1 of *Wahhabism: Doctrine and Development*, edited by Esther Peskes, 33–60. Berlin: Gerlach Press.

Damir-Geilsdorf, Sabine, and Mira Menzfeld. 2016. "'Looking at the Life of the Prophet and How He Dealt with All These Issues': Self-Positioning, Demarcations and Belongingness of German Salafis from an Emic Perspective." *Contemporary Islam* 10, no. 3: 433–54.

Dar-us-Salam Publications. n.d. "About Dar-us-Salam Publications." https://dar-us-salam.com/about_us.htm.

Davis, Gregory M. 2006. *Religion of Peace? Islam's War against the World*. Los Angeles: World Ahead Publishing.

De Bel Air, Francoise. 2014. "Demography, Migration, and Labour Market in Saudi Arabia." Explanatory Note, no. 1/2014. Gulf Labour Markets and Migration. https://gulfmigration .eu/media/pubs/exno/GLMM_EN_2014_01.pdf.

Dekmejian, R. Hrair. 2016. "The Rise of Political Islamism in Saudi Arabia." In vol. 2 of *Wahhabism: Doctrine and Development*, edited by Esther Peskes, 338–53. Berlin: Gerlach Press.

de Konig, Martijn. 2009. "Changing Worldviews and Friendship: An Exploration of the Life Stories of Two Female Salafis in the Netherlands." In *Global Salafism: Islam's New Religious Movement*, edited by Roel Meijer, 404–23. New York: Columbia University Press.

Devji, Faisal. 2008. "The 'Arab' in Global Militancy." In *Kingdom without Borders: Saudi Political, Religious and Media Frontiers*, edited by Madawi al-Rasheed, 283–99. New York: Cambridge University Press.

Doumato, Eleanor Abdella. 2008. "Saudi Arabian Expansion in the United States: Half-Hearted Missionary Work Meets Rock-Solid Resistance." In *Kingdom without Borders: Saudi Political, Religious and Media Frontiers*, edited by Madawi al-Rasheed, 301–21. New York: Cambridge University Press.

Dubaykhī al-, Khālid ibn ʿAbdullāh, and Muḥammad ibn ʿAbd al-Wahhāb. 2011–12. *Minḥat al-ḥamīd fī taqrīb Kitāb al-Tawḥīd li-l-Imām Muḥammad ibn ʿAbd al-Wahhāb*, 1115–1206H. Dammam, Saudi Arabia: Dār Ibn al-Jawzī.

Egerton, Frazer. 2011. *Jihad in the West: The Rise of Militant Salafism*. New York: Cambridge University Press.

Ende, Werner. 2016. "Religion, Politik und Literatur in Saudi-Arabien: Der geistesgeschichtliche Hintergrund der heutigen religiösen und kulturpolitischen Situation." In vol. 2 of *Wahhabism: Doctrine and Development*, edited by Esther Peskes, 230–47. Berlin: Gerlach Press.

Fahad, Abulaziz H. al-. 2016. "From Exclusivism to Accommodation: Doctrinal and Legal Evolution of Wahhabism." In vol. 2 of *Wahhabism: Doctrine and Development*, edited by Esther Peskes, 110–39. Berlin: Gerlach Press.

Farquhar, Michael. 2015. "The Islamic University of Medina since 1961: The Politics of Religious Mission and the Making of a Modern Salafi Pedagogy." In *Shaping Global Islamic Discourses: The Role of Al-Azhar, Al-Medina and Al-Mustafa*, edited by Masooda Bano and Keiko Sakurai, 21–40. Edinburgh: Edinburgh University Press.

2016. *Circuits of Faith: Migration, Education, and the Wahhabi Mission*. Stanford: Stanford University Press.

Fawzān, Sālih al-. n.d. "The Obligation to Ascribe to the Salafiya." Translated by Maaz Qureshi. FatwaIslam.com. www.fatwaislam.com/fis/index.cfm?scn=fd&ID=565.

Hamid, Sadek. 2009. "The Attraction of 'Authentic Islam': Salafism and British Muslim Youth." In *Global Salafism: Islam's New Religious Movement*, edited by Roel Meijer, 384–403. New York: Columbia University Press.

Hasan, Noorhaidi. 2007. "The Salafi Movement in Indonesia: Transnational Dynamics and Local Development." *Comparative Studies of South Asia, Africa and the Middle East* 27, no. 1: 83–94.

2008. "Saudi Expansion, the Salafi Campaign and Arabised Islam in Indonesia." In *Kingdom without Borders: Saudi Political, Religious, and Media Frontiers*, edited by Madawi al-Rasheed, 263–81. New York: Cambridge University Press.

2009. "Ambivalent Doctrines and Conflicts in the Salafi Movement in Indonesia." In *Global Salafism: Islam's New Religious Movement*, edited by Roel Meijer, 169–88. New York: Columbia University Press.

2010. "The Failure of the Wahhabi Campaign: Transnational Islam and the Salafi Madrasa in Post-9/11 Indonesia." *South East Asia Research* 18, no. 4: 675–705.

Hasson, Isaac. 2006. "Les Šī'ites Vus Par Les Néo-Wahhābites." *Arabica* 53, no. 3: 299–330.

Heffelfinger, Christopher. 2011. *Radical Islam in America Salafism's Journey from Arabia to the West*. Washington, DC: Potomac Books.

Hegghammer, Thomas. 2010. *Jihad in Saudi Arabia: Violence and Pan-Islamism since 1979*. Cambridge: Cambridge University Press.

Hegghammer, Thomas, and Stéphane Lacroix. 2007. "Rejectionist Islamism in Saudi Arabia: The Story of Juhayman al-'Utaybi Revisited." *International Journal of Middle East Studies* 39, no. 1: 103–22.

Hilālī, Muhammad Taqi-ud-Din al-, and Muhammad Muhsin Khān, trans. 1996. *The Noble Qur'an: Interpretation of the Meanings of the Noble Qur'an in the English Language*. Riyadh: Dar-us-Salam Publications.

1999. *The Noble Qur'an: Interpretation of the Meanings of the Noble Qur'an in the English Language*. Riyadh: Dar-us-Salam Publications.

Hroub, Khaled. 2009. "Salafi Formations in Palestine: The Limits of a De-Palestinised Milieu." In *Global Salafism: Islam's New Religious Movement*, edited by Roel Meijer, 221–43. New York: Columbia University Press.

Ibn 'Abd al-Wahhāb, Muḥammad. 1979. *Majmū'āt al-fatāwā wa-l-rasā'il wa-l-ajwiba: Khamsūn risāla fī al-tawḥīd*. Cairo: Dār al-Waḥy.

2010a. *Mufīd al-mustafīd fī kufr tārik al-tawḥīd.* Edited by Ḥamad ibn Aḥmad al-ʿAṣlānī. Riyadh: Maktabat al-Rushd Nāshirūn.

2010b. *Majmūʿ muʿallafāt al-Shaykh Muḥammad ibn ʿAbd al-Wahhāb: Mawsūʿa tataḍammanu jamīʿ muʿallafāt wa-rasāʾil wa-khuṭab al-Shaykh Muḥammad ibn ʿAbd al-Wahhāb.* Edited by Rāʾid ibn Ṣabrī and Ibn Abī ʿAlfa. 2 vols. Beirut: Milyār li-l-Istithmār.

Ibn ʿAbd al-Wahhāb, Muḥammad et al. 1926. *Majmūʿāt al-tawḥīd: al-Maʿrūf bi-majmuʿāt al-tawḥīd al-Najdiyya: Majmūʿāt kutub wa-rasāʾil.* Edited by Rashīd Riḍā. Riyadh: al-Amāna al-ʿĀmma li-l-Iḥtifāl bi-Murūr Miʾa ʿĀm ʿalā Taʾsīs al-Mamlaka.

Ibn Bāz, ʿAbd al-ʿAzīz ibn ʿAbdullāh. 1999. *The Ideological Attack.* Translated by Abu Aaliyah Surkheel ibn Anwar Sharif. Hounslow, UK: Message of Islam.

2011. *Subul al-salām sharḥ Nawāqiḍ al-Islām.* Edited by Muḥammad ibn NāṣirFihrī and ʿAbd al-ʿAzīz ibn Muḥammad ibn ʿAlī ʿAbd al-Laṭīf. Cairo: al-Muʾassa al-Saʿūdiyya.

Ibn Bāz, ʿAbd al-ʿAzīz, Muḥammad Ṣāliḥ al-ʿUthaymīn, ʿAbdullāh Ibn Jibrin, and al-Lajna al-Dāʾima. 1988. *Fatāwā Islāmiyya.* Beirut: Dār al-Arqam.

Ibn Ḥammad al-ʿUmar, ʿAbd al-Raḥmān. 1991. *The Religion of Truth.* Riyadh: Maktaba Dar-us-Salam.

Ibn Ḥumayd, ʿAbdullāh ibn Muḥammad. 1995. *Jihad in the Qurʾan and Sunna.* Riyadh: Maktaba Dar-us-Salam.

Ibn Muḥammad ʿAbd al-Wahhāb al-Tamīmī, ʿAbdullāh. 1996. *Al-Kalimāt al-nāfiʿa fī al-mukaffirāt al-wāqiʿa.* Amman: Dār al-Bashīr.

Ibn Qāsim, ʿAbd al-Raḥmān ibn Muḥammad. 1997. *Kitāb al-Durar al-saniyya fī al-ajwiba al-Najdiyya: Majmūʿ rasāʾil wa-masāʾil ʿulamāʾ Najd al-aʿlām.* Mecca: Maṭbaʿa Umm al-Qurā.

International Crisis Group. 2004. "Saudi Arabia Backgrounder: Who are the Islamists?" Middle East Report, no. 31. https://bit.ly/36HyVtL.

2008. "Azerbaijan: Independent Islam and the State." Europe Report, no. 191. www.crisisgroup.org/europe-central-asia/caucasus/azerbaijan/azerbaijan-independent-islam-and-state.

Islamic State. 2014. "A Photo Report on the Destruction of *Shirk* [idolatry or polytheism]." *Dabiq Magazine* 2. July 27.

IslamQA. n.d. "Ruling on Having Intercourse with a Slave Woman When One Has a Wife." No. 10382. http://web.archive.org/web/20160106101656/http://islamqa.info/en/10382.

1998. "Ruling on Photographs." May 15. https://islamqa.info/en/answers/365/ruling-on-photographs.

2002. "Is It Permissible to Put a Marker on a Grave?" No. 8991. July 30. https://islamqa.info/en/answers/8991/is-it-permissible-to-put-a-marker-on-a-grave-so-that-it-will-be-known-whose-grave-it-is.

2003a. "Obligation to Destroy Idols." No. 20894. April 22. https://islamqa.info/en/answers/20894/obligation-to-destroy-idols.

2003b. "Wujūb Taksīr al-Aṣnam." No. 20894. April 22. https://islamqa.info/ar/answers/20894/ال-اصنام-ر-يكسـتـب-وجو.

2010. "Why Is the Apostate to be Executed in Islam?" No. 20327. February 1. https://islamqa.info/en/answers/20327/why-is-the-apostate-to-be-executed-in-islam.

2015. "Li-mādhā lam yaqum ʿAmr ibn al-ʿĀṣ bi-taṭhīm al-tamāthīl al-firʿawniyya?" No. 129769. March 10. https://bit.ly/32OAR2w.

IslamWeb. 2002. "Destruction of Buddhist Statues, Pyramids, Sphinx, etc." Fatwa 84193. May 18. www.islamweb.net/en/fatwa/84193/?Option=FatwaId.

304   *Michael A. Sells*

2004. "Islam and Culture." Fatwa 88060. June 21. www.islamweb.net/en/fatwa/88060/? Option=FatwaId.

2005. "Death as a Punishment for Apostasy." Fatwa 90878. December 12. www.islamweb.net/en/fatwa/90878/death-as-a-punishment-for-apostasy.

2008. "The Punishment for Apostasy Was Applicable and Still Applies." Fatwa 107875. May 8. www.islamweb.net/en/fatwa/107875/the-punishment-for-apostasy-was-applicable -and-still-applies.

2011. "Buddha Statue Destroyed by Taliban." Fatwa 7447. May 8. http://islamweb.net/en/ fatwa/7447/?Option=FatwaId.

2012. "Ḥukm hadam al-athār allatī ʿalā shakl al-aṣnam." Fatwa 193021. December 6, 2012. https://bit.ly/38RfYHR.

2014. "Ruling on Sexual Intercourse with One's Polytheistic Slave-Woman." Fatwa 272452. November 14. www.islamweb.net/en/fatwa/272452/?Option=FatwaId.

2015. "Ruling on Killing an Apostate without the Ruler's permission." Fatwa 17707. August 17. www.islamweb.net/en/fatwa/17707/ruling-on-killing-an-apostate-without-the-rulers-permission.

Jablawi, Hosam al-. 2016. "A Closer Look at the Educational System of ISIS." Atlantic Council. www.atlanticcouncil.org/blogs/syriasource/a-closer-look-at-isis-s-educational-system.

Kéchichian, Joseph A. 1986. "The Role of the Ulama in the Politics of an Islamic State: The Case of Saudi Arabia." *International Journal of Middle East Studies* 18, no. 1: 53–71.

1990. "Islamic Revivalism and Change in Saudi Arabia: Juhayman Al-ʿUtaybi's 'Letters' to the Saudi People." *Muslim World* 18, no. 1: 1–16.

2008. *Faysal: Saudi Arabia's King for All Seasons*. Gainesville: University Press of Florida.

Kramer, Martin. 1990. "Khomeini's Messengers: The Disputed Pilgrimage of Islam." In *Religious Radicalism and Politics in the Middle East*, edited by Emmanuel Sivan and Menachem Friedman, 161–87. Albany: SUNY Press.

Lacroix, Stéphane. 2009. "Between Religion and Apoliticism: Nasir Al-Din Al-Albani and His Impact on the Shaping of Contemporary Salafism." In *Global Salafism: Islam's New Religious Movement*, edited by Roel Meijer, 58–80. New York: Columbia University Press.

2011. *Awakening Islam the Politics of Religious Dissent in Contemporary Saudi Arabia*. Translated by George Holoch. Cambridge, MA: Harvard University Press.

Lauzière, Henri. 2016. *The Making of Salafism: Islamic Reform in the Twentieth Century*. New York: Columbia University Press.

Maqdisī, Abū Muḥammad al-. n.d. *Millat Ibrāhīm – The Religion of Abraham*. Translated by al-Ṭibyān Publications. Al-Ṭibyān Publications.

1994. *Millat Ibrāhīm*. www.tawhed.ws.

Meijer, Roel, ed. 2009. *Global Salafism: Islam's New Religious Movement*. New York: Columbia University Press.

Mouline, Nabil. 2016. "Les Oulémas du Palais: Parcours des Membres du Comité des Grands Oulémas." In vol. 2 of *Wahhabism: Doctrine and Development*, edited by Esther Peskes, 206–29. Berlin: Gerlach Press.

Nordbruch, Götz, Jochen Müller, and Deniz Ünlü. 2014. "Salafismus als Ausweg? Zur Attracktivität des Salafismus unter Jugenlichen." In *Salafismus in Deutschland: Ursprünge und Gefahren einer islamisch-fundamentalistischen Bewegung*, edited by Thorsten Gerald Schneiders, 363–70. Bielefeld, Germany: Transcript Verlag.

Obaid, Nawaf, and Saud al-Sarhan. 2014. "The Saudis Can Crush ISIS." *The New York Times*, September 8. www.nytimes.com/2014/09/09/opinion/the-saudis-can-crush-isis.html.

Pall, Zoltan. 2014. "Kuwaiti Salafism and Its Growing Influence in the Levant." Carnegie Endowment for International Peace. May. http://carnegieendowment.org/2014/05/07/kuwaiti-salafism-and-its-growing-influence-in-levant.

Peskes, Esther. 2016a. "Introduction to Wahhabism: Doctrine and Development." In vol. 1 of *Wahhabism: Doctrine and Development*, edited by Esther Peskes, 1–32. Berlin: Gerlach Press.

Peskes, Esther, ed. 2016b. *Wahhabism: Doctrine and Development*. 2 vols. Berlin: Gerlach Press.

Piscatori, James. 2016. "Managing God's Guests: The Pilgrimage, Saudi Arabia, and the Politics of Legitimacy." In vol. 2 of *Wahhabism: Doctrine and Development*, edited by Esther Peskes, 140–77. Berlin: Gerlach Press.

Rabil, Robert G. 2014. *Salafism in Lebanon: From Apoliticism to Transnational Jihadism*. Washington, DC: Georgetown University Press.

Rasheed, Madawi al-. 2002. *A History of Saudi Arabia*. New York: Cambridge University Press.

    2005b. "Saudi Religious Transnationalism in London." In *Transnational Connections and the Arab Gulf*, edited by Madawi al-Rasheed, 149–67. London: Routledge.

    2007. *Contesting the Saudi State: Islamic Voices from a New Generation*. Cambridge: Cambridge University Press.

    2008a. "The Minaret and the Palace: Obedience at Home and Rebellion Abroad." In *Kingdom without Borders: Saudi Political, Religious and Media Frontiers*, edited by Madawi al-Rasheed, 199–219. New York: Columbia University Press.

Rasheed, Madawi al-, ed. 2005a. *Transnational Connections and the Arab Gulf*. London: Routledge.

    2008b. *Kingdom without Borders: Saudi Political, Religious and Media Frontiers*. New York: Columbia University Press.

Sardar, Ziauddin. 2014. "The Destruction of Mecca." *The New York Times*, September 30. www.nytimes.com/2014/10/01/opinion/the-destruction-of-mecca.html.

Schneiders, Thorsten Gerald, ed. 2014. *Salafismus in Deutschland: Ursprünge und Gefahren einer islamisch-fundamentalistischen Bewegung*. Bielefeld, Germany: Transcript Verlag.

Sells, Michael A. 2006. "War as Worship, Worship as War." Religion and Culture Forum. December. https://divinity.uchicago.edu/sites/default/files/imce/pdfs/webforum/122006/war_as_worship.pdf.

    2013. "'Armageddon' in Christian, Sunni, and Shia Traditions." In *The Oxford Handbook of Religion and Violence*, edited by Mark Juergensmeyer, Margo Kitts, and Michael K Jerryson, 467–95. New York: Oxford University Press.

Shaheed, Shah Ismail. 1995. *Taqwiyat-Ul-Iman* [The strengthening of the faith]. Riyadh: Dar-us-Salam Publications.

Shehabi, Saeed. 2008. "The Role of Religious Ideology in the Expansionist Policies of Saudi Arabia." In *Kingdom without Borders: Saudi Political, Religious and Media Frontiers*, edited by Madawi al-Rasheed, 183–97. New York: Columbia University Press.

Syrian Observatory for Human Rights. 2015. "IS Distributes Its Own New Curriculum in the City of Mayadin." www.syriahr.com/en/2015/02/is-distributes-its-own-new-curriculum-in-the-city-of-al-mayadin/.

Trofimov, Yaroslav. 2007. *The Siege of Mecca: The Forgotten Uprising at Islam's Holiest Shrine and the Birth of Al-Qaeda*. New York: Doubleday.

306   *Michael A. Sells*

US Department of Treasury. 2008. "Kuwaiti Charity Designated for Bankrolling Al Qaida Network." June 13. www.treasury.gov/press-center/press-releases/Pages/hp1023.aspx.

'Uthaymīn, 'Abdullāh al-Ṣāliḥ al-. 2009. *Muhammad Ibn 'Abd al-Wahhab: The Man and His Works*. London: I.B. Tauris.

'Uthaymīn, Muḥammad Ṣāliḥ al-. 2010. *Commentary on the Three Fundamentals of Muhammad Bin 'Abdul-Wahhab = Sharḥ Thalāthat al-uṣūl*. Riyadh: Darussalam.

Wagemakers, Joas. 2009. "The Transformation of a Radical Concept: al-Wala' wa-l-Bara' in the Ideology of Abu Muhammad al-Maqdisi." In *Global Salafism: Islam's New Religious Movement*, edited by Roel Meijer, 81–106. New York: Columbia University Press.

    2012. *A Quietist Jihadi: The Ideology and Influence of Abu Muhammad al-Maqdisi*. Cambridge: Cambridge University Press.

    2015. "'The Kāfir Religion of the West': Tafkīr of Democracy and Democrats by Radical Islamists." In *Accusations of Unbelief in Islam: A Diachronic Perspective on Tafkīr*, edited by Camilla Adang, Hassan Ansari, Maribel Fierro, and Sabine Schmidtke, 327–53. Leiden: Brill.

Wiktorowicz, Quintan. 2001. *The Management of Islamic Activism: Salafis, the Muslim Brotherhood, and State Power in Jordan*. Albany: SUNY Press.

Wilts, Alexandra. 2017. "Donald Trump Signs $110bn Arms Deal Hours after Landing in Saudi Arabia." *The Independent*, May 20. www.independent.co.uk/news/world/amer icas/us-politics/donald-trump-latest-saudi-arabia-billions-arms-deal-military-sales-a7746601.html.

Zaman, Muhammad Qasim. 2007. *The Ulama in Contemporary Islam: Custodians of Change*. Princeton: Princeton University Press.

PART VII

Northern Ireland

12

Protestantism and Settler Identity

The Ambiguous Case of Northern Ireland

David Lloyd [*]

The colonial situation manufactures colonialists, just as it manufactures the colonized.

Albert Memmi, *The Colonizer and the Colonized*

In this chapter, I discuss the ambivalent relation of Protestantism to settler identity in the post-1922 period in Northern Ireland. Whereas in the Republic, Irish Protestants generally, if gradually, learned to accommodate to the new state and the political domination of the majority Catholic population, in Northern Ireland, Protestantism became rapidly identified with the state and saw itself as embattled against a perpetually rebellious or recalcitrant Catholic population. The state that defined itself as "a Protestant state for a Protestant people" took on the political, cultural, and legal forms of a settler-colonial state with a vengeance. Attitudes that might have been thought to be waning during the nineteenth century hardened again and produced a culture of Protestant supremacy that expressed itself in triumphalist cultural forms and in both legalized and informal discrimination against Catholics. In this respect, since the Protestant experience was so different in the south, we can see Northern Ireland as a very clear "laboratory" for the cultural and political formations of the settler colony: the artificiality of the state and of Protestant adherence to and dependence on its institutional forms clarifies the tendencies of settler-colonial entities; the necessary supremacism or racism, even in a racially indistinguishable population; the sectarianization of working-class allegiances; the disproportionately violent response of the state to the demand for rights; and the necessity for the withdrawal of "mother country" support for a peace process to begin – all correlate with similar tendencies in other locations. But the peculiar history of Northern Ireland highlights the extent to which settler mentalities are the effect of a structure of dominance, not an indelible and unchangeable given. Transformation of the structure of domination, whether by internal or external pressures, furnishes space for the transformation of mentalities. The description of Northern Ireland as suffering from religious convictions that determined the form

[*] In memory of Patrick Wolfe, 1949–2016.

309

of the conflict obscures this underlying settler-colonial structure, even as it suggests how religion functions as an alibi for settler mentalities.

In light of this argument, as I argue at the end of the chapter, Northern Ireland and its internal conflicts show remarkable affinities with the situation of Palestine and Israel. While analogies with both Palestine and Israel are frequently invoked by the conflicting parties in Northern Ireland – Republicans and nationalists, on the one hand; Loyalists or Unionists, on the other – this does not mean that the Northern Irish peace process can easily be invoked as a model that would suggest a just way to end Israel's colonization of Palestine. Many of the conditions for the relative success of that process are lacking in the Palestinian-Israeli case, in particular the will of exogenous state actors such as the United States to exert the requisite pressure to end Israel's virtual monopoly of coercive power. What the example of Northern Ireland does offer is an indication that the entrenched structures of racial or ethnic supremacy in settler-colonial societies are not necessarily permanent or endemic, but capable of transformation if and when relations of domination are dismantled. Bleak as prospects for a just resolution of the Palestinian-Israeli conflict may seem at present, the capacity for settler-colonial societies and their supremacist ideologies to undergo structural and institutional transformation is not to be dismissed.

THE SETTLER'S LESSON

No one could have grown up in 1960s Ireland, north or south of the border that the partition of the island imposed in 1922, without feeling at least some of the impact of what was generally cast as religious difference. Partition notoriously created in the small island of Ireland two semi-postcolonial cultures that underwent quite different trajectories of development and quite different relations to the religious questions that, since the Reformation, had been intertwined with British colonial rule and Irish resistance to it. While England from the 1530s became a largely Protestant nation under an established Anglican Church with the monarch as its head, Ireland was divided between a predominantly "native" Catholic population and a predominantly "settler" Protestant population. The latter was formed largely by the so-called plantations, from the time of Elizabeth I in the late sixteenth century through to the Williamite wars of the late seventeenth century, which installed loyal English, Scots, and Welsh settlers on land expropriated from the rebellious Irish. Historically, then, Ireland might be seen as a typical settler colony, complicated by the fact that to a large extent religious adherence took the place of putatively visual marks of racial difference.[1] That aside, the dynamics of settler colonialism – for which, as some have argued, Ireland represented an early laboratory – followed in a modified way the pattern outlined by Patrick Wolfe in his seminal theoretical and historical

---

[1] The literature debating Ireland's colonial status is voluminous, as is that on the racialization of the Irish. For a useful review of both debates, see Murphy (1999, 11–32).

Protestantism and Settler Identity in Northern Ireland

work: the elimination of the natives and seizure of the land – through a mix of genocidal famines and massacres, eviction and transportation – alternated with the exploitation of their labor, primarily in agriculture, and the cultural elimination that took the form of assimilation or "Anglicization."[2]

That blend of or alternation between elimination and exploitation meant that settler colonialism in Ireland came to resemble or anticipate the models familiar from North Africa, as described by Frantz Fanon or Albert Memmi, more than those of the Anglo-Saxon colonies like the United States, Canada, or Australia, which took the genocidal logic of elimination much further.[3] Irish decolonization as articulated through its nationalist movements initially took a nonsectarian, Republican form, inspired by French and American revolutionary ideals: the United Irishmen who led a violently suppressed rebellion in 1798 represented something like the "creole nationalism" that Benedict Anderson describes in Latin America in the same period.[4] But in the course of the nineteenth century, national identity gradually became difficult to separate from religious adherence: to be Irish grew increasingly synonymous with being Catholic, while loyalism or Unionism (loyalty to the Crown and to the Union with the United Kingdom) were regarded as Protestant political positions, despite the genuine and strongly argued commitment of nationalist thinkers to a nonsectarian vision and the high degree of Protestant participation in the mid-century forging of Irish nationalism.[5] In the wake of the Treaty of 1922, which ended a brief but brutal war of independence, the Irish Free State emerged as a conservative Catholic republic, while the statelet of Northern Ireland remained part of the United Kingdom albeit with an independent parliament that managed domestic affairs. The latter was designed by demographic calculus to maintain a Protestant majority, ensuring what one Unionist politician explicitly denominated "a Protestant government for a Protestant people."[6] Sporadic episodes of sectarian violence – of which Catholics were the principal victims, especially in the months immediately following the partition in 1922 – regularly reinforced ethnic or communal segregation in Northern Ireland in a process that might be called

---

[2] See Wolfe (2001). On Ireland as an early site for the articulation of racial capitalism, see C. Robinson (2000, 36–43). On the role of Ireland as a testing ground for later New World colonization, see Canny (1979, 17–44).

[3] Lustick (1993) has usefully compared Ireland and Algeria.

[4] For Benedict Anderson's notion of Creole nationalism, see Anderson (2006, 47–65). On the 1798 uprising in Ireland and its at least aspirational nonsectarian ideology, see R. F. Foster (1989, 264–82).

[5] Protestant leaders within the Young Ireland movement included Thomas Davis, its intellectual inspiration, John Mitchel, the most radical of all, and William Smith O'Brien, the nationalist aristocrat. On the waning of secular nationalism after Young Ireland and 1848, see R. F. Foster (1989, 310–17).

[6] This description of Northern Ireland has known many variations and has a genealogy difficult to pin down. One of its earliest formulations may have been that of James Craig, 1st Viscount Craigavon, Unionist politician and first prime minister: "We are a Protestant Parliament for a Protestant state." This phrase is also attributed to Basil Brooke, later Lord Brookeborough, another leading Unionist politician; the sentiment is also expressed as "a Protestant state" or "a Protestant government." See Bew, Gibbon, and Patterson (2002, 6–7).

David Lloyd

"ethnic cleansing," which continued periodically to reinforce the internal segregation of the state.[7] Nonetheless, Northern Ireland remained home to a large minority
of Catholics, many if not all of whom continued to embrace, if only in principle,
the goal of an independent and united Ireland incorporating the whole island.
That demographic issue, a product of the political artifice by which the state was
constructed, determined the consolidation in Northern Ireland of lines of intercommunal antagonism and containment that would in any other colonial society
be recognized immediately as racially based. In the Republic to the south, on the
contrary, the social and political significance of religion has gradually but indisput-
ably waned, in terms of its practical influence and its cultural salience.

The point that this chapter will elaborate can be illustrated quite graphically by
a personal anecdote that first opened for me a question regarding the different
articulations and roles of religious identity north and south of the Irish border.
My initial encounter with Northern Irish Protestant attitudes came when, in
September 1969, at the very outset of the civil conflict known euphemistically as
"the Troubles," my southern Protestant parents sent me to a boarding school in
Belfast to gain a British education. Soon after I arrived there as a young teenager,
I was taken aside by a schoolmate. "Come here, you," he said. "You're a wee Fenian
from the south; you know nothing. I'm telling you," he asserted, "you can tell
a Catholic. They've got their eyes too close together." He went on to explain in
some detail the inferiority and deficiencies of the Catholic population, but what
struck me even at the time was the conviction with which he maintained the visual
self-evidence of ethnic or racial difference even while admitting that the evidence
would not be perceptible to any outsider.

This lesson – delivered to me by a member of an elite Unionist family – was also,
I discovered much later, my introduction to the very efficacious Northern Irish
practice of "telling," a practice which anthropologists have studied in some detail. As
I rapidly discovered, and as those anthropologists have affirmed, once one is initiated
in the lore, it proves indeed possible to tell, with remarkable accuracy, the religious
and therefore cultural identity of any stranger from a whole complex of audiovisual
markers – from accent to gait and garb (though not, I remain convinced, from the
width of people's brows). "Telling," in a society that was marked by what anthropologist Allen Feldman has called "a proliferation of interfaces" that cut through an
otherwise small and intimate geography, is a practice that becomes critical to
survival.[8] It was a means to negotiate the peculiar geography of a state that contained
an ethnically complex and extensively miscegenated population lacking in salient

---

[7] See Brewer and Higgins (1997, 87–134). See also, for a spatial analysis of the impact of the sectarian
violence of 1922, Cunningham (2013). O'Leary (2017, 821) refers to the "forced displacements" of
Catholics in 1922 as "what today is called ethnic or sectarian cleansing" and remarks that "Since
pogroms had worked, they would be tried again, in 1935 and in 1969."

[8] On both the "interfaces" between sectarian communities and the practice of "telling", see Feldman
(1989, 35, 56–59).

visual racial markers and had, therefore, to *produce* racial differences as an instrument for maintaining and naturalizing what was, to all intents and purposes, a settler-colonial mode of domination. *Religious* difference, as my fellow student was trying to explain, had become the modality through which colonial relations reproduced the appearance of *racial* differences on which power depended. And it had to be made visible, self-evident. I was being taught what one might call settler-colonial common sense: religious differences that were expressed culturally and politically were naturalized as if they could be read from the kinds of phenotypical or biological marks that racist logics assume to be immediately legible, self-evident, or obvious to those in the know.[9]

Of course, the very fact of my being in this particular school – in a state where almost every educational institution was sectarian – marked me as "culturally" Protestant and – in the Irish expression for anyone who is inclined to favor British cultural and political institutions – a "West Briton." It was a school originally founded to educate the sons of Presbyterian ministers and had evolved to the point where it had pretensions to being the "Northern Irish Eton"; certainly, it aimed to prepare the sons of Ulster for entry into British universities. I was expected to absorb and benefit from the advantages of a British education. Ironically, my first lesson was in the contradictions of Britishness, whose problematic status in Ireland I will elaborate below. At the time, that lesson was a little baffling: to a southern Protestant, the modes of quasi-racial differentiation I had just encountered were entirely unfamiliar. Certainly I understood – and could already play – the intricate game of religious and class identification still current in my Dublin childhood, whereby strangers' backgrounds could be identified from the suburb or even street they came from and whence one could therefore "tell" a Catholic from a Protestant. But already the history of the postcolonial Republic had deprived those differentiations of any uniform link to cultural or political domination. If the southern Protestant population to a large degree had retained property and wealth, they no longer enjoyed any monopoly of political power in the Irish Republic. So what shocked me in this Belfast pedagogy was the raw encounter with a form of supremacism that was so unfamiliar and which, from my present vantage, indicates the degree to which Irish postcolonialism – or post-partition Ireland – has to be grasped within the bifurcated context of a process, halting and incomplete, of decolonization within one entity – the south – paralleled by the maintenance and intensification of a very deliberate settler colonialism in the other – the north.

Let me pause here to unfold the terminology that my schoolmate so casually deployed. "Fenian" (from the nineteenth-century Republican movement of that name), like its cognates "*Taig*" (from the Irish *Tadhg*, or poet, often translated as Timothy), or "Mick" (from the commonly Catholic name Michael), or sometimes simply "rebel," was, in common usage, effectively a synonym for Catholic. However,

---

[9] Rifkin (2014) anticipated me in using this expression.

the very fact that I, a southern Protestant, could be interpellated by this term – on this and many subsequent occasions – indicates that the term is more political than religious. Ethnic differentiation in Northern Ireland was not driven in any profound way by religious conviction as such – the vagueness in most people's minds of the theological differences around the nature of transubstantiation in the Eucharist that had preoccupied post-Reformation Europe was evident – but by a series of markers of disloyalty to the state, to the UK, to British polity, or simply to what was initially framed with great deliberateness and artifice as "a Protestant state for a Protestant people." The persisting ambiguity as to whether the Troubles represented religious, civil, or colonial conflict lies in this assertion of the *Protestant* nature of the state, which affirmed the tie to the historically Protestant United Kingdom and opposition to the predominantly Catholic Republic while ensuring the privileging of Northern Irish Protestants over their Catholic counterparts at every level and in every societal domain. Admittedly, Northern Ireland was something of a rump state with purely domestic powers, and likewise in almost every respect an anomaly within the United Kingdom, for both its sectarian constitution and its armed police force. And the very assertion of an explicitly "Protestant state" in twentieth-century Europe was no less anomalous, signaling an identification that was both the expression of a conflict and the institutional means that ensured its prolongation.

Despite these contradictions, whether that conflict was essentially religious – an anachronistic holdover from the confessional wars of post-Reformation Europe – remains a peculiarly vexing question. Some would deny it altogether: As Geoffrey Bell (1976, 13) put it, "Religious affiliation is merely a manifestation of the divisions in Ireland, not its cause." Historian Brian Walker insists rather differently on the inextricability of religion and politics, though without ascribing the political conflict's causes to religious affiliation:

> In Ireland in the late nineteenth century and in Northern Ireland today there was, and is a genuine conflict over religion and nationalism. ... The sharp division in party politics, with Protestant and unionist, on the one side, and Catholic and nationalist, on the other, emerged in Ulster at the general elections of 1885–6 and has remained ever since the nub of our situation, in spite of constitutional and territorial changes. ... Religion and nationalism became firmly intertwined, giving us the special type of politics and sectarian confrontation found today. (Walker 1992, 61)

But Walker's assertion of the "intertwining" of religion and politics, of its imbrication with what are, in fact, two competing nationalisms turns out on reflection to be singularly unhelpful: It does little to clarify the *dynamic* of the conflict, suggesting even a certain parity between both religious and political forces. There is only a short distance between this kind of analytical terminology and the short-lived school of "Two Traditions" thinking that sought for a while to promote the notion of two

Protestantism and Settler Identity in Northern Ireland

equivalent and therefore reconcilable cultural communities in Northern Ireland without interrogating – or even naming – the colonial histories that had defined them.[10]

What, we may well ask, is the nature of this "intertwining" to which Walker refers? Is political unionism or nationalism the expression of religious affiliation, and the conflict therefore a residual phenomenon of seventeenth-century religious wars, lingering long after other nations have resolved or forgotten them? Or is religious affiliation merely one mode in which political positions – ideological and/or structural – get articulated? To riff on Stuart Hall's famous observation that "race is the modality in which class is lived," is religion the modality in which the political is lived, or is politics the modality in which religious difference is lived? (see Hall 1980, 341). Religious difference, or religious sectarianism, would indeed be the more accurate term here than "religion": What is operative is not the positive theological or ritual content of religious belief, but the invocation of *religion as differential*. As in the anecdote I related at the outset, religion is a marker that performs the work that race does in other settler-colonial settings.

In a short narrative, "Question Time," Belfast writer Ciaran Carson (1989) captures very precisely the contours of this mode of racialization through non-visible markers, gathering together the figures of settler-colonial racial positions, the reading of the signs that act as markers of territorialized difference, the repeated experience over time of similar encounters with the inimical other, the threat of violence that attends them, and, above all, the insistently pedagogical form that is required to enforce so performative a system of difference. The first instance recalls a childhood experience of deliberately transgressing the well-inculcated boundary lines between the sectarian communities:

> *Never go by Cupar Street*, my father would say, and I knew this was a necessary prohibition without asking why, for Cupar Street was one of those areas where the Falls and Shankill joined together as unhappy Siamese twins, one sporadically and mechanically beating the other round the head, where the Cullens, Finnegans and Reillys [all considered Catholic or native Irish names] merged with Todds and Camerons and Wallaces [Scotch Irish or Protestant names]. One day I did come home by Cupar Street, egged on by a fellow pupil. Nothing happened, and we felt like Indian scouts penetrating British lines, the high of invisibility. (Carson 1989, 59)

Inevitably, of course, Carson and his companion are eventually spotted and set on by a group of Protestant boys who subject them to a "question time" or interrogation in order to "tell" their identity, "For who knew what we were, who could tell?" (Carson 1989, 59). The subsequent "hiding" by his father reinforces the lesson not to

---

[10] On the two "cultural traditions" of Northern Ireland, see, for example, Crozier (1989). The "Cultural Traditions" group was a British government-sponsored entity that sought to replace the notion of an economically and politically conflicted society with the notion of "cultural pluralism." For a critique of the notion of "parity of esteem" that is the correlative of the "Two Traditions" in the peace process, see S. Kelly (2007).

transgress the invisible yet well-rehearsed interfaces that demarcate the spaces of difference. Nevertheless, many years later, while "out for a harmless spin on the bike," the adult Carson relives that boyhood experience in the midst of the exacerbated violence of the Troubles. This time, it is his own people, suspicious of his coming homeward from a Protestant neighborhood, who submit him to an interrogation that is in fact an investigation into the intimacy with which he knows the sectarian "ghetto" – its streets, denizens, shop names. Carson furnishes a "map," "pieced together bit by bit" (Carson 1989, 63), that is at once a chart of place and street names and a diagram of ethnic differentiation coded in terms that do not appear to be markers of race but that nonetheless function with the same potential for discrimination and ultimately violence. As Feldman (1989, 27) has put it, "Protestant and Catholic communities map themselves into specific historical and spatial arrangements, such as kinship, endogamy, and ethnically defined ethics of residence." These "mappings" are entirely familiar from what Frantz Fanon termed the "compartmentalization" of colonial space, but in Northern Ireland that racially constitutive division of space was organized around religion rather than explicitly around race (Fanon 1968, 37). Indeed, rather than consider race to be the natural foundation of difference articulated in spatial differentiation, we might follow Wolfe (2001, 14) in understanding racialization to be "a response to the crisis occasioned when colonizers are threatened with the requirement to share social space with the colonized."

STATES OF SIEGE

In what remains to my mind one of the most penetrating brief essays on the Northern Irish conflict, "The Limits of Britishness," Jennifer Todd (1988) developed a nuanced and helpful approach to the ways in which religious difference was articulated in Northern Ireland in ways that transformed the acknowledgment of difference into the grounds for a distinctly "settler-colonial" sense of superiority. Todd identifies three aspects of Protestant political formation: its cultural aspect, its state-centered aspect, and its supremacist aspect, though it is important to note that she calls this formation "unionism" and omits any specific religious motives. As I suggested above, Protestantism is the marker of a difference rather than the signifier of any particular theological content. The anecdote with which I began my chapter offers some prompts to analysis that would unpack not only these different "aspects" but also the specific differential introduced by the state's active formalization of them. It stages two quite distinct "Protestant" subject positions. On the one hand, southern Protestants gradually – that is, over a couple of generations at least – assimilated to or, perhaps, simply resigned themselves to the shift in power relations in the Free State that in 1949 became the Republic of Ireland. At first, southern Protestants largely continued to identify with British culture and institutions, giving meaning to the term "Anglo-Irish" that, almost indistinguishable in practice from the designation "Protestant," expressed the difference of the Republic's religious minority on cultural rather than religious grounds. They listened to the BBC, read *The Sunday Times*, and in many cases attended British schools and universities. In many cases, that identification with British cultural institutions stood for a rejection of the conservative, repressive, and insular policies of the Free State in its first decades, but the gradual liberalization of cultural attitudes in the Republic since the 1960s tended to obviate such self-distantiation from Irishness. Such conservative attitudes, associated with the recognition of the Roman Catholic religion as the religion of the majority in the 1937 constitution as well as the close identification of national identity with Catholicism and restrictive social mores, also gave some legitimacy to Unionist arguments for the civic pluralism of the British state, which I discuss below.[11] In recent decades, however, the term Anglo-Irish has virtually vanished from common parlance except as a quaint anachronism or an adjective for interstate relations: Few Protestants born after the mid-1960s would use the term as a self-description, and the social and cultural content of the term has largely evaporated in a society where religion has ceased to be a critical marker of national or even ethnic identity.

Northern Protestants, on the other hand, in establishing and seeking to maintain "a Protestant state for a Protestant people," committed themselves to producing and maintaining those forms of distinction and supremacism, without which – as we know by analogy from Albert Memmi's classic analysis of settler colonialism, *The Colonizer and the Colonized* – the colony has no meaning for the colonist. For reasons that I will address more fully below, I want to emphasize here the notion that in Northern Ireland both the distinction – the religious differential – and its articulation as a mode of supremacism were produced and maintained with a certain degree of effort and artifice. Invocation of the very different experience of southern Protestants suggests the possibility of an equally different, ultimately "postcolonial" relation to the settler-colonial past that the very establishment of Northern Ireland – an artificial entity constituted to ensure sectarian domination by the demographic artifice of the Boundary Commission – was designed to preclude (Laffan 1983, 123). In some respects, then, I am suggesting that, in contrast to the experience of the Free State and Republic of Ireland, the establishment of the state of Northern Ireland consolidated the history and status of the Protestant population – formerly a minority in the island as a whole – as an institutionally and psychically settler-colonial population.[12]

Protestantism functions, then, as a racial-colonial and political differential rather than a theological commitment, however deeply many Protestants maintained their

---

[11] For an excellent account of the cultural divides between Northern Ireland and the Republic, aligned along both religious lines and the tradition-modernity opposition, see Cleary (2002, 66–79).

[12] As Clayton (1998, 56) puts it, from 1922, "Northern Protestants now effectively had their own settler state." In this essay, Clayton reviews the literature on Northern Ireland as a settler colony and emphasizes that paradigm's explanatory power.

FIGURE 12.1 Loyalist mural, Derry, Northern Ireland

interpretations of the Christian faith. There is, indeed, a striking absence of Protestant religious content in most popular expressions of Protestant or Unionist supremacy, an absence that is graphically illustrated by the murals that decorate the gable ends and walls of Loyalist districts of Ulster (see Figures 12.1–12.5).[13] Such murals mobilize a common if highly selective body of historical memories of what are mostly moments of danger and triumph, loyalty and militarism, morphing into images through which the present-day conflict gets interpreted. While their most common icons were of William of Orange at that foundational moment of Protestant triumph, the Battle of the Boyne in 1689, or the sacrifice of loyal Northern Irish volunteers in the Battle of the Somme in 1916, other murals invoked moments of danger and siege, like the "No Surrender" that was the rallying cry of the besieged Protestant citizens of Derry/Londonderry, 1688–89. The more recent murals that emerged in the Troubles tended to blend those motifs with the incidents of the moment, such as the representation of the Loyalist paramilitary Michael Stone, who shot up a Republican funeral in West Belfast, as a latter-day William of Orange. They are, as I shall elaborate further, icons that embody the cultural rather than the religious ambiguities of a settler-colonial psyche, marking the oscillation between the triumphalism that undergirds the sense of supremacy and the defensive siege

---

[13] On this peculiarity, Clayton (1998, 48) remarks that, "actual doctrinal differences are hardly ever seen as fundamental to the conflict." His summary of the literature on religion as a motivating cause of the Troubles concludes, "religion is not an independent variable, and ... causal factors for conflict on the Northern Ireland scale must be sought elsewhere" (Clayton 1998, 49).

Protestantism and Settler Identity in Northern Ireland 319

FIGURE 12.2 Loyalist mural of Michael Stone, Belfast, Northern Ireland

FIGURE 12.3 Loyalist mural of Michael Stone as King William III, Derry, Northern Ireland

FIGURE 12.4 Loyalist Battle of the Somme mural, Belfast, Northern Ireland

FIGURE 12.5 Loyalist paramilitary mural, Belfast, Northern Ireland

mentality that betrays the anxious sense of questionable legitimacy and outnumbered vulnerability. Both psychic poles are mobilized in the peculiar violent outbursts that typify – as Memmi once pointed out – settler-colonial dominance over their subordinate populations (Memmi 1967, 66).

Protestantism and Settler Identity in Northern Ireland 321

Yet – as Todd points out – what is being ambivalently celebrated and defended in these icons of Protestant supremacy, beyond any mere reactiveness to the seemingly irrepressible challenge of Irish nationalism, is an idea that Protestantism is indelibly linked with a commitment to civic culture and its institutional forms. The Unionist faith is that "British institutions embody freedom, individual liberties, democracy, and justice," and the murals as icons appeal to the symbols of those institutions: flag and crown, military sacrifice and pride, and, above all, to that moment of foundation not only of Protestant supremacy, but also of constitutional monarchy and parliamentary government, 1690 and the Glorious Revolution against Stuart absolutism. As Robert L McCartney, then a member of the Ulster Unionist Party, put it: "The true and essential Union is not an exclusive union of loyalists and protestants, but a union between peoples who believe in liberal democracy and civil and religious liberty for all in the fullest sense of a pluralist society."[14] Accordingly, and despite the socially and politically reactionary nature of most Unionist political expression, "being British is progressive." Indeed, as Joe Cleary has observed, even the somewhat more liberal "New Unionists" contended

> that the strongest argument in defence of unionism is that it is premised on a claim to citizenship of the UK, which is, in their view, a multi-ethnic, multi-national, multi-faith society. Unionist allegiance to this pluralist state is, they assert, inherently more progressive than Northern nationalist allegiance to a mono-national Republic of Ireland dominated by one ethnic and religious community. (Cleary 2002, 41)

But this assertion of the progressive nature of the polity irresistibly tends – in a way that is all too familiar from other colonial contexts – to become an assertion of cultural superiority. As Todd (1988, 13) summarizes the Protestant logic, "Protestant culture is more civilised than Catholic culture. Protestant societies are tolerant, liberal and modernising. Catholic societies are superstitious, authoritarian and reactionary."

What begins, then, as no more than "an identification with British social and political institutions" devolves into a constitutive claim to what Edward Said (1979, 7) termed "positional superiority." In Todd's terms, that sense of superiority "involves an essentially relational mode of being British in which British identity is constituted only in opposition to an Other identity – for unionists, the opposition is to Irish identity – and in which the positive qualities of the British are defined in terms of the negative qualities of the Other – the Irish" (Todd 1988, 13). This third aspect of Unionism, she argues, "is inherently supremacist in its conceptual structure; equality between British identity and Irish identity is not possible because Irishness is constituted as the opposite of Britishness and a negative image of the Irish is implicit in the positive self-image of the British" (Todd 1988, 15).

---

[14] Robert McCartney, quoted in Todd (1988, 13). Initially a member of the Ulster Unionist Party, McCartney established the United Kingdom Unionist Party to contest elections to the Northern Ireland Forum and the related talks, which started in 1996. He opposed the subsequent Belfast Agreement in the May 1998 referendum.

An insuperable contradiction thus enters into the claims of political Protestantism that is nonetheless intrinsic to its logic, even in its more liberally inclined advocates. In the unhappy oscillation of the idea of Protestantism in Northern Ireland between the name for a secular and progressive civil society and the name of a religious and sectarian identification, the exclusionary nature of the latter continually infects the practices of the civil or civic. That contradiction found persistent institutional expression in the systemically discriminatory nature of the Protestant state: in the gerrymandering of constituencies that consolidated Unionist political power in what was already a statelet effectively brought into being by gerrymandering; in discrimination in the distribution of public housing; in the workplace, where Protestants were notoriously promoted over more qualified or experienced Catholics; and in access to welfare and education. R. F. Foster (1989, 582–83) summarizes the impact of "structural" discrimination that led to these outcomes: "Catholics were still [in 1971] disproportionately represented in unskilled jobs, and Protestants in skilled employment," while, to cite a few of his examples, Catholics, who made up "31 per cent of the economically active population," accounted for only "7 per cent of 'company secretaries and registrars' and 'personal managers,' 8 per cent of university teachers, 9 per cent of local authority senior officers, 19 per cent of medical practitioners and 23 per cent of lawyers." Similarly, "a 'startlingly high proportion' of alleged discrimination in housing, political representation and employment occurred in the west of the province," the predominantly Catholic region of the state. Discrimination also found expression in the almost exclusively Protestant police force that maintained a constant if often informal surveillance of the Catholic population, purveying a low-level but quotidian intimidation in the process, as Seamus Heaney so memorably recorded in *North*: "all around us, though / We hadn't named it, the ministry of fear."[15]

In a way familiar from other racial states, from the southern states of the USA to South Africa or Israel, these discriminatory practices were required to maintain the vertical integration of working-class Protestants with Unionist landowners and capitalist entrepreneurs, who in all other respects happily exploited their coreligionists.[16] They were requisite to the maintenance of political hegemony and as a means to contain the "demographic time bomb" of a supposedly more concupiscent Catholic population, casually described in colloquial terms as "breeding like rabbits," which threatened eventually to overturn the carefully constructed and maintained Protestant majority that was the statelet's rationale. Above all, and most significant and far-reaching in its implications, was the permanent retention of the Special Powers Act, a British emergency provision dating from the colonial nineteenth century that was never removed from the books from the foundation

[15] Heaney (1975, 84). For an extended discussion of Heaney's poems that deal with the experience of living as a minority under sectarian and potentially violent law, see B. Robinson (2001).

[16] On the necessity for a conservative Unionist leadership to secure the unity of the Protestant population by furnishing social welfare, see Bew, Gibbon, and Patterson (2002, 86–89).

of the state in 1922 until the arrival of British troops in 1969, heralding direct rule from Westminster and effective martial law.[17] The maintenance of the Special Powers Act is symptomatic of the extent to which Northern Ireland has been imagined as a frontier state, one in which – as political scientist Frank Wright succinctly put it – "the hidden violence of metropolitan culture is acted out on the 'ethnic frontier'" (quoted in Todd 1988, 14). The very fact of its remaining in force meant that Northern Ireland substantially represented a continuation of the British colonial state in Ireland, in which, between 1800 and 1922, over 100 emergency powers or "Coercion Acts" had been declared (Tomlinson 1995, 196). The state of exception is, for all intents and purposes, the legal expression of the psychic "state of siege" that afflicts the settler colonial everywhere and at any moment – that sense of always being in a state of emergency, of being surrounded and endangered even when in command of massive superiority of force. It expresses the colonial imaginary of an ever-looming threat of the savage or uncivil Other in one's midst or in one's hinterland.

Historically, Ireland had always been conceived of by its English conquerors as such a space: a wilderness populated by barbarians or savages – the "uncivil Irish" of Elizabethan accounts – who needed to be either subordinated or subjected to genocide.[18] Home to an irreducibly Catholic majority in the heart of the Protestant empire, Ireland did constantly represent a threat to English security and domination, not only in its constant rebellions and indigenous unruliness, but also as the potential back-door for invasions by England's enemies, from Spain in the seventeenth century to France in the eighteenth and nineteenth centuries to Germany in the twentieth century. Ireland could be conceived as at once an essential outwork of empire, an indispensable defense, and a fifth column within the empire, summoning and welcoming the threatening invader.[19] To posit the

---

[17] The Civil Authorities (Special Powers) Act was introduced with the founding of the Northern Irish state in 1922 and remained in force till it was replaced by the Westminster Parliament's Prevention of Terrorism (Emergency Provisions) Act of 1974 and the Northern Ireland (Emergency Provisions) Act of 1978. See von Tangen Page (1998, 40). On the Special Powers Act's Section 2(4), with its broad and vague powers of prosecution, Robin Evelyn, a former CO of the Green Beret's regiment in Northern Ireland, 1972–73, comments: "It is possible to think that merely to be Roman Catholic in Northern Ireland would have been an offence against that section" (Evelyn 1978, 117).

[18] On the constant recurrence of the colonial stereotype of civility vs. barbarity in the Irish context, see Deane (1986, 33–42).

[19] Already in 1811, English political philosopher Samuel Taylor Coleridge, who would become a crucial intellectual resource for liberal Unionism in the 1830s, had expressed this anxiety in response to the post-Union prospect of Catholic emancipation: "Meantime, all agree in the one fact, that, like a fort detached, yet included in the same plan of fortification, Ireland must either remain part of the common defence, or become the most perilous and commanding counterwork for our annoyance.... It is fatal to this branch of the British Empire, that it cannot be severed from the tree but to furnish the axe employed to fell it" (quoted in Colmer 1976, xliv). As this passage eloquently conveys, a destabilizing inversibility constantly haunts this model of Ireland's defensive geographical role at the vulnerable edge of empire: the "outwork" of the empire's intricate system of defenses can all too rapidly flip over into the counterwork that undoes the whole. Coleridge's concern, only thirteen years after the United Irish rebellion of 1798 and in the midst of British campaigns against Napoleon's

David Lloyd

danger of a Catholic "fifth column" in the heart of the Protestant empire is also to signal the intimacy or proximity of the danger, the uncanny closeness of the threat to one's supremacy that plays out as a kind of siege in which the surrounded minority within the state appears phantasmatically as the inimical surrounding threat. So to view the actually defeated colonized as the "existentially threatening besiegers" undermines one's sense of security and supremacy, no matter how much more powerful one's own legal and military apparatus may be.

This insecurity, characteristic of the settler-colonial mentality virtually everywhere, plays out in the perpetual and recurrent siege mentality of the Ulster Protestant to which the permanence of the Special Powers Act of 1922 gave juridical expression. That siege mentality may have found its anachronistic rhetorical anchor in the annually rehearsed popular commemoration of the Siege of Derry by Jacobite forces in the Williamite wars of 1688–89, but as historian Mark McGovern explains:

> The symbol system of "structural opposites", of the Siege as a struggle between two forces, those of imperial civilisation and colonised barbarity . . . became not just an historical touchstone, but the very language through which unionism expressed itself. (McGovern 2004, 49–50)

Accordingly a language of siege that initially celebrated the Williamite wars as the victory of British power and civilization over Irish incivility devolves into an anxious recognition of the "special" nature of the Irish situation that would eventually come to be marked by a sectarian mode of rule that was the means of keeping Ulster British while at the same time constitutively setting Northern Ireland apart from the rest of the United Kingdom as an exception to the evolving liberal state on the other island. Once again, Memmi interprets that contradiction, whereby the settler glorifies the civilization of the "mother country" while at the same time resenting it for abandoning or even criticizing the authoritarian forms of rule that are essential to the maintenance of its colony. Part of this awkward consciousness, as Memmi argues, is an "exaltation-resentment dialectic"; the sense that the motherland – idealized as the source of the values that legitimate the settler and his sense of supremacy – has actually moved on while the settler remains stuck, frozen in reactionary and racist attitudes in which he retrenches more and more deeply, the more evident it becomes that they contradict the virtues of civility and modernity he continues to proclaim (Memmi 1967, 65, 58–66).

The siege mentality so often plangently invoked by Protestant intellectuals is the mark of the continuing settler-colonial status of Northern Ireland in its opposition to the gradually decolonizing integration of Protestants into the social and cultural fabric of the Republic. As Memmi's insights in *The Colonizer and the Colonized* teach us – and as Liam O'Dowd taught me to read it some twenty-five years ago – the northern

France, was explicitly military, but his rhetoric against Catholic emancipation foreshadowed the ways in which the strategic metaphor would be internalized into a psychic structure.

Protestant consciousness oscillates between the enraged desire to annihilate the native with overwhelming power and the awkward consciousness of being at once surrounded by and dependent on the colonized to mean anything at all.[20] Unionist intellectual John Wilson Foster named the dilemma quite explicitly: "We wished, like Memmi's colonialists, the disappearance of the usurped. Indeed, we attempted politically to erase them, imagining, then acting out, a Northern Ireland free from the dormant, sporadically stirring threat of sedition." And yet, as Foster admits, "We defined ourselves over against them which meant that we were in part defined *by* them" (J. W. Foster 1988, 20).

Northern Irish poet John Hewitt had grasped that dilemma as early as 1949, in a deeply anxious poem, "The Colony," which still stands as a marvelous documentation of the psyche of the contemporary settler-colonial, despite its quasi-Roman fancy dress:

> They worship Heaven strangely, having rites
> we snigger at, are known as superstitious,
> cunning by nature, never to be trusted,
> given to dancing and a kind of song
> seductive to the ear, a whining sorrow.
> Also they breed like flies. The danger's there;
> when Caesar's old and lays his sceptre down,
> we'll be a little people, well outnumbered.
>
> (Hewitt 1991, 78)

The quick move from a sense of disdainful superiority to anxious acknowledgement of the "demographic threat" passes very precisely through the contemptuous animalization of the colonized: "they breed like flies." The surrounded are suddenly the surrounding; the marginalized press in on the center. Memmi would have recognized this settler dilemma, trapped among the colonized whom, even when contained in ghettos or pushed back onto the least productive lands, the colonizer still fears surround him, while the "motherland" that he needs for material and moral support and military protection cannot be relied upon to fulfill its protective mission toward the colony.

Memmi's characterizations of the settler help us to grasp the nature and the *peculiarity* of the Northern Irish conflict – unresolved as it remains – in relation to its *typicality*. Northern Ireland is peculiar in relation to the rest of Britain, and, indeed, to the contemporary Republic, where political differences are no longer largely articulated around religious differences. And while religious affiliation still plays some role in other Western European polities, it is not generally a matter of deep conflict regarding the political rights and even the future and survival of those religious communities. In this respect, Northern Ireland seems sui generis and gets represented by British and other European observers as an atavistic holdover from the religious strife that ravaged Europe in the seventeenth century and of which,

---

[20] See Liam O'Dowd, "New Introduction," in Memmi (1990).

indeed, the Protestant triumph of 1690 at the end of Britain's "Glorious Revolution" was already a late expression.

It is that appearance of anachronistic peculiarity that has made it possible for the publics of Britain and beyond, not to mention their pundits, to embrace the notion – telling as it is – that the Irish conflict is "tribal" in nature. That, in itself, is a peculiar expression. On the one hand, it invokes the analogy between Ireland and Britain's other colonies where, in the old Victorian stereotypes, savage tribes from Afghanistan to darkest Africa resisted civility and British rule. But in doing so, it seeks to avoid recognition that the Northern Irish Troubles were in fact a part of the legacy of British colonialism and therefore that the British were participants in, rather than mere spectators of, the conflict. The naturalization of the conflict as "tribal" or as a holdover of obscure doctrinal conflicts wishfully displaces its causes onto the Irish themselves, of whose essentially premodern disposition they are the expression. On the other hand, precisely that ever-so British stereotype bespeaks the contrary *typicality* of Northern Ireland, once grasped, not as a normal part of the United Kingdom, but rather as a familiar settler-colonial entity formed within the long-standing and ongoing history of British imperialism. Religious (tribal) conflict is, as I suggested at the outset, no more than the modality in which the political struggle over that colonial legacy has been lived in Northern Ireland. We need only to add that a willed and adopted settler-colonial identity, one that the history of Protestants in the Republic suggests was never inevitable, was shaped by a state that guaranteed the conditions of its perpetuation and furnished the matrix within which political positions were lived through religion and religious difference expressed through the political. Only within that settler-colonial framework do the apparent peculiarities of Northern Ireland make sense and only thus do they articulate one another. "The colonial situation manufactures colonialists, just as it manufactures the colonized" (Memmi 1967, 56).

To clarify that claim, let me return for a moment to my opening anecdote to stress the significance of the difference of my experience as a southern Protestant, inhabiting the slow trajectory of complete accommodation to and in the postcolonial state, from that of my northern Protestant peer. Since the Protestant experience was so different in the south, we can see Northern Ireland as a very telling "laboratory" for the cultural and political formations of the settler colony: the artificiality of the state and of Protestant adherence to and dependence on its institutional forms clarifies in an almost exemplary way the tendencies of settler-colonial entities. But it also suggests the possibility of their dissolution. The Northern state was an artifice designed to have the shape of a settler colony, and there is something artificial about the assumption of a settler-colonial identity there, something that we would aptly term *performative*. Not only was it the product of a highly *declarative* bringing-into-being of a state that had no natural or naturalizable boundaries; it also depended on and played itself out through the perpetual iteration of its identifications: "I'm telling you" is at once about identifying the Other and pedagogically

Protestantism and Settler Identity in Northern Ireland 327

FIGURE 12.6 Republican murals, Falls Road, Belfast, Northern Ireland

transmitting the performative artifice of difference.[21] Loyalism as an assertion of a paradoxically rebellious adherence to the Crown and the Union continually displays a sense of excess and artifice that Richard Kirkland has nicely grasped as the "camp" of identity.[22]

Indeed, Ulster Protestantism has very flamboyantly performed its identifications with other settler colonies. Just as Irish Republicans have for decades found common cause with the South African ANC and the Palestinian PLO (see Figure 12.6), and have done so in continuity with their understanding of the Irish struggle as a decolonizing one, Loyalists have identified, with a somewhat more strained mythologizing but a no less acute recognition of the colonial dimensions of both conflicts, with Zionism and with the siege mentality of the supposedly beleaguered "Jewish state" of Israel (see Figure 12.7).

To cite a 1973 Ulster Freedom Fighters (UFF) press release:

> We have more in common with the State of Israel, the Star of David on our flag. These brave people fought and won their battle for survival. We intend to win ours. And like the Jewish people, each time an act of aggression is committed against our people, we shall retaliate in a way that only the animals in the IRA can understand. (Quoted in Kirkland 2002, 146)

[21] This collapses Homi Bhabha's important but finally unsustainable distinction between the performative and the pedagogical aspects of national identity (Bhabha 1990, 297). Performativity is the pedagogical mode of the nation. Cleary (2002, 71) comments on the "meandering newly created border" that "lacked the clarity of visual outline" that the island as a whole appears to present.
[22] Kirkland (2002, 125–66).

FIGURE 12.7 Loyalist flag incorporating Ulster Banner and Star of David

The identification in this citation is of course not only with a shared siege mentality, but also with the penchant for disproportionate violence, the rage at resistance, or even just persistence, raised to the technical power of annihilation, compounded by the settler colonial's urge to what John Wilson Foster calls the "erasure" of the animalized Other. With uncanny surety, this UFF paramilitary grasps both the murderous intent and the psychic necessity of Israel's consistent animalization of Palestinians, a rhetorical constant that has only intensified in intervening years.[23]

IMPLICATIONS FOR PEACE AND CONFLICT RESOLUTION: IRELAND AND BEYOND

Is there any productive example to be drawn from this "exemplary" settler-colonial conflict? We are constantly urged to find in the laboratory of Belfast, in the experiment of the Northern Irish peace process, pointers for the resolution of conflicts elsewhere, not least the Israeli/Palestinian conflict.[24] Let me bracket here all the reasons for

---

[23] Consider, as just one example of the animalization of Palestinians that issues from the mouths of Israeli officials, then Minister of Justice Ayelet Shaked's 2014 reference to Palestinian women breeding snakes in an all-out war and therefore as worthy of extermination: "They should go, as should the physical homes in which they raised the snakes. Otherwise, more little snakes will be raised there" (quoted in Abunimah 2014).

[24] For a somewhat skeptical expression of that possibility, see Traub (2010). For an overview of such comparisons, see Byrne (2009), who remarks that Northern Ireland "is fast becoming a conflict-resolution laboratory" and considers in some detail the drawbacks in using it as a model for resolution the Palestinian-Israeli conflict.

misgivings about the Northern Irish peace process – its possibly unintended perpetuation of sectarian difference in the guise of power-sharing; its exclusion of groups that sought to move beyond such divides; its predication on fickle neo-liberal economic investment; its proliferation of the "NGO-ization" of the society as a substitute for effective and durable economic development; its function in pacification of resistance rather than rectification of injustice. Those misgivings find their symbols in the so-called peace walls that still, twenty years into the power-sharing experiment, continue to divide and fence in the working-class sectarian ghettoes of the north. Those misgivings were articulated even before the peace process was long under way, and they have not ceased to have critical power in the present.[25] My tenses will have betrayed my own lack of conviction that the peace process is in any sense an accomplished one: At best, it is a process, but possibly a process of containment and pacification rather than resolution. It is certainly not, unless perhaps by happy or unhappy accident, a process of conscious and deliberate decolonization.

Those drawbacks of the peace process will not be unfamiliar from other contexts. Not dissimilarly, since the Oslo Accords of almost the same period, most of the negative aspects of the Northern Irish peace process have found their analogies in Palestine: in the deliberate consolidation of segregation or apartheid between the two populations; in the promotion of an elite and patriarchal ethno-nationalist Palestinian Authority maintained by externally imposed neo-liberal economic investment and of a right-wing Zionist government that is its counterpart in Israel; in the veneer of rapid economic growth in the urban enclaves of the West Bank, primarily Ramallah, that is supplemented by the peace process industry's proliferation of foreign NGOs whose principal side effect has been to undermine the popular organizations and initiatives of the Palestinians and thereby to contain their resistance.[26]

Those analogies with the utterly failed or sabotaged Oslo Accords aside, there may, nonetheless, be a number of "good things" that have come of the Northern Irish peace process, however provisionally: political power-sharing in Stormont, though reluctant and still troubled, has spelled the end of decades of unrestrained settler-colonial domination by "a Protestant people," even if it has also compromised the Republican movement and its claims to advocate for a complete decolonization of the island. There has been some recognition of civil rights and the passage of

---

[25] For an early compendium of critical responses to the peace process from a variety of perspectives, see P. Kelly and Vince (1996). For a more recent critique of the peace process and its outcomes, see S. Kelly (2007).

[26] See Hilal (2014): "Many NGOs, particularly the larger NGOs, are dependent for their functioning on donor money despite its clear neoliberal political bias and donor priorities to maintain the Oslo-generated 'peace process' at any cost. The significant expansion of the number and types of NGOs has meant, in most cases, the substitution of representative and voluntary associations by professionalized associations with no mandate to represent the interests of any specific constituency. . . . The marginalization of Palestinian national institutions is most clearly seen in the outright sidelining of the Palestine Liberation Organization (PLO) institutions that had previously represented the Palestinian communities inside and outside of historic Palestine . . .. The net result is the loss of a political anchor and a mobilized population that could lead a new *Intifada* against the settler-colonial state."

laws against discrimination, even if that has been performed through artificial declarations of "parity of esteem" and has left in place the very economic injustice and disparity that sectarian domination was instituted to safeguard. These are all tendencies, however small, toward a sense of equality and rights that doubtless any democratic state aspires to.

The difficulty that faces any effort to promote these gains and processes as models or even as possibilities for Israel and Palestine is that Israel is not only not a fully democratic state, but is constitutively founded on and committed to discrimination, as a recent report by a UN body is only the latest official document to demonstrate, and as the recently passed Jewish Nation-State Basic Law has confirmed.[27] To take only one instance upon which the UN report elaborates, Israel maintains the distinction in its Basic Law, unknown in any other modern state, between nationality (*le'om*) and citizenship (*ezrahut*). As a Jewish state, Israel's according of nationality and the highly differential privileges that go with it, on the basis of Jewishness, automatically discriminates against its non-Jewish (i.e., Palestinian) inhabitants, even if they are formally granted citizenship and ostensibly granted civil and political rights.[28] Further, as Adalah (2017), the Legal Center for Arab Minority Rights in Israel, documents, more than sixty-five laws legalize discrimination against the Palestinian minority.[29] (Nothing of this nature was ever so encoded in Northern Irish law, even if many of its discriminatory effects were in force in practice.) Likewise, in order to maintain its identity as "a Jewish state for a Jewish people," Israel must discriminate, ethnically cleanse, or, in the euphemistic terminology of the state, "transfer" Palestinians, in order to maintain the population of Palestinians within Israel and Occupied East Jerusalem at a demographic ratio of 20 percent or less. Israeli Jews continue to construe Palestinians as posing a "demographic danger" or "demographic time bomb" that Catholics similarly represented for the Orange state.[30] In the latter case, however, the containment of the increase of the Catholic population vis-à-vis the Protestants is hard to attribute even to unsystematic government policy but appears rather to have been a side effect of discrimination in employment and housing: higher levels of emigration among Catholics than Protestants can only be inferred to have resulted from such policies and practices, particularly since the Free State and Republic have been historically afflicted with very high levels of out-migration.

[27] See Falk and Tilley (2017). This report was withdrawn by the UN under political pressure by the United States and others, but is archived at www.scribd.com/document/342202464/Israeli-Practices-towards-the-Palestinian-People-and-the-Question-of-Apartheid. For an assessment of the new Jewish Nation-State Basic law, see Adalah (2018).

[28] For a careful and well-documented analysis of this distinction and its implications, see Makdisi (2018, 311–15).

[29] Adalah is an Israel-based human rights organization that maintains a frequently updated database of laws that discriminate against Palestinians within Israel.

[30] For the fear of the Catholic or nationalist minority in Northern Ireland as a "fifth column," see Cleary (2002, 22); on the "demographic problem" Palestinians present to "the Jewish state," see Makdisi (2008, 9–14); for the "demographic time bomb," see Veracini (2006, 30).

Protestantism and Settler Identity in Northern Ireland 331

In both the cases of Northern Ireland and Israel, partition was implemented in the hope of establishing the supremacy of the settler ethnic group over a population that was understood to be "native." In both cases also, the imperative to endow the settler population with what could be considered an adequate territory obliged the incorporation into the states that were forged in partition of a minority population that was larger than desired but nonetheless a minority. In Northern Ireland, despite the absorption of three western and predominantly Catholic counties of the province of Ulster, an artificial majority of Protestants was secured, and emigration helped to maintain that majority even though Catholic birth rates tended to be higher than those of Protestants. At Israel's founding, however, despite the disproportion between the territory granted to Palestinians and that granted to Israel under the UN-imposed partition plan, the Arab Palestinian and Jewish populations would have been virtually equal within the State of Israel. As is well known, the Zionist aspiration to establish a "Jewish state for a Jewish people" could only be secured by the drastic ethnic cleansing of the Palestinian inhabitants of the future Jewish state and the denial of their right of return. Historian Ilan Pappé (2006) has documented both this process and its systematic nature in considerable detail. However, even that act of expulsion was unable to guarantee demographic superiority and, as Israel has continued to expand by appropriating more and more Palestinian land and displacing more and more Palestinians, it faces a dilemma that is unlikely to be resolved insofar as maximalist claims to Eretz Israel continue to drive its governing right-wing coalitions and their refusal to relinquish the expropriated and Occupied Territories. That dilemma is that it proves impossible to incorporate Palestinian territory without incorporating Palestinians, to whom citizenship must be denied even as they are, to all intents and purposes, subjects of the state. What partition and separation sought to secure in the form of two ethnic states can now only be maintained by a systemic imposition of what is a regime of apartheid in all but name, a regime that grows ever more difficult to disguise from international civil society.

This signals what may be the most salient difference between the case of Israel and that of Northern Ireland: rarely if at all, have northern Loyalists expressed irredentist claims to the island as a whole. Their claims to self-determination within the current state are based on historical claims of settlement and residence rather than on any appeal to a destined future: the precariousness of their situation finds expression in the fading strength of the traditional Unionist Party and the rise to power of the more extreme Democratic Unionist Party, formerly the political wing of a paramilitary organization. Zionism, on the contrary, though it grounded its claims to "return" to Palestine in the biblical past of the Promised Land, has always been driven by a messianic, future-oriented project to occupy the whole territory of historic Palestine – including, in the most extreme versions, that of what is now Jordan. As Jacqueline Rose has pointed out, Zionism was a secularization of messianic hopes, "unique in laying one by one the terms of messianic destiny, lifted from a Jewish faith, across its geographical landscape even when that faith has been lost." But as

332   *David Lloyd*

she also points out, the messianic project to restore the Land of Israel as the state of the Jewish people has entailed equally the militarization of Zionism and the necessity for the transfer or ethnic cleansing of the Palestinian population (Rose 2005, 35, 31–57). As Gershom Scholem foresaw, "messianic political Zionism was in danger of triumphing itself to death" (quoted in Rose 2005, 57).

Scholem's anxious foreboding has found its concrete expression in the gradual erosion of partition itself. Currently, only two outcomes of the present stalemate are being entertained by international powers – besides the possibility, condoned in practice by every world power, that Israel will prefer "conflict management," that is, maintaining the situation of stalemate and its disavowed apartheid to any other resolution of their decades-long occupation of Palestine. The alternatives are either a one-state solution that will continue to be predicated on a systematic system of apartheid or segregation (*hafrada*), which is already effectively the de facto case not only under the occupation, but also for the Palestinian second-class citizens of Israel and residents of Occupied East Jerusalem; or a two-state solution in which Palestinian sovereignty over the West Bank and Gaza will be so drastically restricted as to become meaningless and in which Palestinians will continue to face both ethnic cleansing and discrimination within Israel. In other words, in both currently envisaged "resolutions" to the conflict, as well as under the status quo, parity of relation and power-sharing between Palestinians and Israelis, on the models of the Northern Irish peace process, are out of the question, and any proposal that would even attempt to realize equal rights is rejected outright by Israel as portending the "destruction of the Jewish state."

If not a model for any peace process – if indeed, it makes sense to talk of such a thing, given Israeli governmental resistance to serious negotiations and its commitment to maintaining the illegal settlements and other violations of international law – is Northern Ireland exemplary in any other way? Does the specific type of settler-colonial polity that it instances furnish lessons for other sites and, in particular, for Palestine-Israel? I have argued that religious identifications in Northern Ireland formed the modality in which settler-colonial relations are lived. If so, then what appear as primordial identities are in fact politically significant only within a structure that is maintained endogenously and exogenously – within the state and with the support of one or more external states – in order to ensure the supremacy of one segment of the population over another. As the instance of the Republic of Ireland seems to suggest, however, the persistence of settler-colonial mentalities is a function of the structure, not of insuperable primordial attachments. There is nothing "tribal," except for poets and ideologues, about colonial antagonisms: they persist on and through performatively maintained structures of power and do not survive the withdrawal of the material support that sustains them.

How then would it be possible to move toward a just rather than an imposed solution, one that respected rights irrespective of religion or ethnicity? One influential political scientific view of the Northern Irish Peace Process (NIPP) regards it as modeled on consociationality; that is, a process that mediates between conflicting parties by requiring executive power-sharing, some degree of autonomy for each, proportionality of representation, and veto power over decisions that vitally affect their interests. McGarry and O'Leary (2006, 44) emphasize that this process could only have been arrived at in the Irish case through the intervention of what they term an "exogamous actor" or external power capable of wielding both "the carrot and the stick." In the case of Palestine and Israel, only one exogamous actor realistically exists, the US, which furnishes the bulk of Israel's material aid and international diplomatic cover. No other state, or state grouping like the EU, currently has the potential to influence Israel's policies or practices without US engagement. But, as is well known, through every American presidential administration since the 1950s, the US has acted as what in Memmi's terms we might describe as the "mother country": the external defender which, though often stridently decried for being disloyal or treacherous, can be relied on for support, whether in vetoing UN resolutions criticizing Israeli policies or in supplying the munitions by which Israel maintains its occupation and enacts its periodic wars on Gaza.

For this reason the mobilization of an alternative exogamous agency has both become a matter of pressing urgency and proven possible to organize on a global scale. Given the total failure of influential states to act on their own explicit policies with regard to Israel, in recent years the initiative has passed from state actors to US and global civil society, in a process explicitly reminiscent of the anti-apartheid movement that motivated civil society to pressure states to bring an end to South Africa's regime of discrimination and oppression. Over the last decade and a half, a global civil society movement for Boycott, Divestment, and Sanctions (BDS), called for by the vast majority of Palestinian civil society organizations, has begun to exert effective external pressure not only on Israel itself, but also on the political landscape in the US and in Europe. Through its campaigns and organizing, BDS aims at shaping public discourse on Palestine and Israel so as to open the space for political initiatives that will bring the necessary pressure to bear on Israel. In this respect, BDS functions as an "exogamous pressure" toward a peace with justice.

But the secondary impact of BDS may be – as the anti-apartheid campaign was for many South Africans – a means to persuade Israelis themselves of the untenability over the long term of maintaining a settler-colonial relation to Palestine and the wider region. The Israeli human rights organization B'Tselem's recent acknowledgment of the apartheid nature of the Israeli state (Holmes 2021) represents an important opening in that direction. The colonial situation that "manufactures colonialists" (Memmi 1967, 56) may not itself be inevitable. It is at once the wager and the intent of the boycott movement, and intrinsic to its explicitly anti-racist principles, that the exogamous pressure that it supplies in the absence of state-directed interventions stands not as a threat of the "destruction of the state of Israel," but as an invitation to Israelis to abandon the settler-colonial mentality and the privileges that depend on the dispossession and displacement of Palestinians, and to embrace the possibility of cohabitation in the region on equal terms.

If the case of Northern Ireland offers any kind of positive example, then, and if we consider the peace process there to have achieved any transformation of the political landscape, it may be that the artifice of settler colonialism that manufactures colonial mentalities is neither inevitable nor eternal. The colonial racial supremacy currently enjoyed by Israeli Jews over their fellow Palestinian citizens and subjects is, indeed, lived through identification with what are – with a certain deliberate ambiguity – overlapping religious, ethnic, and cultural attachments. But the structures of domination in which identity and difference operate to ensure Jewish supremacy give those identifications their political meaning. Absent the material means to reproduce those structures, the meaning of Jewish identity might cease to entail a system of domination that is, for many Jews, in contradiction with their ethical traditions. In face of the withdrawal of the material, moral, and political support that state powers offer and without which Israel, like Northern Ireland, could scarcely survive, the possibility might open of a withering away of a racial state and the advent of a real and decolonized democracy, as we have witnessed to a very large extent occurring in the Republic of Ireland.

REFERENCES

Abunimah, Ali. 2014. "Israeli Lawmaker's Call for Genocide of Palestinians Gets Thousands of Facebook Likes." *Rights and Accountability* (blog), *The Electronic Intifada*. July 7. https://electronicintifada.net/blogs/ali-abunimah/israeli-lawmakers-call-genocide-palestinians-gets-thousands-facebook-likes.

Adalah. 2017. "The Discriminatory Laws Database." Special Reports. www.adalah.org/en/content/view/7771.

2018. "Israeli Parliament Votes to Approve Nation-State Law That Enshrines Jewish Supremacy Over Palestinian Citizens." Press Releases. www.adalah.org/en/content/view/9565.

Anderson, Benedict. 2006. *Imagined Communities: Reflections on the Origin and Spread of Nationalism*. 2nd ed. London: Verso.

Bell, Geoffrey. 1976. *The Protestants of Ulster*. London: Pluto Press.

Bew, Paul, Peter Gibbon, and Henry Patterson. 2002. *Northern Ireland, 1921–2001: Political Forces and Social Classes*. Rev. ed. London: Serif.

Bhabha, Homi. 1990. "DissemiNation: Time, Narrative and the Margins of the Modern Nation." In *The Nation and Narration*, edited by Homi Bhabha, 291–322. London and New York: Routledge.

Brewer, John D., and Gareth I. Higgins. 1997. "Northern Ireland 1921–1998." In *Anti-Catholicism in Northern Ireland, 1600–1998: The Mote and the Beam*, edited by John D. Brewer and Gareth I. Higgins, 87–134. Basingstoke, UK: Macmillan.

Byrne, Siobhan. 2009. "Women and the Transition from Conflict in Northern Ireland: Lessons for Peace-Building in Israel/Palestine." Working Papers in British-Irish Studies, no. 89. Dublin: Institute for British-Irish Studies. http://irserver.ucd.ie/dspace/bitstream/10197/2416/1/89_byrne.pdf.

Canny, Nicholas. 1979. "The Permissive Frontier: Social Control in English Settlements in Ireland and Virginia, 1550–1650." In *The Westward Enterprise: English Activities in*

Ireland, the Atlantic and America, 1480–1650, edited by Kenneth R. Andrews, Nicholas P. Canny, and P. E. H. Hair, 17–44. Detroit: Wayne State University Press.

Carson, Ciaran. 1989. "Question Time." In *Belfast Confetti*, 57–63. Winston-Salem, NC: Wake Forest University Press.

Clayton, Pamela. 1998. "Religion, Ethnicity and Colonialism as Explanations of the Northern Irish Conflict." In *Rethinking Northern Ireland: Culture, Ideology and Colonialism*, edited by David Miller, 40–54. London: Longman.

Cleary, Joe. 2002. *Literature, Partition, and the Nation State: Culture and Conflict in Ireland, Israel, and Palestine*. Cambridge: Cambridge University Press.

Colmer, John, ed. 1976. Editor's Introduction to *On the Constitution of Church and State: The Collected Works of Samuel Taylor Coleridge*, vol. 10, xxxiii–lxviii. Princeton: Princeton University Press.

Crozier, Maurna, ed. 1989. *Cultural Traditions in Northern Ireland*. Belfast: Institute for Irish Studies, Queen's University.

Cunningham, Niall. 2013. "'The Doctrine of Vicarious Punishment': Space, Religion and the Belfast Troubles of 1920–22." *Journal of Historical Geography* 40: 52–66.

Deane, Seamus. 1986. "Civilians and Barbarians." In *Ireland's Field Day*, edited by Field Day Theatre Company, 33–42. Notre Dame, IN: University of Notre Dame Press.

Evelyn, Robin. 1978. *Peace Keeping in a Democratic Society: The Lessons of Northern Ireland*. London: C. Hurst.

Falk, Richard, and Virginia Tilley. 2017. "Israeli Practices towards the Palestinian People and the Question of Apartheid." Palestine and the Israeli Occupation, no. 1. Report to the United Nations Economic and Social Commission for Western Asia. Beirut: United Nations. www.scribd.com/document/342202464/Israeli-Practices-towards-the-Palestinian-People-and-the-Question-of-Apartheid.

Fanon, Frantz. 1968. *The Wretched of the Earth*. Translated by Constance Farrington. New York: Grove Press.

Feldman, Allen. 1989. *Formations of Violence: The Narrative of the Body and Political Terror in Northern Ireland*. Chicago: Chicago University Press.

Foster, John Wilson. 1988. "Culture and Colonisation: The View from the North." *The Irish Review* 5: 17–26.

Foster, R. F. 1989. *Modern Ireland: 1600–1972*. Harmondsworth, UK: Penguin Books.

Hall, Stuart. 1980. "Race, Articulation and Societies Structured in Dominance." In *Sociological Theories: Race and Colonialism*, edited by UNESCO, 305–45. Paris: UNESCO.

Heaney, Seamus. 1975. "The Ministry of Fear." In *North*, edited by Seamus Heaney, 63–65. London: Faber and Faber.

Hewitt, John. 1991. *Collected Poems*. Belfast: Blackstaff Press.

Hilal, Jamil. 2014. "What's Stopping the 3rd Intifada?" Commentary. Al-Shabaka: The Palestinian Policy Network. https://al-shabaka.org/commentaries/whats-stopping-the-3rd-intifada/.

Holmes, Oliver. 2021. "Israel Is a Non-democratic Apartheid Regime." *The Guardian*, January 11. www.theguardian.com/world/2021/jan/12/israel-is-a-non-democratic-apartheid-regime-says-rights-group.

Kelly, Paddy, and Harry Vince, eds. 1996. "What Peace Process?" Special edition. *Irish Reporter* 21.

Kelly, Susan. 2007. "Ulster Must Be Defended! On the Uses of Cultural Translation in Northern Ireland's Race War." Translate. European Institute for Progressive Cultural Policies. http://translate.eipcp.net/strands/04/kelly-strands01en.html.

Kirkland, Richard. 2002. *Identity Parades: Northern Irish Culture and Dissident Subjects.* Liverpool: Liverpool University Press.

Laffan, Michael. 1983. *The Partition of Ireland, 1911–1925.* Dundalk, Ireland: Dundalgan Press.

Lustick, Ian. 1993. *Unsettled States, Disputed Lands: Britain and Ireland, France and Algeria, Israel and the West Bank and Gaza.* Ithaca, NY: Cornell University Press.

Makdisi, Saree. 2008. *Palestine Inside Out: An Everyday Occupation.* New York: Norton.

2018. "Apartheid, Apartheid, []." *Critical Inquiry* 44, no. 2: 304–30.

McGarry, John, and Brendan O'Leary. 2006. "Consociational Theory, Northern Ireland's Conflict, and Its Agreement: Part 1: What Consociationalists Can Learn from Northern Ireland." *Government and Opposition* 41, no. 1: 43–63.

McGovern, Mark. 2004. "'A Besieged Outpost': The Imagination of Empire and the Siege Myth, 1860–1900." In *Problems and Perspectives in Irish History since 1800*, edited by D. George Boyce and Roger Swift, 32–53. Dublin: Four Courts Press.

Memmi, Albert. 1967. *The Colonizer and the Colonized.* Translated by Howard Greenfeld. Boston: Beacon Books.

1990. *The Colonizer and the Colonized.* Translated by Howard Greenfeld. Introduction by Liam O'Dowd. 3rd rev. ed. London: Earthscan Publications.

Murphy, Andrew. 1999. "'White Chimpanzees': Encountering Ireland." In *But the Irish Sea Betwixt Us: Ireland, Colonialism and Renaissance Literature*, edited by Andrew Murphy, 11–32. Lexington: University of Kentucky Press.

O'Leary, Brendan. 2017. "'Cold House': The Unionist Counter-Revolution and the Invention of Northern Ireland." In *Atlas of the Irish Revolution*, edited by John Crowley, Donal Ó Drisceoil, and Mike Murphy, 818–27. Cork, Ireland: Cork University Press.

Pappé, Ilan. 2006. *The Ethnic Cleansing of Palestine.* Oxford: Oneworld Publications.

Rifkin, Mark. 2014. *Settler Common Sense: Queerness and Everyday Colonialism in the American Renaissance.* Minneapolis: Minnesota University Press.

Robinson, Brian. 2001. "Negotiations: Religion, Landscape and the Postcolonial Moment in the Poetry of Seamus Heaney." In *Mapping the Sacred: Religion, Geography and Postcolonial Literatures*, edited by Jamie S. Scott and Paul Simpson-Housley, 5–36. Amsterdam: Rodopi.

Robinson, Cedric. 2000. *Black Marxism: The Making of the Black Radical Tradition.* Chapel Hill: University of North Carolina Press.

Rose, Jacqueline. 2005. *The Question of Zion.* Princeton: Princeton University Press.

Said, Edward. 1979. *Orientalism.* New York: Vintage Books.

Todd, Jennifer. 1988. "The Limits of Britishness." *The Irish Review* 5: 11–16.

Tomlinson, Mike. 1995. "Imprisoned Ireland." In *Western European Penal Systems: A Critical Anatomy*, edited by Vincenzo Ruggiero, Mick Ryan, and Joe Sim, 194–227. London: Sage.

Traub, James. 2010. "Mixed Irish Blessings." *Foreign Policy*, August 27. https://foreignpolicy.com/2010/08/27/mixed-irish-blessing/.

Veracini, Lorenzo. 2006. *Israel and Settler Society.* London: Pluto.

von Tangen Page, Michael. 1998. *Prisons, Peace and Terrorism: Penal Policy and the Reduction of Political Violence in Northern Ireland, Italy and the Spanish Basque Country, 1968–97.* New York: St. Martin's Press.

Walker, Brian. 1992. "1641, 1689, 1690 and All That: The Unionist Sense of History." *The Irish Review* 12: 61.

Wolfe, Patrick. 2001. "Land, Labor, and Difference: Elementary Structures of Race." *American Historical Review* 106, no. 3: 866–905.

13

Does Religion Still Matter?

Comparative Lessons from the Ethno-national Conflict in Northern Ireland

Liam O'Dowd

Two polarized meta-narratives currently inform debates on the links between religion, nationalism, and violence in Western countries (see, e.g., Armstrong 2014; Cavanagh 2009; Juergensmeyer 1993, 2003). One portrays Western national states as having domesticated or co-opted religion in the interests of peaceful secular democracy. This success is linked to their perceived capacity to consign to the past the "wars of religion" while neutralizing the violent potential of collectivized religion by confining it to the private sphere of individual belief and practice. The second narrative points to contemporary conflict zones where politicized religion, fueled by absolutism and fanaticism, generates violence on a massive scale. Here, the civic and secular nationalism of the West is seen to be ineffectual in the face of the mobilizing power of violent religious nationalism. Moreover, the first narrative is now seen to be under threat, even in its own heartlands, by a politicized religion, driven by the globalization of capitalism, mass immigration, and mass communication.

This chapter falls into two broad sections. Firstly, it elaborates historical and theoretical reflections on what Northern Ireland as a case study can reveal about debates on the links between religion, nationalism, and violence. Secondly, it seeks to advance a deeper and more discriminating analysis of these links by drawing on a research project on the intersection of popular religion and ethno-national conflict in post-conflict Belfast. This research was a module within a much wider, comparative research project, entitled "Conflict in Cities and the Contested State: Everyday Life and the Possibilities of Transformation in Belfast, Jerusalem, and Other Divided Cities" (2007–14).[1]

NORTHERN IRELAND AS A CASE STUDY?

Northern Ireland is a promising case study for challenging the dichotomous thinking behind these two meta-narratives. For nearly three decades of conflict, from the

---

[1] This interdisciplinary project was funded by the ESRC (grant number: RES-060-25-0015) and involved the universities of Cambridge, Exeter, and Queen's University Belfast.

338   *Liam O'Dowd*

1960s to the 1990s, it seemed to be an anomaly – a site of religious nationalist violence in the heartlands of the secular West where the legacy of past religio-political conflict lived on. More recently, however, its peace process and the settlement of 1998 has been celebrated as a rare victory for democratic compromise, negotiation, and secular rationality. As such, it is frequently promoted as a template for peace processes elsewhere.

Of course, it might be suggested that, compared with religious nationalist division elsewhere, for example in parts of the Middle East or South Asia, late twentieth-century conflict in Northern Ireland appears to be driven by the "narcissism of small differences." All the protagonists are "Christian"; they speak the same language; they are not distinguished by racial differences. Moreover, located within the heartland of the imperial West, they have been exposed for centuries to the homogenizing thrust of British state- and nation-building and to the complex of influences associated by social scientists with capitalist industrialization, secularization, and urbanization, sometimes captured under the umbrella term of modernization.

Among close observers of contemporary Northern Ireland, we can discern two diametrically opposed positions: (1) that religion has become largely irrelevant in what is now a secular political conflict between two competing nationalisms; and (2) that the legacy of Northern Ireland's exceptionalism lives on because its political conflict remains rooted in enduring and irreconcilable religious differences. Advocates of the second position argue that religious politics remain largely impervious to the forces that have marginalized religion elsewhere in the modern West.

The bulk of the vast literature on the Northern Ireland conflict leans toward the first position. Most of the social scientific analyses of the contemporary conflict do not even mention religion. Instead, they present the conflict as one between competing (ethno-)nationalisms (e.g., O'Leary and McGarry 1993). Political discourse is suffused by secular terms like security, terrorism, violence, victimhood, civil or human rights, and culture. Identity, social justice, law and order, social inequality, and endless wrangling over governance in a power-sharing administration are the preoccupations of a power-sharing administration prone to periodic collapse and often stymied by mutual communal vetoes.

Religious nationalists[2] as such are hard to find in Northern Ireland. Few seek to identify the nation-state as a collective religious subject; derive its authority from divine writ; or understand it as a potential instrument of God's will with redemptive significance. Certainly the terms "Catholic" and "Protestant"[3] remain in use, but these labels are typically understood as merely nominal and hollowed out of their

---

[2] Gorski and Turkmen-Dervisoglu (2013) define religious nationalism as a social movement that claims to speak for the nation, defining the nation as religiously based, i.e., religion is seen as the key badge of belonging to the nation. They distinguish between macro-cultural approaches to the topic that dominates in sociology and anthropology and the micro-rationalist approach most common in political science, economics, and international relations (Gorski and Turkmen-Dervisoglu 2013, 192).

[3] Social surveys suggest more people prioritize the labels "Catholic" and "Protestant" than other partially overlapping labels that are often used as rough equivalents (Nationalist, Republican, or

substantive religious content. Viewed comparatively, it is clear that there have been no religiously motivated "jihadists" or suicide bombers on the streets of Northern Ireland. Nor are there any contentious sacred sites in Belfast's secular environment that stir passion to the extent of the Haram al-Sharif in Jerusalem or the demolished Babri Mosque in India (Friedland and Hecht 1998; Hassner 2009). Even if the significance of religion in communal division is recognized historically (Wolffe 2011), it is now seen as a relatively benign (Ganiel 2016), if often ineffectual (Brewer, Higgins, and Teeney 2011), force attempting to promote the peace process.

A prominent strand in the second position sees the transition from ethno-religious to ethno-national conflict as incomplete and suggests that Northern Ireland lacks a proper domesticated form of religion suitable for a liberal state. Supporting evidence is found in the anachronistic rhetoric of the Reverend Ian Paisley, a fundamentalist Presbyterian and founder of the now-dominant Democratic Unionist Party, who was to become the iconic Unionist leader during the time of "the Troubles." As the latest in a long tradition of firebrand fundamentalist preachers, Paisley's violent rhetoric appeared to underline the importance of religion to Unionist politics (Bruce 1986) and of anti-Catholicism in the historical formation of Ulster Protestantism (Brewer and Higgins 1998). In post-conflict Northern Ireland, others point to the continued prominence of the politics of sexuality and reproduction (although here divisions span the Protestant-Catholic divide), and continued, deep-rooted religious segregation in education, residential areas, and civil society (e.g., Coulter and Murray 2008).

Both positions, however, tacitly assume that there is a sharp disjuncture between the religious and the secular (exceptions include Mitchell 2006 and Ganiel 2016), and that religious conflict is particularly intractable, resistant to compromise, and prone to violent expression.[4] There is also a general agreement that the conflict in Ireland is about politics rather than theology, except for a small minority (Barnes 2005). According to the first position, religion has been largely sidelined as a primary factor in the contemporary conflict; whereas the second holds that it survives in the exceptional circumstances of Northern Ireland as a potentially obstructive force preventing compromise and conflict transformation. From the perspective of the first position, the Northern Ireland conflict has been effectively secularized; for the second, it has not been secularized enough.

Irish for "Catholic"; Unionist, Loyalist, or British for "Protestant"). Although the various terms are not strictly equivalent, they are typically treated as such in popular discourse. In the 2011 Northern Ireland census, 48 percent defined themselves as Protestant, 45 percent as Catholic, 48 percent as British, 29 percent as Northern Irish, and 28 percent as Irish.

[4] This view is confirmed by observations on the outbreak of religiously influenced conflicts in the Middle East, Africa, and the Balkans (see Cavanaugh 2009; Clarke 2014). A genre of historical research does recognize the role of violent religious politics in Western state-formation (e.g., Wolffe 2011) but typically implies that secular liberal democracies have succeeded in consigning such violence to the past.

RESEARCHING BELFAST: ASSUMPTIONS AND CONTEXT

The Belfast research reported here aims at testing the two positions outlined above. It challenges their shared idea that secularism, or indeed secular nationalism, can be sharply distinguished from religion. Equally, however, it rejects the notion that religion can be simply subsumed into nationalism (see Brubaker 2012, 2013). The detailed primary research summarized below suggests the need for more discriminating accounts of how forms of religion interact with forms of nationalism while focusing on how these intersections generate violent conflict. These interactions and intersections are examined here through the prism of "post-conflict" Belfast focusing on how forms of religion and nationalism are emplaced and embodied in struggles over space and place.

Two key assumptions underlie the following analysis of the links between religion, nationalism, and violence. The first is that religion is understood primarily as a category of *practice* (as vernacular) rather than as a category of *belief*. Here the focus is on everyday material practices rather than on church-state relationships or links between religious doctrine and nationalist ideology. Religion as practice, like nationalism, is centrally concerned with place-making. At the center of everyday religious and nationalist practice are the popular politics of territorial segregation. Secondly, cities, especially capital cities, are now the key sites of often-violent contention involving religion and nationalism. As the Belfast case demonstrates contending claims over place, boundaries and territory are at once intensely local while simultaneously echoing political meta-narratives over who owns the city specifically and Northern Ireland more generally.

The core proposition here is that religion (as practice) remains integral to the Northern Ireland conflict despite the apparently secular form of its contemporary politics. Accepting the views of the scholarly literature on religion that there is no universally agreed-upon, transcultural definition of religion (Cavanaugh 2009), I propose a working distinction between, on the one hand, institutionalized religion as embodied in churches, texts, and formal observance, and, on the other hand, a popular or vernacular religion – understood as a set of lived experiences and practices tied to place and popular memory. This is not the definition of religion implicit in the way that modern secular constitutions accord a proper domain to religion. As Asad (1999, 193) suggests, the practice of vernacular religion may often obscure formal constitutional and theological distinctions – it comprises objects, sites, practices, words, and representation even in the minds and bodies of worshippers (even those who have formally ceased to worship). Religion in this sense is more about "territory" than about text; more about everyday practice and popular memory than about sacred books or theological principle (McAlister 2005).

Popular religion has a changing and variable relationship with formal religious institutions and practices and frequently escapes the analytical frames of theorists of religion and nationalism. Even when formal, institutional religion eschews pro- and anti-state violence or when it may appear to be of little import in nationalist conflicts, popular forms of religion may be involved in commemorating and celebrating representative violence – according meaning and significance to violence, death, victimhood, and sacrifice. Here the practices of popular religion may intersect with those of nationalism.

An emphasis on the grounded nature of the links between vernacular religion and what Billig (1995) terms banal nationalism[5] brings into focus the second major theme of this chapter and of the research project on which it is based – the centrality of cities and urban space in contemporary ethno-religious/ethno-national conflicts. While Belfast is obviously shaped by the politics of state-building in Britain and Ireland generally, it also illuminates the specific role of cities in religious and nationalist conflicts. While ethno-nationalist conflict is by definition about the boundaries, control, or even the existence of the state, cities remain a sine qua non for states' existence. Cities, and particularly capital cities, have become ever more important stakes in ethno-national conflicts (Davis and Libertun de Duren 2011). Ethnic conflict globally has become nationalized and urbanized as political violence over the state is increasingly focused in cities. As Friedland and Hecht (1998, 148) observe, modern territorial collectivities are constituted by their centers as well as by their boundaries. While claimed as centers of secular and religious authority, cities both facilitate and inhibit the homogenizing and transcendental projects of nationalism and religion (see, e.g., Bacchetta 2010; Pullan 2013). Cities are crucibles for creating "peoples" and ritual display, while being shaped simultaneously by secular forms of capitalist accumulation that encourages both violence and cultural diversity. It is in the cities of contested states that we can most clearly see the everyday interaction between religion, nationalism, and violence. This interaction is necessarily embedded and materialized in urban space, territory, and the built environment (see Bollens 2007; Hepburn 2004).

Belfast as a major center of early capitalist industry is ostensibly a secular city located historically in one of the classic Western, liberal, and secular states. However, as much recent scholarship has stressed, cities are more accurately understood as places where the secular and the sacred coexist, interact, and constitute each other (e.g., Goh and van der Veer 2016; van der Veer and Lehmann 1999). Studies of the fundamentalist city (AlSayyad and Massoumi 2011) and the post-secular city (Beaumont and Baker 2011) point to the significance of religious movements in seeking to (re)claim cities or to defend the sacred sites that they contain (Friedland and Hecht 1998; Hassner 2009). Violent struggles over the state expose the processes that link religion and secular nationalism and become

---

[5] Michael Billig's (1995) concept of banal nationalism might be understood as a form of vernacular nationalism, which is often tacit, rather than explicit – it involves everyday representations of the nation that build a sense of collective belonging and is deeply embodied and emplaced in the habits and practices of everyday life.

342 Liam O'Dowd

materialized in the built environment – indeed violence itself does much to sacralize cities by welding popular memories to particular places.

INTERSECTIONS OF IMPERIALISM, URBANISM, AND "RELIGION": THE CREATION OF TERRITORIAL ENCLOSURES

Historically, the creation of a network of urban settlements (alongside land appropriation) has been central to Britain's imperial and settler colonizing project in Ireland. This project, reiterated in many parts of the British Empire, involved selectively co-opting and often consolidating ethno-religious groups. The partition of Ireland in 1920–21 was an imperial arbitration of the so-called Irish Question. It marked the failure (or the reluctance) of British imperial nationalism, after the Act of Union (1801), to assimilate the whole island population to British citizenship. Irish anti-imperial nationalism, on the other hand, was unable to overcome British and Unionist opposition to Irish independence in Northern Ireland. The outcome was two new asymmetrical political jurisdictions centered on Dublin and Belfast, respectively. An alliance of Unionist and British imperial elites carved out a new political unit within the UK state, based on a sectarian headcount aimed at giving Protestants a "permanent" two-to-one majority. Its urban lynchpin was the Protestant and Unionist city of Belfast – the only major industrial center on the island. In the rest of Ireland, the old imperial capital Dublin became the increasingly Catholic capital of a jurisdiction that was overwhelmingly Catholic.

Thus while the role of religion in Irish and British state-formation was incontrovertible, partition ensured that religious division was more comprehensively enshrined in two separate jurisdictions. What was created, therefore, in Ireland were two "territorial enclosures" – one dominated by Catholics (in the Free State, formerly the Republic of Ireland) and one by Protestants (in Northern Ireland). The latter remained part of a British state that retained the powers of taxation and external relations but devolved the policing and micromanagement of intercommunal antagonism and inequality to a local (Protestant) ethnocratic administration. In sum, the most toxic and antagonistic aspects of the long history of British-Irish relationships – its Protestant settler-Catholic native dimensions – were now contained, deepened, and institutionalized within a small six-county area of approximately 1.5 million people and provided with all the superficial trappings of democratic majority rule.

The new Northern Ireland was fractured into a mosaic of internal territorial enclosures. Some, like Belfast, initially had large Protestant majorities; others had Catholic majorities; some were more evenly balanced. This mosaic was rooted in the historic plantation of Ulster and modified and reconstituted by urbanization and industrialization in the nineteenth century. The boundaries – and sometimes the existence – of these enclosures became a matter of periodic, occasionally violent, contention. The exploration of the different meanings of territorialized religion,

Northern Ireland: Does Religion Still Matter?

nationalism, and the links between them are integral to any understanding of violent conflict in Northern Ireland. In what follows, I concentrate on the links between popular religion and the "enclosure" politics of contending nationalisms.

FORMS OF RELIGION AND NATIONALISM AND ASYMMETRIES OF POWER

Contending religious and nationalist politics come in several forms at state and urban levels in Northern Ireland, however, and the underlying structural asymmetries of the Northern Ireland case make it all the more necessary to distinguish among them. If the conflict is to be understood as one of competing Irish and British nationalisms, then the difference between them at the macro-level must be acknowledged. Adopting the distinction used by Charles Tilly (1990), Irish nationalism historically may be characterized as a "nation" in search of a state, whereas British nationalism implies "a state in search of a nation." Northern Ireland is testimony to the limits of both forms. Irish nationalism in Northern Ireland has been largely Republican and anti-imperialist, although historically its constitutional strands contemplated a future within the British empire. The anti-imperialist strand appeals to a secular enlightenment tradition associated with the United Irish movement of the late eighteenth century founded in Belfast. This was a precocious form of nationalism modeled on the French and American revolutions.

Both the imperial and the anti-imperialist forms of Irish nationalism have been influenced throughout the nineteenth and twentieth centuries by the growth of Catholicism, in the shape of a formidable and centralized Church, on the one hand, and a potent melange of popular beliefs and practice, on the other. Irish Republican nationalism appealed for the support of all Irish people regardless of creed in the struggle for national self-determination. In practice, however, the rhetoric of the 1916 insurrection, and more recently the 1980–81 Hunger Strikers, drew on the cultural repertoire of Catholicism, with its myths of sacrifice, victimhood, and redemption.[6]

The UK's long and incomplete journey[7] from imperial to national state is also colored by its religious dimension. Part of this trajectory has been an incomplete transition from a Protestant to a secular state. Contemporary Ulster Unionism does have its British nationalist strands that lay claim to a progressive secularism allegedly enshrined in the contemporary UK state. But the currently dominant strand in Unionism harks back to a settler-colonial past that favors the maintenance of local forms of ethnic dominance and exclusivity under the umbrella of the British state

---

[6] The 1916–22 partially successful movement for Irish independence, hugely influential subsequently for Northern Ireland Republicans, appealed to a hybrid ideology which embraced the tenets of classic eighteenth-century republican nationalism, the romantic nationalism of nineteenth-century Europe, and the cultural repertoire of European Catholicism. In Ireland, however, unlike much of Catholic Europe, the Church was not compromised by formal ties to the British state.

[7] Irish resistance has historically marked the limits of British nation-building as has contemporary support for Scottish separatism within Britain itself.

Liam O'Dowd

(see Todd 1988). More recently, it has found common cause with a renewed British nationalism committed to British sovereignty outside the EU.[8] Whereas the Catholic Church has been a monolithic organizational presence in nationalist Ireland, Protestantism is divided on denominational grounds and builds a common Unionist position based on grassroots practices of the Orange Order that fuse evangelical religion with popular Unionist politics and a reverence for the ritualistic trappings of the British state – notably its monarchy and military.[9]

These asymmetries that pervade the Northern Ireland conflict are rooted in power inequalities – the unequal material and ideological resources available to the protagonists.[10] Too often, these inequalities are obscured by political analyses that erroneously portray two equal, if antagonistic, communities, managed by a British state acting as an "external" neutral arbiter (see O'Dowd 2014).

BELFAST: THE INTERSECTIONS OF IMPERIALISM, POPULAR SECTARIANISM, AND NATIONALISM

In Belfast, the intersections between imperialism, popular sectarianism, and nationalism have become embedded and emplaced in concrete and specific forms. As a postindustrial Western city, by the twenty-first century, Belfast might have been expected to manifest a largely secular rather than religious politics. In the late eighteenth century, it had been the epicenter of a short-lived Republican nationalism inspired by the American and French revolutions and appealing to both Protestants and Catholics. In the nineteenth century, however, Belfast was to become a major industrial city of the British Empire and, by 1920, the focal point of Protestant Unionist and British imperial opposition to the movement for Irish independence.

As Belfast grew rapidly from the 1850s onward, its street politics had become infused by ethno-religious conflict and communal antagonisms translated from the countryside and manifested in periodic riots, intimidation, and contention over Orange parades, political preachers, and local sectarian boundaries (Bardon 1982; Doyle 2009; O'Dowd 1987; Redmond 1961). Sectarian urban conflicts were further exacerbated by evangelical revivals on the Protestant side and the growth of popular devotional practices imported from Europe on the Catholic side. The classic study

---

[8] The Democratic Unionist Party's support of the minority Conservative government in Britain enables the latter to continue to negotiate its exit from the EU.

[9] The Orange Order founded in 1795 is a pan-Protestant organization that has aimed to combat the influence of the Catholic Church while linking defense of the Union with Britain with popular forms of political religion. It has a long tradition of ceremonial marching, which has provoked periodic rioting and intercommunal clashes.

[10] The British state has been the overwhelming repository of economic, political, and military power throughout the conflict. Unionists have sought to draw on this power while asserting popular territorial dominance within Northern Ireland through both official and paramilitary means; Nationalists have relied more on cultural and ideological mobilization punctuated by insurrectionary paramilitary violence.

Northern Ireland: Does Religion Still Matter? 345

of Belfast by Jones (1960) confirmed the longevity and depth of residential segregation on religious grounds. Violence, religion, and nationalism had interacted and become inscribed and emplaced in the spatial and physical fabric of the city – a process further enhanced by the recent thirty-year conflict (Shirlow and Murtagh 2006). In his comparative study of ethno-nationally divided cities in Europe, Hepburn (2004, 158) singles out Belfast, arguing that nowhere has the pattern of ethnic conflict and violence over the past two centuries been so unchanging and unremitting despite the scale of constitutional and economic change.

Localized conflict in Belfast was periodically magnified by grander political and religious conflicts – e.g., the partition of Ireland in 1920–21 induced violence, rioting, and sectarian assassinations in Belfast during that period; the suppression of the Northern Ireland civil rights movement in the 1960s modeled on its US equivalent eventually gave rise to the recent Troubles. During the latter, the major escalations of political violence by pro- and anti-state paramilitaries and the official British state security forces threatened to transcend the localized politics of territorial enclosure.[11] Ultimately, however, these politics remained constrained by ritualized and mutually recognized claims to communal territory and never approached the scale of violent ethnic cleansing or forced population displacement that was to characterize the religious nationalist conflicts in Cyprus, the Balkans, and Palestine. Part of the reason was the overwhelming economic, political, and military power of successive British governments vis-à-vis Ireland. While integral to institutionalizing communal rivalry and inequality in the first place, they were also able to limit the resultant violence while ensuring that the basis of the conflict would endure.[12]

BELFAST IN POST-CONFLICT TRANSITION

Since the 1960s, grander historical forces (capitalist industrialization, imperialism, and nationalism) have been reconfigured and fused in new ways with localized conflicts. Nevertheless, after a period of direct rule by Westminster from 1972 to 1998, a power-sharing executive was eventually installed in 1998. Based on an elite bargain between the two ethno-national communities, and strongly supported by the British, Irish, American, and EU governments, it was legitimized by referenda in both parts of Ireland. The Good Friday Agreement (1998) was both novel and

---

[11] Throughout the conflict, civil rights protesters, Republican paramilitaries, and moderate Nationalists have sought to internationalize the conflict by mobilizing support from "external" sources. Unionists and successive British governments have been much more prone to emphasize territorial containment.

[12] In an interesting comparative study of partition in Northern Ireland and Silesia between 1918 and 1922, Tim Wilson (2010) noted the much greater violence in the Silesian case. His explanation was that communal boundaries were already fixed in Northern Ireland and violence was merely a means of maintaining these boundaries. In Silesia, however (as indeed later in Yugoslavia), there was greater social and residential mixing and integration between ethnic groups – a situation that required more radical violence and displacement to effect a partition and true ethnic separation.

complex, but the process of implementation and consolidation continues to be long and torturous. By 2007, a power-sharing executive was stabilized, even if it remains vulnerable to deadlock and mutual vetoes – most recently exemplified in the collapse of the executive in January 2017. Internationally, however, Northern Ireland appeared as a rare exemplar of a successful "peace process."

Yet, at the time of our research, Belfast's transition appeared even more remarkable than that of Northern Ireland as a whole. For the first time since its foundation, Belfast was no longer a majority Protestant city; rather, today its city council was now finely balanced between Unionists and Nationalists.[13] The last vestiges of its claim to be an industrial city had disappeared as its economy became heavily dependent on services and public expenditure (R. Wilson 2016). New workplaces were more integrated than their predecessors. Urban regeneration was combined with a rebranding of the city as a site of festivals, heritage commemoration, and tourism. Meanwhile the city council and state agencies attempted to promote a "shared city project" to mirror the "power-sharing" arrangements at Northern Ireland level (O'Dowd and Komarova 2013).

The cessation of organized political violence was replaced by low-intensity violence involving periodic rioting at interface areas complemented by criminal activities of disaffected paramilitaries, especially in Loyalist areas, but also involving dissident Republicans. This low-level informal violence coexisted with the intensification of "culture wars" or ideological struggles, most notably in the working-class areas most affected by the conflict. Here, the central issue was how the "conflict" was to be remembered and its outcomes understood. The clash of meta-narratives regarding the ownership of Belfast intensified – whether it was to remain a Protestant, Unionist, and British city, or whether it was to be understood as an increasingly Catholic, Nationalist, and Irish city (Bryan 2015; Jarman 1999; Nolan et al. 2014).

The struggles to control public space were intimately linked to attempts to control "the past." After the paramilitary ceasefires in the mid-1990s, political conflict had intensified over (a) what to remember (and forget); (b) how to remember; and (c) the impact of acts of remembrance (see Stier and Landres 2006, 8). Of course, a divisive politics of memory was scarcely new and had long been central to the history of plantation, state, and nation-building in Ireland. But by the early twenty-first century it had crystallized around the violent thirty-year conflict of the Troubles. It reflected major differences in interpreting what that conflict was about in the first place: For Irish Nationalists, the conflict was variously a struggle for national liberation against

---

[13] Russell (2013, 8) points out that in the 2011 census, Catholics accounted for 49 percent of the Belfast city council area, an increase of 4.3 percent since 2001. The Protestant proportion was 42.3 percent, a decline of 12 percent in the same period. The demographic shift had less to do with violent forms of ethnic cleansing than with "secular" processes of deindustrialization and the greater suburbanization of Protestants from the 1960s onward. Middle-class Protestants and working-class Protestants able to access employment in the smaller "Protestant" towns surrounding Belfast left the Belfast city council areas in greater numbers than Catholics.

the British state and a struggle against a discriminatory ethnocratic regime that monopolized power and denied them civil and human rights. For Unionists, on the other hand, the conflict was rooted either in a "thirty-year crime wave" or in unjustified terrorism that threatened their British citizenship and their survival as a distinct people. Both sides and successive British governments had selectively justified the use of violence (whether by official security forces or pro- or anti-state paramilitaries). This politics of memory had become most sharply manifest in the struggles to claim public space in Belfast through marches, flag protests, memorials, murals, and a range of everyday practices. While, at first glance, religion seemed far less important than nationalism in post-conflict Belfast, nevertheless, like the latter, it served as repository of collective memory; it was deeply involved in commemoration and in giving meaning to violence and victimhood, while its rituals and territorial enclosures ensured that it remained intertwined with the ethno-national division that had materialized in the urban environment.

RESEARCHING RELIGION AND NATIONALISM IN POST-CONFLICT BELFAST

Our study aimed to explore the contemporary political role of popular religion in a Belfast shaped by its interwoven histories of imperialism, nationalism, religion, and partition. More specifically, however, our research project was framed by the overall Good Friday peace settlement, on the one hand, and by the intensification of mainly nonviolent struggles over the legacy of the conflict and over who might now control or "claim" the city, on the other. Informing our research was an underlying question: To what extent did the contemporary city mark a break with its long history of ethno-nationalist and religious conflict?

Empirical Sources

Our study employed several methods of data collection.[14] We began by mapping churches in Belfast, a relatively time-consuming exercise as no single database for religious institutions was available. These churches historically anchor the various sociospatial communities of Belfast in the sectarian geography of the city. They are significant nodes enveloped by more fluid and transient popular struggles over the control of public space. They are, in one sense, a product of institutionalized religion, but even as formal observance declined over time, they have remained key sites and objects of vernacular religion in Asad's (1999) terms and provide a network of physical reference points for everyday urban life.

---

[14] Data were collected by Martina McKnight and Milena Komarova (research officers on the "Conflict in Cities" project) as well as by the author.

348   Liam O'Dowd

Twenty-six semi-structured interviews were conducted with clergy, members of faith-based groups, or community workers linked to faith-based groups. These respondents worked precisely at urban interfaces between popular and institutionalized religion and had direct and immediate experience of dealing with violence on the streets during the conflict and its uneasy aftermath. In their interviews, they were able to reflect on firsthand experience of the grassroots nexus between religion, politics, and violent conflict. In recruiting participants, a form of purposive sampling was used as we sought to engage interviewees who (a) either during the Troubles or currently, ministered or worked in interface areas and had been, or are, actively involved in cross-community activities or peace-building; (b) belonged to organizations such as the Orange Order; or (c) were engaged in displays of religion in public space. These criteria were not mutually exclusive. The interviewees were also chosen to reflect major geographic and denominational differences.[15]

Visual data (video and photographic vignettes) were collected of the intersection of popular religious practices and politics in public space. This was supplemented by direct observation of Orange parades asserting their claim on public space and interfaith marches aimed at promoting a "shared city." This research material further contextualized our interviews, as did the extensive body of secondary empirical research on recent political struggles over public space in Belfast.

STUDY FINDINGS

City of Churches

Our eventual tally of churches in Belfast (2011) was 47 Catholic, 354 "other Christian,"[16] and 7 other faiths. This is probably an underestimate, as it does not include many house churches or more temporary church sites. As Table 13.1 shows, Protestant churches are far more numerous per head of population than their Catholic counterparts. While numbers of churches are not to be confused with the scale or frequency of religious observance or religiosity, they do reveal the extent to which Belfast was constructed as Protestant space while reflecting the different historical trajectories of the Protestant and Catholic population (see Table 13.1). Table 13.1 also suggests a remarkable growth in the density of both Protestant and Catholic churches (i.e., as measured by the number of Protestants and Catholic residents per church) in Belfast. By 2011, density had increased dramatically for both communities but there remained a far greater density among Protestants.

---

[15] Interviews lasted between one and two hours. All interviews focused on the links between religion and politics, the role of religion in encouraging violence and conflict resolution, interchurch collaboration, and everyday priorities and activities.

[16] This included the main Protestant denominations, Church of Ireland, Presbyterian, Methodist, as well as a host of smaller sects professing "reformed" Christianity.

TABLE 13.1 *Average number of Belfast residents per church by religious denomination*

Year	Protestants	Catholics	Total Belfast population
1861	1,300	10,300	121,000
1901	2,248	9,311	349,180
2011	382	2,785	265,691

Sources: Brewer, Keane, and Livingstone (2006, 1); "Conflict in Cities and the Contested State" research project (see note 1); Doyle (2009, 23)

These data should be interpreted cautiously as they are compiled from different sources that are not fully comparable. However, they do indicate clear long-term trends.

At one level, formal religious practice is privatized within church buildings; however, the Catholic churches are typically linked to a network of civil society organizations – charitable organizations, credit unions, and schools. As a minority religion until recently, Catholic churches have served as centers or anchors for clearly defined territorial communities. Because of their political and demographic dominance, Protestant churches were less territorially restricted; their Congregationalist structure and links with the state's educational system presents a pattern of dispersal. Protestantism is highly differentiated and fractured into a number of denominations, whereas Catholicism is represented by a unitary church.

Churches represent continuity in the physical landscape in the midst of radical urban restructuring, demographic change, and deindustrialization that has been occurring since the 1960s. The iconic sites of Belfast's industrial past have disappeared or have been transformed, as have the major commercial outlets now replaced by the chain stores and malls of international corporations. However, the physical infrastructure – what Hayden (2015) terms the religioscape – survives. The greater suburbanization and outmigration of Protestants have left many of their church congregations diminished, even if they periodically return to the city for services.[17] Their clergy also are less likely than Catholics to live in proximity to their churches. In one Protestant view, "the strength of our [Protestant] churches lies in suburban and rural [areas] and the conflict in the city is kept at an arm's length" (interview with the author, June 15, 2011).

[17] Orange lodges historically linked to inner-city localities have many members who have moved out of Belfast inner-city communities but frequently return on days of big Orange marches to "reclaim" the streets. This process is even more marked in Derry, where all but a small number of Protestants live outside the historic walled city.

SHARED THEMES

Beneath the major binary division between two religio-national meta-narratives in our interviews lay a range of diverse practices and opinions. Nonetheless, some common themes emerged. All our respondents tacitly recognized a distinction between religion and secular national politics, even though they varied on how religion and politics were related. Despite their variable views on this relationship, all agreed that the various Christian sects had some responsibility for communal division, violence, and the historical legacies of segregation and communal antagonism. Opinions varied, of course, on the nature and extent of that responsibility.

All our interviewees professed themselves to be opposed to violence, which they attributed mainly to secular politics. However, on closer scrutiny, this rhetorical opposition proved to be far more nuanced and complex. All our respondents were involved in dealing with consequences of violence, death, victimhood, and intimidation at the hands of paramilitaries and/or state security forces. All were governed by abiding affiliations to place – i.e., by a localism shaped and bounded by violent conflict.

The role of churches in commemorating death and officiating at funerals was critically important. Paramilitary funerals were particularly contentious on the Nationalist side when the rituals of paramilitary display and commemoration clashed with British army attempts to prevent them. These clashes also posed sharp dilemmas for local Catholic clergy caught between their churches' formal opposition to paramilitary violence, their local communities' support for the IRA's struggle against the state, and their obligations to organize funeral rituals for the victims of the conflict and their families. Paramilitary displays in churches and church grounds crystallized these tensions. (See Ardoyne Commemoration Project 2002 for detailed accounts of political funerals in one Nationalist area of North Belfast.) The role of Catholic clergy in such funeral commemorations was heavily criticized by some of our Protestant respondents, who distinguished between the "legitimate" violence of the state security forces and the illegitimate violence of the IRA and other paramilitaries.

Thus, our respondents' opposition to violence was nuanced and shaped by the exigencies of local contexts. Opposition was most evident and unambiguous where our respondents combined to sympathize with victims of sectarian killings on both sides by jointly visiting the families affected. However, our respondents varied in terms of their "peace activism" and their perceived capacity to develop cross-communal links. The latter were typically the result of individual initiatives and responses to periods of intense crisis. While none of our respondents openly advocated violence, they were routinely involved in giving it meaning through their ritual commemorations of death. They shared these practices uneasily with secular protagonists of the conflict. In periods of intense conflict, such practices were sometimes assimilated into a celebration of sacrifice and victimhood on behalf of the two contending ethno-national communities.

While much of our data reveals the continuity and resilience of popular religion in the midst of often-violent political change, all our respondents acknowledged that formal religious observance, as measured by popular involvement in rites of passage, births, marriages, and deaths, was in decline. Catholic clergy agreed that church attendance was no longer perceived as compulsory, thereby converging with Protestant practice. This recognition of "secularization" was offset by references to a small number of highly committed, "prophetic" groups who were willing to innovate and take risks in promoting peace, cross-community solidarity, and shared urban space. Ganiel (2016) provides further evidence of the growth of these extra-institutional groups. The decline in formal religious practice, however, has led to a common awareness that clergy and religious activists have lost much of their influence as political intermediaries with state bodies and with the "other" community. They have been largely replaced by community workers, professionals, paramilitaries, and local politicians.

INTERCOMMUNAL ASYMMETRIES AND DIVERGENCES

The deep historical and structural asymmetries of the "two communities" in the Northern Ireland conflict were also clearly evident in our interview material. These were reflected in different understandings of religion and its appropriate relationship to politics; different forms of religious and political mobilization; and divergent experiences of, and attitudes toward, the state. A Protestant respondent from an overwhelmingly Catholic part of the city outlined the practical divergences between the two communities:

> They [the Protestant working-class communities] struggle to have a political voice, they feel themselves sold down the river ... they feel they have gained nothing and lost everything ... There isn't a strong sense of leadership ... I think the church could [help] but ... it is as divided as the Protestant community, and is that why the community is so divided because the church itself struggles to work together in any unified way? That is the strength of the Roman Catholic Church ... [unlike Catholics] we fall out with somebody, and there you go. We have a new church starting down the road. (Interview with the author, May 10, 2011)

Our Catholic respondents broadly agreed with this assessment but were more skeptical of the political influence of the Catholic Church in their communities. They described a different local political configuration than their Protestant counterparts. Unlike their Loyalist counterparts, most Republican paramilitaries had made the transition to politics as elected Sinn Fein representatives, and it was they rather than the clergy who now mediated relationships with official state agencies. The clear tension between the formal Catholic Church leadership and the

Republican movement over the use of violence had also helped reduce the clergy's political role, although at local level, this division was more blurred.

In Protestant areas, paramilitaries largely failed to make the transition to electoral politics; nonetheless, they remained power brokers in their own communities. Never fully committed to the principles of the 1998 settlement, they were keen to mobilize street violence in defense of threats to Protestant "culture and heritage" – threats encapsulated in the rise of Sinn Fein to prominence in the Stormont government and the Belfast city council. Much Protestant paramilitary violence was turned inward in controlling their own communities, often through the drug trade and other criminal activities. The fractured nature of the Protestant churches weakened local opposition to this paramilitary activity. There was recognition on both sides that Catholic working-class areas had more balanced demographic profiles, and benefited from a more effective educational system under the aegis of the Church. Protestant working-class youth, on the other hand, performed poorly in the state-controlled schools.

Remarkably, Catholic clergy, who belonged to a more centralized and hierarchal church, claimed a greater degree of discretion in their everyday activities, whereas the more fractured Protestant clergy were far more directly accountable to their congregations who could get rid of them, if they adopted unacceptable religious or political stances. Alternatively, congregations could join another existing Protestant church or found a new one.

In terms of their overall interpretations, Catholic clergy were unanimous that it was largely a "political" conflict for Catholics, whereas, for Protestants, "religion" was more central. While our Protestant respondents did not disagree with this interpretation, they were less explicit about it as they tended to see "religion" in the plural. Catholics, as a minority in a historically Protestant UK state, seem to have a greater sense of the separateness of church and state, whereas Protestants draw on historical memories of the UK state's identification with "reformed religion."

Moreover, Protestants did recognize explicitly and implicitly that popular Unionist politics were infused by varieties of Protestantism. Mitchell's (2010) close study of working-class Loyalists and paramilitaries – among the least formally observant groups in Northern Ireland – confirmed the shifting and porous boundaries between religion and ethnicity (see also Todd 2010). Mitchell details the tendency of these groups to sometimes combine violent activism with religion. Protestant paramilitary prisoners were more likely also than their Catholic counterparts to embrace "religion" as an alternative to organized violence.

The priority given to cross-communal ties and reconciliation varied, but it was not seen as a practical priority in many local communities and congregations, as they were too busy with the problems of their own followers. Protestant clergy found it difficult to substitute for the lack of a political cadre like Sinn Fein. Like their parishioners, they were often unable to give priority to promoting cross-communal ties. In the words of one of our respondents in Protestant East Belfast, people in the side streets "cannot get through the day, let alone starting to talk to people who [they] don't even like" (interview with the author, August 10, 2011).

A member of the Orange Order contrasted the role of Sinn Fein in preparing their community for peace; he suggested that Protestants had no narrative about the "peace process":

> Protestants, I say, were never prepared for peace ... they woke up one day and Paisley had signed something and it was "whoa, where did that come from?" There was no preparation. (Interview with the author, May 18, 2011)

One of our Catholic respondents confirmed that local Protestant paramilitary commanders thought "the Catholics had everything – credit unions, housing associations, etc." (interview with the author, September 13, 2011).[18] Popular Protestant conviction that they were losing the peace and "in retreat" provided an opportunity for local paramilitaries and young people to take on the mantle of "defending the Protestant people." This took the form of "representative violence" at interfaces or in terms of reclaiming the city center and main roads by populating them with a profusion of British and paramilitary flags, or by murals or graffiti in residential areas.[19] The ongoing struggle to control or claim territory and public space often assumed a zero-sum form. In the aftermath of the 1998 peace settlement, the number of peace walls dividing Catholic and Protestant working-class communities increased substantially. These walls consolidated territorial enclosure and were frequently the site of recurring low-level violence between youths on either side of the communal divide. Middle-class areas remained more mixed, but persisting ethno-national divisions meant that majority electoral support continued to be given to political parties identified with the two ethno-national communities.

INTRA-COMMUNAL DIVERGENCES

There was a wide range of attitudes and practices among our Protestant respondents in how they saw the relationship between religion and politics. One indicator here was in the spectrum of stances vis-à-vis the Orange Order. These ranged from active membership in the Order to celebrating it as a body committed to a fusion of popular religion and politics to condemning it as a divisive force in Northern Ireland. One clergyman, a high-profile member of the Orange Order, saw it as

---

[18] This theme recurred in many of our interviews and resonated with a Protestant sense that they were "losing the peace," whereas Catholics were more highly organized politically and were greater beneficiaries of the "peace settlement." However, this perception has to be set against findings of system social surveys that suggest that overall Catholic working-class communities remain relatively more deprived than their Protestant counterparts, although better served by their educational system.

[19] The flag protests of 2012 caused major disruption and were occasioned by an evenly balanced city council decision not to fly the British "Union" flag over the city hall every day of the year. Rather, the council had decided to fly the Union flag on far fewer days marked by major British national commemorations (see Nolan et al. 2014).

a Christian organization based on four pillars, "religious, political, social, and charitable." He saw a link between preserving Protestant areas and maintaining the right to parade: "If housing goes the wrong way, then we will lose our parade, and that is still a big thing with people." By housing, he meant the preservation of segregated Protestant housing. He also regretted that suburbanite Protestants were forgetting their (inner-city) past (interview with the author, May 18, 2011).

The religion-politics relationship is also affected by varying conceptions of religion. For some, "religion" was mainly about witnessing fundamental and nonnegotiable biblical truths, as well as about salvation. This emphasized the primacy of religious belief and implied a distance from politics, at least in principle. At the other end of the spectrum were those who were highly committed to ecumenism and building Christian unity – a perspective that seemed to imply a degree of political activism in promoting peace. In between there were different views about the degree to which Protestant churches should be engaged in peace activism, social welfare work, and community development.

On the Catholic side, there were divergences between clergy ministering to churches in overwhelming Catholic areas and those attached to churches located in largely Protestant areas. Among the latter, there was a strong sense of being besieged – of needing to "keep your head down" to minimize publicity and the scale and intensity of anti-Catholic sectarianism and attacks on the church. One of our respondents, a Catholic priest with a church in an overwhelmingly Protestant area of the city, detailed the regular attacks on his church and the sectarianism directed at him and his parishioners. While he had good relationships with individual Unionist politicians and Protestant clergy in the area, he generally was reluctant to report physical attacks to the police in case they intensified. He observed "in this part of the city you [i.e., Catholics] are guests; we are tolerated" (interview with the author, July 21, 2011).

Clergy in overwhelmingly Catholic areas by contrast had much less familiarity with sectarian attacks on their churches. They were more involved in ecumenical activities and social welfare work; here, key sites in Catholic West Belfast such as Clonard Monastery were the focal points for local community. This monastery annually hosts the most remarkable public display of popular religion in the city – a ten-day novena or set of devotional practices that drew nonobservant as well as observant Catholics from across the city in the thousands.

In post-conflict Belfast, a precarious form of antagonistic tolerance coexists with middle-class political apathy and rigid working-class segregation. The significance of the politics of territorial closure persists. This has long characterized communal relationships in Belfast and means that violence and the threat of violence remains ever-present. However, for much of the time, violence has been relatively ritualized and constrained and has functioned as a form of mutual deterrence and maintenance of local boundaries. The thirty-year-old conflict has also generated some collaboration between religious activists across the communal divide. This has been facilitated by the crisis of authority in the Irish Catholic Church (Ganiel 2016), making it less of a monolithic threat to many Protestants. Yet, secular ethno-nationalist politics and religious practices have remained mutually reinforcing over time, even if there are signs of a new tension between them in contemporary Belfast.

The links between ritual and territory are shared by both "religion" and nationalism and are strongest where the two overlap. As Koster (2003, 216) observes: "ritual performances create a symbolic territorial model by filling a certain designated space with prescribed ritual actions – but also with symbols." As our observational and photographic research shows, competing territorial enclosures and their respective rituals and symbols collide, both at the level of localities as well as in Belfast and Northern Ireland considered as wholes. When transgressions occur through "ritual overflow" (Koster 2003, 218), violence frequently ensues. Overflow is typically linked to contentious marches, forms of intimidation, rioting, or symbolic claiming, which provoke representative violence. The consequences include antagonistic forms of re-sacralization where memories of violence are enshrined and localized in particular sites, such as churches, memorial gardens, cemeteries, murals, local museums, and interpretative centers (Fraser 2012; Rolston 2010).

The "ownership" of contemporary Belfast is not currently a matter for contending armies. Instead, claims to appropriate its public spaces are made in more indirect, embodied, and everyday ways that signal religious and national allegiance – in the multitude of churches, Orange halls, cemeteries, monuments and memorial gardens, parades, murals, painted curbstones, shrines, flags, medals pinned on prams, body tattoos, and football shirts (see Leonard 2010; Smyth and McKnight 2013). Some claims are fixed and embedded in the physical infrastructure of the city. Others are more fluid and transient. Underlying all these claims are contending meta-narratives, sharpened by thirty years of organized violence: Belfast is a British, Protestant Unionist city or, alternatively, Belfast is an increasingly Irish, Catholic, and Nationalist city. Each side has its iconic localities – for Protestants, those are Shankill, Sandy Row, and Newtownards Road; for Catholics, the Falls Road/West Belfast, the Markets, and the Short Strand. As Mitchell (2006, 91–93) notes, "religious codes, symbols and categorisations litter the landscape and, particularly in everyday life, religion continues to play a role in the creating and maintaining of communities."

Intercommunal antagonisms in post-conflict Belfast are mediated through a politics of contested popular memory and disagreements over the meaning and significance to be accorded to acts of representative violence. For Protestants, official state violence is legitimate, while anti-state Republican violence is illegitimate and morally repulsive. There is less Protestant consensus on pro-state paramilitary violence – that is, the self-proclaimed "breaking of the law to uphold the law" (i.e., the preservation of the Union with Britain). Meanwhile, a strand of Republican nationalism sees anti-state violence as legitimate in principle because

Northern Ireland itself is an illegitimate, antidemocratic, and imperial construction. While there is considerable cross-communal opposition to any return of organized political violence currently, there remains little agreement on the causes of past violence, on victims and perpetrators, or on the hierarchies of significance to be accorded to violent conflict and its victims.

Low-intensity sectarian violence has persisted among young working-class males at interfaces and in defacing physical expressions of the "Other" community (Jarman 2005). When stimulated by communally based political parties in attempts to consolidate their electoral support, they have the potential to erupt into street confrontation and violence. A major example was the four months of popular flag protests by Loyalists (Nolan et al. 2014). On the other side, dissident Republicans are showing signs of "returning to violence," portraying Sinn Fein as traitors as they are now complicit in British state governance of Northern Ireland.

It is in contested localities and the attempts to claim public space that we can most clearly see the interweaving of popular forms of religion and nationalism and how they, in turn, link memory, violence, and "place." It is at this level that the relentless reciprocity of the Northern Ireland conflict persists with the ever-present threat that mutual deterrence will boil over into more extensive violence.

But the relentless reciprocity of mutual antagonism at the locality level has a wider provenance also: It is deeply embedded in the history of settler colonialism, imperialism, and different forms of nationalism. While the links between institutionalized religion and the national state are now less contentious, "religion" conceived as a set of lived experiences and practices drives the politics of memory, violence, and place and remains a political resource for nationalist conflicts over the state. While churches may have radically declining congregations, they remain repositories of collective (communal) memory that is materialized in the enduring sectarian geography of a city with major symbolic significance for Irish and British forms of nationalism.

CONCLUSION

The case of Northern Ireland in general, and Belfast in particular, suggests that the two perspectives outlined at the beginning of this chapter are inadequate. First, the tendency to ignore religion as a factor in contemporary Northern Ireland is misplaced. This tendency is rooted in an excessively narrow definition of religion and nationalist politics that understands both solely in terms of formal relationships between religious institutions and the national state. Our research undermines the proposition that religious division per se is intrinsically violent and intractable. But when convergent and mutually supportive, religion and secular nationalism can sustain enduring violence and division.

Religious change is occurring. Post-conflict Belfast is characterized by two forms of secularization identified by Casanova (2006, 7): the decline in formal religious observance and the compartmentalization of (formal) secular and religious authority. But there is little evidence on its streets of the third form he identifies – the privatization of religion. Instead, popular religion and nationalism overlap and intersect in ways that sustain the binary communal division embedded in the urban environment and underpinning political conflict in Northern Ireland. Popular religion and vernacular (or banal) nationalism have much in common in terms of ritual performance and overspill – i.e., the significance attributed to representative violence and their capacity to sacralize public space. Both "mark space as sacred" (Sinha 2016) even if their object of transcendence differs (i.e., the community of believers and the national state). Religion and nationalism serve as reservoirs of communal memory that can be mutually reinforcing. While popular religion may be a marker of nationalism, this marker is not to be understood as an inert and unchanging badge. Much depends on the form that religious practice takes and how it relates to different forms of nationalism. In times of violent conflict, popular religion and nationalism may converge (or even fuse); at other times, they diverge as their different reference points are exposed.

Evidence from Belfast reveals the necessity of distinguishing between forms of religion and forms of nationalism while exploring the multiple links between them. Understanding such complexities is critical even in an area where nearly all the protagonists are nominally Christian and that has been part of the UK state for over 200 years. Viewed in the round, it might be argued that popular religion and nationalism are "Siamese twins" in Asad's (1999) terms. In this, Northern Ireland is in tune with forms of religious nationalism elsewhere. However, the Siamese twins metaphor needs to be elaborated upon by recognizing that twins can be linked in different ways.

In comparative terms, Belfast might seem like an unlikely location for conflicts driven by religious nationalists. It is hardly a sacred or a holy city in the same sense as Jerusalem, Mecca, or Qom. Nor does it contain high-profile sacred sites central to a conflict over public space. However, the intensification of culture wars in post-conflict Belfast underlines the extent to which capital cities have become "sacred" to the protagonists of ethno-national conflicts.

Belfast's political violence is more localized, ritualized, and limited than the mass slaughter and population displacement associated with religious-nationalist conflicts in the Middle East and South Asia. Its core dynamic is driven less by objectives of assimilation or elimination of the Other than it is by the preservation of both political communities in a mutually defining, antagonistic relationship. However, the antagonistic tolerance and asymmetrical power relationships that have underpinned the stability of Northern Ireland have been undermined by the Troubles, the Good Friday Agreement, and the changing nature of Irish and British nationalisms. Demographic shifts mean that the two communities are now approaching parity. Accordingly, Protestant claims to monopolize power have been abandoned. Instead, Unionist parties have renewed appeals to much older settler myths of a besieged minority facing the inexorable onward march of Irish nationalism.[20] "Culture wars" have intensified in the public domain and in actual urban public space over the right to march, flags, emblems, and, most recently, the Irish language. While religion in a doctrinal or institutional sense is seldom at stake in these conflicts, in its popular forms it reinforces them. Additionally, the leading Protestant party has forged a new alliance with the neo-imperial nationalism of the British Conservative Party intent on gaining independence from the EU.[21]

While conventional academic wisdom suggests that it was the secular ideal of nationalism and the national state that was exported from Western Europe and the US to the rest of the world, the Irish example suggests that particular understandings of religion were deeply inscribed in this ideal from the start (Cavanaugh 2009). In principle, at least, it would appear that the links between religious and nationalist antagonisms first developed in the heartlands of Western imperialism. It follows that they should be examined within the same interpretative frame as contemporary examples of violent religious nationalism elsewhere. Similarly, given intellectual preoccupation with the return of religion to the public domain in the secular West, the Northern Ireland case raises the question of whether it ever left this domain in the first place.

Belfast in particular, and Ireland generally, are reminders of how British imperialism first forged and politicized religious divisions in the formation of the UK state rather than in its overseas territories. Generally, the imperial and anti-imperial violence associated with these strategies were exported and externalized as part of the imperial project. With the disastrous exception of the two World Wars, organized political violence was typically confined to the colonial territories. Meanwhile, in the pacified metropolitan core, this violence was firmly consigned to the past. Belfast provides an uncomfortable and enduring challenge to this narrative – a clue perhaps to why a relatively limited and localized conflict continues to attract disproportionate international attention in Europe and North America.

REFERENCES

AlSayyad, Nezar, and Mejgan Massoumi, eds. 2011. *The Fundamentalist City? Religiosity and the Making of Urban Space*. New York: Routledge.

Ardoyne Commemoration Project. 2002. *Ardoyne: The Untold Truth*. Belfast: Beyond the Pale Publications.

Armstrong, Karen. 2014. *Fields of Blood: Religion and the History of Violence*. London: Vintage.

---

[20] It is instructive that it is Irish Nationalism that is now deemed to be the major cultural and ideological threat to Unionism rather than institutionalized Irish Catholicism – no doubt a testimony to the collapse of the authority of the Catholic Church throughout Ireland over the last four decades.

[21] Even though a majority in Northern Ireland voted to remain in the EU, the DUP now appealed to the majority UK vote in favor of leaving, in effect abandoning their claim to represent a majority of voters in Northern Ireland while taking refuge in the "national majority."

Asad, Talal. 1999. "Religion, Nation-State, Secularism." In *Nation and Religion: Perspectives on Europe and Asia*, edited by Peter van der Veer and Harmut Lehmann, 178–96. Princeton: Princeton University Press.

Bacchetta, Paola. 2010. "The (Failed) Production of Hindu Nationalized Space in Ahmedabad, Gujarat." *Gender, Place and Culture* 17: 551–72.

Bardon, Jonathan. 1982. *Belfast: An Illustrated History*. Belfast: The Blackstaff Press.

Barnes, Philip. 2005. "Was the Northern Ireland Conflict Religious?" *Journal of Contemporary Religion* 20: 55–69.

Beaumont, Justin, and Christopher Baker, eds. 2011. *Postsecular Cities: Space, Theory and Practice*. New York: Continuum.

Billig, Michael. 1995. *Banal Nationalism*. London: Sage.

Bollens, Scott. 2007. *Cities, Nationalism and Democratization*. London: Routledge.

Brewer, John, and Gareth I. Higgins. 1998. *Anti-Catholicism in Northern Ireland 1600–1998: The Mote and the Beam*. London: Macmillan.

Brewer, John, Gareth I. Higgins, and Frances Teeney. 2011. *Religion, Civil Society and Peace in Northern Ireland*. Oxford: Oxford University Press.

Brewer, John, Margaret Keane, and David Livingstone. 2006. "Landscape of Spires." In *Enduring City: Belfast in the Twentieth Century*, edited by Frederick Boal and Stephen Royle, 180–94. Belfast: Blackstaff Press.

Brubaker, Rogers. 2012. "Religion and Nationalism: Four Approaches." *Nations and Nationalism* 18: 2–20.

2013. "Language, Religion and the Politics of Difference." *Nations and Nationalism* 19: 1–20.

Bruce, Steve. 1986. *God Save Ulster: The Religion and Politics of Paisleyism*. Oxford: Oxford University Press.

Bryan, Dominic. 2015. "Parades, Flags, Carnivals and Riots: Public Space Contestation and Transformation in Northern Ireland." *Peace and Conflict: Journal of Peace Psychology* 21: 565–73.

Casanova, José. 2006. "Rethinking Secularization: A Global Comparative Perspective." *The Hedgehog Review* 8: 7–22.

Cavanaugh, William. 2009. *The Myth of Religious Violence: Secular Ideology and the Roots of Modern Conflict*. Oxford: Oxford University Press.

Clarke, Stephen. 2014. *The Justifications of Religious Violence*. London: Wiley-Blackwell.

Coulter, Colin, and Michael Murray, eds. 2008. *Northern Ireland after the Troubles? A Society in Transition*. Manchester: Manchester University Press.

Davis, Diane E., and Nora Libertun de Duren, eds. 2011. *Cities and Sovereignty: Identity Politics in Urban Space*. Bloomington: Indiana University Press.

Doyle, Michael. 2009. *Fighting like the Devil for the Sake of God: Protestants, Catholics and the Origins of Violence in Victorian Belfast*. Manchester: Manchester University Press.

Fraser, Tom G. 2012. "Historical Legacies and the Northern Ireland Peace Process: Issues of Commemoration and Memorialisation." *Shared Space* 12: 41–50.

Friedland, Roger, and Richard Hecht. 1998. "The Bodies of Nations: A Comparative Study of Religious Violence in Jerusalem and Ayodha." *History of Religions* 38: 101–49.

Ganiel, Gladys. 2016. *Transforming Post-Catholic Ireland: Religious Practice in Late Modernity*. Oxford: Oxford University Press.

Goh, Daniel P. S., and Peter van der Veer. 2016. "Introduction: The Sacred and the Urban in Asia." *International Sociology* 31: 367–74.

Gorski, Philip S., and Gulay Turkmen-Dervisoglu. 2013. "Religion, Nationalism and Violence: An Integrated Approach." *Annual Review of Sociology* 39: 191–210.

Hassner, Ron E. 2009. *War on Sacred Grounds*. London: Cornell University Press.

Hayden, Robert M. 2015. "Intersecting Religioscapes and Antagonistic Tolerance: Trajectories of Competition and Sharing of Religious Spaces in the Balkans." In *Religion, Violence and Cities*, edited by Liam O'Dowd and Martina McKnight, 60–74. London: Routledge.

Hepburn, Anthony C. 2004. *Contested Cities in the Modern West*. London: Palgrave.

Jarman, Neil. 1999. *Material Conflicts: Parades and Visual Displays in Northern Ireland*. Oxford: Berg.

   2005. *No Longer a Problem? Sectarian Violence in Northern Ireland*. Belfast: Institute for Conflict Studies.

Jones, Emrys. 1960. *The Social Geography of Belfast*. Oxford: Oxford University Press.

Juergensmeyer, Mark. 1993. *The New Cold War? Religious Nationalism Confronts the Secular State*. Berkeley: University of California Press.

   2003. *Terror in the Mind of God: The Global Rise of Religious Violence*. Rev. ed. Berkeley: University of California Press.

Koster, Jan. 2003. "Ritual Performance and the Politics of Identity: On the Functions and Uses of Ritual." *Journal of Historical Pragmatics* 4: 211–48.

Leonard, Madeleine. 2010. "Parochial Geographies." *Childhood* 17: 329–42.

McAlister, Elisabeth. 2005. "Globalization and the Religious Production of Space." *Journal for the Scientific Study of Religion* 44: 249–55.

Mitchell, Clare. 2006. *Religion, Identity and Politics in Northern Ireland: Boundaries of Belonging and Belief*. Aldershot, UK: Ashgate.

   2010. "The Push and Pull between Religion and Ethnicity: The Case of Loyalists in Northern Ireland." *Ethnopolitics* 9: 53–69.

Nolan, Paul, Dominic Bryan, Katy Hayward, Katy Radford, and Peter Shirlow. 2014. *The Flag Dispute: Anatomy of a Protest*. Belfast: Queen's University Institute of Conflict Transformation and Social Justice.

O'Dowd, Liam. 1987. "Church, State and Women: The Aftermath of Partition." In *Gender in Irish Society*, edited by Chris Curtin, Pauline Jackson, and Barbara O'Connor, 3–6. Galway: Galway University.

   2014. "Symmetrical Solutions, Asymmetical Realities: Beyond the Politics of Paralysis." *Studies in Conflict and Terrorism* 37: 806–14.

O'Dowd, Liam, and Milena Komarova. 2013. "Three Narratives in Search of a City: Researching Belfast's 'Post-conflict' Transitions." *City* 17: 526–46.

O'Dowd, Liam, and Martina McKnight, eds. 2015. *Religion, Violence and Cities*. London: Routledge.

O'Leary, Brendan, and John G. McGarry. 1993. *The Politics of Antagonism: Understanding Northern Ireland*. London: Athlone Press.

Pullan, Wendy. 2013. "Bible and Gun: Militarism in Jerusalem's Holy Places." In *Religion, Violence and Cities*, edited by Liam O'Dowd and Martina McKnight, 75–96. London: Routledge.

Redmond, John. 1961. *Church, State and Industry in East Belfast*. Belfast: self-published.

Rolston, Bill. 2010. "Trying to Reach the Future through the Past: Murals and Memory in Northern Ireland." *Crime, Media, Culture* 6: 285–307.

Russell, Raymond. 2013. *Census 2011: Key Statistics at Northern Ireland and LGD Level*. Belfast: Northern Ireland Assembly Research Paper.

Shirlow, Peter, and Brendan Murtagh. 2006. *Belfast: Segregation, Violence and the City*. London: Pluto Press.

Sinha, Vineeta. 2016. "Marking Spaces as 'Sacred': Infusing Singapore's Urban Landscape with Sacrality." *International Sociology* 31: 467–68.

Smyth, Lisa, and Martina McKnight. 2013. "Maternal Situations: Sectarianism and Civility in a Divided City." *Sociological Review* 61: 304–22.

Stier, Oren B., and J. Shawn Landres, eds. 2006. *Religion, Violence, Memory and Place.* Bloomington: Indiana University Press.

Tilly, Charles. 1990. *Coercion, Capital and European States, A.D. 990–1990.* London: Blackwell.

Todd, Jennifer. 1988. "The Limits of Britishness." *The Irish Review* 5: 11–16.

  2010. "Symbolic Complexity and Political Division: The Changing Role of Religion in Northern Ireland." *Ethnopolitics* 9: 85–102.

van der Veer, Peter, and Harmut Lehmann. 1999. "Introduction." In *Nation and Religion: Perspectives on Europe and Asia*, edited by Peter van der Veer and Harmut Lehmann, 3–15. Princeton: Princeton University Press.

van der Veer, Peter, and Harmut Lehmann, eds. 1999. *Nation and Religion: Perspectives on Europe and Asia.* Princeton: Princeton University Press.

Wilson, Robin. 2016. *The Northern Ireland Peace Monitoring Report: Number Four.* Belfast: Community Relations Council.

Wilson, Tim K. 2010. *Frontiers of Violence: Conflict and Identity in Ulster and Upper Silesia, 1918–1922.* Oxford: Oxford University Press.

Wolffe, John. 2011. "Protestant-Catholic Divisions in Europe and the United States: An Historical and Comparative Perspective." *Politics, Religion and Ideology* 12: 241–56.

PART VIII

Palestine

14

Palestinian Nationalism, Religious (Un)claims, and the Struggle against Zionism

Khaled Hroub

The debates over the comparative use of religion and religious claims by Zionist and Palestinian national narratives and political discourses have followed different lines. A common line of discussion tends to lump and treat both sets of narratives within the universal practice of using religion for political ends (Bunzl 2009; Landau 2009). From this perspective, the fight between Zionism, on one side, and the Arabs and the Palestinians, on the other, is framed within the context of religious national conflicts, typically characterized by a process of conflating religious and nationalist claims. The tactical and strategic use of religious claims by reinventing them in the form of modern national aspirations and proclamations is common practice across all parties involved in such conflicts. However, by offering this understanding, which comingles religion and politics – forms seemingly followed both by mainstream Zionism and the Palestinians – matters are, in fact, simplified and mistakenly cross-equated.

Behind this rather superficial similarity between the Zionist and Palestinian uses of religion lies a complex and differing picture that will be examined in the following discussion. Throughout more than a century of the Palestinian struggle with Zionism, the use of religion and religious claims by the Palestinian national movement has differed profoundly from that practiced by Zionism on two levels: *function* and *centrality*. Function denotes the purpose for which religion and religious claims were deployed by both the Zionists and the Palestinians; centrality refers to how central the place of religion and religious claims has been within these two national movements throughout the struggle.

Functionally, the Zionist movement heavily used and consciously deployed Judaic claims as a *primary* force to invent a strong nationalist Jewish connection with Palestine and to mobilize Jews worldwide behind Zionism. Literature confirming this point is massive; commonly indicating that "even for Ben Gurion and other secularized Jewish nationalists the Hebrew Bible was the spiritual, and cultural touchstone for Jewish identity and the Jewish people's link to the land of Israel" (Landau 2009). By contrast, the Palestinians resorted to religious Islamic claims only *secondarily* by way of affirming their connection with the land of Palestine. For the

365

Palestinians, uninterrupted millennia-long habitation and ownership of Palestine created a natural and uncontested collective connection to the land that warranted no need for imposing meta-religious claims over such links. Even with the alarming rise of Zionist claims over Palestine in the first quarter of the twentieth century, the Palestinians still felt that they neither needed to prove their indigenous status in Palestine nor their subsequent unbroken links with it. Unlike the Palestinians and since its inception, the Zionist movement had been anxious to establish a convincing legitimacy for its "connection," and later for its claim of Jewish "ownership" of the land of Palestine. For the Palestinians, and in the absence of such anxiousness, the overriding concern lay in how to *resist* the military and political actions led by and resulting in the Zionist claims. Thus, there was a great difference in the main function of religion in the cases of Zionism and Palestinian nationalism; for Zionism, to *create ownership* of Palestine; for the Palestinians, to help mobilize and *create resistance* against Zionism.

The *centrality* of religion and religious claims for Zionism and Palestinian nationalism features another fundamental difference. In the case of Zionism, religious claims and discourses have continued to occupy a central position before, during, and after the creation of Israel. Such centrality lies in the concrete materialization of the "promised land" mythology that has permeated most versions of Zionism. In the Palestinian case, the political/religious landscape has always been led and mostly occupied by national forces and claims, allowing only a marginal role for religion and religious discourses. The saliency of a nationalist Palestinian discourse prevailed over decades despite strong religious sentiments about Palestine among Palestinians and Arabs, rooted in the notion of Palestine as a "blessed land." This blessing originated from the Prophet Muhammad's night journey from Mecca to Jerusalem in the year 621 CE, followed by his ascendance there from what would become al-Aqsa Mosque into heaven.[1] Notably, these beliefs were not later manipulated to create a political discourse asserting a religious claim to the land.

Throughout the decades of the struggle, two different trajectories have continued to evolve within the two national movements. Within Zionism and Israel, there has been a continuous process of a further "religionization" of the political (and secular) landscape. If the use of religion by early (secular) Zionists was mostly pragmatic and mobilizing (even among agnostic and atheist Zionist leaders and forces), the trend toward religionized politics at least from the late 1970s onward has offered a new transformation with concrete religious inspirations, foci, and agendas (Pedahzur 2012; Shindler 2015). On the Palestinian side, an inverse trajectory has continued to consolidate a powerful and central process of nationalization that has been able to remold all forces. Within this process, the most religiously oriented groups that

---

[1] Sura al-Isra' of Qur'an 17:1 describes this journey, which, according to Islamic tradition, took place in one night. The site in Jerusalem where Prophet Muhammad ascended to heaven is where the al-Aqsa Mosque was later built by the Caliph 'Umar ibn al-Khattab, then expanded by the Umayyad Caliph al-Walid ibn 'Abd al-Malik in 705 CE.

started out being fundamentally religious, such as Hamas and the Islamic Jihad Movement in 1980s, have gradually and steadily transformed in the direction of Palestinian nationalism. This transformation with respect to Hamas will be closely examined in this chapter.

Paradoxically and from a modernist broader perspective, Zionism's ingrained religious claims molded in ancient mythologies seem to belong to the premodern era, whereas Palestinian nationalism with its embracement of nation-based justifications belongs to the more universal modern precepts of national identity formation. Yet, because the two founding pillars of modern nationalism – a population attached to a single territorial base and a unifying language – were missing when Zionism originated, building an ideology based solely on nationalism would not have been possible. The concerted effort to project Zionism as a modern, Western enterprise was not viable without the armor of religious myths and ancient histories. Adherence to an idea of secular nationalism solely, without the religious claims, would have exposed the inherent vulnerability of Zionism rather than facilitate its consolidation. Zionism needed to find and claim a territory, as well as to reinvent a unifying language, for the massively varied Jewish groups that spoke dozens of languages and lived all over the world. Only this dual effort, requiring the deployment of the mightiest religious arsenal, could have succeeded.

By contrast, on the side of indigenous Palestinian nationalism, the two founding pillars of nationalism were in place, which meant that efforts and aspirations to effect the evolution of a modern nation-state could move forward without the need of religious or other premodern justifications to support their goals. The Palestinians lived on the very same land that their generations-old ancestors inhabited, and all spoke the same Arabic language (Masalha 2018). Their Palestinian nationalism within a framework of an independent nation-state was completely in line with the nationalisms emerging in other Arab nations – the Lebanese, Syrian, Iraqi, Jordanian, and other quests for independence in a modern, postcolonial nation-state.

Although the comparison with Zionism should be kept in mind, this chapter focuses on Palestinian nationalism and the position of religion within it. In order to explore the various aspects and dynamics of this position, the discussion here examines the salient typography of the Palestinian national discourses and practices over decades, before and after the creation of Israel, identifying the religious elements of the Palestinian political milieu and locating and assessing their *function* and *centrality*. This inquiry is divided into three parts. The first part traces the religious elements within the prevailing discourses of the Palestinian national movement during the British Mandate and before the creation of the State of Israel; the second part delves into the decades after the creation of Israel (from the 1950s to the 1980s), scanning the dominant pan-Arab nationalist and leftist discourses that dominated Palestinian politics at the time and evaluating the religious references therein; the third part focuses on the rise of Palestinian Islamism,

368   *Khaled Hroub*

particularly the Hamas movement from the late 1980s with its religious approach
and the fervor that it injected into Palestinian nationalism, pushing the *function* and
centrality of religion into certain heights before both started to gradually wane, even
within Hamas's political milieu.

PALESTINIAN NATIONALISM AND IDENTITY UNTIL 1948

The emergence of an early Palestinian collective national identity and awareness
goes back to the late nineteenth century during Ottoman rule.[2] This national
consciousness continued to take form in the context of, and was further provoked
by, the growing disconnect between the crumbling Turkish-dominated Ottoman
Empire and the repressed Arabs in Palestine and neighboring countries. The advent
of the British military occupation of Palestine and the Mashreq at large from the
early 1920s, coupled with the rise of Zionism in Palestine, further crystallized
a sense of collective national awareness among the Arabs of Palestine. During the
final and desperate years of Ottoman control over the region, as well as during the
early years of British rule, the Palestinian intelligentsia perceived itself as part of
wider Arab elites. Within these elites, the anti-Turkification sentiment culminated
around the turn of the twentieth century with concrete calls for independence and
a complete breakaway from the Ottomans. The same calls for independence and
freedom remained as solid during the British colonial rule and gained vast popularity. Within Arab circles both in Palestine and the wider region, the widespread
resentment of the Turks, who ruled in the name of Islam for centuries, cast
considerable doubts on pan-Islamic alternatives that were promoted by Islamist
reformers. Added to this desire to break away from pan-Islamism came the attract-
iveness of the European model of "nationalism" (Salem 1994, 131–36).

   Under the control of the Ottomans and later the British, individual polity-oriented
nationalism (e.g., Syrian, Iraqi, Palestinian, Jordanian, Saudi, and Lebanese) clearly
emerged, if very much blended with vague calls for pan-Arab nationalism and
unity (Salem 1994, 131–36). For example, the immediate activities of the Arab
Independence Party in Palestine were directed against Zionism and its settlements
while also advocating and working for Arab unity (Choueiri 2000, 93). At the time,
two conflated identities started to emerge: a pan-Arab identity reflecting the centuries-old Arab character of the inhabitants of Palestine and a Palestinian national
identity aligned with the crystallization of the country-based national identities
forming in the region and beyond. This duality has left some unwarranted confusion
inviting unfounded questioning on whether a Palestinian identity and nationhood
ever existed. Rebuking such questions, Khalidi (1997, 145) elaborates that the
"complication" of the Palestinian identity stems from "the difficulty of explaining

---

[2]   There is almost consensus in the literature examining Palestinian nationalism on this point. See, for
      example, Khalidi (1997); Muslih (1988); Schulz (1999).

its interrelation with broad, powerful transnational foci of identity, in particular Arabism and Islam, and with other potent regional and local loyalties." However, in reality, a straightforward and practical understanding of the evolution of Palestinian identity in the first quarter of the twentieth century could be simplified by understanding it as a process of "renaming" rather than "inventing." Facing a new reality within which the Arab region was becoming segmented into smaller entities, the Arabs of Palestine, who had existed and lived there for centuries, started to rename and consider themselves Palestinians, just as their Arab brethren in Lebanon, Syria, Jordan, Iraq, and elsewhere started to rename themselves. In this process of renaming, both identities – the pan-Arab and the country-based ones – were perceived as complementing, rather than rivaling, each other. The Arabs who lived in what would become Syria, Lebanon, Jordan, and Iraq became Syrians, Lebanese, Jordanians, and Iraqis, respectively, with equally strong Arab identities.

The organic overlapping, then gradual decoupling, between the pan-Arab identity of the Arabs of Palestine and their emerging Palestinian identity deserves a closer look, for this shows the early absence of any strong religious identity competing with those two national identities. Palestine was, and continues to be, so central to most if not all strands of Arab nationalism, sincerely or rhetorically, that the radicalization of pan-Arab nationalism itself is linked to the loss of Palestine and the advent of the Zionist project (Salem 1994, 41–9). However, it is worth mentioning that the distinctions between Palestinian nationalism and the wider pan-Arab calls started to appear as early as 1913. In that year, the First Arab Conference was convened in Paris by a group of Arab intellectuals with a focused agenda of seeking Arab independence from the Ottomans. The conference criticized Istanbul's repressive and anti-Arab policies and the treatment of the Arabs as a second-class ethnicity and demanded sovereignty for the Arab countries. Dismayed by the marginalization of the Palestine issue by the Paris conference, the Palestinian press such as *al-Karmil* and Palestine newspapers strongly attacked the conference, indicating that the priority of fighting Zionism in Palestine should have been discussed and pronounced in the documents of the conference as prominently as the other issues (Shoufani 2003, 306).

Over the first four decades of the twentieth century – a crucial and formative period for modern Arab (and Palestinian) identity and nationhood – religious political rhetoric remained marginal as opposed to mainstream nationalist Arab politics in the Arab region. At the Palestinian level, as discussed by Bayan Nuwayhid al-Hout (1986, 27–38) in her landmark historiography of the period, it is revealing that most leading political or politicized organizations and parties that emerged in the same decades were on the nationalist side. One way of understanding the reasons behind the primacy of nationalist tendencies over religious ones is to bear in mind the wide-ranging Arab frustration with the Ottomans/Turks combined with deep doubts over the long-standing religious claims the Turks used to justify their rule over Arabs and others. These early negative attitudes toward the mixed, if not completely tarnished, legacy of the Ottomans in the region during the last half-century of their rule had, in part at least, moved religion and religious politics and discourse from being the principal, let alone sole, vehicle of politics and activism among Arab and Palestinian elites. Additionally, national aspirations and the model of nationalism in the nineteenth and early twentieth centuries were the most attractive political ideas to follow. Although these ideas emerged from Europe, they were globally embraced by countries and national elites elsewhere who were struggling for liberation and independence from foreign and colonial rule.

During the British rule over Palestine, from 1917 through 1948, all Palestinian political parties and organizations shared the goal of resisting the growing influence of Zionism and its increasingly aggressive plans to create a Jewish homeland in Palestine. Leading parties then formulated their resistance and political activism on nationalist bases. Their founding documents and main declarations hardly mentioned any religious references in claiming ownership of Palestine; such references, when they existed, were used to mobilize resistance and jihad against Zionism, as shown below. Their manifestos, political parties' goals, and original pronouncements (as well as throughout the rest of their texts) reveal strong national leaning. For example, in 1923, the Arab National Party's (1923) first goal was "The maintenance of Palestine as an Arab country for her Arab people, purified from any foreign or Zionist right or influence; and as part of the Arab countries" (al-Hout 1986, 721–22). In 1927, the Free Palestine Party's main aspiration was to "Pursue complete independence and fulfill national dreams and sovereignty" (al-Hout 1986, 723). In 1932, the Arab Independence Party's statement of foundation indicated that "Palestine is an Arab country, and natural part of Syria ... [calling for] ... the establishment of parliamentarian Arab rule in Palestine" (al-Hout 1986, 735). In 1934, the National Defense Party's platform asserted, "Seeking full independence for Palestine where Arab sovereignty over it is guaranteed, and without any recognition of any international commitments that lead to foreign control or influence or political condition that compromises independence" (al-Hout 1986, 742–43). In 1935, the Arab Palestinian Party's goals included "The independence of Palestine and the removal of the Mandate ... Protecting the Arabism of Palestine and resisting the establishment of a Jewish homeland ... connecting Palestine with other Arab countries in a political national unity fully independent" (al-Hout 1986, 743–44), and in the same line of expression was the 1935 pronouncement of the National Coalition Party, calling for "the complete political independence of Palestine and the protection of the Arab identity of Palestine using all available political means" (al-Hout 1986, 747–48).

The nationalist arguments and claims presented by individual parties were equally reflected in collective Palestinian action and politics. Evidence from that period abounds, but it suffices here to point to the frequently quoted historical document submitted to the Anglo-American Committee of Inquiry in March 1948. In this document, the Arab Office in Jerusalem, which was the official body

Palestinian Nationalism and Religious (Un)claims

representing the Palestinian viewpoint in all of Palestine, laid out the Arab claims for Palestine in a document that reflected the views of Palestinian notables and leaders. The argument presented in this document entirely reflected nationalist language, aspirations, and demands, with only a few passing lines (out of ten pages) referring to religious elements (Laquer and Schueftan 2016, 57–62). In the aftermath of 1948 and the creation of Israel, the Palestinians formed the short-lived All-Palestine Government in Gaza as a political entity with the hopes of evolving into a state that would control the parts of Palestine that Zionism had not yet occupied – namely, the West Bank and the Gaza Strip. Almost nothing in the documents of this government referred to *any* religious claims justifying their stated aspiration to attain a Palestinian state (Shlaim 2010, 37–53).

RELIGIOUS DISCOURSE AND ACTIVISM WITHIN PALESTINIAN NATIONALISM

Despite the overwhelmingly nationalist discourse that shaped the Palestinian political agenda and aspirations in the pre-1948 era, religion and/or religious references did occasionally appear within the Palestinian political discourse. Yet this rhetoric was mostly directed, as argued above, to mobilize resistance against the British and the Zionist forces, rather than to affirm certain divine links with the land. This religious resistance is exemplified in the cases of Palestinian political or military activism where religion and religious claims were drawn in to the center of action.

The first case was the military group formed and led by Sheikh Izz Eddin al-Qassam in northern Palestine in the first half of the 1930s. Al-Qassam, who was born near Lattakia in Syria in 1882, grew up in an atmosphere filled with anti-French and anti-colonial sentiment in Syria and across the region. Driven by this sentiment and religious motives, he moved to Palestine in 1920, lived an extremely active life, and died in Palestine in a battle against British troops in Ya'bad village near the city of Jenin in 1935.[3]

In Syria, soon after the French occupation of the country began in 1918, al-Qassam promptly engaged in militant activities against the occupier. Immediately he was pursued by the French and fled to Palestine, where he resided in Haifa in 1920 and became the imam of the central al-Istiqlal Mosque.[4] Facing yet more colonial powers, namely the British in Palestine this time, al-Qassam wasted no time and started organizing secret cells to fight both the Zionists and the British. Using his base at the al-Istiqlal Mosque and building on his growing popularity as a respected imam as well as a "nationalist" one, al-Qassam expanded both his religious outreach

---

[3] His months-long efforts to send volunteers to Libya proved a failure after all, as the Turkish authorities held his volunteers for forty days at Alexandria and prevented them from continuing their journey to the Libyan shores.

[4] Al-Qassam acquired religious education first at the hands of his Sufi father and later at al-Azhar in Cairo (Saleh 1988, 231–32).

and sermons and, in later stages, his military activities to the surrounding cities and villages. Obviously, his activities drew British and Zionist attention and placed him atop their most-wanted lists (Lachman 1982, 52–99).

Throughout his short-lived and religiously motivated resistance project, al-Qassam fought on several fronts at a time: militarily against the British and the Zionists; politically against the traditional and timid Palestinian leaders and organizations, notably Hajj Amin al-Husseini of Jerusalem, who believed that achieving Palestinian national goals could be attained through diplomacy and negotiations with the British; and financially and resourcefully, against the Arab governments and leaders, whom al-Qassam contacted in vain to solicit funds and material support. British and Zionist intelligence of the time reported that al-Qassam justified his anti-British and anti-Jewish activism "on religious grounds" (Lachman 1982, 52–99).

To this day, al-Qassam is extolled and idealized by many Palestinians as a true leader who grasped early on that the true and effective way of resisting Zionism was armed struggle. His role is even further exaggerated by Palestinian Islamists, who granted him sainthood status within the Palestinian resistance narrative. This culminated in the early 1990s in Hamas's naming its military wing after him – the "Izz Eddin al-Qassam Brigades." The battle of Ya'bad, which resulted in his "heroic" death alongside his comrades, was one of the early upurks of the April 1936 Palestinian revolt against the British. Despite the significance of al-Qassam and his movement, little literature was left about him – let alone by him – that could elaborate on his ideas and the blend of religion and liberation ideology in his thoughts and activism. A close review of what is written about al-Qassam, based on few and scattered original materials, stories, and statements recorded by his companions, confirms the point argued in this chapter: Although the centrality of religion and religious discourse appeared uncontested in al-Qassam's group, the function of religion by this most religious Palestinian group was primarily to mobilize resistance efforts. Further evidence of this is found in the accounts that chronicled the al-Qassam movement, his mosque sermons, street speeches, and statements quoted during his traveling around villages and rural areas, where his skills as a charismatic orator were used to mobilize people's religious sentiment in the resistance against the British and Zionism (al-Hout 1986, 326–28).

The second case with some religious leaning is that of Hajj Amin al-Husseini (1895–1974), the mufti of Jerusalem in the 1920s and 1930s and a political leader of the Palestinian nationalist movement during that period. Unlike the al-Qassam military action-based movement with its deep religious convictions, al-Husseini's religious aspect was more one of symbolism and traditionalism. Descending from a notable Jerusalemite family, al-Husseini held the position of mufti of Jerusalem with British approval. Despite the religious connotations of the title, the political activities as well as the expectations of the mufti's function were nationalist in essence. Al-Husseini's career and history of activism in Palestine and in the region positioned him as a Palestinian and Arab leader striving for Arab independence.

Al-Husseini's activism went beyond Palestine into Lebanon, Syria, and Iraq, and reflected deep concerns with Arab affairs and aspirations for independence and unity more than an interest in establishing religious order or in Islamism. Yet, even scholars such as historian Youssef Choueiri who refrained from granting al-Husseini the status of an Arab nationalist have also not identified him with any particular religious platform. Instead, Choueiri (2000, 98) sums up al-Husseini's overwhelmingly Palestinian agenda in this way: "His ideological commitments were primarily motivated by the plight of the Palestinian people, tinged with an Islamist tendency which sometimes took on an Arabist colouring." Al-Husseini proved to be a controversial political figure whose political career and politics elicited widely divergent responses – both admiration and condemnation – from different observers. Zionists accused him of being a Nazi collaborator; the British admired him as a faithful politician; and Palestinians on different sides of the political spectrum admired and condemned him.[5] Throughout his active life as a political leader and figure, the mufti had certainly buttressed his politics and political discourse with religious pronouncements. But the core of his message and activism was nationalism and the attempt to achieve national entity and independence. In al-Husseini's case, the function of religion and religious discourse is almost that of al-Qassam: to mobilize Palestinians to face up to, resist, and fight Zionism.[6] Yet his approach to religion differs from al-Qassam's in terms of the decentralization of religion in his politics in contrast to al-Qassam.

The third case of religion playing a central role in the formation and politics of a Palestinian movement struggling against Zionism was the Muslim Brotherhood organization. The mother organization of all Muslim Brotherhood branches in the region was founded in Egypt in 1928 to bring Islam back into personal and public life, fight Westernization amid Egyptian society, and confront British influence in Egypt. By the second half of the 1930s, the Brotherhood had adopted a strategy of expanding into neighboring countries. Thus, the Brotherhood in Egypt sent emissaries to Palestine, Syria, Jordan, and Iraq, who continued to tour these countries helping to establish "national" branches. While the Syrian branch of the organization was founded in 1937, the Iraqi branch around 1944, and the Jordanian branch in 1945, the Palestinian branch of the group was only officially inaugurated in Jerusalem in May 1946. However, the de facto presence of "Palestinian Muslim Brothers" in the form of affiliates and supporters in Palestine had in fact preceded that date by several years (Hroub 2000, 14–19). Nevertheless, smaller chapters in other cities across Palestine were also established.

The political thinking and religious approaches of the Palestinian Brotherhood mostly followed the main organization in Egypt with certain adjustments to fit the

---

[5] A balanced account portraying al-Husseini's political career is found in Mattar (1988).

[6] It should be noted here that al-Husseini opposed al-Qassam's targeting of both the British as well as the Zionists in the first half of the 1930s, because he felt that diplomacy with the British would be more effective.

national context. The Palestinian branch of the organization adopted the main goal of "re-Islamizing" society and appropriated its own other goals drawn from within the Palestinian context, primarily resisting Zionism and its plans in Palestine. Although the Egyptian Muslim Brotherhood took at least a decade to become engaged in Egyptian politics, preferring to focus its activities on religious indoctrination, "preparation of the generations," and preaching, the Palestinian branch found itself involved in hardcore politics in the very first year of its existence (Hroub 2000, 19–36). The early discourse of the Palestinian Brothers deployed a combination of Palestinian national aspirations, Arabism, and pan-Islamism. The main point in relation to our discussion here is that even within the most obvious and religiously centered organization in Palestine, the function of religious discourse and claims were deployed as a means of building resistance, rather than as arguments to justify any unique and divine connection of the Palestinians to Palestine. The literature that has documented the Brotherhood politics and discourse equally shows clear nationalist language, as outlined below.

In October 1946, only a few months after their foundation, the Palestinian Brotherhood convened their first conference in Jerusalem with delegations attending from Jordan and Lebanon as well as many cities across Palestine. One year later, in October 1947, they organized a second and more important convention – the Haifa conference.[7] By the date of this conference, tensions, escalations, and armed clashes between the Palestinians, on one side, and the Zionists and the British, on the other, were showing all signs of an imminent war. The language of "resistance" delivered by the Haifa conference reflected two things: the first is the priority of national politics and resistance over religious discourse and objectives in the Brotherhood's approach at that time; the second is the Brotherhood's shared nervousness and sense of anticipated loss that cut across Arabs and Palestinians. It is worth quoting here at length the elements included in the statement of the Haifa conference in order to further highlight the point that religious references have been used in certain Palestinian discourses by way of mobilization and "resistance" against Zionism, rather than for establishing a religious/historical link with the land. This elaboration on the early Muslim Brotherhood thinking in Palestine is also helpful in understanding the origins of the organization that eventually produced Hamas in the late 1980s. Out of the twelve resolutions in the conference statement, four had direct relevance to what could be seen as mingling religious and political language about Palestine and resistance. The remainder of the statement dealt with organizational, administrative, and general matters. The following is my own translation of the four relevant elements in full:

1. The Muslim Brotherhood announces its determination to defend its country by all possible means, and its readiness to cooperate with all national organizations in this regard.

---

[7] For further history on the Muslim Brotherhood during this period, see el-Awaisi (1998).

Palestinian Nationalism and Religious (Un)claims

2. The delegates of the Muslim Brotherhood in all countries represented at the conference condemn any attempt to delude the Arabs and Muslims that achieving their national goals can be realized through the Security Council or the United Nations; especially after knowing the reality of these organizations to be a mere cloak covering the interests of the great and colonial powers.
3. The delegates to the conference announce that the Muslim Brotherhood organization will fully bear its share of the struggle.
4. The representatives of the Muslim Brotherhood in East Jordan announce their full readiness to bear their share of responsibility in liberating Palestine. (al-Hout 1986, 794)[8]

Examining the cases of the three political or armed agencies discussed above where religion and religious inspirations played a crucial role shows yet again that the use of religion in the discourse and activism of these groups was intended to galvanize mobilization and resistance, not to justify a claim of land ownership. This was the practice of the three most religious-leaning factions involved in Palestinian nationalism: the centrality of religion, within two of them at least – al-Qassam's faction and the Brotherhood – was uncontested. Finally and to reiterate, the significance of the above cases stems from the religious aspect they exhibited, not the weight and role they played within the Palestinian national movement. This applies to both the al-Qassam group and the Muslim Brotherhood: al-Qassam lasted just about two years from 1933 to 1935, and the Brotherhood was very marginal indeed. By contrast, al-Husseini occupied a central role within that movement until 1948.

PALESTINIAN NATIONAL DISCOURSE AND ABSENCE OF RELIGION AFTER 1948

The function and centrality of religion and religious claims within Palestinian nationalism after the creation of the State of Israel continued to remain marginal until the emergence of the Islamic Jihad Movement and Hamas in the 1980s. A mix of nationalist and pan-Arab discourses (often blended with Marxist leanings) dominated the political culture and rhetoric of most, if not all, Palestinian parties post-1948. Likewise, the leading and most influential parties in neighboring Arab countries advocated pan-Arab nationalism, socialism, or a mixture of both. Islamist movements, mainly the Muslim Brotherhood and later Hizb al-Tahrir,[9] grew weaker or more marginalized during the 1950s, 1960s, and 1970s, and never made it to the heart of Palestinian mainstream politics. The main reason behind the marginalization of the Islamist parties along with their low attendant popular

---

[8] The translation of this excerpt and all translations that follow in this chapter are my own.
[9] Hizb al-Tahrir was founded in Jerusalem in 1954 as a pan-Islamic (and not exclusively Palestinian) party. It rejected the gradual bottom-up Islamization process of the Muslim Brotherhood and called for the reestablishment of caliphate. The party competed with the Brotherhood but showed little interest in the Palestinian nationalist movement. See Milton-Edwards (1996, 36–72).

support was the increasing marginalization of Palestine and the liberation cause on those parties' agendas. Both of them invested their effort, time, and resources in religious preoccupations and "bringing back the Palestinians to Islam," paying no particular attention to the nationalist resistance and the direct confrontation with Zionism.[10] By contrast and in the case of the more secular and nationalist movements, Palestine not only topped their agenda, but it also represented the raison d'être of many of these parties' ideologies and political action. The predominant discourses, claims, and ideological precepts were anchored in national foundations. Effectively speaking, religion and religious discourses were pushed to the fringes of mainstream Palestinian nationalism and activism for almost four decades.

Over these decades, Palestine was the overwhelming preoccupation and exclusive issue of the Palestinian movements, and engagement in the struggle for its liberation and resistance against the Zionist project was the basis of political and popular legitimacy. The ideological justifications, claims, and rhetoric that prevailed among the leading and active political Palestinian parties and groups against Zionism clearly reveal profound and ubiquitous national discourses and a near-total absence of religious aspects. Analyzing the discourse of the Fatah movement (which emerged in the late 1950s, and was officially established in 1965) and of the frontline Palestine Liberation Organization (PLO) supports this claim. Over time, from its foundation to the present day, the Fatah movement evolved to become the strongest party within Palestinian politics, led for many years by its charismatic head, Yasir Arafat. Also led by Arafat until his death in 2004 was the PLO, which was officially founded in 1964. This discussion will leave aside dozens of other Palestinian groups and movements whose leftist and Marxist ideologies obviously excluded any notion of religion completely, if not even scorning it outright in certain cases – such as the Popular Front for the Liberation of Palestine and the Democratic Front for the Liberation of Palestine, the two largest political organizations after Fatah. In his monumental work on the history, practice, and political ideas of the Palestinian national movement after the creation of the State of Israel and until 1993, Yezid Sayigh hardly refers to any significant presence of religious claims or discourse. In the historiography that he provides, the dominant political and ideological debates revolved around the role of the Palestinians within the wider Arab nationalist and Marxist movements and whether to consider the liberation of Palestine or Arab unity itself to be the main vehicle against "the Zionist project and its imperial allies."[11]

The ideological principles as well as the political and military practices of Fatah and the PLO confirmed a bold nationalist course of action. The founding

---

[10] In the case of the bigger and more influential Palestinian Muslim Brotherhood, their strategy focused on "building and preparing strong, disciplined, and Islamized generations" capable of fighting Israel. This was projected to need more time to achieve, during which any premature resistance against Israel would be futile. For more on this, see Hroub (2000, 25–41).

[11] This is extensively explained throughout parts 1 and 2 of Sayigh (1997); also see specifically Sayigh (1997, 195–202).

documents for both Fatah and the PLO, principally their charters, stipulate overwhelming nationalist aspirations anchored in fundamental nationalist claims, yet with occasional religious overtones. However, the Fatah/PLO political practice over the years has materialized its nationalist discourse around the idea of Palestinian self-determination and the creation of an independent Palestinian sovereign state on its liberated land. Within the dynamics of practiced politics tied in a nationalist thrust and informed by theoretical principles, it is worth pondering the original documents that greatly directed the national politics of the Palestinians and helped to constitute their national identity. The following discussion of Fatah and PLO charters also helps to provide a broader context to the analysis that will be offered below of Hamas's own charter and the process of nationalizing its own political discourse over time.

In 1968, the Fatah movement issued its "Basic Statute for the Palestinian Liberation National Movement – Fatah." The long and extensive statute covers all aspects relating to the movement's foundation, objectives, organizational structure, strategies, politics, and internal running. The tone and language of the document is totally secular without resorting to religion or any religious references, except in one passing sentence. The document defines Fatah as a "national revolutionary movement . . . and based on being the leading revolutionary organization, it has the right to direct the revolution (of the people)." Under the section "Principles, Objectives, and Approach," the document states that "Palestine is part of the Arab homeland and the Palestinian people is part of the Arab nation ... [and] the Palestinian people enjoy an independent character, and have the right to self-determination and sovereignty over all their land." Denouncing Zionism as "a racist colonial aggressive movement," the document depicts the Israeli presence in Palestine as "a Zionist invasion that constitutes a colonial expansive base [acting as] a natural ally for international imperialism and colonialism." This section goes on to assert the responsibility of the Arab nations to help the Palestinians to liberate their homeland, stating that "the liberation of Palestine and the defense of its holy places is an Arab, religious, and human duty." This latter phrase is the only place in the long document that refers to religion.[12]

In July of the same year, 1968, the National Palestinian Council convened in Cairo and issued another foundational yet more important document, "The Palestinian National Charter." The significance of this document stems from its acclaimed representative and consensual nature. It was embraced by more than a dozen Palestinian factions that belonged to the PLO at that time and has been cherished ever since by the majority of Palestinians as the embodiment of their nationalism and aspirations. As in the case of the Fatah statute, the charter is overwhelmingly national and secular in tone and content. In its thirty-three articles,

---

[12] For the genesis and birth of the Palestinian National Charter, see Horani (2014, 191–230). See the text of the charter (Horani 2014, 345–50). The quotes from the charter used in the text above are taken from Horani's book.

religion and/or religious references are almost absent, let alone near to any centrality. The charter asserts that, "Palestine is the homeland of the Arab Palestinian people and that it constitutes part and parcel of the great Arab homeland, with the Palestinians being part of the Arab nation" (Horani 2014, 345–50). The document draws a nationalist-based definition of the Palestinians, stating they are "the Arab citizens who resided ordinarily in Palestine until 1947, whether they stayed in Palestine or left, and the persons who were born of an Arab Palestinian father after that year either inside or outside Palestine." Following this definition, the charter states that, "The Jews who were ordinarily residing in Palestine prior to the Zionist invasion are considered Palestinians." The charter stipulates the ultimate national objectives of liberating Palestine through armed struggle and a war of the people and declares positions regarding UN resolutions, Arab unity, and cooperation with nations and states. On leadership and representation, the charter makes it clear that the PLO is the representative and leader of the Palestinian people. Throughout the thirty-plus articles of the charter, one needs to search closely for any religious references. Three scant and passing references can be found in the charter, all used rhetorically to solicit Arab and Muslim support in the fight against Zionism and Israel. In Article 7, the text states, "The Palestinians belonging in Palestine and the material, *spiritual*, and historical affiliation to it are established facts. Raising the Palestinian individual along Arab revolutionary lines, it is a national duty to follow all ways of awareness and education to deeply introduce the Palestinian to his homeland *spiritually* and materialistically, and train him for struggle" (emphasis added). Article 15 stresses that the liberation of Palestine is "an Arab duty," and in order to achieve this goal "the [greater] Arab nation should effectively mobilize all its military, human, material, and *spiritual* capacities to contribute to the liberation of Palestine" (emphasis added). Finally, Article 16 states that:

> The liberation of Palestine, from a spiritual perspective, provides the Holy Land with peace and tranquility under which all holy places will be maintained, and freedom of worship and visit will be guaranteed to all without any discrimination based on race, color, language, or religion. Therefore, the people of Palestine long for the support of all spiritual forces in the world.

The uncontested nationalist discourse in the above two documents can hardly be argued against. Alongside this, numerous documents confirm the point that religion and religious references never enjoyed any central position within the main discourses of Palestinian nationalism. The function of using religious rhetoric to mobilize resistance, however, has repeatedly happened in ways unrelated to claiming ownership of the land. Various other commentaries undoubtedly could be drawn out of the above, but two related points deserve to be underlined, particularly for their intimate connection to the next discussion about Hamas. The first one is the almost canonical primacy of "resistance and revolution" in the Palestinian national discourse. Ideas, ideologies, and efforts – national, Arab, or beyond – should be invited to serve resistance. Any political, social, or religious force that stays uninvolved in the national project of resistance loses legitimacy and consequently will languish in disrepute. The function of religion and religious mobilization within this context is no exception; it should serve the Palestinian national effort if it steps into the public domain. The second point is that these charters, along with extensive other national documents issued by the majority of the Palestinian movements, institutions, leaders, and thinkers, have in fact set the tone for Palestinian nationalism for generations to come. In the 1950s, 1960s, and 1970s a process of national identity consolidation happened deeply, profoundly constructing Palestinian nationalism on the foundation of resistance, collective suffering, and experience, and internationalism – with no centrality of religion. Hamas's later attempt to reconstruct this nationalism in a new religio-political model, which tried to pull Palestinian identity closer to religion and farther from pure nationalism, has in fact failed, as we will see next.

NATIONALIZED HAMAS

Announcing itself in December 1987, Hamas was a relative latecomer to the arena of Palestinian national struggle and resistance against Zionism and Israel. Although its roots go back to the Palestinian Muslim Brotherhood (MB) in the 1940s, the effective organization that ultimately emerged in the form of Hamas lagged behind the other national and leftist groups of the 1950s onward. During almost four decades (1948–87), Hamas's mother organization, the Palestinian MB, embraced a nonconfrontational/nonresistance approach toward Israel. The Brothers stayed away from any meaningful involvement in the national resistance struggle, prioritizing instead a strategy of the Islamization of society in line with other MB chapters in the region. As noted earlier, they refrained from adopting or engaging in any confrontation strategy against the Israeli occupation, which they justified on the grounds of lacking sufficient "spiritual" as well as "material" preparedness. In order to redress this, their strategy was to prepare the generations for the coming true battle against Israel; a preparation that had already consumed more than four decades (Hroub 2000, 19–36). This justification was dismissed by many Palestinians and perceived very negatively.

Wanting to distance itself from that detracting past, by the late 1980s, Hamas, as the new transformation of the Palestinian MB, vehemently and ever-increasingly embraced resistance, projected itself into the nationalist fervor, and broke away from the unglorified past that the Islamists had adhered to in Palestine since 1948 – a past that did not include much, if anything, in the way of active resistance. Concomitantly however, Hamas remained committed to the vague and traditional "international Islamism" of the MB maintaining, in its 1988 charter, that it was the MB branch in Palestine. The charter presented a self-image and a worldview molded in religious discourse, claims, and aspirations: The centrality of religion was uncontested and functioned as the principal justification for all intentions, ideas, and practices including the perception of Palestine and its ownership. Religion and resistance were blended together – traditional/nonconfrontational religion was revolutionized and a secular resistance was religionized. In other words,

> Hamas turned to religious and theological concepts deeply ingrained in the Palestinian and Islamic culture in general, emptying them of traditional meaning and infusing them with new revolutionary content. (Aburaiya 2009, 57–67).

Palestine and the Palestinian cause were overtly "religionized" in the charter. Almost all matters, conflicts, individuals, groups, states, histories, and the "end of the world" were framed through a religious perspective. Views spanning from intra-Palestinian rivalries to the French and Communist revolutions all the way to the apocalyptic wars between "truthfulness and falsehood" were delivered from a religious perspective. The density of religiosity in the charter is perhaps only matched by the speed with which Hamas then attempted to leave that charter behind.[13]

Over the three decades after the publication of the charter, Hamas has undergone an intriguing process of Palestinization and nationalization in its political thinking and practice. The previously religious group became more national, and the charter along with its excessive religiosity was effectively abandoned for more pragmatic documents; pan-Islamic overtones and exaggerations were downplayed in the interest of a more patriotic and nationalist agenda. Below is a close review of Hamas's transformative journey from an overwhelmingly religious organization that approached the national cause from the perspective of religion into a national movement that thinks and functions in accordance to nationalist diktats, while maintaining religious references at the level of rhetoric and mobilization.

In her quantitative study on the decline of both religious language and elements in Hamas's discourse in the later period between 2005 and 2112, Neven Bondokji (2014) presents concrete evidence. Bondokji examined a number of binary religious/nationalist terms such as *umma* (with its religious connotations) versus *sha'b* (people) with its nationalist connotations; Jews versus Israelis; and jihad versus resistance. Searching Hamas's statements during those years, she concludes that the word *sha'b*/people was used 282 times in selected communiqués in the year 2006 versus 40 times when *umma* was used. *Sha'b* was used 77 times versus 5 instances of *umma* in 2012. Her research also indicated that during the same period, "Hamas discourse reveals an indifference to Israel's Jewish identity." The use of the word

---

[13] It should be said here that the backstory of Hamas's 1988 charter is equally intriguing. The document was written by one veteran individual, Abdul Fattah Dukhan, and published without proper consultation. Enjoying highly respected status within the Palestinian Muslim Brotherhood prior to the foundation of Hamas, Dukhan seemed to have taken the liberty to write the charter and limit the consultation to a very small circle. Hamas leaders and spokespersons tried their best to mitigate the charter's outlandish naivete and anti-Semitism. See Hroub (2010, 23–28).

Palestinian Nationalism and Religious (Un)claims 381

jihad had sharply declined in favor of the word resistance with its nationalist/secular undertones.

HAMAS'S "NEW CHARTER"[14]

The most recent milestone of Hamas's journey from its mostly religious foundation to its mostly nationalist incarnation is the publication of the "Document of General Principles and Policies" in May 2017.[15] Comparing this document with Hamas's old charter demonstrates the movement's trajectory of nationalization to the present day. The new Hamas document outlines the organization's positions on the fundamentals of the Arab/Palestinian-Israeli conflict in forty-two carefully worded and numbered paragraphs, including a preamble. While asserting the movement's adherence to its founding principles, the document's nationalist discourse exhibits less religiosity and more flexibility. It also leaves gray areas, allowing Hamas political room to maneuver in the future. Because of the significance of its content, the clear measured considerations given to the outlined positions, the style and the timing, along with a de facto abandonment of the 1988 old charter, the new document could in fact be considered as Hamas's new charter. In order to show the considerable nationalist leap taken by the movement and reflected in this new charter, the discussion below highlights the salient themes in both charters and compares their representation.

Basic Definitions

The definition of Palestine that the old charter provides is religiously driven, and the ownership of the land is also perceived from a religious perspective:

> The land of Palestine is an Islamic land entrusted [*waqf*] to Muslim generations until Judgment Day. No one may renounce all or even part of it. No Arab state nor all Arab states combined, no king or president nor all the kings and presidents, and no organization nor all organizations, Palestinian or Arab, have the right to dispose of it or relinquish or cede any part of it. (Hroub 2000, 267–91)

Against this uncompromising religious depiction of the land, the preamble of the new document provides a simpler and geographical nationally bound definition of Palestine: "Palestine is the land of the Arab Palestinian people, from it they originate, to it they adhere and belong, and about it they reach out and communicate." Although the new document reaffirms the Islamic aspect of the land stating that "Palestine is the spirit of the *umma* and its central cause; it is the soul of humanity and its living conscience," the thrust of the text remains focused on Palestine

---

[14] This section draws on, and updates, the author's analysis as detailed in Hroub (2017, 100–111).
[15] For the entire text of the document, see the official English translation on Hamas's website: http://hamas.ps/en/post/678/a-document-of-general-principles-and-policies.

exclusively. Further, "The Land of Palestine" subheading in the new document offers the specific geographical boundaries of Palestine as extending "from the River Jordan in the East to the Mediterranean in the West, and from Ras al-Naqura in the North to Umm al-Rashrash in the South." It also affirms that Palestine "is an integral territorial unit. It is the land and the home of the Palestinian people." Following this clear and concise nationalist definition, a general Islamic reference states, "Palestine is an Arab Islamic land. It is a blessed sacred land that has a special place in the heart of every Arab and every Muslim." However, the new charter clearly asserts the "ownership" of the land from a nationalist rather than religious perspective, where the direct owners are the Palestinians rather than Muslims as a whole.

In the old charter, there is no clear definition of the Palestinian people. In fact, even the term itself, *al-sha 'b al-Filastini* (the Palestinian people), only appears once in the twenty-page document in Arabic compared with numerous references to Muslims and the *umma*. The text incorporates the Muslims of Palestine within the bigger pool of world Muslims using generic religious language. In contrast, in its 2017 charter, a clear national Palestinianist definition is conferred upon the people of Palestine, under the subtitle "The Palestinian People." Tellingly, Hamas borrows the definition of the Palestinian people from the PLO's Palestinian charter of 1968 asserting that

> The Palestinians are the Arabs who had lived in Palestine up to 1947, irrespective of whether they were expelled from it, or stayed in it; and every person that was born to an Arab Palestinian father after that date, whether inside or outside Palestine, is a Palestinian. . . . The Palestinian identity is authentic and timeless; it is passed from generation to generation. (Hamas 2017)

Nowhere in this purely nationalist definition does Hamas conjure up Islam or any religious designation for the Palestinian people.

In a similar vein, Hamas's description of itself in the new document is couched in language quite different from the 1988 charter where Hamas was defined in a heavily religious manner:

> [For] the Islamic Resistance Movement: Islam is its system. From Islam, it reaches for its ideology, fundamental percepts, and view of life, the world, and humanity. It judges all its actions according to Islam, and it is inspired by Islam to correct its errors . . . [it] is a branch of the Muslim Brotherhood chapter in Palestine . . . The structure of [Hamas] is comprised of Muslims who are devoted to God and worship Him verily . . . The Islamic Resistance Movement is a distinct Palestinian move-ment. It gives its loyalty to God, it adopts Islam as a way of life, and it strives to raise the banner of God over every inch of Palestine. (Hroub 2000, 269)

In the three-page definition containing various confirmations of the religious foundations and fundamentals of Hamas, the only clear Palestinianist reference to Hamas comes in this sentence: "[Hamas] is a distinct Palestinian movement." In the new charter, however, Hamas stresses the nationalist and resistance aspects of its purpose far more than the religious and pan-Islamic ones: "The Islamic Resistance Movement 'Hamas' is a Palestinian Islamic national liberation and resistance movement. Its goal is to liberate Palestine and confront the Zionist project. Its frame of reference is Islam, which determines its principles, objectives, and means." In the original Arabic text of the new document, the adjective Islamic clearly comes last – preceded by national, liberation, and resistance.

The Struggle: Against Jews or Zionists?

One of the clearest disconnections between the two charters is the depiction of the struggle as a whole. In the old charter, this struggle is portrayed as part of a perpetual war between Judaism and Islam and between Jews and Muslims historically and universally – a struggle that will only be concluded by the end of time. The anti-Semitism of the old charter was clear, referring to *The Protocols of the Elders of Zion* and conflating Jews and Zionists carelessly:

> Our struggle with the Jews is long and dangerous, requiring all dedicated efforts. It is a phase that must be followed by succeeding phases, a battalion that must be supported by battalion after battalion of the vast Arab and Islamic world until the enemy is defeated and the victory of God prevails. (Hroub 2000, 268)

In the new 2017 charter, all this religious language was left behind. The document frames the struggle in overtly nationalist terms. Steering away from the tenor of the old charter where the struggle against Israel is depicted as a religious one, here Hamas makes plain that the

> conflict is with the Zionist project not with the Jews because of their religion. Hamas does not wage a struggle against the Jews because they are Jewish but wages a struggle against the Zionists who occupy Palestine. Yet, it is the Zionists who constantly identify Judaism and the Jews with their own colonial project and illegal entity. (Hamas 2017)

To be fair, however, Hamas and its leadership have been making this distinction since the 1990s, and that position has been reiterated in many statements and pronouncements since that time.

Justification of Political Positions and Resistance

Hamas's political positions – particularly its rejection to compromises and peace initiatives such as the 1981 peace treaty between Egypt and Israel – were anchored in religious justification. As noted above, giving up any part of the land of Palestine was against religion. In the old charter, Hamas designated an article under the subheading "Initiatives, Peace, and International Conferences," which states:

The initiatives, which are called "a peaceful solution" and "international conferences" to resolve the Palestinian problem, are contrary to the ideology of the Islamic Resistance Movement, because giving up any part of Palestine is like giving up part of religion. (Hroub 2000, 274)

By comparison, this religious justification is abandoned in the 2017 document. Under the subheading "The Position toward Occupation and Political Solutions," the document pronounces a stance that reflects the movement's internal consensus on the two-state solution – that is, the creation of a Palestinian state along the 1967 lines. Such a position breaks away from any of the religious rigidities of the old charter strictly formulating Hamas's positions. Although this shift in position is also not unprecedented, the fact that it is now officially included in what is the de facto Hamas's new charter is of major significance – the subtext being that Hamas acquiesces to a political solution that might bring about a viable Palestinian state.

Conversely, the notion of resistance in the old charter is simply presented as religious duty that is contextualized within the greater battle of defending Islam and its territories. For example:

When an enemy usurps a Muslim land, then jihad is the individual religious duty of every Muslim; and in confronting the unlawful seizure of Palestine by the Jews, it is necessary to raise the banner of jihad. (Hamas 2017)

In the new charter, the portion under the subheading "Resistance and Liberation" is also quite different in its language from the old charter and other past statements. Here, there is a clear assertion of the right to a national liberation struggle on the basis of international law:

Resisting the occupation by all means and methods is a legitimate right guaranteed by divine law and by international norms and laws. At the heart of these lies armed resistance, which is regarded as the strategic choice for protecting the principles and the rights of the Palestinian people. (Hamas 2017)

Significantly, however, the very same passage relaxes the definition of resistance to include the notion of "managing resistance" such that escalation and de-escalation tactics are paired with other "diverse means and methods." Thus,

Hamas rejects any attempt to undermine the resistance and its arms. It also affirms the right of our people to develop the means and mechanisms of resistance. Managing resistance, in terms of escalation or de-escalation, or in terms of diversifying the means and methods, is an integral part of the process of managing the conflict and should not be at the expense of the principle of resistance. (Hamas 2017)

Hamas is not completely abandoning its religious and Islamic pedigree, despite the drastic downplay of such references in its 2017 "charter" when compared with the 1988 charter and other pronouncements. However, compared with Hamas's previous literature, the emphasis on the "Palestinianness" of Palestine, and the Palestinian nationalism articulated in the new document, has never been more clear or obvious. Hamas's particular version of Palestinian nationalism, led by pragmatism and referenced by religion, has moved well past the middle ground between traditional Islamism and secular nationalism. The Palestinianism of the movement and its agenda now takes the overriding priority over other transnational religious utopias, aspirations, and calls.[16]

CONCLUSION

Hamas's evolution and transformation closer to the nationalist course of politics, thought, and action brings the movement in line with the general trend of Palestinian nationalism in terms of deprioritizing religion within the struggle. This transformation of the most influential religious Palestinian movement to date in Palestinian history toward more Palestinian nationalism is indeed paramount. In terms of our discussion here, this shift confirms the line of argument examined above, that is, the *centrality* and *function* of religion within the Palestinian national movement (including its Islamist parties) differs greatly from the case of Zionism and its reliance on religious claims. The place of religion within the Palestinian movement has always been decentered, with its function revolving around mobilization for resistance. Rarely, religion and religious claims represented the foundation for asserting ownership of the land. As a final remark, and within at least the past two decades, it is useful to place the particular case of Hamas within the broader Palestinian national movement and compare the latter with the mainstream Zionist movement. In so doing, it is indeed intriguing to observe how Hamas's shift to the direction of Palestinian nationalism has been taking place in tandem with the shift that mainstream political Zionism has been undertaking in the direction of religious Zionism. While religious parties on the Palestinian side were becoming nationalized, national parties of Zionism were becoming religionized.

REFERENCES

Aburaiya, Issam. 2009. "Islamism, Nationalism, and Western Modernity: The Case of Iran and Palestine." *International Journal of Politics, Culture and Society* 22, no. 1: 57–67.
El-Awaisi, Abd al-Fattah. 1998. *The Muslim Brotherhood and the Palestine Question: 1928–1947.* New York: Tauris Academic Studies.
Bondokji, Neven. 2014. "The Nationalist versus the Religious: Implications for Peace with Hamas." Brookings. March 18. www.brookings.edu/opinions/the-nationalist-versus-the-religious-implications-for-peace-with-hamas/.

---

[16] In certain ways, this "Islamist/Palestinian nationalism" is the one that was observed evolving: "Islamism [in Palestine], while it emerges from a very particular cultural-political milieu within Palestinian society, nevertheless must be understood as a dimension of Palestinian nationalism." See Lybarger (2007, 4).

Bunzl, John, ed. 2009. *Islam, Judaism, and the Political Role of Religions in the Middle East.* Tampa: University Press of Florida.

Choueiri, Youssef M. 2000. *Arab Nationalism: A History.* Oxford: Blackwell Publishers.

Hamas. 2017. "A Document of General Principles and Policies." http://hamas.ps/en/post/678/a-document-of-general-principles-and-policies.

Horani, Faisal. 2014. *Al-Fikr al-Siyasi al-Filastini 1974–1964: Dirasat li-l-Watha'iq al-Ra'isiyya li-Munathamat al-Tahrir al-Filastiniyya* [Palestinian political thought 1964–1974: A study of the main charters of the PLO]. Amman: Dar al-Shorouk.

Al-Hout, Bayan Nuwayhid. 1986. *Political Leadership and Institutions in Palestine 1917–1948.* Beirut: Institute of Palestine Studies.

Hroub, Khaled. 2000. *Hamas: Political Thought and Practice.* Washington, DC: Institute of Palestine Studies.

2010. *Hamas: A Beginner's Guide.* 2nd ed. London: Pluto Press.

2017. "The Revised Charter: A Newer Hamas?" *Journal of Palestine Studies* 46, no. 4: 100–111.

Khalidi, Rashid. 1997. *Palestinian Identity: The Construction of Modern National Consciousness.* New York: Columbia University Press.

Lachman, Shai. 1982. "Arab Rebellion and Terrorism in Palestine 1929–39: The Case of Sheikh Izz al-Din al-Qassam and His Movement." In *Zionism and Arabism in the Palestine and Israel,* edited by Elie Kedourie and Sylvia G. Haim, 52–99. London: Frank Cass.

Landau, Yehezkel. 2009. "Holy Land, Unholy War: The Religious Dimension of the Israeli-Palestinian Conflict." In *Resolving the Israeli-Palestinian Conflict: Perspectives on the Peace Process,* edited by Moises Salinas and Hazza Abu Rabi, 263–85. Amherst, NY: Cambria Press.

Laqueur, Walter, and Dan Schueftan. 2016. *The Israel-Arab Reader: A Documentary History of the Middle East Conflict.* 8th ed. New York: Penguin Books.

Lybarger, Loren D. 2007. *Identity and Religion in Palestine: The Struggle between Islamism and Secularism in the Occupied Territories.* Princeton: Princeton University Press.

Masalha, Nur. 2018. *Palestine: A Four Thousand Year History.* London: Zed Books.

Mattar, Philip. 1988. *The Mufti of Jerusalem: Al-Hajj Amin al-Husayni and the Palestinian National Movement.* New York: Columbia University Press.

Milton-Edwards, Beverly. 1996. *Islamic Politics in Palestine.* London: I.B. Tauris.

Muslih, Muhammad Y. 1988. *The Origin of Palestinian Nationalism.* New York: Columbia University Press.

Pedahzur, Ami. 2012. *The Triumph of Israel's Radical Right.* Oxford: Oxford University Press.

Saleh, Mohsen. 1988. *Al-Tayyar al-Islami fi Filastin 1917–1948* [The Islamic current in Palestine 1917–1948]. Kuwait: Al-Falah.

Salem, Paul. 1994. *Bitter Legacy: Ideology and Politics in the Arab World.* Syracuse: Syracuse University Press.

Sayigh, Yezid. 1997. *Armed Struggle and the Search for State: The Palestinian National Movement, 1949–1993.* Oxford: Clarendon Press.

Schulz, Helena Lindholm. 1999. *The Reconstruction of Palestinian Nationalism: Between Revolution and Statehood.* Manchester: Manchester University Press.

Shindler, Colin. 2015. *Israel: The Rise of the Israeli Right: From Odessa to Hebron.* Cambridge: Cambridge University Press.

Shlaim, Avi. 2010. *Israel and Palestine: Reprisals, Revisions, Refutations.* London: Verso.

Shoufani, Elias. 2003. *Al-Mujaz fi Tarikh Filastin al-Siyasi (Mundhu Fajr al-Tarikh hatta Sanat 1949)* [A digest of Palestine's political history (Since the beginning of history until 1949)]. Beirut: Institute of Palestine Studies.

Index

'Abd al-Wahhāb, 23
abduction of women, 166, 167–68
Abu-Khdeir, Mohammad, 135, 147, 148, 152
Advaita monist philosophy, 174
Afghanistan, Wahhabism in, 23
Ambedkar, Bhimrao Ramji,169, 170
Arabism. *See* pan-Arabism
Arafat, Yasir, 376
Ariel, Yisrael, 137
armed forces. *See* Israel Defense Forces,
    religionization of
Armenian nationalism and Zionism compared,
    73–74
Azarya, Elor, 128

Babri Mosque, demolition of (1992), 172, 177
Balfour, Arthur Balfour, 1st Earl of, 55
Balfour Declaration (1917), 55
Balkan War, First (1912), 223
Balkan Wars (1990s)
    conflicting nationalisms as cause, 216
    human cost of, 215
    ICTY prosecutions, 215
Bandaranaike, Sirimavo, 197, 198, 206
Bandaranaike, Solomon W.R.D., 195, 196
Bano, Asifa, 161
Bar-Yochai, Shimon, 48
Belfast. *See* Northern Ireland
Ben-Gurion, David, 66, 69, 116
Benvenisti, Meron, 137
Bharatiya Janata Party, 163
Bharatmata (Goddess of the Indian Nation), cult
    of, 171
Bible
    nationalism and, 41
    secularism and, 40–44, 67–68
    Zionism and, 22, 39–44, 54–56, 65, 67–68, 79,
    234–35

biopolitics
    demography and, 137
    sacralization by use of, 14
Bishara, Azmi, 78
Bodu Bela Sena (Buddhist Power Force, BBS),
    190, 204–5
Buddhist nationalism. *See* Sinhalese Buddhist
    nationalism

capitalism, Hindutva and, 173
caste divisions in India, 125, 169–70
Catholicism. *See* Christianity; Northern Ireland
Ceylon. *See* Sri Lanka
Chelvanayakam, Samuel J.V., 196
Christianity. *See also* Bible
    Christian Zionism in US, 142–44
    colonialism equated with, 173
    Hindutva narratives against, 173
    Ireland's Catholic identity, erosion of, 23–24
    Protestantism in Northern Ireland. *See*
    Northern Ireland; Ulster Unionism
    Serbian Orthodoxy and nationalism. *See*
    Serbian nationalism
    Sinhalese Buddhist nationalism, and,
    193–94, 197
    Tamil separatism, and, 191
    Zionism and, 37, 42
    Zionism and Christian millenarianism, 16, 42
    Zionism and Protestant theological imagin-
    ation, 39
Cohen, Itamar, 122
colonialism
    Christianity equated with, 173
    decolonization, and, 79
    elimination of native society as organizing prin-
    ciple of, 75
    geopolitics and sacralized colonialism, 153–54
    Hindutva (Hindu nationalism) and, 20

387

Index

colonialism (cont.)
  indispensibility of religious legitimation, 79–80
  nationalism and, 54, 62
  Northern Ireland and settler colonialism. *See*
    Northern Ireland; Ulster Unionism
  racialized structure of, 136–38
  religion and, 23–24, 54
  religious legitimation of, 72–75
  resistance to, 75–78
  secularism and, 35, 41
  secularization and, 54
  supremacy, notions of, 10
  waning of, 62
  Zionism and settler colonialism. *See* East
    Jerusalem; Zionism
consciousness
  domination and, 10
  sacralized politics and management of, 9–11
Convention on the Elimination of All Forms of
    Racial Discrimination, 142

Dalits (Untouchables). *See* caste divisions in India
Danon, Danny, 54–56, 66
da ʻwā. See pan-Islamism
Dawabshe family, 147, 148
decolonization, Zionism and, 79
demography
  biopolitics and, 137
  racialized sense of demographic threat, 15
  religionization of armed forces, and, 113
  religious violence, and, 167–68
Dharmapala, Anagarike, 193, 198
discrimination
  Convention on the Elimination of All Forms of
    Racial Discrimination, 142
  religious justification of legalized, 138–42
domination, consciousness and, 10
Durga Vahini movement, 173, 177

East Jerusalem
  al-Aqsa Mosque, Israeli settler attack on
    (2019), 134
  colonialism and racialized violence, 135
  colonization of space, 136–38
  demographic biopolitics in, 137
  Foucault's theory of governance, and, 134
  geopolitics and sacralized colonialism, 153–54
  international law, Israeli violation of, 142
  land policies, racialized, 137–38
  legalized discrimination against Palestinians,
    religious justification of, 138–42
  sacralized violence in, 134, 135
  Sivuv Shearim (Encircling the Gates), 151
  US support for Israel's position, 19, 135, 142–44

Eisenkot, Gadi, General, 127
ethnicity. *See* racialization
exclusivity
  exclusive sovereignty, concept of, 68
  Jewish secularism, of, 39
  narrative power of, 10
  politics of religious conversion, 97–98
  privilege and, 10
  religion and, 9
  sacralized narrations of, 9
  self-identity and, 9–11
  supremacy, notions of, 10
  Zionism and, 60, 63

Fanon, Frantz, 153
Fascism, Hindutva and, 165
Fatah, 376–77
Federal Party (Sri Lanka), 196
festivals, religious-nationalistic, 11, 21–22, 178–79
Fonseka, Sarath, 190
forced conversion of women, 166, 167–68
Foucault, Michel, theorization on governance,
    19, 134
Friedman, David, 147–49, 153

Gandhi, Mahatma, 169
Gandhi, Rajiv, 201
Gaza Strip, 126
  Israeli withdrawal from, 123
  March of Return (2018), 39, 144
Global Centre for Combating Extremist Ideology
    (Saudi Arabia), 275
Gnanasara, Galagoda Aththe, 190
Golwalkar, Madhav Sadashiv, 165, 170, 173, 175–76
governance. *See* state policies
Gramsci, Antonio, 180
Greater Serbia. *See* Serbian nationalism
Gush Emunim movement, 119–20, 122

Haʻam, Aḥad, 104, 105
Ha-Ari. *See* Luria, Isaac
Hamas
  charter, 379, 381, 382, 383, 384–85
  definition of Palestine, 381–83
  definition of Palestine people, 382
  definition of Palestinian struggle, 383
  military wing, 372
  nationalization of, 25, 366, 379–81, 385
  origins of, 374
  political positions and resistance, justification
    of, 383–85
  religion, role of, 2–3, 25
  self-identity, 382
Harel, Israel, 126

Index

Hariri, Saad, 275
Heaney, Seamus, 322
Hedgewar, Keshav Baliram, 169
Herzl, Theodore, 72, 104, 105
hesder. See yeshivot hesder
Hindu Mahasabha movement, 169
Hindutva (Hindu nationalism)
  Advaita monist philosophy, and, 174
  anti-Christian narratives, 173
  anti-Muslim narratives, 9, 164, 166–68, 170,
    171–73
  anti-Muslim violence, examples of, 161
  Babri Mosque, demolition of (1992), 172, 177
  Bharatmata (Goddess of the Nation), cult of, 171
  blurred distinction between religion and state
    politics, 20
  capitalism, and, 173
  caste divisions, 125, 169–70
  colonialism and, 20
  demography and, 167–68
  exclusivity, 164
  festivals, 178–79
  historical background, 169–73
  historical/ideological sources of religious vio-
    lence, 166–67
  ideology, 164
  Indian democracy, and, 165
  Indian independence and partition violence,
    and, 171–72
  Nazism as inspiration, 165, 170
  pan-Hindu mobilization of violence, 176–79
  political parties within, 163
  religious nationalism, 161–63
  religious violence as organizational feature
    of, 165
  ritual practices, 176–79
  sacralization of land of India, 12
  sacralized exclusivity, 9
  Sangh Parivar movement, 163–66, 174, 180
  self-representation, 179–81
  Serbian nationalism compared with, 235
  theology of, 174–76
  women activists, 177
  women's organizations, 173
  youth movement (Bajrang Dal), 176–79
  Zionism and, 170
human rights conventions, Israeli violation of, 142

ideology
  idealization of sacred places, 235
India. *See also* Hindutva
  Bharatmata (Goddess of the Nation), cult of, 171
  caste divisions, 169–70
  democracy in, 165

independence and partition violence, 171–72
Pakistan, and, 171
sacralization of land of, 12
Sri Lanka civil war, and, 200
Indian National Congress, 169, 171
International Covenant on Civil and Political
  Rights, 142
international law
  basis for Jewish claim to Israel, 55
  Israeli violation of, 142
Iran
  distinctiveness of Iranian nationalism, 265–67
  forms of nationalism in, 265
  Iran-Iraq War (1980–88), 247
  Mosaddeq era, 22
  nationalism and Islamic foreign policy, 22
  nationalism and Islamic revolution, 22, 247,
    264–65
  nationalism and politics in, 250
  nationalism and religion in, 22, 247
  nationalism in late nineteenth century, 252
  Pahlavi dynasty, 22, 247
  sacralized politics, 4
  secular nationalism, rise of, 22, 247, 258–59
Ireland
  Catholic identity, erosion of, 23–24
  Catholic nationalism in, 311
  colonial legacy of politicized religious
    divisions, 358
  English colonialism in, 311
  English racialized attitudes to, 323–24
  Irish Free State, 311
  mutual legitimation of religion and politics,
    6
  Partition (1922), and, 310–12
  Protestant assimilation to Catholic Ireland,
    309, 316
  Protestant plantations in, 310
Islam. *See also* Iran; Muslims; Saudi Arabia;
    Wahhabism
  da'wā (pan-Islamism). *See* pan-Islamism
  incompatibility with nation-state, 109
Islamophobia. *See* Muslims
Israel, 42. *See also* East Jerusalem; Zionism
  armed forces. *See* Israel Defense Forces, reli-
    gionization of
  Balfour Declaration (1917), 55
  Basic Law, 98–99
  biblical basis for Jewish claim to, 55, 65
  conscription into armed forces, 113
  demographic control policies, 67
  denationalization of politics, 115, 120–23
  displacement of Palestinians, 60
  East Jerusalem, sacralized politics in, 134–54

Index

Israel (cont.)
ethno-national societal religionization, 115, 117–20
exclusive sovereignty, concept of, 68
exclusivity of Jewish secularism, 39
exile of Jews from, perceptions of, 46–50
Gush Emunim movement, 119–20, 122
historical basis for Jewish claim to, 55
history of the land of, 46
incompatibility of Jewish and Zionist conceptions of, 109–10
international law basis for Jewish claim to, 55
international law, violation of, 142
international recognition of, 76
Israel Defense Forces. *See* Israel Defense Forces, religionization of
Israeli national identity, denial of, 99
Jewish identities in, 102–5, 107–8
Jewish state or state of the Jews, whether, 105–6
Jewish state, as, 35
land control, 67–68
legitimation of social power by, 76
messianism and nationalism, 34
nationalism and religion in, 33, 36
nationalist politics in, 2, 95–99
Northern Ireland compared with, 24, 310, 329–34
Palestinian secularism, and, 39
peace and security basis for Jewish claim to, 55
PLO recognition of (1993), 77, 115
politics of religious conversion in, 97–98
pre-Zionist Jewish settlement (Old Yishuv), 46–50
recognition as Jewish state, demand for, 78
relationship between politics and tradition in, 101–2
relationship between religion and politics in, 99–101
religionization of armed forces, 18–19, 113–30
religionization of politics, 115–17, 123–29
religious basis of citizenship, 34
religious identity in, 107–8
religious legitimation of, 65–69, 77–78
religious/secular political agreement, 69, 116
Safedian cultural legacy, 47–50
Second Intifada (2000), 127–28
secular identity in, 107–8
secularism and secularization in, 33–36, 38–39, 50
settler-colonial regime in East Jerusalem, 19
statist ideology (*mamlachtiyut*), 117–18
Supreme Court, 63, 99, 141
Third Intifada (2015), 128
US support for, 19, 135, 142–44

West Bank settlements, religious legitimation of, 77–78
West Bank, religious claim to, 11, 54
Israel Defense Forces, religionization of
conscription into armed forces, 113
correlation with societal religionization, 114
creation of IDF, 115
demographic aspects of, 113
denationalization of politics, and, 115, 120–23
ethno-national societal religionization, and, 115, 117–20
Gaza Strip, withdrawal from, 123
Identity and Purpose (document), 125
Military Rabbinate, 116, 125, 127
nationalism in relation to, 114
partial religionization, 115–17
premilitary Torah academy (*mechina*), 121, 122
process of, 113
receptiveness to religious influences, 114
religionization of politics, and, 115, 123–29
religious education program (*yeshivot hesder*), 118, 119, 120, 122
religious groups' status within armed forces, 114
Second Intifada (2000), 127–28
stages of, 18–19, 115
Third Intifada (2015), 128
Israeli Independence War (1948). *See* wars (Arab/Israeli)

Janata. *See* Bharatiya Janata Party
Jayewardene, Junius R., 200
Jerusalem as global symbol, 235
Jerusalem, East. *See* East Jerusalem
Jevtić, Atanasije, 219
Jewish nationalism. *See* Israel; Zionism
Jewish reform movement (Reform Judaism), 37, 102
Joseph, Rayappu, 201

Kahane, Meir, 145
Kandyan Kingdom in Ceylon (1739–1815), 193
Karađorđević, Alexander, 217
Karo, R. Yosef, 47
The King's Torah (*Torat ha-Melekh*), 145
Kosovo. *See also* Serbia
historic Serbian monasteries in, 224
sacralization of land of, 22
Kosovo, Battle of (1389), 12, 216, 218, 222, 224

land
colonization of space, 136–38
geopolitics and sacralized colonialism, 153–54
idealization of sacred places, 235
land control policies, 67–68

Index

legalized discrimination, religious justification
of, 138–42
racialized policies, 137–38
religiously legitimated territorial expansion,
11
sacralization of, 11–13
sacralized land-related policies, 13
language and religion, 191–92
Lazar, Prince of Serbia, 222, 224
legalized discrimination, religious justification of,
138–42
legitimation
social power by religion, of, 5
state policies by religious sacralization, of, 5
Liberation Tigers of Tamil Eelam
capability for violence, 201
Christian support for, 191
civil war, and, 187, 200–2
defeat of, 201
Indian Peace Keeping Force, and, 201
secularism of, 191
Luria, Isaac (Ha-Ari), 47

Mahavamsa (*Great Chronicle*), 12, 189–90, 192
mamlachtiyut (Israeli statist ideology), 117–18
maternalism, violence and, 173
McCartney, Robert L., 321
mechina (premilitary Torah academy), 121, 122
Mendelssohn, Moses, 102
messianism
nationalism and, 34, 38
Safedian rabbinic scholarship, and, 48
secularism and, 38
Zionism and, 38, 44–46
military forces. *See* Israel Defense Forces, religionization of
millenarianism, Zionism, and Christian, 16
Mitzna, Amram, Major General, 121
Modi, Narendra Damodardas, 169
Mohammad Reza Shah, Shah of Iran, 22, 247
monist Advaita philosophy, Hindutva and, 174
Mosaddeq, Mohammad, 22
Muḥammad bin Salmān, Crown Prince of Saudi
Arabia, 275
Muḥammad ibn Saʿūd, 23
Muslim League, 171
Muslims
Hindutva narratives against, 9, 164, 166–68, 170,
171–73
Hindutva violence against, 161
opposition to Tamil separatism, 203
Serb nationalist narratives against, 12
Sinhalese Buddhist nationalist violence against,
203–6

narrative
authority of, 10
exclusivity and, 9
power of, 10
National Democratic Assembly (Palestinian),
75–78
nationalism. *See also* sacralized politics
Bible and, 41
colonialism and, 54, 62
denationalization of politics, 115
festivals, religious-nationalistic, 178–79
messianism and, 34, 38
politics and, 1
populist nationalism, global growth of, 275
religion and, 1–4, 15, 33, 36–37, 64–65, 358, 366
religionization of, 115, 123–29
religious-like influences, 3
research on religion/nationalism relationship,
340–42
secularism and, 1, 36–37
Wahhabism and, 23, 276
Western meta-narratives of, 337
Zionism and, 62–64
nation-state
incompatibility with religious conceptions of
state, 109
religious-secular dichotomy, and, 89
secular legitimization of state violence, 89
secularism and, 91
theopolitics of, 90–92
NATO bombing of Serbia (1999), 215, 220
Nazism, Hindutva and, 165, 170
necropolitics, sacralization by use of, 13–15
Netanyahu, Benjamin, 42, 55, 66
New Historians, 58
Nissim, Yitzhak, 123
Northern Ireland. *See also* Ulster Unionism
case study, as, 337–39
colonial legacy of politicized religious divisions, 358
colonial origins of anti-Catholic discrimination,
322–23
common perspectives on religion/nationalism
relationship, inadequacy of, 356
continued colonialist influences in, 344–45
discrimination against Catholics, 322
forms of religion/nationalism interaction, 25,
343–45
Good Friday Agreement, 24
Israel compared with, 24, 310, 329–34
Partition of Ireland (1922), and, 310–12
peace process, prospects for, 328–34
peculiarity of conflict in, 325
political violence, distinctive features of, 357

Index

Northern Ireland (cont.)
  post-partition religious territorial enclosures, 342–43
  post-conflict relevance of religion, 24–25
  post-conflict transition, 345–47
  power inequalities, 344
  racial and religious difference, conflation of, 311–16
  religion, territoriality, and violence in relation, 25
  religious change in, 356
  religious identity in, 310–16
  research on religion/nationalism relationship, 340–42, 347–56
  sacralization of land of, 357
  sectarianism in, 344–45
  secularization, forms of, 356
  settler-colonial, 309, 326
  settler-colonial origins of conflict, 23, 310–16

Olmert, Ehud, 123
Orientalism
  secularism and, 34, 35, 37
  Zionism and, 44
Oslo Accords (1993), 75–78, 115

Pahlavi dynasty (Iran), 22
Pakistan, foundation of (1947), 171
Palestine Liberation Organization
  charter (1968), 382
  founding of (1964), 57, 376
  Palestinian state as objective, 57
  recognition of Israel (1993), 77
  Research Centre, 57
Palestinian nationalism. See also East Jerusalem;
    Gaza Strip; Hamas; Palestine Liberation
    Organization
  British rule (1917–48), and, 326, 370
  consolidation of nationalization, 366
  displacement of Palestinians from Israel, and, 60
  equal citizenship claims in Israel, 64, 75–78
  Fatah, 376–77
  Israeli army religionization, and, 125, 126
  Israeli Independence (1948), and, 144–49, 371
  modern movement, as, 367
  National Democratic Assembly, 75–78
  national discourse post-1948, 375–79
  National Palestinian Council, 377
  Palestinian National Charter (1968), 377–78
  Palestinian state as objective, 57
  pan-Arabism, and, 25
  PLO. See Palestinian Liberation Organization
  political aims of, 57
  pre-1948, 368–71

recognition of Israel (1993), 75–78, 115
  religion and, 25
  religious claims, centrality of, 365, 366
  religious claims, function of, 365–66
  religious claims, use of, 365
  religious discourse and activism pre-1948, 371–75
  religious discourse, decline after 1948, 375–79
  resistance to Zionism, 75–78
  secularism and, 39
  view of Zionism as settler-colonial project, 56–62
  Zionism compared with, 25, 365–68
  Zionist narratives against Palestinians, 13
pan-Arabism, Palestinian nationalism, and, 25
pan-Islamism (da'wā)
  advancement of, 23
  radicalization after 1979 , 288–91
  rise of, 282–87
  transnational, 292–96
PLO. See Palestine Liberation Organization
political violence
  religious legitimation of, 6–7
  sacralization by use of, 13–15
politics. See also sacralized politics; state policies
  denationalization of, 115
  geopolitics and sacralized colonialism, 153–54
  narratives as codes for power politics, 10
  nationalism and, 1
  partial religionization of, 115–17
  religion and, 1–4, 88
  religionization of, 115, 123–29
  religious conversion, of, 97–98
  religiously legitimated politics, 1
  theopolitics of nation-state, 90–92
Popović, Jovan S., 222
populist nationalism, global growth of, 275
power
  inequalities in Northern Ireland, 344
  land policies and sacralized hierarchies of power, 13
  narrative power of exclusivity, 10
  narratives as codes for power politics, 10
  racialization in structural relations of power, 9
  sensory power regime, 149–53
  social power legitimated by religion, 5
Prabhakaran, Velupillai, 191, 201
privilege
  exclusivity and, 10
  racialized institutionalization of, 15
Protestantism. See Christianity; Ulster Unionism
racialization
  Convention on the Elimination of All Forms of Racial Discrimination, 142
  demographic threat, sense of, 15

Index

ethno-national societal religionization, 115, 117–20
ethno-religious violence, reasons for, 205
institutionalized privilege, and, 15
racialized structure of colonialism, 136–38
sacralized politics, and, 9
secularism and, 89

Rahula, Walpola, 199
Rajapaksa, Mahinda, 191, 201, 202, 204–5, 208
Ramakrishna Mission, 175, 176
Ramasamy Naicker, E. V., 169
Ramjanambhoomi movement, 177
Rashidi, Sibghatulla, 161
Rashtrasevika Samiti movement, 173
Rashtriya Swayam Sevak Sangh (RSS), 163–66, 174, 180
Reform Judaism. *See* Jewish reform movement
religion. *See also* sacralized politics
   armed forces, and. *See* Israel Defense Forces, religionization of
   colonialism and, 23–24, 54, 72–75
   decolonization, and, 79
   ethno-national societal religionization, 115, 117–20
   ethno-religious violence, reasons for, 205
   exclusivity and, 9
   festivals, religious-nationalistic, 178–79
   geopolitics and sacralized colonialism, 153–54
   idealization of sacred places, 235
   indispensibility of religious legitimation, 79–80
   influences on state policies, 1
   language and, 191–92
   legalized discrimination, religious justification of, 138–42
   legitimation of social power by, 5
   nationalism and, 1–4, 15, 33, 36–37, 64–65, 358
   nation-state, and, 89, 109
   partial religionization of politics, 115–17
   politics and, 1–4, 88
   politics of religious conversion, 97–98
   religionization of politics, 115, 123–29
   research on religion/nationalism relationship, 340–42
   sacralization distinguished from, 5
   secularism and, 34, 36–37, 39, 88
   theopolitics of nation-state, 90–92
   Western meta-narratives of, 337
Reza Shah Pahlavi, Shah of Iran, 22, 247
Rithambara, Sadhvi Nisha, 177
Rothschild, Lionel Rothschild, 2nd Baron, 55
Roumi, Nassim Abu, 134, 154
RSS. *See* Rashtriya Swayam Sevak Sangh

sacralized politics. *See also* state policies
   colonialism and, 10

concept of, 4, 43, 46
definition of, 8
definitions of sacralization, 4
distinction between sacralization and religion, 5
framed politics of sacredness, 1
interaction between religion and nationalism, 8
modes of, 9–13
political violence, 6–7
process of sacralization, 4, 7
racialization and, 9
religious claims and, 4–7, 10, 321
religious exclusivity, 9
religiously based sacralized politics, 7–12
religiously legitimated politics, 1
sacred places, idealization of, 235
Sadan, Eli, 122, 123, 127
Safed, 47–50
Salafism, 23
Salmān ibn ʿAbd al-ʿAzīz, King of Saudi Arabia, 275
Sanatan Dharm, 177
Sangh Parivar movement, 163–66
Saraswati, Swami Chinmayananda, 176
Saudi Arabia. *See also* pan-Islamism (*daʿwā*); *Wahhabism*
   extremist ideology, and, 297–300
   foundational agreement (1744), 23
   historical timeline, 299
   nationalism and religion in, 23
   religiously legitimated authoritarianism, 23
   Salafism, 23
   US collaboration in Afghanistan, and, 23
Savarkar, Vinayak Damodar, 9, 164, 165, 168, 170, 173, 179
Sayegh, Fayez, 57
Scholem, Gershom, 44–46
secularism
   anti-multiculturalism of Western secularism, 34
   Bible and, 40–44, 67–68
   binary thinking within, 91
   colonialism and, 35, 41, 54
   conceptual critique of, 33–36
   decolonization, and, 79
   legitimization of state violence, 89
   messianism and, 38
   nationalism and, 1, 36–37
   nation-state, and, 89, 91
   Orientalism and, 34, 35, 37
   Palestinian nationalism, and, 39
   racialization and, 89
   religion and, 34, 36–37, 39, 88
   secularization paradigm, 1
   Zionism and, 35, 37, 38, 65–67

394 *Index*

self-identity
  exclusivity and, 9–11
  sacralized politics and construction of, 9–11
Senanayake, Don Stephen, 194, 196
sensory power regime, 149–53
Serbia
  Balkan War, First (1912), 223
  claim to Kosovo, 223
  early history of, 223
  NATO bombing of (1999), 215, 220
Serbian nationalism
  anti-Muslim narratives, 12
  fusion of ethnic and religious nationalism, 216
  Greater Serbia, concept of, 21
  Hindutva (Hindu nationalism) compared
    with, 235
  ICTY prosecutions, 215
  international support, bids for, 217–18
  rise of, 218–22
  sacralization of land, 12
  Zionism, and, 22, 79, 234–35
Serb-Jewish Friendship Society, 218
settler colonialism. *See* colonialism
al-Sharif, Yusri, 128
Sharma Prem, Baikunth Lal, 177
Sheikh, Hammouda Khader, 134
Shivaji, King, 178
Sinhalese Buddhist nationalism
  anti-Catholic measures, 197
  anti-Muslim violence, 203–6
  beginnings of, 188
  beginnings of Sinhala-Buddhist settlement, 188
  Christianity and, 193–94
  civil service reforms, and, 206
  civil war, and, 187, 200–2
  competing influences within, 199
  consequences of, 202–3
  consolidation of, 194–97
  construction of Sinhala-Buddhist identity, 189
  early riots (1883, 1915), 194
  ethno-religious demography in Sri Lanka,
    and, 188
  exclusive nationalist claims, 21
  fusion of language and religion, 191–92
  ideology, 189, 190–91
  Indian Peace Keeping Force, and, 201
  Mahavamsa (*Great Chronicle*), and, 189–90, 192
  Muslims, and, 195
  political Buddhism, 199
  political decay resulting from, 206–7
  post-civil war measures against Tamils, 201
  religious claims to Sinhalese domination, 21
  religious impetus for nationalism, 192–94
  religious legitimation of political violence, 199

  rise to political supremacy, 197–200
  sacralization of land of Sri Lanka, 12, 21
  siege mentality, 199
  success of, 207–8
  violence, legitimation of, 21
al-Sīsī, 'Abd al-Fattāḥ, 275
Sivuv Shearim (Encircling the Gates), 151
Six-Day War (1967). *See* wars (Arab/Israeli)
SLPF. *See* Sri Lanka Freedom Party
social power, religious legitimation of, 5
Sokolof, Nahum, 42
Sri Lanka. *See also* Liberation Tigers of Tamil
    Eelam; Sinhalese Buddhist nationalism;
    Tamil separatism
  British unification of Ceylon (1815), 193
  civil service reforms, 206
  civil war, 187, 191
  colonization of, 188
  constitution (1948), 194
  constitution (1972), 198, 206
  constitution (1978), 198
  ethno-religious conflict in, 20, 187–88
  ethno-religious demography, 188
  ethno-religious tension, rise under British rule,
    193–94
  independence (1948), 187
  Kandyan Kingdom (1739–1815), 193
  pro-Western relations, 200
  religious tolerance, 193
  sacralization of land of, 12, 21
  Sinhala as official language, 187, 195–96, 197
Sri Lanka Freedom Party, 195, 205
state policies
  Foucault's theory of governance, 19, 134
  religious influences on, 1, 3–4
  religious sacralization and legitimation, 5
Stone, Michael, 318
Suez War (1956). *See* wars (Arab/Israeli)
supremacy, exclusivist notions of, 10

Tamil separatism. *See also* Liberation Tigers of
    Tamil Eelam
  Bandaranaike governments, and, 196–97
  Christian support for, 191
  civil war, 187
  denial of Sri Lankan citizenship to Tamils, 195
  ethno-religious demography in Sri Lanka,
    and, 188
  growth of Sinhalese Buddhist supremacy, and,
    197–200
  India and, 200
  Muslim opposition to, 203
  origins of, 187
  post-civil war measures against, 201

Index 395

Sri Lankan independence, and, 194
Tamil deaths in civil war, 201
tawḥīd. See Wahhabism
territory. *See* land
Tiran, Strait of, Israeli claim to, 117
Tito, Josip Broz, 218
Trump, Donald, 19, 135, 142, 153, 275
Turkey, sacralized politics, 4

Ulster Freedom Fighters, 327
Ulster Unionism
  belief in superiority of British institutions, 319
  cultural superiority over Catholicism, belief
    in, 321
  exclusionary nature of, 322
  future of peace process, and, 328–34
  Good Friday Agreement, and, 24
  historical foundations, 310–16
  ideology, 316–28
  murals as visual expression of, 317–18, 327
  political formation, aspects of, 316
  Protestant nationalism, and, 23–24
  Protestantism as marker of tribal difference,
    316, 317
  settler-colonialism, and, 23–24, 309
  siege mentality, 324–25
  state identified with, 309
  supremacism, 317
  Zionism and, 327
United Kingdom. *See also* Northern Ireland;
    Ulster Unionism
  Balfour Declaration (1917), 55
  colonial legacy of politicized religious divi-
    sions, 358
  Palestine Mandate (1917–48), 370
  Sri Lanka, and, 193–94
United National Party (Sri Lanka), 195
United States
  Christian Zionism in, 142–44
  Israel Defense Forces, religionization of, 114
  sacralized politics, 5
  Saudi collaboration in Afghanistan, and, 23
  support for Israel's position on Jerusalem, 19, 135,
    142–44
Untouchables (Dalits). *See* caste divisions in India

Vikramaditya, King, 178
violence
  ethno-religious violence, reasons for, 205
  maternalism and, 173
  populist nationalism, global growth of, 275
  religious legitimation of political violence,
    6–7
  secular legitimization of state violence, 89

sensory power regime, 149–53
Western meta-narratives of, 337
Vishwa Hindu Parishad (VHP), 163, 171, 176–79

Wahhabism
  Afghanistan, in, 23
  anti-nationalist ideology, 23, 276
  da'wā (pan-Islamism). *See* pan-Islamism
  origins of, 276–78
  Salafism and, 23
  tawḥīd, doctrine of, 278–82
wars (Arab/Israeli)
  1948 (Israeli Independence War), 57, 58, 76
  1956 (Suez War), 117
  1967 (Six-Day War), 18, 57, 58, 70, 117
  1973 (Yom Kippur War), 57, 118, 119, 120
West Bank. *See* Israel
Winter, Ofer, Colonel, 126
women
  abduction and forced conversion of, 166, 167–68
  clothing and body covering, 92
  Hindutva and, 173, 177
  maternalism and violence, 173
Wriggins, William Howard, 187

yeshivot hesder, 118, 119, 120, 122
Yom Kippur War (1973). *See* wars (Arab/Israeli)
Yudhisthira, King, 178
Yugoslavia, breakup of, 218–22, 235–38

Zimmermann, Warren, 225
Zionism, 38, 39
  anti-Palestinian narratives, 13
  Armenian nationalism compared with, 73–74
  Bible and, 39–44, 67–68
  binary of, 17–18
  Christian millenarianism, and, 16, 42
  Christian Zionism in US, 142–44
  Christianity and, 37, 42
  colonialism and, 11, 35
  decolonization, and, 79
  distinctiveness of, 15, 16
  exclusively Jewish state, aim of, 60
  exclusivity of, 63
  exile from Israel, perceptions of, 46–50
  fusion of religion and nationalism, 2–3, 64–65
  Hindutva and, 170
  history of the Land of Israel, and, 46
  incompatibility with Jewish conceptions of state,
    109–10
  Israeli national identity, denial of, 63, 99
  Jews and, 36, 43
  justifications for, 59
  messianism and, 38, 44–46

Index

Zionism (cont.)
modern movement, as, 367
national movement, as, 62–64
Orientalism and, 44
origins of, 16, 59
Palestinian nationalism compared with, 25,
365–68
Palestinian resistance to, 75–78
politics of jewish identity, and, 105–6
pre-Zionist Jewish settlement in Israel (Old
Yishuv), and, 46–50
Protestant theological imagination, and, 39
religious legitimation, 65–69, 116–17
religious legitimation, indispensibility of,
79–80
rise of religious influences in, 69–78
sacralization of land, 13

Safedian cultural legacy, and, 47–50
secularization and, 16, 17, 35, 37, 38
secularism and, 65–67
Serbian nationalism, and, 22, 79, 234–35
settler colonialism, and, 16–17, 54–80
settler-colonial dimension of, obscuring of, 56,
72–75, 79
settler-colonial paradigm, Israeli view of, 58
settler-colonial project, as, 56–62
settler-colonialism as process and structure,
75–77
settler-colonialism, continuance of, 61–62
settler-colonialism, religious legitimation of, 79
theopolitics of, 92–94
Uganda, proposed Jewish state in (1903), 38,
72–73, 227–29
Ulster Unionism, and, 327

CPSIA information can be obtained
at www.ICGtesting.com
Printed in the USA
LVHW011609030821
694401LV00006B/364